Twentieth-Century Artists on Art

An Index to Artists' Writings,
Statements, and Interviews

Twentieth-Century Artists on Art

An Index to Artists' Writings,
Statements, and Interviews

JACK ROBERTSON

G.K.HALL&CO.

70 LINCOLN STREET, BOSTON, MASS.

Library of Congress Cataloging in Publication Data

Robertson, Jack.
    Twentieth-century artists on art.

    1. Artists—Addresses, essays, lectures—Indexes.
2. Artists—Interviews—Indexes.   3. Arts, Modern—
20th century—Indexes.   I. Title.
NX456.R59   1985   016.7'0092'2   85-21895
ISBN 0-8161-8714-2

This publication is printed on permanent/durable acid-free paper
MANUFACTURED IN THE UNITED STATES OF AMERICA

This book is dedicated to my parents, Jean and James Robertson, for all of their known and unknown support; and to my wife, Diane Dale, for her presence and the promise of the future.

Contents

Preface

In art historical research there are two distinct types of primary documents. The painter's paintings, the designer's chairs, the architect's buildings, or the photographer's images may be studied and analyzed directly and seen to reveal very much of the visual artist's working premises. The second type of primary document is an artist's own words. The artist's comments and writings form a very important portion of the verbal cloud which surrounds any work of art. Spoken and written words create a welter of commentaries and criticisms, appreciations and appraisals, relating to the artwork, and when words by the creator of the work can be sifted from this encompassing cloud, the import of the work itself may be enhanced. Frequently, an artist will speak and write about not only his art, but also about his life and training, his influences and associates, his tastes and aesthetic theories, and technical procedures in such a way that things otherwise unknown and unknowable are revealed. All too frequently an artist's words will seem to be only obliquely or tangentially pertinent to the speaker and his work; sometimes a visual artist's writings will appear to be expression through metaphor; and sometimes an artist will write cryptically in puzzles and paradoxes. But always an artist's words are revealing and potentially useful in showing how his or her mind and creative spirit work. It is the task of the student of modern art--the researcher, scholar, and curator--to consider an artist's personal commentary and to reconcile these primary documents with the rest of the verbal cloud and especially with the observable physical facts, that is, the works of art themselves.

Artists' writings and comments are not a unique or new phenomenon in twentieth-century art. In this century, however, there has been a proliferation of art publications in which a visual artist's writings may appear: anthologies of writings, essays, manifestos, etc.; anthologies of transcribed interviews; many more specialized art periodicals and serials; group exhibition catalogs with extensive documentation. The problem for the researcher is that much of this literature falls outside the coverage of the standard art indexing tools, and it is frequently not cataloged in such a way that each individual artist's name is listed. This difficulty is addressed by this Index: approximately 5,000 artists active in the twentieth-century are listed alphabetically with 14,000 citations to primary documents published in 495 sources. Of this material, 80% is listed in its original (and usually only) place of publication; the remaining 20% includes previously published pieces, translations from original pieces, and a small number of cases of multiple listings for the same piece, e.g., all or portions of Picasso's 1935 comments to Christian Zervos are cited in nine sources, and Jackson Pollock's statement entitled "My Painting" published in 1947/48 is listed in nine sources. The importance of a certain few artists' comments is such that, to facilitate accessibility to these words, as many published sources as possible have been cited.

The major working premise of this Index has been to provide easy and direct access to twentieth-century artists' words. The fact that almost all of the 495 published sources indexed are not otherwise analyzed by individual artist's name (nor are very many of them cataloged with indication that they contain this form of primary document) has created the first and biggest difficulty in compiling the Index. Only by browsing, by guessing, by following clues in one source to others, by suggestions and tips from individuals well-acquainted with the field of twentieth-century art, have these nearly 500 sources been discovered. When a researcher is interested in an individual artist, the Index provides the first step in acquiring primary documents by the artist. The second step is provided by the standard library cataloging and interlibrary loan networking tools. The bibliographical listing of the sources indexed includes OCLC and LC card numbers to facilitate retrieval on the various library networks. Compiling the Index required that every source be examined very closely and completely, and about 40% of them were borrowed for this purpose through interlibrary loan services. In the case of the periodicals and serials, the Index provides sufficient details to submit photocopy requests for the specific volume and page numbers to the specialized art libraries, such as the Museum of Modern Art Library, which have strong collections on twentieth-century art.

Preface

The scope of coverage of the Index has been made as inclusive as possible. Artists of over 60 nationalities are included; artists practicing all visual art media including painting, sculpture, architecture, photography, video, performance, all forms of crafts, and earthworks have been included. For practical reasons only material in Western European languages is cited: 75% is in English, the rest in German, French, Italian, Spanish, or Dutch. A few major nineteenth-century artists, e.g., Cezanne, Monet, Gauguin, I. Repin, are included in the Index because citations to any artist's words written in the twentieth-century are included. No sources published after 1983 are included in the Index. No sources of artists' interviews on audio/video tape which have not been transcribed or published in the traditional sense are included in the Index.

This indexing project was extended to all forms of artists' words including not only statements and interviews but also poems, stories, essays, group discussions, etc., and the types of publications containing artists' words were extended to include anthologies, monographs, group exhibition catalogs, periodicals, and serials. The resulting publication is, therefore, a large-scale and unique compilation of this type of information, but, at the same time, it must be viewed as a preliminary step in gaining control of this form of primary art document. There are many more publications which must be given similar indexing coverage as they are discovered, and, of course, many new publications since 1983 will fall within the scope guidelines of this publication. It is pleasing to have accomplished so much in this preliminary effort, and it is exciting to look forward to future improvements and expansions.

Jack Robertson
July 1985
Nashville, TN

Acknowledgments

Many individuals assisted me in the compilation of this Index; some helped without knowing it, such as many interlibrary loan personnel; some helped with concrete suggestions, tips, comments, questions; and some helped with moral support, eager interest, enthusiasm. The few people's names I have taken the liberty to list here helped most markedly of the many, and I do wish to acknowledge my appreciation for their time, energy, intelligence, and care. They are: Paula Baxter, Fran Hardie, Diane Kirkpatrick, Geoff Lee, Janice Meagher, Skip Sickles, Elizabeth Stewart, Jim Toplon, and Jane Wagner.

Key to Information in Citations

This sample artist entry and citations exemplifies the content and the format of the information contained in the Index.

BALDESSARI, John[1] (1931)[2] Amer;[3] instal, photo, video[4]

    ART AND TECHNOLOGY[5] 53[6] (project proposal)[7]

    ART-WRITE no.7[8] 22-23 ("TV Like 1. A Pencil 2. Won't Bite Your Leg"); 1 ill[9]

    DAVIS 108-111 (statement, p.p.); port[10]

    SKIRA 1980 104-105 (statement); 3 ill

(1) Artist's name, including also-known-as names and name/spelling variations in parentheses.

(2) Artist's birthdate and, if applicable, death date.

(3) Artist's nationality in four letter abbreviation--see "Key to Abbreviations."

(4) Artist's principal artistic medium, or up to three media--see "Key to Abbreviations."

(5) Short form of the main entry of the published source containing the artist's words--see the "Bibliography" at the front of the Index for the full bibliographic details.

(6) Page number(s) containing the artist's words.

(7) Descriptive phrase for the form of the artist's words--including titles of essays or statements where applicable.

Key to Information in Citations

(8) For serials and periodicals, the edition year or volume and issue numbers are specified.

(9) Indication of number of illustrations of reproductions of the artist's works.

(10) Indication of portrait(s) or self portrait(s) of the artist.

Key to Abbreviations

<u>Abbreviations</u> <u>for</u> <u>Artist's</u> <u>Nationality</u>.

Two nationalities are noted for an artist when it is clearly documented that a substantial amount of that individual's life was spent in one country and another substantial amount, frequently marked by change in citizenship, was spent in a second country. Change of citizenship is not a necessary factor in noting double nationality for an artist; when an artist was born and educated in one country and then spends most or all of his creative life in another, double nationality is attributed.

Alge = Algerian
Amer = American
Atrl = Australian
Aust = Austrian
Belg = Belgian
Boli = Bolivian
Braz = Brazilian
Brit = British (including English &
　　other British Isles unless
　　specified as Irish, Scottish,
　　or Welsh)
Bulg = Bulgarian
Cana = Canadian
Chil = Chilean

Chin = Chinese
Colo = Colombian
Cuba = Cuban
Czec = Czechoslovakian
Dani = Danish
Dutc = Dutch
Egyp = Egyptian
Esto = Estonian
Fili = Filipino
Finn = Finnish
Fren = French
Germ = German
Gree = Greek
Guat = Gautamalan

Key to Abbreviations

Hung = Hungarian

Icel = Icelandic

Indi = Indian

Iran = Iranian

Iraq = Iraqi

Iris = Irish

Isra = Israeli

Ital = Italian

Japa = Japanese

Latv = Latvian

Lith = Lithuanian

Luxe = Luxembourger

Mala = Malaysian

Malt = Maltese

Mexi = Mexican

Moro = Moroccan

NewZ = New Zealander

Norw = Norwegian

Para = Paraguayan

Peru = Peruvian

Poli = Polish

Port = Portuguese

Puer = Puerto Rican

Ruma = Rumanian

Russ = Russian

Scot = Scottish

Sing = Singaporean

SoAf = South African

Span = Spanish

Suri = Surinamese

Swed = Swedish

Swis = Swiss

Thai = Thai

Turk = Turkish

Ukra = Ukranian

Urug = Uruguayan

Vene = Venezuelan

Wels = Welsh

Yugo = Yugoslavian

Abbreviations for Artistic Media

Many twentieth-century artists have practiced more than one artistic technique or medium, and many artists have combined media or invented new forms and formats for expression; the listing of artistic medium or media for individuals has been limited to three at most, and the designations have been based on the following definitions:

arch = architect, including landscape architect and urban and regional planner

calli = calligrapher

cart = cartoonist

coll = collage maker

design = interior and industrial designer

envir = environmental artist, including sculpture out of doors encompassing and/or interacting with the environment, also, earthworks artist

Key to Abbreviations

film	=	filmmaker
glass	=	glassmaker
illus	=	illustrator
instal	=	installation artist, including sculpture/painting, etc. encompassing and/or interacting with the interior gallery/room setting
light	=	artist using light and light sources such as fluorescent, neon, lasers
metal	=	metal artist, including jeweler
mosaic	=	mosaic and tile artist
paper	=	paper maker
perf	=	performance artist, including happenings and staged artist's events
photo	=	photographer
pott	=	potter
print	=	print maker
ptr	=	painter
sclp	=	sculptor
sound	=	artist using sound sources as elements of sculpture or performance
text	=	textile artist, including artist practicing weaving, macrame, fiber arts, stitchery
video	=	video artist, including audio-visual pieces

Other Abbreviations

no.	=	number
o.p.	=	originally published
p.p.	=	previously published
v.	=	volume

Bibliography

Bibliography

ABSTRACT. American Abstract Artists. Three Yearbooks (1938, 1939, 1946). Reprint edition, New York: Arno Press, 1969. OCLC # 1185761.

ABSTRACTION. Abstraction, Creation, Art Non-Figuratif. Paris: Edition Paule Nemours, 1932-1936; reprint edition, New York: Arno Press, 1968. OCLC # 1460578. LC # 68-9226. (Numbers 1-5 indexed, all published.)

ACKLAND. Ackland Art Museum, University of North Carolina at Chapel Hill. Some Recent Art from Chicago. Chapel Hill, N.C.: Ackland Art Museum, 1980. OCLC # 6706492. LC # 79-92884. (Unpaginated; artists arranged alphabetically.)

ADACHI. Adachi, Barbara. The Living Treasures of Japan. Tokyo: Kodansha International, 1973. OCLC # 1124505. LC # 73-80959.

ADLERS. Adlers, Bengt. Interviews of Internews; Intrrvjuer om Interna Vyer. Ahus: Kalejdoskop, 1978. OCLC # 6489099. LC # 80-478518 (Interviews in English and Swedish.)

ADVERSARY. Artist as Adversary. New York: Museum of Modern Art, 1971. OCLC # 161234. LC # 76-164876.

ALBRIGHT-KNOX. Albright-Knox Art Gallery. Contemporary Art 1942-1972; Collection of the Albright-Knox Art Gallery. New York: Praeger Publishers, 1972. OCLC # 590643. LC # 70-189296.

ALLEY. Alley, Ronald. New British Sculpture/Bristol. Bristol: Arnolfini Gallery, 1968. OCLC # 91319. LC # 68-30372.

ALLOWAY. Alloway, Lawrence. Topics in American Art Since 1945. New York: W. W. Norton and Co., 1975. OCLC # 1818064. LC # 74-34361.

AMERICAN PRINTS. American Prints Today, 1962. New York: Print Council of America, 1962. OCLC # 2056970. LC # 59-16916.

ANDREWS. Andrews, Oliver. Living Materials; A Sculptor's Handbook. Berkeley, CA.: University of California Press, 1983. OCLC # 7835858. LC # 77-71057.

ANGEL. Angel, Felix. Nosotros. Museo El Castillo, 1976/77. OCLC # 2977058. LC # 77-556108.

APOLLONIO. Apollonio, Umbro, editor. Futurist Manifestos. The Documents of 20th-Century Art. New York: The Viking Press, 1973. OCLC #

643909. LC # 72-89124. (All entries in this anthology were previously published.)

APPLE. Apple, Jacki. Alternatives in Retrospect; An Historical Overview, 1969-1975. New York: The New Museum, 1981. OCLC # 8395968. LC # 81-81185.

ARCHER. Archer, B. J. and Anthony Vidler. Follies; Architecture for the Late-Twentieth-Century Landscape. New York: Rizzoli, 1983. OCLC # 10696522 & 10416487. LC # 83-42958.

ARCHITECTURES. Architectures en France, Modernite, Post-Modernite. Paris: Centre de Creation Industrielle, Centre Georges Pompidou, 1981. OCLC # 10559242 & 8760116. LC # 83-104795.

ARMORY SHOW. The 1913 Armory Show in Retrospect. Amherst, MA.: Amherst College, 1958. OCLC # 1266968.

ART AND ARTIST. Art & Artist. Berkeley and Los Angeles: University of California Press, 1956. OCLC # 1024136 & 977317. LC # 56-8104.

ART AND TECHNOLOGY. Art and Technology; A Report on the Art and Technology Program of the Los Angeles County Museum of Art. Los Angeles: Los Angeles County Museum of Art, 1971. OCLC # 163470. LC # 74-146884.

ART ATTACK. Art Attack Gallery. Sam Francis. Boise, ID.: Art Attack Gallery, 1983.

ART D'AUJOURD'HUI. L'Art d'Aujourd'hui. Paris: Editions Albert Morance, 1924-1929; reprint edition, New York: Arno Press, 1968. OCLC # 2778521 & 2445007 & 6239666. LC # 68-9225 & 43-40138. (Volume 1 no.1/2-volume 6 indexed, all published.)

ART NETWORK. Art Network. Sydney, Australia: Art Network, 1979-. (Numbers 1-11 indexed.)

ART NOW. Art Now: New York. New York: University Galleries, Inc., 1969-1972. OCLC # 1514299. LC # 82-3142. (Volume 1 no.1-volume 4 no.2 indexed, all published; each issue an unpaginated double-fold pamphlet with loose-leaf color reproductions.)

ART PARTRON ART. Southeastern Center for Contemporary Art. Art Patron Art. Winston-Salem, N.C.: Southeastern Center for Contemporary Art, 1979. OCLC # 5730900.

ART SINCE. Art Since Mid-Century; The New Internationalism. 2 volumes. Greenwich, CT.: New York Graphic Society, 1971. OCLC # 175371. LC # 70-154332. (All entries in these volumes were previously published.)

ART VOICES. Art Voices from Around the World. New York: Art Voices Publishing Co., 1962-. OCLC # 2058695 & 1514312. LC # 67-51521 & 83-3031.

ARTFORUM. Artforum. San Francisco: 1962-. OCLC # 1514329. LC # 65-8747. (Volume 1 no.1-volume 7 no.4 indexed; subsequent issues indexed in Art Index.)

ARTHUR. Arthur, John. Realists at Work. New York: Watson-Guptill, 1983. OCLC # 9762314. LC # 83-14545.

ARTIST AND CAMERA. Artist and Camera. London: Arts Council of Great Britain, 1980. OCLC # 10557798 & 7259111. LC # 81-174098.

ARTISTS. Artists' Forum; The Reader Written Arts Magazine. Beverly Hills, CA.: The Center for Contemporary Art, 1980-. (Numbers 1-5 indexed.)

ART-LANGUAGE. Art-Language; The Journal of Conceptual Art. Leamington Spa, England: Art and Language Press, 1969-. OCLC # 2243756 & 1780087. LC # 75-647499. (Volume 1 no.1-volume 4 no.4 indexed.)

ARTPARK. Artpark; The Program in Visual Arts. Lewiston, N.Y.: Artpark, 1976 (includes annual exhibitions for 1974, 1975, and 1976), 1977, 1978, 1979, 1980, 1981, 1982, 1983. OCLC # 3819051 (1974-1976), 5126710 (1977), 5430715 (1978), 6720083 (1979), 9109528 (1980), 10095968 (1981), 9927428 (1982). LC # 82-642102 & 79-1429 (1974-1976), 76-1160 (1977), 80-85317 (1980), 83-70801 (1982). (Volumes for 1978, 1979, 1980, and 1981 are unpaginated; artists arranged alphabetically.)

ART-RITE. Art-Rite. New York: Art-Rite Publishing Co., 1973-. OCLC # 3949627. LC # 83-9002. (Numbers 1-21 indexed; numbers 10 and 11/12 unpaginated.)

ARTS YEARBOOK. Arts Yearbook. New York: Art Digest, Inc., 1957-. OCLC # 2059515. LC # 57-11409. (Volumes 1-11 indexed.)

AUPING I. Auping, Michael. Common Ground: Five Artists in the Florida Landscape. Sarasota, FL.: The John and Mable Ringling Museum of Art, 1982. OCLC # 8628474. LC # 82-81122.

AUPING II. Auping, Michael. <u>Jess:</u> <u>Paste-Ups</u> <u>(and</u> <u>Assemblies)</u> <u>1951-1983.</u> Sarasota, FL.: The John and Mable Ringling Museum, 1983. OCLC # 10518671. LC # 83-82281.

AVALANCHE. <u>Avalanche.</u> New York: Kineticism Press, 1970-. OCLC # 1518926. LC # 76-23823. (Numbers 1-13 indexed.)

AVANT-GARDE. <u>The</u> <u>Avant-Garde:</u> <u>12</u> <u>in</u> <u>Atlanta.</u> Atlanta: The High Museum of Art, 1979. OCLC # 6143597. LC # 79-90349.

AWARDS. <u>Cincinnati</u> <u>Invitational</u> <u>Awards</u> <u>Exhibition.</u> Cincinnati: Cincinnati Art Museum, 1974. OCLC # 951873 & 2930546 & 6682806. LC # 76-369535.

AXIS. <u>Axis;</u> <u>A</u> <u>Quarterly</u> <u>Review</u> <u>of</u> <u>Contemporary</u> "Abstract" <u>Painting</u> <u>and</u> <u>Sculpture.</u> London: 1935-1937; reprint edition, New York: Arno Press, 1968.) OCLC # 1518956. LC # 68-9236. (Numbers 1-8 indexed, all published.)

BANN. Bann, Stephen. <u>The</u> <u>Tradition</u> <u>of</u> <u>Constructivism.</u> <u>The</u> <u>Documents</u> <u>of</u> <u>20th-Century</u> <u>Art.</u> New York: The Viking Press, 1974. OCLC # 862847. LC # 72-75748. (Most entries in this anthology were previously published; some entries translated into English for the first time.)

BARBER. Barber, Noel. <u>Conversations</u> <u>with</u> <u>Painters.</u> London: Collins, 1964. OCLC # 2186099. LC # 66-37674.

BARRON. Barron, Stephanie, editor. <u>California:</u> <u>5</u> <u>Footnotes</u> <u>to</u> <u>Modern</u> <u>Art</u> <u>History.</u> Los Angeles: Los Angeles County Museum of Art, 1977. OCLC # 2743741. LC # 77-70284.

BARROW. Barrow, Thomas F., Shelley Armitage, and William E. Tydeman, editors. <u>Reading</u> <u>into</u> <u>Photography;</u> <u>Selected</u> <u>Essays,</u> <u>1959-1980.</u> Albuquerque: University of New Mexico Press, 1982. OCLC # 8587951. LC # 81-52051.

BATTCOCK I. Battcock, Gregory, editor. <u>The</u> <u>New</u> <u>Art,</u> <u>A</u> <u>Critical</u> <u>Anthology.</u> New York: E. P. Dutton, 1966. OCLC # 331023. LC # 66-3422. (Most entries in this anthology were previously published.)

BATTCOCK II. Battcock, Gregory, editor. <u>Idea</u> <u>Art,</u> <u>A</u> <u>Critical</u> <u>Anthology.</u> New York: E. P. Dutton, 1973. OCLC # 741642. LC # 73-174858. (Most entries in this anthology were previously published.)

BATTCOCK III. Battcock, Gregory, editor. Super Realism, A Critical Anthology. New York: E. P. Dutton, 1975. OCLC # 1734086. LC # 75-324335. (Most entries in this anthology were previously published.)

BATTCOCK IV. Battcock, Gregory. Why Art. New York: E. P. Dutton, 1977. OCLC # 2955890. LC # 72-122777.

BATTCOCK V. Battcock, Gregory, editor. Minimal Art, A Critical Anthology. New York: E. P. Dutton, 1968. OCLC # 68389 & 378256. LC # 77-457118 & 68-5528. (Most entries in this anthology were previously published.)

BATTCOCK VI. Battcock, Gregory, editor. New Artists Video; A Critical Anthology. New York: E. P. Dutton, 1978. OCLC # 3900002. LC # 77-73146. (Entries in this anthology were previously published.)

BATTCOCK VII. Battcock, Gregory, editor. New Ideas in Art Education; A Critical Anthology. New York: E. P. Dutton, 1973. OCLC # 696819. LC # 73-166189. (All entries in this anthology were previously published.)

BAYON. Bayon, Damian and Paolo Gasparini. The Changing Shape of Latin American Architecture; Conversations with Ten Leading Architects. Chichester, New York, Brisbane, Toronto: John Wiley and Sons, 1979. OCLC # 4549954. LC # 78-31583.

BELFORD. Belford, Marilyn and Jerry Herman, editors. Time and Space Concepts in Art. New York: Pleiades Gallery, 1980. OCLC # 6625317. LC # 78-89746.

BERCKELAERS. Berckelaers, Ferdinand L. L'Art Abstrait; Ses Origines, Ses Premiers Maitres. Paris: Maeght, 1950. OCLC # 3333105 & 1015248. LC # 52-28830.

BETHERS I. Bethers, Ray. Pictures, Painters, and You. New York: Pitman Publishing Co., 1948. OCLC # 700015. LC # 48-10532.

BETHERS II. Bethers, Ray. How Paintings Happen. New York: W. W. Norton and Co., 1951. OCLC # 732745. LC # 51-1933.

BIENNALE. La Biennale di Venezia; Settore Arti Visive; Catalogo Generale 1980. Venezia: Edizioni La Biennale di Venezia, 1980.

BOOTH. Booth, Pat, editor. Master Photographers; The World's Great Photographers on Their Art and Technique. New York: Clarkson N. Potter, Inc., 1983. OCLC # 9575392. LC # 83-10903.

BOSHIER. Boshier, Derek. <u>Lives; An Exhibition of Artists Whose Work is Based on Other People's Lives.</u> London: Arts Council of Great Britain, 1979. OCLC # 6789318 & 5397633. LC # 80-492223. (Unpaginated; artists arranged alphabetically.)

BOSTON I. <u>Boston Now: Figuration.</u> Boston: Institute of Contemporary Art, 1982. (Unpaginated; artists arranged alphabetically.)

BOSTON II. <u>Boston Now: Abstract Painting.</u> Boston: Institute of Contemporary Art, 1981. (Unpaginated; artists arranged randomly.)

BOSTON III. <u>Boston: Now.</u> Boston: Institute of Contemporary Art, 1983. (Unpaginated; artists arranged alphabetically.)

BOSWELL. Boswell, Peyton. <u>Modern American Painting.</u> New York: Dodd, Mead and Co., 1939. OCLC # 280081. LC # 39-27892.

BOWLT. Bowlt, John E., editor. <u>Russian Art of the Avant-Garde; Theory and Criticism 1902-1934.</u> New York: Viking Press, 1976. OCLC # 1365848. LC # 73-17687. (Most entries in this anthology have been translated by the editor.)

BOWNESS. Bowness, Alan. <u>Contemporary British Painting.</u> New York and Washington, D.C.: Frederick A. Praeger, 1968. OCLC # 440794 & 170899. LC # 68-19133.

BRAKKE. Brakke, Michael, Michiko Itatani, and Auste, editors. <u>Art Book 2.</u> Chicago: N.A.M.E. Gallery, 1980. OCLC # 7715064. LC # 80-81214.

BREICHA. Breicha, Otto and Gerhard Fritsch, editors. <u>Finale und Auftakt Wien 1898-1914.</u> Salzburg: Otto Muller Verlag, 1964. OCLC # 4385989. LC # 66-57477.

BRENTANO. Brentano, Robyn, editor. <u>112 Workshop/112 Greene Street.</u> New York: New York University Press, 1981. OCLC # 7460666. LC # 78-71391.

BRITANNICA. Pagano, Grace. <u>Contemporary American Painting; The Encyclopedia Britannica Collection.</u> New York: Duell, Sloan and Pearce, 1945. OCLC # 1014860. LC # 45-35086. (Unpaginated; artists arranged alphabetically. The numbers listed are the catalog entry numbers.)

BRITISH. <u>British Sculptors' Attitudes to Drawing.</u> Sunderland, England: Sunderland Arts Centre and the Arts Council of Great Britain, 1974. OCLC # 7665901. (Unpaginated; artists arranged alphabetically.)

BRUMME. Brumme, C. Ludwig. <u>Contemporary</u> <u>American</u> <u>Sculpture.</u> New York: Crown Publishers, 1948. OCLC # 1202433. LC # 48-9357.

BUILDINGS. <u>Buildings</u> <u>for</u> <u>Best</u> <u>Products.</u> New York: Museum of Modern Art, 1979. OCLC # 5946889.

CALIFORNIA--COLLAGE. Long Beach Museum of Art. <u>Arts</u> <u>of</u> <u>Southern</u> <u>California.</u> Volume 10--Collage. Long Beach: Long Beach Museum of Art, 1961. (Unpaginated; artists arranged alphabetically.)

CALIFORNIA--DRAWING. Long Beach Museum of Art. <u>Arts</u> <u>of</u> <u>Southern</u> <u>California.</u> Volume 8--Drawing. Long Beach: Long Beach Museum of Art, 1960. (Unpaginated; artists arranged alphabetically.)

CALIFORNIA--PAINTING. Long Beach Museum of Art. <u>Arts</u> <u>of</u> <u>Southern</u> <u>California.</u> Volume 2--Painting. Long Beach: Long Beach Museum of Art, 1957.

CALIFORNIA--PHOTOGRAHY. Long Beach Museum of Art. <u>Arts</u> <u>of</u> <u>Southern</u> <u>California.</u> Volume 7--Photography. Long Beach: Long Beach Museum of Art, 1960. (Unpaginated; artists arranged alphabetically.)

CALIFORNIA--PRINTS. Long Beach Museum of Art. <u>Arts</u> <u>of</u> <u>Southern</u> <u>California.</u> Volume 16--Prints. Long Beach: Long Beach Museum of Art, 1965. (Unpaginated; artists arranged alphabetically.)

CAMERON D. Cameron, Daniel J. <u>Extended</u> <u>Sensibilities:</u> <u>Homosexual</u> <u>Presence</u> <u>in</u> <u>Contemporary</u> <u>Art.</u> New York: The New Museum, 1982. OCLC # 9504555. LC # 82-61279.

CAMERON E. Cameron, Elisabeth and Philippa Lewis. <u>Potters</u> <u>on</u> <u>Pottery.</u> New York: St. Martin's Press, 1976. OCLC # 3186568 & 3017670 & 2725656 & 2707800. LC # 77-359493 & 76-11329.

CAMPBELL. Campbell, Bryan, editor. <u>World</u> <u>Photograpy.</u> New York: Ziff-Davis Books, 1981. OCLC # 7883325. LC # 81-50869.

CANADA. Cameron, Dorothy. <u>Sculpture</u> <u>'67.</u> Toronto: National Gallery of Canada, 1967. OCLC # 14118. LC # 70-390014. (Texts in English and French.)

CANADIAN. <u>Building</u> <u>with</u> <u>Words;</u> <u>Canadian</u> <u>Architects</u> <u>on</u> <u>Architecture.</u> Toronto: The Coach House Presss, 1981. OCLC # 8551242 & 9111004. LC # 82-106584.

CELANT. Celant, Germano. Art Povera. New York and Washington, D.C.: Praeger Publishers, 1969. OCLC # 45609. LC # 70-84095.

CELEBRATION. American Artists '76, A Celebration. San Antonio, TX.: Marion Koogler McNay Art Institute, 1976. OCLC # 2914068 & 2416793. LC # 76-367903. (Unpaginated; artists arranged alphabetically.)

CENTERBEAM. Piene, Otto and Elizabeth Goldring. Centerbeam. Cambridge: M. I. T., Center for Advanced Visual Studies, 1980. OCLC # 7134502. LC # 80-68325.

CHARBONNIER. Charbonnier, Georges. Le Monologue du Peintre; Entretiens avec.... 2 volumes. Paris: Rene Julliard, 1959, 1960. OCLC # 9312947 & 10164512.

CHIPP. Chipp, Herschel B. Theories of Modern Art; A Source Book by Artists and Critics. Berkeley, CA.: University of California Press, 1968. OCLC # 1029913. LC # 68-12038. (Entries in this anthology were previously published.)

CHOIX. Choix pour Aujourd'hui. Paris: Centre Georges Pompidou, 1982. OCLC # 10123012. LC # 83-119583. (Most entries in this source were previously published.)

CHRYSALIS. Chrysalis; A Magazine of Women's Culture. Los Angeles: Chrysalis, 1977-. OCLC # 3128311. LC # 79-643087. (Numbers 1-10 indexed.)

CINCINNATI. Mel Bochner, Barry LeVa, Dorothea Rockburne, Richard Tuttle. Cincinnati: The Contemporary Arts Center, 1975. OCLC # 2993636.

CIRCLE. Martin, J. L., Ben Nicholson, and Naum Gabo, editors. Circle; International Survey of Constructive Art. New York: Weyhe, 1937; reprint edition, New York: Praeger, 1971. OCLC # 3512363 & 329180 & 153663. LC # 78-118819 & 72-178918.

CLAIR. Clair, Jean. Nouvelle Subjectivite. Bruxelles: Lebeer Hossamann, 1979. OCLC # 6488647. LC # 80-476785.

CLARK. Clark, Garth, editor. Ceramic Art; Comment and Review 1882-1977. New York: E. P. Dutton, 1978. OCLC # 4834780. LC # 78-53107. (Entries in this anthology were previously published.)

CLAUS. Claus, Jurgen. Theorien Zeitgenossischer Malerei in Selbstzeugnissen.

Hamburg: Rowohlt, 1963. OCLC # 7029370. LC # 64-6803. (Some entries in this anthology were previously published.)

COLLABORATION. Diamonstein, Barbaralee, editor. Collaboration: Artists and Architects. New York: Whitney Library of Design, 1981. OCLC # 7172360. LC # 80-27526.

COLLARD. Collard, Jacques. 50 (i.e., Cinquante) Artistes de Belgique. Bruxelles: Louis Musin, 1976. OCLC # 3892302. LC # 78-341350.

COMPUTER. The Computer and Its Influence on Art and Design. Lincoln, Nebraska: Sheldon Memorial Art Gallery, 1983. OCLC # 11743127. (Unpaginated; artists arranged randomly.)

CONCEPT. Concept. Poughkeepsie, N.Y.: Vassar College Art Gallery, 1969. OCLC # 5294345.

CONCEPTUAL ART. Conceptual Art and Conceptual Aspects. New York: The New York Cultural Center, 1970. OCLC # 89986. LC # 70-122334.

CONRADS. Conrads, Ulrich, editor. Programs and Manifestoes on 20th-Century Architecture. Cambridge, MA.: M. I. T. Press, 1970. OCLC # 154224 & 167099 & 142041. LC # 71-143178 & 70-563039. (Entries in this anthology were previously published.)

CONTEMPORARY. Contemporary British Artists, with Photographs by Walia. New York: St. Martin's Press, 1979. OCLC # 6426644 & 5951917. LC # 80-476899 & 79-87712. (Unpaginated; artists arranged alphabetically.)

CONTEMPORARY AFRICAN. Contemporary African American Crafts. Memphis, TN: Brooks Memorial Art Gallery, n.d. OCLC # 5660788. (Unpaginated; artists arranged alphabetically.)

COOK. Cook, John Wesley. Conversations with Architects. New York: Praeger, 1973. OCLC # 842700 & 570573. LC # 74-157095 & 72-85972.

COOPER-HEWITT I. Cooper-Hewitt Museum. Urban Open Spaces. New York: Rizzoli, 1981. OCLC # 7836396 & 7503196. LC # 81-65547.

COOPER-HEWITT II. Cooper-Hewitt Museum. Cities; The Forces that Shape Them. New York: Rizzoli, 1982. OCLC # 9685398 & 9092179 & 9224494. LC # 81-51718.

CORCORAN. Corcoran Gallery of Art. Five Washington Artists.

Washington, D.C.: Corcoran Gallery of Art, 1976. OCLC # 3532786. LC # 76-42079. (Interviews conducted by Jane Livingston.)

COTT. Cott, Jonathan. Forever Young. New York: Random House, 1977. OCLC #.3205606 & 4037613. LC # 77-21488 & 77-5963.

COUNTERPOINT. California Counterpoint: New West Coast Architecture 1982. New York: Rizzoli, 1982. OCLC # 9152255. LC # 82-42533.

CRISPO I. Andrew Crispo Gallery. Twelve Americans: Masters of Collage. New York: Andrew Crispo Gallery, 1977. OCLC # 4099576. LC # 77-93025. (Unpaginated; artists arranged alphabetically. Entries were previously published.)

CRISPO II. Andrew Crispo Gallery. Ten Americans. New York: Andrew Crispo Gallery, 1974. OCLC # 980434. LC # 74-81596. (Unpaginated; artists arranged alphabetically. Entries were previously published.)

CRISS-CROSS. Criss-Cross Art Communications. Boulder, CO.: Criss-Cross Foundation, 1974-. OCLC # 4183309 & 4186498. LC # 80-1776 & 80-1777. (Numbers 1-13 indexed.)

CRONE. Crone, Rainer F. Numerals, 1924-1977. New Haven: Yale University Art Gallery, 1978. OCLC # 4183804. (Unpaginated; artists arranged alphabetically.)

CUBAN. Center for Inter-American Relations. 6 Cuban Painters Working in New York. New York: Center for Inter-American Relations, 1975. OCLC # 1960667 & 3745829. (Unpaginated; artists arranged alphabetically.)

CUMMINGS. Cummings, Paul. Artists in Their Own Words: Interviews. New York: St. Martin's Press, 1979. OCLC # 5171656. LC # 79-16474.

DADA. Dada; Francis Picabia, Clement Pansaers. Verviers: Temps Meles, 1958. OCLC # 9503063.

DANOFF. Danoff, I. Michael. Emergence and Progression; Six Contemporary American Artists. Milwaukee: The New Milwaukee Art Center, 1979. OCLC # 6014999. LC # 79-5166.

DANZIGER. Danziger, James and Barry Conradd III. Interviews with Master Photograhers. New York and London: Paddington Press, 1977. OCLC # 2614212. LC # 76-53315.

DAUGHERTY.   Daugherty, Charles M., editor.   6 Artists Paint a Portrait. Westport, CT.:   North Light Publishers, 1974.   OCLC # 1144826.   LC # 74-81928.

DAVIS.   Davis, Douglas and Allison Simmons, editors.   The New Television: A Public/Private Art.   Cambridge: M. I. T. Press, 1977.   OCLC # 3051635 & 5981330 & 3004190.   LC # 76-29198.

DE GROEN.   De Groen, Geoffrey.   Conversations with Australian Artists. Melbourne: Quartet Books, 1978.   OCLC # 5209923.   LC # 79-312901.

DEMARNE.   Demarne, Pierre.   Art, Artistes: 1947-1977, trente ans d'ecrits et conversations sur les arts plastiques contemporains.   Paris: Union Nationale des Polios de France, 1977.   OCLC # 6446954.   LC # 80-474144.

DESIGN.   Design Since 1945.   Philadelphia: Philadelphia Museum of Art, 1983.   OCLC # 9895284.   LC # 83-17414.

DIAMONSTEIN I.   Diamonstein, Barbaralee.   Inside New York's Art World. New York: Rizzoli, 1979.   OCLC # 6100160.   LC # 79-64991.

DIAMONSTEIN II.   Diamonstein, Barbaralee.   American Architecture Now. New York: Rizzoli, 1980.   OCLC # 7069560.   LC # 80-51175.

DIAMONSTEIN III.   Diamonstein, Barbaralee.   Visions and Images; American Photographers on Photography.   New York: Rizzoli, 1981.   OCLC # 8387011 & 8268481 & 8147278.   LC # 81-51236.

DIAMONSTEIN IV.   Diamonstein, Barbaralee.   Handmade in America; Conversations with Fourteen Craftmasters.   New York: Abrams, 1983. OCLC # 8709028.   LC # 82-13941.

DIAMONSTEIN V.   Diamonstein, Barbaralee.   Interior Design; The New Freedom.   New York: Rizzoli, 1982.   OCLC # 10360501 & 8590391.   LC # 82-50501.

DICCIONARIO.   Diccionario Biografica Enciclopedico de la Pintura Mexicana; Biographic Encyclopedic Dictionary of Mexican Painting.   Pintores Contemporaneos, Siglos XX (1940-1978).   Mexico: Quinientos Anos, 1979-. OCLC # 5724171.   (Bilingual—Spanish and English; volumes 1-3 indexed.)

DIRECTIONS I.   Milwaukee Art Center.   Directions 1: Options.   Milwaukee: Milwaukee Art Center, 1968.   OCLC # 38473.   LC # 72-454.

Bibliography

DOUZE ANS. Douze Ans d'Art Contemporain en France. Paris: Editions des Musees Nationaux, 1972. OCLC # 547187. LC # 72-353768.

DOUZE PEÍNTRES. 12 [i.e., Douze] Peintres et Sculpteurs Americains Contemporains. Paris: Musee National d'Art Moderne, 1953. OCLC # 7932278. (Unpaginated; artists arranged alphabetically.)

DOWNTOWN. Downtown L. A. in Santa Barbara. Santa Barbara: Santa Barbara Contemporary Arts Forum, 1980. OCLC # 8528081. (Unpaginated; artists arranged alphabetically.)

DRAWING. Drawing Distinctions; American Drawings of the Seventies. Munich: Alfred Kren, 1981. OCLC # 8437867.

DUGAN. Dugan, Thomas. Photography Between Covers; Interviews with Photo-Bookmakers. Rochester, N.Y.: Light Impresssions, 1979. OCLC # 5101830. LC # 79-9260.

DUNOYER. Dunoyer, Lise. La Peinture et Son Double; Ecrits de Peintres. Paris: Galerie Le Bateau Lavoir, 1974. OCLC # 1257941. LC # 75-500352. (Unpaginated; artists arranged chronologically by birthdate.)

EARLY WORK. Early Work by Five Contemporary Artists. New York: The New Museum, 1977. OCLC # 5002390. LC # 77-92326. (Unpaginated; artists arranged alphabetically.)

EDDY. Eddy, Arthur Jerome. Cubists and Post-Impressionists. Second edition. Chicago: A. C. McClurg and Co., 1919. OCLC # 1261635. LC # 19-19061.

EIGHT. Man, Felix H., editor. Eight European Artists. London: William Heinemann Ltd., 1954. OCLC # 689133 & 7376147 & 3308914 & 3489731 & 8822327. LC # 54-14709. (Unpaginated; artists arranged alphabetically.)

EMANUEL I. Emanuel, Muriel, editor. Contemporary Architects. New York: St. Martin's Press, 1980. OCLC # 6936100 & 6483421. LC # 81-451933 & 79-67803.

EMANUEL II. Emanuel, Muriel, et al. Contemporary Artists. Second edition. New York: St. Martin's Press, 1983. OCLC # 9154607. LC # 82-25048.

ENGLISH. English Art Today, 1960-1976. New York: Rizzoli, 1976. OCLC # 2524368 & 2333471 & 2802132 & 3701518 & 4567017. LC # 76-19195 & 76-464746.

ENVIRONMENT. The Artists' Environment: West Coast. Fort Worth, TX.: Amon Carter Museum of Western Art, 1962. OCLC # 1037843. LC # 62-20199.

EUROPE. Europe in the Seventies: Aspects of Recent Art. Chicago: Art Institute of Chicago, 1977. OCLC # 3653543. LC # 77-88802.

EVANS. Evans, Myfanwy, editor. The Painter's Object. London: Gerald Howe, Ltd., 1937. OCLC # 2942747 & 3486297. LC # 38-14581 & 73-109022.

EVENTS I. Events: Fashion Moda, Taller Boricua, Artists Invite Artists. New York: The New Museum, 1981. OCLC # 8784011. LC # 81-81184.

EVENTS II. Events: En Foco, Heresies Collective. New York: The New Museum, 1983. OCLC # 10521158. LC # 83-50565.

EXPOSICION. Exposicion Phases. Buenos Aires: Museo Nacional de Bellas Artes, 1963. (Unpaginated; artists arranged alphabetically; statements in French.)

FACE IT. Face It: 10 Contemporary Artists. Columbus, OH.: Ohio Foundation on the Arts, 1982. OCLC # 10726262 & 10006930. LC # 82-60394.

FAMOUS. Famous Artists Annual 1; A Treasury of Contemporary Art. New York: Hastings House, 1969. OCLC # 6804832 & 1568805. LC # 78-97767. (Volume 1 indexed; all published.)

FAX I. Fax, Elton C. Seventeen Black Artists. New York: Dodd, Mead and Co., 1971. OCLC # 221530. LC # 72-165671.

FAX II. Fax, Elton C. Black Artists of the New Generation. New York: Dodd, Mead and Co., 1977. OCLC # 2984385. LC # 77-7053.

FERRIS. Ferris, William. Local Color; A Sense of Place in Folk Art. New York: McGraw-Hill Book Co., 1982. OCLC # 8494407. LC # 82-10052.

FIBER. Fiber: The Artist's View. Greenvale, N.Y.: Hillwood Art Gallery, C. W. Post Center of Long Island University, 1983. OCLC # 9902196.

FIFIELD. Fifield, William. In Search of Genius. New York: William Morrow and Co., 1982. OCLC # 8532461. LC # 82-8193.

FIFTY. Fifty Contemporary American Artists. New York: Greenwich Gallery, 1957. OCLC # 4220772. LC # 57-59420. (Unpaginated; artists arranged alphabetically.)

FIGURES. Figures, Forms and Expressions. Buffalo: Buffalo Fine Arts Academy, 1981. OCLC # 8667953. LC # 81-70792.

FINCH COLLEGE. Art in Progress IV. New York: Finch College Museum of Art/Contemporary Wing, 1970. OCLC # 1992637. LC # 67-21455. (Unpaginated; artists arranged alphabetically.)

FINE. Fine, Elsa Honig. The Afro-American Artist; A Search for Identity. New York: Holt, Rinehart and Winston Inc., 1973. OCLC # 716302. LC # 73-1235. (Some entries in this source were previously published.)

FIRST AMERICAN. First American Artists' Congress. American Artists' Congress Against War and Facism. New York: 1936. OCLC # 4059354 & 1957542. LC # 37-164.

FIVE. Five from Louisiana. New Orleans: New Orleans Museum of Art, 1977 (published as ·NOMA Supplement to the Times-Picayune, January 30, 1977·). OCLC # 2982946. OCLC # 76-52639.

FORD/VIEW. Ford, Charles Henri, editor. View. New York: View Inc., 1940-1947; reprint edition, Kraus Reprints, 1969. OCLC # 1769132 & 4902694. LC # 45-31664. (Volume 1 number 1-volume 7 no.3 indexed; all published.)

FORMA. Forma, Warren. 5 British Sculptors (Work and Talk). New York: Grossman Publishers, 1964. OCLC # 514080 & 711021. LC # 64-7807.

FORTY. 40 American Painters, 1940-1950. Minneapolis: University of Minnesota, University Gallery, 1951. OCLC # 7970955 & 5071341. LC # 51-9543.

FORUM 1916. The Forum Exhibition of Modern American Painters. New York: M. Kennerly, 1916; reprint edition, New York: Arno Press, 1968. OCLC # 1170913 & 112095 & 11732717. LC # 68-9240.

FOUNDERS. Washington Women's Arts Center. The Founders. Washington, D. C.: Washington Women's Arts Center, 1980. OCLC # 7596725. LC # 80-53589.

FOX. Fox, Howard N. Metaphor; New Projects by Contemporary Sculptors.

Washington, D. C.: Smithsonian Institution Press, 1982. OCLC # 7945934. LC # 81-607122.

FRALIN. Fralin, Frances. Washington Photography: Images of the Eighties. Washington, D. C.: Corcoran Gallery of Art, 1982. OCLC # 8393466. LC # 81-71615.

FRAMPTON. Frampton, Kenneth, editor. Modern Architecture and the Critical Present. London: Architectural Design Profile, 1982. OCLC # 9205221. LC # 83-109219.

FRASCINA. Frascina, Francis and Charles Harrison, editors. Modern Art and Modernism: A Critical Anthology. New York: Harper and Row Publishers, 1982. OCLC # 8846178. LC # 82-48153. (All entries in this anthology were previously published.)

FRASNAY. Frasnay, Daniel. The Artist's World. New York: Viking Press, 1969. OCLC # 50974. LC # 69-10630.

FRIEDENTHAL. Friedenthal, Richard. Letters of the Great Artists. Volume 2: from Blake to Pollock. New York: Random House, 1963. OCLC # 507728. LC # 63-14981. (All entries in this anthology were previously published.)

FRY. Fry, Edward F. Cubism. New York: McGraw-Hill Book Co., 1966. OCLC # 3842633 & 954226 & 295043. LC # 66-24888 & 78-7541 & 67-71328.

FRYM. Frym, Gloria. Second Stories: Conversations with Women Whose Artistic Careers Began After Thirty-five. San Francisco: Chronicle Books, 1979. OCLC # 5196957. LC # 79-9390.

FUGITIVE. Fugitive Color; A National Invitational Show of Color Photography. Ann Arbor: School of Art, University of Michigan, 1982. OCLC # 11289824 & 8436322. LC # 83-233068. (Unpaginated; artists arranged alphabetically.)

FULBRIGHT. Fulbright Painters. Washington, D. C.: Smithsonian Institution, 1958; New York: Institute of International Education, 1958. OCLC # 3226790. LC # 59-535.

GA DOCUMENT. GA [Global Architecture] Document. Tokyo: A.D.A. EDITA Tokyo Co., Ltd., 1980-. OCLC # 7982779 & 7099622. LC # 83-4082 & 81-6042. (Numbers 1-7 indexed; texts in English and Japanese.)

GA HOUSES. <u>GA</u> [Global Architecture] <u>Houses.</u> Tokyo: A.D.A. EDITA Tokyo Co., Ltd., 1976-. OCLC # 3514959. LC # 77-373487. (Volumes 1-14 indexed.)

GALLERY STUDIES I. <u>Gallery Studies I.</u> Buffalo: Buffalo Fine Arts Academy, 1977. OCLC # 3798494 & 5629653. LC # 77-23725.

GASSNER. Gassner, John and Sidney Thomas, editors. <u>The Nature of Art.</u> New York: Crown Publishers, Inc., 1964. OCLC # 350777. LC # 63-21126.

GEOMETRIC. <u>Geometric Art: An Exhibition of Paintings and Constructions by Fourteen Contemporary New Jersey Artists.</u> Trenton: The New Jersey State Museum, 1967. OCLC # 72335. LC # 68-63639. (Unpaginated; artists arranged alphabetically.)

GEORGIA. <u>Open to New Ideas; A Collection of New Art for Jimmy Carter.</u> <u>Georgia Museum of Art Bulletin,</u> volume 2 number 3 & volume 3 numbers 1-3, 1976-1977.

GIEDION-WELCKER. Giedion-Welcker, Carola. <u>Poetes a l'Ecart; Anthologie der Abseitigen.</u> Bern: Verlag Bentelli, 1946. OCLC # 6361354. LC # 48-3154. (All poems in this anthology were previously published.)

GLASS. <u>New American Glass: Focus West Virginia.</u> Huntington, W.V.: Huntington Galleries, 1976. OCLC # 2507789. LC # 76-20377 (volume 1) & 77-76747 (volume 5). (Volumes 1 & 5 indexed; volume 5 is unpaginated.)

GOLDAINE. Goldaine, Louis and Pierre Astier. <u>Ces Peintres Vous Parlent.</u> Paris: Les Editions du Temps, 1964. OCLC # 11527150. LC # 67-46410.

GOLDWATER. Goldwater, Robert and Marco Treves, editors. <u>Artists on Art, From the XIV to the XX Century.</u> New York: Pantheon Books, 1945 & 1974. OCLC # 878312 & 3150052. LC # 50-2433 & 74-176211. (Entries in this anthology were previously published; some entries translated into English for the first time.)

GOODMAN. Goodman, Lisl Marburg. <u>Death and the Creative Life; Conversations with Prominent Artists and Scientists.</u> New York: Springer Publishing Co., 1981. OCLC # 8764834 & 7282815 & 7716597. LC # 81-1045 & 82-16617.

GOODRICH. Goodrich, Lloyd and John I. H. Baur. <u>Four American Expressionists.</u> New York: Praeger, 1959. OCLC # 1101287 & 510489. LC # 59-7363.

GOODYEAR. Goodyear, Frank H. <u>Seven</u> <u>on</u> <u>the</u> <u>Figure.</u> Philadelphia: Pennsylvania Academy of the Fine Arts, 1979. OCLC # 5940834. LC # 79-90199.

GRAHAM. Graham, Mayo. <u>Some</u> <u>Canadian</u> <u>Women</u> <u>Artists.</u> Ottawa: National Gallery of Canada, 1975. OCLC # 2315847. LC # 76-379326. (Statements in English and French.)

GRAY. Gray, Camilla. <u>The</u> <u>Great</u> <u>Experiment;</u> <u>Russian</u> <u>Art</u> <u>1863-1922.</u> New York: Abrams, 1962. OCLC # 511799. LC # 62-14462.

GRAYSON. Grayson, John, editor. <u>Sound</u> <u>Sculpture;</u> <u>A</u> <u>Collection</u> <u>of</u> <u>Essays</u> <u>by</u> <u>Artists</u> <u>Surveying</u> <u>the</u> <u>Technique;</u> <u>Applications;</u> <u>and</u> <u>Future</u> <u>Directions</u> <u>of</u> <u>Sound</u> <u>Sculpture.</u> Vancouver, B. C.: A.R.C. Publications, 1975. OCLC # 2082885. LC # 77-373278.

GREENHALGH. Greenhalgh, Michael and Vincent Megaw, editors. <u>Art</u> <u>in</u> <u>Society;</u> <u>Studies</u> <u>in</u> <u>Style,</u> <u>Culture</u> <u>and</u> <u>Aesthetics.</u> New York: St. Martin's Press, 1978. OCLC # 4766069. LC # 78-69954.

GRENIER. Grenier, Jean. <u>Entretiens</u> <u>avec</u> <u>dix-sept</u> <u>peintres</u> <u>non-figuratifs.</u> Paris: Calmann-Levy, 1963. OCLC # 3624020. LC # 63-47449.

GROH. Groh, Klaus, editor. <u>If</u> <u>I</u> <u>had</u> <u>a</u> <u>Mind...</u> <u>(ich</u> <u>stelle</u> <u>mir</u> <u>vor...),</u> <u>Concept-Art</u> <u>Project-Art.</u> Koln: Verlag Dumont Schauberg, 1971. OCLC # 273640. LC # 75-586742. (Unpaginated; artists arranged alphabetically.)

GROHMANN. Grohmann, Will. <u>Bildende</u> <u>Kunst</u> <u>und</u> <u>Architektur.</u> Berlin: Suhrkamp Verlag, 1953. OCLC # 4810401. LC # 54-786. (Most entries in this anthology were previously published.)

GROTE. Grote, Ludwig. <u>Deutsche</u> <u>Kunst</u> <u>im</u> <u>Zwanzigsten</u> <u>Jahrhundert.</u> Munchen: Prestel Verlag, 1953. OCLC # 7808460 & 849705. LC # 54-1182.

GRUEN. Gruen, John. <u>Close-Up.</u> New York: Viking Press, 1968. OCLC # 1137815. LC # 67-26916.

GUENTHER. Guenther, Bruce. <u>50</u> <u>Northwest</u> <u>Artists.</u> San Francsico: Chronicle Books, 1983. OCLC # 9621825. LC # 83-10159.

GUGGENHEIM I. <u>Guggenheim</u> <u>International</u> <u>Award</u> <u>1964.</u> New York: The Solomon R. Guggenheim Foundation, 1963. OCLC # 847634. LC # 63-14482.

GUGGENHEIM II. Guggenheim, Peggy, editor. <u>Art of this Century.</u> New York: Art of this Century, 1942. OCLC # 1075452. LC # 42-17126. (Some entries in this source were previously published.)

GUITAR. Guitar, Mary Anne. <u>22 Famous Painters and Illustrators Tell How They Work.</u> New York: David McKay Co., 1964. OCLC #510667. LC # 63-19334.

GUMPERT I. Gumpert, Lynn and Ned Rifkin. <u>Persona.</u> New York: The New Museum, 1981. OCLC # 8962257. LC # 81-81190.

GUMPERT II. Gumpert, Lynn and Ned Rifkin. <u>New Work New York.</u> New York: The New Museum, 1982. OCLC # 9988872. LC # 81-81188.

GUMPERT III. Gumpert, Lynn. <u>The End of the World; Contemporary Visions of the Apocalypse.</u> New York: The New Museum, 1983. OCLC # 10521176. LC # 83-43253.

GUMPERT IV. Gumpert, Lynn and Allan Schwartzman. <u>Investigations: Probe Structure Analysis.</u> New York: The New Museum, 1980. OCLC # 7359956. LC # 80-8341.

GUSSOW. Gussow, Alan. <u>A Sense of Place; The Artist and the American Land.</u> New York: Seabury Press, 1972. OCLC # 287058. LC # 79-154250.

HAAR I. Haar, Francis and Prithwish Neogy. <u>Artists of Hawaii; Volume One, Nineteen Painters and Sculptors.</u> Honolulu: The State Foundation on Culture and the Arts, and the University Press of Hawaii, 1974. OCLC # 1185874. LC # 74-78861.

HAAR II. Haar, Francis. <u>Artists of Hawaii; Volume Two.</u> Honolulu: The State Foundation on Culture and the Arts, and the University Press of Hawaii, 1977. OCLC # 1185874. LC # 74-78861.

HALLWALLS. <u>Hallwalls: Five Years.</u> New York: The New Museum, 1980. OCLC # 11225501. (Unpaginated.)

HAND COLORED. <u>The Hand Colored Photograph.</u> Philadelphia: Philadelphia College of Art, 1979. OCLC # 5068182 & 5263638. LC # 79-87708.

HAUSSER. Hausser, Robert. <u>Kunst, Landschaft, Architektur.</u> Bad Neuenahr-Ahrweiler: Ahrtal-Verlag, 1983. OCLC # 11043624. LC #83-237803.

HAYSTACK. Art in Craft Media; The Haystack Tradition. Brunswick, ME.: Bowdoin College Museum of Art, 1981. OCLC # 7399844. LC # 81-65685.

HAYWARD. Hayward Gallery, London. Hayward Annual. London: Arts Council of Great Britain, 1977-. OCLC # 3794641. LC # 80-646607. (Volumes for 1978 and 1979 indexed.)

HERMAN. Herman, Lloyd E. American Porcelain: New Expressions in an Ancient Art. Forest Grove, OR.: Timber Press, 1980. OCLC # 7048805. LC # 81-124691.

HESS. Hess, Thomas B. and Elizabeth C. Baker, editors. Art and Sexual Politics. New York: Macmillan, 1971. OCLC # 2182038 & 677065. LC # 72-85182. (Some entries in this source were previously published.)

HEYER. Heyer, Paul. Architects on Architecture. New York: Walker and Co., 1966. OCLC # 914138 & 41632 & 3715279. LC # 76-355733 & 66-22504.

HIGHRISE. Highrise of Homes. New York: Rizzoli, 1982. OCLC # 9001144 & 9556121. LC # 82-50645.

HILL. Hill, Paul and Thomas Cooper. Dialogue with Photography. New York: Farrar, Straus, and Giroux, 1979. OCLC # 4492971. LC # 78-25851. (Entries in this source were previously published.)

HODIN. Hodin, Josef Paul. Modern Art and the Modern Mind. Cleveland and London: The Press of Case Western Reserve University, 1972. OCLC # 357417. LC # 75-81831.

HOPKINS. Hopkins, Henry. 50 West Coast Artists. San Francisco: Chronicle Books, 1981. OCLC # 7732666. LC # 81-12269.

HOUSE. The House that Art Built. Fullerton, CA.: Visual Arts Center, California State University, Fullerton, 1983. OCLC # 11361394. LC # 83-72931.

HOUSTON. Contemporary Arts Museum, Houston. 4 Painters. Houston: Contemporary Arts Center, 1981. OCLC # 9115943. LC # 81-69447.

HOW FAMOUS. How Famous Photographers Work. New York: Amphoto, 1983. OCLC # 9371238. LC # 82-63163.

HOWARD. Howard, David. Perspectives. San Francisco: The San Francisco

Center for Visual Arts, 1978. OCLC # 136631. LC # 77-90787. (Unpaginated; interviews arranged randomly.)

HUGHES. Hughes, Sukey. Washi; The World of Japanese Paper. Tokyo: Kodansha International, 1978. OCLC # 11061858 & 4889396 & 4003748. LC # 77-74831.

HUMAN. The Human Clay. London: Arts Council of Great Britain, 1976. OCLC # 3071308. LC # 77-361148. (Unpaginated.)

HUNTER. Hunter, Sam, editor. Monumenta; A Biennial Exhibition of Outdoor Sculpture, Newport, Rhode Island, 1974. Newport: Monumenta Newport Inc., 1974. OCLC # 1093376. LC # 74-14395.

IDENTITE. Identite-Identifications. Bordeaux: Centre d'Arts Plastique Contemporains, 1976. OCLC # 4438649. LC # 78-376115.

ILLINOIS. University of Illinois, College of Fine and Applied Arts. University of Illinois Exhibition of Contemporary American Painting. (Title varies.) Urbana: University of Illinois, 1948-1974. OCLC # 1714608. LC # 48-340. (Volumes for the following years indexed: 1948, 1949 (unpaginated), 1950, 1951, 1952, 1953, 1955, 1957, 1959, 1961, 1963, 1965, 1967, 1969, 1974, all published.)

ILLUSTRATION. Society of Illustrators. Illustration in the Third Dimension; The Artist Turned Craftsman. New York: Hastings House Publishers, 1978. OCLC # 2964955. LC # 77-7316.

IMAGE COLOR FORM. Image, Color and Form; Recent Paintings by Eleven Americans. Toledo: Toledo Museum of Art, 1975. OCLC # 1256121. LC # 74-31742.

IMAGES. Images of the 70's: 9 Washington Artists. Washington, D.C.: Corcoran Gallery of Art, 1979. OCLC # 6806198. LC # 79-91187.

IN A PICTORIAL. In a Pictorial Framework. New York: The New Museum, 1979. OCLC # 6365967. LC # 79-89195.

IN SITU. In Situ; 12 Artistes pour les Galeries Contemporaines. Paris: Centre Georges Pompidou, 1982. OCLC # 9468938. LC # 82-166719.

INTERVIEWS. Interviews with Women in the Arts. Part 2. New York: Women in the Arts Publication, The School of Visual Arts, 1976.

IRVINE. University of California, Irvine, 1965-1975. La Jolla, CA.: La Jolla Museum of Contemporary Art, 1975. OCLC # 2005462. LC # 75-37097.

ISSUE. Issue; Social Strategies by Women Artists. London: Institute of Contemporary Arts, 1980. OCLC # 10548419. LC # 83-103093. (Unpaginated.)

IT IS. It Is; A Magazine of Abstract Art. New York: Second Half Publishing Co., 1958-1965. OCLC # 1754047. (Numbers 1-6 indexed; all published.)

JANIS I. Janis, Sidney. Abstract and Surrealist Art in America. New York: Reynal and Hitchcock, 1944. OCLC # 1183922. LC # 44-51180.

JANIS II. Janis, Sidney. They Taught Themselves; American Primitive Painters of the Twentieth Century. New York: The Dial Press, 1942. OCLC # 1064435. LC # 42-36065.

JEAN. Jean, Marcel, editor. The Autobiography of Surrealism. The Documents of 20th-Century Art. New York: Viking Press, 1980. OCLC # 2523403. LC # 76-46637. (Entries in this anthology were previously published.)

JOHNSON. Johnson, Ellen H., editor. American Artists on Art, from 1940 to 1980. New York: Harper and Row, 1982. OCLC # 7460461. LC # 80-8702. (Most entries in this anthology were previously published.)

JOURNAL OF THE AAA. Journal of the Archives of American Art. Detroit: Archives of American Art, 1960-. OCLC # 2239423 & 1780073. LC # 73-903 & 80-365. (Volumes 1-10 indexed.)

KARDON. Kardon, Janet. Photography: A Sense of Order. Philadelphia: Institute of Contemporary Art, University of Pennsylvania, 1981. OCLC # 8376034. LC # 81-85346.

KATZ. Katz, Jane. Artists in Exile. New York: Stein and Day, 1983. OCLC # 8667274. LC # 81-48457.

KEPES I. Kepes, Gyorgy, editor. Sign, Image, Symbol. New York: George Braziller, 1965. OCLC # 649780 & 954808. LC # 66-13045 & 67-78662.

KEPES II. Kepes, Gyorgy, editor. Arts of the Environment. New York: George Braziller, 1972. OCLC # 723269 & 495529. LC # 72-161569 & 73-169203.

KEPES III. Kepes, Gyorgy, editor. The Man-Made Object. New York: George Braziller, 1966. OCLC # 652233 & 7747504. LC # 66-13046.

KEPES IV. Kepes, Gyorgy, editor. Module, Proportion, Symmetry, Rhythm. New York: George Braziller, 1966. OCLC # 541945 & 886050. LC # 66-13044.

KEPES V. Kepes, Gyorgy, editor. The New Landscape in Art and Science. Chicago: Paul Theobald and Co., 1956. OCLC # 507258. LC # 57-576.

KEPES VI. Kepes, Gyorgy, editor. Structure in Art and Science. New York: George Braziller, 1965. OCLC # 529250 & 8610655. LC # 65-10807.

KEPES VII. Kepes, Gyorgy, editor. The Nature and Art of Motion. New York: George Braziller, 1965. OCLC # 665722. LC # 65-5600.

KEPES VIII. Kepes, Gyorgy, editor. Education of Vision. New York: George Braziller, 1965. OCLC # 692823. LC # 65-5601.

KEPES IX. Kepes, Gyorgy, editor. The Visual Arts Today. Middletown, CT.: Wesleyan University Press, 1960. OCLC # 1345957 & 204139. LC # 60-13159.

KERBER. Kerber, Bernhard. Amerikanische Kunst seit 1945. Stuttgart: Philipp Reclam jun., 1971. OCLC # 1188106. LC # 72-300695.

KINETIC. Selz, Peter. Directions in Kinetic Sculpture. Berkeley, CA.: University of California, Berkeley, 1966. OCLC # 1862554. LC # 66-63482.

KINETISCHE. Kinetische Kunst. Zurich: Kunstgewerbemuseum Zurich, 1960. OCLC # 4323913. (Unpaginated; artists arranged alphabetically.)

KIRBY. Kirby, Michael. Happenings; an Illustrated Anthology. New York: E. P. Dutton, 1965. OCLC # 965399 & 332943. LC # 65-16289.

KNOWLES. Knowles, Roderic, editor. Contemporary Irish Art. New York: St. Martin's Press, 1982. OCLC # 9557198. LC # 83-10619.

KNOXVILLE. Knoxville Artists. Knoxville, TN., 1960. OCLC # 4682537. LC # 60-64167. (Unpaginated; artists arranged alphabetically.)

KONZEPT. Konzept--Kunst. Basel: Kunstmuseum Basel, 1972. OCLC # 2987512. LC # 72-362292. (Unpaginated; artists arranged alphabetically.)

KORNFELD. Kornfeld, Lisbet. 23 (i.e., dreiundzwanzig) Atelierbesuche. Bern: L. Kornfeld, 1973. OCLC # 6303666. LC # 79-396127.

KRESGE. Kresge Art Gallery, Michigan State University, East Lansing, Michigan. Eighth Michigan Biennial. East Lansing, Ml.: Kresge Art Gallery, 1983. OCLC # 11477299. (Unpaginated; artists arranged alphabetically.)

KUFRIN. Kufrin, Joan. Uncommon Women. Piscataway, N.J.: New Century Publishers, 1981. OCLC # 7597231. LC # 81-11097.

KUH. Kuh, Katharine. The Artist's Voice; Talks with Seventeen Artists. New York: Harper and Row, 1962. OCLC # 510888 & 837875 & 710851. LC # 62-9893.

KUNG. Kung, David. The Contemporary Artist in Japan. Honolulu: The East-West Center Press, 1966. OCLC # 458670 & 1187155. LC # 68-82314 & 66-31499.

KUNST BLEIBT KUNST. Kunst bleibt Kunst. Katalog + Dokumentation. Koln: Kunsthalle, 1974. OCLC # 7274396 & 1545367. LC # 75-544252. (Statements in English and German except where noted.)

KUNST UND POLITIK. Kunst und Politik. Basel: Kunsthalle, 1970. OCLC # 4974791. LC # 71-577622. (Unpaginated; artists arranged alphabetically.)

LA JOLLA. The California Condition; A Pregnant Architecture. La Jolla, CA.: La Jolla Museum of Contemporary Art, 1982. OCLC # 9266900. LC # 82-83257.

LAPLANTE. La Plante, Jerry C. Photographers on Photography. New York: Sterling Publishing Co., 1979. OCLC # 4004805. LC # 78-7063.

LEAVITT. Leavitt, Thomas W. Painting Up Front. Ithaca, N.Y.: Herbert F. Johnson Museum of Art, Cornell University, 1981. OCLC # 7725107. LC # 81-80250. (Unpaginated; artists arranged alphabetically.)

LEEKELY. Leekley, Sheryle and John Leekley. Moments: The Pulitzer Prize Photographs. Updated edition: 1942-1982. New York: Crown Publishers, 1982. OCLC # 8846083. LC # 82-18252.

LEITE. Leite, George and Bern Porter, editors. Circle. 1944-1948. Reprint edition, New York: Arno Press, 1974. OCLC # 4188172 & 1554743. LC # 49-20741 & 74-646211. (Numbers 1-10 indexed, all published.)

LETTERS. Moore, Ethel, editor. Letters from 31 Artists to the Albright-Knox Art Gallery. Buffalo: Buffalo Fine Arts Academy, 1970. OCLC # 1868252. (Issued as: Gallery Notes, vol. XXXI no. 2 & vol. XXXII no. 2.)

LEWIS I & LEWIS II. Lewis, Samella S. and Ruth G. Waddy. Black Artists on Art. 2 volumes. Los Angeles: Contemporary Crafts Publishers, 1969, 1971. OCLC # 1231174 & 48813. LC # 76-97788.

LEWIS I REVISED. Lewis, Samella S. and Ruth G. Waddy. Black Artists on Art. Revised edition of volume 1. Los Angeles: Contemporary Crafts Publishers, 1976. OCLC # 2644712. LC # 76-150523.

LHOTE. Lhote, Andre. De la Palette a l'Ecritoire. Paris: Editions Correa, 1946. OCLC # 6427702. LC # 47-28355.

LIBERMAN. Liberman, Alexander. The Artist in His Studio. New York: Viking Press, 1960. OCLC # 513585. LC # 60-13244.

LICHT. Licht, Jennifer. Eight Contemporary Artists. New York: Museum of Modern Art, 1974. OCLC # 1551161. LC # 74-84690.

LIFE. Life Experiences in Environmental Design. Washington, D. C.: Association of Collegiate Schools of Architecture, 1975. OCLC # 1341768. LC # 75-308766.

LIGHT. Tucker, Jean S. Light Abstractions. St. Louis, MO.: University of Missouri--St. Louis, 1980. OCLC # 6433638. LC # 80-65032.

LIPPARD. Lippard, Lucy R., editor. Surrealists on Art. Englewood Cliffs, N.J.: Prentice-Hall, Inc., 1970. OCLC # 98274. LC # 78-104858. (Selections in this anthology are translated by the editor for the first time unless otherwise noted.)

LIVE. Live, Performance Art Magazine. New York: Performing Arts Journal Publications, 1980-. OCLC # 6729317. LC # 82-22134. (Numbers 3 through 6/7 indexed; continues Performance Art Magazine.)

LOCATION. Location. New York: Longview Foundation Inc., 1963-1964. OCLC # 3360128. (v.1 no.1, Spring 1963, and v.1 no.2, Summer 1964 indexed.)

LOGAN I. Logan, Susan and Allan Schwartzman and Kathleen Thomas. Dimensions Variable. New York: The New Museum, 1979. OCLC # 6231935. LC # 79-90825.

LOGAN II. Logan, Susan and Allan Schwartzman. New Work/New York. New York: The New Museum, 1980. OCLC # 11225508. LC # 79-92412.

LONDON BULLETIN. London Bulletin. London: The London Gallery, 1938-1940; reprint edition, New York: Arno Press, 1969. OCLC # 1645781 & 8878043 & 2917203 & 4512642. LC # 77-96917. (Numbers 1-20 indexed, all published.)

LONDON COUNTY. Sculpture 1850-1950. London: London County Council, 1957. OCLC # 2904259. (Unpaginated; artists arranged alphabetically.)

LUMIERE. Lumiere et Mouvement. Paris: Musee d'Art Moderne de la Ville de Paris, 1967. OCLC # 2723357. (Unpaginated; artists arranged alphabetically.)

M. H. DE YOUNG. M. H. de Young Memorial Museum. Meet the Artist. San Francisco: M. H. de Young Memorial Museum, 1943. OCLC # 1018394. LC # 44-1509.

MADE FOR BUFFALO. Made for Buffalo. Buffalo: Albright-Knox Art Gallery, 1980. OCLC # 9477724. (Unpaginated pamphlet/poster.)

MAGIC. Society of Illustrators Library of American Illustrations. Magic and Other Realism; The Art of Illusion. New York: Hastings House, 1980. OCLC # 5239678. LC # 79-18013.

MARAINI. Maraini, Dacia. E Tu Chi Eri? Milano: Bompiani, 1973. OCLC # 1215893. LC # 75-569433.

MARSHALL. Marshall, Richard. New Image Painting. New York: Whitney Museum of American Art, 1978. OCLC # 4136011. LC # 78-13760.

MAYWALD. Maywald, Wilhelm. Portrait + Atelier. Zurich: Verlags AG "Die Arche," 1958. OCLC # 3353920 & 895491. LC # 60-10050. (Unpaginated; artists arranged randomly.)

MCCAUSLAND. McCausland, Elizabeth, editor. Work for Artists; What? Where? How? New York: American Artists Group, Inc., 1947. OCLC # 732650. LC # 47-5013.

MCCLINTIC. McClintic, Miranda. Directions 1981. Washington, D. C.: Smithsonian Institution, 1981. OCLC # 7318032. LC # 81-601576.

MCCOUBREY. McCoubrey, John W. American Art 1700-1960, Sources and

Documents. Englewood Cliffs, N.J.: Prentice-Hall, 1965. OCLC # 503223. LC # 65-23063. (All entries in this anthology were previously published.)

MEILACH. Meilach, Dona Z. Woodworking; The New Wave. New York: Crown Publishers, 1981. OCLC # 7248565. LC # 81-190.

MEISEL. Meisel, Louis K. Photo-Realism. New York: Abrams, 1980. OCLC # 4495935. LC # 78-10768.

METALWORKS. Metalworks Invitational. Muncie, IN.: Ball State University Art Gallery, 1979. (Unpaginated; artists arranged alphabetically.)

MEYER. Meyer, Ursula. Conceptual Art. New York: E. P. Dutton, 1972. OCLC # 489115. LC # 72-195118. (Some entries in this anthology were previously published.)

MICHIGAN. Michigan Artists 80-81. Detroit: Detroit Institute of Arts, 1982. OCLC # 10204816.

MIESEL. Miesel, Victor, editor. Voices of German Expressionism. Englewood Cliffs, N. J.: Prentice-Hall, Inc., 1970. OCLC # 57504. LC # 71-90968. (Selections indexed from this source have been translated from German publications by the editor except where noted.)

MIKELLIDES. Mikellides, Byron, editor. Architecture for People; Explorations in a New Humane Environment. New York: Holt, Rinehart, and Winston, 1980. OCLC # 6691965 & 6674977. LC # 79-48067.

MILLER. Miller, Lynn F. and Sally S. Swenson. Lives and Works; Talks with Women Artists. Metuchen, N. J.: The Scarecrow Press, Inc., 1981. OCLC # 7576158. LC # 81-9043.

MILLER 1942. Miller, Dorothy C., editor. Americans, 1942; 18 Artists from 9 States. New York: Museum of Modern Art, 1942. OCLC # 918551. LC # 42-36115.

MILLER 1943. Miller, Dorothy C. and Alfred H. Barr, editors. American Realists and Magic Realists. New York: Museum of Modern Art, 1943. OCLC # 1540548 & 86050. LC # 48-40268.

MILLER 1946. Miller, Dorothy C., editor. Fourteen Americans. New York: Museum of Modern Art, 1946. OCLC # 1134755 & 845556. LC # 47-1397.

MILLER 1952. Miller, Dorothy C., editor. 15 Americans. New York: Museum of Modern Art, 1952. OCLC # 847704. LC # 52-2347.

Bibliography

MILLER 1956. Miller, Dorothy C., editor. <u>12 Americans.</u> New York: Museum of Modern Art, 1956. OCLC # 510514. 56-3810.

MILLER 1959. Miller, Dorothy C., editor. <u>Sixteen Americans.</u> New York: Museum of Modern Art, 1959. OCLC # 543761 & 510515. LC # 59-15966.

MILLER 1963. Miller, Dorothy C., editor. <u>Americans 1963.</u> New York: Museum of Modern Art, 1963. OCLC # 1036693. LC # 63-17994.

MINOTAURE. <u>Minotaure.</u> Paris: A. Skira, 1933-1939; reprint edition, New York: Arno Press, 1968. OCLC # 7437761 & 7927141 & 3691844. LC # 68-9227 & 70-232906 & 82-641292. (Numbers 1-13 indexed, all published.)

MISE EN SCENE. <u>Mise en Scene.</u> Vancouver: Vancouver Art Gallery, 1982. OCLC # 10006764. LC # 82-218087.

MITCHELL. Mitchell, Margaretta K. <u>Recollections; Ten Women of Photography.</u> New York: Viking Press, 1979. OCLC # 5007272. LC # 79-13980.

MOMA 1959. <u>The New American Painting; as Shown in Eight European Countries, 1958-1959.</u> New York: Museum of Modern Art, 1959. OCLC # 1280867 & 2720866 & 3425038. LC # 59-2812.

MORRIS. Morris, Jack A., Jr. <u>Contemporary Artists of South Carolina.</u> Greenville, S.C.: Greenville County Museum of Art, 1970. OCLC # 149357. LC # 70-94681.

MOTHERWELL. Motherwell, Robert and Ad Reinhardt, editors. <u>Modern Artists in America.</u> First Series. New York: Wittenborn Schultz, Inc., 1951. OCLC # 2159804. LC # 52-2111.

MULLER. Muller, Gregoire. <u>The New Avant-Garde; Issues for the Art of the Seventies.</u> New York: Praeger Publishers, 1972. OCLC # 539061. LC # 72-166514.

MUNRO. Munro, Eleanor. <u>Originals; American Women Artists.</u> New York: Simon and Schuster, 1979. OCLC # 4569966. LC # 78-31814.

MURS. <u>Murs.</u> Paris: Centre Georges Pompidou, 1981/82. OCLC # 9438125.

MYLAR. <u>The Mylar Method Manifesto.</u> Grafton, Vermont: Atelier North Star, 1979. OCLC # 7286380.

NAYLOR. Naylor, Colin and Genesis P-Orridge, editors. <u>Contemporary</u> <u>Artists.</u> New York: St. Martin's Press, 1977. OCLC # 3511363. LC # 76-54627.

NELSON. Nelson, James. <u>Wisdom; Conversations with the Elder Wise Men of Our Day.</u> New York: W. W. Norton and Co., 1958. OCLC # 366183. LC # 58-11109.

NEMSER. Nemser, Cindy. <u>Arttalk; Conversations with 12 Women Artists.</u> New York: Charles Scribner's Sons, 1975. OCLC # 948137. LC # 74-11302.

NEW DECADE. <u>The New Decade; 35 American Painters and Sculptors.</u> New York: Whitney Museum of American Art, 1955. OCLC # 2625837 & 529361. LC # 55-3046.

NEW DECORATIVE. <u>New Decorative Works from the Collection of Norma and William Roth.</u> Orlando, FL.: Loch Haven Art Center, 1983. OCLC # 10572483.

NEW VISIONS. <u>New Visions.</u> Amarillo, TX.: Amarillo Art Center, 1981. OCLC # 10644449. (Unpaginated; portfolio of loose pamphlets on each artist.)

NEWMAN. Newman, Oscar. <u>New Frontiers in Architecture; CIAM '59 in Otterlo.</u> New York: Universe Books, Inc., 1961. OCLC # 2161654. LC # 61-14470.

NORTH LIGHT. <u>The North Light Collection; The Views, Beliefs, and Working Methods of 49 Prominent Artists.</u> Westport, CT.: Fletcher Art Services, Inc., 1972. OCLC # 827688. LC # 72-76379.

NORTH P. North, Percy. <u>Abstractions from the Phillips Collection.</u> Fairfax, VA.: George Mason University, 1983. OCLC # 10008972. LC # 83-82427. (Unpaginated; artists arranged alphabetically.)

NOSANOW I. Nosanow, Barbara Shissler. <u>More than Land or Sky; Art from Appalachia.</u> Washington, D.C.: Smithsonian Institution Press, 1981. OCLC # 7741600. LC # 81-13566.

NOSANOW II. Nosanow, Barbara Shissler. <u>Sawtooths and Other Ranges of Imagination: Contemporary Art from Idaho.</u> Washington, D.C.: Smithsonian Institution Press, 1983. OCLC # 9919048. LC # 83-16889.

O'HARA. O'Hara, Frank. <u>Art Chronicles, 1954-1966.</u> New York: Braziller, 1975. OCLC # 1426123 & 1176133. LC # 74-77526.

OK ART. <u>OK Art; Artists from Ohio and Kentucky.</u> Cincinnati, OH.: The Contemporary Arts Center, 1975. OCLC # 3837252. (Unpaginated; artists arranged randomly.)

O'KANE. O'Kane Gallery, University of Houston Downtown College. <u>Impressions of Houston.</u> Houston: O'Kane Gallery, University of Houston Downtown College, 1981?. OCLC # 10394204. (Unpaginated; artists arranged alphabetically.) OCLC # 10394204.

ON SITE. <u>On Site.</u> New York: Site, Inc., 1972-. (Numbers 1-6 indexed; number 1 unpaginated.)

100 CONTEMPORARY. <u>100 Contemporary American Jewish Painters and Sculptors.</u> New York: YKUF Art Section, 1947. OCLC # 6366983. LC # 51-21530. (Statements in English and Hebrew.)

OPEN AIR. <u>Sculpture in the Open Air.</u> London: London County Council, 1954, 1960. OCLC # 3929386 (1954) & 465142 (1960). LC # 68-125357 (1960). (Unpaginated; artists arranged alphabetically.)

OUTSIDE I. <u>Outside New York.</u> New York: The New Museum, 1978. OCLC # 5344474. LC # 78-64750.

OUTSIDE II. <u>Outside New York: The State of Ohio.</u> New York: The New Museum, 1980. OCLC # 6960754. LC # 80-81411.

PAINTING. <u>Painting in Post-War Italy, 1945-1957.</u> New York: The Casa Italiana of Columbia University, 1957. OCLC # 1608630. (Unpaginated; artists arranged randomly; numbers cited are catalog entry numbers.)

PAOLETTI. Paoletti, John T., editor. <u>No Title.</u> Middletown, CT.: Wesleyan Universiy, 1981. OCLC # 8079176.

PAPERWORKS. <u>Paperworks: An Exhibition of Texas Artists.</u> San Antonio, TX.: San Antonio Museum Association, 1979. OCLC # 5678432. LC # 79-66426. (Statements in English and Spanish.)

PARACHUTE. <u>Parachute.</u> Montreal, Canada: Artdata Enr., 1975-. OCLC # 2851563 & 3348789. LC # 77-30069. (Numbers 1-11 indexed; entries in French unless otherwise specified.)

PERFORMANCE. Performance Art Magazine. New York: Performing Arts Journal, Inc., 1979. OCLC # 5313869. LC # 82-22133. (Numbers 1-2 indexed; all published; continued by Live, q.v.)

PERSONAL. Personal Statement, Painting Prophecy, 1950. Washington, D.C.: David Porter Gallery, 1945. OCLC # 8054490. LC # 45-5270. (Unpaginated; artists arranged randomly.)

PHELPS. Phelps, Robert, editor. Twentieth-Century Culture; The Breaking Up. New York: George Braziller, 1965. OCLC # 2360244 & 832595. LC # 65-23182.

PHILLPOT. Phillpot, Clive. Artists' Books; From the Traditional to the Avant-Garde. New Brunswick, N.J.: Archibald Stevens Alexander Library, Rutgers University, 1982. OCLC # 8788397. (Unpaginated; artists arranged alphabetically.)

PHOTOGRAPHY. Photography Here and Now; 15 Artists from the Washington-Baltimore Area. College Park, MD.: University of Maryland, Department of Art, 1972. OCLC # 2284333. LC # 76-362195. (Unpaginated; artists arranged alphabetically.)

PLASTIQUE. Plastique. Paris, New York: 1937-1939; reprint edition, New York: Arno Press, 1969. OCLC # 8288310 & 2156142 & 5660092. LC # 74-91379. (Numbers 1-5 indexed, all published.)

PLATSCHEK. Platschek, Hans. Dichtung Moderner Kunst. Wiesbaden: Limes Verlag, 1956. OCLC # 6466982. LC # 57-4286. (Entries in this source were previously published.)

POENSGEN. Poensgen, Georg and Leopold Zahn. Abstrakte Kunst iene Weltsprache. Baden-Baden: Woldemar Klein Verlag, 1958. OCLC # 1029853. LC # 59-2274. (Entries in this source were previously published.)

POINT OF VIEW. From This Point of View; 60 British Columbia Painters, Sculptors, Photographers, Graphic, and Video Artists. Vancouver: Vancouver Art Gallery, 1977. OCLC # 3758115.

PORCEL I. Porcel, Baltasar. La Palabra del Arte. Madrid: Ediciones Rayuela, 1976. OCLC # 2816742. LC # 77-451598.

PORCEL II. Porcel, Baltasar. Personajes Excitantes. Barcelona: Plaza & Janes, 1978. OCLC # 5832550. LC # 79-388494.

RAICES. Raices Antiguas/Visiones Nuevas; Ancient Roots/New Visions. Tucson, AZ.: Tucson Museum of Art, 1977. OCLC # 4423553. LC # 77-78902. (Statements in Spanish and English.)

RAYNAL. Raynal, Maurice. Anthologie de la Peinture en France de 1906 a nos Jours. Paris: Editions Montaigne, 1927. OCLC # 1994371. LC # 27-22311. (Also available in English translations, with different pagination: OCLC # 106420 & 1002728. LC # 28-25752 & 76-91374.)

READ. Read, Herbert, editor. Unit 1; The Modern Movement in English Architecture Painting and Sculpture. London: Cassell and Co., 1934. OCLC # 1320458. LC # 35-2657.

REALLIFE. Reallife Magazine. New York: Pictures Production, 1979-. OCLC # 8576392. LC # 83-11398. (Numbers 1-10 indexed.)

REFLECTION. Reflection and Reality-Reflexion und Realitat. Amsterdam: Visual Arts Office, 1976. OCLC # 4667059 & 4118723. LC # 78-326924.

REGIONALISM. Regionalism: Seven Views. Omaha, NB.: Joslyn Art Museum, 1979. OCLC # 5632200 & 6447243. LC # 79-89283.

RE-VIEW. Re-view; Artists on Art. New York: 1977-. OCLC # 6741657. LC # 80-2144. (Volumes 1-3 indexed.)

REVOLUTION. Revolution Place and Symbol. New York: International Congress on Religion, 1969. OCLC # 13782. LC # 70-80740.

REVOLUTION SURREALISTE. La Revolution Surrealiste. Paris: 1924-1929; reprint edition, Paris: Editiona Jean-Michel Place, 1975. OCLC # 5365474 & 3574574 & 1645675. LC # 77-643983 & 68-28660. (Numbers 1-12 indexed; all published.)

RICKERT. Rickert-Ziebold Trust Award Exhibition. Carbondale, IL.: University Museum and Art Galleries, University of Southern Illinois, 1974-. OCLC # 8390890. (Volumes for 1974-1980 indexed; unpaginated; artists arranged alphabetically.)

RIPS. Rips in Reality. Akron, OH.: Akron Art Institute, 1978. OCLC # 7292998. (Unpaginated; artists arranged alphabetically.)

RISENHOOVER. Risenhoover, Morris and Robert T. Blackburn. Artists as Professors; Conversations with Musicians, Painters, Sculptors. Urbana: University of Illinois Press, 1976. OCLC # 1945538. LC # 75-38681.

RITCHIE. Ritchie, Andrew Carnduff. The New Decade; 22 European Painters and Sculptors. New York: Museum of Modern Art, 1955. OCLC # 1253143. LC # 55-2214.

RODITI. Roditi, Edouard. Dialogues on Art. New York: Horizon Press, 1961. OCLC # 1177977 & 517622. LC # 60-51855 & 61-14760.

RODMAN I. Rodman, Selden. Conversations with Artists. New York: Devin-Adair Co., 1957. OCLC # 510655 & 1183882 & 893672 & 3145927. LC # 57-5945.

RODMAN II. Rodman, Selden. Mexican Journal; The Conquerors Conquered. New York: Devin-Adair Co., 1958. OCLC # 242623 & 962268. LC # 58-12620.

RODMAN III. Rodman, Selden. The Insiders. Baton Rouge: Louisiana State University Press, 1960. OCLC # 510622. LC # 60-15433.

ROSE I. Rose, Barbara. A New Aesthetic. Washington, D.C.: The Washington Gallery of Modern Art, 1967. OCLC # 45440. LC # 67-22134.

ROSE II. Rose, Barbara, editor. Readings in American Art Since 1900, A Documentary Survey. New York: Frederick A. Praeger, 1968. OCLC # 439432 & 1422463. LC # 68-16421. (All entries in this anthology were previously published.)

ROSE II REVISED. Rose, Barbara, editor. Readings in American Art, 1900-1975. Revised edition. New York: Praeger Publishers, 1975. OCLC # 1422463 & 5230187. LC # 74-17891. (Most entries in this anthology were previously published.)

ROSNER. Rosner, Stanley and Lawrence E. Abt, editors. The Creative Experience. New York: Dell Publishing Co., 1970. OCLC # 5867018 & 2683927 & 142908 & 1141241. LC # 76-86116.

ROSS. Ross, David A. Southland Video Anthology 1976-77. Long Beach, CA.: Long Beach Museum of Art, 1977. OCLC # 3855318. LC # 75-17356.

ROTH. Roth, Leland M., editor. America Builds; Source Documents in American Architecture and Planning. New York: Harper and Row, 1983. OCLC # 9131833. LC # 82-48151. (Entries in this anthology were previously published.)

ROTHENSTEIN. Rothenstein, Michael. Looking at Pictures. London: George Routledge and Sons, Ltd., 1947. OCLC # 2898841. LC # 47-28522.

ROYER. Royer, Jean. Pays Intimes; Entretiens, 1966-1976. Montreal: Editions Lemeac Inc., 1976. OCLC # 3326605. LC # 77-477165.

RUDDICK. Ruddick, Sara and Pamela Daniels. Working It Out; 23 Women Writers, Artists, Scientists, and Scholars Talk about Their Lives and Work. New York: Pantheon Books, 1977. OCLC # 2984655. LC # 76-54624.

RUSSELL F. Russell, Frank, editor. Architecture in Progress. New York: St. Martin's Press, 1983. OCLC # 9869088. LC # 82-62087.

RUSSELL J. Russell, John and Suzi Gablik, editors. Pop Art Redefined. London: Thames and Hudson, 1969. OCLC # 29388 & 44556. LC # 74-85330 & 70-429377.

SANDBERG. Sandberg, Willem, editor. An Annual of New Art and Artists. New York: Abrams, 1974. OCLC # 1791367. LC # 76-640593.

SAO PAULO. Sao Paulo 9; United States of America/Estados Unidos da America. Washington, D.C.: Smithsonian Institution Press, 1967. OCLC # 236456. LC # 67-29477.

SAYLER. Sayler, Oliver M. Revolt in the Arts. New York: Brentano's, 1930. OCLC # 848298 & 494269. LC # 30-29442.

SCHAPIRO. Schapiro, Miriam. Art: A Woman's Sensibility. Valencia, CA.: Feminist Art Program, California Institute of the Arts, 1975. OCLC # 3115769.

SCHIMMEL. Schimmel, Paul, editor. American Narrative/Story Art: 1967-1977. Houston: Contemporary Arts Museum, 1977. OCLC # 8766394. LC # 77-88112.

SCHMIDT. Schmidt, Diether, editor. In Letzter Stunde, 1933-1945. Dresden: Verlag Der Kunst, 1964. OCLC # 8995053. (Some entries in this source were previously published.)

SCHNEIDER. Schneider, Pierre. Louvre Dialogues. New York: Atheneum, 1971. OCLC # 156700. LC # 72-135572.

SCRIPPS COLLEGE. The Gallery as Studio. Claremont, CA.: Lawrence Rand Lang Art Gallery, Scripps College, 1975. OCLC # 2096581. (Unpaginated; artists arranged alphabetically.)

SCULPTURE OUTSIDE. Sculpture Outside in Cleveland. Cleveland: New Organization for the Visual Arts, 1981. OCLC # 8380878. LC # 81-84553. (Unpaginated; artists arranged alphabetically.)

SEARING. Searing, Helen. New American Art Museums. New York: Whitney Museum of American Art, 1982. OCLC # 8727526. LC # 82-8412.

SEGHERS. Seghers, Pierre, editor. The Art of Painting in the Twentieth Century. New York: Hawthorne Books, 1965. OCLC # 10097390 & 756168. LC # 64-19203. (Entries in this anthology have been previously published.)

SEITZ I. Seitz, William C. Art Israel; 26 Painters and Sculptors. New York: Museum of Modern Art, 1964. OCLC # 951583. LC # 64-8870. (Unpaginated; artists arranged alphabetically.)

SEITZ II. Seitz, William C. Abstract Expressionist Painting in America. The Ailsa Mellon Bruce Studies in American Art. Cambridge, MA.: Harvard University Press, 1983. OCLC # 8927994. LC # 82-18734.

SEITZ III. Seitz, William. The Art of Assemblage. New York: Museum of Modern Art, 1961. OCLC # 510626. LC # 61-17803. (Some entries in this source were previously published.)

SELZ. Selz, Peter. New Images of Man. New York: Museum of Modern Art, 1959. OCLC # 492063 & 83212. LC # 59-14221.

SEUPHOR. Seuphor, Michel [i.e., F. L. Berckelaers]. Dictionary of Abstract Painting. New York: Paris Book Center, Inc., 1957. OCLC # 3592677 & 1043886 & 2566325 & 1025468. LC # 58-1975.

SEXTANT. Sextant; Six Artistes Suedois Contemporains. Paris: Centre Georges Pompidou, 1981. OCLC # 9758670. LC # 81-210116.

SHAFER. Shafer, Thomas. The Professional Potter. New York: Watson-Guptill Publications, 1978. OCLC # 4036612. LC # 78-16547.

SHEARER. Young American Artists; 1978 Exxon National Exhibition. New York: Solomon R. Guggenheim Foundation, 1978. OCLC # 4293606. LC # 78-54030. (Interviews conducted by Linda Shearer.)

SIX PEINTRES. Six Peintres Americains. Paris: M. Knoedler and Cie, 1967. OCLC # 8829901. LC # 67-68410. (Entries in this source were previously published.)

SKIRA. Art Actuel. Actual Art. Geneve: Editions d'Art Albert Skira, 1975-. OCLC # 3881540. LC # 80-642930. (Annual editions for 1975-1980 indexed, all published; 1975-1977 in French; 1978-1980 in French and English.)

SLEEPING. Sleeping Beauty—Art Now, Scandinavia Today. New York: Solomon R. Guggenheim Foundation, 1982. OCLC # 9556221. LC # 82-60793.

SOBY. Soby, James Thrall. Modern Art and the New Past. Norman, OK.: University of Oklahoma Press, 1957. OCLC # 511490. LC # 57-5959.

SOME. Some Points of View--'62. Stanford, CA.: Stanford University Art Gallery, 1962. OCLC # 6698422.

SONDHEIM. Sondheim, Alan, editor. Individuals: Post-Movement Art in America. New York: E. P. Dutton, 1977. OCLC # 2967399. LC # 76-151894.

SOUTHEAST. Southeastern Center for Contemporary Art. The Southeast 7. Winston-Salem, N.C.: Southeastern Center for Contemporary Art, 1977. OCLC # 4565603 & 4573561 & 8779579. LC # 82-8141. (Unpaginated; artists arranged alphabetically.)

SPENCER. Spencer, Harold, editor. American Art; Readings from the Colonial Era to the Present. New York: Charles Scribner's Sons, 1980. OCLC # 6087754. LC # 80-12325. (All entries were previously published.)

SPIRIT. Spirit and Invention. London: Architectural Associatiaon, 1982. OCLC # 11029490 & 9457533. LC # 83-199529.

SPIRITUAL. Musei Vaticani and the Smithsonian Institution. The Influence of Spiritual Inspiration on American Art. Rome: Libreria Editrice Vaticana, 1977. OCLC # 5288060 & 4294498. LC # 79-310368.

SPURLOCK. Spurlock, William, editor. 16 Projects/4 Artists. Dayton: Wright State University, 1977. OCLC # 6261475 & 4212546.

STEDELIJK. Stedelijk Museum. Amsterdam. '60 '80 Attitudes/Concepts/ Images. Amsterdam: Stedelijk Museum, 1982. OCLC # 8983002 & 10073311. LC # 82-235052. (Texts in English and Dutch.)

STEWART. Stewart, Virginia. 45 Contemporary Mexican Artists. Stanford, CA.: Stanford University Press, 1951. OCLC # 1390423 & 917308. LC # 51-14200.

STRAND. Strand, Mark. Art of the Real; Nine American Figurative Painters. New York: Clarkson N. Potter, Inc., 1983. OCLC # 9325099. LC # 83-4034.

STRUCTURED. Structured Sculpture. New York: Galerie Chalette, 1968. OCLC # 129490. LC # 76-271753. (Unpaginated; artists arranged alphabetically.)

STURM. Der Sturm; Herwath Walden und die Europaische Avantgarde Berlin 1912-1932. Berlin: Nationalgalerie, 1961. OCLC # 1081291. LC # 68-40055.

SULTAN. Sultan, Donald and Nancy Davidson, editors. Statements on Art. Name Book 1. Chicago: N.A.M.E. Gallery, 1977. OCLC # 3294098. LC # 77-152093.

SUPERREAL. San Antonio Museum Association. Real, Really Real, Superreal. San Antonio, TX.: San Antonio Museum Association, 1981. OCLC # 7698810. LC # 80-54876.

SURREALISME. Le Surrealisme au Service de la Revolution. Paris: 1930-1933; reprint edition, New York: Arno Press, 1968. OCLC # 6569584 & 1715858 & 4019324. LC # 68-28661 & 79-648571 & 82-3181. (Numbers 1-6 indexed, all published.)

SYMBOLS. Symbols and Images; Contemporary Primitive Artists. New York: American Federation of Arts, 1970. OCLC # 100186. LC # 70-134912. (Unpaginated; artists arranged alphabetically.)

SYSTEMATIC. Solomon R. Guggenheim Museum. Systematic Painting. New York: Solomon R. Guggenheim Foundation, 1966. OCLC # 510492. LC # 66-28425.

TECHNOLOGIES. 5 Artists/5 Technologies. Grand Rapids, MI.: Grand Rapids Art Museum, 1979. OCLC # 6485665 & 5910022. LC # 79-89216. (Unpaginated; artists arranged randomly.)

TEMOIGNAGES I. Temoignages pour l'Art Abstrait 1952. Boulogne (Siene): Editions "Art d'Aujourd'hui," 1952. OCLC # 1263021. LC # 53-17728.

TEMOIGNAGES II. Temoignages Pour La Sculpture Abstraite. Boulogne (Siene): Editions "Art d'Aujourd'hui," 1956. OCLC # 6970111 & 4888700.

TEXAS. San Antonio Museum Association. What's Up in Texas? San Antonio, TX.: Witte Museum, 1978. OCLC # 4136253. LC # 78-13558.

THORN. Thorn, Eduard. Kunstler uber Kunst; ein Ewiger Dialog uber die Probleme der Kunst von Leonardo bis Picasso. Baden-Baden: Woldemar Klein, 1951. OCLC # 7978922. LC # 52-8238. (Entries in this anthology were previously published.)

TIGER. The Tiger's Eye; on Arts and Letters. New York: The Tiger's Eye Publishing Co., 1947-1949. OCLC # 1767488 & 6512827. LC # 54-29272. (Numbers 1-9 indexed, all published.)

TIME-LIFE I. Time-Life Books. Photography as a Tool. Revised edition. Alexandria, VA.: Time-Life Books, 1982. OCLC # 8219272. LC # 82-3174.

TIME-LIFE II. Time-Life Books. Documentary Photography. Revised edition. Alexandria, VA.: Time-Life Books, 1983. OCLC # 8952545. LC # 82-19411.

TIME-LIFE III. Time-Life Books. Great Photographers. Revised edition. Alexandria, VA.: Time-Life Books, 1983. OCLC # 9216991. LC # 83-415.

TIME-LIFE IV. Time-Life Books. The Art of Photography. Revised edition. Alexandria, VA.: Time-Life Books, 1981. OCLC # 7795798. LC # 81-14433.

TIME-LIFE V. Time-Life Books. Photographing Nature. Revised edition. Alexandria, VA.: Time-Life Books, 1981. OCLC # 7462661. LC # 81-5346.

TIME-LIFE VI. Time-Life Books. Travel Photography. Revised edition. Alexandria, VA.: Time-Life Books, 1982. OCLC # 7978162. LC # 81-21206.

TOMASEVIC. Tomasevic, Nebojsa, editor. Jugoslawische Naive Kunstler uber sich Selbst. Konigstein im Taunus: K. R. Langewiesche Nach., 1974. OCLC # 1380736. (In German.)

TOMKINS. Tomkins, Calvin. The Bride and the Bachelors. New York: Viking Press, 1962. OCLC # 1744250 & 517779 & 3172639, etc. LC # 65-14512. ("Except for the Introduction, the text of this book appeared originally in somewhat different form, in The New Yorker.")

TRACKS. George, Herbert, editor. Tracks; a Journal of Artists' Writings. New York: 1974-1977. (Volume 1 number 1-volume 3 number 3 indexed, all published.)

TRANSPERSONAL. Transpersonal Images. San Diego, CA.: International Transpersonal Association, 1983. (Statements in English, German, French, and Japanese.)

TUCHMAN. Tuchman, Maurice, editor. American Sculpture of the Sixties. Los Angeles: Los Angeles County Museum of Art, 1967. OCLC # 166545. LC # 67-18143.

TUCKER I. Tucker, Marcia. The Structure of Color. New York: Whitney Museum of American Art, 1971. OCLC # 156802. LC # 73-154613.

TUCKER II. Tucker, Marcia. Not Just for Laughs. New York: The New Museum, 1981. OCLC # 9484971. LC # 81-81189.

VAN DER MARCK. Van Der Marck, Jan. American Art, Third Quarter Century. Seattle: Seattle Art Museum, 1973. OCLC # 790555. LC # 73-86482.

VANCOUVER. 17 Canadian Artists: A Protean View. Vancouver: Vancouver Art Gallery, 1976. OCLC # 2613995. LC # 76-378957. (Unpaginated; artists arranged alphabetically.)

VARIAN I. Varian, Elayne H. Art in Process; The Visual Development of a Collage. New York: Finch College Museum of Art, 1967. OCLC # 1992637. LC # 67-21455. (Unpaginated; artists arranged alphabetically.)

VARIAN II. Varian, Elayne H. Art in Process; The Visual Development of a Structure. New York: Finch College Museum of Art, 1966. OCLC # 613906. LC # 72-184004. (Unpaginated; artists arranged alphabetically.)

VARIAN III. Varian, Elayne H. Art in Process; The Visual Development of a Painting. New York: Finch College Museum of Art, 1965. OCLC # 659889. LC # 73-155868. (Unpaginated; artists arranged alphabetically.)

VARIAN IV. Varian, Elayne H. Schemata 7. New York: Finch College Museum of Art, 1967. OCLC # 2790710. LC # 67-25560. (Unpaginated; artists arranged alphabetically.)

VASSAR COLLEGE. New American Abstract Painting. Poughkeepsie, N.Y.: Vassar College Art Gallery, 1972. OCLC # 2651532. (Unpaginated; artists arranged alphabetically.)

VEHICULE. Vehicule Art Montreal Inc. Real Live Art. Montreal: Vehicule Art Inc., 1976. OCLC # 4015647. (Unpaginated; artists arranged randomly.)

VERDET. Verdet, Andre. Entretiens; Notes et Ecrits sur la Peinture. Paris: Editions Galilee, 1978. OCLC # 4883022. LC # 79-337558.

VERZOCCHI. Verzocchi, Giuseppe. Il Lavoro; Nella Pittura D'Oggi. Milano: Raccolte Verzocchi, 1950. OCLC # 500232. LC # 53-34991. (Statements in Italian, French, Spanish, English, and German.)

VICTORIA. Victoria and Albert Museum. London. Personal Choice. London: Victoria and Albert Museum, 1983. OCLC # 10540220 & 11289853. LC # 83-233508.

VIEW. View. Oakland, CA.: Crown Point Press, 1978.1980. OCLC # 4544851. LC # 79-1235. (Interviews conducted by Robin White.)

VIEWPOINT. Viewpoint: Ceramics. El Cajon, CA.: Grossmont College Gallery, 1977-1981. OCLC # 8440570. (Annual editions for 1977-1981 indexed, all published; 11981 edition unpaginated; artists arranged alphabetically.)

VINGTIEME. XXe Siecle. Paris: Chroniques du Jour, 1938-1939, 1951- (new series). OCLC # 1605791. LC # 60-1544. (Volumes 1-2, 1938-1939 and number 1-13 new series indexed; volumes 1-2 in French and English, numbers 1-13 new series in French only.)

VISION. Vision. Oakland, CA.: Crown Point Press, 1975-. OCLC # 3127150 & 5168208. LC # 84-11391. (Numbers 1-3 indexed.)

VISUAL. Visual Dialog. Los Altos, CA.: 1975-. OCLC # 2244577. LC # 75-648825. (Volume 1 number 1-volume 4 number 4 indexed.)

VRIES. Vries, Gerd de, editor. On Art, Uber Kunst; Artists' Writings on the Changed Notion of Art After 1965; Kunstlertexte zum veranderten Kunstverstandnis nach 1965. Koln: Verlag M. DuMont, 1974. OCLC # 1099013. LC # 74-338055. (Entries in English and German.)

WALDMAN. Waldman, Diane. Italian Art Now: An American Perspective; 1982 Exxon International Exhibition. New York: Solomon R. Guggenheim Foundation, 1982. OCLC # 8639932 & 8737589. LC # 81-86563.

WALSH. Walsh, George, Colin Nalyor and Michael Held, editors. Contemporary Photographers. New York: St. Martin's Press, 1982. OCLC # 8283869. LC # 82-3337.

WEBB. Webb, Peter. The Erotic Arts. New York: Farrar Straus Giroux, 1983. OCLC # 9466017 & 10513960. LC # 83-8896.

WEBER. Weber, Annina Nosei. Discussion. New York: Out of London Press, 1980. OCLC # 7727551. LC # 78-19533. (This work is an anthology of transcripts of artists' pieces presented on film or in person at the exhibition entitled ■Discussion■ held at New York University, Washington Square, May 9th to 20th, 1977.)

WECHSLER. Wechsler, Susan. Low-Fire Ceramics. New York: Watson-Guptill Publications, 1981. OCLC # 7739833. LC # 81-13086.

WHELDON. Wheldon, Huw, editor. Monitor; An Anthology. London: Macdonald, 1962. OCLC # 1540413. LC # 64-825.

WHITE WALLS. White Walls; A Magazine of Writings by Artists. Chicago: White Walls, Inc., 1978. OCLC # 6741708. LC # 80-2149. (Numbers 1-9 indexed.)

WHITNEY. Whitney Museum of American Art. Forty Artists Under Forty. New York: Whitney Museum of American Art, 1962. OCLC # 510507 & 3675810. LC # 62-19111 & 62-51153. (Unpaginated; artists arranged alphabetically.)

WIGHT. Wight, Frederick S. Transparency, Reflection, Light, Space: Four Artists. Los Angeles: UCLA Art Galleries, 1971. OCLC # 160111. LC # 79-198215.

WINGLER. Wingler, Hans Maria. Wie Sie Einander Sahen. Munchen: Georg Muller, 1957. OCLC # 7115961. (Entries in this source were previously published.)

WINSTON-SALEM. Awards in the Visual Arts 2. Winston-Salem, N.C.: Southeastern Center for Contemporary Art, 1983. OCLC # 9619446. LC # 83-061570.

WISCONSIN I. Wisconsin Directions. Milwaukee: Milwaukee Art Center, 1975. OCLC # 2586457. (Unpaginated loose portfolio; artists arranged alphabetically.)

WISCONSIN II. Wisconsin Directions Two: Here and Now. Milwaukee: The New Milwaukee Art Center, 1978. OCLC # 4834640. LC # 78-64517. (Unpaginated; artists arranged alphabetically.)

WOMANART. Womanart. Brooklyn, N.Y.: Womanart Enterprises, 1976-. OCLC # 2531831. LC # 76-646271. (Volume 1 number 1-volume 2 number 3 indexed.)

WOODWORKING. Woodworking in the Rockies. Colorado Springs: Colorado Springs Fine Arts Center, 1982. OCLC # 8638157. LC # 82-71534.

YALE. Yale French Studies. New Haven. OCLC # 1770272. LC # 59-38386. (Number 19/20, 1957/58, indexed.)

YAMADA. Yamada, Chisaburoh, editor. Dialogue in Art; Japan and the West. Tokyo and New York: Kodansha International, 1976. OCLC # 2624187 & 3738132 & 2629802 & 4430998. LC # 73-79772 & 78-302260.

YOUNG 1957. Young America 1957; Thirty American Painters and Sculptors under Thirty-five. New York: Whitney Museum of American Art, 1957. OCLC # 5538846. LC # 57-1835. (Unpaginated; artists arranged alphabetically.)

YOUNG 1960. Goodrich, Lloyd and John I. H. Baur. Young America 1960; Thirty American Painters Under Thirty-Six. New York: Praeger, 1960. OCLC # 1675204. (Unpaginated; artists arranged alphabetically.)

YOUNG 1965. Goodrich, Lloyd. Young America 1965; Thirty Americans Under Thirty-five. New York: Praeger, 1965. OCLC # 1865684 & 2594910 & 174537 & 5538846. LC # 57-1835. (Unpaginated; artists arranged alphabetically.)

ZAIDENBERG. Zaidenberg, Arthur, compiler. The Art of the Artist; Theories and Techniques of Art by the Artists Themselves. New York: Crown Publishers, 1951. OCLC # 853937.

ZEITLIN. Zeitlin, Marilyn A. Messages: Words and Images. Reading, PA.: Freedman Gallery, Albright College, 1981. OCLC # 8661941. (Unpaginated; artists arranged alphabetically.)

Index of Artists' Writings, Statements, and Interviews

AACH, Herbert (1923-) Germ/Amer; ptr
ILLINOIS 1961 59 (response); port; 1 ill

AARON, George (1896-) Amer; sclp
100 CONTEMPORARY 2-3 (statement); port; 1 ill

ABADI, Fritzie (1915-) Amer; ptr
ILLINOIS 1952 161 (statement)
ILLINOIS 1955 173 (statement)

ABAKANOWICZ, Magdalena (1930-) Poli; sclp, text
EMANUEL II 6-8 (statement); 1 ill
NAYLOR 10-11 (statement); port; 1 ill
SKIRA 1975 113 (extract from interview with Jean-Luc Daval); 1 ill
SKIRA 1976 102 (statement); 1 ill
SKIRA 1979 115-116 (statement); 1 ill
SKIRA 1980 130-131 (statement); 3 ill

ABASCAL, Graciela (1939-) Mexi; ptr
DICCIONARIO v.1 17-19 (statement); port; 1 ill

ABBOTT, Berenice (1898-) Amer; photo
MITCHELL 12-29 (statement); ports; 17 ill
TIME-LIFE IV 20 (statement, p.p.)

ABE, Eishiro ( ) Japa; paper
ADACHI 10-13 (statement); 7 ill

ABE, Satoru (1926-) Amer; sclp
HAAR I 19-25 (interview with Prithwish Neogy); ports; 3 ill

ABERCROMBIE, Gertrude (1909-) Amer; ptr
ILLINOIS 1951 157 (statement); 1 ill

ABERCROMBIE, Stanley ( ) Amer; arch
COOPER-HEWITT I 39-41 (essay: "Places for Play")

ABISH, Cecile Gelb ( ) Amer; instal, sclp
APPLE 45 (statement); 1 ill
NAYLOR 11-12 (statement); 1 ill

ABRAHAM, Raimund (1933-) Swis/Amer; arch
ARCHER 76-79, 94 (statement); port; 14 ill

ABRAHAM RIOS, Jose (1938-) Mexi; ptr
DICCIONARIO v.1 21-23 (statement); port; 1 ill

ABRAHAMS, Ivor (1935-) Brit; sclp
ENGLISH 38-43 (statement); ports; 6 ill

ABRAMOCHKIN, Yuri V. (1936-) Russ; photo
WALSH 10-11 (statement); 1 ill

ABRAMOVIC, Marina (1946-) Yugo; perf, photo
SKIRA 1976 14-15 (statement); 5 ill
VISION no.2 27-30 (statement); 5 ill

ABRAMOVITZ, Albert (1879-) Russ/Amer; ptr
100 CONTEMPORARY 4-5 (statement); port; 1 ill

ABRAMOWITZ, Max (1908-) Amer; arch
EMANUEL I 10-12 (statement); 1 ill

ABRAMSON, Charles ( ) Amer; sclp
EVENTS I 39 (poem); 1 ill

ABUGARADE, Emilio (1938-) Mexi; ptr
DICCIONARIO v.1 25-27 (statement); port; 1 ill

ABULARACH, Rodolfo (1933-) Guat/Amer; print
RAICES 63 (statement); 1 ill

ADAMI, Valerio (1935-) Ital; ptr
ART SINCE v.2 328 (statement, o.p.
1968)
CHOIX 9 (statement, 1980); 1 ill
SKIRA 1975 68 (statement); 1 ill

ADAMS, Alice (1930-) Amer; envir, sclp
ART NOW v.1 no.4 (statement); 1 ill
ARTPARK 1978 10-13 (statement); 8 ill
HOUSE 24-25 (statement); 1 ill

ADAMS, Ansel (1902-1984) Amer; photo
BETHERS I 216-217 (statement); 1 ill
BOOTH 8-21 (interview); port; 8 ill
HOWARD (interview)
TIME-LIFE IV 12 (statement, p.p.)
WALSH 11-13 (statement); 1 ill

ADAMS, Jude ( ) perf
ART NETWORK no.2 44 (interview); 1
ill

ADAMS, Kim (1951-) Cana; instal, sclp
MISE EN SCENE 19, 22-39 (statement);
23 ill

ADAMS, Mac (1943-) Brit; coll, envir,
ptr
GEORGIA 2-3 (statement and
interview); 1 ill
GEORGIA 118-166 (group discussion:
"Artists' Convention," in Athens, GA.,
1/7/1977, moderated by Jan van der
Marck)
SKIRA 1977 79 (statement); 1 ill
SKIRA 1979 99 (statement); 1 ill

ADAMS, Norman (1927-) Brit; ptr
CONTEMPORARY (statement); port; 2
ill

ADAMS, Pat (1928-) Amer; ptr
ART NOW v.4 no.2 (statement); 1 ill
FULBRIGHT 13 (statement)
SCHAPIRO 3 (statement); port; 1 ill

ADAMS, Robert Hickman (1937-) Amer;
photo
BARROW 49-50 ("Introduction" to *The
New West*, o.p. 1974)
DUGAN 169-178 (interview, 1977); port
WALSH 14-15 (statement); 1 ill

ADAMS, Ron (1934-) Amer; ptr, illus
LEWIS I REVISED 99-100 (statement);
port; 2 ill

ADER, Mary Sue ( )
AVALANCHE no.13 26-27 (interview); 2
ill

ADKINS, J. R. (1907-) Amer; ptr
SYMBOLS (statement); 1 ill

ADLER, Samuel Marcus (1898-1979)
Amer; ptr
ART VOICES v.4 no.2 92 (statement); 1
ill
ILLINOIS 1951 157-158 (statement); 1 ill
ILLINOIS 1952 161-162 (statement); 1 ill
ILLINOIS 1953 161 (statement); 1 ill
ILLINOIS 1957 169 (response)
ILLINOIS 1959 189 (statement); 1 ill
ILLINOIS 1961 220-221 (response); port;
1 ill
ILLINOIS 1963 130-131 (statement); 1 ill
ILLINOIS 1965 76-77 (statement); 1 ill
ILLINOIS 1967 144-145 (statement); 1 ill

ADZAK, Roy (1927-) Amer; print, sclp
NAYLOR 15-16 (statement); 1 ill
SKIRA 1979 46 (statement); 1 ill

AFFLECK, Ray (1922-) Cana; arch
CANADIAN 18-21 (statement); 5 ill
EMANUEL I 14-15 (statement); 1 ill

AFRICANO, Nicholas (1948-) Amer; ptr
JOHNSON 260-262 (extract from letter
to Ellen Johnson, 1980); 1 ill
MARSHALL 14 (statement); port; 5 ill

AFRO (Basaldella) (1912-) Ital; ptr
PREMIER BILAN 279 (statement); port
RITCHIE 78-81 (statement); port; 4 ill
VERZOCCHI 33-37 (statement); self
port; 1 ill

AGAM, Yaacov (1928-) Isra; sclp, ptr
ART SINCE v.1 294 (statement, o.p.
1967)
DIRECTIONS I 75 (response); 1 ill
LUMIERE (statement); port; 2 ill
SEITZ I (statement, o.p. 1962); 10 ill
SKIRA 1975 88-89 (statement); 1 ill

AGNETTI, Vincenzo (1926-) Ital; perf,
photo
NAYLOR 17-18 (statement)
SKIRA 1976 12 (statement); 1 ill

AGOSTI, Jean-Paul (1948-) Fren; ptr
SKIRA 1979 20 (statement); 1 ill

AGOSTINI, Peter (1913-) Amer; sclp
ART NOW v.2 no.10 (statement); 1 ill
IT IS no.4 15 (statement)
IT IS no.5 51-56 (group discussion)

AGREST, Diana ( ) Arge/Amer; arch
ARCHER 38-41, 94 (statement); port; 8
ill

AGROS (Jose Ernesto Matanzo Rojas) ( )
Mexi; ptr
DICCIONARIO v.1 41-43 (statement);
port; 1 ill

AGUAYO, Miguel (1934-) Mexi; ptr
DICCIONARIO v.1 45-47 (statement);
port; 1 ill

AGUAYO, Ramon Carlos ( ) Mexi; ptr
DICCIONARIO v.1 49-51 (statement);
port; 1 ill

AGUERREGERE, Jose Luis (1927-)
Mexi; ptr
DICCIONARIO v.1 53-55 (statement);
port; 1 ill

AGUILA HERRERA, Jose de Jesus
(1942-) Mexi; ptr
DICCIONARIO v.1 57-59 (statement);
port; 1 ill

AGUILAR COVARRUBIAS, Salvador
(1943-) Mexi; ptr
DICCIONARIO v.1 61-63 (statement and
interview); port; 1 ill

AGUILAR OLEA, Oscar (1951-) Mexi;
ptr
DICCIONARIO v.1 65-67 (statement);
port; 1 ill

AGUILAR RODRIGUEZ, Jose
Encarnacion (1950-) Mexi; ptr
DICCIONARIO v.1 69-71 (statement);
port; 1 ill

AGUILAR SURO, Teresa (1931-) Mexi;
ptr
DICCIONARIO v.1 73-75 (statement);
port; 1 ill

AGUINACO LLANO, Jorge Pablo (1950-
) Mexi; ptr, print
DICCIONARIO v.1 77-79 (statement);
port; 1 ill

AGUIRRE TINOCO, Rodolfo (1927-)
Mexi; ptr
DICCIONARIO v.1 81-83 (statement);
port; 1 ill

AHEARN, John ( ) Amer; sclp
FACE IT 8-9 (statement); 1 ill

AHLERS-HESTERMANN, Friedrich
(1883-) Germ; ptr

WINGLER 15-26 (essay: "Der Deutsche Kunstlerkreis des Cafe du Dome in Paris," p.p.)
WINGLER 26-30 (essay: "Bei Henri Matisse," p.p.)

AHRENDS BURTON AND KORALEK (arch firm)
EMANUEL I 17-18 (statement); 1 ill

AHRENDS, Peter ( ) Brit; arch
SEE: AHRENDS BURTON AND KORALEK

AHRENDS, Steffen (1907-) SoAf; arch
EMANUEL I 15-16 (statement); 1 ill

AHUATZI, Alberto Armando (1950-) Mexi; ptr
DICCIONARIO v.1 85-87 (statement); port; 1 ill

AIDA, Takefumi (1937-) Japa; arch
EMANUEL I 18-19 (statement); 1 ill

AIGNER, Lucien (1901-) Amer; photo
WALSH 15-17 (statement); 1 ill

AIKA (1915-) Isra; sclp, ptr
SEITZ I statement); 3 ill

AILLAUD, Gilles (1928-) Fren; ptr
SANDBERG 12-15 (statement); 3 ill

AIN, Gregory (1908-) Amer; arch
EMANUEL I 19-20 (statement); 1 ill

AIRHART, David W. (1953-) Amer; ptr
NOSANOW II 21, 38 (statement); 2 ill

AIVALIOTIS, Stak ( ) photo
HOW FAMOUS 180-183 (statements); port; 5 ill

AKAWIE, Thomas F. (1935-) Amer; ptr
ILLINOIS 1967 84-85 (statement); 1 ill

AKERS, Adela (1933-) Amer; text
FIBER 28-29 (statement); 1 ill

AKHRR (group)
SEE: ASSOCIATION OF ARTISTS OF REVOLUTIONARY RUSSIA

ALANDRADE, Ismael Davidson De
SEE: D'ALA

ALANIZ PASTRANA, Gustavo (1921-) Mexi; ptr
DICCIONARIO v.1 89-91 (statement); port; 1 ill

ALBARRAN, G. Gerardo (1929-) Mexi; ptr
DICCIONARIO v.1 93-95 (statement); port; 1 ill

ALBERS, Josef (1888-1976) Germ/Amer; print, ptr
ABSTRACT 239-241 (essay: "Abstract----Presentational"); 1 ill
ART SINCE v.1 289-290 (statement, o.p. 1965)
ART VOICES v.4 no.1 38-39 (interview with Jacqueline Barnitz)
HAUSSER 34-35 (statement, o.p. 1968); 3 ill
ILLINOIS 1952 162-163 (statement); 1 ill
ILLINOIS 1953 161-162 (statement)
ILLINOIS 1955 174 (statement)
ILLINOIS 1965 103 (statement); 1 ill
JANIS I 80-81 (statement); 1 ill
KEPES IX 105 (statement); 1 ill
KINETISCHE (statement); 1 ill
KUH 11-22 (interview); 5 ill
PREMIER BILAN 277 (statement); port
ROSE II 172-173 (extract from *Homage to the Square*, o.p. 1964)

ROSE II 173-174 (extract from interview with Katharine Kuh, o.p. 1960)
ROSE II REVISED 166-167 (statement, o.p. 1964)
ROSE II REVISED 167-169 (extract from interview with Katharine Kuh, o.p. 1960)

ALBERTOS LUNA, Maria de Jesus (1949-) Mexi; ptr
DICCIONARIO v.1 97-99 (statement); port; 1 ill

ALBERTY, John ( ) envir
CRISS-CROSS no.4 14-19 (interview with Donald Lipski and Joe Hobbs); 8 ill

ALBINET, Jean Paul (1951-) Fren
SEE: GROUPE UNTEL

ALBRECHT D (Dieter) (1944-) Germ; perf, print, ptr
NAYLOR 21-22 (statement); 1 ill
NAYLOR 845-846 (statement on the artist Gunter Saree)
SKIRA 1978 64 (statement); 1 ill

ALBRIGHT, Ivan Le Lorraine (1897-) Amer; ptr
ART SINCE v.2 154 (statement, o.p. 1959)
CUMMINGS 48-63 (interview, 1972); self port; 2 ill
DOUZE PEINTRES (statement); 1 ill
EMANUEL II 17-19 (poem); 1 ill
ILLINOIS 1953 162-163 (statement); 1 ill
KUH 23-37 (interview); 7 ill
MILLER 1943 24-25 (statement); self port; 2 ill
ROSE II 112-113 (statement, o.p. 1943)
ROSE II REVISED 92-93 (statement, o.p. 1943)

ALBRIGHT, Malvin Marr
SEE: ZSISSLY

ALBUQUERQUE, Lita (1946-) Amer; sclp, instal, ptr
CELEBRATION (statement); 1 ill
MCCLINTIC 40-43 (statement); 4 ill

ALCALAY, Albert (1917-) Fren/Amer; ptr
ILLINOIS 1955 174-175 (statement); 1 ill
ILLINOIS 1957 170-171 (response); 1 ill
ILLINOIS 1959 189-190 (statement); 1 ill

ALCAZAR PARTIDA, Crispin (1942-) Mexi; ptr
DICCIONARIO v.1 101-103 (statement); port; 1 ill

ALDACO SALIDO, Esther (1924-) Mexi; ptr
DICCIONAIO v.1 105-107 (statement); port; 1 ill

ALDANA MIJARES, Miguel (1920-) Mexi; ptr
DICCIONARIO v.1 109-111 (statement); port; 1 ill

ALDAPA ABARCA, Ignacio (1948-) Mexi; ptr
DICCIONARIO v.1 113-115 (statement); port; 1 ill

ALDINGTON AND CRAIG (arch firm)
SEE: CRAIG, John

ALECHINSKY, Pierre (1927-) Belg; ptr
EXPOSICION (statement); port; 1 ill
QUADRUM no.1 43-52 (essay: "Calligraphie Japonaise"); port
SKIRA 1975 105 (extract from interview with Jean-Luc Daval, o.p. 1971); 1 ill

ALEIX, Montserrat Pecanins (1909-)
Mexi; ptr
DICCIONARIO v.1 117-119 (poem); port;
1 ill

ALEKSIC, Dragutin (1947-) Yugo; sclp
TOMASEVIC 15-19 (statement); port; 1
ill

ALEXANDER, Christopher (1936-)
Amer; arch
KEPES III 96-107 (essay: "From a Set of
Forces to a Form")

ALEXANDER, Dorothy ( )
TRACKS v.2 no.2 45 (poem: "Peril")
TRACKS v.3 no.1/2 91-93 ("Fishing")

ALEXANDER, Peter (1939-)
Fren/Amer; sclp, instal
WIGHT 9-39 (interview); ports

ALEXANDER, Robert E. (1907-) Amer;
arch
EMANUEL I 26-27 (statement); 1 ill

ALF, Martha (1930-) Amer; sclp
CELEBRATION (statement); 1 ill

ALFARO, Andreu ( ) Span
PORCEL I 9-18; port

ALFARO HERNANDEZ, Rafael (1938-)
Mexi; ptr
DICCIONARIO v.1 123-125 (statement);
port; 1 ill

ALFIERI, Bruno ( )
ART VOICES v.1 no.1 17 (essay:
"Where is Modern Art Heading?")

ALFONSO LORENZO, Santos (1951-)
Mexi; ptr
DICCIONARIO v.1 127-129 (statement);
port; 1 ill

ALFORD, Gloria (1938-) Amer; print,
sclp
WISCONSIN I (statement); 1 ill

AL HILALI, Neda (1938-) Czec/Amer;
sclp
ARTPARK 1979 (statement); 1 ill

ALINGTON, William Hildebrand (1929-
) NewZ; arch
EMANUEL I 27-28 (statement); 1 ill

ALIS PUERTA, Rene ( ) Cuba/Mexi; ptr
DICCIONARIO v.1 131-133 (statement);
port; 1 ill

ALIX, Yves (1890-) Fren; ptr
RAYNAL 43-47 (statement); 3 ill
ART D'AUJOURD'HUI v.6 16
(statement); 4 ill

ALLAN, Jody (1920-) Brit/Mexi; ptr
DICCIONARIO v.1 135-137 (statement);
port; 1 ill

ALLAN, William (1936-) Amer; ptr
HOPKINS 22-23 (statement); port; 1 ill

ALLEN, Gerald ( ) Amer; arch
COOPER-HEWITT I 68-69 (essay:
"Architectural Elements")
COOPER-HEWITT II 57-58 (essay:
"Urbanity")

ALLEN, Marie Enriquez de (1907-)
Mexi/Amer; sclp
RAICES 32 (statement); 1 ill

ALLEN, Rebecca ( ) Amer; print
COMPUTER (statements); 1 ill

ALLEN, Richard (1933-) Brit; illus
SKIRA 1976 55 (statement); 1 ill

ALLEN, Roberta (1945-) Amer; envir
ART-RITE no.14 5-6 (response)
SKIRA 1979 32 (statement); 1 ill
WHITE WALLS no.8 14-23 (text piece)

ALLEN, Terry (1943-) Amer; perf, sclp,
video
WHITE   WALLS   no.5   6-10
("Anterabbit/Bleeder")

ALLEY FRIENDS (group) sclp
ARTPARK 1975 50-53 (statement); port;
14 ill

ALLEYN, Edmund (1931-) Cana; ptr
ROYER 109-114 (interview 1974)

ALMARAZ LOPEZ, Salvador (1930-)
Mexi; ptr
DICCIONARIO v.1 139-141 (statement);
port; 1 ill

ALMASY, Paul (1906-) Fren; photo
WALSH 18-20 (statement); 1 ill

ALMEIDA, Helena (1934-) Span; print
SKIRA 1977 87 (statement); 1 ill

ALMEIDA RAMIREZ, Laura (1954-)
Mexi; ptr
DICCIONARIO v.1 143-145 (statement);
port; 1 ill

ALMELA   ESPINOSA   DE   LOS
MONTEROS, Mario (1940-) Mexi; ptr
DICCIONARIO v.1 147-149 (statement);
port; 1 ill

ALMQUIST, Don ( ) Amer; sclp
ILLUSTRATION 90-93 (statement); port;
4 ill

ALONSO CAMPOS, Alicia (1943-)
Mexi; ptr

DICCIONARIO v.1 151-153 (statement);
port; 1 ill

ALPERT, Bill (1934-) Amer; ptr, sclp
RE-VIEW v.1 47-49 (poem); 2 ill

ALSTON, Charles Henry (1907-) Amer;
ptr
FINE 139-142 (statements, o.p. 1968,
1969); 4 ill

ALTAMIRANO COZZI, Salvador (1943-
) Mexi; ptr
DICCIONARIO v.1 155-157 (statement);
port; 1 ill

ALTMAN, Edith ( ) Amer; ptr
BRAKKE 157-162 (text piece: "The
Play—Proper Perspective")

ALTMAN, Harold (1924-) Amer; ptr,
print
AMERICAN PRINTS 13, 64 (statement);
1 ill
RISENHOOVER 13-30

ALTMAN, Natan (1889-1970) Russ; ptr,
sclp
BOWLT 161-164 (essay: "'Futurism'
and Proletarian Art," o.p. 1918); 2 ill

ALTOLAGUIRRE,   Paloma   (1935-   )
Mexi; ptr
DICCIONARIO v.1 159-161 (statement);
port; 1 ill

ALVARENGA, Tuno ( ) Mexi; ptr
DICCIONARIO v.1 163-165 (statement);
port; 1 ill

ALVAREZ, Mario Roberto (1913-) Arge;
arch
EMANUEL I 29-32 (statement); 1 ill

ALVAREZ AMAYA, Jesus (1925-) Mexi; ptr
DICCIONARIO v.1 167-169 (statement); port; 1 ill

ALVAREZ BRAVO, Manuel (1902-) Mexi; photo
CAMPBELL 228-237 (statement, o.p. 1945); port; 10 ill
HILL 224-236 (interview, 1976); port

ALVAREZ DAVALOS, Manuel (1912-) Mexi; ptr
DICCIONARIO v.1 171-173 (statement); port; 1 ill

ALVAREZ GOLZARRI DE SALAZAR, Rosa (1925-) Mexi; ptr
DICCIONARIO v.1 175-177 (statement); self port; 1 ill

ALVAREZ KENNY, Herminio (1947-) Mexi; ptr
DICCIONARIO v.1 179-181 (statement); port; 1 ill

ALVAREZ LOPEZ, Francisco (1903-) Mexi; ptr
DICCIONARIO v.1 183-185 (statement); port; 1 ill

ALVAREZ MARTIN DEL CAMPO, Alicia Josefina ( ) Mexi; ptr
DICCIONARIO v.1 187-189 (statement); port; 1 ill

ALVAREZ MENDEZ, Raymundo (1934-) Mexi; ptr
DICCIONARIO v.1 191-193 (statement); port; 1 ill

ALVAREZ PORTUGAL, Antonio (1948-) Mexi; ptr
DICCIONARIO v.1 195-197 (statement); port; 1 ill

ALVERMANN, H. P. (1931-) Germ; sclp
KUNST UND POLITIK (statement); port; 5 ill

AMADO, Jean (1922-) Fren; sclp
SKIRA 1977 101 (statement); 1 ill

AMARAL CHAVEZ, Manuel (1932-) Mexi; ptr
DICCIONARIO v.1 199-201 (statement); port; 1 ill

AMATO, Sam (1924-) Amer; ptr
CALIFORNIA--PAINTING 33 (statement); 1 ill
ILLINOIS 1959 191 (statement); 1 ill

AMBASZ, Emilio (1943-) Arge/Amer; arch
ARCHER 34-37, 94 (statement); port; 7 ill
COLLABAORATION 130-135 (essay: "The Four Gates to Columbus"); 4 ill

AMBRIS, Isaac (1942-) Mexi; ptr
DICCIONARIO v.1 203-205 (statement); port; 1 ill

AMEIJIDE, Raymond ( ) Amer; sclp
ILLUSTRATION 62-67 (statement); port; 10 ill

AMEN, Woody van (1936-) Dutc; print
NAYLOR 26-27 (statement); 1 ill

AMENDOLLA GASPASO, Luis (1928-) Mexi; ptr
DICCIONARIO v.1 207-209 (statement); port; 1 ill

AMEVOR, Charlotte (1932-) Amer; ptr, illus
FAX I 112-127 (statements); port; 2 ill

AMINO, Leo (1911-) Amer; sclp
NEW DECADE 8-9 (statement); 3 ill

AMIS, Stanley F. (1924-) Brit; arch
SEE: HOWELL KILLICK
PARTRIDGE AND AMIS

AMOR, Martinez Gallardo (1951-) Mexi;
ptr
DICCIONARIO v.1 211-213 (statement);
port; 1 ill

ANA ROSA (Ana Rosa Barrios de Diaz)
(1940-) Mexi; ptr
DICCIONARIO v.1 215-217 (statement);
port; 1 ill

ANASTASI, William (1933-) Amer;
photo
GEORGIA 118-166 (group discussion:
"Artists' Convention," in Athens, GA.,
1/7/1977, moderated by Jan van der
Marck)

ANATOL (1931-) Germ; sclp
HAUSSER 36-37 (statement, o.p. 1972);
2 ill

ANCHER, Sydney (1904-) Atrl; arch
EMANUEL I 32-33 (statement); 1 ill

ANCONA OJEDA, Fernando (1924-)
Mexi; ptr
DICCIONARIO v.1 219-221 (statement);
port; 1 ill

ANDERSEN, Eric (1943-) Dani; envir,
sclp
GROH (statement); 1 ill

ANDERSON, Adrienne (1949-) Amer;
ptr, sclp
NOSANOW I 34 (statement); 1 ill

ANDERSON, Carl (1856-) Amer; cart
M.H. DE YOUNG 10 (response); self port

ANDERSON, Doug (1954-) Amer; ptr
BOSTON I (interview); 1 ill
BOSTON III (interview); 1 ill

ANDERSON, Guy Irving (1906-) Amer;
ptr
GUENTHER 16-17 (statement); port; 1
ill

ANDERSON, Jeremy Radcliffe (1921-)
Amer; sclp
ENVIRONMENT 34-35 (statement); 2 ill
ILLINOIS 1955 175 (statement); 1 ill
SOME 30 (statement); 1 ill

ANDERSON, John (1923-) Amer; ptr
ILLINOIS 1953 163 (statement); 1 ill

ANDERSON, Judith (1952-) Amer; ptr
RICKERT 1980 (statement); port; 3 ill

ANDERSON, Laura (1902-) Amer; pott
HERMAN 25 (statement); port; 1 ill

ANDERSON, Laurie (1947-) Amer; perf,
sound
ARTPARK 1977 6-8 (statement); port; 4
ill
ART-RITE no.5 6 (response)
ART-RITE no.6 5 ("Take Two")
ART-RITE no.19 34-35
("Autobiography: The Self in Art")
AVALANCHE no.12 22-23 ("Confessions
of a Street Talker")
GEORGIA 6-8 (statement); port; 2 ill
JOHNSON 240-244 (interview with
Robin White, o.p. 1980); 1 ill
LIVE no.5 2-9 (interview); port; 7 ill
PERFORMANCE no.1 22 (statement)
PERFORMANCE no.2 16-18 (interview);
port
SCHIMMEL 24-25, 87 (statement); 3 ill

SONDHEIM 68-83 (extract from "For Instants"); 1 ill
VIEW v.2 no.8 (interview); port; 5 ill

ANDERSON, Lawrence B. (1906-) Amer; arch
KEPES IV 102-117 (essay: "Module: Measure, Structure, Growth, and Function")

ANDERSON, Lennart (1928-) Amer; ptr
COLLABORATION 126-129 (essay: "Bacchanal"); 5 ill
GUSSOW 112-113 (interview, 1970); 1 ill
STRAND 136-159 (interview); port; 18 ill

ANDERSON, Ruthadell (1922-) Amer; text
HAAR II 3-7 (interview); ports; 2 ill

ANDERSON, Torsten (1926-) Swed; ptr
SEXTANT 33-51 (poem: "A Dream," in French and English); 25 ill

ANDO, Tadao ( ) Japa; arch
GA DOCUMENT no.7 68-89 (statements); 53 ill
GA HOUSES no.6 172-205 (statement); 111 ill; port

ANDRE, Carl (1935-) Amer; sclp, instal
ART SINCE v.1 293 (statement, o.p. 1966)
ARTFORUM v.5 no.2 14-17 (statements); 7 ill
ART-RITE no.9 18 (statement)
AVALANCHE no.1 18-27 (interview); port; 8 ill
CELANT 204-210 (statement); 5 ill
CHOIX 10 (statement, o.p. 1982); 1 ill
CUMMINGS-195 (interview, 1972); port; 2 ill
DIRECTIONS I 75 (response); 1 ill

FINCH COLLEGE (extract form interview with Dodie Gust, o.p. 7/18/68); port; 1 ill
JOHNSON 120-123 (extract from interview with Phylis Tuchman, o.p. 1970)
NAYLOR 29 (statement); 1 ill
PAOLETTI 16-19 (statements, p.p.); 1 ill
ROSE II REVISED 189 (statement: "Art Is What We Do/Culture Is What Is Done To Us," o.p. 1967)
SKIRA 1975 44 (extract from interview with Irmeline Lebeer, o.p. 6/74); 1 ill
SKIRA 1979 64 (statement); 1 ill
STEDELIJK 80 (statement); 3 ill
TRACKS v.2 no.2 71-76 ("Billy Builder, or the Painful Machine, a Novel of Velocity")
TRACKS v.2 no.3 53-67 ("Billy Builder, or the Painful Machine, a Novel of Velocity")
TRACKS v.3 no. 1/2 145-157 ("Billy Builder, or the Painful Machine, a Novel of Velocity")
VRIES 26-27 ("Questions and Answers," o.p. 1969)

ANDREA (1940-) Brit/Mexi; ptr
DICCIONARIO v.1 223-225 (statement); port; 1 ill

ANDREJEVIC, Milet (1925-) Yugo/Amer; ptr
ART NOW v.1 no.10 (statement); 1 ill

ANDREWS, Benny (1930-) Amer; ptr
FAX I 236-252 (statements); port; 1 ill
LEWIS II 4 (statement); port; 3 ill

ANDREWS, John (1933-) Atrl; arch
EMANUEL I 33-35 (statement); 1 ill

ANGEL (Angel Salinas Mendez) (1948-) Mexi; ptr

DICCIONARIO v.1 227-229 (statement); port; 1 ill

ANGEL, Felix (1949-) ptr
ANGEL 19-41 (statement); port; 1 ill

ANGEL, Heather (1941-) Brit; photo
CAMPBELL 144-155 (statement); port; 8 ill
HOW FAMOUS 96-101 (statements); port; 9 ill

ANGELO, Nancy (1953-) Amer; perf, video
CHRYSALIS no.4 26-27 (interview with Ruth Iskin); 1 ill
ROSS 38-39 (statement); 1 ill

ANGLES (Fela Tejado de Angles) ( ) Mexi; ptr
DICCIONARIO v.1 231-233 (statement); port; 1 ill

ANGNIANO, Raul (1909-) Mexi; ptr
STEWART 108-111 (statement); port; 3 ill

ANGUIA BECERRIL, Ricardo (1951-) Mexi; ptr
DICCIONARIO v.1 235-237 (statement); port; 1 ill

ANGUIANO VALDEZ, Armando (1920-) Mexi; ptr
DICCIONARIO v.1 239-241 (statement); port; 1 ill

ANKER, Suzanne ( ) Amer; paper
CRISS-CROSS no.3 16-19 ("The Genital Handicap")
CRISS-CROSS no.3 38-40 (text piece); 3 ill

ANLIKER, Roger William (1924-) Amer;
ptr
ILLINOIS 1952 163 (statement); 1 ill

ANSELMO, Giovanni (1934-) Ital; sclp
CELANT 109-114 (statement); 6 ill

ANT FARM (group)
ARTPARK 1975 54-57 (statement); 9 ill
ON SITE no.5/6 57-65 (essay: "Autorama")

ANTES, Horst (1936-) Germ; ptr, print, sclp
SKIRA 1975 68 (extract from interview with Eva Stanke, 1973); 1 ill

ANTHONY, Carol ( ) Amer; ptr, sclp
ILLUSTRATION 76-81 (statement); port; 5 ill
NORTH LIGHT 12-17 (statement); port; 8 ill

ANTHONY, Lawrence Kenneth (1934-) Amer; sclp
MORRIS 14-19 (statements); ports; 4 ill

ANTIN, Eleanor (1935-) Amer; perf, instal
APPLE 21 (statement); 1 ill
ART-RITE no.7 23-24 ("Dialogue with a Medium")
CHRYSALIS no.8 43-51 (statements, p.p.); 22 ill
CHRYSALIS no.10 6-7 (letter)
EMANUEL II 28-29 (statement); 1 ill
GUMPERT I 37 (statement); port
HESS 86-87 (statement)
IRVINE 53, 88 (statement); 1 ill
MUNRO 417-430 (interview); port; 3 ill
NAYLOR 32-33 (statement); 1 ill
NEMSER 266-301 (interview); self port; 14 ill
PAOLETTI 20-23 (statements, p.p.); 2 ill
PROFILE v.1 no.4 (interview); port

SCHAPIRO 4 (statement); port; 1 ill
SCHIMMEL 26-28, 88 (statement); 3 ill
VISION no.1 52-53 (extract from "The King's Meditations")

ANTONAKAKIS, Dimitris (1933-) Gree; arch
EMANUEL I 36-38 (statement); 1 ill

ANTONAKAKIS, Suzana (1935-) Gree; arch
EMANUEL I 36-38 (statement); 1 ill

ANTONAKOS, Stephen (1926-) Gree/Amer; instal, light, sclp
ART AND TECHNOLOGY 50 (project proposal)
ARTFORUM v.7 no.2 4 (letter)

ANTRAGNE, Paul (1931-) Mexi; ptr
DICCIONARIO v.1 243-245 (statement); port; 1 ill

ANTUN, Bahunek (1912-) Yugo; ptr
TOMASEVIC 20-25 (statement); port; 1 ill

ANTUNEZ, Nemesio (1918-) Chil; ptr
REVOLUTION 134-135 (statement)

ANTUNEZ REBOLLAR, Jesus (1939-) Mexi; ptr
DICCIONARIO v.1 247-249 (statement); port; 1 ill

ANUSZKIEWICZ, Richard Joseph (1930-) Amer; ptr
ILLINOIS 1961 82 (response); port; 1 ill
ILLINOIS 1963 71 (statement); 1 ill
MILLER 1963 6-11 (statement); port; 5 ill
TUCKER I 14 (statement)
VARIAN III (statement); port

ANZURES TORRES, Javier (1950-) Mexi; ptr
DICCIONARIO v.1 251-253 (statement); port; 1 ill

APOLLONIO, Marina ( ) instal
GROH (statement); 2 ill

APPEL, Karel (1921-) Dutc; ptr
ART NOW v.1 no.10 (statement); 1 ill
ART SINCE v.2 151 (letters)
EMANUEL II 31-33 (statement)
FRASNAY 287-297 (statement); ports; 8 ill
NAYLOR 34-36 (statement); 1 ill
RITCHIE 98-101 (statement); port; 4 ill
SELZ 16-22 (statement, from letters); 5 ill

APPLE, Billy (1935-) Amer; sclp
APPLE 22, 24, 27 (statements); 6 ill

APPLE, Jacqueline B. (Jacki) ( ) Amer
APPLE 5-7 ("Introduction")
TRACKS v.3 no.1/2 102-109 ("Tracings")

APPLETON, Alanson ( ) print
VISUAL v.1 no.3 22-23 (essay: "Technique and Scholarship in Etching: In Defense of Appletree"); port; 1 ill

APPLEYARD, Donald (1928-) Brit/Amer; arch
KEPES VII 176-192 (essay: "Motion, Sequence and the City")

AQUINO, Edmundo (1939-) Mexi; print; ptr
DICCIONARIO v.1 259-261 (statement); port; 1 ill

AQUINO CASAS, Arnulfo (1942-) Mexi;

ptr
DICCIONARIO v.1 255-257 (statement);
port; 1 ill

ARAGON, Luis Y. (1930-) Mexi; ptr,
print
DICCIONARIO v.1 267-269 (statement);
port; 1 ill

ARAGON ECHEAGARAY, Enrique ( )
Mexi; ptr
DICCIONARIO v.1 263-265 (statement);
port; 1 ill

ARAI, Sachi ( ) Mexi; ptr
DICCIONARIO v.1 271-273 (statement);
port; 1 ill

ARAIZA PADILLA, Maria Teresa (1936-
) Mexi; ptr
DICCIONARIO v.1 275-277 (statement);
self port; 1 ill

ARAKAWA, Shusaku (1936-)
Japa/Amer; ptr
ALLOWAY 213-217 ("Stolen (with
Arakawa: An Interview)"); 1 ill
ILLINOIS 1965 96 (interview with John
Weber); 1 ill
ILLINOIS 1967 98 (statement); 1 ill
TRACKS v.3 no.3 32-35 ("Some
Words")
TRACKS v.3 no.3 109 ("Obituary for
Oyvind Fahlstrom")
WHITE WALLS no.5 11-17 (text piece)

ARANGO DE POSADA, Leticia (1952-)
Mexi; ptr
DICCIONARIO v.1 279-281 (statement);
port; 1 ill

ARANGUREN VALLE, Gustavo (1934-)
Mexi; print, ptr
DICCIONARIO v.1 283-285 (statement);
self port; 1 ill

ARAUJO SUAREZ, Rolando (1943-)
Mexi; ptr
DICCIONARIO v.1 287-289 (statement);
port; 1 ill

ARBEITSRAT FUR KUNST (group)
SEE: WORK COUNCIL FOR ART

ARBUS, Diane (1923-1971) Amer; photo
TIME-LIFE III 222-225 (statements,
p.p.); 4 ill

ARCHIPENKO, Alexander (1887-1964)
Russ/Amer; sclp, ptr
ARMORY SHOW 13 (statement)
JOURNAL OF THE AAA v.7 no.2 7
(statements)
ZAIDENBERG 165-169 (essay: "The
Extension of Creativity"); 4 ill

(THE) ARCHITECTS
COLLABORATIVE
SEE: TAC

ARCHITECTS' CO-PARTNERSHIP
INC. (arch firm)
EMANUEL I 39-41 (statement); 1 ill

ARCIER, Joseph William (1909-) Amer;
ptr
NORTH LIGHT 83 (statement); 1 ill

ARDALAN, Nader (1939-) Iran/Amer;
arch
EMANUEL I 41-43 (statement); 1 ill

ARDEN QUIN, Carmelo (1913-) Urug;
ptr
SEUPHOR 122 (statement)

ARDON, Mordecai (1896-) Isra; ptr
ART SINCE v.2 149 (statement, o.p.
1967)
SEITZ I (extract from letter to
W. Sandberg, 1960); 2 ill

ARELLANO FISCHER, Jose (1911-)
Mexi; ptr, print
DICCIONARIO v.1 291-293 (statement);
port; 1 ill

ARENTZEN, Glenda ( ) Amer; metal
HAYSTACK 1 (statement); 1 ill
METALWORKS (statement); 1 ill

AREVALO SUAREZ, Javier ( ) Mexi; ptr
DICCIONARIO v.1 299-301 (statement);
port; 1 ill

ARIAS, Alfredo Rodriguez (1944-) sclp
PREMIO NACIONAL 1966 40-41
(statement); port; 1 ill

ARIAS BELTRAN, Francisco (1945-)
Mexi; ptr
DICCIONARIO v.1 303-305 (statement);
port; 1 ill

ARIAS DE ALBA, Ruben (1917-) Mexi;
ptr
DICCIONARIO v.1 309-311 (statement);
port; 1 ill

ARIAS-MISSION, Alain (1936-)
Belg/Amer; print
NAYLOR 39-40 (statement); 1 ill

ARIAS-MISSION, Nela (1925-)
Cuba/Amer; ptr
NAYLOR 40-41 (statement); 1 ill

ARIKHA, Avigdor (1929-) Ruma/Isra;
envir, ptr, sclp
ART AND TECHNOLOGY 50-51 (project
proposal); 2 ill
CLAIR 48-49 (extract from interview
with Germain Viatte, 1974); 1 ill

ARIOSTO (Ariosto Otero Reyes) (1945-)
Mexi; ptr

DICCIONARIO v.1 313-315 (statement);
1 ill

ARISTOVULOUS, Nick ( ) Gree/Amer;
sclp
ILLUSTRATION 54-55 (statement); port;
3 ill

ARJONA AMABILIS, Rolando (1920-)
Mexi; ptr
DICCIONARIO v.1 317-319 (statement);
port; 1 ill

ARLEN, Nancy (1947-) Amer; instal,
sclp
LOGAN II 12-15 (statement); port; 5 ill

ARMAJANI, Siah (1939-) Iran/Amer;
sclp, instal
FOX 36-43 (statement); 9 ill
HOUSE 26-27 (statement); 2 ill
QUINTESSENCE 41-49 (statement);
ports; 17 ill
SHEARER 14-18 (interview); 3 ill

ARMAN, (Fernandez Armand) (1928-)
Fren/Amer; sclp, ptr
ART SINCE v.2 327 (statement, o.p.
1969)
LETTERS 5 (letter); 1 ill
PREMIO NACIONAL 1964 44-45
(statement); port; 1 ill
SKIRA 1975 15 (statement, 1964); 1 ill

ARMER, Ruth ( ) Amer; ptr
ART AND ARTIST 3-8 ("notes of an
interview with Ernest Mundt"); 2 ill

ARMIJO, Federico (1946-) Amer; wood
WOODWORKING 6-7 (statement); ports;
2 ill

ARMITAGE, Kenneth (1916-) Brit; sclp
ART SINCE v.2 150 (statement, o.p.
1960)

CONTEMPORARY (statement); port; 2 ill

FORMA 73-97 (statement); ports; 3 ill

RITCHIE 56-59 (statement); port; 4 ill

SELZ 23-27 (statement); 5 ill

ARMSTRONG, John (1893-1973) Brit; ptr

READ 37-45 (statement); port; 5 ill

ARMSTRONG-JONES, Antony Charles Robert

SEE: SNOWDON, Lord

ARNAL, Francois (1924-) Fren; ptr

PREMIER BILAN 277 (statement); port

ARNATT, Keith (1930-) Brit; photo, perf

CONTEMPORARY (statement); port; 1 ill

ENGLISH 346-351 (statement); port; 4 ill

SANDBERG 16-19 (statement); port; 8 ill

ARNATT, Raymond (1934-) Brit; sclp

CONTEMPORARY (statement); port; 2 ill

ARNAUTOFF, Jacob Victor (1930-) Amer; ptr

BETHERS II 56-57 (statement); 2 ill

ARNESON, Robert Carston (1930-) Amer; pott, sclp

EMANUEL II 38-39 (statement); 1 ill

HOPKINS 24-25 (statement); port; 1 ill

VISUAL v.2 no.1 5-8 (interview and poems); 3 ill

ARNOLD, Anne (1925-) Amer; sclp

CELEBRATION (statement); 1 ill

ARNOLD, Eve (1913-) Amer; photo

BOOTH 22-33 (interview); port; 5 ill

HOW FAMOUS 12-15 (statements); port; 4 ill

ARNOLDI, Charles (1946-) Amer; ptr, sclp

HOPKINS 80-81 (statement); port; 1 ill

ARNOULD, Marcel (1928-1974) Belg; sclp

COLLARD 12-15 (interview, 1972); port; 1 ill

AROFFO, Armando ( ) sclp

ART VOICES v.2 no.6 26-27 (interview with Susan Drysdale); 11 ill

ARONSON, Boris (1900-) Russ/Amer; ptr

100 CONTEMPORARY 6-7 (statement); port; 1 ill

ARONSON, David (1923-) Lith/Amer; ptr

ILLINOIS 1955 175-176 (statement); 1 ill

MILLER 1946 10-14 (statement); 6 ill

WHITNEY (statement); 1 ill

ARONSON, Hahum (1872-1943) Russ/Amer; sclp

100 CONTEMPORARY 8-9 (statement); port; 1 ill

ARP, Jean (Hans) (1887-1966) Fren; ptr, sclp

BANN 51-52 ("A Call for Elementarist Art," o.p. 1922)

BERCKELAERS 99-100 (essay: "Kandinsky," o.p. 1948)

BERCKELAERS 109-111 (essay: "Sophie Taeuber-Arp," o.p. 1948)

BERCKELAERS 169-171 (poems: "...et des Etoiles, des Etoiles...," "Place Blanche")

VINGTIEME N.S. no.8 13-16 (essay: "Encyclopedia Arpadienne"); 9 ill
VINGTIEME N.S. no.10 88 (poem: "Josef Albers")
VINGTIEME N.S. no.13 24-26 (essay: "Tibiis Canere," o.p. 1938); port; 2 ill
WINGLER 82-83 (essay: "Der Dichter Kandinsky," p.p.)
WINGLER 83-85 (essay: "Franz Muller's Drahtfruhling," p.p.)

ARQUITECTONICA (arch firm)
GA DOCUMENT no.7 42-43 (statement); 1 ill

ARRANZ BRAVO, Eduardo (1941-) Span; ptr
PORCEL I 49-58; port

ARRIETA AUPART, Manuel (1925-) Mexi; ptr
DICCIONARIO v.1 321-323 (statement); port; 1 ill

ARROYO, Eduardo (1937-) Span; ptr
KUNST UND POLITIK (statement); port; 5 ill

ARROYO, Jose Garcia (1934-) Mexi; ptr
DICCIONARIO v.1 329-331 (statement); port; 1 ill

ARROYO BORNSTEIN, Alexis (1938-) Mexi; ptr
DICCIONARIO v.1 325-327 (statement); port; 1 ill

ART AND LANGUAGE PRESS (group)
CONCEPTUAL ART 10-11 (essay: "Notes on Substance Concepts")
CONCEPTUAL ART 11-12 (essay: "368 Year Old Spectator")
CONCEPTUAL ART 12-13 (essay: "Notes: Harold Hurrell")

CONCEPTUAL ART 16-30 (essay: "Sunnybank")
KONZEPT (statement)
VRIES 28-49 ("Introduction," o.p. 1969)

ART CONCRET (group)
BANN 191-193 ("The Basis of Concrete Painting," o.p. 1930)

ARTEMIS, Maria (1945-) sclp, instal
AVANT-GARDE 10-11 (statement); 1 ill

ARTHUR, Revington ( ) ptr
BETHERS II 58-59 (statement); 2 ill

ARTIGAS, Josep Llorens ( ) Span
PORCEL I 123-131; port

ARTIGAU, Francesc ( ) Span; ptr
PORCEL I 39-48; ports

ARTSCHWAGER, Richard Ernst (1924-) Amer; sclp, ptr, envir
DIRECTIONS I 75 (response); 1 ill
EMANUEL II 43 (statement); 1 ill
NAYLOR 45-46 (statement); 1 ill
SKIRA 1979 31 (statement); 1 ill
SKIRA 1980 64 (statement); 3 ill
SULTAN 15-24 (statements: "Mirror" and "Revolving Door (Sine of Life)")
VARIAN II (statement); port

ARVIZU (Gertrudis Ybarra De Moctezuma) ( ) Mexi; ptr
DICCIONARIO v.1 333-335 (statement); port; 1 ill

ASAWA, Ruth (1926-) Amer; sclp
HOPKINS 26-27 (statement); port; 1 ill

ASCENCIO, Pedro (1951-) Mexi; ptr
DICCIONARIO v.1 337-339 (statement); port; 1 ill

ASHER, Elise (1914-) Amer; ptr, sclp
ART NOW v.2 no.4 (statement); 1 ill
SCHAPIRO 5 (statement); port; 1 ill

ASHER, Michael (1943-) Amer; light, ptr
ART AND TECHNOLOGY 52 (project proposal)

ASHIHARA, Yoshinobu (1918-) Japa; arch
EMANUEL I 45-46 (statement); 1 ill

ASHLEY, Robert (1930-) Amer; video
LIVE no.3 3-7 (interview); port; 7 ill

ASIS, Antonio (1932-)
LUMIERE (statement); port; 1 ill

ASKEVOLD, David (1940-) Amer; ptr, video
ROSS 96-97 (extract from interview with Carol Williams)
SONDHEIM 84-103 ("Four Selections"); 27 ill

ASKIN, Walter Miller (1929-) Amer; illus, print
CALIFORNIA--DRAWING (statement); 2 ill
VISUAL v.4 no.3 12-14 (interview); 3 ill

ASO, Saburo (1913-) Japa; ptr
KUNG 44-47 (statement); port; 2 ill

ASSOCIATION OF ARTISTS OF REVOLUTIONARY RUSSIA (group)
BOWLT 264-267 ("The Immediate Tasks," o.p. 1924)
BOWLT 264-267 ("Declaration," o.p. 1922)
BOWLT 271-272 ("Declaration," o.p. 1928)

ASTMAN, Barbara Anne (1950-) Amer;

photo
WALSH 26-27, 29 (statement); 1 ill

ATELIER 5 (arch firm)
EMANUEL I 49-52 (statement); 1 ill

ATHERTON, John C. (1900-1952) Cana; ptr
ILLINOIS 1950 155-156 (statement); 1 ill
ILLINOIS 1951 158 (statement); 1 ill
ILLINOIS 1952 164-165 (statement); 1 ill
ILLINOIS 1953 164 (statement); 1 ill
M.H. DE YOUNG 12 (response); self port
MILLER 1943 26-27 (statement); 2 ill

ATHFIELD, Ian Charles (1940-) NewZ; arch
EMANUEL I 52-53 (statement); 1 ill

ATKINS, Dorothy (1936-) Amer; ptr, sclp
LEWIS II 43 (statement); port; 1 ill

ATKINSON, Conrad (1940-) Brit; photo, print, ptr
BOSHIER (statement); port; 10 ill
CONTEMPORARY (statement); port; 1 ill
MCCLINTIC 64-66 (statement); 3 ill
EMANUEL II 45-46 (statement); port
SKIRA 1977 138-141 (essay: "Realisme Capitaliste ou Socialisme a une Personne")

ATKINSON, Terry (1939-) Brit
ART-LANGUAGE v.1 no.2 25-60 ("From an Art and Language Point of View")
ART-LANGUAGE v.1 no.2 61-71 ("Concerning Interpretation of the Bainbridge/Hurrell Models")
ART-LANGUAGE v.1 no.4 25-50 (essay: "Art Teaching")
ART-LANGUAGE v.1 no.4 51-69 ("La Pensee avec Images," in English)

ART-LANGUAGE v.2 no.1 1-27 ("Unnatural Rules and Excuses")

ART-LANGUAGE v.2 no.1 51-55 (essay: "On the Material-Character/Physical-Object Paradigm of Art")

ART-LANGUAGE v.2 no.2 11-20 ("Information")

ART-LANGUAGE v.3 no.2 1-6 ("For Thomas Hobbes--I")

ART-LANGUAGE v.3 no.2 41-43 ("Art and Language")

ART-LANGUAGE v.3 no.2 44-45 ("Community Work")

MEYER 8-21 (essay, o.p. 1969); 1 ill

MEYER 22-25 ("Lecher System," o.p. 1970)

SEE ALSO: ART AND LANGUAGE PRESS

ATLAN, Jean (1913-1960) Alge/Fren; ptr
GOLDAINE 183-185 (interview); port
PREMIER BILAN 277 (statement); port
SEUPHOR 123-124 (statement); 1 ill
VINGTIEME N.S. no.9 33 (statement); 1 ill
YALE 55-56 (statement)

ATTALAI, Gabor (1934-) Hung; ptr
NAYLOR 48-49 (statement); 1 ill

ATTAR, Hamdi El ( ) Germ; instal
PRADEL 58 (statement, o.p. 1982); 1 ill

ATTIE, Dotty (1938-) Amer; ptr
WHITE WALLS no.5 18-24 (text piece)

AUBERT, Jean ( ) Fren; arch
ARCHITECTURES 62-67 (essay: "L'Enigme du Dessin Premonitoire"); 4 ill

AUBERTIN, Bernard (1934-) Fren; ptr
DOUZE ANS 125-127 (statement); port; 6 ill
EMANUEL II 47-48 (statement); 1 ill

NAYLOR 49-50 (statement); 1 ill

AUERBACH, Frank (1931-) Germ/Brit; ptr
BOWNESS 12, 108-110 (statement); 2 ill
NAYLOR 50-51 (statement); 1 ill

AUERBACH-LEVY, William (1889-) Amer; ptr
100 CONTEMPORARY 122-123 (statement); port; 1 ill

AUGER, Jean L. ( ) ptr
ART VOICES v.4 no.1 81 (statement); 1 ill

AUGUSTE, Simon ( )
GOLDAINE 180-182 (interview); port

AULENTI, Gae ( ) Ital; arch
MARAINI 145-151 (interview)

AULONT, George (1888-) Amer; ptr
JANIS II 192-195 (statements); port; 1 ill

AURORINA (Aurorina Suarez) ( ) Mexi; ptr
DICCIONARIO v.1 341-343 (statement); port; 1 ill

AUSLOOS, Paul (1927-)Belg; photo
WALSH 31-32 (statement); 1 ill

AUSTIN, Darrel (1907-) Amer; ptr
ILLINOIS 1949 (statement)
MILLER 1942 11-17 (statement); port; 6 ill

AUTH, Robert R. (1926-) Amer; ptr
NOSANOW II 40 (statement); 1 ill

AUYON (Eduardo Auyon Gerardo) (1935-) Chin/Mexi; ptr

DICCIONARIO v.1 345-347 (statement and interview); port; 1 ill

AVEDON, Richard (1923-) Amer; photo
WALSH 32-34 (statement); 1 ill

AVERY, Milton (1893-1965) Amer; ptr
CRISPO II (statement); 13 ill
ILLINOIS 1951 158-159 (statement)
ILLINOIS 1955 176-177 (statement); 1 ill
ILLINOIS 1957 172 (response); 1 ill
ILLINOIS 1959 192 (statement); 1 ill
ILLINOIS 1961 103 (statement); port; 1 ill
ILLINOIS 1963 156-157 (statement); 1 ill

AVILA MARTINEZ, Elizabeth ( ) Mexi; ptr
DICCIONARIO v.1 349-351 (statement); port; 1 ill

AXEL, Jan (1946-) Amer; pott
HERMAN 26 (statement); port; 1 ill

AXELROD, Dee ( ) sclp
REALLIFE no.1 7 (essay: "Post-Modern Art: The Personal Perplex")

AYAKO (Ayako Tsuru Kayaba) (1941-) Japa/Mexi; ptr
DICCIONARIO v.1 353-355 (statement); port; 1 ill

AYALA GRESS, Carlos (1942-) Mexi; ptr
DICCIONARIO v.1 361-363 (statement); port; 1 ill

AYCOCK, Alice (1946-) Amer; envir, instal, sclp
ARTPARK 1977 9-11 (statement); 6 ill
AVALANCHE no.4 28-31 (statements)
COLLABORATION 152-155 (essay: "Two Fantasies of a Mythical Waterworks"); 6 ill

FOX 44-51 (statement); 8 ill
HOUSE 28-29 (statement); 1 ill
JOHNSON 221-223 (extract from "Work 1972-74," o.p. 1977); 1 ill
KUNST BLEIBT KUNST 114-117 (statement); 6 ill
NAYLOR 52-53 (statement); 1 ill
PROJECTS (statement); 8 ill
QUINTESSENCE 1-12 (project proposal); ports; 19 ill
SKIRA 1978 126 (statement); 1 ill
SKIRA 1980 134-135 (statement); 4 ill
SONDHEIM 104-121 ("Work 1972-74"); 19 ill
TRACKS v.2 no.2 23-26 ("Project for Five Wells Descending a Hillside"); 1 ill
TRACKS v.3 no.1/2 141-144 ("For Granny (1881-) Whose Lamps Are Going Out: A Short Lecture on the Effects of Afterimages")

AYERS, Doug ( ) Amer; wood
MEILACH 195 (statement); 1 ill

AYLON, Helane (1931-) Amer; ptr
FRYM 16-35 (interview); port
VISUAL v.2 no.3 44-46 ("Politics and Fear of Feminism")
WOMANART v.2 no.1 10-15, 20-21 ("Interview with Betty Parsons")

AYMONINO, Carlo (1926-) Ital; arch
EMANUEL I 53-55 (statement); 1 ill

AY-O (Takao Iijima) (1931-) Japa; sclp
DIRECTIONS I 75 (response); 1 ill

AYRES, Gillian (1930-) Brit; ptr
BOWNESS 21, 98-99 (statement); 2 ill
CONTEMPORARY (statement); port; 2 ill

AYRES, Tony ( )
ART NETWORK no.8 49 (essay)

AYRTON, Michael (1921-1975) Brit; ptr
  NAYLOR 54-55 (statement); 1 ill
  ROTHENSTEIN 62 (statement)
  WHELDON 38-43 (essay: "On the Last
  Michelangelo")

AZEVEDO, Fernando (1923-) Port
  PREMIER BILAN 278 (statement); port

AZUMA, Takamitsu (1933-) Japa; arch
  EMANUEL I 55-56 (statement); 1 ill

BABER, Alice (1928-) Amer; ptr
CELEBRATION (statement); 1 ill
NAYLOR 56-57 (extract from "Color"
in *Color Forum*, 1972); port
SCHAPIRO 6 (statement); port; 1 ill

BABOU (1946-) Fren; ptr
SKIRA 1978 104-105 (extract from
interview with Bernard Noel); 1 ill

BACKSTRAND, Jay (1934-) Amer; ptr
GUENTHER 18-19 (statement); port; 1
ill

BACON, Edmund Norwood (1910-)
Amer; arch
EMANUEL I 58-59 (statement); 1 ill

BACON, Francis (1909-) Brit; ptr
ART SINCE v.2 152 (statement, o.p.
1967)
CHIPP 620-621 (statements, o.p. 1952,
1953, 1955)
CHIPP 621-622 (extract from interview
with David Sylvester, o.p. 1963)
FRASNAY 279-285 (statement); port; 2
ill
PROTTER 246 (statement, 1962)
RITCHIE 60-64 (statements, 1952-1955);
port; 4 ill

BADAMI, Andrea (1913-) Amer; ptr
SYMBOLS (statement); 1 ill

BADEN, Mowry (1936-) Cana; envir,
instal, sclp
ARTPARK 1982 24-25, 44 (statement);
port; 1 ill
MISE EN SCENE 19, 40-57 (statement);
15 ill

BADER, Evriah ( ) ptr
ART-RITE no.9 20 (letter); 1 ill

BADGER, Gerry (1948-) Brit; photo
WALSH 35-36 (statement); 1 ill

BADILLO, Fernando Ortiz (1936-) Mexi;
ptr
DICCIONARIO v.1 365-367 (statement);
port; 1 ill

BADOT, Marco (1957-) Amer; ptr
BOSTON I (interview); 1 ill

BADURA, Michael (1938-) Germ; coll,
perf, sclp
KUNST BLEIBT KUNST 118-121
(statement); 3 ill
SKIRA 1976 33 (statement); 1 ill
SKIRA 1978 34 (statement); 1 ill
SKIRA 1980 62-63 (statement); 6 ill

BAEDER, John (1938-) Amer; ptr
SUPERREAL 112-113 (statement); 1 ill

BAER, Jo (1929-) Amer; ptr
PAOLETTI 24-26 (statements, p.p.); 1
ill
REALLIFE no.10 16-17 ("Beyond the
Pale"); 1 ill
SYSTEMATIC 23 (statement); 1 ill

BAER, Martin (1894-) Amer; ptr
M.H. DE YOUNG 13 (response); self port

BAER, Steve ( )
CRISS-CROSS no.1 2-8 ("Chapter
One"); 2 ill
CRISS-CROSS no.2 23-29 ("D Zone")

BAERMANN, Walter (1903-) arch
MCCAUSLAND 87-96 (essay:
"Technology and the Artist")

BAERTLING, Olle (1911-) Swed; ptr
NAYLOR 59-61 (statement); 1 ill

BAEZ, Concepcion (1933-) Mexi; ptr
DICCIONARIO v.1 369-371 (statement);
port; 1 ill

BAGOT, Francoise ( ) Fren/Mexi; ptr
DICCIONARIO v.1 373-375 (statement);
port; 1 ill

BAHUNEK, Branko (1935-) Yugo; ptr
TOMASEVIC 26-29 (statement); port; 1
ill

BAILEY, Clayton (1939-) Amer; pott,
sclp
HERMAN (statement); port; 1 ill
VIEWPOINT 1977 6 (extract of
interview with Lewis Stewart); 3 ill
WISCONSIN I (statement); 1 ill

BAILEY, David (1938-) Brit; photo
BOOTH 34-43 (interview); port; 6 ill
CAMPBELL 78-89 (statement); port; 11
ill
VICTORIA 16-17 (statement)

BAILEY, Marsha
SEE: MARSHA

BAILEY, Oscar (1925-) Amer; photo
ARTPARK 1977 12-16 (statement); port;
7 ill
WALSH 37-38 (statement); 1 ill

BAILEY, William (1930-) Amer; ptr
COLLABORATION 118-125 (essay:
"The Hexagonal Room: A Door, Two
Windows, and Three Paintings"); 15 ill
ILLINOIS 1961 69 (response); port; 1 ill
STRAND 12-39 (interview); port; 26 ill

BAIM, Richard ( )
REALLIFE no.4 26-28 (essay: "Ericka
Beckman, Movies for the New
American Adult")

BAIN, Elizabeth ( ) Amer; sclp
DOWNTOWN (statement); 1 ill

BAINBRIDGE, David (1941-) Brit
ART-LANGUAGE v.1 no.1 19-22 ("Notes
on M1")
ART-LANGUAGE v.1 no.1 30-32 ("Notes
on M1(2)")
ART-LANGUAGE v.1 no.2 5-7 (essay)
ART-LANGUAGE v.2 no.2 31 ("Lupus in
Fabula")
ART-LANGUAGE v.2 no.3 78
("'Praxisectomy' and
'Theoryorrhaphy'")
MEYER 22-25 ("Lecher System," o.p.
1970)
MEYER 26-31 ("Notes on M1," o.p.
1969)
SEE ALSO: ART AND LANGUAGE
PRESS

BAIRD, George (1939-) Cana; arch
CANADIAN 22-25 (statement); 6 ill

BAIZERMAN, Saul (1889-1957)
Russ/Amer; sclp
FIFTY (statement); port; 1 ill
ILLINOIS 1957 172-173 (response); 1 ill
TRACKS v.1 no.2 8-23 (journal entry:
"The Journal, May 10, 1952")

BAJ, Enrico (1924-) Ital; ptr
NAYLOR 61-63 (statement)

BAJONERO GIL, Octavio ( ) Mexi; ptr
DICCIONARIO v.1 377-379 (statement);
port; 1 ill

BAKANOWSKY, Louis J. (1930-) Amer;
arch, sclp
EMANUEL I 133-135 (statement); 1 ill

BAKEMA, Jacob B. (1914-) Dutc; arch
EMANUEL I 60-64 (statement); 1 ill
NEWMAN 21-22, 106 (statements)

NEWMAN 50-52, 60-63, 94-97, 169, 218-221 (group discussion)
NEWMAN 140-149 (essay); port; 24 ill

BALABUCK, Richard (1952-) Amer; print
COMPUTER (statements); 1 ill

BALAN, Marija (1923-) Yugo; ptr
TOMASEVIC 30-33 (statement); port; 2 ill

BALDACINI, Cesar (1921-) Fren
PREMIER BILAN 278 (statement); port

BALDESSARI, John (1931-) Amer; instal, photo, video
ART AND TECHNOLOGY 53 (project proposal)
ARTIST AND CAMERA 16-17 (statement: *Blasted Allegories*--An Explanation*); 2 ill
ART-RITE no.7 22-23 (*TV Like 1. A Pencil 2. Won't Bite Your Leg*); 1 ill
ART-RITE no.14 5-6 (response)
CALIFORNIA--COLLAGE (statement); 1 ill
CALIFORNIA--DRAWING (statement); 2 ill
DAVIS 108-111 (statements, p.p.); port
EMANUEL II 59-60 (statement); 1 ill
KONZEPT (statement: *Two Artists*)
KUNST BLEIBT KUNST 122-125 (statement); 10 ill
MEYER 32-33 (text piece)
SKIRA 1976 25 (statement); 1 ill
SKIRA 1980 104-105 (statement); 3 ill
WALSH 38-39 (statement); 1 ill

BALDI, Roland (1942-) Fren; video
NAYLOR 63-64 (statement); 1 ill

BALDICCINI, Cesar
SEE: CESAR

BALDWIN, Michael (1945-) Brit
ART-LANGUAGE v.1 no.1 23-30 (*Notes on M1*)
ART-LANGUAGE v.1 no.2 14-21 (*Plans and Procedures*)
ART-LANGUAGE v.1 no.3 30-35 (*General Notes*)
ART-LANGUAGE v.1 no.4 25-50 (essay: *Art Teaching*)
ART-LANGUAGE v.1 no.4 51-69 (*La Pensee avec Images,* in English)
ART-LANGUAGE v.2 no.1 1-27 (*Unnatural Rules and Excuses*)
ART-LANGUAGE v.2 no.1 51-55 (essay: *On the Material-Character/Physical-Object Paradigm of Art*)
ART-LANGUAGE v.2 no.2 11-20 (*Information*)
ART-LANGUAGE v.3 no.2 1-6 (*For Thomas Hobbes--I*)
ART-LANGUAGE v.3 no.2 41-43 (*Art and Language*)
ART-LANGUAGE v.3 no.2 46-51 (*Rambling: To Partial Correspondents*)
ART-LANGUAGE v.3 no.2 59-62 (*Little Grey Rabbit Goes to Sea*)
ART-LANGUAGE v.3 no.2 68-80 (*'Mr. Lin Yutang Refers to *Fair Play*...?'*)
ART-LANGUAGE v.3 no.2 93-94 (*Accidental Synopsis*)
MEYER 22-25 (*Lecher System,* o.p. 1970)
SEE ALSO: ART AND LANGUAGE PRESS

BALFOUR, Alan H. ( ) arch
ON SITE no.5/6 26-27 (essay: *Solar Energy and Survival*)

BALJEU, Joost (1925-) Dutc; sclp
BANN 287-295 (essay: *The Constructive Approach Today,* o.p. 1964); 1 ill
NAYLOR 65-66 (statement); 1 ill

BALL, George (1929-) Amer; ptr
ILLINOIS 1963 74 (statement); 1 ill

BALL, Hugo ( )
ON SITE no.4 45 (statement and poem,
1917)

BALL, Lillian ( ) Amer; sclp
ARTPARK 1979 (statement); 1 ill

BALL, Sydney (1953-) Atrl; ptr, print
ART NETWORK no.1 12 (interview);
port

BALLA, Giacomo (1871-1958) Ital; ptr,
sclp
APOLLONIO 24-27 ("Manifesto of the
Futurist Painters," o.p. 1910)
APOLLONIO 27-31 ("Futurist
Paintings: Technical Manifesto," o.p.
1910)
APOLLONIO 45-50 ("The Exhibitors to
the Public," o.p. 1912)
APOLLONIO 132-134 ("Futurist
Manifesto of Men's Clothing," o.p.
1913)
APOLLONIO 197-200 ("Futurist
Reconstruction of the Universe," o.p.
1915)
CHIPP 289-293 ("Futurist Painting:
Technical Manifesto," o.p. 1910)
CHIPP 294-298 ("The Exhibitors to the
Public," o.p. 1912)
GUGGENHEIM II 135-137 ("Manifesto of
the Futurist Painters," o.p. 1910)

BALLENTINE, Jene (1942-) Amer; ptr
LEWIS I REVISED 43-46 (statement);
port; 2 ill

BALLESTER, Bonilla (1941-) ptr
SEE: EQUIPO REALIDAD

BALMER, Jean (1905-) Amer; print
CALIFORNIA--PRINTS (statement)

BALSLEY, John G. (1944-) Amer; sclp,
ptr
ILLINOIS 1969 70-71 (statement); 1 ill

BALSON, Ralph (1890-) Brit/Atrl
SEUPHOR 126 (statement)

BALTAUSS, Richard (1946-) Fren;
photo
WALSH 40 (statement); 1 ill

BALTH, Carel (1939-) Dutc; photo
SKIRA 1979 26 (statement); 2 ill

BALTHUS (Balthazar Klossowski de
Rola) (1908-) Fren; ptr
PROTTER 245-246 (extract from
interview with Georges Bernier, 1956);
1 ill

BALTZ, Lewis (1945-) Amer; photo
BARROW 57-60 (essay: "Review of *The
New West*," o.p. 1975)

BAMA, James E. (1926-) Amer; ptr, illus
MAGIC 12-15 (statement); port; 10 ill

BAND, Max (1900-) Lith/Amer; ptr
100 CONTEMPORARY 10-11
(statement); port; 1 ill

BANDAU, Joachim (1936-) Germ; sclp
HAUSSER 38-39 (statement); 1 ill

BANGERT, Charles J. ( ) Amer; print
COMPUTER (statements); 1 ill

BANGERT, Colette (1934-) Amer; print
COMPUTER (statements)

BANJO, Casper (1937-) Amer; sclp
LEWIS II 113 (statement); port

BANKS, Catherine C. (1898-) Amer; ptr
SYMBOLS (statement); 1 ill

BANKS, Ellen (1938-) Amer; ptr
BOSTON II (statement); 1 ill

BANNARD, Walter Darby (1934-) Amer; ptr
ART NOW v.2 no.7 (statement); 1 ill
ARTFORUM v.4 no.8 34-37 (essay: "Color, Paint and Present-Day Painting"); 5 ill
ARTFORUM v.5 no.4 30-35 (essay: "Present-Day Art and Ready-Made Styles")
ARTFORUM v.6 no.6 4 (letter)
ARTFORUM v.6 no.8 22-32 (essay: "Cubism, Abstract Expressionism, David Smith")
ARTFORUM v.7 no.3 4 (letter)
ROSE II REVISED 192 (statement: "The Mainstream and the Avant-Garde," o.p. 1967)
ROSE II REVISED 195-200 (extract from essay: "Notes on American Painting of the Sixties," o.p. 1970)
TUCKER I 12 (statement)

BANNON, Tony ( ) Amer; film
ARTPARK 1975 58-61 (statement); port; 9 ill

BANTING, John (1902-1972) Brit; ptr
LONDON BULLETIN no.18/19/20 2 (essay: "The Careless Have Inherited the Earth")

BARACKS, Barbara ( ) perf, video
TRACKS v.3 no.1/2 48-53 ("Chapter 4, from Pleasure, A Novel in Progress")

BARAJAS-TONDRE, Calvin ( )
RAICES 26 (statement); 1 ill

BARANDIARAN, Rafael ( ) Mexi; ptr
DICCIONARIO v.1 381-383 (statement); port; 1 ill

BARANIK, Rudolph (1920-) Lith/Amer; ptr
ART-RITE no.6 25 (statement)
ART-RITE no.9 18 (statement)
GUMPERT III 45, 55-56 (statement and text piece)
NAYLOR 69-70 (statement); 1 ill
TRACKS v.2 no.2 30-31 ("A Statement"; "From a Response to a Critic's Letter")

BARATELLA, Paolo (1935-) Ital; ptr
KUNST UND POLITIK (statement with Giangiacomo Spadari); port; 1 ill

BARBASH, Steven A. (1933-) Amer; ptr
NOSANOW I 35-36 (statement); 2 ill

BARD, Gayle (1936-) Amer; ptr
WISCONSIN II (statement); 1 ill

BARDIN, Jesse Redwin (1923-) Amer; ptr
ART PATRON ART 11-12 (statement); port; 1 ill

BARINGER, Richard (1921-) Amer; ptr
ILLINOIS 1963 119 (statement); 1 ill
VARIAN II (statement); port

BARK, Jared (1944-) Amer; perf, photo
GROH (statement)

BARKER, Walter (1921-) Amer; ptr, sclp
ILLINOIS 1963 62 (statement); 1 ill

BARLACH, Ernst (1870-1938) Germ; sclp
ART AND ARTIST 9-32 ("selected letters," 1889-1938, o.p. 1947); 1 ill
FRIEDENTHAL 209-212 (letter to Reinhard Piper, 1911); 2 ill
GROTE 62 (statement); 1 ill
MIESEL 91-93 ("From a Notebook,1916")

MIESEL 93-96 (letter to Reinhard Piper, 1911)
MIESEL 127-136 (play: "Dead Day," 1912)
MIESEL 207-208 (letters, 1934, 1938)
SCHMIDT 31, 33-37, 59-60, 68-72, 75-76, 88, 110-114, 116, 119, 151, (letters and statements, 1933-1938)
THORN 44, 50, 110, 112, 132, 165, 171, 194, 201-202, 206, 210, 236, 261, 267-268, 286, 289, 292, 294, 298, 305, 308-310, 329, 335 (statements, p.p.)

BARLOW, Phyllida (1944-) Brit; sclp
BRITISH (statement); 1 ill
CONTEMPORARY (statement); port; 1 ill

BARNES, Edward Larrabee (1915-)Amer; arch
DIAMONSTEIN I 13-27 (interview); ports
DIAMONSTEIN II 16-32 (interview); port; 2 ill
HEYER 324-335 (interview); 18 ill
SEARING 86-91 (statement); 5 ill

BARNES, Robert M. (1934-) Amer; ptr
YOUNG 1965 (statement); 2 ill

BARNET, Will (1911-) Amer; ptr
ART NOW v.2 no.6 (statement); 1 ill
GUITAR 2-11 (interview]; port; 4 ill
ILLINOIS 1969 147 (statement); 1 ill
SPIRITUAL 123-129 (essay: "A Personal Reflection on the Spiritual Aspects in American Art")
SPIRITUAL 138-140 (group discussion)

BARNETT, Elizabeth Bradford ( ) Amer/Mexi; ptr
DICCIONARIO v.1 389-391 (statement); port; 1 ill

BARNETT, Jonathan (1937-)Amer; arch

COLLABORATION 90-95 (essay: "Beyond Revivalism and the Bauhaus: A New Partnership in the Arts")
DIAMONSTEIN II 208-228 (interview); port; 2 ill
EMANUEL I 69-71 (statement); 2 ill

BARON, Richard ( )
AVALANCHE no.13 7 (statement); 1 ill

BARON ARCE, Jose (1928-) Mexi; ptr
DICCIONARIO v.1 393-395 (statement); port; 1 ill

BARRADAS MORENO, Noe (1942-) Mexi; ptr
DICCIONARIO v.1 397-399 (statement); port; 1 ill

BARRAGAN, Luis (1902-) Mexi; arch
EMANUEL I 71-73 (statement); 1 ill
RODMAN II 96-97 (statements)

BARRE, Martin (1924-) Fren; ptr
CHOIX 11 (statement, o.p. 1979); 1 ill

BARRETT, Neil (1915-) Amer; ptr
ILLINOIS 1959 192 (statement); 1 ill
ILLINOIS 1961 155 (response); 1 ill

BARRETT-DANES, Alan (1936-) Amer; pott
CAMERON E 8-17 (response); 11 ill

BARRETT-DANES, Ruth ( ) Amer; pott
CAMERON E 8-17 (response); 11 ill

BARRIENTOS OLIVARES, Evangelina (1951-) Mexi; ptr
DICCIONARIO v.1 401-403 (statement); port; 1 ill

BARRIOS, Ignacio ( ) Mexi; ptr
DICCIONARIO v.1 405-407 (statement); port; 1 ill

BARRIOS DE DIAZ, Ana Rosa
SEE: ANA ROSA

BARRON MIRANDA, Luis (1938-)
Mexi; ptr
DICCIONARIO v.1 409-411 (statement);
port; 1 ill

BARROW, Thomas F. (1938-) Amer;
photo
BARROW vii-viii ("Preface")
WALSH 44-45 (statement); 1 ill

BARRY, Judith (1949-) Amer; video
REALLIFE no.6 33-35 (essay: "Building
Conventions")

BARRY, Robert Thomas (1936-) Amer;
sclp, ptr
BATTCOCK II 141-142 (interview with
Arthur Rose, o.p. 1969)
BELFORD 129-157 (group discussion)
CELANT 115-119 (statement); 2 ill
CONCEPTUAL ART 32, 38, 41, 45
(statements)
GEORGIA 118-166 (group discussion:
"Artists' Convention," in Athens, GA.,
1/7/1977, moderated by Jan van der
Marck)
KONZEPT (statement)
MEYER 34-41 (interview with Ursula
Meyer); 1 ill
VIEW v.1 no.2 (interview); port; 8 ill

BARTHELEMY, Gerard (1937-) Fren;
ptr
SKIRA 1977 12 (statement); 1 ill

BARTHELME, Frederic ( )
ART-LANGUAGE v.1 no.2 8-10 ("Three
from May 23rd 1969")

BARTLETT, Jennifer (1941-) Amer; ptr,
design
MARSHALL 20 (statement); port; 5 ill

MUNRO 396-408 (interview); port; 3 ill
TRACKS v.3 no.3 64-98 ("Falling in
Love")

BARTOLI NATINGUERRA, Amerigo
(1891-) Ital; ptr
VERZOCCHI 39-43 (statement); self
port; 1 ill

BARTOLINI, Luciano (1948-) Ital; coll
ART-RITE no.14 5-6 (response)

BARTOLINI, Luigi (1892-) Ital; ptr
VERZOCCHI 45-49 (statement); self
port; 1 ill

BARTOLOZZI, Rafael Lozano (1943-)
Span; ptr
PORCEL I 49-58 (interview); port

BARTON, Frank (1931-) Amer; ptr
DICCIONARIO v.1 413-415 (statement);
port; 1 ill

BARTON, Loren (1893-) Amer; ptr
BRITANNICA 1 (statement); port; 1 ill

BARTON, Peter (1943-) Amer; video
ROSS 12-15 (statement); 5 ill

BARUCHELLO, Gianfranco (1924-) Ital;
ptr
SKIRA 1976 66-67 (statement); 1 ill

BASALDELLA, Afro
SEE: AFRO

BASALDELLA, Mirko (1910-) Ital; sclp
SEE: MIRKO

BASCHET, Bernard (1917-) Fren;
sclp,sound
GRAYSON 1-12 (essay: "Structures
Sonores," o.p. 1968); 6 ill

BASCHET, Francois (1920-) Fren; sclp, sound
GRAYSON 13-15 (essay: "Structures Sonores and Future"); port

BASELITZ, Georg (1938-) Germ; ptr
CHOIX 12 (statement, o.p. 1982); 1 ill
STEDELIJK 88-89 (statement); 4 ill

BASKIN, Leonard (1922-) Amer; sclp
ILLINOIS 1961 162 (response); port; 1 ill
QUADRUM no.3 150-151 (statement); 3 ill
RODMAN I 169-177 (interview)
RODMAN III 91-96 (statements)
SELZ 34-38 (statement); 5 ill

BASQ, Carlos (1929-)
FRASNAY 238 (statement)

BASS, Joel (1942-) Amer; ptr
ART-RITE no.19 25-26 (statements); 1 ill
TUCKER I 20 (statement)

BASS, Saul (1923-) Amer; print, film
KEPES I 200-205 (essay: "Movement, Film, Communication"); 5 ill

BASSFORD, Wallace (1900-) Amer; ptr
ILLINOIS 1950 156 (statement); 1 ill
ILLINOIS 1951 159 (statement); 1 ill

BASSI, Sofia Celorio de ( ) Mexi; ptr
DICCIONARIO v.1 417-419 (statement); port; 1 ill

BASSING, Carolyn (1937-) Amer; pott
HERMAN 29 (statement); port; 1 ill

BATES, Leo (1944-) Amer; ptr, film
BRENTANO 150-151 (statement); 1 ill

BATESON, Gregory ( )

MOTHERWELL 24-37 (group discussion: "The Western Round Table on Modern Art," San Francisco, 1949)

BATEY, Andrew (1944-) Amer; arch
ARCHER 24-27, 95 (statement); port; 6 ill
COUNTERPOINT 22-35 (statements); 29 ill
GA HOUSES no.10 94-95 (statement); 7 ill

BATHO, Claude (1935-) Fren; photo
WALSH 45-46 (statement); 1 ill

BATHO, John (1939-) Fren; photo
WALSH 46-47 (statement); 1 ill

BATMANIS, Cynthia Morgan (1939-) Amer; ptr
O'KANE (statement); 1 ill

BATSON, Margaret (1899-) Amer; ptr
SYMBOLS (statement); 1 ill

BATT, Miles G. (1933-) Amer; ptr
ART PATRON ART 13-14 (statement); port; 1 ill

BATTAGLIA, Carlo (1933-) Ital; ptr
EMANUEL II 68, 70 (statement); 1 ill
NAYLOR 74-75 (statement); 1 ill
SKIRA 1979 51-52 (statement); 1 ill

BATTEN, Mark ( ) Brit; sclp, ptr
OPEN AIR 1960 (statement); 1 ill

BATTENBERG, John (1931-) Amer; sclp
VISUAL v.2 no.4 6-11 (interview); 4 ill

BATTKE, Heinz (1900-1966) Germ; ptr
THORN 13, 80, 91, 167, 168, 190, 237, 332 (statements, p.p.)

BAT-YOSEF, Myriam (1931-) Icel/Isra; sclp, ptr
NAYLOR 75-76 (statement); 1 ill

BAUCHANT, Andre (1873-1958) Fren; ptr
RAYNAL 49-52 (statement); 2 ill

BAUERMEISTER, Mary (1934-) Germ/Amer; sclp, ptr
ALBRIGHT-KNOX 284-285 (letter, 7/1971); 1 ill
VARIAN II (statement); port

BAUGHMAN, Ross ( ) Amer; photo
LEEKLEY 120-123 (statement); 3 ill

BAUM, Donald (1922-) Amer; sclp
ACKLAND 20-37, 46-47 (group discussion, 10/29/79); 1 ill
HOUSE 30-31 (statement); 2 ill

BAUMBACH, Harold (1905-) Amer; ptr
ILLINOIS 1952 165-166 (statement); 1 ill

BAUMEISTER, Willi (1889-1955) Germ; ptr
ABSTRACTION no.1 3 (statement); 2 ill
ALBRIGHT-KNOX 246-247 (letter, 4/1953); 1 ill
ART SINCE v.1 159 (statement, o.p. 1960)
CLAUS 22-27 (statement)
GROHMANN 416-417 ("Gedanken," p.p. 1947)
PLATSCHEK 109-113 ("Zigarren," 1944)
PLATSCHEK 114-115 ("Ohne Titel"); 2 ill
POENSGEN 122-123 ("Die Vision," 1947)
PREMIER BILAN 280 (statement); port
QUADRUM no.8 65-68 (extracts from *L'Inconnu dans Art*, in German and English)

THORN 10, 17, 28, 34, 36, 40, 41, 45, 47, 48, 50, 51-54, 58, 86, 92, 105, 109, 112, 118, 120, 121, 126, 151, 153, 155, 161, 177, 184, 190, 197, 202-204, 219, 223, 224, 233, 234, 237, 251, 277, 281, 282, 288, 306, 326 (statements, p.p.)
WINGLER 101 (essay: "Oskar Schlemmer," p.p.)
WINGLER 102-106 (essay: "Fernand Leger," p.p.)

BAXTER, Iain (1936-) Cana; design,sclp
ART AND TECHNOLOGY 53 (project proposal)
CANADA 84-85 (statement); port; 1 ill
CONCEPTUAL ART 31, 38, 41, 42, 44 (statements)
VIEW v.2 no.4 (interview); port; 21 ill
SEE ALSO: N. E. THING CO., LTD.

BAXTER, Ingred (1938-)
SEE: N. E. THING CO., LTD.

BAXTER, John (1912-) Amer; sclp
ARTFORUM v.1 no.3 32 (statement); 1 ill
ILLINOIS 1963 50 (statement); 1 ill
SOME 32 (statement); 1 ill

BAXTER, Robert (1933-) Amer; ptr
DAUGHERTY 86-105 (statements); ports; 2 ill
NORTH LIGHT 18-23 (statement); port; 7 ill

BAY, Didier (1944-) Fren; photo
SKIRA 1976 13 (statement); 4 ill
SKIRA 1978 67 (statement); 1 ill

BAYER, Herbert (1900-) Aust/Amer; photo, ptr, design
HAUSSER 40-41 (statement, o.p. 1974); 1 ill
HILL 111-131 (interview, 1977); port
JANIS I 110 (statement); 1 ill

WALSH 48-51 (statement); 1 ill

BAYER, Svend (1946-)Amer; pott
CAMERON E 18-29 (response); 14 ill

BAYLINSON, A.S. (1882-) Amer; ptr
100 CONTEMPORARY 12-13 (statement); port; 1 ill

BAYLISS, George V. (1931-) Amer; ptr
KRESGE (statement); port; 1 ill

BAYRLE, Thomas (1937-) Germ; ptr, print
KUNST UND POLITIK (statement); port; 3 ill

BAZAINE, Jean (1904-) Fren; ptr
ART SINCE v.1 157-158 (statement, o.p. 1960)
CHARBONNIER v.1 95-106 (interview)
GOLDAINE 129-133 (interview); port
GROHMANN 444-445 ("Anmerkungen zur Malerei," o.p. 1953)
PREMIER BILAN 280 (statement); port
RITCHIE 12-16 (statement); port; 3 ill
SEGHERS 262-265 (essay: "Art of Painting," p.p.)
SEUPHOR 129 (statement); 1 ill
VINGTIEME N.S. no.9 26 (statement)
YALE 56-57 (statement)

BAZILE, Bernard (1952-) Fren; sclp, instal
IN SITU 13-23 (statement); 19 ill

BAZIOTES, William (1912-1963) Amer; ptr
ART SINCE v.1 156 (poem, o.p. 1948; statement, o.p. 1959)
CHIPP 565 (statement, o.p. 1951)
IT IS no.4 11 ("Notes on Painting")
JANIS I 101 (statement); 1 ill
MILLER 1952 12-14 (statement); 4 ill

MOTHERWELL 8-22 (three group discussions: "Artists' Sessions at Studio 35," New York, 1950)
NEW DECADE 10-11 (statement); 2 ill
PERSONAL (statement)
POSSIBILITIES 2-6 (essay: "I Cannot Evolve any Concrete Theory"); 6 ill
ROSE II 142-143 (statements, o.p. 1945, 1947)
ROSE II REVISED 142-145 (group discussion, o.p. 1952)

BEAL, Gifford (1879-1956) Amer; ptr
BRITANNICA 2 (statement); port; 1 ill

BEAL, Jack (1931-) Amer; ptr
ART NOW v.2 no.3 (statement); 1 ill
ART VOICES v.5 no.3 36 (statement); 1 ill
ARTHUR 10-23 (interview); port; 22 ill
COLLABORATION 96-103 (essay: "Restaurant Pavilions for Bryant Park: Musings on Variety"); 10 ill
GOODYEAR 16-23 (interview); 3 ill
STRAND 40-59 (interview); port; 19 ill
SUPERREAL 64-65 (statement); 1 ill

BEALL, Dennis Ray (1929-) Amer; print
VISUAL v.1 no.3 14-16 ("An Open Letter to Art Critics"); ports

BEARD, Peter (1938-) Amer; photo
WALSH 51-52 (statement); 1 ill

BEARDEN, Romare (1914-) Amer; ptr, coll
ART NOW v.2 no.4 ("The Poetics of Collage"); 1 ill
CRISPO I (statement); 17 ill
DIAMONSTEIN I 28-39 (interview); ports
FAX I 128-145 (statements); port; 2 ill
FAX II ("Foreword")
FINE 156-159 (statements, o.p. 1960, 1964, 1971); 3 ill

BEASLEY, Bruce (1939-) Amer; sclp
ILLINOIS 1969 107 (statement); 1 ill

BEATON, Cecil (1904-) Brit; photo
HILL 21-32 (interview, 1976); port

BEATTIE, Basil (1935-) Brit; ptr
CONTEMPORARY (statement); port; 2 ill

BEATTIE, George (1919-) Amer; ptr
FULBRIGHT 12-13 (statement); 1 ill

BEAUCHAMP, Robert (1923-) Amer; ptr
ART NOW v.1 no.8 (statement); 1 ill

BEAUDIN, Andre (1895-) Fren; ptr
GOLDAINE 99-101 (interview); port
RAYNAL 53-59 (statement); 2 ill

BEAUDOUIN, Eugene (1898-) Fren; arch
EMANUEL I 79-81 (statement); 1 ill

BECHER, Bernhard (Bernd) (1931-) Germ; photo
ARTIST AND CAMERA 18-19 (extract from interview with Lynda Morris, o.p. 1974); 2 ill
EUROPE 27 (statement); 2 ill
IDENTITE 21-22 (interview with Jacques Clayssen); port
MEYER 46-49 (text piece: "The Function"); 3 ill
PAOLETTI 30-32 (statements, p.p.); 2 ill
SKIRA 1976 10 (statement); 9 ill

BECHER, Hilla (1934-) Germ; photo
ARTIST AND CAMERA 18-19 (extract from interview with Lynda Morris, o.p. 1974); 2 ill
EUROPE 27 (statement); 2 ill

IDENTITE 21-22 (interview with Jacques Clayssen); port
MEYER 46-49 (text piece: "The Function"); 3 ill
PAOLETTI 30-32 (statements, p.p.); 2 ill
SKIRA 1976 10 (statement); 9 ill

BECHTLE, Robert Alan (1932-) Amer; ptr
EMANUEL II 78-79 (statement); 1 ill
HOPKINS 28-29 (statement); port; 1 ill
IMAGE COLOR FORM 8-9 (statement); 1 ill
JOHNSON 151-157 (interview with Brian O'Doherty); 1 ill
MEISEL 25-54 (statement, 1973); port; 95 ill
NAYLOR 81 (statement); 1 ill

BECHTOLD, Erwin (1925-) Germ; ptr
NAYLOR 82 (statement); 1 ill
SKIRA 1978 80 (statement); 1 ill

BECK, Rosemarie (1923-) Amer; ptr
YOUNG 1957 (statement); 2 ill

BECK, Stephen ( ) Amer; video
DAVIS 48-52 (statement: "Video Synthesis"); port

BECKER, Carolyn Berry
SEE: BERRY, Carolyn

BECKER, Fred (1913-) Amer; print
AMERICAN PRINTS 15, 64 (statement); 1 ill

BECKER, Maurice (1889-) Amer; ptr
100 CONTEMPORARY 14-15 (statement); port; 1 ill

BECKER, Nan ( )
WHITE WALLS no.7 2-11 (text piece)

BECKLEY, Bill (1946-) Amer; photo, ptr
APPLE 31 (statement); 1 ill
ARTIST AND CAMERA 20-21 (extract from interview with Chantal Darcy-Lette, o.p. 1980); 2 ill
AVALANCHE no.3 18-21 (statement); 28 ill

BECKMAN, Susan ( ) Amer; pott
HERMAN 30 (statement); port; 1 ill

BECKMAN, William (1942-) Amer; ptr
ARTHUR 24-37 (interview); port; 21 ill
GOODYEAR 24-30 (interview); self port; 3 ill
MCCLINTIC 16-18 (statement); 3 ill
SUPERREAL 66-67 (statement); 1 ill

BECKMANN, Max (1884-1950) Germ/Amer; ptr, print
ART SINCE v.2 148 (statement, o.p.1959)
CHIPP 187-192 (essay: "On My Painting," o.p. 1941; originally a speech given in London, 1938); self port
FRIEDENTHAL 213-215 (letters, 1915; statement, o.p. 1948); 2 ill
GOLDWATER 447-448 (statement, 1938)
GROHMANN 366-369 ("Bekenntnis," o.p. 1920)
GROTE 60 (statement, 1950)
ILLINOIS 1951 160-161 (statement)
MIESEL 106-107 ("The New Program" 1914); 107-109 ("Creative Credo" 1920)
PROTTER 211-212 (extract from talk: "On My Painting," given at the Burlington Galleries, London, 1938)
SCHMIDT 161-163, 176, 185-186, 196, 205, 211 (journal entries, 1940-1945)
THORN 59-60, 79, 80, 110, 179 (statements, p.p.)

BECKWITH, William (1952-) Amer; sclp
NOSANOW I 37 (statement); 1 ill

BEDFORD, Chris ( ) Amer; design, film
LIFE 202-214 (interview); port

BEDI, Mitter (1926-) Indi; photo
WALSH 56-57 (statement); 1 ill

BEEBE, Tina ( ) Amer; arch
GA HOUSES 7 158-165 (essay: "Coloring Space"); port

BEEBY, Thomas Hall (1941-) Amer; arch
EMANUEL I 82-83 (statement); 1 ill
GA HOUSES 8 126-127 (statement); 7 ill

BEERE, Susan (1944-) Brit; sclp
HAYWARD 1978 74-77 (statement); 4 ill

BEERE, Tommy ( ) ptr
ZAIDENBERG 131-132 (essay: "The Derivation of Impulses"); 2 ill

BEHAN, John (1932-) Iris; sclp
KNOWLES 118-119 (statement); 4 ill

BEHL, Wolfgang (1918-) Germ/Amer; sclp
ILLINOIS 1957 174-175 (response); 1 ill

BEHNE, Adolf (1895-1948) arch
CONRADS 47-48 ("New Ideas on Architecture," o.p. 1919)

BEHNISCH, Gunter (1922-) Germ; arch
EMANUEL I 83-84 (statement); 1 ill

BEHNKE, Leigh (1946-) Amer; ptr
SUPERREAL 116-117 (statement); 1 ill

BEHRENS, Peter C. (1868-1940) Germ; arch

GROHMANN 458-459
("Stadtebauliches," p.p. 1914)

BEHRENS, Roy R. (1946-) Amer; ptr
WISCONSIN II (statement); 1 ill

BEIGNEUX, Ariane ( ) Amer; ptr
DAUGHERTY 66-85 (statements); ports;
2 ill

BEINART, Julian (1932-) SoAf; arch
KEPES VIII 184-200 (essay: "Visual
Education")

BEIRNE, Bill ( ) perf
APPLE 52 (statement, o.p. 1975); 2 ill

BEJAR, Feliciano (1920-) Mexi; ptr
DICCIONARIO v.1 429-431 (statement);
port; 1 ill

BEKEN, Lewis (1924-) Amer; ptr
ILLINOIS 1969 181 (statement); 1 ill

BEKKER, David (1897-) Russ/Amer;
ptr
100 CONTEMPORARY 16-17
(statement); port; 1 ill

BEKMAN, Diana (1947-) Mexi; ptr
DICCIONARIO v.1 433-435 (statement);
port; 1 ill

BEL GEDDES, Norman (1893-1958)
Amer; arch
SAYLER 334-336 (essay: "The
Challenge of Industrial Design")

BELAIN PENA, Fernando (1921-) Mexi;
ptr
DICCIONARIO v.1 437-439 (statement);
port; 1ill

BELANGER, Gerard ( ) Cana; sclp
ROYER 103-105 (interview, 1974)

BELINE, George (1887-) Amer; ptr
100 CONTEMPORARY 18-19
(statement); port; 1 ill

BELING, Helen (1914-) Amer; sclp
ILLINOIS 1957 175 (response); 1 ill

BELKIN, Arnold (1930-) Cana; print,
ptr
DICCIONARIO v.1 441-443 (statement);
port; 1 ill

BELKOVIC, Dragica (1931-) Yugo; sclp
TOMASEVIC 34-36 (statement); port; 1
ill

BELL, Charles (1935-) Amer; ptr
MEISEL 55-82 (statement); port; 44 ill

BELL, Larry Stuart (1939-) Amer; sclp
ART VOICES v.5 no.4 61, 64 (response);
1 ill
ARTFORUM v.3 no.5 28 (statement,
1963); 9 ill
EMANUEL II 81-82 (statement)
IRVINE 31, 82 (statement); 1 ill
NAYLOR 85-86 (statement); 1 ill
ROSE I 21-25 (statement); 4 ill
ROSE II REVISED 175-176 (extract from
essay: "Andy Warhol," o.p. 1965)
RUSSELL J 115-116 (essay: "Andy
Warhol," o.p. 1965)
SPURLOCK 28-37 (statement); ports
WIGHT 41-65 (interview); ports

BELL, Robert ( )
AVALANCHE no.9 28-29 (interview); 3
ill

BELLANY, John (1942-) Brit; ptr
CONTEMPORARY (statement); port; 1
ill

BELLEGARDE, Claude (1927-) Fren;

ptr
SKIRA 1977 31 (statement); 1 ill
SKIRA 1977 132-134 (essay: "Pour une Sociobiologie de la Coleur")

BELLING, Rudolph ( ) sclp
SCHMIDT 47-48 (letter, 1933)

BELLMER, Hans (1902-1975) Germ; ptr
ART SINCE v.2 154 (statement, o.p. 1957)
JEAN 304-305 (statement)
LIPPARD 63-66 (essay: "Birth of the Doll," o.p. 1936)
WEBB 366-370 (interview, 1972); 2 ill

BELLO GOMEZ, Alberto (1925-) Mexi; ptr
DICCIONARIO v.1 445-447 (statement); port; 1 ill

BELLON SOBRINO, Alberto (1952-) Mexi; ptr
DICCIONARIO v.1 449-451 (statement); port; 1 ill

BELLOW, Cleveland (1946-) Amer; ptr
LEWIS II 102-103 (statement); port; 1 ill

BELLOWS, George (1882-1925) Amer; ptr
GOLDWATER 460-462 (statement)
PROTTER 206 (extract from *The Paintings of George Bellows*)
SEGHERS 203-207 (statement, p.p.)

BELLUSCHI, Pietro (1899-) Ital/Amer; arch
EMANUEL I 86-88 (statement); 1 ill
HEYER 224-233 (interview); 14 ill
KEPES IX 62-73 (extract from "private communications" with John E. Burchard)

BELMOOD, Husny
SEE: NEAGU, Paul

BELSKY, Franta (1921-) Czec; sclp
LONDON COUNTY (statement); 1 ill

BELTRAN, Amelia I. de ( ) Mexi; ptr
DICCIONARIO v.1 453-455 (statement); port; 1 ill

BELTRAN, Esteban Aguirre (1916-) Mexi; ptr
DICCIONARIO v.1 457-459 (statement); port; 1 ill

BEMBERG, Georges ( ) ptr
TIGER no.1 41-42 (essay: "As a View of Human Freedom")

BEN (1935-) Ital/Fren
CHOIX 13 (extract from poem: "J'attends la guerre"); 1 ill

BENAVIDES, Ruben Garcia (1934-) Mexi; ptr
DICCIONARIO v.1 461-463 (statement); port; 1 ill

BENAYOUN, Robert (1926-) ptr
EXPOSICION (statement); port; 1 ill

BENDER, Eleanor ( ) print
VISUAL v.1 no.3 9-11 (interview); 3 ill

BENEDETTO, Angelo di
SEE: DI BENEDETTO, Angelo

BENEDICT-JONES, Linda (1947-) Amer; photo
WALSH 59-60 (statement); 1 ill

BENEDIT, Luis Fernando (1937-) Arge; sclp, instal, print
EMANUEL II 84-86 (statement); 1 ill
NAYLOR 87-88 (statement); 1 ill

BENET, Rafael ( ) Span; ptr
PORCEL I 59-80 (interview); 1 ill

BENGELSDORF, Rosalind (1916-)
Amer; ptr
ABSTRACT 21-22 (essay: "The New
Realism"); 1 ill

BENGLIS, Lynda (1941-) Amer; sclp,
ptr, video
ART-RITE no.5 6 (response)
ART-RITE no.7 11-12 (response); 1 ill
CELEBRATION (statement); 1 ill
EMANUEL II 86-88 (statement); 1 ill
FINCH COLLEGE (statement); port; 3 ill
HESS 96-97 (statement)
NAYLOR 88-89 (statement); 1 ill
PARACHUTE no.6 9-11 (interview in
English)
ROSS 42-43 (statement)

BENGSTON, Billy Al (1934-) Amer; ptr
ART VOICES v.5 no.4 61, 66 (response);
1 ill

BENJAMIN, Karl Stanley (1925-) Amer;
ptr
CALIFORNIA--PAINTING 34 (statement);
1 ill

BENN, Ben (1884-1983) Russ/Amer; ptr
FORUM 1916 44 (statement); 1 ill
100 CONTEMPORARY 20-21
(statement); port; 1 ill

BENNETT, Derek (1944-) Amer; photo
WALSH 60-61 (statement); 1 ill

BENNETT, James (1948-) Amer; metal
METALWORKS (statement); 1 ill

BENNETT, Rainey (1907-) Amer; ptr
ILLINOIS 1951 161 (statement); 1 ill
ILLINOIS 1957 175-176 (response); 1 ill
ILLINOIS 1959 193-194 (statement); 1 ill

ILLINOIS 1961 66 (response); port; 1 ill
ILLINOIS 1963 85 (statement); 1 ill

BENNETT, Ward ( ) design
DIAMONSTEIN V 16-31 (interview);
ports; 9 ill

BENNING, James ( ) Amer; sclp, envir,
film
ARTPARK 1978 14-17 (statement); port;
8 ill

BENNY, Robert ( ) ptr
BETHERS I 218-219 (statement); 1 ill

BENNYWORTH, Steve ( ) Amer; sclp
ART PATRON ART 15-16 (statement);
port; 1 ill

BENOFF, Miki (1922-) Amer; sclp
CELEBRATION (statement); 1 ill

BENOIT, Jean (1922-) Cana; sclp
NAYLOR 92 (statement); 1 ill

BENRATH, Frederic (1930-) Fren; ptr
NAYLOR 92-93 (statement); 1 ill

BENRIMO, Tom (1887-1958) Amer; ptr
ILLINOIS 1951 161-162 (statement); 1 ill
ILLINOIS 1957 176-177 (response); 1 ill

BENTLEY, Claude R. (1915-) Amer; ptr
ILLINOIS 1950 158 (statement)
ILLINOIS 1951 162 (statement); 1 ill
ILLINOIS 1952 166-167 (statement)
ILLINOIS 1957 177-178 (response); 1 ill

BENTON, Fletcher (1931-) Amer; sclp
DIRECTIONS I 75 (response); 1 ill
HOPKINS 30-31 (statement); port; 1 ill
KINETIC 18-19 (statement); port; 2 ill

BENTON, Suzanne ( ) Amer; sclp

ARTPARK 1975 62-63 (statement); port; 4 ill

BENTON, Thomas Hart (1889-1975) Amer; ptr
BRITANNICA 3 (statement); port; 1 ill
CUMMINGS 24-46 (interview, 1973); self port; 2 ill
FORUM 1916 48 (statement); 1 ill
M.H. DE YOUNG 14-15 (response); self port
MCCAUSLAND 21-26 (essay: "Business and Art")
MCCOUBREY 201-207 (essay: "On Regionalism," o.p. 1951)
ROSE II 106-108 (statement, o.p. 1916)
ROSE II 108-111 (extract from *An Artist in America,* o.p. 1951)
ROSE II REVISED 87-90 (extract from *An Artist in America,* o.p. 1951)
SPENCER 263-274 (extract from *An Artist in America*); 1 ill

BENTON-HARRIS, John (1939-) Amer; photo
WALSH 61-62 (statement); 1 ill

BENY, Roloff (1924-) Cana
NAYLOR 94 (statement)

BEN-ZION (1897-) Russ/Amer; ptr
ILLINOIS 1950 158-159 (statement); 1 ill
ILLINOIS 1955 178 (statement); 1 ill

BENZLE, Curtis (1949-) Amer; pott
HERMAN 31 (statement); port; 1 ill

BEOTHY, Etienne (1897-) Hung; sclp
ABSTRACTION no.1 4 (statement); 2 ill
ABSTRACTION no.2 3 (statement); 2 ill
TEMOIGNAGES I 22-27 (statement); port; 4 ill

BEOTHY, Karl ( ) sclp
ABSTRACTION no.3 4 (statement); 1 ill

ABSTRACTION no.4 (essay: "L'Abstraction est la Qualite Specifique de l'Homme"); 1 ill
ABSTRACTION no.5 3 ("L'Objet Vivant"); 2 ill

BERDECIO, Roberto (1916-) Mexi; ptr
DICCIONARIO v.1 465-467 (statement); port; 1 ill

BERDYSZAK, Jan (1934-) Poli; sclp
NAYLOR 95-96 (statement); 1 ill

BEREAL, Ed (1937-) Amer; sclp
IRVINE 68, 80-81 (statement)

BEREND-CORINTH, Charlotte (1880/81-) Germ; ptr
THORN 266, 274 (statements, p.p.)
WINGLER 37-41 (essay: "Vom Leben und Schaffen Corinths," p.p.)

BERENICE (Berenice Garmendia Ramirez) (1947-) Mexi; ptr
DICCIONARIO v.1 469-471 (statement); port; 1 ill

BERENSOHN, Paulus ( ) Amer
IRVINE 86 (statement)

BERG, Adrian (1929-) Brit; ptr
CONTEMPORARY (statement); port; 1 ill

BERGALLO, Armando
SEE: TALLER DE MONTEVIDEO

BERGAMI, Aldo (1903-) Ital; ptr
VERZOCCHI 51-55 (statement); self port; 1 ill

BERGEN, Emiel ( ) ptr
DADA 113, 116-117 (statement)

BERGHAUER-RAYMOND, Helene ( )
ptr
DADA 113-114 (statement)

BERGHE, Frits van den (1883-1939)
Belg; ptr
RAYNAL 61-64 (statement); 2 ill

BERGSTEIN, Gerry (Gary) (1945-)
Amer; ptr
BOSTON I (interview); 1 ill
BOSTON III (interview); 1 ill

BERKEY, John C. ( ) Amer; illus, ptr
MAGIC 16-19 (statement); port; 5 ill

BERKMAN, Phil ( ) Amer; perf
BRAKKE 150-156 (text piece: "6
Sketches for Architectural Graffiti")
WHITE WALLS no.7 26-43 (statements);
9 ill

BERKO, Ferenc (1916-) Amer; photo
WALSH 64-65 (statement); 1 ill

BERKOWITZ, Leon (1915-) Amer; ptr
NAYLOR 97-98 (statement); port

BERLAGE, Hendrik Petrus (1856-1934)
Dutc; arch
ROTH 399-402 (essay: "The New
American Architecture," o.p. 1912)

BERLANDINA, Jane (1898-) Amer; ptr
ILLINOIS 1955 178-179 (statement); 1 ill

BERLANT, Tony (1941-) Amer; sclp
HOUSE 32-33 (statement, o.p. 1982); 2
ill

BERLEWI, Henryk (1894-1967) Poli; ptr
LUMIERE (statement); port; 1 ill

BERLIE, Christiane (1938-) Mexi; ptr

DICCIONARIO v.1 473-475 (statement);
port; 1 ill

BERLIN, Beatrice (1922-) Amer; print
FRYM-53 (interview); port

BERMAN, Eugene (1899-1972)
Russ/Amer; ptr
ILLINOIS 1950 159 (statement); 1 ill
ILLINOIS 1955 179-180 (statement); 1 ill
ILLINOIS 1963 116 (statement); 1 ill
ILLINOIS 1965 54 (statement); 1 ill

BERMAN, Fred J. (1926-) Amer;
ptr,photo
WISCONSIN II (statement); 1 ill
YOUNG 1960 (statement); 2 ill

BERMEN, Leonid
SEE: LEONID

BERNARD, Emile (1868-1941) Fren;
illus,ptr
EDDY 36,43 (extracts from *Souvenirs
Sur Paul Cezanne*, o.p. 1912)
LHOTE 293-298 (essay: "Les Palettes
d'Eugene Delacroix," o.p. 1910)

BERNARDES, Sergio (1919-) Braz; arch
EMANUEL I 90-93 (statement); 1 ill

BERNASCONI, Ugo (1874-) Ital; ptr
VERZOCCHI 57-61 (statement); self
port; 1 ill

BERNDT, Randall (1944-) Amer; ptr
WISCONSIN II (statement); 1 ill

BERNEA, Horia (1938-) Ruma; ptr
NAYLOR 100-101 (statement); 1 ill

BERNER, Bernd (1930-) Germ; ptr
NAYLOR 101-102 (statement); 1 ill

BERNHARD, Ruth (1905-) Amer; photo
MITCHELL 30-47 (statement); ports; 15 ill
WALSH 65-67 (statement); 1 ill

BERNHARDT, John ( ) sclp
ARTFORUM v.1 no.5 30-34 (group discussion); port; 2 ill

BERNIK, Janez (1933-) Yugo; ptr
SKIRA 1976 67 (statement); 1 ill

BERNOFSKY, Gene ( )
CRISS-CROSS no.1 19-20 ("Lunar Power"); 1 ill

BERNSTEIN, Judith (1942-) Amer; ptr
CRISS-CROSS no.4 28-33 (interview with Jeanie Weiffenbach); 6 ill
SCHAPIRO 8 (statement); port; 1 ill

BERNSTEIN, Lou ( ) photo
TIME-LIFE II 102-103 (statement); 2 ill

BERNSTEIN, Saul ( ) Amer; illus
CALIFORNIA--DRAWING (statement); 2 ill

BERNSTEIN, Theresa ( ) Amer; ptr
100 CONTEMPORARY 22-23 (statement); self port; 1 ill

BERROCAL, Miguel-Ortiz (1933-) Span; sclp
NAYLOR 102-104 (statement); 1 ill
SKIRA 1977 68 (statement); 1 ill

BERRUECOS, Juan (1948-) Mexi; ptr
DICCIONARIO v.1 477-479 (statement); port; 1 ill

BERRY, Arthur (1923-) Amer; sclp
LEWIS I REVISED 27 (statement); port; 1 ill

BERRY, Carolyn (Carolyn Berry Becker) (1930-) Amer; ptr
VISUAL v.2 no.3 44 (letter)

BERRY, Ian (1934-) Brit; photo
CAMPBELL 260-271 (statement); port; 13 ill

BERRY, Paul ( )
GROH (statement)

BERTHA ALICIA (Bertha Alicia Cruz) (1935-) Mexi; ptr
DICCIONARIO v.1 481-483 (statement); port; 1 ill

BERTHOLIN, Jean-Marie (1936-) Fren; sclp
EMANUEL II 92-94 (statement); 1 ill
NAYLOR 104-105 (statement); 1 ill
SKIRA 1977 51 (statement); 1 ill

BERTHOLLE, Jean (1909-1970) Fren; ptr
PREMIER BILAN 280 (statement); port

BERTHOLO, Rene (1935-) Port; ptr
ART SINCE v.2 327 (statement, o.p. 1965)
SKIRA 1978 107 (statement); 1 ill

BERTINI, Gianni (1922-) Ital; ptr
ART SINCE v.2 327 (statement, o.p. 1962)

BERTOIA, Harry (1915-1978) Amer; sclp
DIRECTIONS I 75 (response); 1 ill
ILLINOIS 1961 48 (response); port; 1 ill
ILLINOIS 1963 94-95 (statement); 1 ill
JANIS I 72 (statement); 1 ill
KEPES IX 62-73 (extract from "private communications" with John E. Burchard)
LETTERS 6-7 (letter); 2 ill
NAYLOR 105-106 (statement); 1 ill

BERTOLO, Diane ( ) Amer; sclp, instal
ARTPARK 1983 12-13 (statement); port; 5 ill

BERTONCINI, Mario ( ) perf, sound
PARACHUTE no.4 10-15 (interview, in English); 4 ill

BERTRAND, Gaston (1910-) Belg
PREMIER BILAN 281 (statement); port

BERTRAND, Huguette (1925-) Fren; ptr
SEUPHOR 132-133 (statement); 1 ill

BERTRAND, Jean-Pierre (1937-) Fren; ptr, instal, film
EMANUEL II 95-96 (statement); 1 ill
NAYLOR 106-107 (statement); 1 ill

BESNARD, Paul Albert (1849-1934) Fren; ptr
THORN 40, 97 (statements, p.p.)

BEST, David (1945-) Amer; sclp, pott
VISUAL v.4 no.1 13-15 (interview); port; 3 ill

BEST, Sue (1953-) sound,light
BOSHIER (statement); port; 20 ill

BETANCOURT CUEVAS, Jorge (1927-) Mexi; ptr
DICCIONARIO v.1 485-487 (statement); port; 1 ill

BETETA QUINTANA, Ignacio M. (1888-) Mexi; ptr
DICCIONARIO v.1 489-491 (statement); port; 1 ill

BETSBERG, Ernestine Osver (1909-) Amer; ptr
ILLINOIS 1959 194 (statement); 1 ill

BEUYS, Joseph (1921-) Germ; print, sclp, ptr
ART SINCE v.2 324 (extract from interview, o.p. 1964)
AVALANCHE no.5 12-15 (statement); port
AVALANCHE no.9 4-7 (interview: "public dialogue"); ports
CELANT 48-55 (statement); 7 ill
KUNST UND POLITIK (statement); port; 1 ill
MULLER 128-139 (statement); ports; 15 ill
PARACHUTE no.4 22-23 (statement in English); port
PROFILE v.1 no.1 (interview); port
SCHWEBEL 15-42 (interview); port
SKIRA 1975 42 (interview with Hans van der Grinten, 12/70); 2 ill
WEBER 21-31 ("Public Dialogue"); port; 1 ill

BEVERLOO, Cornelis van
SEE: CORNEILLE

BEYDLER, Gary Earl (1944-) Amer; film, photo
AVALANCHE no.13 8 (statement); 1 ill

BEYER, Steven J. (1951-) Amer; sclp
WHITE WALLS no.5 25-31 (text piece)

BEZ, Frank ( ) Amer; photo
CALIFORNIA--PHOTOGRAPHY (statement); port; 4 ill

BEZEM, Naphtali (1924-) Isra; ptr
SEITZ I (statement); 3 ill

BHAVSAR, Natvar (1934-) Indi/Amer; ptr
CONCEPT 22-24 (statement); 1 ill
NAYLOR 108-109 (statement); 1 ill
SKIRA 1979 51, 53 (statement); 1 ill

BIALA, Janice (1903-) Poli/Amer; ptr
MOTHERWELL 8-22 (three group
discussions: "Artists' Sessions at
Studio 35," New York, 1950)

BIASI, Guido (1933-) Ital; print
SKIRA 1977 70 (statement); 1 ill

BICKHAM, Helen (1935-) Amer; ptr
DICCIONARIO v.1 493-495 (statement);
port; 1 ill

BIDDLE, George (1885-1973) Amer; ptr
BOSWELL 115-116 (statement)
BRITANNICA 5 (statement); port; 1 ill
FIRST AMERICAN 21-22 (essay:
"Artists' Boycott of Berlin Olympics
Art Exhibition")

BIEDERMAN, Charles (1906-) Amer;
ptr, sclp
ARTFORUM v.3 no.7 34-38 (essay:
"The Visual Revolution of Structurist
Art"); 7 ill
BANN 223-234 (extract from *Art as the
Evolution of Visual Knowledge*, o.p.
1948)
EMANUEL II 97-98 (statement); 1 ill
NAYLOR 109-110 (statement); 1 ill

BIEDERMAN, James (1947-) Amer; sclp
CHOIX 14 (statement, o.p. 1982); 1 ill

BIELER, Ted (1938-) Cana; sclp
CANADA 36-37 (statement); port; 1 ill

BIGGE, John (1892-) Brit; ptr
READ 47-56 (statement); port; 4 ill

BIGGERS, John (1924-) Amer; ptr
FAX I 267-282 (statements); port; 1 ill

BIGOT, Gary (1949-) Belg; coll
SKIRA 1979 25 (statement); 1 ill

BILL, Max (1908-) Swis; sclp, ptr, arch
ART SINCE v.1 291 (statement, o.p.
1967)
DESIGN 2 (interview)
EMANUEL II 99-100 (statement); 1 ill
GROHMANN 418-419 ("Die
Mathematische Denkweise in der
Kunst Unserer Zeit," o.p. 1949)
GROHMANN 419 ("Konkrete Kunst,"
o.p. 1943)
KEPES VI 150-151 (essay: "Structure
as Art? Art as Structure?"); 1 ill
NAYLOR 111-112 (statement, 1974)
POENSGEN 112-113 ("Ein
Standpunkt," 1944)
PREMIER BILAN 281 (statement); port
SKIRA 1975 87 (extract from essay:
"Art, a non-changeable fact." 1968); 1
ill
VINGTIEME v.1 no.4 29 (essay: "Swiss
Peasants and Absolute Form")
VINGTIEME v.2 no.1 51-52 (essay:
"The Mastery of Space"); 7 ill

BILLEN, Andre ( ) Belg; ptr
COLLARD 16-19; port; 1 ill

BILLGREN, Ola (1940-) Dani; ptr
SANDBERG 26-27 (statement); 3 ill

BILLINGS, Henry (1901-) Amer; ptr,
illus
BOSWELL 119 (statement)
FIRST AMERICAN 94-96 (essay:
"Survey of Painters' Organizations")

BILLMAN, Blaine A. (1953-) Amer; illus
NOSANOW II 41 (statement); 1 ill

BINDE, Gunar (1933-) Latv; photo
WALSH 70-71 (statement); 1 ill

BINDER, Ursula (1941-) Germ; sclp
SKIRA 1979 60 (statement); 2 ill

BINDER/FISCHER/FIALA (arch firm)
GA HOUSES 168-173 (statements); 21 ill

BINFORD, Julien (1908-) Amer; ptr
ILLINOIS 1952 167-168 (statement); 1 ill

BINKS, Ronald (1934-) Amer; ptr
FULBRIGHT 14-15 (statement); 1 ill

BIRCH, Janett Rozillio de (1949-) Mexi;
ptr
DICCIONARIO v.1 497-499 (statement);
port; 1 ill

BIRDWELL, Robert (1924-) Amer; ptr
KNOXVILLE (statement); port; 9 ill

BIRES, Mihaijlo (1912-) Yugo; ptr
TOMASEVIC 37-39 (statement); port; 1
ill

BIRGE, Priscilla ( ) Amer; coll, photo
VISUAL v.2 no.3 38-40 (essay: "Women
Artists in New York City: Getting
Their Act Together"); 1 ill

BIRKERTS, Gunnar ( ) arch
GA   DOCUMENT   no.2   92-107
(statements); 21 ill

BIRMELIN, August Robert (1933-)
Amer; ptr
ILLINOIS 1965 122 (statement); 1 ill
WHITNEY (statement); 1 ill

BIRNBAUM, Dara (1946-) Amer; video,
perf
REALLIFE   no.3   15   ("Inserted
Realities")

BIROLLI, Renato (1906-) Ital; ptr
PAINTING 11 (statement); port; 1 ill
PREMIER BILAN 281 (statement); port
VERZOCCHI 63-67 (statement); self
port; 1 ill

BISCHOFF, Elmer Nelson (1916-) Amer;
ptr
ENVIRONMENT 38-39 (statement); 1 ill
GUSSOW 52-53 (letter, 1971); 1 ill
HOPKINS 32-33 (statement); port; 1 ill
ILLINOIS 1959 194-195 (statement); 1 ill
ILLINOIS 1961 65 (response); port; 1 ill

BISHOP, Isabel (1902-) Amer; ptr
BRITANNICA 6 (statement); port; 1 ill
DIAMONSTEIN I 40-53 (interview); ports
ILLINOIS 1963 110 (statement); 1 ill
ILLINOIS 1965 204-205 (statement); 1 ill
ILLINOIS 1967 75 (statement); 1 ill
M.H. DE YOUNG 19 (response); self port
MUNRO 145-153; ports; 2 ill

BISHOP, Jeffrey Britton (1949-) Amer;
ptr
GUENTHER 20-21 (statement); port; 1
ill

BISHOP, Joseph ( )
REALLIFE no.4 8-10 (essay: "Desperate
Character")

BISSIERE, Roger (1886-1964) Fren; ptr
FRASNAY 151-155 (statement)
GOLDAINE 33-35 (interview); port
PREMIER BILAN 282 (statement); port
SEUPHOR 134 (statement)

BITKER, Colette ( ) Belg; ptr
COLLARD 20-24 (interview); port; 1 ill

BJORGE, Nancy Loo (1939-) Amer; sclp
WISCONSIN I (statement); 1 ill

BLACK, David Evans (1928-) Amer; sclp
ILLINOIS 1969 135 (statement); 1 ill

BLACK, Harold (1913-) Amer; ptr
DICCIONARIO v.1 501-503 (statement);
port; 1 ill

DICCIONARIO v.2 37-38 (statement, on the painter Kent Bowman)

BLACK TARANTULLA ( ) Video
ART-RITE no.7 11 (response)

BLACKADDER, Elizabeth (1931-) Brit; ptr
CONTEMPORARY (statement); port; 2 ill

BLACKBURN, Ed (1947-) Amer; pott, sclp
VIEWPOINT 1978 6-9 (statement); 4 ill

BLACKBURN, Morris (1920-1979) Amer; print, ptr
BETHERS II 60-61 (statement); 2 ill

BLACKWELL, Thomas Leo (1938-) Amer; ptr
MEISEL 83-108 (statement); port; 48 ill
SUPERREAL 118-119 (statement); 1 ill

BLADEN, Ronald (1918-) Cana/Amer; sclp
ART AND TECHNOLOGY 55 (project proposal); 2 ill
CANADA 14-15 (statement); port; 1 ill
ROSE II REVISED 260 (statement, o.p. 1965)

BLAINE, Julien ( )
GROH (statement); 6 ill

BLAINE, Nell Walden (1922-) Amer; ptr
ART NOW v.2 no.1 (statement); 1 ill
GUSSOW 136-138 (interview, 1970); 1 ill
MUNRO 261-271 (interview); port; 2 ill
NAYLOR 113-115 (statement); 1 ill
SCHAPIRO 9 (statement); port; 1 ill

BLAIR, Carl Raymond (1932-) Amer; ptr
MORRIS 26-31 (statements); ports; 3 ill

BLAKE, Peter Jost (1920-) Amer; arch
COOPER-HEWITT I 11-12 (essay: "Warning: The Surgeon General has determined that Open Space...")
COOPER-HEWITT II 158-159 (essay: "The End of Cities?")
EMANUEL I 96-97 (statement); 1 ill
ON SITE no.2 10-11 (response)

BLAKE, Peter Thomas (1932-) Brit; ptr
CONTEMPORARY (extract from interview with Colin Painter, p.p.); port; 2 ill
ENGLISH 44-49 (statement); port; 9 ill

BLAKEMORE, John (1936-) Brit; photo
CAMPBELL 56-67 (statement); port; 11 ill
WALSH 74-75 (statement); 1 ill

BLAMEY, Norman (1914-) Brit; ptr
CONTEMPORARY (statement); port; 2 ill

BLANCARTE OSUNA, Alvaro (1934-) Mexi; ptr
DICCIONARIO v.1 505-507 (statement); port; 1 ill

BLANCH, Arnold (1896-1968) Amer; ptr, illus
BRITANNICA 7 (statement); port; 1 ill
FIRST AMERICAN 63-64 (essay: "Tendencies in American Art")
FORTY (statement); 2 ill
GUITAR 12-23 (interview); port; 4 ill
ZAIDENBERG viii ("Foreword")
ZAIDENBERG 53-57 (essay: "The Creative Incentive"); 4 ill

BLANCH, Lucile Linquist (1895-) Amer; ptr
ZAIDENBERG 157-160 (essay: "Transferrance of Ideas to the Canvas"); 1 ill

BLANCHARD, Carol (1918-) Amer; ptr
ILLINOIS 1950 160 (statement); 1 ill
ILLINOIS 1952 169 (statement); 1 ill

BLANCHE, Jacques Emile (1861-1943) Fren; ptr
THORN 131 (statement, p.p.)

BLANCO, Lazaro (1938-) Mexi; photo
WALSH 75-77 (statement); 1 ill

BLANCO FUENTES, Margarita (1889-1972) Mexi; ptr
DICCIONARIO v.1 513-515 (statement); port; 1 ill

BLANCO VENEGAS, Adolfo Xavier (1915-) Mexi; ptr
DICCIONARIO v.1 504-511 (statement); port; 1 ill

BLANE, Marc ( ) Amer
CRISS-CROSS no.7/8/9 56-61 (project proposal)

BLASHFIELD, Edwin Howland (1848-1936) Amer;ptr
ROSE II 88-90 (extract from essay: "The Painting of Today," o.p. 1914)

BLATAS, Arbit (1908-) Lith/Amer; ptr
100 CONTEMPORARY 26-27 (statement); port; 1 ill

BLAUE REITER (group)
GROHMANN 403 ("Programmatisches," o.p. 1911/12)
GROHMANN 403-404 ("Vorwort der Aussteller," o.p. 1913)

·BLAUVELT, Melinda (1949-) Amer; photo
FRALIN 28-29, 42 (statement); 1 ill

BLAYTON, Betty (1937-) Amer; ptr
FINE 239-241 (poem: "Tune Into Yourself"); 2 ill

BLAZEJE, Zbigniew (1942-) Russ/Cana; sclp
CANADA 78-79 (statement); port; 1 ill

BLEE, Michael J. (1931-) Brit; arch
KEPES III 76-89 (essay: "The Meeting: Man and Man-Made Object, Architectural Implications")

BLITCHTEIN, Martha (1937-) Mexi; ptr
DICCIONARIO v.1 517-519 (statement); port; 1 ill

BLOC, Andre (1896-1966) Fren; sclp, ptr
OPEN AIR 1960 (statement); 1 ill
TEMOIGNAGES I 28-35 (statement); port; 5 ill
TEMOIGNAGES II 10-13 (statement); port; 8 ill

BLOCH, Albert (1882-1961) Amer; ptr
EDDY 202-205 (statements)

BLOCHER, Heidi ( ) ptr
WOMANART v.1 no.4 13-17 (essay: "On Paula Modersohn-Becker, German Painter")

BLODGETT, Peter ( ) Amer; metal
HAYSTACK 2 (statement); 1 ill

BLOEDEL, Joan Stuart Ross (1942-) Amer; ptr
GUENTHER 22-23 (statement); port; 1 ill

BLOK (group)
BANN 103-106 (essay: "What Is Constructivism," o.p. 1924)

BLOM, Holger (1906-) Swed; arch
EMANUEL I 98-99 (statement); 1 ill

BLOMSTEDT, Aulis (1906-) Finn; arch
EMANUEL I 99-100 (statement); 1 ill

BLONDEL, Michel (1942-) Fren; ptr
SKIRA 1978 68-69 (statement); 1 ill

BLOW, Sandra (1925-) Brit; ptr
CONTEMPORARY (statement); port; 2 ill

BLUE SKY
SEE: SKY, Blue

BLUEMNER, Oscar (1867-1938) Germ/Amer; ptr
FORUM 1916 52 (statement); 1 ill
ROSE II 56-57 (statement, o.p. 1916)

BLUHM, Norman (1920-) Amer; ptr
FRASNAY 238 (statement)
IT IS no.2 41 (statement)
IT IS no.3 59-62 (group discussion: "5 Participants in a Hearsay Panel")
IT IS no.5 40 ("A Cahier Note")

BLUM, Andrea (1950-) Amer; sclp, instal
ARTPARK 1982 8-11, 44 (statement); port; 6 ill

BLUM, June (1939-) Amer; ptr
WOMANART v.1 no.3 26, 32 (response); port

BLUMBERG, Donald (1935-) Amer; photo
WALSH 81-83 (statement); 1 ill

BLUMBERG, Feiga Yuli (1894-1964) Lith/Amer; ptr
M.H. DE YOUNG 21 (response)

BLUME, Peter (1906-) Russ/Amer; ptr
ADVERSARY 11-12 (extract from interview at the Museum of Modern Art, New York, 1943)
ART SINCE v.2 154 (statement, o.p. 1968)
FIRST AMERICAN 27-30 (essay: "The Artist Must Choose")
100 CONTEMPORARY 30-31 (statement); port; 1 ill
PROTTER 244 (statement, 1963)

BO, Jorgen (1919-) Dani; arch
EMANUEL I 100-102 (statement); 1 ill

BOBB, Victor ("Hickory Stick Vic") (1892-1978) Amer; wood
FERRIS 1-31 (statement); ports; 3 ill

BOB-E BEHIND THE VEIL ( ) perf
ART-RITE no.6 20 (statement)

BOBOVEC, Dragan (1950-) Yugo; ptr
TOMASEVIC 40-42 (statement); port; 2 ill

BOBROWICZ, Mark (1955-) Amer; arch
SPIRIT 28-33 (statement); 8 ill

BOCCACCI, Marcello (1914-) Ital; ptr
VERZOCCHI 69-73 (statement); self port; 1 ill

BOCCIA, Edward Eugene (1921-) Amer; ptr
ILLINOIS 1957 180-181 (response); 1 ill

BOCCIONI, Umberto (1882-1916) Ital; ptr, sclp
APOLLONIO 24-27 ("Manifesto of the Futurist Painters," o.p. 1910)
APOLLONIO 27-31 ("Futurist Paintings: Technical Manifesto," o.p. 1910)

APOLLONIO 45-50 (*The Exhibitors to the Public,* o.p. 1912)

APOLLONIO 51-52, 61-65 (*Technical Manifesto of Futurist Sculpture,* o.p. 1912)

APOLLONIO 88-90 (*The Plastic Foundations of Futurist Sculpture and Painting,* o.p. 1913)

APOLLONIO 92-95 (*Plastic Dynamism,* o.p. 1913)

APOLLONIO 107-110 (*Futurist Dynamism and French Painting,* o.p. 1913)

APOLLONIO 150-154 (*Absolute Motion + Relative Motion = Dynamism,* o.p. 1914)

APOLLONIO 172-181 (extract from *Futurist Painting and Sculpture,* o.p. 1914)

CHIPP 289-293 (*Futurist Painting: Technical Manifesto,* o.p. 1910)

CHIPP 294-298 (*The Exhibitors to the Public,* o.p. 1912)

CHIPP 298-304 (*Technical Manifesto of Futurist Sculpture,* o.p. 1912); self port

GOLDWATER 434-437 (statements, 1910, 1912)

GUGGENHEIM II 135-137 (*Manifesto of the Futurist Painters,* o.p. 1910)

POENSGEN 87, 89-90 (*Der Futurismus,* 1910)

PROTTER 207-208 (extract from *The Second Futurist Manifesto,* o.p. 1910)

BOCHNER, Mel (1940-) Amer; ptr
ART VOICES v.5 no.4 44-51 (*The Domain of the Great Bear*)
ARTFORUM v.6 no.4 28-33 (*The Serial Attitude*); 1 ill
BATTCOCK II 180-181 (text piece, o.p.1970)
BATTCOCK V 92-102 (essay: *Serial Art, Systems, Solipsism,* o.p. 1967)
CONCEPTUAL ART 34 (statement)

JOHNSON 127-130, 133-134 (extract from essay: *Serial Art Systems: Solipsism,* o.p. 1967)
KONZEPT (statement)
MEYER 50-59 (*Excerpts from Speculation (1967-1970)* o.p. 1970); 3 ill
MURS 6 (statement); 1 ill
PAOLETTI 33-35 (statements, p.p.); 1 ill
ROSE II REVISED 254-257 (extract from essay: *Serial Art, Systems, Solipsism,* o.p. 1967)

BOCK, Walter (1919-) Amer; illus
CALIFORNIA--DRAWING (statement); 2 ill

BODE, Barbara ( )
CRISS-CROSS no.7/8/9 100-104 (*Mercury*); 13 ill

BODEN, Neville (1929-) Brit; sclp
BRITISH (statement); 1 ill

BODMER, Walter (1903-) Swis; ptr
PREMIER BILAN 282 (statement); port

BOERO, Renata (1936-) Ital; photo, coll
SKIRA 1979 104 (statement); 2 ill

BOEZEM, Marinus Lambertus van den (1934-) Dutc; ptr, video
CELANT 198-203 (statement); 5 ill
EMANUEL II 111 (statement); 1 ill
GROH (statement); 1 ill
NAYLOR 119 (statement); 1 ill

BOFILL, Ricardo (1939-) Span; arch
ARCHER 58-61, 95 (statement); port; 8 ill
EMANUEL I 103-105 (statement); 1 ill
GA DOCUMENT no.3 48-57, 64-67 (statements, in French and Japanese); 27 ill

BOMAR, Bill (1919-) Amer; ptr
ILLINOIS 1955 181 (statement); 1 ill

BON, Christoph (1921-) Brit; arch
SEE: CHAMBERLIN POWELL AND BON

BONAND, Jenny ( )
REALLIFE no.7 19 (poem: "Elk Grazed as if Nothing Had Happened")

BONDREAU, Catharine (1922-) Cana; sclp
CANADA 38-39 (statement); port; 2 ill

BONET, Jordi (1932-) Cana; ptr, sclp
ROYER 93-98 (interview, 1974)

BONET, Pep (1941-) Span; arch
EMANUEL I 111-112 (statement); 1 ill

BONEVARDI , Marcelo (1929-) Amer; ptr, sclp
VARIAN I (statement, "translated from a notebook page"); port

BONILLA, Jorge Valencia Ballester (1941-) Span; ptr
SEE: EQUIPO REALIDAD

BONILLA, Miguel Antonio (1954-) Mexi; ptr
DICCIONARIO v.1 521-523 (poem); self port; 1 ill

BONILLA CORTES, Rafael ( ) Mexi; ptr
DICCIONARIO v.1 525-527 (statement and interview); port; 1 ill

BONNARD, Pierre (1867-1947) Fren; ptr
FRIEDENTHAL 242-246 (extract from conversation with M. Teriade, 1942; extract from conversation with Angele Lamotte, 1943); 2 ill
PROTTER 177-178 (letters, 1915)

PROTTER 178 ("The Primary Conception," 1943)
SEGHERS 243-244 (statement, p.p.)

BONNEFOI, Christian (1948-) Fren; ptr
SKIRA 1978 74 (statement); 1 ill

BONNELL, Mary ( ) sclp
IT IS no.4 15 (statement)

BONSET, I. K.
SEE: DOESBURG, Theo van

BONTECOU, Lee (1931-) Amer; sclp
MILLER 1963 12-19 (statement); port; 9 ill
MUNRO 377-387 (interview); port; 2 ill
PREMIO NACIONAL 1964 48-49 (statement); port; 1 ill

BOOGAERTS, Pierre (1946-) Belg; photo, coll
PARACHUTE no.1 12-15 (statement); 6 ill
SKIRA 1979 24-25 (statement); 1 ill
VEHICULE (statement); 4 ill
WALSH 86-88 (statement); 1 ill

BOOKATZ, Samuel (1910-) Amer; ptr, sclp
ILLINOIS 1952 170-171 (statement)
ILLINOIS 1953 167-168 (statement); 1 ill

BOOTH, Cameron (1892-) Amer; ptr
FORTY (statement); 2 ill

BOOTH, Laurence Ogden (1936-) Amer; arch
GA HOUSES 8 12-36 (statement); port; 59 ill

BOOTH, Robert Alan ( ) Amer; sclp, envir
ARTPARK 1983 14-15 (statement); 2 ill

BOOTH HANSEN (arch firm)
SEE: BOOTH, Laurence

BOPPEL, Todd (1934-) Amer; ptr
WISCONSIN II (statement); 1 ill

BORACK, Stanley ( ) Amer; ptr, illus
MAGIC 24-27 (statement); port; 4 ill

BORDUAS, Paul Emile (1905-1960)
Cana; ptr
ART SINCE v.1 158-159 (statement, o.p.
1960/61)

BORES, Francisco (1898-) Span; ptr
GOLDAINE 96-98 (interview); port

BORGESE, Leonardo (1904-) Ital; ptr
VERZOCCHI 75-79 (statement); self
port; 1 ill

BORI, Christl ( ) Amer; arch, design
LIFE-89; port

BORIANI, Davide (1936-) Ital; sclp
CHIPP 623 (statement, o.p. 1966)
KINETIC 20-23 (statement); port; 3 ill

BORKOWSKI, Mary (1916-) Amer; text
SYMBOLS (statement); 1 ill

BORNSTEIN, Harry (1923-) Amer; illus
CALIFORNIA--DRAWING (statement); 2
ill

BORNSTEIN, Ruth Lecher (1927-)
Amer; illus
CALIFORNIA--DRAWING (statement); 2
ill

BOROFSKY, Jonathan (1942-) Amer;
ptr
JOHNSON 262-264 (extract from letter
to Ellen Johnson, 1980); 1 ill
SKIRA 1980 125 (statement); 1 ill

BORONAT, Modesto (1928-) Mexi; ptr
DICCIONARIO v.2 17-19 (statement);
port; 1 ill

BORRA, Pompeo (1898-) Ital; ptr
VERZOCCHI 81-85 (statement); self
port; 1 ill

BORSTEIN, Elena (1946-) Amer; ptr
CELEBRATION (statement); 1 ill
WOMANART v.1 no.4 4-5 (essay:
"Why Have There Been No Great
Women Architects?")

BORY, Jean-Francois (1938-) Fren; sclp
SKIRA 1976 96-97 (statement); 1 ill

BOSA, Louis (1905-) Ital/Amer; ptr
BETHERS I 222-223 (statement); 1 ill
BRITANNICA 9 (statement); port; 1 ill
ILLINOIS 1950 160-161 (statement); 1 ill
ILLINOIS 1953 168-169 (statement); 1 ill
ILLINOIS 1959 196-198 (statement); 1 ill

BOSCH GARCIA, Carlos (1919-) Mexi;
ptr
DICCIONARIO v.2 21-23 (statement);
port; 1 ill

BOSCOTT-RIGGS, Hilary ( ) instal
ART NETWORK no.2 37 (statement); 2
ill

BOSHIER, Derek (1937-) Brit; ptr,
photo, film
BOWNESS 23, 148-150 (statement); 2 ill
CONTEMPORARY (statement); port; 1
ill
NAYLOR 126-127 (statement); 1 ill

BOSLSTERLY, Walther (1955-) Mexi;
ptr
DICCINARIO v.2 25-27 (statement);
port; 1 ill

BOSMAN, Richard (1944-) Amer; ptr
GUMPERT III 56-57 (statement)

BOSSHARD, R.T. (1889-) Fren; ptr
RAYNAL 75-79 (statement); 2 ill

BOSTELMANN, Enrique (1939-) Mexi; photo
WALSH 88-89 (statement); 1 ill

BOTELLO, Telma (1934-) Mexi; ptr
DICCIONARIO v.2 29-31 (statement); port; 1 ill

BOTERO, Fernando (1932-) Colo; ptr
SKIRA 1975 76 (extract from interview with Wibke von Bonin); 1 ill

BOTKIN, Henry A. (1896-) Amer; ptr
ART VOICES v.4 no.4 67 (statement); 1 ill
ILLINOIS 1951 163-164 (statement); 1 ill
ILLINOIS 1952 171-172 (statement)
M.H. DE YOUNG 23 (response); self port
100 CONTEMPORARY 34-35 (statement); port; 1 ill

BOTO, Martha (1925-) Arge; sclp, ptr
EMANUEL II 124-125 (statement); 1 ill
LUMIERE (statement); port; 2 ill

BOTT, Peter ( ) Amer; text
HAYSTACK 3 (statement); 1 ill

BOTTA, Mario (1943-) arch
GA DOCUMENT no.6 6-9 (interview); ports
GA HOUSES 1 162-167 (statement); 23 ill
GA HOUSES 3 60-93 (statement); 84 ill
GA HOUSES 6 160-167 (statement); 22 ill
RUSSELL F 64-65 (project proposal); 9 ill

BOTTO, Otto (1903-) Swis/Amer; ptr
ILLINOIS 1952 172 (statement)

BOTTON, Jean de ( ) ptr
BETHERS II 64-65 (statement); 2 ill

BOUBAT, Edouard (1923-) Fren; photo
WALSH 89-91 (statement); 1 ill

BOUCHE, Louis (1896-1969) Amer; ptr
BRITANNICA 10 (statement); port; 1 ill

BOUCHER, Pierre (1908-) Fren; photo
WALSH 90, 92 (statement); 1 ill

BOUL'CH, Jean-Pierre Le (1940-) Fren; ptr
SKIRA 1978 68-69 (statement); 1 ill

BOULETT, Yvette ( ) Mexi; ptr
DICCIONARIO v.2 33-35 (statement); port; 1 ill

BOUMEESTER, Christine ( ) ptr
DADA 13, 115-116 (statement)

BOURDEAU, Robert (1931-) Cana; photo
WALSH 92-93 (statement); 1 ill

BOURDELLE, Emile Antoine (1861-1929) Fren; ptr, sclp, design
GOLDWATER 405-406 (statements, 1910)

BOURDON, Robert ( ) Amer; wood
MEILACH 151-153 (statement); 7 ill

BOURGEOIS, Louise (1911-) Fren/Amer; sclp
ART NOW v.1 no.7 (statement); 1 ill
BRENTANO 162-163 (statement); 1 ill
MILLER 2-14 (interview with Sally Swenson); port; 1 ill

MOTHERWELL 8-22 (three group discussions: "Artists' Sessions at Studio 35," New York, 1950)
MUNRO 154-169 (interview); port; 3 ill
PERSONAL (statement)

BOURKE-WHITE, Margaret (1904-1971) Amer; photo
FIRST AMERICAN 17-18 (essay: "An Artist's Experience in the Soviet Union")

BOURN, Ian (1953-) Brit; film, perf
HAYWARD 1979 138 (statement); port

BOUVIER (1926-) Fren; ptr
YALE 57-58 (statement)

BOVA, Joe (1941-) Amer; pott, sclp
VIEWPOINT 1979 10-11 (statement); 4 ill

BOVE, Richard (1920-) Amer; ptr
FULBRIGHT 14 (statement)

BOWMAN, Boris (1943-) Amer; wood
WOODWORKING 8-9 (statement); port; 2 ill

BOWMAN, Geoffrey (1928-) Amer; ptr
ILLINOIS 1963 129 (statement); 1 ill
SOME 3 (statement); 1 ill

BOWMAN, Kent C. (1923-) Amer; ptr
DICCIONARIO v.2 37-39 (statement); port; 1 ill

BOXER, Stanley Robert (1926-) Amer; ptr, sclp
SKIRA 1980 54-55 (statement); 2 ill

BOYADJIAN, Micheline Erard (1923-) Belg; ptr
COLLARD 32-35 (interview); port; 1 ill

BOYCE, Richard (1920-) Amer; sclp
ILLINOIS 1965 55 (statement); 1 ill
ILLINOIS 1967 110 (statement); 1 ill

BOYD, Fionnuala (1944-) Brit
SEE: BOYD AND EVANS

BOYD AND EVANS (group) ptr
CONTEMPORARY (statement); port; 2 ill

BOYLE, Mark (1934-) Scot; ptr, light, photo
EMANUEL II 127-128 (statement)
ENGLISH 50-55 (statement); port; 5 ill
NAYLOR 131-132 (statement); 1 ill

BOYLEN, Michael ( ) Amer; glass
HAYSTACK 4 (statement); 1 ill

BOZZOLINI, Silvano (1911-) Ital; ptr, print
TEMOIGNAGES I 36-41 (statement); port; 5 ill

BRACH, Paul Henry (1924-) Amer; ptr, print
ARTFORUM v.4 no.1 32 (statement); 1 ill
IT IS no.3 26 (statement)
ROSE II REVISED 191 (statement: "It's Still Lonely in the Studions," o.p. 1967)
VARIAN III (statement); port

BRACHO, Angel (1911-) Mexi; ptr, print
DICCIONARIO v.2 41-43 (statement); port; 1 ill

BRACKETT, Ward ( ) Amer; ptr
NORTH LIGHT 24-29 (statement); port; 7 ill

BRACKMAN, Robert (1898-) Russ/Amer; ptr

BRITANNICA 11 (statement); port; 1 ill
ILLINOIS 1952 173 (statement); 1 ill

BRADFORD, David Philip (1937-) Amer; ptr
LEWIS I REVISED 70-71 (statement); port; 2 ill

BRADLEY, Stewart (1951-) Cana; photo
POINT OF VIEW 52 (statement); 1 ill

BRADY, Caroline (1937-) Amer; ptr
CELEBRATION (statement); 1 ill
SUPERREAL 120-121 (statement); 1 ill

BRAGA, Philip F. (1925-) Amer/Mexi; ptr, print
DICCIONARIO v.2 45-47 (statement); port; 1 ill

BRAGABLIA, Anton Giulio ( ) Ital; photo
APOLLONIO 38-45 ("Futurist Photodynamism," o.p. 1912)

BRAGHIERRI, Gianni ( ) arch
RUSSELL F 94-97 (project proposal); 11 ill

BRAINARD, Joe (1942-) Amer; ptr, coll
ILLINOIS 1969 95 (statement); 1 ill
RUSSELL J 58-59 ("extract from a diary")

BRAKHAGE, James Stanley (1933-) Amer; film
CRISS-CROSS no.2 9 ("Manifest")
CRISS-CROSS no.6 42-56 (debate with Malcolm Le Grice); port
CRISS-CROSS no. 7/8/9 69-70 ("Western History")

BRAKHAGE, Jane ( )
CRISS-CROSS no.7/8/9 66-67 ("News from the Art World")

BRAKKE, Michael ( ) Amer; photo, perf
BRAKKE 82-110 (text piece); 20 ill

BRAMSON, Phyllis (1941-) Amer; ptr
IN A PICTORIAL 32-39 (statements); 5 ill

BRANCA, Glenn ( ) perf, sound
LIVE no.6/7 4-10 (interview); port; 3 ill

BRANCACCIO, Giovanni (1903-) Ital; ptr
VERZOCCHI 87-91 (statement); self port; 1 ill

BRANCUSI, Constantin (1876-1957) Ruma; sclp
CHIPP 364-365 ("Aphorisms," o.p. 1925)
GUGGENHEIM II 34-37 (statement, o.p. 1926); 2 ill
LIBERMAN 47-48 (statements)
MINOTAURE no.3/4 41 (statement); 1 ill

BRANDL, Eva ( ) Cana; instal
VEHICULE (statement); 4 ill

BRANDT, Bill (1904-) Brit; photo
BOOTH 44-57 (statements); port; 7 ill
HOW FAMOUS 214-217 (statements); port; 9 ill
VICTORIA 32-35 (statements)
WALSH 96-99 (statement); 1 ill

BRANDT, Warren (1918-) Amer; ptr
ART NOW v.4 no.2 (statement); 1 ill

BRAQUE, Georges (1882-1963) Fren; ptr
CHARBONNIER v.1 7-18 (interview)
CHIPP 259-260 (statements, o.p. 1910)
CHIPP 260-262 (essay: "Thoughts and Reflections on Art," o.p. 1917); port
CHIPP 262 (statement, o.p. 1954)

EIGHT (handwritten statement in French; statement in English, French and German); ports
FRIEDENTHAL 264-266 (extract from conversation with Dora Vallier, 1954); 1 ill
FRY 53 (statement, o.p. 1910)
FRY 147-148 (essay: "Thoughts on Painting," o.p. 1917)
GOLDAINE 18-21 (interview); port
GOLDWATER 421-423 (statement, 1917)
GROHMANN 384-386 ("Gedanken," p.p. 1948)
GUGGENHEIM II 62-64 (statement, o.p. 1917); 1 ill
LHOTE 386-391 ("Reflexions," o.p. 1946)
LIBERMAN 37-42 (statements)
MAYWALD (statement in English, German, and French; handwritten statement in French); ports
PROTTER 209-210 (extract from *Aphorisms*; and statement, 1949); 1 ill
RAYNAL 85-92 (statement); 3 ill
SEGHERS 148-150 ("Aphorisms on Painting," p.p.)
THORN 68, 93, 125, 349, 350 (statements, p.p.)
VERDET 11-50 (interview)
VINGTIEME N.S. no.4 34 ("Nouvelles Pensees"); 1 ill

BRASIC, Janko (1906-) Yugo; ptr
TOMASEVIC 43-49 (statement); port; 1 ill

BRASSAI (1899-) Fren; photo
CAMPBELL 202-215 (statements); port; 8 ill
HILL 37-43 (interview, 1974); port
MINOTAURE no.3/4 6-7 ("Du Mur des Cararnes au Mur d'Usine"); 2 ill
MINOTAURE no.3/4 105 ("Enquete")
VINGTIEME N.S. no.10 21-24 (essay: "Graffiti Parisiens")

TIME-LIFE III 140-141 (statements, p.p.); 2 ill
WALSH 99-101 (statement); 1 ill

BRAUER, Erich (Arik) (1929-) Atrl; ptr
EMANUEL II 130-131 (statement); 1 ill

BRAUN; Werner (1918-) Isra; photo
WALSH 101-102 (statement); 1 ill

BRAUNER, Victor (1903-1966) Ruma; ptr
ART VOICES v.2 no.7 20-21 (interview with Edouard Roditi); self port; 4 ill
GUGGENHEIM II 125 (statement, o.p. 1941); 1 ill
LIPPARD 67-69 ("On the Fantastic," o.p. 1943/44)

BRAUN-REINITZ, Janet ( ) Amer
ARTISTS no.1 3-6, 12 ("Looking for an Audience: A Soap Opera in 1700 Words")

BRAVO, Claudio (1936-) Chil; ptr, print, sclp
EMANUEL II 132-133 (statement); 1 ill
NAYLOR 136-137 (statement); 1 ill

BRAVO, Manuel Alvarez
SEE: ALVAREZ BRAVO, Manuel

BRAVO GARCIA, Daniel (1938-) Mexi; ptr
DICCIONARIO v.2 49-51 (statement); port; 1 ill

BRAVO HIDALGO, Sergio (1929-) Mexi; ptr
DICCIONARIO v.2 53-55 (statement); port; 1 ill

BRAWER, Gladys R. ( ) Arge; glass
DICCIONARIO v.2 57-59 (statement); port; 1 ill

BRAWNE, Michael (1925-) Brit; arch
EMANUEL I 115-117 (statement); 1 ill

BRAY, Bob ( ) design
DIAMONSTEIN V 32-47 (interview);
port; 9 ill

BRAYER, Yves (1907-) Fren; ptr
ART VOICES v.3 no.1 12-13 (interview
with Gordon Brown); port; 3 ill
GOLDAINE 138-140 (interview); port

BREAKWELL, Ian (1943-) Brit; coll,
photo
CONTEMPORARY (statement); port; 1
ill
NAYLOR 137-138 (statement); 1 ill

BRECHER, Samuel (1897-) Amer; ptr
100   CONTEMPORARY   36-37
(statement); port; 1 ill

BRECHT, George (1926-) Amer; ptr,
sclp
ADLERS 32-35 (interview); 3 ill
ART AND TECHNOLOGY 56-57 (project
proposal); 1 ill
RUSSELL J 59 ("A Questionnaire on
Pop")
RUSSELL J 60 ("Event Scores")

BRECKENRIDGE, Bruce (1929-) Amer;
pott
WISCONSIN I (statement); 1 ill

BREDDO, Gastone (1915-) Ital; ptr
VERZOCCHI 93-97 (statement); self
port; 1 ill

BREDER, Hans (1935-) Germ/Amer;
sclp, video
DIRECTIONS I 75 (response); 1 ill

BREER, Robert C. (1926-) Amer; film,
sclp, ptr

EMANUEL II 135-136 (statement)
NAYLOR 138-139 (statement); 1 ill

BREHMER, K.P. (1938-) Germ; ptr,
print
EMANUEL II 136 (statement)
KUNST UND POLITIK (statement); port;
3 ill
NAYLOR 139-140 (statement); 1 ill

BREININ, Raymond (1910-) Russ/Amer;
ptr
BRITANNICA 12 (statement); port; 1 ill
M.H. DE YOUNG 25 (response); self port
MILLER 1942 24-29 (statement); port; 6
ill

BREIVIK, Bard (1948-) Norw; sclp
PRADEL 38 (statement, o.p. 1981); 2 ill
SLEEPING 32-41 (statement); 9 ill

BREKKE, John P. (1955-) Amer; glass
WISCONSIN II (statement); 1 ill

BREMER Y DE MARTINO, Cristina
(1937-) Mexi; ptr
DICCIONARIO v.2 61-63 (statement);
port; 1 ill

BREMS, Robert ( ) Belg; ptr
COLLARD 36-40 (interview); port; 1 ill

BRENDEL, Bettina (1923-) Germ/Amer;
illus, ptr
CALIFORNIA--DRAWING (statement); 2
ill

BRENER, Roland (1942-) Cana/SoAf;
sclp, instal
MISE EN SCENE 13, 58-75 (statement);
15 ill

BRENNAN, Daniel
SEE: DANIEL

BRENNER, Susan ( ) Amer; ptr
SCHAPIRO 10 (statement); port; 1 ill

BRENTANO, Robyn ( ) Amer; film
BRENTANO 166-167 (statement); 1 ill

BRESCHI, Karen Lee (1941-) Amer;
pott, sclp
NAYLOR 140-141 (statement); 1 ill

BRESLOW, Norman ( ) photo
ARTISTS no.1 17-23 ("On Photographic
Schizophrenia")
ARTISTS no.2 16, 23 ("A Bedtime
Story")

BRETT, Dorothy (1883-) Brit/Amer; ptr
ILLINOIS 1953 169-170 (statement); 1 ill

BRETT, Guy (1942-) Brit
BOSHIER (statement); port; 6 ill

BRETT, Nancy (1946-) Amer; ptr
LEAVITT (statement); port; 5 ill

BRETTEVILLE, Shiela Levrant de ( )
print, design
CHRYSALIS no.9 33-45 (essay: "The
'Polarization' of Our Homes and
Ourselves")

BREUER, Marcel (1902-) Hung/Amer;
arch, design
CIRCLE 193-202 (essay: "Architecture
and Material"); 24 ill
EMANUEL I 117-119 (statement); 1 ill
HEYER 264-277 (interview); 29 ill
KEPES III (essay: "Genesis of Design");
5 ill

BREUSTE, H. J. (1933-) sclp
KUNST UND POLITIK (statement, with
Asmus Petersen); port; 1 ill

BREWSTER, Michael (1946-) Amer;
sclp, envir
ARTPARK 1982 24-25, 45 (statement);
port; 1 ill

BRIANCHON, Maurice (1899-1979) Fren;
ptr
CHARBONNIER v.2 109-118 (interview)
GOLDAINE 126-128 (interview); port

BRICE, Olivier (1933-) Fren; sclp
SKIRA 1977 18 (statement); 1 ill

BRICE, William (1921-) Amer; illus, ptr
CALIFORNIA--DRAWING (statement); 2
ill
HOPKINS 84-85 (statement); port; 1 ill

BRIGANTE, Nicholas (1895-)
Ital/Amer; illus, ptr, print
CALIFORNIA--DRAWING (statement); 2
ill

BRIGGS, Austin (1908-1973) Amer; illus
FAMOUS v.1 170-172 (statement); 4 ill
GUITAR 24-33 (interview); port; 4 ill
NORTH LIGHT 30-31 (statement); port

BRIGGS, Ernest (1923-) Amer; ptr
MILLER 1956 6-12 (statement); port; 6
ill

BRIGGS, Peter (1950-) Brit; sclp
CHOIX 16 (statement); 1 ill

BRIGHAM, Joan (1935-) Amer; envir
CENTERBEAM 69-70, 99-100
("Steam"); port; 3 ill

BRIHAT, Denis (1928-) Fren; photo
WALSH 102-103 (statement); 1 ill

BRISEL, Bella (1929-) Isra; ptr
PREMIER BILAN 283 (statement); port

BRISEPIERRE, Christian (1947-) Amer; wood
WOODWORKING 10-11 (statement); port; 2 ill

BRISLEY, Stuart (1933-) Brit; perf
ENGLISH 416-421 (statement); port; 12 ill

BRITT, Arthur L. (1934-) Amer; ptr
LEWIS I REVISED 19-20 (statement); port; 2 ill

BRITTON, Benjamin (1958-)
SEE: SUBTERRANEAN VIDEO

BRITTON, Louise (1953-) Germ/Mexi; ptr
DICCIONARIO v.2 65-67 (statement); self port; 1 ill

BROCQUY, Louis le (1916-) Fren; ptr
SKIRA 1977 27 (statement); 1 ill

BRODERSON, Morris (1928-) Amer; ptr
ILLINOIS 1963 137 (statement); 1 ill
ILLINOIS 1965 100-101 (statement); 1 ill
YOUNG 1960 (statement); 2 ill

BRODIE, Gandy (1924-) Amer; ptr
WHITNEY (statement); 1 ill

BRODSKY, Judith Kapstein (1933-) Amer; print, ptr
MILLER 15-36 (interview with Sally Swenson); port; 1 ill
VISUAL v.2 no.3 2-3 (essay: "Reflections on the Women's Art Movement")
WOMANART v.1 no.4 10-12 ("Women's Caucus for Art, Report from the President")

BRODY, Sherry (1932-) Amer; coll, print, ptr

CELEBRATION (statement); 1 ill
SCHAPIRO 11 (statement); port; 1 ill

BROEMEL, Carl (1891-) Amer; ptr, illus
NORTH LIGHT 32-37 (statement); port; 7 ill

BROGGER, Stig (1941-) Dani; coll, photo, sclp
SKIRA 1978 65 (statement); 1 ill
SKIRA 1979 84 (statement); 2 ill

BROKAW, Lucile (1915-) Amer; coll, ptr
CALIFORNIA--COLLAGE (statement); 2 ill

BROOK, Alexander (1898-1980) Amer; ptr
BETHERS II 68-69 (statement); 2 ill
BRITANNICA 13 (statement); port; 1 ill

BROOKE, Anne P. ( ) Amer; text
HAYSTACK 5 (statement); 1 ill

BROOKS, Ellen (1946-) Amer; coll, instal, photo
SCRIPPS COLLEGE (statement); 1 ill

BROOKS, James (1906-) Amer; ptr
ALBRIGHT-KNOX 55, 57 (letter, 7/1968); 1 ill
ART NOW v.3 no.2 (statement); 1 ill
EMANUEL II 138-139 (statement); 1 ill
FORTY (statement); 2 ill
FRASNAY 237 (handwritten statement)
ILLINOIS 1952 174 (statement); 1 ill
ILLINOIS 1953 170 (statement); 1 ill
ILLINOIS 1955 182 (statement); 1 ill
ILLINOIS 1961 67 (response); port; 1 ill
LETTERS 8-9 (letter); 2 ill
MILLER 1956 14-20 (statement); port; 6 ill
MOMA 1959 24-27 (statement); port; 3 ill

MOTHERWELL 8-22 (three group discussions: "Artists' Sessions at Studio 35," New York, 1950)
NEW DECADE 12-14 (statement); 4 ill

BROOKS, Jon ( ) Amer; sclp
ARTPARK 1975 64-65 (statement); port; 4 ill
ARTPARK 1976 140-141 (statement); port; 4 ill

BROOKS, Mona ( ) Amer; pott
HERMAN 33 (statement); port; 1 ill

BROOKS, Turner ( ) Amer; arch
GA HOUSES 8 150-153 (statement); 12 ill

BROOKS, Walter ( ) Amer; design, print
NORTH LIGHT 38-43 (statement); port; 9 ill

BROSK, Jeffrey Owen (1947-) Amer; envir, sclp
ARTPARK 1983 16-17 (statement); 1 ill

BROSTERMAN, Norman (1952-) Amer; envir
PROJECTS (statement); 6 ill

BROUWN, Stanley ( )
AVALANCHE no.4 32-33 (text piece: "Steps")
KONZEPT (statement)

BROWN, Aika
SEE: AIKA

BROWN, Carlyle (1919-1964) Amer; ptr
ILLINOIS 1952 174 (statement); 1 ill
NEW DECADE 15-17 (statement); 2 ill

BROWN, Denise Scott
SEE; SCOTT BROWN, Denise

BROWN, Fred (1941-) Amer; ptr
LEWIS I REVISED 29 (statement); port; 1 ill

BROWN, James A. ( ) Amer; video
EVENTS I 41 (poem); 1 ill

BROWN, Joan (1938-) Amer; ptr
GOODYEAR 31-37 (interview); 3 ill
HOPKINS 34-35 (statement); port; self port
ILLINOIS 1961 58 (response); port; 1 ill
PROFILE v.2 no.3 (interview); port; 3 ill
SCHAPIRO 12 (statement); port; 1 ill
VISUAL v.1 no.2 15-18 (interview); 2 ill
YOUNG 1960 (statement); 2 ill

BROWN, Kathan (1935-) Amer; print
VISION no.1 62-67 ("The Underground Gardens of Baldasare Forestiere")

BROWN, Kay Bell ( ) Amer; print, ptr
FAX II 165-180 (statements); port; 1 ill
FINE 210 (poem, o.p. 1971); 1 ill

BROWN, Lynne (1951-) Amer; photo
FUGITIVE (statement); 1 ill

BROWN, Robert ( )
ART-LANGUAGE v.1 no.2 23-24 ("Moto-Spiritale")

BROWN, Robert Delford (1930-) Amer; print
ART-RITE no.14 5, 7 (response)
NAYLOR 236-237 (statement); 1 ill

BROWN, Roger (1941-) Amer; ptr
ACKLAND 20-37, 54-55 (group discussion, 10/27/79); 2 ill
GUMPERT III 57-58 (statement)

BROWN, Winifred (1936-)Amer; metal
CONTEMPORARY AFRICAN (statement); port; 1 ill

WISCONSIN I (statement); 1 ill

BROWNE, Byron (1907-) Amer; ptr
FIFTY (statement); port; 1 ill
JANIS 56 (statement); 1 ill
ILLINOIS 1950 161-162 (statement); 1 ill
ILLINOIS 1951 164-165 (statement); 1 ill

BROWNE, Vivian E. (1929-) Amer;
print, ptr
EVENTS I 41 (statement); 1 ill
LEWIS II 10 (statement); port; 3 ill

BROWNING, Colleen (1929-) Amer; ptr
ILLINOIS 1952 174-175 (statement); 1 ill
ILLINOIS 1953 171 (statement); 1 ill
ILLINOIS 1955 182-183 (statement); 1 ill
ILLINOIS 1959 198-199 (statement); 1 ill

BROWNLEE, Edward M. (1929-) Amer;
sclp
HAAR I 26-30 (interview with Prithwish
Neogy); ports; 3 ill

BROWNLEE, Henry (1940-) Amer; ptr
LEWIS I 38 (statement); port; 1 ill

BROWNSON, Jacques (1923-) Amer;
arch
HEYER 37-40 (interview); 9 ill

BROZON, Guadalupe Vallejo de (1940-)
Mexi; ptr
DICCIONARIO v.2 69-71 (statement);
port; 1 ill

BRUBAKER, Charles William (1926-)
Amer; arch
EMANUEL I 122-123 (statement); 1 ill

BRUCKMAN, Lodewyk K. (1903-)
Amer; ptr
ILLINOIS 1952 175 (statement); 1 ill

BRUDER, Harold Jacob (1930-) Amer;
ptr
GUSSOW 88-89 (interview, 1970); 1 ill
NAYLOR 143-144 (statement); 1 ill

BRUGUERA, Mayoli V. (1952-) Mexi;
ptr
DICCIONARIO v.2 73-75 (statement);
port; 1 ill

BRUMER, Miriam (1939-) Amer; ptr
ARTS YEARBOOK v.10 96-98 (essay:
"The First Lignano Biennale")

BRUMFIELD, John (1934-) Amer; photo
FIGURES 6-7 (statement, o.p. 1981); 1
ill

BRUN, Adrian (1939-) Mexi; ptr
DICCIONARIO v.2 77-79 (statement);
port; 1 ill

BRUNET SARDA, Gabriel (1933-) Mexi;
ptr
DICCIONARIO v.2 81-83 (statement);
port; 1 ill

BRUNING, Peter (1929-) Germ; sclp
HAUSSER 44-45 (statement, o.p. 1972);
1 ill

BRUNIUS, Jacques B. (1906-) ptr
EXPOSICION (statement); port; 1 ill

BRUNNER, Edy (1943-) Swis; sclp
SKIRA 1977 102 (statement); 1 ill

BRUNO, Jose Rosales (1950-) Mexi; ptr
DICCIONARIO v.2 85-87 (statement);
port; 1 ill

BRUNORI, Enzo (1924-) Ital; ptr
PAINTING 4 (statement); port; 1 ill

BRURIA (1932-) Amer; pott
HERMAN 34 (statement); port; 1 ill

BRUS, Gunter (1938-) Aust; film, perf, ptr
NAYLOR 144-145 (statement); 1 ill

BRUSCA, Jack (1939-) Amer; ptr
NAYLOR 145 (statement); 1 ill

BRUSH, Daniel (1947-) Amer; ptr
CORCORAN 24-37 (interview); port; 6 ill

BRUSSE, Mark (1937-) Dutc; sclp
FRASNAY 238 (statement)
PREMIO NACIONAL 1965 50-51 (extract from interview with Pierre Restany); port; 1 ill

BRUTE, Dr. (Eric W. Metcalfe) (1940-) Cana; cart, video
AVALANCHE no.8 34-39 (group discussion); 14 ill

BRUTE, Lady ( )
AVALANCHE no.8 34-39 (group discussion); 14 ill

BRYAN, Jack ( ) Amer; print
PHILLPOT (statement)

BRYCE, Jose Garcia (1928-) Peru; arch
BAYON 170-189 (interview); 19 ill

BRYEN, Camille (1907-) Fren; ptr
CLAUS 39-42 (statement)
GOLDAINE 76-79 (interview); port
GRENIER 37-43 (interview)
SEUPHOR 140 (statement); 1 ill

BRYSON, Edwin F.
SEE: EDWIN

BRZOZOWSKI, Tadeusz Alexander (1918-) Poli; ptr
NAYLOR 145-146 (statement); 1 ill

BUBEROFF, Beatriz (1939-) Arge/Mexi; ptr
DICCIONARIO v.2 89-91 (statement); port; 1 ill

BUCCI, Anselmo (1887-) Ital; ptr
VERZOCCHI 99-103 (statement); self port; 1 ill

BUCHANAN, Nancy ( ) Amer; instal
IRVINE 43, 85-86 (statement); 1 ill

BUCHEN, Bill ( ) Amer; sclp, sound, envir
ARTPARK 1981 (statement); port; 3 ill

BUCHEN, Mary ( ) Amer; sclp, sound, envir
ARTPARK 1981 (statement); port; 3 ill

BUCHER, Carl (1935-) Swis; sclp, ptr
SKIRA 1976 100 (statement); 1 ill

BUCHHEISTER, Karl (1890-) Germ; sclp, ptr
ABSTRACTION no.1 5 (statement); 2 ill
ABSTRACTION no.2 5 (statement); 2 ill
PREMIER BILAN 283 (statement); port

BUCHNER, Saumitra Lewis ( ) Amer; wood
MEILACH 66, 224 (statement); 2 ill

BUCHWALD, Stella (1900-) Amer; ptr
100 CONTEMPORARY 38-39 (statement); port; 1 ill

BUCK, John E. (1946-) Amer; ptr, sclp, instal
GUENTHER 24-25 (statement); port; 1 ill

HOUSE 34-35 (statement); 1 ill

BUDD, David (1927-) Amer; ptr
ART NOW v.2 no.1 (statement); 1 ill

BUDNEY, Virginia (1944-) Amer; pott
HERMAN 35 (statement); port; 1 ill

BUENO, Jose
SEE: GOODE, Joe

BUENO HERRERA, Jose Manuel (1946-
) Mexi; ptr
DICCIONARIO v.2 93-95 (statement);
port; 1 ill

BUFF, Conrad (1886-1975) Swis/Amer;
ptr
BRITANNICA 14 (statement); port; 1 ill

BUFFET, Bernard (1928-) Fren; ptr
ART VOICES v.2 no.4 24-25 (interview
with Edouard Roditi); port; 2 ill
CHARBONNIER v.2 119-130 (interview)
CONTEMPORARY (statement); port; 1
ill
FRASNAY 299-311 (statement); port; 6
ill
GOLDAINE 199-200 (interview); port

BUISMAN, Sjoerd (1948-) Dutc; sclp
NAYLOR 148-149 (statement); 1 ill

BUJAIDAR, Francisco Zenteno (1933-)
Mexi; ptr
DICCIONARIO v.2 97-99 (statement); 1
ill

BUKTENICA, Eugen (1914-) Yugo; ptr
TOMASEVIC 50-53 (statement); port; 1
ill

BULLER, Audrey (1902-) Amer; ptr
MILLER 1943 34 (statement); 1 ill

BULLOCK, Wynn (1902-1975) Amer;
photo
HILL 313-337 (interview, 1975); port

BULTMAN, Fritz Orbes (1919-) Amer;
ptr
ILLINOIS 1952 175-176 (statement)
ILLINOIS 1953 171-172 (statement); 1 ill
IT IS no.3 53 ("A Cahier Leaf")

BUNCE, Louis DeMott (1907-) Amer;
print
AMERICAN PRINTS 17, 64-65
(statement); 1 ill
GUENTHER 26-27 (statement); port; 1
ill
ILLINOIS 1967 134 (statement); 1 ill

BUNJEVACKI, Dragisa (1925-) Yugo;
ptr
TOMASEVIC 54-58 (statement); port;
self port

BUNSHAFT, Gordon (1909-) Amer; arch
EMANUEL I 126-127 (statement); 1 ill

BUONAGURIO, Edgar (1946-) ptr
TRANSPERSONAL 20-29 (statement);
port; 4 ill

BURAGLIO, Pierre (1939-) Fren; ptr
MURS 7 (statement); 1 ill
SKIRA 1977 36 (statement); 1 ill

BURCHARD, Jerry (1931-) Amer; photo
WALSH 114-115 (statement); 1 ill

BURCHFIELD, Charles (1893-1967)
Amer; ptr
BRITANNICA 15 (statement); port; 1 ill
CRISPO II (statement, 1963); 12 ill
ILLINOIS 1959 199-200 (statement); 1 ill
ILLINOIS 1961 96-97 (response); port; 1
ill

SKIRA 1979 85 (statement); 2 ill
TRACKS v.3 no.3 36-44 (essay: "Looking at Photographs")
VRIES 76-89 (essay: "Situational Aesthetics," o.p. 1969)
WALSH 115-117 (extract from interview with Tony Godfrey); 1 ill
WEBER 81-91 ("Videotape")

BURGOS, Inocencio (1926-1978) Mexi; ptr
DICCIONARIO v.2 101-103 (statement); self port; 1 ill

BURGY, Donald Thomas (1937-) Amer
CONCEPTUAL ART 36 (statement)
MEYER 88-91 (text piece)

BURI, Samuel (1935-) Swis; sclp, ptr
SKIRA 1978 30 (statement); 1 ill
SKIRA 1980 68-69 (statement); 3 ill

BURKE, Ainslie (1922-) Amer; ptr
FULBRIGHT 14 (statement)

BURKE, Kenneth ( ) Amer
MOTHERWELL 24-37 (group discussion: "The Western Round Table on Modern Art," San Francisco, 1949)

BURKERT, Heribert (1953-) Germ; photo
SKIRA 1977 85 (statement); 4 ill

BURKERT, Nancy Ekholm (1933-) Amer; illus, ptr
WISCONSIN I (statement); 1 ill

BURKERT, Robert Randall (1930-) Amer; print, ptr
WISCONSIN I (statement); 1 ill

BURKET, Le Roy (1920-) Amer; ptr
FULBRIGHT 16 (statement)

BURKHARDT, Hans Gustav (1904-) Swis/Amer; ptr, illus
CALIFORNIA--PAINTING 12 (statement); 1 ill
CALIFORNIA--DRAWING (statement); 2 ill

BURKHARDT, Linde ( )
GROH (statement); 3 ill

BURKO, Diane (1945-) Amer; ptr
SCHAPIRO 13 (statement); port; 1 ill

BURLE MARX, Roberto (1909-) Braz; arch
BAYON 38-61 (interview); port; 29 ill
EMANUEL I 127-130 (statement); 1 ill

BURLIK, David (1882-1967) Russ; ptr
BOWLT 8-11 (extract from "The Voice of an Impressionist: In defense of Painting," o.p. 1908); 1 ill
BOWLT 69-77 (essay: "Cubism (Surface-Plane)," o.p. 1912); port; 1 ill

BURLIN, Paul (1886-1969) Amer; ptr
BRITANNICA 17 (statement); port; 1 ill
FORTY (statement); 2 ill
ZAIDENBERG 79-81 (essay: "Creative Painting"); 4 ill

BURN, Ian (!939-) Brit
ART NETWORK no.5 37-38 (essay: "ACTU National Conference: Art and Working Life")
ART NETWORK no.6 42-44 (essay: "Painting,Interpreting, and Other Hazards")
ART NETWORK no.8 39-43 (essay: "The Australian National Gallery: Populism or a New Federalism?")
ART-LANGUAGE v.1 no.2 22 ("Dialogue")
ART-LANGUAGE v.1 no.3 1-3 ("The

Society for Theoretical Art and Analyses Proceedings*)
ART-LANGUAGE v.2 no.1 28-37 ("Four Wages of Sense*)
ART-LANGUAGE v.2 no.2 1-10 (essay: "Some Questions on the Characterization of Questions*)
ART-LANGUAGE v.2 no.2 21-28 (essay: "Art Language and Art-Language*)
ART-LANGUAGE v.2 no.3 53-72 (essay: "Problems of Art and Language Space*)
ART-LANGUAGE v.3 no.1 1-110 ("Draft for an Anti-textbook*)
ART-LANGUAGE v.3 no.2 31-40 ("Brainstorming--New York*)
ART-LANGUAGE v.3 no.2 46-51 ("Rambling: To Partial Correspondents*)
ART-LANGUAGE v.3 no.2 81-86 ("Strategy is Political: Dear M...*)
MEYER 92-95 (text pieces); 2 ill
MEYER 96-103 ("Excerpts from the Grammarian," o.p. 1971)
VRIES 90-95 (essay: "The Role of Language," o.p. 1968)
VRIES 96-103 (essay: "Some Notes on Practice and Theory," o.p. 1969)
VRIES 104-115 (talk: "The Artist as Victim," given in Melbourne, 1972)
SEE ALSO: SOCIETY FOR THEORETICAL ART AND ANALYSES

BURNETT, Calvin (1921-) Amer; ptr, print
LEWIS I REVISED 6 (statement); port; 1 ill

BURNHAM, Daniel H. (1846-1912) Amer; arch
ROTH 439-445 (extract from *Plan of Chicago*, o.p. 1909)

BURNS, Maurice (1937-) Amer; ptr
FAX II 1-18 (statements); port; 1 ill

BURNS, Pamela (1938-) Brit; ptr
HAYWARD 1978 34-37 (statement); 5 ill

BURR, F. Andrus ( ) Amer; arch
COOPER-HEWITT II 144-145 (essay: "Urban Graveyards*)
GA HOUSES 7 173-179 (essay: "learning under Moore*); port

BURRI, Alberto (1915-) Ital; ptr
QUADRUM no.7 79-90 (statements); 8 ill
RITCHIE 82-85 (statement); port; 4 ill

BURRI, Rene (1933-) Swis; photo
CAMPBELL 112-123 (statement); port; 8 ill

BURROUGHS, Margaret T.G. (1917-) Amer; sclp
LEWIS II 57 (statement); port; 2 ill

BURROWS, Larry (1926-1971) Brit; photo
WALSH 118 (extract of interview)

BURROWS, Tom (1940-) Amer; sclp
CANADA 34-35 (statement); port; 1 ill

BURT, Lawrence (1925-) Brit; sclp
NAYLOR 152-154 (statement); 1 ill

BURTIN, Will ( ) Germ/Amer; print
KEPES VIII 78-95 (essay: "Design and Communication*)

BURTON, Cecil (1941-) Amer; sclp
LEWIS I REVISED 13 (statement); port; 1 ill

BURTON, James ( ) Amer; sclp, envir
ARTPARK 1978 18-19 (statement); port; 6 ill

BURTON, Richard ( ) Brit; arch
SEE: AHRENDS BURTON AND KORALEK

BURTON, Scott (1939-) Amer; sclp
ARTPARK 1983 18-21 (statement); port; 8 ill
ART-RITE no.6 24-25 (statement)
PERFORMANCE no.2 7-10 (interview); port
SHEARER 19-23 (interview); 3 ill

BURY, Pol (1922-) Belg; sclp
ART NOW v.3 no.3 ("A Way Out"); 1 ill
ART SINCE v.1 295 (statements, o.p. 1964, 1967)
DADA 79 ("Picabia")
DOUZE ANS 149-151 (statement); port; 6 ill
LUMIERE (statement); port; 1 ill
SKIRA 1975 88-89 (extract from "Le petit commencement," 1966); 1 ill

BUSA, Peter (1914-) Amer; ptr; sclp
IT IS no.4 14 (statement)

BUSCHKE, Frances ( )
PHILLPOT (statement)

BUSHNELL, Kenneth (1931-) Amer; ptr
HAAR I 34-40 (interview with Prithwish Neogy); port; 3 ill

BUSSARD, Ken ( ) Amer; arch, design
LIFE 91-114 (interview); port

BUSSE, Fritz (1903-) Germ; ptr
GRENIER 47-57 (interview)

BUSSE, Jacques (1922-) Fren; ptr
YALE 58 (statement)

BUSTAMANTE, Maris ( ) Mexi; print, ptr
DICCIONARIO v.2 105-107 (statement); port; 1 ill

BUSTION, Nathaniel (1942-) Amer; ptr
LEWIS II 114 (statement); port; 1 ill

BUSZKO, Henryk (1924-) Poli; arch
EMANUEL I 130-131 (statement); 1 ill

BUTCHER, Larry D. (1944-) Amer; ptr
MICHIGAN 8-9 (statement); 2 ill

BUTHE, Michael (1944-) Germ; ptr, coll
CHOIX 17 (extract from poem, o.p. 1982); 1 ill

BUTLER, Katherine ( ) Amer; paper, print
FOUNDERS 6-7 (statement); 1 ill

BUTLER, Reginald Cottrell (1913-) Brit; sclp
ALBRIGHT-KNOX 138-139 (letter, 1/1956); 1 ill
ART SINCE v.2 150 (statement, o.p. 1953)
FORMA 99-123 (statement); ports; 1 ill
KEPES IX 62-73 (extract from "private communications" with John E. Burchard)
PREMIER BILAN 284 (statement); port
RITCHIE 65-69 (statement); port; 4 ill
SELZ 39-44 (statement: from a conversation recorded in England in 1959); 4 ill

BUTLER, Sheryle (1947-) Amer; text
LEWIS II 31 (statement); port; 1 ill

BUTTER, Tom (1952-) Amer; sclp
GUMPERT II 4-7, 30 (statements); port; 6 ill

BUTTERFIELD, Deborah (1949-) Amer;
 sclp
 GUENTHER 28-29 (statement); port; 1
 ill

BUTTON, John (1929-) Amer; ptr
 ART NOW v.1 no.6 (statement); 1 ill
 GUSSOW 120-121 (interview, 1970); 1 ill

BYARD, Carole (1941-) Amer; ptr
 FAX II 61-78 (statements); port; 1 ill

BYARS, James Lee (1932-) Amer
 ART AND TECHNOLOGY 58-67 (project
 proposal); 7 ill
 CONCEPTUAL ART 36,43 (statement)

BYRD, D. Gibson (1923-) Amer; ptr
 WISCONSIN I (statement); 1 ill

BYRNE, David ( )
 CRISS-CROSS no.7/8/9 4 (statement)

BYRNE, James (1950-) Amer; photo
 MCCLINTIC 19-20 (statement); 1 ill

BYRNE, Peter ( ) Brit; ptr
 BOSHIER (statement); port; 3 ill

BYTLACIL, Vaclav ( ) ptr
 BETHERS I 256-257 (statement); 1 ill

BYZANTIOS, Constantin (1924-) Gree;
 ptr
 SKIRA 1978 106 (statement); 1 ill

SHAFER 10-29 (statements); port; 24 ill

CAILLAND, Aristide (1902-) Fren; ptr
RAGON 119-122 (statement)

CAIN, Michael
SEE: PULSA

CAIRE GOMEZ, Benjamin (1916-)
Mexi; ptr
DICCIONARIO v.2 141-143 (statement);
port; 1 ill

CAIRN (group)
CRISS-CROSS no.11/12 42-45
(statements); 13 ill

CALCAGNO, Lawrence (1916-) Amer;
ptr
ILLINOIS 1959 200-201 (statement); 1 ill

CALDER, Alexander (1898-1976) Amer;
sclp
ABSTRACTION no.1 6 (statement); 2 ill
CHIPP 561-562 ("What Abstract Art
Means to Me," o.p. 1951)
DOUZE PEINTRES (poem); 2 ill
EVANS 62-67 (essay: "Mobiles"); 3 ill
GROHMANN 453-454 ("Zu den
'Mobliles'," o.p. 1932)
GUGGENHEIM II 96-97 (statement, o.p.
1932); 1 ill
HAUSSER 46-47 (statement, 1932, o.p.
1953); 1 ill
KUH 38-51 (interview); 7 ill
MCCOUBREY 208-210 ("What Abstract
Art Means to Me," o.p. 1951)
POENSGEN 111-112 ("Wie ich zur
Abstraktion Kam," 1952)
QUADRUM no.6 9-11 (interview with
George W. Staemfli); port; 3 ill
RODMAN I 136-142 (interview)
ROSE II 184-185 (extract from interview
with Katharine Kuh, o.p. 1960)

ROSE II REVISED 243-244 (extract from
interview with Katharine Kuh, o.p.
1960)
SPENCER 293-295 ("What Abstract
Art Means to Me," o.p. 1951); 1 ill
TEMOIGNAGES I 42-49 (statement);
port; 5 ill
TIGER no.4 74, 99 (statement); 1 ill

CALDERARA, Antonio (1903-) Ital; ptr
SKIRA 1977 34 (statement); 1 ill

CALDERON, Federico (1951-) Mexi; ptr
DICCIONARIO v.2 149-151 (statement);
port; 1 ill

CALHAU, Fernando (1948-) Port; print
SKIRA 1977 82 (statement); 1 ill

CALKINS, Earnest Elmo ( ) print
MCCAUSLAND 14-20 (essay: "Artist
into Advertising Man")

CALLAHAN, Harry (1912-) Amer; photo
BOOTH 58-69 (interview); port; 6 ill
DIAMONSTEIN III 11-22 (interview); 6 ill

CALLAHAN, Kenneth (1907-) Amer; ptr
ENVIRONMENT 42-43 (statement); 1 ill
GUENTHER 30-31 (statement); port; 1
ill
ILLINOIS 1959 203 (statement); 1 ill
M. H. DE YOUNG 28 (response)

CALLAS, Peter (1952-) Atrl; video,
instal
ART NETWORK no.9 70 (essay)

CALLE, Paul (1928-) Amer; ptr, illus
MAGIC 28-31 (statement, extracts from
The Pencil by Paul Calle); port; 3 ill
NORTH LIGHT 44-49 (statement); port;
6 ill

CALLEJAS, Rodrigo (1937-) ptr
ANGEL 43-57 (interview); port; 1 ill

CALLERY, Mary (1903-1977) Amer; sclp
ILLINOIS 1955 183-184 (statement); 1 ill
TIGER no.4 74-75, 88 (statement); 1 ill

CALLIGAS, Alexander ( ) arch
PORPHYRIOS 114-117 (essay: "Houses at Monemvasia, Greece"); 8 ill

CALLIGAS, Charis ( ) arch
PORPHYRIOS 114-117 (essay: "Houses at Monemvasia, Greece"); 8 ill

CALLIS, Jo Ann (1940-) Amer; photo
WALSH 123-125 (statement); 1 ill

CALLISTER, Charles Warren (1917-) Amer; arch
HEYER 102-109 (interview); 12 ill

CALLIYANNIS, Manolis (1923-) Gree
PREMIER BILAN 284 (statement); port

CALMIS, Charlotte ( )
WOMANART v.2 no.2 12-13 (essay: "Seraphine De Senlis")

CALOS, Nino (1926-)
LUMIERE (statement); port; 1 ill

CALOUTSIS, Valerios (1927-) Gree; sclp
EMANUEL II 162 (statement)
NAYLOR 159-160 (statement)

CALWELL, Ben L. (1918-) Amer; ptr
MILLER 1946 15-19 (statement); 6 ill

CALZADA, Rafael (1951-) Mexi; ptr
DICCIONARIO v.2 153-155 (statement); port; 1 ill

CALZOLARI, Pier Paolo (1943-) Ital
CELANT 120-125 (statement); 6 ill

CAMACHO HERNANDEZ, Juan Jose (1950-) Mexi; ptr
DICCIONARIO v.2 157-159 (statement); port; 1 ill

CAMARATA, Martin L. (1934-) Amer; print
VISUAL v.1 no.3 20-21 (essay: "Lithography"); port; 2 ill

CAMARENA ESPINOSA, Hector (1927-) Mexi; ptr
DICCIONARIO v.2 161-163 (statement); port; 1 ill

CAMARGO, Sergio de (1930-) Braz; sclp
LUMIERE (statement); port; 1 ill

CAMBLIN, Robert (1928-) Amer; ptr
FULBRIGHT 17 (statement)

CAMBRIDGE SEVEN ASSOCIATES INC. (firm) Amer; arch
EMANUEL I 133-135 (statement); 1 ill

CAMERON, Shirley (1944-) Brit
SEE CAMERON AND MILLER

CAMERON AND MILLER (group) Brit; perf
CONTEMPORARY (statement); port; 2 ill

CAMESI, Gianfredo (1940-) Swis; ptr
SKIRA 1978 113 (statement); 2 ill

CAMP, Jeffery (1923-) Brit; ptr
CONTEMPORARY (statement); port; 2 ill

CAMPBELL, Bryn (1933-) Brit; photo
VICTORIA 36-39 (statements)
WALSH 124-125 (statement); 1 ill

CAMPBELL, Colin Keith (1942-) Cana;
video
GUMPERT I 38-39 (statement); port

CAMPBELL, Elizabeth (1893-) Amer;
ptr
ILLINOIS 1965 62 (statement); 1 ill

CAMPBELL, Gretna (1923-) Amer; ptr
FULBRIGHT 17 (statement)
SCHAPIRO 14 (statement); port; 1 ill

CAMPBELL, Kenneth (1913-) Amer;
sclp
ILLINOIS 1965 74 (statement); 1 ill
IT IS no.3 79 (statement)

CAMPENDONK, Heinrich (1889-1957)
Germ; ptr
STURM 22-23 (letter, 1916); 1 ill

CAMPIGLI, Massimo (1895-) Ital; ptr
VERZOCCHI 117-121 (statement); self
port; 1 ill

CAMPILLO SAENZ, Hilda ( ) Mexi; ptr
DICCIONARIO v.2 169-171 (statement);
port; 1 ill

CAMPION, Frank (1949-) Amer; ptr
BOSTON II (statement); 1 ill

CAMPOLI, Cosmo (1922-) Amer; sclp
SELZ 45-49 (statement); 4 ill

CAMPOS, Maria Teresa ( ) Mexi; ptr
DICCIONARIO v.2 173-175 (statement);
port; 1 ill

CAMPOS, Susana ( ) Mexi; ptr
DICCIONARIO v.2 177-179 (statement);
port; 1 ill

CAMPUS, Peter (1937-) Amer; film,
light, video

ARTPARK 1974 10-11 (statement); port;
2 ill
ART-RITE no.7 11, 15 (response)
ART-RITE no.8 3 (response)
EMANUEL II 163-164 (statement)
NAYLOR 163 (statement)
TECHNOLOGIES (statement: *Man's
Head*); port; 3 ill

CAMUS, Gustave ( ) Belg; ptr
COLLARD 46-50 (interview); port; 1 ill

CANCELA, Elia (1940-) envir
PREMIO NACIONAL 1966 28-29
(statement); port; 1 ill

CANCINO, Victor (1929-) Mexi; ptr
DICCIONARIO v.2 181-183 (statement);
port; 1 ill

CANDELA, Felix (1910-) Span/Amer;
arch
RODMAN II 56-59 (statements)

CANDELL, Victor (1903-1977)
Hung/Amer; ptr
ILLINOIS 1952 175-177 (statement); 1 ill
ILLINOIS 1955 184-185 (statement); 1 ill
ILLINOIS 1957 185-186 (response); 1 ill

CANDILIS, Georges (1913-) Fren; arch
EMANUEL I 137-138 (statement); 1 ill
NEWMAN 114-127 (essay); port; 50 ill

CANE, Louis (1943-) Fren; ptr
EMANUEL II 164-165 (statement); 1 ill
NAYLOR 162-163 (statement); 1 ill
SKIRA 1978 83 (statement); 1 ill
SKIRA 1979 102-103 (statement); 1 ill
SKIRA 1980 52-53 (statement); 2 ill

CANIARIS, Vlassis (1928-) Gree; sclp
KUNST UND POLITIK (statement); port;
3 ill

CANIFF, Milton (1907-) Amer; illus
M.H. DE YOUNG 29 (response); self port

CANOGAR, Rafael Garcia (1935-) Span;
ptr
EMANUEL II 165-166 (statement); 1 ill
KUNST UND POLITIK (statement); port;
4 ill
NAYLOR 163-165 (statement); 1 ill

CANTATORE, Domenico (1906-) Ital;
ptr
VERZOCCHI 123-127 (statement); self
port; 1 ill

CANTE-PACOS, Francois (1946-) Fren;
illus
SKIRA 1976 46 (statement); 1 ill

CANTU, Gerardo (1934-) Mexi; print,
ptr
DICCIONARIO v.2 189-191 (statement);
port; 1 ill

CANTU FABILA, Federico (1929-)
Mexi; ptr
DICCIONARIO v.2 185-187 (statement);
port; 1 ill

CAPA, Cornell (1918-) Amer; photo
DANZIGER 56-77 (interview); port; 3 ill
DIAMONSTEIN III 23-38 (interview); 12
ill
MITCHELL 7 ("Foreword")
WALSH 125-127 (statement); 1 ill

CAPARN, Rhys Steel (1909-) Amer; sclp
SCHAPIRO 15 (statement); port; 1 ill

CAPDEVIELLE LICASTRO, Rene
(1925-) Mexi; ptr
DICCIONARIO v.2 193-195 (statement);
port; 1 ill

CAPDEVILA, Francisco Moreno (1926-)
Mexi; print, ptr
DICCIONARIO v.2 197-199 (statement);
port; 1 ill

CAPEHART, Noyes (1933-) Amer; ptr
NOSANOW I 38 (statement); 1 ill

CAPOGROSSI, Giuseppe (1900-1972)
Ital; ptr
RITCHIE 86-89 (statement); port; 4 ill
VERZOCCHI 129-133 (statement); self
port; 1 ill

CAPONIGRO, Paul (1932-) Amer;
photo
TIME-LIFE III 212-215 (statements,
p.p.); 3 ill

CAPRALOS, Christos (1909-) Gree; sclp
NAYLOR 166 (statement); 1 ill

CARAN, Steluca (1940-) Yugo; ptr
TOMASEVIC 59-61 (statement); port; 1
ill

CARBAJAL REJON, Miguel Angel
(1948-) Mexi; ptr
DICCIONARIO v.2 201-203 (statement);
port; 1 ill

CARBONE, David (1949-) Amer; ptr
BOSTON I (interview); 1 ill

CARCAN (1925-) Belg; ptr
COLLARD 42-45 (interview) port; 1 ill

CARD, Greg (1945-) Amer
ART AND TECHNOLOGY 67 (project
proposal)

CARDENAS BARAJAS, Federico (1926-
) Mexi; ptr
DICCIONARIO v.2 205-207 (statement);
port; 1 ill

CARDEW, Michael (1901-) Brit; pott
CAMERON E 47-53 (response); 13 ill
CLARK 89-95 (essay: "Industry and the Studio Potter," o.p. 1942); 3 ill
CLARK 95-99 (essay: "Stoneware Pottery," p.p.); 5 ill
CLARK 100-104 (essay: "Potters and Amateur Potters," o.p. 1972)
GREENHALGH 15-20 (essay: "Design and Meaning in Preliterate Art")

CARDINAL, Douglas Joseph (1934-) Cana; arch
CANADIAN 26-29 (statement); 5 ill
EMANUEL I 139-140 (statement); 1 ill

CARDINALE, Robert L. ( ) metal
VISUAL v.4 no.2 2-3 (essay: "The Aesthetics of Contemporary Crafts")
VISUAL v.4 no.3 24 (essay)

CARENA, Felice (1879-) Ital; ptr
VERZOCCHI 135-139 (statement); self port; 1 ill

CAREWE, Sylvia ( ) text
ART VOICES v.2 no.4 26-27 (interview with Susan Drysdale); port; 2 ill

CAREY, Ellen (1952-) Amer; photo, ptr
FIGURES 8-9 (statement); 1 ill

CARLIN, David ( ) Amer; wood
MEILACH 228 (statement); port

CARLINI, Alessandro ( ) Ital
GROH (statement); 4 ill

CARLOTA, Bertha (Berta Carlota Valdes de Sola) (1920-) Mexi; ptr
DICCIONARIO v.2 209-211 (statement); port; 1 ill

CARLSIN, Frederick Wilhelm
SEE: FREDDIE, Wilhelm

CARLSON, Cynthia (1942-) Amer; sclp
ARTPARK 1977 17-19 (statement); 7 ill
JOHNSON 249-251 (statement, o.p. 1979); 1 ill
WHITE WALLS no.9 57-79 ("Insects: A Guide"); 11 ill

CARLSON, Susana Munoz de Cote de (1933-) Mexi; ptr
DICCIONARIO v.2 213-215 (statement); port; 1 ill

CARMEAN, Harry ( ) Amer; illus
CALIFORNIA--DRAWING (statement); 2 ill

CARMEN (Carmen Sanchez Montoya) (1913-) Mexi; ptr
DICCIONARIO v.2 217-219 (statement); port; 1 ill

CARMI, Eugenio (1920-) Ital; ptr
NAYLOR 168-169 (statement); 1 ill

CARMI, Lisetta (1924-) Ital; photo
WALSH 131-132 (statement); 1 ill

CARMICHAEL, Jae (1925-) Amer; illus, ptr
CALIFORNIA--DRAWING (statement); 2 ill

CARMICHAEL JIMENEZ, Elio J. (1935-) Mexi; ptr
DICCIONARIO v.2 221-223 (statement); port; 1 ill

CARMONA FLORES, Antonio (1932-) Mexi; ptr
DICCIONARIO v.2 225-227 (statement); port; 1 ill

CARNEIRO, Alberto (1937-) Port; envir
SKIRA 1977 54 (statement); 1 ill

CARNEY, Georges (1902-1953) Fren; ptr
PREMIER BILAN 285 (statement); port

CARO, Anthony (1924-) Brit; sclp
ALLEY (statement); 1 ill
CONTEMPORARY (extract from interview with Peter Fuller, p.p.); port; 3 ill
ENGLISH 234-239 (interview with Noel Channon, 1974); port; 11 ill
SKIRA 1975 101 (statement); 1 ill

CARO ENG, Aurora (1951-) Mexi; ptr
DICCIONARIO v.2 229-231 (statement); port; 1 ill

CARONE, Nicolas (1917-) Amer; ptr
FULBRIGHT 18 (statement)

CAROOMPAS, Carole ( ) Amer; ptr, sclp
SCHAPIRO 16 (statement); port; 1 ill
WHITE WALLS no.5 32-37 (text piece)

CARPENTER, James ( ) Amer; film
ARTPARK 1979 (statement); 1 ill

CARPENTER, Jamie (1949-) Amer; glass
GLASS v.1 20-21 (statement); port; 1 ill
GLASS v.5 (group discussion)

CARPI, Aldo (1886-) Ital; ptr
VERZOCCHI 141-145 (statement); self port; 1 ill

CARPI, Cioni (1923-) perf
PARACHUTE no.1 35-41 (statements in English and French); 22 ill
TRACKS v.3 no.1/2 124-129 ("Man (=1, That is, Plus or Minus Being = X) An Interlinked Commentary to Seven Masked Masks in Thirty-five Areas of Memory, or: Thirty-five Palimpsests from the Imperfect Memory to the Imaginary")

CARRA, Carlo (1881-1966) Ital; ptr
APOLLONIO 24-27 ("Manifesto of the Futurist Painters," o.p. 1910)
APOLLONIO 27-31 ("Futurist Paintings: Technical Manifesto," o.p. 1910)
APOLLONIO 45-50 ("The Exhibitors to the Public," o.p. 1912)
APOLLONIO 91-92 ("Plastic Planes as Spherical Expansions in Space," o.p. 1913)
APOLLONIO 111-115 "The Painting of Sounds, Noises, and Smells," o.p. 1913)
APOLLONIO 202-205 (extract from "Warpainting," o.p. 1915)
CHIPP 289-293 ("Futurist Painting: Technical Manifesto," o.p. 1910)
CHIPP 294-298 ("The Exhibitors to the Public," o.p. 1912)
CHIPP 304-308 (essay: "From Cezanne to Us, the Futurists," o.p. 1913)
CHIPP 453-456 (essay: "The Quadrant of the Spirit," o.p. 1919)
GUGGENHEIM II 135-137 ("Manifesto of the Futurist Painters," o.p. 1910)
PAINTING 9 (statement); port; 1 ill
VERZOCCHI 147-151 (statement); self port; 1 ill

CARRADE, Michel (1923-) Fren; ptr
GRENIER 61-72 (interview)
PREMIER BILAN 285 (statement); port

CARRASCO VELAZQUEZ, Humberto (1929-) Mexi; ptr
DICCIONARIO v.2 233-235 (statement); port; 1 ill

CARRAWAY, Arthur (1927-) Amer; ptr
LEWIS I REVISED 5 (statement); port; 1 ill

CARRENO, Alfredo (1955-) Mexi; ptr
DICCIONARIO v.2 241-243 (statement); port; 1 ill

CARRENO, Jorge (1929-) Mexi; print, ptr, cart
DICCIONARIO v.2 237-239 (statement); 1 ill

CARRENO, Mario (1913-) Cuba; ptr
TIGER no.2 37-41, 45 (statement); 4 ill

CARREON, Martha Lavalle de ( ) Mexi; ptr
DICCIONARIO v.2 245-247 (statement); port; 1 ill

CARR-HARRIS, Ian (1941-) Cana; sclp
SKIRA 1979 85 (statement); 2 ill

CARRILLO, Lilia (1930-1974) Mexi; print, ptr
DICCIONARIO v.2 249-251 (statement); self port; 1 ill

CARRILLO, Ricardo Joel (1957-) Mexi; ptr
DICCIONARIO v.2 257-259 (statement); port; 1 ill

CARRILLO GONZALEZ, David (1920-) Mexi; ptr
DICCIONARIO v.2 253-255 (statement); self port; 1 ill

CARRINGTON, Leonora (1917-) Brit; ptr
CIRCLE no.6 73-79 (play: "Flannel Night Shirt")
FORD/VIEW v.1 no.9/10 7 (story: "White Rabbits")
FORD/VIEW v.1 no.11/12 7-8 (story: "The Sisters")
FORD/VIEW v.2 no.1 13 (essay: "The Bird Superior, Max Ernst"); 1 ill
GUGGENHEIM II 132 (statement, o.p. 1939); 1 ill
JEAN 386-389 ("The Seventh Horse," o.p. 1943)

PLASTIQUE no.5 2-9 (story: "L'Homme Qui a Perdu Son Squelette," with Marcel Duchamp, Jean Arp, Max Ernst, et al.)

CARRINO, Nicola (1932-) Ital; instal, ptr, sclp
EMANUEL II 169-170 (statement); 1 ill
NAYLOR 171-172 (statement); 1 ill

CARRION SAMANIEGO, Hector E. (1938-) Mexi; ptr
DICCIONARIO v.2 261-263 (statement); port; 1 ill

CARRIZALEZ ESCOBEDO, Jose (1925-) Mexi; ptr
DICCIONARIO v.2 265-267 (statement); port; 1 ill

CARROLL, James F.L. ( ) Amer; ptr
BRENTANO 172-173 (statement); 1 ill

CARROLL, John (1892-1959) Amer; ptr
BRITANNICA 19 (statement); port; 1 ill

CARSKI, Leticia (1947-) Mexi; ptr
DICCIONARIO v.2 269-271 (statement); port; 1 ill

CARSMAN, Jon (1944-) Amer; ptr
ART NOW v.2 no.4 (statement); 1 ill

CARSON, Karen (1943-) Amer; print, ptr, coll
CELEBRATION (statement); 1 ill
SCHAPIRO 17 (statement); 1 ill

CARTER, Brian ( )
ARTISTS no.4 10-11 ("Programmed")

CARTER, Cecil (1908-) Amer; ptr
ILLINOIS 1959 203-204 (statement); 1 ill

CARTER, Clarence Holbrook (1904-)
Amer; ptr
GEOMETRIC (statement); 1 ill
M.H. DE YOUNG 32-33 (response); self
port
MCCAUSLAND 60-64 (essay: "Artist-
Advertiser Relations")
MILLER 1943 32-33 (statement); 2 ill

CARTER, Eliot (1908-) Amer; sound,
perf
STEDELIJK 98 (statement, o.p. 1971)

CARTER, Harry ( ) Amer; ptr
NORTH LIGHT 50-55 (statement); port
6 ill

CARTER, Katharine T. (1950-) ptr
OUTSIDE I 4-7, 29 (statement); port; 3
ill

CARTER, Lucius ( ) Amer; sclp
ART PATRON ART 19-20 (statement);
port; 1 ill

CARTER, Whitford (-1973) Amer/Mexi;
ptr, print
DICCIONARIO v.2 273-275 (statement);
port; 1 ill

CARTIER, Ferdinand (1893-) Amer; ptr
MILLER 1943 35 (statement); 1 ill

CARTIER-BRESSON, Henri (1908-)
Fren; photo
HILL 74-79 (interview, 1977); port
TIME-LIFE IV 21 (statement, p.p.)
WALSH 132-135 (statement); 1 ill

CARTON, Norman (1908-) Amer; ptr
ILLINOIS 1961 56 (response); port; 1 ill

CARTWRIGHT, Virginia (1943-) Amer;
pott
HERMAN 37 (statement); port; 1 ill

CARZOU, Jean (1907-) Fren; ptr
GOLDAINE 157-159 (interview); port

CASADESUS, Beatrice ( ) Fren; ptr
SKIRA 1978 99 (statement); 3 ill

CASANOVA MENDEZ, Felipe (1942-)
Mexi; ptr
DICCIONARIO v.2 277-279 (statement);
port; 1 ill

CASARIEGO, Florencio Mendez ( ) sclp
PREMIO NACIONAL 1966 30-31
(statement); port; 1 ill

CASAS, Mel (1929-) Amer; ptr
RAICES 39 (statement); 1 ill

CASAS CASTANO, Fernando (1905-)
Mexi; ptr
DICCIONARIO v.2 285-287 (statement);
port; 1 ill

CASAS CASTANOZ, Enrique (1897-)
Mexi; ptr
DICCIONARIO v.2 281-283 (statement);
port; 1 ill

CASDIN-SILVER, Harriet (1935-) Amer;
photo, film
CENTERBEAM 75-81, 102
("'Centerbeam' documenta 6--
"'Centerbeam' Washington, D.C.");
port; 7 ill
TECHNOLOGIES (statement: "On the
Creative Process and Holography");
port; 8 ill

CASEBERE, James (1953-) Amer; sclp,
light, photo
ARTPARK 1983 22-23 (statement); 2 ill

CASEY, Bernie (1939-) Amer; ptr
LEWIS I REVISED 17-18 (statement);
port; 2 ill

CASHWAN, Samuel (1900-) Russ/Amer; sclp
MILLER 1942 30-37 (statement); port; 10 ill

CASO LOMBARDO, Alejandro (1926-) Mexi; ptr
DICCIONARIO v.2 289-291 (statement); port; 1 ill

CASO RAPHAEL, Pablo (1958-) Mexi; ptr
DICCIONARIO v.2 293-295 (statement); port; 1 ill

CASORATTI, Felice (1886-) Ital; ptr
VERZOCCHI 153-157 (statement); self port; 1 ill

CASSEN, Jackie (1938-) Amer; sclp
DIRECTIONS I 75 (response); 1 ill

CASSINARI, Bruno (1912-) Ital; ptr
VERZOCCHI 159-163 (statement); self port; 1 ill

CASSON, Hugh (1910-) Brit; arch
EMANUEL I 140-141 (statement); 1 ill

CASSON, Michael (1925-) Amer; pott
CAMERON E 54-61 (response); 11 ill
SHAFER 30-49 (statements); port; 25 ill

CASSY DE GOENAGA, Cristina ( ) Mexi; ptr
DICCIONARIO v.2 297-299 (statement); self port; 1 ill

CASTANEDA, Pilar ( ) Mexi; ptr
DICCIONARIO v.2 305-307 (statement); port; 1 ill

CASTANIS, Muriel (1926-) Amer; sclp
NAYLOR 173 (statement); 1 ill

CASTANON RANGEL, Heliodoro (1943-) Mexi; ptr
DICCIONARIO v.2 309-311 (statement); port; 1 ill

CASTANOS, Magdalena Martinez de (1919-) Mexi; ptr
DICCIONARIO v.2 313-315 (statement); port; 1 ill

CASTELLANI, Enrico (1930-) Ital; ptr, arch
GUGGENHEIM I 98 (essay: "Totality in the Art of Today," o.p. 1963)

CASTELLANOS RIVERA, Albino (1918-) Mexi; ptr
DICCIONARIO v.2 317-319 (statement); port; 1 ill

CASTELLI, Luciano (1951-) Swis; perf, ptr, sclp
EMANUEL II 172-173 (extract from interview with Jacques Clayssen); 1 ill
IDENTITE 27-30 (interview with Jacques Clayssen); port
NAYLOR 174-175 (extract from interview with Jacques Clayssen); 2 ill
SANDBERG 38-41 (statement); 6 ill

CASTIGLIONI, Achille (1918-) Ital; design
DESIGN 139-142 (interview with Raffaella Crespi); 1 ill

CASTILLO, Consuelo Mendez (1952-) Vene; ptr
RAICES 54 (statement); 1 ill

CASTILLO, Jorge (1933-) Span; ptr
SKIRA 1980 76-77 (statement); 3 ill

CASTILLO ELIZONDO, Angel (1923-) Mexi; ptr

DICCIONARIO v.2 325-327 (statement); port; 1 ill

CASTLE, Wendell Keith (1932-) Amer; sclp, wood
DIAMONSTEIN IV 24-37 (interview); port; 16 ill

CASTLES, John (1946-) sclp
ANGEL 59-81 (interview); port; 1 ill

CASTORO, Rosemarie (1939-) Amer; envir, instal, sclp
ARTPARK 1979 (statement); 1 ill
CELEBRATION (statement); 1 ill
HESS 98-99 (statement)
MCCLINTIC 67-69 (statement); 3 ill
MEYER 104-107 (text piece: "Eclipse"); 1 ill
SKIRA 1979 62 (statement); 1 ill
TRACKS v.1 no.2 24-25 (poem)

CASTRO, Alex (1943-) Amer; instal, ptr
CORCORAN 38-53 (interview); port; 9 ill

CASTRO LENERO, Alberto (1951-) Mexi; ptr
DICCIONARIO v.2 329-331 (statement); port; 1 ill

CASTRO LENERO, Francisco (1954-) Mexi; ptr
DICCIONARIO v.2 333-335 (statement); port; 1 ill

CASTRO LENERO, Miguel (1956-) Mexi; ptr
DICCIONARIO v.2 341-343 (statement); port; 1 ill

CASTRO SILVA, Roberto (1920-) Mexi; ptr
DICCIONARIO v.2 345-347 (statement); port; 1 ill

CASTRO VALDES, Oscar H. (1913-) Mexi; ptr
DICCIONARIO v.2 349-351 (statement); port; 1 ill

CASTRO-CID, Enrique (1937-) Chil/Amer; ptr, sclp
DIRECTIONS I 75 (response); 1 ill
ILLINOIS 1965 50 (statement); 1 ill

CASTRUITA CHAPA, Humberto (1945-) Mexi; ptr
DICCIONARIO v.2 353-355 (statement); port; 1 ill

CATALA DESCARREGA, Rosa (1922-) Mexi; ptr
DICCIONARIO v.2 357-359 (statement); port; 1 ill

CATALANO, Eduardo (1917-) Arge/Amer; arch
EMANUEL I 141-142 (statement); 1 ill
HEYER 234-241 (interview); 8 ill

CATANY, Toni (1942-) Span; photo
WALSH 135 (statement); 1 ill

CATCHINGS, Yvonne Parks (1935-) Amer; ptr
LEWIS II 25 (statement); port; 1 ill

CATLETT, Alice Elizabeth (1915-) Amer; print, sclp
FAX I 14-31 (statements); port; 2 ill
LEWIS II 107 (statement); port; 4 ill

CATLING, Brian (1948-) Brit; sclp
BRITISH (statement); 1 ill

CATON, Mitchell (1930-) Amer; ptr
LEWIS II 122 (statement); port; 3 ill

CAUDILL, William Wayne (1914-) Amer; arch

EMANUEL I 142-144 (statement); 1 ill

CAVALLON, Giorgio (1904-) Amer; ptr
ART NOW v.3 no.3 (statement); 1 ill

CAVANAUGH, James ( ) photo
LAPLANTE 9-16 (interview); port; 1 ill

CAVANAUGH, Tom Richard (1923-)
Amer; ptr
FULBRIGHT 18-19 (statement); 1 ill

CAVANNA, Elise ( ) Amer; illus
CALIFORNIA--DRAWING (statement); 2
ill

CAVAT, Irma (1928-) Amer; ptr
ILLINOIS 1959 204-205 (statement); 1 ill

CAVAZOS, Alberto (1939-) Mexi; ptr
DICCIONARIO v.2 365-367 (statement);
port; 1 ill

CAVE, Leonard Edward (1944-) Amer;
sclp, wood
MEILACH 109, 226 (statement); ports; 2
ill

CAVELLINI, Guglielmo Achille (1914-)
Ital; photo, ptr
NAYLOR 177-178 (statement); 1 ill
SKIRA 1976 18 (statement); 1 ill

CAZAL, Philippe (1948-) Fren
SEE: GROUPE UNTEL

CAZARES, Jorge (1937-) Mexi; ptr
DICCIONARIO v.2 369-371 (statement);
port; 1 ill

CEDILLO RODRIGUEZ, Enrique (1937-
) Mexi; ptr
DICCIONARIO v.2 373-375 (statement);
self port; 1 ill

CELENDER, Donald Dennis (1931-)
Amer; ptr
ON SITE no.2 10, 12 (response)

CELENTANO, Francis Michael (1928-)
Amer; ptr
GUENTHER 32-33 (statement); port; 1
ill
LETTERS 10-11 (letter); 2 ill

CELMINS, Vija (1939-) Amer; ptr, sclp
HOPKINS 86-87 (statement); port; 1 ill

CENICEROS, Guillermo (1939-) Mexi;
ptr
DICCIONARIO v.2 377-379 (statement);
port; 1 ill

CERNY, George (1905-) Amer; ptr, sclp
ILLINOIS 1953 173-174 (statement); 1 ill

CERVANTES CERVANTES, Noe (1951-
) Mexi; ptr
DICCIONARIO v.2 381-383 (statement);
port; 1 ill

CERVANTES PALOMINO, Juan (1940-
) Mexi; ptr
DICCIONARIO v.2 385-387 (statement);
port; 1 ill

CESAR (Cesar Baldiccini) (1921-) Fren;
sclp
ART SINCE v.2 149 (statement, o.p.
1953)
ART VOICES v.4 no.2 116-121
(interview with Edouard Roditi); 5 ill
FRASNAY 359-369 (handwritten
statement, in French, with English
translation); ports; 2 ill
VINGTIEME N.S. no.9 32-33 (statement);
1 ill
VINGTIEME N.S. no.12 57-61, 96
(interview with Yvon Taillandier, in
French and English); 5 ill

CETTO, Max (1903-) Mexi; arch
EMANUEL I 1441-46 (statement); 1 ill

CEZANNE, Paul (1839-1906) Fren; ptr
CHIPP 18-23 (letters, 1902, 1903, 1904, 1905, 1906)
FRIEDENTHAL 180-185 (letters to Emile Bernard, 1904, 1905); 3 ill
GOLDWATER 363-367 (letters, 1904, 1905, 1906)
GROHMANN 359-362 ("Aus Gesprachen," p.p.)
POENSGEN 73 ("Kunst und Natur")

CHACALLIS, Louis (1943-) Fren; sclp
SKIRA 1976 98 (statement); 1 ill

CHACON PINEDA, Alejandro (1942-) Mexi; ptr
DICCIONARIO v.3 89-91 (statement); port; 1 ill

CHACON REYES, Abel (1937-) Mexi; ptr
DICCIONARIO v.3 85-87 (statement); port; 1 ill

CHADBOURN, Alfred ( ) Amer; ptr
DAUGHERTY 10-29 (statements); ports; 2 ill

CHADIRJI, Rifat (1926-) Iraq; arch
EMANUEL I 146-147 (statement); 1 ill

CHADWICK, Lynn (1914-) Brit; sclp
FORMA 28-49 (statement); ports; 7 ill
OPEN AIR 1954 (statement)
RITCHIE 70-73 (statement); port; 3 ill

CHAET, Bernard (1924-) Amer; ptr
ILLINOIS 1951 166-167 (statement)
ILLINOIS 1953 174 (statement); 1 ill

CHAGALL, Marc (1887-) Russ/Fren; ptr
ART SINCE v.2 148 (statements, o.p. 1952, 1957)
ART VOICES v.4 no.2 130-136 (interview with Miklos Hubay); 4 ill
CHARBONNIER v.2 39-49 (interview)
CHIPP 440-443 (extract from interview with James Johnson Sweeney, o.p. 1944); self port
EIGHT (handwritten statement in French; statement in English, French, and German, and two poems); ports
FIFIELD 245-252 (interview)
FORD/VIEW v.5 no.6 7, 12, 14 (essay: "My Life: Two Excerpts," extracts from *Ma Vie*); 1 ill
FRASNAY 53-63 (statement); ports; 4 ill
FRIEDENTHAL 261-263 (statement, o.p. 1931); 1 ill
GOLDAINE 22-25 (interview); port
GOLDWATER 432-434 (extract from interview, 1944)
JANIS I 132 (statement); 1 ill
LIBERMAN 63-67 (statements)
MAYWALD (statement in English, German, and French; handwritten poem: "A Bella," in French); ports
MINOTAURE no.3/4 106 ("Enquete")
PROTTER 215-216 (extract from *Reflections on My Work*); 1 ill
RODITI 16-38 (interview); port; self port
RAYNAL 93-98 (statement); 3 ill
SCHNEIDER 136-157 (interview); 1 ill
SEGHERS 208-215 (essay: "Some Impressions on Paintinng," p.p.)
THORN 47, 49, 55, 56, 96 (statements, p.p.)
VINGTIEME N.S. no.9 23-24 (statement)

CHAIKEN, William (1921-) Amer; ptr
ILLINOIS 1957 186-187 (response); 1 ill
ILLINOIS 1959 205-206 (statement); 1 ill

CHAIMOWICZ, Marc Camille (1947-) Fren; perf, instal

HAYWARD 1978 70-73 (statement); 3 ill

CHAISSAC, Gaston ( ) Fren; ptr
RAGON 112-118 (statement)

CHAMBERLAIN, John Angus (1927-)
Amer; sclp, ptr
ART AND TECHNOLOGY 68-77 (project
proposal)
TUCHMAN 44-45 (letter)

CHAMBERLAIN, Wynn (1928-) Amer;
ptr
ART VOICES v.5 no.3 43 (statement); 1
ill

CHAMBERLAND, Claude ( ) film
PARACHUTE no.10 18-20 (interview);
port

CHAMBERLIN, Peter (1919-1978) Brit;
arch
SEE: CHAMBERLIN POWELL AND
BON

CHAMBERLIN, Wesley (1932-) Amer;
illus
CALIFORNIA--DRAWING (statement)

CHAMBERLIN POWELL AND BON
(arch firm)
EMANUEL I 148-149 (statement); 1 ill

CHAMBERS, Nancy (1952-) Amer;
paper
PAPERWORKS 6-7 (statement); 5 ill

CHAMIZO, Juan Ruiz (1921-) Mexi; ptr
DICCIONARIO v.3 93-95 (statement);
port; 1 ill

CHANDLER, Dana C.W. (1941-) Amer;
ptr, sclp
FAX II 345-361 (statements); port; 1 ill

FINE 203-204 (statements, o.p. 1969,
1970); 2 ill
LEWIS I REVISED 39-42 (statement);
ports; 7 ill

CHANG, Ching-Yu ( ) sclp, envir
ARTPARK 1974 12-15 (statement); port;
11 ill

CHAO FODERE, Roberto Jorge (1949-)
Mexi; ptr
DICCIONARIO v.3 97-99 (poem); port; 1
ill

CHAP, Yeap Poh (1927-) pott
CAMERON E 156-164 (response); 8 ill

CHAPA, Martha (1946-) Mexi; ptr
DICCIONARIO v.3 101-103 (statement);
port; 1 ill

CHAPELAIN-MIDY, Roger (1904-)
Fren; ptr
GOLDAINE 144-146 (interview); port

CHAPIN, Francis (1899-1965) Amer; ptr
ILLINOIS 1957 187-188 (response); 1 ill
MILLER 1942 38-42 (statement); port; 5
ill

CHAPIN, James Ormsbee (1887-) Amer;
ptr
BRITANNICA 20 (statement); port; 1 ill

CHAPMAN, George (1908-) Brit; ptr
WHELDON 168-173 (statement); port

CHAPMAN, Tjae (1947-) Amer; metal
WISCONSIN I (statement); 1 ill

CHAPOI DE LOS SANTOS, Sergio
(1938-) Mexi; ptr
DICCIONARIO v.3 105-107 (statement);
port; 1 ill

CHAPOVAL, Jules (1919-1951) Fren; ptr
PREMIER BILAN 286 (statement); port
TEMOIGNAGES I 50-57 (statement);
port; 6 ill

CHAPPELL, Walter (1952-) Amer;
photo
WALSH 139-141 (statement); 1 ill

CHARBONNIER, Jean-Philippe (1921-)
Fren; photo
WALSH 141 (statement); 1 ill

CHARCHOUNE, Serge (1888-) Russ; ptr
BERCKELAERS 282-285 (statement);
port; 2 ill

CHARLES, Milton ( ) Amer; pott
ILLUSTRATION 56-59 (statement); port;
7 ill

CHARLESWORTH, Bruce (1950-)
Amer; video
GUMPERT I 39 (statement); port
GUMPERT III 60-61 (statement)

CHARLESWORTH, Sarah ( )
ART-LANGUAGE v.3 no.2 68-80 ("'Mr.
Lin Yutang Refers to "Fair Play"...?'")
SEE ALSO: INTERNATIONAL
LOCAL

CHARLOT, Jean (1898-1979)
Fren/Amer; ptr
HAAR I xi-xviii ("Introduction")
HAAR I 42-49 (interview with Prithwish
Neogy); ports; 3 ill

CHARNEY, Melvin (1935-) Cana; arch
CANADIAN 30-35 (statement); 13 ill
EMANUEL I 150-151 (statement); 1 ill

CHAROUX, Siegfried (1896-) sclp
LONDON COUNTY (statement); 1 ill
OPEN AIR 1960 (statement); 1 ill

CHARPENTIER, Louis (1947-) Cana;
ptr, illus
PRADEL 138 (statement, o.p. 1982); 2
ill

CHASE, Louisa (1951-) Amer; ptr
LOGAN II 16-19 (statement); port; 5 ill

CHASE-RIBOUD, Barbara Dwayne
(1939-) Amer; sclp
MUNRO 370-376 (interview); port
NAYLOR 185 (statement); 1 ill

CHASTEL, Roger (1897-) Fren; ptr
SEUPHOR 147-148 (statement); 1 ill

CHASTELLAIN, Maribel (1954-) Mexi;
ptr
DICCIONARIO v.3 109-111 (statement);
port; 1 ill

CHAVARRIA, Jose Ramirez (1942-)
Mexi; ptr
DICCIONARIO v.3 117-119 (statement);
port; 1 ill

CHAVARRIA RUIZ, Enrique (1957-)
Mexi; ptr
DICCIONARIO v.3 113-115 (statement);
port; 1 ill

CHAVES BARCELLOS, Vera (1938-)
Braz; photo
SKIRA 1977 91 (statement); 2 ill

CHAVEZ, Edward Arcenio (1917-)
Amer; ptr
FULBRIGHT 19 (statement)
ILLINOIS 1952 179 (statement); 1 ill
ILLINOIS 1955 186 (statement); 1 ill
ZAIDENBERG 124-127 (essay: "The
Artist and His Environment"); 7 ill

CHAVEZ BARRAGAN, Carlos Antonio
(1935-) Mexi; ptr

DICCIONARIO v.3 121-123 (statement); port; 1 ill

CHAVEZ ESPARZA, Carlos (1953-) Mexi; ptr
DICCIONARIO v.3 125-127 (statement); port; 1 ill

CHAVEZ MENDEZ, Ricardo (1953-) Mexi; ptr
DICCIONARIO v.3 129-131 (statement); port; 1 ill

CHAVEZ MENDOZA, Hugo (1943-) Mexi; ptr
DICCIONARIO v.3 133-135 (statement); port; 1 ill

CHELIMSKY, Oscar ( ) ptr
ARTS YEARBOOK v.6 24-27 (essay: "A Memoir of Brancusi," o.p. 1958)

CHEMALY SAYEG, Magdalena (1951-) Mexi; ptr
DICCIONARIO v.3 143-145 (statement); port; 1 ill

CHEMETOV, Paul ( ) Fren; arch, sclp
ARCHITECTURES 98-103 (essay: "Une Rude Epreuve"); 11 ill

CHEN, Chi (1912-) Chin/Amer; ptr
ILLINOIS 1957 188 (response); 1 ill

CHEN, Valeria W. (1950-) Amer; metal, wood
WISCONSIN II (statement); 1 ill

CHEN YU LOPEZ, Juan (1934-) Chin/Mexi; ptr
DICCIONARIO v.3 147-149 (statement); port; 1 ill

CHERMAYEFF, Peter ( ) Amer; arch
EMANUEL I 133-135 (statement); 1 ill

CHERMAYEFF, Serge Ivan (1900-) Russ; ptr, arch, design
BATTCOCK VII 3-10 (essay: "The Shape of Humanism," o.p. 1971)
COOPER-HEWITT I 100-101 (essay: "Graphic Design in Public")
EMANUEL I 151-153 (statement); 1 ill
ILLINOIS 1951 167 (statement); 1 ill

CHERNIKOV, Jakob Georgiyevich (Chernikhov, Yakov) (1889-1951) Russ; ptr, print
BANN 152-169 (essay: "The Constitution, Study, and Form of Constructivism," o.p. 1931); 2 ill
BOWLT 254-261 (extract from *The Construction of Architectural and Machine Forms*, o.p. 1931); 1 ill

CHERNITSKY, Shirley (1944-) Mexi; ptr
DICCIONARIO v.3 151-153 (statement); port; 1 ill

CHERRY, Catherine ( ) perf
ART NETWORK no.2 45 (statement); 1 ill
ART NETWORK no.2 48 (statement)

CHERRY, Herman (1909-) Amer; ptr
ILLINOIS 1955 186-187 (statement)
RODMAN I 97-98 (interview)
TRACKS v.2 no.1 26-27 (poems: "Show Biz," "O,Velvetius!")
WINSTON-SALEM 16-22 (statement); 6 ill
ZAIDENBERG 92-94 (essay: "The State of Painting"); 4 ill

CHESSAL RAMIREZ, Antonio (1939-) Mexi; ptr
DICCIONARIO v.3 155-157 (statement); port; 1 ill

CHESTER, Robert C. ( ) Amer; pott
HAYSTACK 7 (statement); 1 ill

CHET, Florika
SEE: KEC, Florika

CHEVALIER, Jack ( ) Amer; sclp
GUENTHER 34-35 (statement); port; 1 ill

CHEW, C. T. ( ) Amer; coll, ptr
GUENTHER 36-37 (statement); port; 1 ill

CHIA, Sandro (1946-) Ital; ptr
WALDMAN 10-33 (statement); 17 ill

CHIARENZA, Carl (1935-) Amer; photo
BARROW 209-236 (essay: "Notes Toward an Integrated History of Picturemaking," o.p. 1979)

CHIARI, Giuseppe (1926-) Ital; photo, film
SKIRA 1977 63 (statement)
WEBER 178-216 ("Discussione/ Discussion," Italian and English); ports

CHIBA, Anyano ( ) Japa; text
ADACHI 14-16 (statement); ports; 2 ill

CHICAGO, Judy (Judy Gerowitz) (1939-) Amer; sclp, ptr, instal
ART-RITE no.5 6 (response)
CELEBRATION (statement); 1 ill
CHRYSALIS no.4 89-102 (interview with Arlene Raven and Susan Rennie); 5 ill
EMANUEL II 183-185 (statement); 1 ill
HOPKINS 88-89 (statement); port; 1 ill
NAYLOR 186-187 (statement)
TUCKER I 18 (statement)
VISUAL v.2 no.3 14-17 (interview); 3 ill

CHICO CHAVEZ, Julio (1947-) Mexi; ptr
DICCIONARIO v.3 159-161 (statement); port; 1 ill

CHIEN-SHIN, Lin (1918-) Cana; ptr
POINT OF VIEW 16 (statement); 1 ill

CHIHULY, Dale (1941-) Amer; glass
DIAMONSTEIN IV 38-53 (interview); port; 13 ill
GLASS v.5 (group discussion)
HAYSTACK 8 (statement); 1 ill

CHILLIDA, Eduardo (1924-) Span; sclp
HAUSSER 48-49 (statement, 1967, o.p. 1981); 1 ill
KEPES IX 62-73 (extract from "private communications" with John E. Burchard)

CHILTON, Helen Z. (1946-) Amer; ptr
NOSANOW I 39 (statement); 1 ill

CHIMACOFF AND PETERSON (arch firm)
GA HOUSES no.1 110-119 (statement); 22 ill

CHIMES, Thomas (1921-) Amer; ptr
ILLINOIS 1965 49 (statement); 1 ill

CHINCHILLA CHINCHILLA, Antonio (1950-) Mexi; ptr
DICCIONARIO v.3 163-165 (statement); port; 1 ill

CHINN, Yuen Yuey (1922-) Chin/Amer; ptr
FULBRIGHT 21 (statement)

CHIRICO, Giorgio de (1888-1978) Ital; ptr
CHIPP 397-401 (essay: "Meditations of a Painter," o.p. 1955)

100   CONTEMPORARY   40-41
(statement); port; 1 ill

CIVITELLO, John (1939-) Amer; ptr
GEOMETRIC (statement); 1 ill

CLAASS, Arnaud (1949-) Fren; photo
WALSH 147-149 (statement); 1 ill

CLAIRE (Claire Jalil) (1938-) Mexi; ptr
DICCIONARIO v.2 389-391 (statement);
port; 1 ill

CLAREBOUDT, Jean (1944-) Fren;
photo, perf, envir
SKIRA 1978 33 (statement); 3 ill
SKIRA 1979 36 (statement); 1 ill

CLARIDGE, John (1944-) Brit; photo
WALSH 148-149 (statement); 1 ill

CLARK, Claude Lockhart, Jr. (1945-)
Amer; wood, ptr, sclp
CONTEMPORARY   AFRICAN
(statement); port; 1 ill

CLARK, Fiona ( ) NewZ; photo
ART NETWORK no.9 56 (statement)

CLARK, Irene (1927-) Amer; ptr
LEWIS I REVISED 107 (statement); port;
1 ill

CLARK, Larry (1943-) Amer; photo
DUGAN 65-77 (interview, 1978); port

CLARK, Leon "Peck" (1906-) Amer;
wood
FERRIS 33-51 (statements); ports; 3 ill

CLARK, Lygia (Lygia Pimental Lins)
(1920-) Braz; sclp, perf
EMANUEL II 189-190 (statement)
NAYLOR 194-195 (statement); 1 ill

CLARK, Michael Vinson (1946-) Amer;
ptr
IMAGES 10-17 (interview with Clair
List); port; 5 ill

CLARK, Ron ( ) video
ART-RITE no.7 11 (response)

CLARKE, Dale ( ) Amer; arch, design
LIFE 116-119 (interview); port

CLARKE, John Clem (1937-) Amer; ptr
ART NOW v.2 no.5 (statement); 1 ill

CLARKE, Richard (1923-) Amer; ptr
KNOXVILLE (statement); port; 7 ill

CLARKE, Wendy ( ) sclp, video
ARTPARK 1983 24-25 (statement); port;
3 ill

CLAUGHTON, R. B. (1917-) sclp
OPEN AIR 1960 (statement); 1 ill

CLAUS, Hugo (1929-) ptr
QUADRUM no.10 142-143 (poem); 3 ill

CLAUS, Jurgen (1935-) Germ; ptr
GROH (statement); 1 ill

CLAVE, Antoni (1913-) Span/Fren;
design, illus, ptr
GOLDAINE 192-194 (interview); port

CLAY, Ed (1948-) Amer; wood
WOODWORKING   14-15   (statement);
port; 2 ill

CLEARY, Manon Catherine (1942-)
Amer; ptr, illus
IMAGES 18-25 (interview with Clair
List); port; 5 ill

CLELLAND, Doug ( ) arch

RUSSELL F 103-108 (project proposal); 35 ill

CLEMENTE, Francesco (1952-) Ital; illus, print, ptr
VIEW v.3 no.6 (interview); port; 12 ill

CLEMENTZ, Jon ( ) ptr
BRAKKE 184-186 ("Why I Paint"); 1 ill

CLERGUE, Lucien (1934-) Fren; photo
WALSH 151-152 (statement); 1 ill

CLIFFORD, Kathy ( ) Amer; ptr
KRESGE (statement); port; 1 ill

CLOAR, Carroll (1913-) Amer; ptr
ILLINOIS 1957 189-190 (response); 1 ill
ILLINOIS 1959 206-207 (statement); 1 ill
ILLINOIS 1963 81 (statement); 1 ill

CLOSE, Chuck (Charles) (1940-) Amer; ptr
ART NOW v.3 no.4 ("After Four Years of Working in Black and White");1 ill
ARTHUR 38-53 (interview); port; 26 ill
BATTCOCK III 145-162 (statements, o.p. 1974); 3 ill
DIAMONSTEIN I 68-80 (interview); ports
EMANUEL II 191-193 (statement); 1 ill
JOHNSON 160-164 (interview with Linda Chase and Robert Feldman, o.p. 1972); 1 ill
NAYLOR 196-197 (statement); 1 ill
ROSE II REVISED 225-227 (extract from interview o.p. 1972)
VAN DER MARCK 46, 49 (statement); 1 ill

CLOSE, Cynthia (1946-) Amer; ptr
BOSTON I (interview); 1 ill

CLOSON, Henri J. (1888-) Belg; ptr
ABSTRACTION no.3 7-8 (statement); 2 ill

ABSTRACTION no.4 7 (statement); 1 ill

CLOTET, Lluis (1941-) Span; arch
EMANUEL I 155-157 (statement); 1 ill

CLOUGH, Charles ( ) Amer; coll, ptr
HALLWALLS (statement)

CLUSMANN, G. H.
SEE: HENGHES

CLUTTON, Robert (1932-) Amer; coll
CALIFORNIA--COLLAGE (statement); 1 ill

COATES, Wells Wintemute (1895-1958) Cana; arch
READ 105-115 (statement); port; 8 ill

COATS, Marvin S. (1943-) Amer; sclp
NOSANOW I 40 (statement); 1 ill

COBB, Charles B. ( ) Amer; wood
MEILACH 228-229 (statement); port

COBB, Henry N. (1926-) arch
SEARING 98-105 (statement); 7 ill

COBIAN CASTRO, Raquel (1931-) Mexi; ptr
DICCIONARIO v.2 397 (statement); port; 1 ill

COBRA (group)
ART SINCE v.2 150 (statement, o.p. 1967)
CHIPP 601-603 ("Our Own Desires Build the Revolution," o.p. 1949)

COBURN, Alvin Langdon (1882-1966) Amer; photo
LIGHT 24-29 (extract from essay: "The Future of Pictorial Photography," o.p. 1916); 5 ill

COCHRAN, Malcolm ( ) Amer; sclp
ARTPARK 1981 (statement); port; 2 ill

CODERCH Y DE SENTMENAT, Jose
Antonio (1913-) Span; arch
EMANUEL I 158-161 (statement); 1 ill
NEWMAN 36-41 (essay); 14 ill

COEN, Arnaldo (1940-) Mexi; ptr
DICCIONARIO v.2 405-407 (statement);
port; 1 ill

COFFEEN SERPAS, Carlos (1932-)
Mexi; ptr
DICCIONARIO v.2 409-411 (statement);
port; 1 ill

COGHLAN, Edgardo ( ) Mexi; ptr
DICCIONARIO v.2 417-419 (statement);
self port; 1 ill

COGSWELL, Barry (1939-) Cana; sclp
POINT OF VIEW (project proposal); 1 ill

COHAN, Suzanne ( ) Amer; coll, ptr
ARTPARK 1981 (statement); port; 3 ill

COHEN, Adele (1922-) Amer; envir, ptr,
sclp
ARTPARK 1978 20-21 (statement); port;
8 ill

COHEN, Bernard (1933-) Brit; ptr
BOWNESS 22, 128-130 (statement); 2 ill
ENGLISH 68-73 (statement); port; 6 ill
NAYLOR 197-198 (statement)

COHEN, Eduardo (1939-) Mexi; ptr
DICCIONARIO v.2 421-423 (statement);
port; 1 ill

COHEN, Judy
SEE: CHICAGO, Judy

COHN, Julie (1955-) Amer; sclp, instal
HOUSE 40-41 (statement); 1 ill

COINER, Charles T. (1897-) Amer; ptr
MCCAUSLAND 36-41 (essay: ■Full
Employment and the Artist■)

COLDSTREAM, William (1908-) Brit;
ptr
ROTHENSTEIN 55 (statement, p.p.)

COLE, Robert (1952-) Amer; arch
SPIRIT 34-37 (statement); 6 ill

COLEMAN, John E. (1923-) Amer; illus
CALIFORNIA--DRAWING (statement); 2
ill

COLEMAN, Tom (1945-) Amer; pott
HERMAN 39 (statement); port; 1 ill

COLES, Donald E. (1947-) Amer; ptr
LEWIS I REVISED 88-89 (statement);
port; 2 ill

COLESCOTT, Robert (1925-) Amer; ptr
TUCKER II 29-30 (statement); port

COLESCOTT, Warrington W. (1921-)
Amer; print, ptr
FULBRIGHT 21 (statement)
WISCONSIN I (statement); 1 ill
WISCONSIN II (statement); 1 ill

COLETTE (1947-) Amer; perf
GUMPERT I 40 (statement); port

COLIN, Jean (1927-) Fren; ptr
YALE 59-60 (statement)

COLLET, Louis ( ) Belg; ptr
COLLARD 52-55 (interview); port; 1 ill

COLLIGNON, Georges (1923-) Belg; ptr
COLLARD 56-59 (interview); port; 1 ill

COLLINS, Catherine (1950-) Amer; paper
NOSANOW II 42 (statement); 1 ill

COLLINS, Cecil (1908-) Brit; ptr
CONTEMPORARY (statement); port; 2 ill

COLLINS, James (1939-) Brit/Amer; photo, ptr
EMANUEL II 197-198 (statement); 1 ill
PARACHUTE no.8 17 (statement, in English)
SKIRA 1976 24 (statement); 1 ill

COLLINS, Jess
SEE: JESS

COLLOM, Jack ( )
CRISS-CROSS no.1 10-11 ("Prose Poems")

COLOMBINO, Carlos (1937-) Para; arch
BAYON 154-169 (interview); port; 6 ill

COLOMBO, Gianni (1937-) Ital; ptr, sclp
KINETIC 32-33 (statement); port; 2 ill
NAYLOR 200 (statement); 1 ill

COLOMBO, Paolo ( )
WHITE WALLS no.9 53-56 (poems); 2 ill

COLP, Norman B. ( )
PHILLPOT (statement)

COLQUHOUN, Alan ( ) Brit; arch
FRAMPTON 47-49 (essay: "Modern Architecture and the Liberal Conscience")
SEE ALSO: COLQUHOUN AND MILLER

COLQUHOUN, Ithell (1906-) Brit; ptr

LONDON BULLETIN no.7 23 ("The Double-Village")
LONDON BULLETIN no.10 11 ("The Moths")
LONDON BULLETIN no.17 13 ("What do I Need to Paint a Picture?")
LONDON BULLETIN no.17 15-16 ("The Volcano"); 1 ill
LONDON BULLETIN no.17 17-18 ("The Echoing Bruise"); 1 ill

COLQUHOUN AND MILLER (arch firm) Brit
EMANUEL I 161-162 (statement); 1 ill

COLQUITT, Clair ( ) Amer; perf
ARTPARK 1977 20-23 (statement); 12 ill

COLT, John N. (1925-) Amer; ptr
WISCONSIN I (statement); 1 ill

COLVIG, William ( ) sclp, sound
GRAYSON 162-169 (essay: "A Western Gamelan"); port; 10 ill

COLVILLE, Alex (1920-) Cana; ptr
ART VOICES v.4 no.4 102-105 (statements); 5 ill

COLVIN, Brenda (1897-) Brit; arch
EMANUEL I 162-164 (statement); 1 ill

COLVIN, Marta (1917-) Chil; sclp
OPEN AIR 1960 (statement); 1 ill

COMPTON, Candace (1950-) Amer; video
ROSS 38-39 (statement); 1 ill

COMPTON, William Lawrence
SEE: KOLAWOLE, William Lawrence

CONCHOLAR, Dan (1939-) Amer; ptr

LEWIS I REVISED 119-120 (statement); port; 2 ill

CONE, Marvin (1891-1964) Amer; ptr
ILLINOIS 1957 190-191 (response); 1 ill

CONE-SKELTON, Annette (1942-) Amer; sclp, instal, ptr
AVANT-GARDE 14-15 (statement); 1 ill

CONGDON, William G. (1912-) Amer; ptr
ILLINOIS 1952 179-181 (statement)
ILLINOIS 1953 174-175 (statement); 1 ill
ILLINOIS 1955 187-188 (statement); 1 ill
ILLINOIS 1957 191-192 (response); 1 ill
ILLINOIS 1959 207 (statement); 1 ill
NEW DECADE 17-19 (statement); 3 ill

CONGRES INTERNATIONAUX D'ARCHITECTURE MODERNE
SEE: CIAM

CONGRESS OF INTERNATIONAL PROGRESSIVE ARTISTS (group)
BANN 58-62 ("A Short Review of the Proceedings," o.p. 1922)

CONKLIN, William J. ( ) Amer; arch
REVOLUTION 93-97 (essay: "Emerging New Cities of the U.S.A.")

CONN, Laurence L. (1945-) Amer; ptr
WISCONSIN II (statement); 1 ill

CONNELL, Amyas Douglas (1901-) NewZ; arch
EMANUEL I 164-165 (statement); 1 ill

CONNELLY, Arch (1950-) Amer; coll, ptr
CAMERON D 49-50 (statement)

CONNER, Bruce (1933-) Amer; ptr, sclp

CRISS-CROSS no.7/8/9 72-85 ("Spunk"); 25 ill
ILLINOIS 1961 55 (response); port; 1 ill

CONNOR, Linda S. (1944-) Amer; photo
WALSH 159-161 (statement); 1 ill

CONNOR, Maureen ( ) Amer; text, sclp
RE-VIEW v.2/3 76-81 (statement); 4 ill
WHITE WALLS no.9 6-13 ("Homage to Sadness: A Memorial to Charles M. Connor"); 3 ill

CONNORS, Betsy (1950-) Amer; photo, video
BOSTON III (interview); 1 ill

CONRAD, Tony (1940-) film
KUNST BLEIBT KUNST 386 (statement); 1 ill

CONSTANT (Constant A. Nieuwenhys) (1920-) Dutc; ptr, sclp, arch
ART SINCE v.2 151 (statement, p.p.)
CONRADS 161-162 ("Situationist Definitions," o.p. 1958)
CONRADS 177-178 (extract from "New Babylon," o.p. 1960)

CONSTRUCTIVIST GROUPS OF RUMANIA, SWITZERLAND, SCANDINAVIA, AND GERMANY (group)
BANN 66-67 (statement, o.p. 1922)

CONSUEGRA, Hugo (1929-) Cuba; ptr
CUBAN (statement); 2 ill

CONTI, Primo (1900-) Ital; ptr
VERZOCCHI 165-169 (statement); self port; 1 ill

CONTIS, Peter (1890-) Amer; ptr
SYMBOLS (statement); 1 ill

CONTRERAS, Victor Manuel (1941-)
Mexi; ptr
DICCIONARIO v.2 431-433 (statement);
port; 1 ill

CONTRERAS PENA, Jesus (1920-)
Mexi; ptr
DICCIONARIO v.2 427-429 (statement);
port; 1 ill

CONWAY, Frederick E. (1900-) Amer;
ptr
ILLINOIS 1951 167-168 (statement); 1 ill
ILLINOIS 1952 181 (statement)
ILLINOIS 1955 188 (statement); 1 ill
ILLINOIS 1957 192-193 (response); 1 ill

COOGAN, Jay ( ) Amer; sclp, envir
ARTPARK 1983 26-27 (statement); 3 ill

COOK, Howard N. (1901-) Amer; ptr
BETHERS II 72-73 (statement); 2 ill
ILLINOIS 1952 181-182 (statement); 1 ill

COOK, Jeffrey ( ) arch
ON SITE no.5/6 86-87 (essay:
"Architecture for a New Era")

COOK, Judith A. (1948-) Amer; ptr
NOSANOW II 22-23, 43 (statement); 3 ill

COOK, Lia (1942-) Amer; text
DIAMONSTEIN IV 54-65 (interview);
port; 10 ill
FIBER 26-27 (statement); 1 ill

COOK, Michael (1953-) Amer; video, ptr
GUMPERT III 61-62 (statement)

COOK, Peter (1936-) Brit; arch
ARCHER 20-23, 96 (statement); port; 6
ill
EMANUEL I 165-166 (statement); 1 ill
SPIRIT 4-7 (essay: "Art Has
Returned"); 2 ill

COOK, Ted ( )
ARTISTS no.2 17, 20 ("MOMA/Reno")

COOKE, Jean (1927-) Brit; ptr
CONTEMPORARY (statement); port; 2
ill

COOKE, Judy Hanson (1940-) Amer;
ptr
GUENTHER 38-39 (statement); port; 1
ill

COOKE, Michael (1932-) Cana; sclp
CANADA 80-81 (statement); port; 2 ill

COOLING, Janet (1951-) Amer; ptr
CAMERON D 50 (statement)
FACE IT 10-11 (statement); 1 ill

COOPER, Frank Lee (1941-) Iris; light,
sclp, instal
KNOWLES 176 (statement); 2 ill

COOPER, Michael Ashford (1943-)
Amer; ptr
ILLINOIS 1974 36 (statement); 1 ill

COOPER, Thomas Joshua (1946-)
Amer; photo
WALSH 161-162 (statement); 1 ill

COPLEY, William (1919-) Amer; ptr
JEAN 414-415 (poems: "Paramyths")

COPNALL, John (1928-) Brit; ptr
CONTEMPORARY (statement); port; 2
ill

CORA, Vladimir (1951-) Mexi; ptr
DICCIONARIO v.2 435-437 (statement);
port; 1 ill

CORAL REVELO, Flaviano E. (1929-)
Mexi; ptr

DICCIONARIO v.2 439-441 (statement); port; 1 ill

CORBETT, Edward (1919-1971) Amer; ptr
ILLINOIS 1955 189 (statement); 1 ill
ILLINOIS 1965 104 (statement); 1 ill

CORBINO, Jon (1905-1964); Ital/Amer; ptr
BRITANNICA 22 (statement); port; 1 ill

CORCUERA, Patricia P. (1929-) Mexi; ptr
DICCIONARIO v.2 443-445 (statement); port; 1 ill

CORDERO, Moises (1926-) Mexi; ptr
DICCIONARIO v.2 447-449 (statement); port; 1 ill

CORDERO DE BEDOLLA, Graciela (1938-) Mexi; ptr
DICCIONARIO v.2 425-427 (statement); port; 1 ill

CORDIER, Pierre (1933-) Belg; photo
WALSH 162-164 (statement); 1 ill

CORDIOLI, Marco (1934-) Ital; ptr
NAYLOR 205 (statement); 1 ill

CORDOVA, Gloria Lopez (1942-) Amer; sclp
RAICES 29 (statement); 1 ill

CORDOVA, Herminio (1936-) Amer; sclp
RAICES 29 (statement); 1 ill

CORINTH, Lovis (1858-1925) Germ; print, ptr
THORN 11, 18, 26, 55, 98, 100, 110, 113, 122, 135, 169, 199, 201, 204, 208, 209, 243, 252, 262, 265, 276, 288, 308, 309, 324, 340, 344 (statements, p.p.)

CORITA, Sister Mary ( ) Amer; ptr, print
RODMAN I 21-26 (interview)

CORMAN, Don (1951-) Cana; photo
POINT OF VIEW 55 (statement); 1 ill

CORMIER, Don ( ) Amer; arch, design
LIFE 51-53 (interview); port

CORNEILLE (Cornelis Guillaume van Beverloo) (1922-) Dutc; ptr
ART NOW v.2 no.8 (statement); 1 ill
GUGGENHEIM I 100 (poem, p.p.)
RAGON 190-192 (statement)
YALE 60 (statement)

CORNELIUS, Philip (1934-) Amer; pott
HERMAN 40 (statement); port; 1 ill
VIEWPOINT 1980 6-7 (statement); 3 ill

CORNELL, Allela (1914-) Amer; ptr
M.H. DE YOUNG 35 (response); self port

CORNELL, Joseph (1903-1972) Amer; sclp, ptr, coll
ART SINCE v.2 154 (statement, o.p. 1948)
CRISPO I (statement); 17 ill
FORD/VIEW v.1 no.9/10 3 ("'Enchanted Wanderer,' Excerpt from a Journey Album for Hedy Lamar")
FORD/VIEW v.2 no.4 10-16 (text piece: "The Crystal Cage")
LIPPARD 79-85 ("Monsieur Phot (Scenario)," o.p. 1936)
TRACKS v.1 no.2 32-35 (card and letter to Eleanor Ward)

CORNING, Merv ( ) Amer; print
MYLAR 18-21 (statement); 2 ill

CORONA, Victoria ( ) Mexi; ptr
DICCIONARIO v.2 455-457 (statement);
port; 1 ill

CORONA NORIEGA, Jorge A. (1912-)
Mexi; ptr
DICCIONARIO v.2 451-453 (statement);
port; 1 ill

CORONADO ORTEGA, Carlos (1947-)
Mexi; ptr
DICCIONARIO v.2 459-461 (statement);
port; 1 ill

CORPORA, Antonio (1909-) Ital; ptr
PAINTING 38 (statement); port; 1 ill
PREMIER BILAN 287 (statement); port
VERZOCCHI 171-175 (statement); self
port; 1 ill

CORPRON, Carlotta M. (1901-) Amer;
photo
LIGHT 78-83 (statement); 5 ill
MITCHELL 48-65 (statement); ports; 15
ill
WALSH 164-166 (statement); 1 ill

CORRALES, Raul (1925-) Cuba; photo
WALSH 166-167 (statement); 1 ill

CORREA, Charles Mark (1930-) Indi;
arch
EMANUEL I 166-168 (statement); 1 ill

CORRIGAN, Peter (1941-) Atrl; arch
EMANUEL I 168-169 (statement); 1 ill

CORRIS, Michael ( )
ART-LANGUAGE v.2 no.3 34-37 ("The
Fine Structure of Collaboration")
ART-LANGUAGE v.2 no.3 38-52 (essay:
"Frameworks and Phantoms")

CORRO FERRER, Jesus (1933-) Mexi;

ptr
DICCIONARIO v.2 475-477 (statement);
port; 1 ill

CORSAUT, Share (1947-) Cana; photo
POINT OF VIEW 8, 56 (statement); 2 ill

CORTEZ, Diego ( ) film
ART-RITE no.6 20-21 ("Bugs Dela")
ART RITE no.10 ("Notes on
'Painter/Patient' Performance")
AVALANCHE no.13 35-37 (interview);
port; 6 ill

CORTOR, Eldzier (1915-) Amer; ptr
FAX I 79-94 (statements); port; 2 ill
FINE 166-170 (statements, o.p. 1954,
1971); 5 ill
ILLINOIS 1951 168 (statement); 1 ill

CORTRIGHT, Steven (1942-) Amer;
print
TUCKER II 30 (statement); port

CORY, Fanny Y. (1877-) Amer; illus
M.H. DE YOUNG 36-37 (response); self
port

CORZAS, Francisco (1936-) Mexi; ptr
DICCIONARIO v.2 479-481 (statement);
port; 1 ill

COSEY FANNI TUTTI (1951-) Brit;
perf
HAYWARD 1979 139 (statement); 1 ill
SKIRA 1977 61 (statement); 1 ill

COSTA, Claudio (1942-) Ital; sclp
EMANUEL II 206-207 (statement); 1 ill
KUNST BLEIBT KUNST 166-169
(statement); port; 6 ill
NAYLOR 207-208 (statement); 1 ill
SKIRA 1979 108 (statement); 1 ill

COSTA, Luciano ( ) photo
IDENTITE 31-34 (interview with Clayssen, Jacques); port

COSTA, Lucio (1902-) Braz; arch
EMANUEL I 169-170 (statement); 1 ill

COSTIGAN, John Edward (1888-) Amer; ptr
BRITANNICA 23 (statement); port; 1 ill

COTE, Alan (1937-) Amer; ptr
TUCKER I 18 (statement)

COTERO PONCE, Agustin (1949-) Mexi; ptr
DICCIONARIO v.2 483-485 (statement); port; 1 ill

COTTIER, Keith Eric (1938-) Atrl; arch
EMANUEL I 170-171 (statement); 1 ill

COTTINGHAM, Robert (1935-) Amer; ptr, print
ART NOW v.3 no.4 (statement); 1 ill
ARTHUR 54-67 (interview); port; 18 ill

COUBINE, Othon (1883-) Czec/Fren; ptr
RAYNAL 105-108 (statement); 2 ill

COUCH, Jane (1944-) ptr
CRISS-CROSS no.6 16-19 (statement)

COUNHAYE, Charles (1884-1971) Belg
COLLARD 60-67 (interview, 1970); port; 1 ill

COUNTY TIMES (group)
BOSHIER (statement); ills.

COURCHESNE, Luc (1952-) Amer; video
BOSTON III (interview); 1 ill

COURTRIGHT, Robert (1926-) Amer; coll, ptr, sclp
CRISPO I (statement); 11 ill
ILLINOIS 1965 97 (statement); 1 ill
MORRIS 62-67 (statements); ports; 4 ill

COUTAUD, Lucien (1904-) Fren; ptr, design
CHARBONNIER v.1 41-51 (interview); 1 ill

COVANTES, Hugo (1935-) Mexi; ptr
DICCIONARIO v.2 487-489 (statement); port; 1 ill

COVINO, Frank ( ) Amer; ptr
NORTH LIGHT 56-59 (statement); port; 6 ill

COWGILL, Molly (1948-) Amer; pott
HERMAN 41 (statement); port; 1 ill

COWIN, Eileen (1947-) Amer; photo
FUGITIVE (statement); 1 ill

COWLES, Russell (1887-1979) Amer; ptr
BETHERS II 74-75 (statement); 2 ill
BRITANNICA 24 (statement); port; 1 ill

COX, J. Halley (1910-) Amer; ptr
HAAR I 50-56 (interview with Prithwish Neogy); ports; 3 ill

COX, Kenyon (1856-1919) Amer; ptr, illus
MCCOUBREY 193-196 (essay: "The 'Modern' Spirit in Art, Some Reflections Inspired by the Recent International Exhibition," o.p. 1913)
ROSE II 80-86 (extract from essay: "The 'Modern' Spirit in Art," o.p. 1913)
ROSE II 86-87 (extract from essay: "The Illusion of Progress," o.p. 1913)

ROSE II REVISED 71-74 (extract from essay: "The 'Modern' Spirit in Art," o.p. 1913)

COX, Kris ( ) Amer; pott
VIEWPOINT 1981 (statement); 3 ill

COX, Philip Sutton (1939-) Atrl; arch
EMANUEL I 171-173 (statement); 1 ill

COX, Stephen (1946-) Brit; sclp, ptr
HAYWARD 1978 42-45 (statement); 5 ill
SKIRA 1978 75 (statement); 1 ill

COX, Warren Jacob (1935-) Amer; arch
EMANUEL I 173-175, 349 (statement); 1 ill

COYLE, Jill ( ) Amer; pott
HAYSTACK 9 (statement); 1 ill

CRAFT, David R. (1945-) Amer; ptr
NOSANOW I 42-43 (statement); 3 ill

CRAGG, Tony (1949-) Brit; sclp, instal
CHOIX 19 (statement, o.p. 1982); 1 ill
PRADEL 87 (statement, p.p.); 2 ill

CRAIG, John ( ) arch
MIKELLIDES 27-33 (essay: "Understanding People and Developing a Brief"); 5 ill

CRAIG, Tom (1908-) Amer; ptr
M. H. DE YOUNG 38 (response); self port

CRAIG-MARTIN, Michael (1941-) Brit; sclp, ptr
BRITISH (statement); 1 ill
EMANUEL II 209-210 (statement)
SKIRA 1977 71 (statement); 1 ill

CRAIN, Walter Hagel (1955-) sclp
SCULPTURE OUTSIDE (statement); 4 ill

CRAMPTON, Rollin McNeil (1886-1970) Amer; ptr
ZAIDENBERG 90-91 (essay: "Intuition"); 2 ill

CRANE, David Alford (1927-) Amer; arch
EMANUEL I 175-177 (statement); 1 ill

CRANE, Mikel ( ) perf
WHITE WALLS no.1 20-21 (text piece)

CRANE, Stanley William (1905-) Amer; ptr
ILLINOIS 1950 166 (statement); 1 ill

CRANHAM, Gerry (1929-) Brit; photo
HOW FAMOUS 124-129 (statements); port; 10 ill
WALSH 168-169 (statement); 1 ill

CRAWFORD, Cair Wegerski (1944-) Amer; ptr
CELEBRATION (statement); 1 ill

CRAWFORD, Ralston (1906-1977) Cana/Amer; ptr
ART NOW v.3 no.4 (statement); 1 ill
BOSWELL 137 (statement)
BRITANNICA 25 (statement); port; 1 ill
FORTY (statement); 2 ill
JANIS I 64 (statement); 1 ill

CREEL, Alejandro (1945-) Mexi; ptr
DICCIONARIO v.2 491-493 (statement); port; 1 ill

CREELEY, Robert ( )
CRISS-CROSS no.7/8/9 68-69 ("Notes on Film")

CREFFIELD, Dennis (1931-) Brit; ptr
CONTEMPORARY (statement); port; 2 ill

CREHAN, Hubert ( ) ptr
IT IS no.3 28-31 ("A Little Room For Feeling")

CREMER, Marva (1942-) Amer; print
LEWIS I REVISED 94 (statement); port; 2 ill

CREMONINI, Leonardo (1925-) Ital; ptr
SKIRA 1978 15 (statement); 1 ill
SKIRA 1979 101 (statement); 1 ill
SKIRA 1980 74 (statement); 2 ill

CRESS, Fred (1938-) Atrl; ptr
DE GROEN 63-73 (interview); port

CRESS, George Ayers (1921-) Amer; ptr
NOSANOW I 44 (statement); 1 ill

CRESSMAN, Larry (1945-) Amer; ptr
MICHIGAN 10-11 (statement); 2 ill

CREUZ, Serge ( ) Belg; ptr
COLLARD 68-73 (interview); port; 1 ill

CRIACH, F. Enrique (1930-) Mexi; ptr
DICCIONARIO v.2 495-497 (statement); port; 1 ill

CRISS, H. Francis (1901-1973) Brit/Amer; ptr
BRITANNICA 26 (statement); port; 1 ill
100 CONTEMPORARY 42-43 (statement); port; 1 ill

CRISTOFANETTI, Francesco (1901-1951) Ital; ptr
JANIS I 109 (statement); 1 ill

CRIVELLI, Elaine ( ) Amer; sclp, perf
ARTPARK 1982 20-21, 45 (statement); port; 3 ill

CROAK, James L. ( ) Amer; sclp
DOWNTOWN (statement); 1 ill

CROISET, Nicole (1950-) Fren
ISSUE (statement, in French); 7 ill

CRONICA
SEE: EQUIPO CRONICA

CROSBY, Theo (1925-) Brit; arch
COOPER-HEWITT II 26-27 (statement)
EMANUEL I 177-179 (statement); 1 ill

CROWE, Sylvia (1901-) Brit; arch
EMANUEL I 179-180 (statement); 1 ill

CROWLEY, Don ( ) Amer; ptr, illus
MAGIC 32-35 (statement); port; 5 ill

CROWLEY, Harry (c.1900-) Amer; ptr
ILLINOIS 1951 169 (statement)

CROZIER, William (1930-) Brit; ptr
CONTEMPORARY (statement); port; 1 ill

CRUDUP, Doris (1933-) Amer; ptr
LEWIS I 61 (statement); port; 1 ill

CRUIKSHANK, Alan (1953-) Atrl; photo
ART NETWORK no.9 66-67 (essay: "Portrait of Elizabeth")

CRUMPLER, Dewey (1949-) Amer; ptr
LEWIS I REVISED 75-76 (statement); port; 2 ill

CRUZ, Angeles (1952-) Mexi; ptr
DICCIONARIO v.2 503-505 (statement); port; 1 ill

CRUZ, Bertha Alicia
SEE: BERTHA ALICIA

CRUZ, Emilio (1938-) Amer; ptr
FINE 241-242 (letter, 1972); 2 ill

SULTAN 75-76 ("Torrid Notes Strewn from the Pen of a Bipedal Predator of Dreams While Digesting Fossils")

CRUZ, Esteban (1935-) Mexi; ptr
DICCIONARIO v.2 511-513 (statement); port; 1 ill

CRUZ, Jose Garcia Rocha (1948-) Mexi; ptr
DICCIONARIO v.2 499-501 (statement); port; 1 ill

CRUZ BENITEZ, Maria Guadalupe (1914-) Mexi; ptr
DICCIONARIO v.2 507-509 (statement); port; 1 ill

CRUZ GARCIA, Francisco Javier (1952-) Mexi; ptr
DICCIONARIO v.2 515-517 (statement); port; 1 ill

CRUZ RAMIREZ, Julio (1937-) Mexi; ptr
DICCIONARIO v.2 519-521 (statemnt); port; 1 ill

CRUZ RODRIGUEZ, Aaron (1947-) Mexi; ptr
DICCIONARIO v.2 523-525 (statement); port; 1 ill

CRUZ ZERON ESPANA, Fernando (1922-) Mexi; ptr
DICCIONARIO v.3 21-23 (statement); port; 1 ill

CRUZADO, Salvador (1934-) Mexi; ptr
DICCIONARIO v.3 25-27 (statement); port; 1 ill

CRUZ-DIEZ, Carlos (1923-) Vene; ptr, sclp

ART SINCE v.1 294 (statement, o.p. 1967)
LUMIERE (statement); port; 1 ill

CUAXILOA, Francisco Xavier (1921-) Mexi; ptr
DICCIONARIO v.3 29-31 (statement); port; 1 ill

CUBITT, James William Archibald (1914-) Brit; arch
EMANUEL I 180-182 (statement); 1 ill

CUE GONZALEZ, Fernando Salvador (1955-) Mexi; ptr
DICCIONARIO v.3 33-35 (statement); port; 1 ill

CUE MIER, Maria de las Nieves (1935-) Mexi; ptr
DICCIONARIO v.3 37-39 (statement); port; 1 ill

CUELLAR, Marcos (1935-) Mexi; ptr
DICCIONARIO v.3 45-47 (statement); port; 1 ill

CUELLAR HIDALGO, Carlos (1943-) Mexi; ptr
DICCIONARIO v.3 41-43 (statement); port; 1 ill

CUENCA Y CORTINA, Ignacio (1930-) Mexi; ptr
DICCIONARIO v.3 49-51 (statement); port; 1 ill

CUERVO MARTINEZ, Jose (1936-) Mexi; ptr
DICCIONARIO v.3 53-55 (statement); port; 1 ill

CUESTA ULEY, Dulce Maria (1936-) Mexi; ptr

CURTIS, Dolly ( ) Amer; text
FIBER 24-25 (statement); 1 ill
HAYSTACK 10 (statement); 1 ill

CURTIS, George A. (1921-) Amer; sclp
ILLINOIS 1957 194 (response); 1 ill

CURTIS, John Cates ( ) Amer; coll
IRVINE 45, 89 (statement); 1 ill

CURTIS, Robert (1948-) Amer; sclp
WISCONSIN II (statement); 1 ill

CURTIS, Samuel (1919-) Amer; ptr
LEWIS I REVISED 109 (statement); port;
1 ill

CURTIS, Stuart (1894-) Amer; ptr
ILLINOIS 1957 194-195 (response); 1 ill

CURTIS, William (1939-) Amer; ptr
LEWIS I REVISED 92 (statement); port;
1 ill

CURTO LOPEZ, Consuelo (1916-) Mexi;
ptr
DICCIONARIO v.3 81-83 (statement);
port; 1 ill

CUSUMANO, Stefano (1912-1975) Amer;
ptr
ILLINOIS 1965 86 (statement); 1 ill

CUTFORTH, Roger (1944-) Brit/Amer;
photo
ART-LANGUAGE v.1 no.3 1-3 ("The
Society for Theoretical Art and
Analyses Proceedings")
CONCEPTUAL ART 22-25 (essay:
"Elements in Reference To")
MEYER 108-115 (text piece: "The
Empire State Building")
SKIRA 1977 95 (statement); 1 ill

CUTHBERT, Virginia I. (1908-) Amer;
ptr
ILLINOIS 1950 166-167 (statement); 1 ill

CYWINSKI, ( ) arch
GA HOUSES no.9 42-43 (statement);
port

DABROWSKY, Iwan
SEE: GRAHAM, John D.

D'ACQUARONE DIERIEX DE TEN HAMMEN Y CELORIO, Claire ( )
Mexi; ptr
DICCIONARIO v.3 167-169 (statement); port; 1 ill

DACRE, Winifred
SEE: NICHOLOSON, Winifred

DADA (Daniel Davila Helmer) (1918-)
Mexi; ptr, print
DICCIONARIO v.3 179-181 (statement); port; 1 ill

DADAMAINO (Eduardo Dada Maino) (1935-) Ital; sclp
GROH (statement); 1 ill

DADZU (1926-) Fren; sclp
LUMIERE (statement); port; 1 ill

DAEN, Lindsay (1924-) NewZ/Amer; sclp
RODMAN I 154-163 (interview)

DAHINDEN, Justus (1925-) Swis; arch
EMANUEL I 184-186 (statement); 1 ill
REVOLUTION 177-183 (essay)

DAHL-WOLFE, Louise (1895-) Amer; photo
BOOTH 70-79 (interview); port; 5 ill
MITCHELL 66-83 (statement); ports; 14 ill
WALSH 175-176 (statement); 1 ill

DAHMEN, Karl Fred (1917-) Germ; ptr
NAYLOR 216-217 (statement); 1 ill

D'ALA, (Ismael Davidson De Alandrade) (1942-) Mexi; ptr

DICCIONARIO v.3 171-173 (statement); port; 1 ill

D'ALESSANDRO, Robert (1942-) Amer; photo
WALSH 176-177 (statement); 1 ill

DALI, Salvador (1904-) Span; ptr
ART NOW v.2 no.5 (statement); 1 ill
BRITANNICA 28 (statement); port; 1 ill
CHARBONNIER v.2 25-37 (interview)
FIFIELD 211-241 (interview)
FRASNAY 127-139 (statement, in French and English); ports; 1 ill
GOLDAINE 92-95 (interview); port
JEAN 267-269 ("The Putrescent Donkey," o.p. 1930); port
JEAN 269-270 (poem: "The Visible Woman," o.p. 1930)
JEAN 272-275 ("Reverie," o.p. 1931)
JEAN 296-297 ("Psycho-atmospheric-anamorphic Objects," o.p. 1933)
JEAN 302-303 ("Honor to the Objects," p.p.)
JEAN 339 ("The Spectral Surrealism of the Pre-Raphaelite Eternal Feminine," o.p. 1934)
LIPPARD 87-97 (essay: "The Object as Revealed in Surrealist Experiment," o.p. 1932)
LIPPARD 97-100 ("The Stinking Ass," o.p. 1932)
LIPPARD 101-107 ("An Andalusian Dog," o.p. 1929)
MINOTAURE no.1 65-67 (essay: "Interpretation Paranoiaque-Critique de l'Image Obsedante 'L'Angelus' de Millet")
MINOTAURE no.3/4 69-76 (essay: "De la Beaute Terrifiante et Comestible, de l'Architecture Modern Style")
MINOTAURE no.3/4 76-77 ("Le Phenomene de l'Extase"); 1 ill
MINOTAURE no.5 20-22 (essay: "Les

Nouvelles Couleurs du Sex Appeal Spectral"); 2 ill

MINOTAURE no.6 32-34 (essay: "Apparitions Aerodynamiques des Etres-Objets"); 3 ill

MINOTAURE no.7 56-57 (essay: "Psychologie Non-Euclidienne d'une Photographie")

MINOTAURE no.8 46-49 (essay: "Le Surrealisme Spectral de l'Eternel Feminin Preraphaelite")

MINOTAURE no.9 60-61 (essay: "Premiere Loi Morphologique sur les Poils dans les Structures Molles")

PORCEL I 91-100 (interview); port

PORCEL II 13-29 (interview)

PROTTER 239 (statement)

REVOLUTION SURREALISTE no.12 34-37 ("Un Chien Andalou," with Luis Bunuel)

SEGHERS 258-259 (extract from *The Conquest of the Irrational*)

SEITZ III 58-59 (extract from *The Secret Life of Salvador Dali*, o.p. 1942); 1 ill

SURREALISME no.1 9-12 ("L'Ane Pourri")

SURREALISME no.2 7-9 ("Intellectuels Castillians et Catalans--Expositions-- Arrestation d'un Exhibitionniste dans le Metro")

SURREALISME no.3 17 ("Objects Surrealistes")

SURREALISME no.3 40 ("Communication: Visage Paranoique"); 3 ill

SURREALISME no.4 31-36 ("Reverie")

SURREALISME no.5 45-48 ("Objets Psycho-Atmospheriques- Anamorphiques"); 1 ill

SURREALISME no.6 10-23 ("Recherches Experimentales" (questions and responses))

SURREALISME no.6 40-41 ("Notes-- Communications")

VINGTIEME N.S. no.3 69 (statement, o.p. 1932)

DALKE, Michael (1946-) Amer; sclp
ILLINOIS 1969 178 (statement); 1 ill

DALLEGRET, Francois (1937-) Fren/Cana; sclp
ART AND TECHNOLOGY 80 (project proposal); 3 ill
DIRECTIONS I 75 (response); 1 ill

DALLMANN, Daniel (1942-) Amer; ptr
SUPERREAL 68-69 (statement); 1 ill

DALTON, John (1927-) Atrl; arch
EMANUEL I 186-188 (statement); 1 ill

DALTON, Stephen Neale (1937-) Brit; photo
CAMPBELL 166-177 (statement); port; 10 ill
HOW FAMOUS 116-121 (statements); port; 8 ill

DALY, Norman D. (1911-) Amer; ptr
ILLINOIS 1950 167 (statement); 1 ill

DAMASDY, Julius (1937-) Cana; sclp
CANADA 50-51 (statement); port; 1 ill

DAMIAN, Horia (1922-) Ruma; sclp
SKIRA 1977 115 (statement); 1 ill

D'AMICO, Alicia (1933-) ARge; photo
WALSH 177-178 (statement); 1 ill

D'AMICO, Oskar (1923-) Mexi; ptr
DICCIONARIO v.3 175-177 (statement); port; 1 ill

DAMON, Elizabeth (1940-) Amer; ptr
CAMERON D 50-51 (statement)
CONCEPT 27-29 (statement); 1 ill

DANBY, Ken (1940-) Amer; ptr, print
EMANUEL II 221 (statement)
NAYLOR 218-219 (statement); 1 ill

DANESE, Bruno ( ) Ital; design
DESIGN 165-167 (essay: "Plastics")

DANIEL (Daniel Brennan) ( ) Amer; ptr
DICCIONARIO v.3 183-185 (statement);
port; 1 ill

DANIEL, Lewis C. (1901-1952) Amer; ptr
ILLINOIS 1950 168 (statement); 1 ill

DANIELE, Mario (1944-) Ital; sclp
SKIRA 1978 87 (statement); 1 ill
SKIRA 1979 110 (statement); 1 ill

DANIELI, Edie ( ) Amer; sclp
SCHAPIRO 18 (statement); port; 1 ill

DANNATT, James Trevor (1920-) Brit;
arch
EMANUEL I 188-189 (statement); 1 ill

DANNER, Robert W. (1948-) Amer; ptr
WISCONSIN II (statement); 1 ill

DANTU, Andree (1941-) Fren; sclp
LUMIERE (statement); port; 1 ill

DANZIGER, Itzhak (1916-) Isra; sclp
SEITZ I (statement); 2 ill

DANZIGER, Joan (1934-) Amer; sclp
IMAGES 26-33 (interview with Clair
List); port; 5 ill

DAPHNIS, Nassos (1914-) Gree/Amer;
ptr
ALBRIGHT-KNOX 398-399 (letter, 1970);
1 ill
ART NOW v.4 no.2 (statement); 1 ill

DARBOURNE, John ( ) Brit; arch
MIKELLIDES 34-37 (essay: "Social
Needs and Landscape Architecture"); 4
ill

DARBOURNE AND DARKE (arch firm)
SEE: DARBOURNE, John

DARBOVEN, Hanne (1941-) Germ
AVALANCHE no.4 42-51 (text piece:
"Words")
LICHT 27-32 ("in correspondence with
Lucy Lippard"); 4 ill

D'ARCANGELO, Allan (1930-) Amer;
ptr
ART NOW v.1 no.2 (statement); 1 ill

DARLING, Lowell (1942-) Amer; video
AVALANCHE no.7 24-29 (interview); 9
ill
AVALANCHE no.8 74 (interview); 2 ill
ROSS 76-87 (statement); 30 ill

DA ROZA, Gustavo (1933-) Cana; arch
EMANUEL I 189-191 (statement); 1 ill

D'ARRIGO, Elisa ( ) Amer; sclp
ARTPARK 1979 (statement); 1 ill

D'ARTISTA, Robert (1929-) Amer; ptr
PROTTER 258-260 (statement, 1963); 1
ill

DASBURG, Andrew M. (1887-1979)
Amer; ptr
FORUM 1916 56 (statement); 1 ill
ROSE II 90-94 (extract from essay:
"Cubism--Its rise and Influence," o.p.
1923)
ROSE II REVISED 75-78 (extract from
essay: "Cubism--Its Rise and
Influence," o.p. 1923)

DASH, Robert Warren (1934-) Amer; ptr
ART NOW v.2 no.9 (statement); 1 ill

DATER, Judy (1941-) Amer; photo
VISUAL v.1 no.4 10-12 (interview); 2 ill
WALSH 179-180 (statement); 1 ill

DAUDELIN, Charles (1921-) Cana; sclp
ROYER 99-102 (interview, 1974)

DAUNIS-DUNNING, Patricia ( ) Amer; metal
HAYSTACK 11 (statement); 1 ill

DAURIAC, Jacqueline (1945-) Fren; illus
SKIRA 1976 43 (statement); 1 ill

DAVALOS, G. Felipe (1942-) Mexi; ptr
DICCIONARIO v.3 187-189 (statement); port; 1 ill

DAVE, Prafull (1934-) ptr
TRANSPERSONAL 30-39 (statement); port; 4 ill

DAVENPORT, Rebecca (1943-) Amer; ptr
IMAGES 34-41 (interview with Clair List); port; 5 ill
SUPERREAL 43, 124, 125 (interview); 1 ill

DAVEY, Randall (1887-1964) Amer; ptr
BRITANNICA 29 (statement); port; 1 ill

DAVID, Michael ( ) ptr, sclp
RE-VIEW v.2/3 160-161 (poem); 2 ill

DAVIDOVICH, Jaime (1936-) Amer; video, ptr
APPLE 51 (statement); 1 ill

DAVIDSON, Morris (1898-1979) Amer; ptr
BETHERS I 224-225 (statement); 1 ill

DAVIDSON, Phyllis ( ) ptr
VISUAL v.4 no.1 10-12 (interview); port; 3 ill

DAVIE, Alan (1920-) Scot; ptr
ART SINCE v.1 159 (statement, o.p. 1960)
CONTEMPORARY (statement); port; 3 ill
FRASNAY 327-337 (letter); ports
PROTTER 253 (statement, 1961)

DAVIES, John (1949-) Brit; sclp
BRITISH (statement); 1 ill

DAVIES, Kenneth (1925-) Amer; ptr, illus
ILLINOIS 1951 170 (statement); 1 ill
ILLINOIS 1952 183 (statement); 1 ill
MAGIC 36-39 (statement); port; 4 ill

DAVIES, Peter (1944-) Amer; sclp
BRITISH (statement); 1 ill

DAVILA, Juan ( ) Chil/Atrl; ptr
ART NETWORK no.7 44-45 ("Love of Australia"); 1 ill

DAVILA HELMER, Daniel
SEE: DADA

DAVIS, Alonzo (1942-) Amer; ptr
LEWIS II 105 (statement); port; 2 ill

DAVIS, Bing (1937-) Amer; sclp, design
CONTEMPORARY AFRICAN (statement); port; 1 ill
LEWIS II 47 (statement); port; 1 ill

DAVIS, Bradley Darius (1942-) Amer; ptr
APPLE 33 (statement); 1 ill

DAVIS, Dale (1945-) Amer; sclp
LEWIS II 63 (statement); port; 2 ill

DAVIS, Douglas (1933-) Amer; perf, video, film
APPLE 47 (statement); 2 ill
ARTPARK 1976 144-145 (statement); 4 ill
BATTCOCK VI 24-35 (essay: "The End of Video: White Vapor," p.p.); 3 ill
DAVIS 72-79 (statement: "Time! Time! Time! The Context of Immediacy")
EMANUEL II 226-227 (statement)
GEORGIA 17-20, 112 (statement); 3 ill
KUNST BLEIBT KUNST 410 (statement); 2 ill
NAYLOR 222 (statement); 1 ill

DAVIS, Emma Lu (1905-) Amer; ptr, sclp
MILLER 1942 43-50 (statement); port; 8 ill

DAVIS, Gene (1920-) Amer; ptr
ART NOW v.2 no.2 (statement); 1 ill
DIRECTIONS I 76 (response); 1 ill
NORTH P (interview); port; 1 ill
TUCKER I 16 (statement)

DAVIS, Gladys Rockmore (1901-) Amer; ptr
BRITANNICA 31 (statement); port; 1 ill

DAVIS, Harry ( ) Brit; pott
CLARK 105-109 (essay: "Some Thoughts on Attitudes," o.p. 1971)

DAVIS, Jerrold (1926-) Amer; ptr
ILLINOIS 1959 208 (statement); 1 ill
ILLINOIS 1961 62 (response); port; 1 ill

DAVIS, John (1936-) Atrl; sclp
DE GROEN 199-202 (interview); port
EMANUEL II 229-230 (statement); 1 ill

DAVIS, Palli Davene (1948-) Amer; sclp
WISCONSIN I (statement); 1 ill

DAVIS, Robert James (1944-) Atrl; photo
WALSH 183-184 (statement); 1 ill

DAVIS, Ronald W. (1937-) Amer; ptr, sclp
EMANUEL II 230-231 (statement)
NAYLOR 224-225 (statement); 1 ill
ROSE I 26-33 (statement); 6 ill

DAVIS, Stuart (1894-1964) Amer; ptr
ARMORY SHOW 15 (statement)
ARTS YEARBOOK v.3 47 ("Foreword: New York")
ARTS YEARBOOK v.4 66-68 (essay: "Memo on Mondrian")
BETHERS I 226-227 (statement); 1 ill
BRITANNICA 32 (statement); port; 1 ill
CHIPP 466-470 (essay: "The Artist Today," o.p. 1935)
CHIPP 521-523 (letter to Henry McBride, o.p. 1930); port
CHIPP 523 (extract from essay: "Abstract Art in the American Scene," o.p. 1941)
CHIPP 524 (extract from essay: "Cube Root," o.p. 1943)
CHIPP 524-525 (extracts from *Stuart Davis*, o.p. 1945)
DOUZE PEINTRES (statement); 2 ill
FIRST AMERICAN 3-6 (essay: "Why an Artists' Congress?")
FORTY (statement); 2 ill
GUITAR 34-43 (interview); port; 4 ill
ILLINOIS 1952 183-185 (statement); 1 ill
ILLINOIS 1961 44-45 (response); port; 1 ill
JANIS I 53 (statement); 1 ill
KUH 52-67 (interview); 8 ill
MCCOUBREY 207-208 (statements, o.p. 1940, 1943)
PERSONAL (statement)
PROTTER 229-230 (statement, 1961); 1 ill

ROSE II 122-125 (essay: "On Abstract Art," o.p. 1935)

ROSE II 125-126 (extract from interview with Katharine Kuh, o.p. 1960)

ROSE II REVISED 100-102 (essay: "On Abstract Art," o.p. 1935)

ROSE II REVISED 102 (extract from "Abstract Art in the American Scene," o.p. 1941)

SPENCER 227-228 ("Stuart Davis on Robert Henri", tape-recorded interview, 1962)

DAVISON, David P. ( ) Amer; pott
HAYSTACK 12 (statement); 1 ill

DAVISON, Kendra J. ( ) Amer; pott
HAYSTACK 13 (statement); 1 ill

DAY, Esther Worden (1916-) Amer; ptr
ILLINOIS 1950 169 (statement); 1 ill

DAY, Fred (1937-) Amer; photo
PHOTOGRAPHY (statement); 1 ill

DAY, John (1932-) Amer; ptr
ILLINOIS 1965 110 (statement; from a letter to "T.P." 1963); 1 ill
VARIAN I (extract from a letter); port

DAY, Worden (1916-) Amer; ptr, sclp, print
AMERICAN PRINTS 20, 65 (statement); 1 ill

DAYEZ, Georges (1907-) Fren; ptr
PREMIER BILAN 288 (statement); port

DE AMELIO, Gloria Carrillo (1934-) Mexi; ptr
DICCIONARIO v.3 191-193 (statement); port; 1 ill

DEAN, Nat ( )

WHITE WALLS no.8 24-31 ("Dictionary")

DE ANDREA, John (1941-) Amer; sclp, ptr
GOODYEAR 38-44; 3 ill

DE BIASI, Mario ( ) Ital; photo
HOW FAMOUS 228-233 (statements); 6 ill

DE BLASI, Anthony (1933-) Ital/Amer; ptr
MICHIGAN 12-13 (statement); 2 ill

DEBLE, Colette (1944-) Fren; prt
SKIRA 1979 24 (statement); 1 ill

DEBORD ( ) arch
CONRADS 161-162 ("Situationist Definitions," o.p. 1958)

DEBOURG, Narciso (1925-) Vene/Fren; sclp
LUMIERE (statement); port; 1 ill

DEBRE, Olivier (1920-) Fren; ptr
GRENIER 75-86 (interview)
SKIRA 1976 84 (statement); 1 ill

DE CARAVA, Roy (1919-) Amer; ptr, print, photo
FAX I 167-187 (statements); port; 1 ill

DE CARLO, Giancarlo (1919-) Ital; arch
NEWMAN 80-91 (essay); port; 14 ill
NEWMAN 147-149 (group discussion)

DE CASTRO, Robert (1923-) Cana; sclp
CANADA 30-31 (statement); port; 1 ill

DECHELETTE, Louis-Auguste (1894-1964) Fren; ptr
PREMIER BILAN 275 (letter); port

DECKER, Richard (1907-) Amer; illus, ptr
M. H. DE YOUNG 45 (response); self port

DE COSTER, Miles ( )
WHITE WALLS no.8 82-89 ("Iconomies")

DE DIEGO, Julio (1900-1979) Span/Amer; illus, ptr
ILLINOIS 1951 170-171 (statement); 1 ill

DEE, John (1938-) Brit; sclp
ALLEY (statement); 1 ill
BRITISH (statement); 1 ill

DEEM, George (1932-) Amer; ptr
EMANUEL II 235-236 (statement); 1 ill
ILLINOIS 1965 112 (statement); 1 ill
WHITE WALLS no.6 2-22 ("Extra Genre"); 8 ill

DE ERDELY, Francis (1904-) Hung/Amer; ptr
CALIFORNIA--PAINTING 13 (statement); 1 ill

DE FAZIO, Raymond (1936-) Amer; ptr
NOSANOW I 46-47 (statement); 1 ill

DE FEO, Jay (1929-) Amer; ptr
HOPKINS 36-37 (statement); port; 1 ill
MILLER 1959 8-12 (statement); port; 5 ill

DEFFEBACH, Lee (1928-) Amer; ptr
FULBRIGHT 22 (statement)

DE FILIPPI, Fernando (1940-) Ital; illus, perf
NAYLOR 228-229 (statement); 1 ill
SKIRA 1976 51-52 (statement); 1 ill

DE FOREST, Roy Dean (1930-) Amer;

ptr
EMANUEL II 236-237 (statement)
HOPKINS 38-39 (statement); port; 1 ill
ILLINOIS 1965 135 (statement); 1 ill
NAYLOR 229-231 (statement); 1 ill

DEFRAOUI, Cherif (1932-) Swis; photo, video
EUROPE 48-49 (statement); 1 ill
SKIRA 1978 91 (statement); 1 ill

DEFRAOUI, Sylvie (1935-) Swis; coll, perf
SKIRA 1976 32 (statement); 1 ill

DE FREITAS, Iole (1945-) Braz/Ital; photo
SKIRA 1976 14-15 (statement); 1 ill

DEGOTTEX, Jean (1918-) Fren; ptr
ART SINCE v.1 159 (statement, o.p. 1961)
PREMIER BILAN 288 (statement); port
QUADRUM no.10 99-110 (interview with Julien Alvard); 7 ill
SKIRA 1977 35 (statement); 1 ill
SKIRA 1979 58 (statement); 1 ill

DE GRADA, Raffaele (1885-) Ital; ptr
VERZOCCHI 183-187 (statement); self port; 1 ill

DE GROOT, Nanno ( ) print
TIGER no.8 58-59 (statement)

DEHN, Adolf A. (1895-1968) Amer; illus, print, ptr
AMERICAN PRINTS 21, 65 (statement); 1 ill
BRITANNICA 34 (statement); port; 1 ill
GUITAR 44-53 (interview); port; 4 ill
ILLINOIS 1952 185-186 (statement); 1 ill

DEHNER, Dorothy (1908-) Amer; print,

sclp
ILLINOIS 1965 99 (statement); 1 ill
TRACKS v.3 no.1/2 76-77 (poems: "Past Tense," "Two Lives")

DEILMANN, Harald (1920-) Germ; arch
EMANUEL I 195-198 (statement); 1 ill

DEKEIJSER, Andre ( ) Belg; sclp
COLLARD 74-78 (interview); port; 1 ill

DEKKERS, Ad (1938-1974) Dutc; ptr
STEDELIJK 109 (statement, in Dutch, o.p. 1967); 2 ill

DEKKERS, Gerrit H. (1929-) Dutc; photo
EMANUEL II 239-240 (statement)
KUNST BLEIBT KUNST 174-177 (statement); 29 ill
SKIRA 1976 28-29 (statement); 11 ill
WALSH 187-189 (statement); 1 ill

DE KOONING, Elaine (1920-) Amer; ptr
CHIPP 571 (essay: "Subject: What, How, or Who?" o.p. 1955)
HESS 56-70 (interview with Rosalyn Drexler)
IT IS no.1 19 (essay: "Prejudices, Preferences, and Preoccupations")
IT IS no.2 72 ("All-Over Painting")
IT IS no.3 59-62 (group discussion: "5 Participants in a Hearsay Panel")
IT IS no.4 29-30 (statement)
MILLER 1956 58 (statement, from an unpublished foreword for the catalog of Franz Kline's first exhibition, Egan Gallery, 1950)
MUNRO 248-260 (interview); ports; 4 ill
VARIAN III (statement); port

DE KOONING, Willem (1904-) Amer; ptr
ART NOW v.1 no.3 (statement); 1 ill

ART SINCE v.1 154 (statement, o.p. 1960)
CHIPP 555-556 (extract from talk: "The Renaissance and Order," given in New York, 1950)
CHIPP 556-561 (statement: "What Abstract Art Means to Me," o.p. 1951); port
CHIPP 565 (statement, o.p. 1951)
CLAUS 113-117 (statement)
FRASNAY 221-233 (statements); ports; 5 ill
JOHNSON 19-23 (extract from interview with David Sylvester, o.p. 1963); 1 ill
LOCATION v.1 no.1 45-53 ("Content is a Glimpse..." extract from interview with David Sylvester, B.B.C.); 6 ill
MOTHERWELL 8-22 (three group discussions: "Artists' Sessions at Studio 35," New York, 1950)
PROTTER 240 (statement, 1951)
PROTTER 241 (extract from interview, 1956); 1 ill
RODMAN I 100-105 (interview)
ROSE II 153-154 ("What Abstract Art Means to Me," o.p. 1951)
ROSE II REVISED 125-127 (extract from "What Abstract Art Means to Me," o.p. 1951)
ROSE II REVISED 127-128 (extract from interview with David Sylvester, o.p. 1963)
ROSE II REVISED 128 (extract from interview with Thomas B. Hess, o.p. 1958)
ROSE II REVISED 128-129 (extract from essay: "The Renaissance and Order," o.p. 1951)
ROSE II REVISED 130 (extract from interview with Harold Rosenberg, o.p. 1972)
ROSE II REVISED 142-145 (group discussion, o.p. 1952)
SIX PEINTRES (extract from "What

Abstract Art Means to Me," o.p. 1951); port; 2 ill

DELABANO, Martin (1957-) Amer; sclp
NEW VISIONS (statement); 3 ill

DE LA COLINA, Sonia M. (1937-) Mexi; ptr
DICCIONARIO v.3 199-201 (statement); port; 1 ill

DELACOUR, John ( ) photo
ART NETWORK no.7 32-35 (essay: "Julie Brown's Disclosures")
ART NETWORK no.9 33-39 (essay: "Merlin and Bayliss: Work from the Hill End Studio")

DE LA GARZA, Manuel (1903-) Mexi; ptr
DICCIONARIO v.3 203-305 (statement); port; 1 ill

DELANEY, Beauford (1901-1979) Amer; ptr
FINE 133-134 (statements, o.p. 1948); 1 ill

DELANGHE, Jan ( ) Belg; illus
COLLARD 80-85 (interview); port; 1 ill

DELAP, Tony (1927-) Amer; sclp, coll, ptr
ART-RITE no.19 17-20 (group discussion)
HOPKINS 90-91 (statement); port; 1 ill
ILLINOIS 1965 142 (statement); 1 ill
IRVINE 52, 81-82 (statement); 1 ill
SOME 8 (statement); 1 ill

DE LA PENA, Dora
SEE: DORA

DE LA PENA, Margarita ( ) Mexi; ptr

DICCIONARIO v.3 211-213 (statement); port; 1 ill

DE LA PENA ANGUIANO, Francisco Javier (1951-) Mexi; ptr
DICCIONARIO v.3 207-209 (statement); port; 1 ill

DE LA TORRE CALDERON, Nicolas (1923-) Mexi; ptr
DICCIONARIO v.3 221-223 (statement); port; 1 ill

DE LA TORRE VILLALPANDO, Felipe (1950-) Mexi; ptr
DICCIONARIO v.3 225-227 (statement); port; 1 ill

DE LA VEGA, Horacio (1943-) Mexi; ptr
DICCIONARIO v.3 233-235 (statement); port; 1 ill

DE LA VEGA, Jorge (1929-) Mexi; ptr
DICCIONARIO v.3 229-231 (statement); port; 1 ill

DE LAS CASAS, Maueel (1924-) Mexi; ptr
DICCIONARIO v.3 241-243 (statement); port; 1 ill

DELAUNAY, Robert (1885-1941) Fren; ptr
ABSTRACTION no.1 7 (statement); 2 ill
ABSTRACTION no.2 9 (statement)
BERCKELAERS 179 (statement, 1912)
CHIPP 317-318 (letter to August Macke, 1912, o.p. 1958)
CHIPP 318-319 (letter to Wassily Kandinsky, 1912, o.p. 1958)
CHIPP 319-320 (essay: "Light," o.p. 1912)
GUGGENHEIM II 66-67 (statement); 1 ill
POENSGEN 86-87 ("Uber das Licht," 1913)

RAYNAL 113-118 (statement); 3 ill

DELAUNAY, Sonia (1885-1979) Russ/Fren; ptr
ABSTRACTION no.1 8 (statement); 2 ill
ALBRIGHT-KNOX 218-219 (letter, 8/1970); 1 ill
FRASNAY 33-39 (statement); ports
NEMSER 34-51 (interview); port; 9 ill
TEMOIGNAGES I 58-67 (statement); port; 7 ill
VINGTIEME N.S. no.6 19-20 (essay: "Collages de Sonia et de Robert Delaunay"); 2 ill

DELAY, Alexandre (1941-) Swis; ptr, photo
IDENTITE 35-38 (interview with Jacques Clayssen); port
SKIRA 1976 42 (statement); 1 ill
SKIRA 1978 25 (statement); 2 ill

DELFINO, Leonardo (1928-) Ital/Fren; sclp
SKIRA 1976 93 (statement); 1 ill

DELFORD BROWN, Robert
SEE: BROWN, Robert Delford

DELGADO, Adolfo (1927-) Mexi; ptr
DICCIONARIO v.3 269-271 (statement); port; 1 ill

DELGADO GUERRERO, Humberto
SEE: DELGUER

DELGUER (Humberto Delgado Guerrero) (1947-) Mexi; ptr
DICCIONARIO v.3 261-263 (statement); port; 1 ill

DE LIMA, Viana ( ) Port; arch
NEWMAN 132-135 (statement); 9 ill

DE LISIO, Michael (1911-) Amer; sclp
NAYLOR 237-238 (statement); 1 ill

DELLER, Harris (1947-) Amer; pott
HERMAN 42 (statement); port; 1 ill

DELMAR, Eduardo (1914-1977) Mexi; ptr
DICCIONARIO v.3 273-275 (statement); port; 1 ill

DELMARLE, Felix Mac (1889-) Fren; ptr
FRY 131-132 ("Some Notes on Simultaneity in Painting," o.p. 1914)
TEMOIGNAGES I 68-75 (statement); port; 5 ill

DEL MORAL, Enrique (1905-) Mexi; arch
EMANUEL I 201-203 (statement); 1 ill

DEL MORAL LOPEZ, Fernando (1942-) Mexi; ptr
DICCIONARIO v.3 253-255 (statement); port; 1 ill

DELOS, (Julio de los Reyes Merino) (1937-) Mexi; ptr
DICCIONARIO v.3 277-279 (statement); port; 1 ill

DEL PEZZO, Lucio (1933) Ital; sclp
SKIRA 1979 74 (statement); 1 ill

DEL RE, Marco (1950-) Ital; photo
SKIRA 1976 18 (statement); 1 ill

DELVAUX, Paul (1897-) Belg; ptr
DUNOYER (manuscript: "Venise," 1965); 1 ill
FRASNAY 193-201 (statement); ports; 4 ill

DEMARCO, Hugo (1932-) Arge/Fren; sclp
LUMIERE (statement); port; 1 ill

DE MARIA, Walter (1935-) Amer; sclp
CELANT 13-18 (statement); 5 ill
DIRECTIONS I 75-76 (response); 1 ill

DE MARS, Vernon Armand (1908-) Amer; arch
EMANUEL I 204-205 (statement); 1 ill
HEYER 94-101 (interview); 11 ill

DE MARTELLY, John Stockton (1903-) Amer; print, ptr
BRITANNICA 35 (statement); port; 1 ill

DEMARTINI, Hugo (1931-) Czec; sclp
NAYLOR 241-242 (statement); 1 ill

DEMATTIO, Bruno (1938-) Germ; film, perf
GROH (statement)
NAYLOR 242-243 (statement); 1 ill

DE MOTT, Helen ( ) Amer; ptr
BRENTANO 176-177 (poem); 1 ill

DE MOULPIED, Deborah (1933-) Amer; sclp
STRUCTURED (statement); 3 ill

DEMUTH, Charles (1883-1935) Amer; ptr
CRISPO II (statement); 18 ill

DENBY, Jillian (1944-) Amer; ptr
CELEBRATION (statement); 1 ill

DENDY, J. Brooks III (1936-) Amer; ptr
LEWIS I REVISED 116 (statement); port; 1 ill

DENES, Agnes (1938-) Amer; envir, sclp, ptr
ARTPARK 1977 24-27 (statement); port; 6 ill
ARTPARK 1979 (statement); 1 ill
ART-RITE no.6 25 (statement)
ART-RITE no.14 5, 7-8 (response)
BELFORD 129-157 (group discussion)
BRENTANO 178-179 (statement); 2 ill
EMANUEL II 247, 249 (statement)
GUMPERT IV 20-23, 40-41 (extract from talk: "Evolution and the Creative Mind," given at the Smithsonian Institution, Washington, D.C.); port; 7 ill
JOHNSON 137-141 (extract from talk: "Evolution and the Creative Mind," given at the Smithsonian Institution, Washington, D.C.); 2 ill
KUNST BLEIBT KUNST 178-181 (statement); 4 ill
NAYLOR 244-246 (statement); 1 ill
SKIRA 1978 111 (statement); 1 ill
SKIRA 1979 73 (statement); 1 ill
SKIRA 1980 96-97 (statement); 3 ill
VISUAL v.1 no.1 6-7 (text piece: "Human Dust"); 1 ill
WHITE WALLS no.1 22-27 ("Rice/Tree/Burial Project")
WHITE WALLS no.5 38-45 (text piece)
ZEITLIN (statement, o.p. 1970)

DE NIRO, Robert (1922-) Amer; ptr
ART NOW v.2 no.6 (statement); 1 ill
TRACKS v.1 no.3 48-49 ("Corot, Verlaine, and Greta Garbo, or the Melancholy Syndrome (March 1975)")

DENIS, Maurice (1870-1943) Fren; ptr
CHIPP 100-105 (essay: "The Influence of Paul Gauguin," o.p. 1903)
CHIPP 105 (extract from essay: "Cezanne," o.p. 1907)
CHIPP 105-107 (extract from essay: "De Gauguin et de Van Gogh au Classicisme," in English, o.p. 1909)

FRASCINA 51-55 (essay: "From Gauguin and Van Gogh to Classicism," o.p. 1909)

FRASCINA 57-63 (essay: "Cezanne," o.p. 1907)

LHOTE 398-405 (extracts from *Theories 1890-1910 du Symbolisme et de Gauguin vers un Nouvel Ordre Classique*)

SEGHERS 246-247 (essay: "Definition of Neotraditionalism," p.p.)

DENNINGHOFF, Brigitte (1923-) Germ; sclp
HAUSSER 124-125 (statement, o.p. 1977); 1 ill

DENNIS, Charles ( ) Amer; perf
BRENTANO 180-181 (statement); 1 ill

DENNIS, Donna (1942-) Amer; sclp, instal
HOUSE 42-43 (statement); 1 ill

DE PAOLA, Alex ( ) Amer; photo
CALIFORNIA--PHOTOGRAPHY (statement); port; 4 ill

DEPERO, Fortunato (1892-) Ital; ptr
APOLLONIO 197-200 ("Futurist Reconstruction of the Universe," o.p. 1915)
VERZOCCHI 189-193 (statement); self port; 1 ill

DEPILLARS, Murry N. (1938-) Amer; ptr, illus, print
LEWIS II 27 (statement); port; 4 ill

DE PISIS, Filippo (1896-) Ital; ptr
VERZOCCHI 195-199 (statement); self port; 1 ill

DERAIN, Andre (1880-1954) Fren; ptr, sclp

FRIEDENTHAL 198-200 (letter to Maurice Vlaminck, 1909)

LHOTE 393-395 (statement, p.p.)

MINOTAURE no.3/4 8 ("Criterium des As")

SEGHERS 250-253 (essay: "On the Art of Painting," p.p.)

DEREN, Maya ( ) Russ/Amer; film
KEPES IX 154-171 (essay: "Cinematography: The Creative Use of Reality")

DERGES, Susan (1955-) Brit; sclp
HAYWARD 1978 92-95 (statement); 5 ill

DE RIVERA, Jose (1904-) Amer; sclp
EMANUEL II 249-250 (statement); 1 ill
NAYLOR 246-247 (statement)
ILLINOIS 1953 176-177 (statement); 1 ill
ILLINOIS 1955 190 (statement); 1 ill
ILLINOIS 1957 195-196 (response); 1 ill

DE ROCCHI, Francesco (1902-) Ital; ptr
VERZOCCHI 201-205 (statement); self port; 1 ill

DEROUX, Charles ( ) Belg; ptr
COLLARD 86-89 (interview); port; 1 ill

DERZIPILSKI, Kathleen ( )
PHILLPOT (statement)

DE SANDO, Sandra (1946-) Amer; sclp
EVENTS II 34-35 (statement); 1 ill

DESCAMPS, Bernard (1947-) Fren; photo
WALSH 195-196 (statement); 1 ill

DESCOMBES, Roland J. ( ) Amer; ptr, illus
MAGIC 40-43 (statement); port; 6 ill

DESCOMBIN, Maxime (1909-) Fren; sclp
TEMOIGNAGES II 14-17 (statement); port; 5 ill

DESHAIES, Arthur (1920-) Amer; print
AMERICAN PRINTS 22, 65-66 (statement); 1 ill

DE SILVA, Jenaro (1952-) Mexi; ptr, sclp
DICCIONARIO v.3 245-247 (statement); port; 1 ill

DESLAUGIERS, Francois ( )
ARCHITECTURES 114-119 (essay: "Architecture et Technologie"); 7 ill

DESNOS, Robert (1900-1945) print
JEAN 92-93 ("Penalties of Hell," o.p. 1922); port
JEAN 166-168 ("Mourning for Mourning," o.p. 1924)

DESOUCHES, Marie Claire (1912-) Mexi; ptr
DICCIONARIO v.3 281-283 (statement); port; 1 ill

DESPIAU, Charles (1874-1946) Fren; sclp
MINOTAURE no.3/4 107-108 ("Enquete")

DESPIERRE, Jacques (1912-)
PREMIER BILAN 289 (statement)

DE STAEBLER, Stephen (1933-) Amer; pott
VIEWPOINT 1979 12-13 (extract from the National Council on education for the Ceramic Arts' *NCECA Newsletter*, v.2 no.2, Jan. 1979); 3 ill

DE STIJL (group)
BANN 64-66 (statement; and "Manifesto I," 1918)
CONRADS 39-40 ("Manifesto I," o.p. 1918)
CONRADS 64 ("Creative Demands," o.p. 1922)
CONRADS 66 ("Manifesto V," o.p. 1923)

DETRE, Roland (1903-) Amer; ptr
ILLINOIS 1959 209-210 (statement); 1 ill

DETRELL DIAZ, Miguel Angel (1952-) Mexi; ptr
DICCIONARIO v.3 285-287 (statement); port; 1 ill

DE TRINIDAD SOLIS, Alberto (1916-) Mexi; ptr
DICCIONARIO v.3 249-251 (statement); port; 1 ill

DETWILER, Joseph (1951-) Amer; pott
HERMAN 43 (statement); port; 1 ill

DEUTSCH, Boris (1892-) Lith/Amer; ptr
ILLINOIS 1951 171 (statement)
100 CONTEMPORARY 44-45 (statement); port; 1 ill

DEUTSCH, Richard (1953-) Amer; pott
HERMAN 44 (statement); port; 1 ill

DEVADE, Marc (1943-) ptr
TRACKS v.2 no.2 51-65 ("Painting and its Double")

DEVELIN, John (1950-) Iris; ptr
KNOWLES 40-41 (statement); 2 ill

DE VREE, Paul (1909-) Belg; ptr, sclp
EMANUEL II 252-253 (statement); 1 ill
NAYLOR 249 (statement); 1 ill

DE VRIES, Erwin Jules (1929-)
Suri/Dutc; sclp
NAYLOR 249-250 (statement); 1 ill

DE VRIES, Herman (1931-) Dutc; ptr
EMANUEL II 253-255 (statement); 1 ill

DEWASNE, Jean (1921-) Fren; ptr, sclp
ART SINCE v.1 290-291 (statement, o.p. 1959)
CHARBONNIER v.1 53-62 (interview)
DOUZE ANS 185-188 (statement); port; 5 ill
EMANUEL II 255-256 (statement); 1 ill
POENSGEN 119-120 ("Ein Gesteigertes Bewusstsein des Kunstlerischen Handelns," 1952)
PREMIER BILAN 289 (statement); port
QUADRUM no.7 115-120 (essay: "Reflexions sur l'Art 'Abstraite'"); 6 ill
SKIRA 1975 86 (statement); 1 ill
TEMOIGNAGES I 76-85 (statement); port; 8 ill
VINGTIEME N.S. no.4 78-79 (essay: "Jacobsen")

DEYROLLE, Jean Jacques (1911-1967)
Fren; ptr
GRENIER 89-94 (interview)
PREMIER BILAN 289 (statement); port
TEMOIGNAGES I 87-93 (statement); port; 7 ill

DEZEUZE, Daniel (1942-) Fren; ptr, instal
MURS 8 (statement); 1 ill
SKIRA 1979 79 (statement); 1 ill
SKIRA 1980 61 (statement); 3 ill

D'HAESE, Roel (1921-) Belg; sclp
SKIRA 1976 92 (statement); 1 ill

D'HUE, Robert Raleigh, Jr. (1917-)
Amer; ptr

LEWIS I REVISED 24, 141 (statement); port; 1 ill

DIAMOND, Abel Joseph (1932-) Cana; arch
EMANUEL I 205-207 (statement); 1 ill

DIAMOND, Jack (1932-) Cana; arch
CANADIAN 36-39 (statement); 5 ill

DIAS, Antonio (1944-) Braz; ptr
KUNST UND POLITIK (statement); port; 4 ill

DIAS, Cicero (1908-) Braz; ptr
PREMIER BILAN 290 (statement); port
TEMOIGNAGES I 94-99 (statement); port; 5 ill

DIAS, Pavel (1938-) Czec; photo
WALSH 196-197 (statement); 1 ill

DIAZ, Daniel Vazquez ( ) Span; ptr
PORCEL I 189-198 (interview); 1 ill

DIAZ, Ricardo Rodrigo (1939-) Amer; print
RAICES 15 (statement); 1 ill

DIAZ ADAME, Daniel (1916-) Mexi; ptr
DICCIONARIO v.3 289-291 (statement); port; 1 ill

DIAZ CORTES, Antonio (1935-) Mexi; ptr
DICCIONARIO v.3 293-295 (statement); port; 1 ill

DIAZ DE LA SERNA, Fernando (1949-)
Mexi; ptr
DICCIONARIO v.3 297-299 (statement); port; 1 ill

DIAZ PAYAN, Jorge (1946-) Mexi; ptr

DICCIONARIO v.3 305-307 (statement); port; 1 ill

DIAZ-MORALES, Ignacio ( ) Mexi; arch
RODMAN II 254-259 (statement)

DIAZSOLORZANO, Sergio (1938-) Mexi; ptr
DICCIONARIO v.3 309-311 (statement); port; 1 ill

DIBBETS, Jan (1941-) Dutc/Amer; photo
AVALANCHE no.1 34-39 (interview); port; 6 ill
CELANT 103-108 (statement); 5 ill
CONCEPTUAL ART 31, 37, 44 (statement)
MEYER 116-121 (text piece); 7 ill
PAOLETTI 41-43 (statements, p.p.); 1 ill

DI BELLO, Bruno (1938-) Ital; ptr
SKIRA 1979 50 (statement); 1 ill

DI BENEDETTO, Angelo (1913-) Amer; ptr
BRITANNICA 36 (statement); port; 1 ill

DIB LATORRE, Rosario (1946-) Mexi; ptr
DICCIONARIO v.3 313-315 (statement); port; 1 ill

DICK, Robert ( ) Amer; sclp
ARTPARK 1983 28-29 (statement); 1 ill

DICKERSON, Daniel Jay (1922-) Amer; ptr
FULBRIGHT 22 (statement)
VARIAN III (statement); port

DICKERSON, Kenneth (1935-) Amer; ptr
LEWIS II 95 (statement); port; 1 ill

DICKERSON, Vera M. (1946-) Amer; ptr
NOSANOW I 48 (statement); 1 ill

DICKEY, Dan (1910-) Amer; illus
CALIFORNIA--DRAWING (statement); 2 ill

DICKINSON, Edwin Walter (1891-1978) Amer; ptr
GUSSOW 152-153 (interview, 1970); 1 ill
KUH 68-80 (interview); 7 ill
PROTTER 223 (statement, 1963)

DICKINSON, Eleanor (1931-) Amer; video, paper, ptr
VISUAL v.1 no.1 38-40 (essay: "Technical Information")
VISUAL v.1 no.2 11-14 (interview); 3 ill
VISUAL v.1 no.2 38-39 (essay: "Technical Information")
VISUAL v.1 no.3 33-34 (essay: "Technical Information")
VISUAL v.1 no.4 21 (essay)
VISUAL v.1 no.4 29-30 (essay: "Technical Information")
VISUAL v.2 no.4 34-35 (essay: "Technical Information")
VISUAL v.3 no.3 43-44 (essay: "Technical Information")
VISUAL v.4 no.1 36-37 (essay: "Technical Information")
VISUAL v.4 no.2 33-34 (essay: "Technical INformation")
VISUAL v.4 no.4 36-37 (essay: "Technical Information")

DI DONNA, Profirio ( )
ART-RITE no.9 29-34 (group discussion)

DIEBENKORN, Richard (1922-) Amer; ptr
ART NOW v.2 no.1 (interview); 1 ill
ART SINCE v.2 151 (statement, o.p. 1964)

ARTFORUM v.1 no.10 26-28 (interview); 1 ill
GUSSOW 142-143 (letter, 1970); 1 ill
ILLINOIS 1955 191 (statement); 1 ill
ILLINOIS 1961 91 (response); port; 1 ill
SKIRA 1975 103 (statement); 1 ill

DIEGO, Julio de (1900-) ptr
BRITANNICA 33 (statement); port; 1 ill
ZAIDENBERG 161-162 (essay: "Painting Free Association"); 2 ill

DIEHL, Hans-Jurgen (1940-) Germ; print, ptr
EMANUEL II 262 (statement); 1 ill
NAYLOR 254 (statement); 1 ill

DIENES, Sari (1899-) Amer; ptr, sclp, print
IT IS no.4 62-63 ("Notes on Japan")
MUNRO 97-99 (interview)
TRACKS v.1 no.2 38, 64 (poems)

DIENST, Rolf Gunter (1942-) Germ; ptr
SKIRA 1979 51-52 (statement); 1 ill

DIERICKX, Karel (1940-) Belg; ptr
SKIRA 1978 102 (statement); 1 ill

DIERICX, Hadelin (1942-) Mexi; ptr
DICCIONARIO v.3 317-319 (statement); port; 1 ill

DIESTE, Eladio (1917-) Urug; arch
BAYON 190-213 (interview); port; 18 ill
EMANUEL I 207-208 (statement); 1 ill

DIETMANN, Erik (1937-) Swed; ptr
ADLERS 20-23 (interview); ports; 2 ill

DIETRICH, Paul E. ( ) Amer; arch
EMANUEL I 133-135 (statement); 1 ill

DIEUZAIDE, Jean (1921-) Fren; photo
WALSH 198-200 (statement); 1 ill

DIEZ DE SOLLANO, Dolores Ortega de (1907-) Mexi; ptr
DICCIONARIO v.3 321-323 (statement); port; 1 ill

DIEZ DE SOLLANO, Maria Elena (1944-)Mexi; ptr
DICCIONARIO v.3 325-327 (statement); port; 1 ill

DIFFRIENT, Niels ( ) design
DESIGN 11-16 (essay: "Design and Technology")

DIJULIO, Charles ( ) ptr
CRISS-CROSS no.5 8-11 (statement); 4 ill
CRISS-CROSS no.10 4-5 (essay: "Criss-Cross and Pattern")
CRISS-CROSS no.10 10-11 (essay: "A Definition of Pattern"); port; 1 ill

DILL, Guy Giraro (1946-) Amer; sclp
HOPKINS 94-95 (statement); port; 1 ill

DILL, Jane Anne ( ) Amer; ptr
ART PATRON ART 23-24 (statement); port; 1 ill

DILL, Laddie John (1943-) Amer; ptr
HOPKINS 96-97 (statement); port; 1 ill

DILLER, Burgoyne (1900-1965) Amer; ptr, sclp
ROSE II 117-118 (extract from essay: "Poverty, Politics, and Artists, 1930-45," o.p. 1965)
ROSE II REVISED 95-96 (extract from essay: "Poverty, Politics, and Artists, 1930-45," o.p. 1965)

DILLEY, Barbara ( ) perf
AVALANCHE no.11 33-35 (interview); port; 4 ill

DIXON, Maynard (1875-1946) Amer; ptr
BRITANNICA 37 (statement); port; 1 ill

DJORDJEVIC, Miodrag Borislav (1919-)
Yugo; photo
WALSH 201-202 (statement); 1 ill

DOBRIC, Dorde (1931-) Yugo, ptr
TOMASEVIC 62-65 (statement); port; 2
ill

DODD, Lamar (1909-) Amer; ptr
BETHERS II 76-77 (statement); 1 ill
ILLINOIS 1951 172 (statement); 1 ill
ILLINOIS 1955 191-192 (statement); 1 ill
ILLINOIS 1961 78 (response); port; 1 ill

DODD, Lois (1927-) Amer; ptr, print
ART NOW v.4 no.2 (statement); 1 ill

DOELL, Glenn E. (1951-) Amer; pott
HERMAN 46 (statement); port; 1 ill

DOESBURG, Theo van (C.
E. M. Kupper) (1883-1931) Dutc; ptr,
arch
ABSTRACTION no.1 39 (statement); 2
ill
ART SINCE v.1 290 (statement, o.p.
1966/67)
BANN 91-93 ("Elemental Formation,"
o.p. 1923); 1 ill
BANN 109-112 (essay: "Toward a
Constructive Poetry," o.p. 1923); 1 ill
BANN 115-118 (essay: "Toward a
Collective Construction," o.p. 1924)
BERCKELAERS 179 (statements, 1916,
1930)
CHIPP 324-325 ("Introduction to
Volume II of *De Stijl*," o.p. 1919)
CONRADS 67 ("Towards Collective
Building," o.p. 1923)
CONRADS 78-80 (essay: "Towards a
Plastic Architecture," o.p. 1924)

GIEDION-WELCKER 117-124 (poems:
"Vollmond," 1913, "Nacht," "Hort!
Hort!," 1915, in German; "Der
Missetater," 1916, "Voorbijtrekkende
Troep," 1916, in Dutch); port
GROHMANN 417 ("Das Verhaltnis des
Betrachters zum Kunstwerk," p.p.
1924)
GUGGENHEIM II 86-87 (statement, o.p.
1920); 1 ill

DOHANOS, Stevan (1907-) Amer; ptr,
illus
GUITAR 54-65 (interview); port; 4 ill
MAGIC 44-47 (statement); port; 4 ill
NORTH LIGHT 60-65, 81 (statement);
port; 7 ill

DOHANY, Jack ( ) Amer; wood
MEILACH 232-235 (statement); port

DOISNEAU, Robert (1912-) Fren; photo
BOOTH 80-89 (interview); port; 6 ill
HILL 80-110 (interview, 1977); port
TIME-LIFE IV 98-99 (statement); 1 ill
WALSH 203-205 (statement); 1 ill

DOKLEAN, Sofija (1931-) Yugo; ptr
TOMASEVIC 66-68 (statement); port; 1
ill

DOLE, William (1917-) Amer; illus, ptr,
coll
CALIFORNIA--DRAWING (statement); 2
ill
CRISPO I (statement); 14 ill
ILLINOIS 1965 81 (statement); 1 ill
ILLINOIS 1967 79 (statement); 1 ill

DOLK, Michiel ( )
ART NETWORK no.5 17 (essay:
"Aspects of Socially Engaged and
Community Art")

DOLORES (Dolores Rocha) (1929-) Mexi; ptr
DICCIONARIO v.3 329-331 (statement); port; 1 ill

DOLOVSKI, Mladen (1932-) Yugo; ptr
TOMASEVIC 69-72 (statement); port; 1 ill

DOMELA-NIEUWENHUIS, Cesar (1900-) Dutc; ptr, sclp
BERCKELAERS 291-292 (statement); port; 1 ill
EMANUEL II 268-270 (statement); 1 ill
NAYLOR 259-260 (statement); 1 ill
SEUPHOR 162-163 (statement); 1 ill
TEMOIGNAGES I 100-107 (statement); port; 6 ill

DOMINGUEZ, Benjamin (1942-) Mexi; ptr
DICCIONARIO v.3 333-335 (statement); port; 1 ill

DOMINGUEZ, Oscar (1906-1957) Span; ptr
GUGGENHEIM II 126, 128 (statement, o.p. 1939); 1 ill
LIPPARD 108-110 (essay: "The Petrification of Time," o.p. 1942)

DOMINGUEZ ORTIZ, Jorge (1952-) Mexi; ptr
DICCIONARIO v.3 337-339 (statement); port; 1 ill

DOMINGUEZ RODRIGUEZ, Conrado (1950-) Mexi; ptr
DICCIONARIO v.3 341-343 (statement); port; 1 ill

DOMINIS, John (1921-) Amer; photo
WALSH 206-207 (statement); 1 ill

DOMMISSE, Durwood (1938-) Amer; ptr
WISCONSIN I (statement); 1 ill

DONAGH, Rita (1939-) Brit; ptr
HAYWARD 1978 78-81 (statement); 3 ill

DONATI, Enrico (1909-) Amer; ptr, sclp
ILLINOIS 1959 211 (statement); 1 ill
IT IS no.3 27 (statement)

DONDE, Olga (1937-) Mexi; ptr
DICCIONARIO v.3 345-347 (statement); port; 1 ill

DONGHI, Antonio (1897-) Ital; ptr
VERZOCCHI 207-211 (statement); self port; 1 ill

DONGHIA, Angelo ( ) design
DIAMONSTEIN V 64-79 (interview); port; 12 ill

DONHAUSER, Paul S. (1936-) Germ/Amer; pott, sclp
WISCONSIN I (statement); 1 ill

DONINI, Marilyn J. ( ) Amer; paper, print
HAYSTACK 15 (statement); 1 ill

DONNELL-VOGT, Radka ( ) Bulg/Amer; text
MILLER 37-56 (statement); port; 1 ill

DONNELLY, James (1955-) Amer; ptr, coll
WISCONSIN II (statement); 1 ill

DONOVAN, Terence ( ) Brit; photo
HOW FAMOUS 26-31 (statements); port; 5 ill

DORA (Dora de la Pena) (1930-) Mexi; ptr

DICCIONARIO v.3 351-353 (statement); port; 1 ill

DORANTES, Antonio (1942-) Mexi; ptr
DICCIONARIO v.3 355-357 (statement); port; 1 ill

DORAZIO, Piero (1927-) Ital; ptr
ART SINCE v.1 292 (statement, o.p. 1965)
PAINTING 40 (statement); port; 1 ill
SKIRA 1976 78 (statement); 1 ill
TRACKS v.1 no.2 53-57 (statement: "Notes on the Art of Painting," 1961)

DORESIC, Vilma (1936-) Yugo; ptr
TOMASEVIC 73-75 (statement); port; 1 ill

DORFMAN, Elsa (1937-) Amer; photo
BOSTON III (interview); 1 ill

DORNE, Albert (1904-) Amer; ptr
GUITAR 66-77 (interview); port; 4 ill

DORR, Nell (1893-) Amer; photo
MITCHELL 84-101 (statement); ports; 15 ill

DORYS, Benedykt Jerzy (1901-) Poli; photo
WALSH 207-208 (statement); 1 ill

DOSHI, Balkrishna Vithaldras (1927-) Indi; arch
EMANUEL I 210-212 (statement); 1 ill
REVOLUTION 86-92 (essay: "The Proliferating Unplanned Cities: The Case of India")

DOSSI, Ugo (1943-) Germ; print
SKIRA 1977 69 (statement); 1 ill

DOTSON, Louis (1917-) Amer; wood
FERRIS 53-67 (statements); ports

DOUCET, Jacques (1924-) Fren; ptr
YALE 61 (statement)

DOUGLAS, Aaron (1899-1979) Amer; ptr, print
FINE 85-88 (statements, o.p. 1943, 1960); 6 ill
FIRST AMERICAN 12-16 (essay: "The Negro in American Culture")

DOUGLAS, Christine (1949-) Amer; paper
WISCONSIN II (statement); 1 ill

DOUGLAS, Edward (1943-) Amer; photo
WALSH 208-209 (statement); 1 ill

DOUGLAS, Emory (1943-) Amer; ptr, print
FAX II 256-278 (statements); port; 1 ill

DOVA, Gianni (1925-) Ital; ptr
PAINTING 12 (statement); port; 1 ill

DOVE, Arthur Garfield (1880-1946) Amer; ptr, coll
CRISPO I (poem); 12 ill
CRISPO II (statement); 15 ill
EDDY 48-49 (letter)
FORUM 1916 60 (statement); 1 ill
MCCOUBREY 196-197 (letter to Arthur Jerome Eddy, 1912)
ROSE II 54 ("The Meaning of 291," o.p. 1917)
ROSE II 56 (statement, o.p. 1916)
ROSE II 70-71 (letter to Arthur Jerome Eddy)
ROSE II REVISED 50-51 ("The Meaning of 291," o.p. 1917)
ROSE II REVISED 52 (statement, o.p. 1916)
ROSE II REVISED 64-65 (extract from letter to Arthur Jerome Eddy, 1912, p.p.)

DOW, Harold (1902-) sclp
OPEN AIR 1960 (statement); 1 ill

DOW, Jane M. (1945-) Amer; ptr
CORCORAN 54-67 (statement and interview); port; 11 ill

DOWLER GOW, Isobel ( ) Cana; instal
VEHICULE (statement); 3 ill

DOWNES, Rackstraw (1939-) Brit; ptr
SUPERREAL 70-71 (statement); 1 ill
TRACKS v.2 no.3 70-73 (essay: "Post-Modernist Painting")

DOWNEY, Juan (1940-) Chil; video
BRENTANO 184-185 (statement); 1 ill
NAYLOR 263-264 (statement); 1 ill
ON SITE no.4 6-7 ("Invisible Architecture"); 4 ill
ON SITE no.4 8-9 ("Energy Fields"); 3 ill

DOWNING, Robert James (1935-) Cana; sclp
CANADA 108-109 (statement); port; 3 ill

DOWNS, Barry Vance (1930-) Cana; arch
CANADIAN 40-43 (statement); 5 ill
EMANUEL I 212-213 (statement); 1 ill

DOWNSBOROUGH, Peter (1940-)
ART-RITE no.14 5,8 (response)
TRACKS v.3 no.3 21-31 (text pieces, poems)

DOWSON, Philip Manning (1924-) Brit; arch
EMANUEL I 213-214 (statement); 1 ill

DOXFUD, Rem
SEE: HILL, Anthony

DOYLE, Tom (1928-) Amer; sclp
DIRECTIONS I 76 (response); 1 ill

DOZIER, Otis (1904-) Amer; ptr
ILLINOIS 1952 186-187 (statement); 1 ill

DRAHOS, Tom (1947-) Fren; photo
WALSH 209-210 (statement); 1 ill

DRAKE, John (1946-) Amer; sclp
NEW VISIONS (statement); 3 ill

DRAPER, William F. (1912-) Amer; ptr
ART VOICES v.1 no.2 16 (interview); port; 1 ill

DREIER, Paul Uwe (1939-) Germ; ptr
ABSTRACTION no.2 10 (statement); 2 ill

DREISBACH, Fritz (1941-) Amer; glass
GLASS v.1 16-17 (statement)
GLASS v.5 (group discussion); port; 1 ill

DRESKIN, Jeanet S. (1921-) Amer; ptr, print
MORRIS 68-73 (statements); ports; 1 ill

DRESSLER, Jack ( ) photo
LAPLANTE 17-21 (interview); port; 1 ill

DRESSLER, Otto (1930-) Germ; ptr
NAYLOR 264-265 (statement); 1 ill

DREW, Jane Beverley (1911-) Brit; arch
EMANUEL I 215-216 (statement); 1 ill

DREXLER, Henry J. (1947-) Amer; ptr
NOSANOW I 50-51 (statement); 2 ill

DREXLER, Rosalyn ( ) Amer; ptr
LOCATION v.1 no.2 75-81 ("The Drexlers at Home"); 7 ill

DREXLER, Sherman ( ) ptr
ART VOICES v.5 no.3 42 (statement); 1 ill

DRISKELL, David C. (1931-) Amer; ptr
LEWIS I REVISED 95 (statement); port; 1 ill

DROPE, McCleary (1931-) Cana; sclp
CANADA 72-73 (statement); port; 2 ill

DRUIK, Don (1945-) Cana; video
POINT OF VIEW 45 (statement); 1 ill

DRUKS, Michael (1940-) Brit; photo, print
SKIRA 1977 90 (statement); 4 ill

DRUMLEVITCH, Seymour (1923-) Amer; ptr
WHITNEY (statement); 1 ill

DRUMMOND, Sally Hazelet (1924-) Amer; ptr
MILLER 1963 26-31 (statement); port; 6 ill

DUARTE, Angel (1930-) Span; sclp
LUMIERE (statement); port; 4 ill

DUBAIL, Berthe ( ) Belg; ptr
COLLARD 94-97 (interview); port; 1 ill

DUBANIEWICZ, Paula (1954-) sclp
SCULPTURE OUTSIDE (statement); 4 ill

DU BOIS, Guy Pene (1884-1958) Amer; ptr
BRITANNICA 38 (statement); port; 1 ill
ROSE II 43-46 (extract from essay: "George B. Luks and Flamboyance," o.p. 1923)
ROSE II 46-47 (extract from essay: "William Glackens," o.p. 1914)

ROSE II REVISED 41-43 (extract from essay: "George B. Luks and Flamboyance," o.p. 1923)
ROSE II REVISED 43-44 (extract from essay: "William Glackens," o.p. 1914)

DUBOIS, Macy (1929-) Cana; arch
CANADIAN 44-47 (statement); 5 ill
EMANUEL I 216-217 (statement); 1 ill

DUBOWSKI, Donald E. ( ) Amer; ptr, illus
MAGIC 48-51 (statement); port; 4 ill

DUBUFFET, Jean (1901-) Fren; sclp, ptr
ART AND TECHNOLOGY 86-94 (project proposal); 3 ill
ART SINCE v.1 154-155 (statements, o.p. 1944, 1956/57)
ART SINCE v.2 152 (statement, o.p. 1960)
CHIPP 606-616 (essay: "Empreintes," o.p. 1957, in English); port
CLAUS 132-136 (statement)
GOLDAINE 102-105 (interview); port
PROTTER 233-234 (statement, 1961); 1 ill
RITCHIE 17-21 (statement); port; 5 ill
SEGHERS 266-267 (statement, p.p.)
SEITZ III 93-95 (statement, o.p. 1961); 4 ill
SELZ 60-67 (statement); 7 ill
SKIRA 1979 90 (statement); 1 ill
STEDELIJK 113-115 (statement, in French); 5 ill
TRACKS v.1 no.2 26-29 ("More Modest")
VINGTIEME N.S. no.9 24-25 (statement); 1 ill

DUCA, Alfred Milton (1920-) Amer; ptr
ILLINOIS 1951 172-173 (statement); 1 ill
ILLINOIS 1953 177 (statement); 1 ill

"La Vase des Mares," in French and English); 6 ill

DUFRANE, Paul ( ) Belg; ptr
COLLARD 98-103 (interview); port; 1 ill

DUFY, Raoul (1877-1953) Fren; ptr
SEGHERS 254-255 (statement, p.p.)
THORN 83 (statement, p.p.)

DUGGER, John (1948-)
BOSHIER (statement); port; 2 ill

DUHALQUE, Albert (1925-) Fren
PREMIER BILAN 291 (statement); port

DUHART, Emilio (1917-) Chil; arch
BAYON 108-129 (interview); 20 ill

DUHRESSEN, Alfred ( ) ptr
IT IS no.5 27 ("On the Absurd and Painting")

DUJOVNY, Gregorio (1925-) Arge; sclp
NAYLOR 268-269 (statement); 1 ill

DULCHE PEDROZA, Guillermina (1939-) Mexi; ptr
DICCIONARIO v.3 359-361 (statement); port; 1 ill

DUMBRELL, Lesley (1941-) Atrl; ptr
DE GROEN 121-130 (interview); port

DUMONT, Pierre-Jean ( ) Fren; ptr
EDDY 180 (statement)

DUNAS, William ( ) Amer; sclp
ARTPARK 1974 26-27 (statement); port; 1 ill

DUNCAN, Frank Davenport, Jr. (1915-) Amer; ptr
ILLINOIS 1951 173 (statement)
ILLINOIS 1955 193 (statement); 1 ill

DUNCAN, Tom ( ) Amer; wood
MEILACH 166 (statement); 2 ill

DUNFORD, Mike (1946-) Brit; film
ENGLISH 444-445 (statement); port; 1 ill

DUNLAP, William R. (1944-) Amer; ptr
ART PATRON ART 25-26 (statement); port; 1 ill
NOSANOW I 52-53 (statement); 2 ill

DUNLAVEY, Rob (1955-) Amer; sclp
RICKERT 1980 (statement); port; 3 ill

DUNN, Alan Cantrell (1900-1974) Amer; cartoonist
M.H. DE YOUNG 48 (response); self port

DUNN, Alfred C. (1909-) Amer; ptr
NOSANOW II 44-45 (statement); 2 ill

DUNN, Douglas ( )
LIVE no.4 2-9 (interview); 8 ill

DUNN, Eugenia V. (1918-1971) Amer; ptr
LEWIS I 103 (statement); port; 1 ill

DUNN, Richard (1944-) Atrl; ptr
DE GROEN 102-114 (interview); port

DUNN, Robert (1932-) Amer; ptr
ILLINOIS 1959 211-212 (statement); 1 ill

DUNSTAN, Bernard (1920-) Brit; ptr
CONTEMPORARY (statement); port; 2 ill

DUPAIN, Max (1911-) Atrl; photo
WALSH 213-214 (statement); 1 ill

DUPUY, Jean (1925-) Fren/Amer; perf
ART AND TECHNOLOGY 95-100 (project proposal)

TRACKS v.2 no.1 35-50 (statement)

DURAN MENDEZ, Luis Gabriel (1948-1979) Mexi; ptr
DICCIONARIO v.3 363-365 (statement); port; 1 ill

DURAN VAZQUEZ, Alfonso (1930-) Mexi; ptr
DICCIONARIO v.3 367-369 (statement); port; 1 ill

DURANTE, Armando (1934-) Arge; video
LUMIERE (statement); port; 1 ill

DURCHANEK, Louis W. (Ludvik) (1902-) Aust/Amer; sclp
ILLINOIS 1963 75 (statement); 1 ill

DURFEE, Hazard (1915-) Amer; ptr
BETHERS II 42-43 (statement); 3 ill
ILLINOIS 1952 187 (statement); 1 ill

DURHAM, Robert L. ( ) arch
REVOLUTION 248-249 (statement)

DURRANT, Jennifer (1942-) Brit; ptr
CONTEMPORARY (statement); port; 1 ill
HAYWARD 1979 66-69 (statement); 10 ill

D'URSO, Joseph Paul ( ) design
DIAMONSTEIN V 80-95 (interview); port; 8 ill

DURST, Alan Lydiat (1883-) Brit; sclp
OPEN AIR 1960 (statement); 1 ill

DURYEA, Lynn ( ) Amer; pott
HAYSTACK 16 (statement); 1 ill

DUTTON, Allen A. (1922-) Amer; photo
WALSH 215 (statement); 1 ill

DUVAL, Alex (1920-) Mexi; ptr
DICCIONARIO v.3 371-373 (statement); self port; 1 ill

DWYER, Nancy ( ) Amer; ptr
FACE IT 12-13 (statement); 1 ill

DYE, David (1945-) Brit; film, instal, sclp
CONTEMPORARY (statement); port; 2 ill
EMANUEL II 277-278 (statement); 1 ill
ENGLISH 368-373 (statement); port; 18 ill
NAYLOR 271 (statement)

DYER, Carolyn ( ) text
VISUAL v.4 no.2 32-33 (essay: "Contemporary Crafts"); 1 ill

DZUBAS, Friedel (1915-) Germ/Amer; ptr
ART NOW v.3 no.4 (statement); 1 ill
ARTFORUM v.4 no.1 49-52 (interview with Max Kozloff); 4 ill
IT IS no.2 78 (statement)

EADES, Luis (1923-) Span/Amer; ptr
WHITNEY (statement); 1 ill

EARL, Clifford (1945-) Amer; sclp
SOUTHEAST (statement); port; 4 ill

EARL, Jack Eugene (1934-) Amer; pott,
sclp
VIEWPOINT 1980 8-9 (statement); 3 ill

EARLS, Paul (1934-) Amer; instal, sclp,
sound
CENTERBEAM 72-74, 104-105 ("Laser
and Music/Sound Lines"); port; 4 ill
GRAYSON 170-175 (essay: "Sounding
Space: Drawing Room Music"); 2 ill
TECHNOLOGIES (statements:
"Compute Generated Imagery," and
"Laser Chamber: Zero Point,
Sketches, Scores"); port; 6 ill

EASLEY, Annette Lewis (1948-) Amer;
sclp
LEWIS I 38 (statement); port; 1 ill

EASTWICK-FIELD, Elizabeth (1919-)
arch
SEE: STILLMAN AND EASTWICK-
FIELD

EASTWICK-FIELD, John (1919-) arch
SEE: STILLMAN AND EASTWICK-
FIELD

EATHERLEY, Gill ( ) film
KUNST BLEIBT KUNST 387 (statement);
1 ill

EBENDORF, Robert ( ) Amer; metal
METALWORKS (statement); 1 ill

EBIHARA, Kinosuke (1904-) Japa; ptr
KUNG 52-55 (statement); port; 2 ill

ECHAURREN, Roberto Sebastian
Antonio Matta
SEE: MATTA

ECKBO, Garrett (1910-) Amer; arch
EMANUEL I 223-226 (statement); 1 ill

ECKE, Betty Tseng Yu-Ho
SEE: TSENG YU-HO

ECKERT, Tom (1942-) Amer; wood
WOODWORKING 16-17 (statement);
port; 2 ill

EDA (EDAW), Eugene (1939-) Amer; ptr
LEWIS II 119 (statement); port; 1 ill

EDDY, Don (1944-) Amer; ptr
EMANUEL II 280-281 (statement); 1 ill
ILLINOIS 1974 44-45 (statement); 1 ill
IMAGE COLOR FORM 14-15 (statement);
1 ill
NAYLOR 273-274 (statement); 1 ill
SUPERREAL 156-157 (statement); 1 ill

EDELHEIT, Martha (1931-) Amer; ptr
NAYLOR 272-273 (statement); 1 ill
SCHAPIRO 19 (statement); port; 1 ill

EDENS, Stephanie ( )
ART-RITE no.5 2-4 (essays: "Whitney
Downtown," and "Artists Space")

EDER, Susan (1950-) Amer; envir
PROJECTS (statement); 6 ill

EDEY, Maitland A. ( ) photo
TIME-LIFE V 160-179 (essay: "Trophies
from a Photographic Safari"); 19 ill

EDGERTON, Harold E. (1903-) Amer;
photo
WALSH 216-218 (statement); 1 ill

EDIE, Stuart (1908-1974) Amer; ptr
ZAIDENBERG 82-85 (essay: "On Painting"); 4 ill

EDIT DE AK ( ) REALLIFE no.8 2-4 (interview)

EDMONDS, Nicholas B. (1937-) Amer; sclp
ILLINOIS 1974 46-47 (statement); 1 ill

EDMONDS, Ron ( ) Amer; photo
LEEKLEY 150-153 (statement); 7 ill

EDMONDSON, Leonard (1916-) Amer; print, ptr
AMERICAN PRINTS 23, 66 (statement); 1 ill
CALIFORNIA--PAINTING 14 (statement); 1 ill
CALIFORNIA--PRINTS (statement); 1 ill
ILLINOIS 1953 178 (statement); 1 ill
ILLINOIS 1955 194 (statement); 1 ill
ILLINOIS 1969 170-171 (statement); 1 ill

EDWARDS, John (1938-) Brit; ptr
CONTEMPORARY (statement); port; 2 ill

EDWARDS, Mark (1947-) Brit; photo
WALSH 218-219 (statement); 1 ill*

EDWARDS, Mel (1937-) Amer; sclp
ART-RITE no.9 18 (statement)
FINE 265-267 (statements; o.p. 1970, 1971); 2 ill

EDWARDS, Roger ( ) Amer; sclp
ARTPARK 1975 70-71 (statement); port; 6 ill

EDWARDS, Wendy (1950-) Amer; ptr
TEXAS 4-7 (statement); 9 ill

EDWIN (Edwin F. Bryson) (1930-) Cana/Mexi; ptr
DICCIONARIO v.3 379-381 (statement); port; 1 ill

EESTEREN, Cornelis van ( ) arch
BANN 115-118 (essay: "Toward a Collective Construction," o.p. 1924); port
CONRADS 67 ("Toward Collective Building," o.p. 1923)

EGAS, Eric ( ) Amer; instal
ARTPARK 1982 32-35, 47 (statement); port; 5 ill

EGELIUS, Mats ( ) arch
MIKELLIDES 134-148 (essay: "Housing and Human Needs: the Work of Ralph Erskine")

EGGENSCHWILER, Franz (1930-) Swis; envir, sclp
KORNFELD 10-13 (statement); port; 7 ill
SKIRA 1979 107 (statement); 1 ill

EGIDO, Melquiades ( ) Mexi; ptr
DICCIONARIO v.3 383-385 (statement); port; 1 ill

EGINTON, Meg ( ) perf
LIVE no.6/7 73-76 (interview); port

EGLESTON, Truman (1931-) Amer; ptr
BOSTON III (interview); 1 ill

EGLOFF, Frank (1948-) Amer; ptr
BOSTON I (interview); 1 ill
BOSTON III (interview); 1 ill

EGNER, John (1940-) Amer; sclp
SHEARER 24-27 (interview); 3 ill

EGRI, Ted (1913-) Amer; ptr
ILLINOIS 1952 187-188 (statement); 1 ill
ILLINOIS 1953 178-179 (statement); 1 ill
ILLINOIS 1955 194-195 (statement); 1 ill
ILLINOIS 1961 64 (response); port; 1 ill

EGURROLA MINAUR, Agustina
F. (1923-) Mexi; ptr
DICCIONARIO v.3 387-389 (statement);
port; 1 ill

EHM, Josef (1909-) Czec; photo
WALSH 219-221 (statement); 1 ill

EHRENBERG, Felipe (1943-) Mexi; ptr
DICCIONARIO v.3 391-393 (statement);
port; 1 ill

EHRENKRANTZ, Ezra D. (1933-)
Amer; arch
KEPES IV 118-127 (essay: "Modular
Materials and Design Flexibility")

EHRENZWEIG, Anton ( ) Aust/Brit; ptr
ART AND ARTIST 33-52 (essay: "The
Mastering of Creative Anxiety"); 1 ill

EINS, Stefan ( )
SEE: FASHION MODA

EINSEL, Naiad ( ) design, illus, sclp
NORTH LIGHT 66-71 (statement); port;
13 ill

EINSEL, Walter ( ) Amer; sclp
ILLUSTRATION 32-39 (statement); port;
6 ill

EINSTEIN, William ( ) ptr
ABSTRACTION no.1 10 (statement); 2
ill

EISENMAN, Peter D. (1932-) Amer;
arch

ARCHER 54-57, 96 (statement); port; 6
ill
EMANUEL I 229-232 (statement); 1 ill
ON SITE no.4 41-44 ("Notes on
Conceptual Architecture"); 4 ill
RUSSELL F 91-93 (project proposal); 6
ill

EISENSTADT, Alfred (1898-)
Germ/Amer; photo
DIAMONSTEIN III 39-54 (interview); 8 ill

EK, Bo (1924-) sclp
KINETISCHE (statement); 1 ill

EKKS, Robert Rasmussen (Redd) (1937-
) Amer; perf
GUMPERT I 40 (statement); port

ELDRED, Charles J. (1938-) Amer; illus,
sclp
NOSANOW 54-55 (statement); 5 ill

ELDRED, Dale (1934-) Amer; light
PRADEL 32-33 (statement, o.p. 1982);
12 ill

ELENES, Laura ( ) Mexi; ptr
DICCIONARIO v.3 395-397 (statement);
port; 1 ill

ELETA, Sandra (1942-) Pana; photo
WALSH 222-223 (statement); 1 ill

ELIAS, Etienne (1936-) Belg; ptr
NAYLOR 276-277 (statement); self port

ELISOFON, Eliot (1911-1973) Amer;
photo, ptr
TIME-LIFE II 96-97 (statement); 2 ill

ELIZONDO, Evangelina (1929-) Mexi;
ptr
DICCIONARIO v.3 399-401 (statement);
port; 1 ill

ELK, Ger van (1941-) Dutc; photo, ptr, sclp
ARTIST AND CAMERA 28-29 (interview with Gijs van Tuyl, o.p. 1976); 3 ill
CELANT 67-72 (statement); 5 ill
REFLECTION 10-13 (interview); 6 ill

ELLER, Evelyn S. (1933-) Amer; coll, ptr
FULBRIGHT 23 (statement)

ELLIOTT, Julian (1928-) SoAf; arch
EMANUEL I 232-233 (statement); 1 ill

ELLIOTT, Lester ( ) Amer; ptr
ART VOICES v.4 no.1 82-83 (interview); port

ELLIS, Dean ( ) Amer; illus, ptr
NORTH LIGHT 72-77 (statement); ports; 6 ill

ELLIS, Rennie (1940-) Atrl; photo
WALSH 223-224 (statement); 1 ill

ELLIS, Robert (1922-) Amer; ptr
CALIFORNIA--PAINTING 36 (statement); 1 ill

ELLWOOD, Craig (1922-) Amer; arch
EMANUEL I 233-234 (statement); 1 ill

ELLWOOD, Craig (1922-) arch
HEYER 146-156 (interview); 16 ill

EL' NIGOUMI, Siddig A. (1931-) pott
CAMERON 118-125 (response); 10 ill

ELORDUY, Hortensia (1947-) Mexi; ptr
DICCIONARIO v.3 403-405 (statement); port; 1 ill

ELOUL, Kosso
SEE: KOSSO

ELSHIN, Jacob A. (1892-) Russ/Amer; ptr
ILLINOIS 1952 188-189 (statement)

ELSKEN, Edward van der (1925-) Dutc; photo
WALSH 780 (statement); 1 ill

ELSKUS, Albinas ( ) Amer; glass
HAYSTACK 19 (statement); 1 ill

ELTZBACHER ( ) ptr
ABSTRACTION no.2 11-12 (statement); 2 ill

EMBREE, Lea (1934-) Amer; pott
HERMAN 49 (statement); port; 1 ill

EMERIC ( )
DEMARNE 212-215 (interview)

EMIGHOLZ, Heinz (1948-) film
KUNST BLEIBT KUNST 388-389 (statement); 1 ill

EMSHWILLER, Ed ( ) video
DAVIS 53-57 (statement: "Image Maker Meets Video, or, Psyche to Physics and Back")

ENARD, Andre (1926-) Fren
PREMIER BILAN 291 (statement); port

ENGEL, Harry (1901-) Amer; ptr
ILLINOIS 1955 195-196 (statement); 1 ill

ENGELS, Pieter Gerardus Maria (1938-) Dutc; ptr
NAYLOR 277-278 (statement); 1 ill

ENGLAND, Richard (1937-) Malt; arch
EMANUEL I 234-236 (statement); 1 ill

ENGMAN, Robert (1927-) Amer; sclp
ROSNER 343-354 (interview); port

STRUCTURED (statement); 3 ill

ENGSTROM, Deirdre ( ) Amer; coll
IRVINE 27, 79 (statement); 1 ill

ENO, Brian (1948-) Brit; perf, sound
STEDELIJK 118 (statement, o.p. 1981);
1 ill

ENOS, Chris (1944-) Amer; photo
BOSTON III (interview); 1 ill

ENRIQUE (Mondragon) (1947-) Mexi;
ptr
DICCIONARIO v.3 407-409 (statement);
port; 1 ill

ENRIQUEZ ROCHA, Luis Fernando
(1950-) Mexi; ptr

ENSOR, James (1860-1949) Belg; ptr
CHIPP 110-111 (extract from the
Preface to his collected writings, o.p.
1921)
CHIPP 111-112 (extract from talk given
in 1923); 1 ill
CHIPP 112-114 (extract from talk given
in 1932); 1 ill
DUNOYER (manuscript: "Sur La
Beaute des Dunes"); 1 ill
GOLDWATER 387 (statement, 1915)
PROTTER 167-168 ("Reflections on
Art," o.p. 1922)

ENTE, Lily (1905-) Russ/Amer; sclp,
print
ILLINOIS 1957 196 (response); 1 ill

ENVAS, Tom (1943-) Amer; ptr
GUMPERT II 8-11, 30 (statement); port;
6 ill

EPP, William Harold (1930-) Cana; sclp
CANADA 26-27 (statement); port; 2 ill

EPSTEIN, Dave ( ) Amer; sclp
ILLUSTRATION 70-71 (statement); port;
2 ill

EPSTEIN, Jacob (1880-1959) Brit; sclp,
ptr
GOLDWATER 462-465 (statements,
1931, 1940); 1 ill
OPEN AIR 1954 (statement)

EPTING, Marion (1940-) Amer; print
LEWIS I REVISED 117-118 (statement);
port; 3 ill

EQUIPO CRONICA (group: Rafael
Solbes and Manuel Valdes) Span; ptr
KUNST UND POLITIK (statement); 5 ill
SKIRA 1978 62 (statement); 1 ill

EQUIPO REALIDAD (Jorge Valencia
Ballester Bonilla) Span; ptr
SKIRA 1978 62 (statement); 1 ill

ERBEN, Ulrich (1940-) Germ; ptr,
photo, coll
SKIRA 1976 70 (statement); 1 ill
SKIRA 1978 115 (statement); 1 ill
SKIRA 1980 58 (statement); 4 ill

ERICKSON, Arthur (1924-) Cana; arch
CANADIAN 48-51 (statement); 5 ill
EMANUEL I 236-238 (statement); 1 ill
GA HOUSES no.2 110-145 (statement);
74 ill

ERIKA (Erika Schedel Schauwecker)
(1898-) Germ/Mexi;ptr
DICCIONARIO v.3 415-417 (statement);
self port; 1 ill

ERIKSON, Joan M. ( ) Amer; design,
metal
KEPES III 50-61 (essay: "Eye to Eye")

ERNI, Hans (1909-) Swis; ptr, print
AXIS no.2 27-28 (essay: "The Lucerne Exhibition")

ERNST, Jimmy (1920-) Germ/Amer; ptr
ART NOW v.4 no.1 (statement); 1 ill
ILLINOIS 1953 179-180 (statement); 1 ill
ILLINOIS 1961 99 (response); port; 1 ill
ILLINOIS 1963 46 (statement); 1 ill
JANIS I 103 (statement); 1 ill
JOURNAL OF THE AAA v.4 no.1 12-16 (talk: "The Artist and the Wonderful World of International Provincialism," given at the Detroit Institute of Arts, 1963)
JOURNAL OF THE AAA v.4 no.2 10, 12-14 (talk: "The Artist and the Wonderful World of International Provincialism," given at the Detroit Institute of Arts, 1963)
KEPES IX 62-73 (extract from "private communications" with John E. Burchard)
MOTHERWELL 8-22 (three group discussions: "Artists' Sessions at Studio 35," New York, 1950)
NEW DECADE 22-24 (statement); 2 ill
PERSONAL (statement)

ERNST, Max (1891-1976); Germ; ptr, print
ART SINCE v.2 153 (statement, o.p. 1959)
CHARBONNIER v.1 29-40 (interview)
CHIPP 427 (essay: "What is the Mechanism of Collage?" o.p. 1936)
CHIPP 428-431 (essay: "On Frottage," o.p. 1936); port; 1 ill
DUNOYER (poem: "Wieviel Farben Hat Die Hand," handwritten), 2 ill
EVANS 74-79 (essay: "Inspiration to Order"); 3 ill
FORD/VIEW v.1 no.7/8 "poetry supplement" 3 ("The Hundred Headless Woman")

FORD/VIEW v.2 no.1 28-30 (essay: "Some Data on the Youth of Max Ernst, as Told by Himself," o.p. 1948); ports
GOLDAINE 43-45 (interview); port
GROHMANN 428-429 ("Autobiographisches," p.p. 1948)
GUGGENHEIM II 139-142 (essay: "Inspiration to Order," 1932)
JANIS I 136 (statement); 1 ill
DEMARNE 34-36 (radio interview, 1950)
JEAN 78 (extract from poem: "Arp," o.p. 1921)
JEAN 264-265 ("Danger of Pollution," o.p. 1931)
JEAN 271-272 ("Inspiration to Order," o.p. 1933)
JEAN 334-335 ("The Mysteries of the Forest," o.p. 1934)
JEAN 401-403 (essay: "Some Data on the Youth of Max Ernst as Told by Himself," o.p. 1948)
JEAN 410-411 (extract from interview with James Johnson Sweeney, o.p. 1946)
LIPPARD 118-134 (essay: "Beyond Painting," o.p. 1937)
LIPPARD 134-137 (essay: "What Is Surrealism?" o.p. 1934)
LIPPARD 138-140 ("Dream of a Little Girl Who Wanted to Become a Carmelite: Preface," o.p. 1930)
MINOTAURE no.5 6-7 ("Les Mysteres de la Foret"); 3 ill
PLASTIQUE no.4 2-6 (story: "L'Homme Qui a Perdu Son Squelette," with Marcel Duchamp, Jean Arp, et al.)
PLASTIQUE no.5 2-9 (story: "L'Homme Qui a Perdu Son Squelette," with Marcel Duchamp, Jean Arp, Leonora Carrington, et al.)
PLATSCHEK 84-85 ("Lisbeth," 1920)
PLATSCHEK 87-91 ("Visionen Im Halbschlaf," 1927)

PLATSCHEK 92-93 ("Tag und Nachtgleich"); 3 ill
REVOLUTION SURREALISTE no.9/10 7 ("Visions de Demi-Sommeil")
REVOLUTION SURREALISTE no.12 65, 72 ("Enquete")
SEGHERS 216-222 (extract from *Beyond Painting and Other Writings*, 1948)
SKIRA 1975 63 (extract from interview with Robert Lebel, 1969); 1 ill
SURREALISME no.3 22-25 ("Danger de Pollution")
SURREALISME no.6 43-45 ("Comment on Force L'Inspiration")
WHELDON 160-167 (interview with Roland Penrose); port

ERNST, Wolfgang ( )
GROH (statement); 3 ill

ERRO (Gudmundur Gudmundsson) (1932-) Icel; ptr
EMANUEL II 289-290 (statement); 1 ill
KUNST UND POLITIK (statement); port; 4 ill
SKIRA 1976 65 (statement); 1 ill
SKIRA 1978 62 (statement); 1 ill

ERSKINE, Ralph (1914-) Brit; arch
NEWMAN 60-63, 182 (group discussion)
NEWMAN 160-169 (essay: "The Sub-Arctic Habitat"); 2 ill
RUSSELL F 44-47 (project proposal); 8 ill

ERWITT, Elliott (1928-) Amer; photo
BOOTH 90-99 (interview); port; 7 ill
CAMPBELL 102-111 (statement); port; 12 ill
DANZIGER 78-95 (interview); port 79; 3 ill
DIAMONSTEIN III 55-66 (interview); 7 ill

ERY (Ery Camara) (1952-) Vene; ptr

DICCIONARIO v.3 419-421 (statement); port; 1 ill

ESCARZAGA, Irma Graciela (1932-) Mexi; ptr
DICCIONARIO v.3 423-425 (statement); port; 1 ill

ESCOBAR, Marisol
SEE: MARISOL

ESCOBAR LEON, Carlos (1914-) Mexi; ptr
DICCIONARIO v.3 427-429 (statement); port; 1 ill

ESCOBEDO, Helen (1934-) Mexi; ptr
DICCIONARIO v.3 431-433 (statement); port; 1 ill

ESCUTIA, Manuel Luis (1940-) Mexi; ptr
DICCIONARIO v.3 435-437 (statement); port; 1 ill

ESHERICK, Joseph (1914-) Amer; arch
EMANUEL I 241-243 (statement); 1 ill
HEYER 110-116 (interview); 11 ill

ESHOO, Robert (1926-) Amer; ptr
ILLINOIS 1957 198 (response); 1 ill

ESPADAS REYES ESPINDOLA, Rafael (1934-) Mexi; ptr
DICCIONARIO v.3 439-441 (statement); port; 1 ill

ESPANA SANTIAGO, Miguel Angel (1943-) Mexi; ptr
DICCIONARIO v.3 443-445 (statement); port; 1 ill

ESPARZA LOPEZ, Tomas (1941-) Mexi; ptr

DICCIONARIO v.3 451-453 (statement); port; 1 ill

ESPINOSA CARRIZALES, Jorge (1942-) Mexi; ptr
DICCIONARIO v.3 455-457 (statement); port; 1 ill

ESPOSITO, Enzo (1946-) Ital; photo
SKIRA 1978 61 (statement); 1 ill

ESQUEDA, Xavier (1943-) Mexi; ptr
DICCIONARIO v.3 459-461 (statement); port; 1 ill

ESQUENAZI, Becky Levy de ( ) Mexi; ptr
DICCIONARIO v.3 463-465 (statement); port; 1 ill

ESQUIVEL, Carmen Alcocer de (1937-) Mexi; ptr
DICCIONARIO v.3 467-469 (statement); port; 1 ill

ESQUIVEL HERNANDEZ, Carlos (1938-) Mexi; ptr
DICCIONARIO v.3 471-473 (statement); port; 1 ill

ESTEBAN (Esteban Garcia Rodriguez) (1924-1977) Mexi; ptr
DICCIONARIO v.3 475-477 (statement); port; 1 ill

ESTERE, Maurice (1904-)
GOLDAINE 160-163 (interview); port

ESTES, Richard (1936-) Amer; ptr
JOHNSON 146-151 (interview with Linda Chase and Ted McBurnett, o.p. 1972); 1 ill
SUPERREAL 126-127 (statement); 1 ill
VAN DER MARCK 48-49 (statement); 1 ill

ESTEVES, Sandra Maria ( ) ptr
CHRYSALIS no.7 37 (poem: ■For Tulani,■ o.p. 1978)
DICCIONARIO v.3 487-489 (statement); port; 1 ill

ESTRADA, Aurora (1940-) Mexi; ptr, print
DICCIONARIO v.3 483-485 (statement); port; 1 ill

ESTRADA, Enrique (1942-) Mexi; ptr
ETNIER, Stephen M. (1903-) Amer; ptr
BETHERS II 78-79 (statement); 2 ill
ILLINOIS 1951 173-174 (statement)
ILLINOIS 1957 198-199 (response); 1 ill

ETROG, Sorel (1933-) Ruma/Cana; sclp, ptr, print
ART VOICES v.2 no.4 20 (statement); port; 1 ill
CANADA 76-77 (statement); port; 2 ill

EULALIA (1946-) Span; photo
SKIRA 1978 65 (statement); 8 ill

EURICH, Richard (1903-) Brit; ptr
CONTEMPORARY (statement); port; 2 ill

EUSTON, Andrew F. ( ) Amer; arch
COOPER-HEWITT I 96-97 (essay: ■Urban Environmental Design■)

EVANS, Chuck ( ) Amer; metal
METALWORKS (statement); 1 ill

EVANS, Dennis ( ) Amer; perf, envir
GUENTHER 40-41 (statement); port; 1 ill

EVANS, Dick (1941-) Amer; pott, sclp
HERMAN 50 (statement); port; 1 ill
WISCONSIN II (statement); 1 ill

EVANS, Garth (1934-) Brit; sclp
ALLEY (statement); 1 ill
HAYWARD 1979 115-116, 120-123 (interview with David Robson); port; 9 ill

EVANS, Leslie (1945-) Brit; ptr
SEE: BOYD AND EVANS

EVANS, Minnie (1883/92-) Amer; ptr, coll
SYMBOLS (statement); 1 ill

EVANS, Susan S. (1952-) Amer; pott
WISCONSIN II (statement); 1 ill

EVANS, Walker (1903-1975) Amer; photo
CUMMINGS 82-100 (interview, 1971); port; 2 ill

EVERGOOD, Philip (1901-1973) Amer; ptr
ART VOICES v.2 no.10 8-9 (interview with Gordon Brown); port; 4 ill
BRITANNICA 39 (statement); port; 1 ill
FIFTY (statement); port; 1 ill
FORTY (statement); 2 ill
ILLINOIS 1951 174-175 (statement)
ILLINOIS 1953 180-181 (statement); 1 ill
ILLINOIS 1955 196-197 (statement); 1 ill
ILLINOIS 1961 160-161 (response); port; 1 ill
ILLINOIS 1965 139 (statement); 1 ill
M.H. DE YOUNG 51-52 (response); self port
PROTTER 235-236 (statements, 1961, 1963)

EVERSLEY, Frederick (1941-) Amer; sclp
ART AND TECHNOLOGY 101 (project proposal)

EVERTS, Connor (1928-) Amer; illus, ptr
CALIFORNIA--DRAWING (statement); 2 ill
CALIFORNIA--PAINTING 37 (statement); 1 ill

EVESONG, Saribenne ( )
PHILLPOT (statement)

EVETT, Kenneth W. (1913-) Amer; ptr
ILLINOIS 1951 175 (statement); 1 ill
NOSANOW 57 (statement); 1 ill
RISENHOOVER 53-67

EWING, C. Kermit (1910-) Amer; ptr
KNOXVILLE (statement); port; 8 ill

EWING, Edgar (1913-) Amer; ptr
CALIFORNIA--PAINTING 15 (statement); 1 ill
ILLINOIS 1957 200-201 (response); 1 ill
ILLINOIS 1961 70 (response); port; 1 ill
ILLINOIS 1963 89 (statement); 1 ill

EWING, Lauren (1946-) Amer; film, sclp, envir
FOX 52-57 (statement); 7 ill
GUMPERT IV 24-27, 42 (statement); port; 6 ill

EXPORT, Valie (1940-) Aust; perf
SKIRA 1978 41 (statement); 2 ill
SKIRA 1980 114 (statement); 4 ill

EYTON, Anthony (1923-) Brit; ptr
CONTEMPORARY (statement); port; 2 ill

FABERT, Jacques (1925-) Amer; ptr
ILLINOIS 1969 49 (statement); 1 ill

FABIAN-SANCHEZ (1935-) ptr
SEE: SANCHEZ, Fabian

FABIO, Cyril (1921-) Amer; sclp
LEWIS II 104 (statement); port; 1 ill

FABRE, Karmen (1929-) Mexi; ptr
DICCIONARIO v.3 495-497 (statement);
port; 1 ill

FABRI, Stella Maris (1943-) Mexi; ptr
DICCIONARIO v.3 491-493 (statement);
port; 1 ill

FABRIS LUNA, Vicente (1929-) Mexi;
ptr
DICCIONARIO v.3 499-501 (statement);
port; 1 ill

FABRO, Luciano (1936-) Ital; sclp,
photo
SKIRA 1976 17 (statement); 1 ill

FACIO, Sara (1932-) Arge; photo
WALSH 231-232 (statement); 1 ill

FAGER, Charles (1936-) Amer; pott
HERMAN 51 (statement); port; 1 ill

FAHLEN, Charles (1939-) Amer; sclp,
envir
ARTPARK 1976 146-147 (statement);
port; 4 ill

FAHLSTROM, Oyvind (1928-1976)
Braz/Amer; ptr, sclp, perf
ART AND TECHNOLOGY 102-113
(project proposal); 17 ill
ART SINCE v.2 328 (statement, o.p.
1969)
ARTFORUM v.5 no.6 27 (statement)

ARTS YEARBOOK v.9 83, 86 (response);
1 ill
DIRECTIONS I 76 (response); 1 ill
NAYLOR 288-289 (statement); 1 ill
RUSSELL J 66-68 (essay: "Jime Dine,"
o.p. 1963)
RUSSELL J 68-71 (essay: "Take Care
of the World")
TRACKS v.1 no.2 43-52 ("The Black
Room, a theatre play")
TRACKS v.1 no.3 52-73 ("The Black
Room, a theatre play" part 2)
TRACKS v.2 no.1 59-73 ("The Black
Room, a theatre play")

FAHRENHOLZ, Chr. ( ) Germ; arch
NEWMAN 64-67 (essay); 12 ill

FAHS, Phil ( ) Amer; photo
CALIFORNIA--PHOTOGRAPHY
(statement); port; 4 ill

FALANA, Kenneth (1940-) Amer; ptr,
print
LEWIS II 36 (statement); port; 1 ill

FALCON GARZA, Adolfo (1942-) Mexi;
ptr
DICCIONARIO v.3 503-505 (statement);
port; 1 ill

FALCONER, H. Ricardo (1944-) Mexi;
ptr, print
DICCIONARIO v.3 507-509 (statement);
port; 1 ill

FALCONI VERA, Leonel (1905-)Mexi;
ptr
DICCIONARIO v.3 511-513 (statement);
port; 1 ill

FALK, Gathie (1928-) Cana; sclp, perf,
instal
GRAHAM 25-40 (statement); 18 ill
POINT OF VIEW 11 (statement); 1 ill

FALKENSTEIN, Claire (1909-) Amer; sclp, ptr
HOPKINS 98-99 (statement); port; 1 ill

FALLEMBAUM DE GATENO, Toni (1950-) Pana/Mexi; ptr
DICCIONARIO v.3 519-521 (statement); port; 1 ill

FANGOR, Wojciech (Vox) (1922-) Poli/Amer; ptr
ART NOW v.2 no.8 (statement); 1 ill
EMANUEL II 297 (statement)
NAYLOR 289-290 (statement); 1 ill

FANTI, Lucio (1946-) Ital; ptr
KUNST UND POLITIK (statement); port; 3 ill

FANTINA (Fantina Caballero de Lasso de la Vega) (1931-) Mexi; ptr
DICCIONARIO v.3 523-525 (statement); port; 1 ill

FARINA, Ralston (1948-) Amer; perf
BRENTANO 192-193 (statement); 1 ill
PERFORMANCE no.1 24-28 (interview)

FARNSWORTH, Donald ( ) paper
VISUAL v.2 no.2 33-35 (interview); port
VISUAL v.3 no.4 40-41 (essay: "Technical Information"); port

FARNSWORTH, Jerry (1895-) Amer; ptr
BRITANNICA 40 (statement); port; 1 ill
M. H. DE YOUNG 53 (response); self port

FARR, Fred (1914-1973) Amer; sclp
ILLINOIS 1959 213 (statement); 1 ill

FARRELL, Michael (1945-) Iris; print, ptr, instal
KNOWLES 54-57, 111 (statement); 5 ill

FARRER, Julia (1950-) Brit; illus
HAYWARD 1978 54-57 (statement); 4 ill

FARRUGGIO, Remo M. (1906-) Ital/Amer; ptr
ILLINOIS 1957 201 (response); 1 ill

FASHION MODA (group)
REALLIFE no.3 7-9 (interview with Thomas Lawson)

FAUCON, Bernard (1950-) Fren; photo
IN SITU 61-71 (statement); port; 6 ill
WALSH 232-233 (statement)

FAULKNER, Frank (1946-) Amer; ptr
ART PATRON ART 27-28 (statement); port; 1 ill
SOUTHEAST (statement); port; 6 ill
TRANSPERSONAL 40-49 (statement); port; 4 ill

FAUSETT, William Dean (1913-) Amer; ptr, print
BETHERS II 80-81 (statement); 2 ill

FAUTRIER, Jean (1898-1964) Fren; ptr
ART SINCE v.1 154 (statement, o.p. 1960)
CLAUS 128-132 (statement)
GOLDAINE 106-108 (interview); port
VINGTIEME N.S. no.9 30-31 (statement); 2 ill

FAVRO, Murray (1940-) Cana; sclp, ptr
KUNST BLEIBT KUNST 194-197 (statement); 5 ill

FAWCETT, Robert (1903-1967) Brit/Amer; ptr
GUITAR 78-87 (interview); port; 4 ill

FAWKES, Judith Poxson ( ) Amer; text
FIBER 30-31 (statement); 1 ill

FAY, Joe (1950-) Amer; print, ptr
DOWNTOWN (statement); 1 ill

FEARING, Kelly (1918-) Amer; ptr
ILLINOIS 1955 197-198 (statement); 1 ill
ILLINOIS 1963 97 (statement); 1 ill

FEATHERSTON, William (1927-) Cana;
sclp
CANADA 48-49 (statement); port; 2 ill

FEDERIGHI, Christine ( ) Amer; pott
VIEWPOINT 1981 (statement); 3 ill

FEDERLE, Helmut (1944-) Swis; ptr,
illus
SKIRA 1979 75-76 (statement); 1 ill

FEELINGS, Thomas (1933-) Amer; ptr,
illus
LEWIS II 111 (statement); port; 2 ill

FEHER, Joseph (1908-) Hung/Amer; ptr
HAAR II 8-13 (interview); ports; 3 ill

FEHN, Sverre (1924-) Norw; arch
EMANUEL I 245-246 (statement); 1 ill

FEICHTMEIR, Kurt ( )
CRISS-CROSS   no.7/8/9   96-99
("Temporal Relativity"); 7 ill

FEIGENBAUM, Harriet (1939-) Amer;
sclp, envir
ARTPARK 1977 31-34 (statement); 5 ill

FEILDEN, Bernard Melchior (1919-)
Brit; arch
EMANUEL I 246-248 (statement); 1 ill

FEIN, Sherry Karver ( ) Amer; pott
VIEWPOINT 1980 10-11 (statement); 4
ill

FEINE, Ernest (1894-) Amer; ptr
ILLINOIS 1950 173 (statement); 1 ill

FEININGER, Andreas (1906-) Fren;
photo
WALSH 233-235 (statement); 1 ill

FEININGER, Lyonel (1871-1956) Amer;
print, ptr
GROHMANN   411-413   ("Brief,"   p.p.
1931)
M. H. DE YOUNG 54 (response); self port
POENSGEN 86 (statement)
PROTTER 185-186 (letters, 1905, 1906,
1907, 1914); 1 ill
SCHMIDT 74-76, 109, 164 (letters, 1935,
1936, 1937, 1942)
WINGLER   94-95   (letter   to   Georg
Muche)

FEITELSON, Lorser (1898-1978) Amer;
ptr
ARTFORUM v.1 no.2 20-25 (group
discussion); port
CALIFORNIA--PAINTING 16 (statement);
1 ill
ILLINOIS 1950 173 (statement); 1 ill
ILLINOIS 1951 176 (statement); 1 ill
ILLINOIS 1965 48 (statement); 1 ill

FEKNER, John ( ) Amer; ptr, envir
GUMPERT II 12-15, 31 (statement);
port; 9 ill

FELDMAN, Bella Tabak (1930-) Amer;
sclp
FRYM 86-102 (interview); port

FELL, Sheila (1931-) Brit; ptr
CONTEMPORARY (statement); port; 2
ill

FENICCHIA, Concetta (1949-) Amer;
pott
HERMAN 52 (statement); port; 1 ill

FENOSA, Apelles (1899-) Span; sclp
PORCEL I 19-28 (interview); ports

FENSTER, Fred (1934-) Amer; metal
METALWORKS (statement); 1 ill
WISCONSIN I (statement); 1 ill

FENTON, Julia Ann (1937-) Amer
AVANT-GARDE 18-19 (text piece)

FENZI, Warren S. (1947-) Amer; wood
WOODWORKING 18-19 (statement);
port; 2 ill

FERBER, Herbert (1906-) Amer; sclp
ART NOW v.3 no.1 (statement); 1 ill
CHIPP 554-555 (essay: *On
Sculpture,* o.p. 1954)
CHIPP 566 (statement, o.p. 1951)
IT IS no.6 7-16, 57-64, 73-75 (group
discussion)
MILLER 1952 10-11 (statement); 2 ill
MOTHERWELL 8-22 (three group
discussions: *Artists' Sessions at
Studio 35,* New York, 1950)
TIGER no.2 44 (statement)
TIGER no.4 75-76, 103 (essay: *On
Sculpture and Painting*); 1 ill

FERGUSON, Ken (1920-) Amer; pott
HERMAN 53 (statement); port; 1 ill

FERGUSON, Steve (1946-) Amer; ptr
NOSANOW I 58 (poem); 1 ill

FERNANDEZ, ( ) ptr
ABSTRACTION no.2 14-15 (statement);
2 ill

FERNBACH-FLARSHEIM, Carl ( )
GROH (statement)
MEYER 122-125 (text piece)

FERNIE, John Chipman (1945-) Amer;
photo, coll

CRISS-CROSS no.3 36-37 (statement); 2
ill
NAYLOR 293-294 (statement); 1 ill
TRACKS v.3 no.3 10-12 (*22 January
1977*)
TRACKS v.3 no.3 13-14 (*From
Journals (1974)*)

FERRANDINI, Robert (1948-) Amer;
ptr
BOSTON I (interview); 1 ill

FERRARA, Jackie ( ) Amer; sclp
HOUSE 46-47 (statement); 1 ill

FERRARI, Virginio (1937-) Ital/Amer;
sclp
ILLINOIS 1969 84 (statement); 1 ill

FERREN, John (1905-1970) Amer; sclp,
ptr
ART NOW v.1 no.5 (statement); 1 ill
ART VOICES v.4 no.2 91 (statement); 1
ill
CHIPP 573-574 (essay: *Epitaph for an
Avant-Garde,* o.p. 1958)
FORTY (statement); 2 ill
IT IS no.1 45 (statement)
IT IS no.2 12 (*On Innocence in
Abstract Painting*)
JANIS I 73 (statement); 1 ill
ROSE II 135-138 (extract from essay:
*Epitaph for an Avant-Garde,*o.p.
1958)

FERRER, Rafael (1933-) Puer; sclp
FINCH COLLEGE (statement); port; 1 ill
SKIRA 1978 31 (statement); 1 ill

FICHTER, Robert Whitten (1939-)
Amer; photo
GUMPERT III 62-63 (statement)
WALSH 236-237 (statement); 1 ill

FICHTER, Toma ( )
PHILLPOT (poem)

FIELDS, Mitchell (1900-) Amer; sclp
100 CONTEMPORARY 46-47 (statement); port; 1 ill

FIENE, Ernest (1894-1965) Germ/Amer; ptr
BRITANNICA 41 (statement); port; 1 ill
GUITAR 88-97 (interview); port; 4 ill
ILLINOIS 1951 176-177 (statement); 1 ill

FIFIELD, Mary L. (1946-) Amer; ptr, design
VISUAL v.2 no.3 34-37 (essay: "Affirmative Action in Academia: An Unfulfilled Promise"); 1 ill

FIGUEROA FLORES, Gabriel (1952-) Mexi; photo
WALSH 237-238 (statement); 1 ill

FIKE, Felice (1947-) Amer; photo
ARTISTS no.3 10-11 ("An Invested Interest in Photography")

FILGUEIRAS LIMA, Joao (1932-) Braz; arch
EMANUEL I 249-251 (statement); 1 ill

FILIGER, Charles (1863-1953)
DUNOYER (letter, c.1910); 1 ill

FILIPOVIC, Franjo (1930-) Yugo; ptr
TOMASEVIC 76-79 (statement); port; 2 ill

FILIPPOV, Alexei Vasilevich (1882-1956) Russ
BANN 22-25 (essay: "Production Art," o.p. 1921)

FILKO, Stano (1937-) Czec; instal, sclp
NAYLOR 294-295 (statement); 1 ill

FILLION, John (1933-) Cana; sclp
CANADA 106-107 (statement); port; 2 ill

FILLIOU, Robert (1926-) Fren; sclp
ADLERS 11-15 (interview); 4 ill

FILLON, Jacques ( ) arch
CONRADS 155 ("New Games!," o.p. 1954)

FILMUS, Tully (1908-) Amer; ptr
100 CONTEMPORARY 48-49 (statement); port; 1 ill

FILO, John ( ) Amer; photo
LEEKLEY 78-79 (statement); 1 ill

FILONOV, Pavel (1883-1941) Russ; ptr
BOWLT 284-287 (extract from essay: "Ideology of Analytical Art," o.p. 1930); 2 ill

FILSON, Ron ( ) Amer; arch
GA HOUSES no.7 128-131 (essay: "Charles Moore and Company Evolution"); port

FIMA (1916-) Isra; ptr
SEITZ I (statement); 2 ill

FINCH, Keith Bruce (1920-) Amer; ptr
CALIFORNIA--PAINTING 17 (statement); 1 ill

FINCHER, Terry ( ) Brit; photo
HOW FAMOUS 66-71 (statements); port; 8 ill

FINDLAY, Kathryn (1953-) Scot; arch
SPIRIT 38-43 (statement); 5 ill

FINDS, Dudley ( )
AVALANCHE no.8 74 (interview); 2 ill

FINE, A. M. ( )
TRACKS v.1 no.3 50-51 (poem: "Chamber Music")

FINE, Jud (1944-) Amer; sclp
NAYLOR 296-297 (statement); 1 ill
TRACKS v.2 no.2 46-49 ("Discourse, A Parody")

FINE, Perle (1908-) Amer; ptr
ILLINOIS 1951 177-178 (statement); 1 ill
IT IS no.2 14 (statement)
SCHAPIRO 20 (statement); port; 1 ill

FINI, Leonor (1908-) Arge/Ital; ptr
ART VOICES v.2 no.10 20-21 (interview with Edouard Roditi); port; 2 ill
GOLDAINE 186-188 (interview); port
NAYLOR 297-299 (statement); 1 ill

FINK, Aaron (1955-) Amer; ptr
BOSTON I (interview); 1 ill
BOSTON III (interview); 1 ill

FINK, Shirley (1932-) Amer; text
FIBER 48-49 (statement); 1 ill

FINKEL, Alan ( ) Amer; sclp, envir
ARTPARK 1981 (statement); port; 2 ill

FINKELSTEIN, Louis (1923-) Amer; ptr
CHIPP 572-573 (essay: "New Look: Abstract-Impressionism," o.p. 1956)
FULBRIGHT 23-24 (statement); 1 ill

FINLAY, Ian Hamilton (1925-) Brit; sclp
CONTEMPORARY (statement); port; 2 ill
SKIRA 1978 85 (statement); 1 ill
SKIRA 1980 98 (statement); 3 ill

FINSTERLIN, Herman (1887-) arch
CONRADS 83-86 ("Casa Nova," o.p. 1924)

FIORE, Joseph A. (1925-) Amer; ptr
ILLINOIS 1961 106 (response); port; 1 ill

FIORINI, William R. (1942-) Amer; metal
WISCONSIN I (statement); 1 ill

FIRST WORKING GROUP OF CONSTRUCTIVISTS (group)
BOWLT 241-243 (statement, o.p. 1924)

FIRST WORKING ORGANIZATION OF ARTISTS (group)
BOWLT 243 ("Basic Tenets," o.p. 1924)

FISCHER, Corey ( ) perf
GRAYSON 150-152 ("Transitions"); port

FISCHER, Herve (1941-) Fren; photo, perf, sclp
NAYLOR 299-301 (statement); 1 ill
PARACHUTE no.5 26-27 (statements, in French and English)
PARACHUTE no.7 25-29 (interview)
SKIRA 1976 20-21 (statement); 3 ill

FISCHER, Sam (1921-) Amer; ptr
FULBRIGHT 23 (statement)

FISCHL, Eric ( ) Amer; ptr
VANCOUVER (statement); 2 ill

FISH, Janet (1938-) Amer; ptr
ARTHUR 68-81 (interview); 21 ill
INTERVIEWS 2 (interview); 1 ill
SUPERREAL 72-73 (statement); 1 ill

FISH, Mary ( ) Amer; ptr
ART-RITE no.14 5, 8 (response)

FISH, Richard (1925-) Amer; ptr, illus
MAGIC 52-55 (statement); port; 3 ill

FISHER, Ethel (1923-) Amer; ptr
VISUAL v.3 no.2 8-11 (interview); port;
4 ill

FISHER, Frederick (1949-) Amer; arch
COUNTERPOINT 36-49 (statement); 27
ill

FISHER, Joel A. (1947-) Amer; ptr, sclp,
instal
AVALANCHE no.10 28-31 (interview);
11 ill
BRENTANO 194-195 (statement); 1 ill
CHOIX 20 (statement, o.p. 1980); 1 ill
EMANUEL II 305-306 (statement)
GEORGIA 21-27 (statement); port; 5 ill
GEORGIA 118-166 (group discussion:
"Artists' Convention," in Athens, GA,
1\7\1977, moderated by Jan van der
Marck)
NAYLOR 301-302 (statement); 1 ill
VIEW v.3 no.4 (interview); port; 12 ill

FISHER, Leonard Everett (1924-) Amer;
ptr, illus
MAGIC 56-59 (statement); port; 6 ill

FISHER, Vernon (1943-) Amer; ptr, coll,
photo
GUMPERT IV 28-31, 43-44 (statement
and text piece); port; 5 ill
MCCLINTIC 44-47 (statement); 4 ill
PAPERWORKS 10-11 (text piece); 4 ill
WHITE WALLS no.2 16-17 ("Dairy
Queen"); 1 ill
WHITE WALLS no.2 18-19 ("Space
Time"); 2 ill
WHITE WALLS no.2 20-21 ("Seashell");
2 ill
WHITE WALLS no.2 22-23 ("Bottles"); 2
ill
WHITE WALLS no.2 24-25 ("Baseball
Cap"); 2 ill
WHITE WALLS no.5 46-47 (text piece)

FISHMAN, Louise (1939-) Amer; ptr
CELEBRATION (statement); 1 ill

FITCH, Steve (1949-) Amer; photo
WALSH 241-242 (statement); 1 ill

FITZGERALD, Tom (1939-) Iris; sclp
KNOWLES 154-155 (statement); 2 ill

FITZGIBBON, Colleen ( ) film
AVALANCHE no.13 11-13 (interview);
port; 4 ill

FITZPATRICK, Jim (1948-) Iris; ptr
KNOWLES 34-35 (statements); 3 ill

FLACK, Audrey (1931-) Amer; ptr
CELEBRATION (statement); 1 ill
IMAGE COLOR FORM 16-17 (statement);
1 ill
JOHNSON 157-160 (extract from
Audrey Flack on Painting, 1981); 1 ill
NEMSER 302-325 (interview); port; 8 ill
SCHAPIRO 21 (statement); port; 1 ill
SUPERREAL 158-159 (statement); 1 ill

FLANAGAN, Barry (1941-) Brit; sclp
CELANT 133-138 (statement); 6 ill
CONTEMPORARY (statement); port; 2
ill
FINCH COLLEGE (statement); port; 4 ill

FLANAGAN, John B. (1895-1942) Amer;
sclp
ROSE II 183 (statement, 1939, o.p.
1965)
ROSE II 183-184 (extract from *Letters
of John B. Flanagan*, o.p. 1942)
ROSE II REVISED 242 (statement, o.p.
1965)
ROSE II REVISED 242-243 (letter, o.p.
1942)

FLANNERY, Vaughn ( ) ptr
BETHERS I 228-229 (statement); 1 ill

FLAVIN, Dan (1933-) Amer; sclp, light, instal
ART AND TECHNOLOGY 114 (project proposal)
ART NOW v.1 no.3 (statement); 1 ill
ARTFORUM v.4 no.4 20-24 (essay: "'...In Daylight or Cool White' an Autobiographical Sketch"); port; 7 ill
ARTFORUM v.5 no.4 27-29 ("Some Remarks...Excerpts from a Spleenish Journal"); 5 ill
ARTFORUM v.6 no.4 20-25 ("Some Other Comments...More Pages from a Spleenish Journal"); 5 ill
ARTFORUM v.6 no.6 4 (letter)
ARTFORUM v.6 no.7 28-32 (essay: "On an American Artist's Education")
ARTFORUM v.7 no.2 4 (letter)
BATTCOCK V 401-402 (statement, o.p. 1967)
CONCEPTUAL ART 48, 57, 59 (statements)
ROSE I 34-42 (statement); 7 ill
ROSE II REVISED 182-183 (statement, o.p. 1969)
ROSE II REVISED 183 (extract from "Some Remarks," o.p. 1966)
SKIRA 1975 44-45 (statement); 1 ill
VARIAN II (extract from "Record" pp. 197-8, 1963); port

FLEISCHMANN, Adolf Richard (1902-1968) Germ/Amer; ptr
ILLINOIS 1955 198-199 (statement)
TEMOIGNAGES I 108-113 (statement); port; 4 ill

FLEISCHMANN, Arthur ( ) Brit; sclp
LONDON COUNTY (statement); 1 ill

FLEISCHNER, Richard (1944-) Amer; envir, sclp
ARTPARK 1976 148-149 (statement); 5 ill

SKIRA 1978 122 (extract from interview with Hugh M. Davies); 2 ill
SKIRA 1980 146 (statement); 4 ill

FLEMING, Dean (1933-) Amer; ptr
ILLINOIS 1967 118 (statement); 1 ill
SYSTEMATIC 23 (statement); 1 ill

FLEMING, Frank (1940-) Amer; pott
NOSANOW I 61 (statement); 1 ill

FLEMING, Linda ( ) sclp
CRISS-CROSS no.5 22-25 (interview with Jalal Quinn); 3 ill

FLEMMONS, Quentin T. (1959-) Amer; wood
CONTEMPORARY AFRICAN (statement); port; 1 ill

FLETCHER, Kenneth ( ) Cana; photo
POINT OF VIEW 59 (statement); 1 ill

FLETCHER, Mikele Egozi (1945-) Amer; print
LEWIS I REVISED 77 (statement); port; 1 ill

FLETCHER, Robin ( ) Brit; photo
HOW FAMOUS 102-105 (statements); port; 5 ill

FLEURY, Claude ( ) Cana; ptr
ROYER 120-126 (interview, 1975)

FLOCH, Joseph (1895-1977) Aust/Amer; ptr
BRITANNICA 42 (statement); port; 1 ill

FLORSHEIM, Lillian ( ) Amer; sclp
ILLINOIS 1967 107 (statement); 1 ill

FLOYD, J. P. Chadwick ( ) arch
GA HOUSES no.13 106-111 (statement); 5 ill

FLYR, Diane (1947-) Amer; pott
HERMAN 55 (statement); port; 1 ill

FOLEY, Marie (1959-) Iris; sclp
KNOWLES 164-165 (extracts from notebook); 4 ill

FOLKARD, Edward (1911-) Brit; sclp
LONDON COUNTY (statement); 1 ill

FOLON, Jean-Michel (1934-) Belg; print
DOUZE ANS 209-211 (statement); port; 5 ill

FONDAW, Ron (1954-) Amer; pott
HERMAN 56 (statement); port; 1 ill

FONTANA, Franco (1933-) Amer; photo
WALSH 242-244 (statement); 1 ill

FONTANA, Lucio (1899-1968) Arge/Ital; ptr, sclp
ART SINCE v.1 160 (statement, o.p. 1946)

FONTCUBERTA, Joan (1955-) Span; photo
WALSH 244-245 (statement); 1 ill

FONTENE, Robert (1892-) Fren; ptr
GRENIER 97-109 (interview)

FOOTE, John, Jr. (1921-1968) Amer; ptr
ILLINOIS 1951 178 (statement); 1 ill

FORAKIS, Peter (1927-) Amer; sclp
ILLINOIS 1967 82 (statement); 1 ill

FORD, Sue (1943-) Atrl; photo
DE GROEN 32-46 (interview); port

FOREMAN, Richard ( )
PERFORMANCE no.1 29-34 ("Auto-Interview"); 7 ill

FOREST, Fred (1933-) Alge/Fren; perf, photo, video
NAYLOR 305-306 (statement); 1 ill
SKIRA 1976 20 (statement); port; 1 ill
SKIRA 1980 93 (statement); port

FORMAN, Alice (1931-) Amer; ptr
YOUNG 1960 (statement); 2 ill

FORMAN, Cecile ( ) ptr
ZAIDENBERG 118-120 (essay: "What Makes a Painting?"); 3 ill

FORMAN, Stan ( ) Amer; photo
LEEKLEY 104-107 (statement); 4 ill

FORRESTER, Jay W. (1918-) Amer; arch
KEPES II 152-166 (essay: "Planning Under the Dynamic Influences of Complex Social Systems")

FORRESTER, Michael ( )
ARTISTS no.4 7-8 (letter)
ARTISTS no.5 2 (letter)

FORRESTER, Patricia Tobacco (1940-) Amer; ptr
SUPERREAL 128-129 (statement); 1 ill

FORT-BRESCIA, Bernardo ( ) arch
GA DOCUMENT no.7 4-14 (interview); port; 6 ill
SEE ALSO: ARQUITECTONICA

FORTESS, Karl E. (1907-) Belg/Amer; ptr
ILLINOIS 1950 174 (statement)
ILLINOIS 1955 199 (statement); 1 ill
ZAIDENBERG 48-52 (essay: "On the Nature of Things or the Things of Nature"); 8 ill

FORTHAL, Barbara ( ) Amer; ptr
IRVINE 70, 85 (statement); 1 ill

FORTI, Simone (1935-) Ital; perf, video
AVALANCHE no.10 20-23 (statement); 15 ill
KUNST BLEIBT KUNST 358-359 (statement); 2 ill
STEDELIJK 122 (statement); 1 ill

FOSS, Oliver (1920-) Amer; ptr
ILLINOIS 1952 190-191 (statement); 1 ill

FOSTER, Norman Robert (1935-) Brit; arch
EMANUEL I 255-256 (statement); 1 ill

FOSTER, Steven Douglas (1945-) Amer; photo
WISCONSIN II (statement); 1 ill

FOUGERON, Andre (1913-) Fren
PREMIER BILAN 292 (statement); port

FOUJITA, Tsougharu (1886-1968) Japa/Fren; ptr, print
ART D'AUJOURD'HUI v.4 13-18 (statement); 19 ill
GOLDAINE 40-42 (interview); port

FOULKES, Llyn (1934-) Amer; ptr, perf
EMANUEL II 310-311 (statement); 1 ill
NAYLOR 307 (statement); 1 ill
SAO PAULO 70-71 (statement); port; 1 ill

FOUR ARTS SOCIETY OF ARTISTS (group)
BOWLT 281-284 ("Declaration," o.p. 1929)

FOWOWE, Moses O. (1947-) Amer; pott
CONTEMPORARY AFRICAN (statement); port; 1 ill

FOX, Lorraine ( ) Amer; ptr, design
FAMOUS v.1 176-177 (statement); 3 ill

FOX, Sandi ( ) Amer; text
DIAMONSTEIN IV 66-79 (interview); port; 12 ill

FOX, Terry (1943-) Amer; sclp, perf, print
AVALANCHE no.2 70-81 (interview); 10 ill
AVALANCHE no.2 96-99 (group discussion)
AVALANCHE no.10 32-33 (interview); 20 ill
VIEW v.2 no.3 (interview); port; 5 ill

FRAAS, Gayle ( ) Amer; sclp
ARTPARK 1980 (statement); 3 ill

FRAME, Robert (1924-) Amer; ptr
ILLINOIS 1957 202-203 (response); 1 ill
ILLINOIS 1961 85 (response); port; 1 ill
ILLINOIS 1965 73 (statement); 1 ill

FRAMPTON, Hollis (1935-) Amer; film, video
BARROW 35-44 (essay: "Meditations Around Paul Strand," o.p. 1972)
DAVIS 24-35 (statement: "The Withering Away of the State of the Art")
KUNST BLEIBT KUNST 390-391 (statement); 1 ill

FRANCAIS, Jacques ( ) Amer; wood
DIAMONSTEIN IV 80-91 (interview); port; 13 ill

FRANCES, Juana (1926-) Span; sclp
NAYLOR 309-310 (statement); 1 ill

FRANCIA, Peter de (1921-) Brit; ptr, illus
CONTEMPORARY (statement); port; 2 ill

FRANCIS, Jean Thickens (1943-) Amer; coll, paper
NOSANOW I 62-63 (statement(; 2 ill

FRANCIS, Ke (1945-) Amer; sclp
NOSANOW I 64 (statement); 1 ill

FRANCIS, Linda ( ) ptr, illus
WHITE WALLS no.6 23-32 (text piece)

FRANCIS, Miriam B. Dixon (1930-) Amer; sclp
FAX II 238-255 (statements); port; 1 ill

FRANCIS, Sam (1923-) Amer; ptr, print
ART SINCE v.1 157 (statements, o.p. 1958, 1962)
ENVIRONMENT 54-55 (statement); 1 ill
HOPKINS 100-101 (statement); port; 1 ill
MOMA 1959 28-31 (statement); port; 3 ill
SCHNEIDER 175-190 (interview); 1 ill
SEUPHOR 174 (statement); 1 ill
VISUAL v.3 no.1 4-8 (interview); port; 2 ill

FRANCK, Martine (1938-) Belg; photo
WALSH 246-247 (statement); 1 ill

FRANCKS, Frederick S. (1909-) Dutc/Amer; ptr
BETHERS II 36-37 (statement); 1 ill
ILLINOIS 1950 174-175 (statement); 1 ill
ILLINOIS 1951 178-179 (statement); 1 ill
ILLINOIS 1952 190-191 (statement); 1 ill
ILLINOIS 1953 181-182 (statement); 1 ill

FRANK, Barbara ( ) ptr, illus
FOUNDERS 8-9 (statement); 1 ill

FRANK, Ellen ( ) ptr
WHITE WALLS no.9 42-48 (extracts from "Minoan Series"); 3 ill

FRANK, Jeremie ( ) Amer; arch
SPIRIT 44-49 (statement); 6 ill

FRANK, Mary (1933-) Brit/Amer; ptr, sclp
MUNRO 289-308 (interview); ports; 7 ill

FRANK, Peter ( )
CRISS-CROSS no.7/8/9 62-63 (project proposal)
LIVE no.3 16 (statement)

FRANK, Robert (1924-) Amer; photo
WALSH 247-249, 251 (statement); 1 ill

FRANKENBERGER, Scott (1949-) Amer; pott
HERMAN 57 (statement); port; 1 ill

FRANKENTHALER, Helen (1928-) Amer; ptr
ART NOW v.1 no.3 (statement); 1 ill
ARTFORUM v.4 no.2 28-36 (interview with Henry Geldzahler); 3 ill
ILLINOIS 1959 215-216 (statement); 1 ill
JOHNSON 52-55 (extract from interview with Cindy Nemser, o.p. 1971); 1 ill
MUNRO 207-224 (interview); port; 3 ill
ROSE II REVISED 161-162 (extract from interview with Henry Geldzahler, o.p. 1965)
YOUNG 1957 (statement); 1 ill

FRANSIOLI, Thomas Adrian (1906-) Amer; ptr
ILLINOIS 1950 175 (statement); 1 ill
ILLINOIS 1951 179-180 (statement); 1 ill
ILLINOIS 1952 191 (statement); 1 ill
ILLINOIS 1957 203-204 (response); 1 ill

FRANTA, Aleksander (1925-) Poli; arch
EMANUEL I 130-131 (statement); 1 ill

FRANZEN, Ulrich (1921-) Amer; arch
EMANUEL I 259-260 (statement); 1 ill

GA HOUSES no.6 106-109 (statement); 10 ill
ROSNER 161-172 (interview); port

FRARY, Michael (1918-) Amer; ptr
ILLINOIS 1953 182-183 (statement); 1 ill

FRASCONI, Antonio (1919-) Urug/Amer; print
TIGER no.8 59-61 (statement)

FRASER, Betty ( ) Amer; illus
NORTH LIGHT 86-91 (statement); ports; 3 ill

FRASER, Donald Hamilton (1929-) Brit; ptr
BARBER 129-144 (interview); port
CONTEMPORARY (statement); port; 2 ill

FRASER, Juliette May (1887-) Amer; ptr, illus
HAAR I 58-64 (interview with Prithwish Neogy); ports; 3 ill

FRASIER, Debra ( ) Amer; text, sclp, envir
ARTPARK 1981 (statement); port; 2 ill

FRASS, Gayle J. ( ) Amer; text
HAYSTACK 20 (statement); 1 ill

FRATINO, Cesare (1886-) Ital; ptr
VERZOCCHI 213-217 (statement); self port; 1 ill

FRAZER, James Nesbit (1949-) Amer; photo
ART PATRON ART 29-30 (statement); port; 1 ill
AVANT-GARDE 20-21 (statement); 1 ill

FRAZIER, Charles (1930-) Amer; sclp, video
ARTFORUM v.1 no.5 30-34 (group discussion); port; 3 ill
ARTFORUM v.5 no.10 88-92 ("From a Work Journal of Flying Sculpture"); 14 ill
ROSS 20-23 (extract from "Mimbres Journal")

FRAZIER, Paul D. (1922-) Amer; sclp
VARIAN II (statement); port
YOUNG 1957 (statement); 2 ill

FRECKELTON, Sondra (1936-) Amer; ptr
COLLABORATION 96-103 (essay: "Restaurant Pavilions for Bryant Park: Musings on Variety"); 10 ill

FREDDIE, Wilhelm (1909-) Dani; ptr
EXPOSICION (statement); port; 1 ill

FREED, Ernest (1908-) Amer; print, ptr
CALIFORNIA--PRINTS (statement)

FREED, Hermine (1940-) Amer; video
GEORGIA 28-30, 114 (statement); 3 ill
SCHAPIRO 22 (statement); port; 1 ill

FREED, James Ingo (1930-) Amer; arch
COLLABORATION 152-155 (essay: "Two Fantasies of a Mythical Waterworks"); 6 ill

FREEDENTHAL, David (1914-) Amer; ptr
BETHERS II 48-53 (statement); 8 ill
100 CONTEMPORARY 52-53 (statement); port; 1 ill

FREEDMAN, Deborah S. (1947-) Amer; ptr
MILLER 57-73 (interview with Sally Swenson); port

ILLINOIS 1959 216-217 (statement); 1 ill
ILLINOIS 1961 95 (response); port; 1 ill
VARIAN I (statement); port
YOUNG 1957 (statement); 2 ill

FRIEDLAENDER, Johnny (1912-)
Germ; illus, print
PREMIER BILAN 293 (statement); port

FRIEDLANDER, Lee (1934-) Amer;
photo
CAMPBELL 216-227 (interview with
Bryan Campbell); port; 13 ill

FRIEDMAN, Benno (1945-) Amer; photo
HAND COLORED 22-23 (statement); 1 ill
WALSH 256-258 (statement); 1 ill

FRIEDMAN, Ken ( )
LIVE no.3 30-32 (essay: "Between the
Covers")

FRIEDMAN, Martin (1896-) Amer; ptr
ILLINOIS 1951 180 (statement)
ILLINOIS 1953 183 (statement); 1 ill

FRIEDMAN, Yona (1923-) Hung/Fren;
arch
CONRADS 183-184 ("Ten Principles of
Space Town Planning," o.p. 1962)
EMANUEL I 264-265 (statement); 1 ill

FRIESZ, Othon (1879-1949); Fren; ptr
RAYNAL 151-155 (statement); 3 ill

FRINK, Elisabeth (1930-) Brit; sclp
WHELDON 24-28 (interview with Laurie
Lee); port

FRISSELL, Toni (1907-) Amer; photo
MITCHELL 102-119 (statement); ports;
17 ill

FRITSCH, Elizabeth (1940-) Brit; pott
CAMERON E 62-69 (response); 9 ill

FRIZZELL, Julianne ( ) sclp
VISUAL v.2 no.4 21 (statement); 1 ill

FRODL, Richard (1950-) Amer; ptr
WISCONSIN II (statement); 1 ill

FROESE, Dieter (1937-) Germ; film,
video
APPLE 48, 51 (statements); 1 ill

FROMANGER, Gerard (1939-) Fren;
ptr
SKIRA 1978 68-69 (statement); 1 ill

FROST, Terry (1915-) Brit; ptr
CONTEMPORARY (statement); port; 2
ill

FROUCHTBEN, Bernard (1872-) Amer;
ptr
JANIS II 154-159 (statements); port; 1
ill

FRUHTRUNK, Gunter (1923-) Germ;
ptr
HAUSSER 56-59 (statement, o.p. 1971);
6 ill

FRY, Edwin Maxwell (1899-) Brit; arch
EMANUEL I 265-266 (statement); 1 ill

FRYER, Finley (1952-) Amer; ptr, instal
IN A PICTORIAL 16-23 (statements);
port; 4 ill

FRYER, Flora (1892-) Amer; ptr
SYMBOLS (statement); 1 ill

FUCHS, Bernie ( ) Amer; illus
FAMOUS v.1 172-173 (statement); 4 ill

FUCHS, Douglas ( ) Amer; sclp, text
ARTPARK 1980 (statement); port; 2 ill
FIBER 32-33 (statement); 1 ill

FUDGE, John (1941-) Amer; ptr
CRISS-CROSS no.3 3-7 (interview); port;
3 ill

FUENTE, Larry (1947-) Amer; sclp
RAICES 27 (statement); 1 ill

FUJI, Hiromi (1935-) Japa; arch
EMANUEL I 267-269 (statement); 1 ill

FUJII, Hideki (1934-) Japa; photo
HOW FAMOUS 58-63 (statements); port;
7 ill

FUJIWARA, Kei (1899-) Japa; pott
ADACHI 17-19 (statement); port; 2 ill

FUKUZAWA, Ichiro (1898-) Japa; ptr
KUNG 56-59 (statement); port; 2 ill

FULFORD, Patricia (1935-) Cana; sclp
CANADA 68-69 (statement); port; 2 ill

FULLER, Craig ( )
CRISS-CROSS no.10 12-13 (statement);
port; 1 ill

FULLER, Richard Buckminster
(1895-1983) Amer; arch, design
CONRADS 128-136 ("Universal
Architecture" o.p. 1932)
CONRADS 179-180 (extract from talk:
"The Architect as World Planner,"
given in 1961)
HEYER 378-387 (interview); 14 ill

FULLER, Sue (1914-) Amer; sclp
CELEBRATION (statement); 1 ill

FULTON, Don Hendry (1925-) Atrl;
arch
EMANUEL I 270-271 (statement); 1 ill

FULTON, Hamish (1946-) Brit; photo,
ptr, perf

AUPING I 16-32, 86-96 (interview; 11 ill
VICTORIA 50-53 (statements)
WALSH 260-261 (statement); 1 ill

FUMAGALLI, Orazio (1921-) Amer; sclp
WISCONSIN II (statement); 1 ill

FUNDI, Ibibio (1929-) Amer; sclp
LEWIS I REVISED 14-16 (statement);
port; 3 ill

FUNDINGSLAND, Stephen Rinn
(1945-1978); ptr
CRISS-CROSS no.7/8/9 86-89 (journal
entries, 1975-1978); 4 ill

FUNI, Achille (1890-) Ital; ptr
VERZOCCHI 219-223 (statement); self
port; 1 ill

FUNK, Verne (1932-) Amer; pott, sclp
VIEWPOINT 1980 12-13 (statement); 3
ill

FURLONGER, Steve (1939-) Brit; sclp
HAYWARD 1978 66-69 (statement); 4 ill

FURMAN, David (1945-) Amer; pott,
sclp
VIEWPOINT 1977 8 (statement); 3 ill

FURNIVAL, John (1933-) Brit; print,
ptr
NAYLOR 321-322 (statement)

FURUTA, An (1915-) Japa; ptr
KUNG 60-63 (statement); port; 3 ill

GABLIK, Suzi (1934-) Amer; ptr
HESS 88-89 (statement)
RUSSELL J 9-20 ("Introduction")
RUSSELL J 72 (extract from essay: "Fahlstrom: A Place for Everything," o.p. 1966)
RUSSELL J 85 (essay: "Ray Johnson," o.p. 1964)
RUSSELL J 88 ("Edward Keinholz," o.p. 1965)

GABO, Naum (1890-1977) Russ/Amer; sclp
ABSTRACTION no.1 14 (statement); 2 ill
ALBRIGHT-KNOX 182-183 (letter, 8/1971,); 1 ill
BANN 3-11 ("The Realistic Manifesto," o.p. 1920)
BANN 202-204 ("Editorial" from *Circle*, o.p. 1937)
BANN 204-214 (essay: "The Constructive Idea in Art," o.p. 1937)
BANN 214-220 (letter to Herbert Read, 1942, o.p. 1944)
BOWLT 208-214 ("The Realistic Manifesto," o.p. 1920)
BANN 234-248 (talk: "On Constructive Realism," given as the Trowbridge Lecture, Yale University, 1948); 1 ill
CHIPP 325-330 ("The Realistic Manifesto," o.p. 1920, with Antoine Pevsner); port
CHIPP 330-337 (essay: "Sculpture: Carving and Construction in Space," o.p. 1937); 2 ill
CIRCLE 1-10 (essay: "The Constructive Idea in Art")
CIRCLE 103-111 (essay: "Sculpture: Carving and Construction in Space")
CONRADS 56 ("Basic Principles of Construction," o.p. 1920)
GOLDWATER 454-455 (statement, 1920)
GROHMANN 450 ("Konstrucktive Plastik," o.p. 1930)

GUGGENHEIM II 138 ("Realistic Manifesto," with Antoine Pevsner)
KEPES V 60-63 (essay: "Art and Science"); 2 ill
KUH 94-104 (interview); 5 ill
POENSGEN 91-92 ("Aus dem Realistischen Manifest," 1920)
POENSGEN 114-115, 117 ("Ruckblick," 1948)
PROTTER 221 (extract from the Trowbridge Lecture, 1948)
ROTHENSTEIN 63 (statement, p.p.)
TEMOIGNAGES I 114-129 (extract from Trowbridge Art Lecture, Yale University, 1948); port; 7 ill
VINGTIEME v.1 no.5/6 47 (extract from letter)
VINGTIEME N.S. no.13 44-45 (extract from letter, o.p. 1939)

GABOURY, Etienne (1930-) Cana; arch
CANADIAN 52-55 (statement); 5 ill

GABY, Nina (1950-) Amer; pott
HERMAN 58 (statement); port; 1 ill

GAFFORD, Alice (1886-) Amer; ptr
LEWIS II 84 (statement); port; 1 ill

GAFGEN, Wolfgang (1936-) Germ; illus
NAYLOR 325-326 (statement); 1 ill

GAGLIANI, Oliver L. (1917-) Amer; photo
WALSH 263-264 (statement); 1 ill

GAGNAIRE, Aline (1922-) Fren; ptr
PREMIER BILAN 294 (statement); port

GAGNON, Charles (1934-) Cana; photo
WALSH 264-265 (statement); 1 ill

GAGREN, Verena von
SEE: VON GAGREN, Verena

GAILLIARD, Jean-Jacques (1890-) Belg; ptr
COLLARD 104-110 (interview); port; 1 ill
DADA 27-30 (extract from diary, 1915); 1 ill

GAINES, Charles (1944-) photo
CRONE (statement); 3 ill
PAOLETTI 48-51 (statement); 1 ill

GALANIS, Demetrios (1882-) Gree/Fren; print, ptr
ART VOICES v.2 no.9 12-13 (interview with Edouard Roditi); 5 ill

GALBRAITH, Gary ( ) Amer; wood
MEILACH 71 (statement); 1 ill

GALE, Denise ( ) ptr
ART-RITE no.19 25-26 (statements); 1 ill

GALE, West (1942-) Amer; ptr
LEWIS I 104 (statement); port; 1 ill

GALLATIN, Albert Eugene (1882-1952) Amer; ptr
ABSTRACT 219-220 (essay: "Museum-Piece"); 1 ill
PLASTIQUE no.3 6-10 (essay: "Abstract Painting and the Museum of Living Art"); 1 ill

GALLETTI, Bepi (1911-) Ital; ptr
VERZOCCHI 225-229 (statement); self port; 1 ill

GALLI, Stanley W. (1912-) Amer; ptr, illus
MAGIC 60-63 (statement); port; 6 ill

GALLIBERT, Genevieve ( ) Fren; ptr
ART D'AUJOURD'HUI v.4 6 (statement); 5 ill

GALLIEN, Pierre-Antoine ( ) print
DADA 100-102 ("L'Accoucheur irreverencieux"); 1 ill

GALLO, Frank (1933-) Amer; sclp
ILLINOIS 1965 79 (statement); 1 ill

GALOS, Ben (1899-) Amer; ptr
100 CONTEMPORARY 56-57 (statement); port; 1 ill

GALVAN, Jesus Guerrero (1910-) Mexi; ptr
STEWART 116-119 (statement); port; 3 ill

GAMBOA, Harry, Jr. (1951-) Amer; sclp
RAICES 43 (statement); 1 ill

GAMBONE, Bruno ( )
GROH (statement); 1 ill

GAN, Alexei (1893-1942) Russ; print
BANN 32-42 (extracts from *Constructivism*, o.p. 1922)
BANN 127-132 (essay: "Constructivism in the Cinema," o.p. 1928)
BOWLT 214-225 (extract from *Constructivism*, o.p. 1922); port; 1 ill
GRAY 284-286 (extract from *Constructivism*, o.p. 1922)

GANDELSONAS, Mario ( ) Arge/Amer; arch
ARCHER 38-41, 94 (statement); port; 8 ill

GANIS, John (1951-) Amer; photo
FUGITIVE (statement); 1 ill

GARAY, Miguel ( ) arch
PORPHYRIOS 36-39 (essay: "Architecture as Discipline," with Jose-Ignacio Linazasoro); 9 ill

PORPHYRIOS 80-83 (essay: "School at Ikastola, Basque Country," with Jose-Ignacio Linazasoro); 9 ill
PORPHYRIOS 84-89 (essay: "Casa Mendiola, Andoian, Basque Country"); 12 ill

GARCIA ROCHA, Jose Cruz
SEE: CRUZ, Jose Garcia Rocha

GARCIA RODRIGUEZ, Esteban
SEE: ESTEBAN

GARCIE-ROSSI, Horacio (1929-) Arge/Fren; sclp
LUMIERE (statement); port; 1 ill

GARCIN, Laure ( ) Fren; ptr
ABSTRACTION no.2 17 (statement); 2 ill
ABSTRACTION no.4 9 (statement); 1 ill
ABSTRACTION no.5 11 (statement); 2 ill

GARDELLA, Ignazio (1905-) Ital; arch
NEWMAN 98-101 (essay); 14 ill

GARMENDIA RAMIREZ, Berenice
SEE: BERENICE

GAROUSTE, Gerard (1946-) Fren; ptr
CHOIX 23 (statement, o.p. 1982); 1 ill
IN SITU 73-83 (statement); 9 ill

GARRARD, Rose ( ) Brit; perf, film, instal
BOSHIER (statement); port; 3 ill

GARRETT, John (1950-) Amer; text
FIBER 34-35 (statement); 1 ill

GASPARI, Luciano (1913-) Ital; ptr
VERZOCCHI 231-235 (statement); self port; 1 ill

GASTINI, Marco (1938-) Ital; ptr
SKIRA 1979 78 (statement); 1 ill

GATCH, Harry Lee (1902-1968) Amer; ptr
ILLINOIS 1951 180-181 (statement); 1 ill
ILLINOIS 1953 184 (statement)
ILLINOIS 1961 46 (response); port; 1 ill
ILLINOIS 1963 188-189 (statement); 1 ill

GATES, Robert F. (1906-) Amer; ptr
ILLINOIS 1961 57 (response); port; 1 ill

GATEWOOD, Charles (1942-) Amer; photo
WALSH 268-269 (statement); 1 ill

GATHA, Ashvin ( ) Indi; photo
HOW FAMOUS 82-87 (statements); port; 8 ill

GATTI, Ana Maria (1939-) Arge/Fren; sclp
LUMIERE (statement); port; 1 ill

GAUDIER-BRZESKA, Henri (1891-1915) Fren; sclp
EDDY 210-211 (letter)

GAUDIN, Henri ( ) Fren; arch
ARCHITECTURES 144-147 (essay: "Bric a Brac"); 8 ill

GAUGUIN, Paul (1848-1903) Fren; ptr
CHIPP 84-86 (letters, 1903); 1 ill
FRIEDENTHAL 165-167 (letters to Georges de Monfried, 1903); 3 ill

GAUL, Winfred (1928-) Germ; sclp, ptr
ART SINCE v.1 159-160 (statement, o.p. 1967)
EMANUEL II 325-327 (statement); 1 ill
HAUSSER 60-61 (statement); 3 ill
NAYLOR 327-329 (statement); 1 ill

GAUTHIER, Oscar (1921-) Fren; ptr
GRENIER 113-125 (interview)

GAUTRAND, Jean-Claude (1932-) Fren;
photo
WALSH 269-270 (statement); 1 ill

GAZI, Dragan (1930-) Yugo; ptr
TOMASEVIC 80-84 (statement); port; 1
ill

GAZZERA, Romano (1908-) Ital; ptr
VERZOCCHI 237-241 (statement); self
port; 1 ill

GEAM (Groupe d'Etudes d'Architecture
Mobile) (group)
CONRADS 167-168 ("Program for a
Mobile Architecture," o.p. 1960)

GEAR, William (1915-) Scot; ptr
SEUPHOR 177 (statement)

GEBHARDT, Eduard von (1838-1925)
Germ; ptr
THORN 237 (statement, p.p.)

GEBHARDT, Roland (1939-) Amer; sclp
RE-VIEW v.2/3 64-66 (statement); 2 ill

GECCELLI, Johannes (1925-) Germ; ptr
EMANUEL II 327-329 (statement); 1 ill
NAYLOR 329-330 (statement); 1 ill

GECHTOFF, Sonia (1926-) Amer; ptr
ILLINOIS 1955 200 (statement)
SCHAPIRO 24 (statement); port; 1 ill
YOUNG 1960 (statement); 2 ill

GEDDES, Norman Bel (1893-1958);
Amer; design
SEE: BEL GEDDES, Norman

GEDDES, Robert (1923-) Amer; arch
EMANUEL I 276-277 (statement); 1 ill

GEHRY, Frank O. (1929-) Cana/Amer;
arch
ARCHER 51-53, 96 (statement); port; 5
ill
COLLABORATION 156-159 (essay:
"Connections"); 8 ill
COUNTERPOINT 50-63 (statements); 38
ill
DIAMONSTEIN II 34-46 (interview);
port; 4 ill
EMANUEL I 278-280 (statement); 1 ill
GA DOCUMENT no.5 82-87 (statement);
12 ill
GA HOUSES no.6 19-20, 57-83
(statements; and "Frank O. Gehry on
Stanley Tigerman," p20); 86 ill
LA JOLLA 40-45 (statement); port; 13
ill

GEIGER, Robert H. ( ) Amer; coll
CALIFORNIA--COLLAGE (statement); 1
ill
SKIRA 1977 35 (statement); 1 ill

GEIGER, Rupprecht (1908-) Germ; ptr
HAUSSER 62-63 (statement); 2 ill

GEIS, William, III (1940-) Amer; sclp
ILLINOIS 1969 123 (statement); 1 ill
ILLINOIS 1974 50 (statement); 1 ill
TUCHMAN 45 (extract from interview
with Joe Raffaele)

GEISSMANN, Robert (1909-) Amer; ptr,
illus, design
NORTH LIGHT 92-97 (statement); port;
6 ill

GEIST, Sidney (1914-) Amer; sclp
ARTS YEARBOOK v.6 71-73 (essay:
"The Contribution of 'The Eight',"
o.p. 1958)
ARTS YEARBOOK v.6 96-98 (essay:
"Salut! Apollinaire," o.p. 1961)

ARTS YEARBOOK v.6 124-126 (essay: "A New Sculpture by Mark di Suvero," o.p. 1960)
ARTS YEARBOOK v.8 92-98 (essay: "Color It Sculpture")
CHIPP 581 (essay: "The Private Myth," o.p. 1961)
CHIPP 582 (essay: "Sculpture and Other Trouble," o.p. 1961)
IT IS no.3 32-33 ("Face Front")

GELBER, Sam (1929-) Amer; ptr
GUSSOW 102-103 (interview, 1970); 1 ill

GELDMAN, Stephen S. ( ) Amer; ptr, coll
IRVINE 55, 88 (statement); 1 ill

GELLER, Todros (1889-) Amer; ptr
100 CONTEMPORARY 58-59 (statement); port; 1 ill

GELLERT, Hugo (1892-) Hung/Amer; ptr, print
FIRST AMERICAN 76-79 (essay: "Fascism, War and the Artist")

GELON, Diane ( )
CHRYSALIS no.4 91-94, 96, 99 (statements)

GELPKE, Andre (1947-) Germ; photo
WALSH 270-272 (statement); 1 ill

GENERAL IDEA (group)
AVALANCHE no.7 14-21 (interview); 12 ill

GENERALIC, Ivan (1914-) Yugo; ptr
TOMASEVIC 85-102 (statement); port; 5 ill

GENERALIC, Josip (1936-) Yugo; ptr
TOMASEVIC 103-108 (statement); port; 1 ill

GENERALIC, Mato (1920-) Yugo; sclp
TOMASEVIC 109-111 (statement); port; 1 ill

GENERATIVE ART GROUP
SEE: NEAGU, Paul

GENESIS P-ORRIDGE (1950-) Brit; perf, instal
HAYWARD 1979 14-15 (interview with William Furlong)
HAYWARD 1979 24-27 (statement); 5 ill

GENOVES, Juan (1930-) Span; ptr
KUNST UND POLITIK (statement); port; 5 ill
SKIRA 1978 60 (statement); 1 ill

GENTILINI, Franco (1909-) Ital; ptr
PAINTING 14 (statement); port; 1 ill

GENTILLE, Thomas ( ) Amer; metal
HAYSTACK 22 (statement); 1 ill

GENTILS, Vic ( )
ART SINCE v.2 323 (statement, o.p. 1970)

GENTLEMAN, Ross (1949-) Cana; video
POINT OF VIEW 46 (statement); 1 ill

GEORGE, Dan ( ) Amer; sclp
ARTPARK 1982 12-13, 46 (statement); port; 4 ill

GEORGE, Patrick (1923-) Brit; ptr
CONTEMPORARY (statement); port; 2 ill

GEORGE, Thomas (1918-) Amer; ptr
ILLINOIS 1965 127 (statement); 1 ill

GERAN, Joseph (1945-) Amer; ptr, sclp

LEWIS I REVISED 61-62 (statement); port; 1 ill

GERARD, Francoise (1951-) Belg; ptr
COLLARD 112-115 (interview); port; 1 ill

GERARDIA, Helen (1913-) Russ/Amer; ptr
ILLINOIS 1959 217-218 (statement); 1 ill

GERARDLAENEN ( ) Belg; ptr
COLLARD 116-120 (interview); port; 1 ill

GERARDO, Eduaro Auyon
SEE: AUYON

GERBARG, Darcy (1949-) Amer; print
COMPUTER (statement); 1 ill

GERD, Abigail ( )
ART-RITE no.5 6 (response)

GERMAIN, Jacques (1915-) Fren; ptr
GRENIER 129-135 (interview)

GERNSHEIM, Helmut (1913-) Germ/Brit; photo
HILL 160-210 (interview, 1977); port
WALSH 273-275 (statement); 1 ill

GERRARD, A. H. (1899-) sclp
OPEN AIR 1960 (statement); 2 ill

GERSTEN, Gerry ( ) Amer; sclp
ILLUSTRATION 68-69 (statement); port; 2 ill
NORTH LIGHT 98-103 (statement); port; 8 ill

GERSTER, Georg (1928-) Swis; photo
WALSH 275-276 (statement); 1 ill

GERSTNER, Karl (1930-) Swis; ptr
EMANUEL II 330-331 (statement); 1 ill
KEPES VII 128-141 (essay: "Structure and Movement")
KINETISCHE (statement); port
NAYLOR 332-333 (statement); 1 ill

GERTSCH, Franz (1930-) Swis; ptr
KUNST BLEIBT KUNST 206-209 (statement); 4 ill
SKIRA 1975 23 (extract from interview with Michael S. Cullen, o.p. 1974)

GERVAIS, Lise (1933-) Cana; sclp, ptr
CANADA 102-103 (statement); port; 2 ill

GERZ, Jochen (1940-) Germ; sclp, ptr, instal
EMANUEL II 332-334 (statement); 1 ill
GROH (statement); 2 ill
SKIRA 1977 92 (statement); 3 ill
SKIRA 1980 93 (statement); 1 ill

GESSNER, Albert ( ) arch
SCHMIDT 39-40 (letter, 1933)

GETTE, Paul-Armand (1927-) Fren; print, photo
IDENTITE 39-41 (interview with Jacques Clayssen); port
SKIRA 1977 82 (statement); 1 ill

GETZ, Arthur ( ) Amer; illus, ptr
NORTH LIGHT 104-109 (statement); port; 7 ill

GEVA, Avital (1941-) Isra
SANDBERG 88-91 (project proposal); 8 ill

GHEN, Dina ( ) Amer; ptr
BRENTANO 202-203 (statement); 1 ill

GHIKA, Nicolas (1909-) Gree; ptr
NAYLOR 334-335 (statement); 1 ill

GHIKAS, Panos (1924-) Amer; ptr
FULBRIGHT 25 (statement)

GHIRRI, Luigi (1943-) Ital; photo
TIME-LIFE IV 100-101 (statement); 1 ill
WALSH 276-277 (statement); 1 ill

GHOBERT, Bernard (1914-1975) Belg;
ptr
COLLARD 122-125 (interview); port; 1
ill

GIACOMETTI, Alberto (1901-1966)
Swis; sclp, ptr
ART SINCE v.2 149 (statement, p.p.)
CHARBONNIER v.1 159-170 (interview,
1951)
CHARBONNIER v.1 171-183 (interview,
1957)
CHIPP 598-601 (letter to Pierre
Matisse, o.p. 1948); port
FRASNAY 203-211 (statement); 6 ill
GOLDAINE 86-88 (interview); port
GUGGENHEIM II 120-121 (statement,
o.p. 1933); 2 ill
JEAN 292 ("Moving and Mute
Objects," o.p. 1931)
JEAN 293 ("Yesterday, Quicksands,"
o.p. 1933)
LIBERMAN 69-70 (statements)
LIPPARD 141-143 (essay: "Yesterday,
Moving Sands," o.p. 1933)
LIPPARD 144-145 ("1 + 1 = 3...," o.p.
1936)
LIPPARD 145-148 ("A Letter" to Pierre
Matisse, o.p. 1948)
MINOTAURE no.3/4 46-47 (statement);
3 ill
MINOTAURE no.3/4 109 ("Enquete")
SCHNEIDER 191-208 (interview); 5 ill
SELZ 68-75 (statement); 7 ill

SURREALISME no.3 18-19 ("Objects
Mobiles et Muets"); 7 ill
SURREALISME no.5 15 ("Charbon
d'Herbe")
SURREALISME no.5 44-45 ("Hier, Sables
Mouvants")
SURREALISME no.6 10-23 ("Recherches
Experimentales" (questions and
responses))
TIGER no.4 76-78, 85 (statement); 1 ill
TRACKS v.1 no.1 50-51 ("May 1920")
TRACKS v.1 no.1 52-58 ("The Dream,
the Sphinx, and the Death of T")
TRACKS v.1 no.2 36-37 (essay: "The
Automobile Demystified," o.p. 1957)
VINGTIEME N. S. no.9 36 (statement)

GIANALCOS, Steve ( ) ptr
REALLIFE no.2 2-4 (interview with
Susan Morgan); 1 ill

GIANELLA, Victor (1918-) Swis; photo
WALSH 279-280 (statement); 1 ill

GIBBERD, Frederick (1908-) Brit; arch
EMANUEL I 280-282 (statement); 1 ill

GIBBONS, Dan (1943-) Amer; sclp
OK ART (statement); 1 ill

GIBBS, Howard (1904-) Amer; ptr
ILLINOIS 1952 192 (statement)

GIBSON, Jon ( ) Amer; perf, sound
ART-RITE no.14 5, 8 (response)
AVALANCHE no.10 41 (interview); ports

GIBSON, Lloyd (1945-) Brit; sclp
BRITISH (statement); 1 ill

GIBSON, Ralph (1939-) Amer; photo
BOOTH 100-111 (interview); port; 6 ill
CAMPBELL 238-249 (statement); port;
10 ill
DUGAN 47-63 (interview, 1975); port

HOWARD (interview)
WALSH 280-282 (statement); 1 ill

GIBSON, Robin (1930-) Atrl; arch
EMANUEL I 282-283 (statement); 1 ill

GIDAL, Peter ( ) Brit; film
ENGLISH 448-449 (statement); port; 1 ill

GIDAL, Tim N. (1909-) Germ; photo
WALSH 282-284 (statement); 1 ill

GIESE, David F. (1944-) Amer; coll
NOSANOW II 25, 47 (statement); 3 ill

GIESELMANN, Reinhard ( ) arch
CONRADS 165-166 ("Towards a New Architecture," o.p. 1960)

GIGUERE, Roland (1929-) Cana; ptr
ROYER 127-130 (interview, 1975)

GIKOW, Ruth (1915-) Amer; ptr
ILLINOIS 1950 176 (statement); 1 ill
ILLINOIS 1955 201 (statement); 1 ill
ILLINOIS 1957 205 (response); 1 ill

GILARDI, Piero (1942-) sclp
DIRECTIONS I 76 (response); 1 ill

GILBERT AND GEORGE (George Passmore, 1943- , and Gilbert Proesch, 1942-) (group) Brit; perf, sclp, instal
AVALANCHE no.8 26-33 (text piece); 8 ill
CONTEMPORARY (statement, 1971); port; 2 ill
EMANUEL II 336-337 (statement); 1 ill
EUROPE 56-57 (textpiece: "Red Morning"); 1 ill
HAYWARD 1979 96-101 (statement); 5 ill
KONZEPT (statements: "The Pencil on Paper Descriptive Works of Gilbert and George," and "To be with Art is all we ask...," and "A Day in the Life of Gilbert and George")
PAOLETTI 52-54 (statements, p.p.); 1 ill
SKIRA 1980 101 (statement); 1 ill
STEDELIJK 123 (statement); 2 ill

GILBERT-ROLFE, Jeremy ( ) Brit; ptr
ART-RITE no.9 6-7 (statement)
ART-RITE no.10 ("Performance: A Comment from Outside")
TRACKS v.2 no.2 66-69 ("On Some Criticisms of My Criticism, with Particular Regard to Those of the Confessional and Exculpatory Variety")

GILHOOLY, David (1943-) Cana; pott, sclp
HOPKINS 40-41 (statement); port; 1 ill
NAYLOR 338-339 (statement); 1 ill
VIEWPOINT 1978 10-13 (statement); 4 ill
VISUAL v.2 no.1 13-17 (interview); 2 ill

GILI, Katherine (1948-) Brit; sclp
HAYWARD 1979 116-117, 124-127 (interview with David Robson); port; 8 ill

GILIOLI, Emile (1911-) Fren; sclp
TEMOIGNAGES I 130-137 (statement); port; 5 ill
TEMOIGNAGES II 18-21 (statement); port; 7 ill
VINGTIEME N. S. no.9 29 (statement)
YALE 25-26 (statement)

GILL, Andrea (1948-) Amer; pott
WECHSLER 76-81 (statement); port; 5 ill

GILL, Eric (1882-1940) Brit; sclp, print
GOLDWATER 455-457 (statement, 1940)

GILLAIREAU, Georges (1884-) Fren
PREMIER BILAN 299 (statement); port

GILLESPIE, Gregory (1936-) Amer; ptr
SUPERREAL 76-77 (statement); self
port

GILLETTE, Frank (1941-) Amer; video,
film
DAVIS 65-70 (group discussion); port
KUNST BLEIBT KUNST 412 (statement);
2 ill

GILLIAM, Sam (1933-) Amer; ptr, envir
ARTPARK 1977 35-37 (statement); port;
2 ill
FINE 224-226 (statements, o.p. 1970); 2
ill
NORTH P (interview); port; 2 ill

GILLIAM, Scott ( ) Amer; sclp
ARTPARK 1981 (statement); port; 2 ill

GILLIES, Mary Ann (1935-) Amer; sclp
WOMANART v.1 no.3 26, 28 (response);
port

GILLIS, Paul ( ) ptr
CRISS-CROSS no.6 20-23 (statement); 4
ill

GILMOUR, Gina ( ) Amer; ptr
ART PATRON ART 31-32 (statement);
port; 1 ill

GILOTH, Copper (1952-) Amer; print
COMPUTER (statement); 1 ill

GILPIN, Laura (1891-1979) Amer; photo
HILL 282-292 (interview, 1975); port
MITCHELL 120-139 (statement); ports;
18 ill

GINNEVER, Charles (1931-) Amer; sclp
SCULPTURE OUTSIDE (statement); 4 ill

GINS, Madeline ( )
TRACKS v.3 no.3 15-20 ("Excerpts")
TRACKS v.3 no.3 109 ("Obituary for
Oyvind Fahlstrom")

GIOBBI, Edward (1926-) Amer; ptr
ILLINOIS 1957 205-206 (response); 1 ill
VARIAN I (statement); port
WHITNEY (statement); 1 ill
YOUNG 1960 (statement); 2 ill

GIOLI, Paolo (1942-) Ital; photo
WALSH 285-287 (statement); 1 ill

GIORGINI, Vittorio ( ) arch
ON SITE no.5/6 76-79 (text piece:
"Spatiology")

GIROUARD, Tina (1946-) Amer; ptr,
design, perf
APPLE 40 (statement); 1 ill
AVALANCHE no.5 36-45 (group
discussion); 8 ill
AVALANCHE no.8 48-53 (interview);
port; 11 ill
FIVE 6-9 (interview with Liza Bear,
1976); 6 ill
PARACHUTE no.6 12-14 (interview, in
English); port

GISCHIA, Leon (1903-) Fren; ptr
CHARBONNIER v.2 145-158 (interview)
GOLDAINE 164-167 (interview); port

GIUFFREDA, Mauro ( ) print
MYLAR 4-5 (statement); port

GIULIANI, Vin ( ) Amer; illus
ILLUSTRATION 27-31 (statement); port;
3 ill

GIURGOLA, Romaldo (1920-)
Ital/Amer; arch
EMANUEL I 285-287 (statement); 1 ill

GIUSTI, George ( ) Ital/Amer; ptr
FAMOUS v.1 174-175 (statement); 3 ill
GUITAR 98-109 (interview); port; 4 ill

GLACKENS, William James (1870-1938)
Amer; ptr
ROSE II 72-74 (interview, o.p. 1913)
ROSE II REVISED 66-67 (extract from
interview, o.p. 1913)

GLADSTONE, Gerald (1925-) Cana;
sclp
ART VOICES v.3 no.1 18 (interview
with Raul Furtado); port; 2 ill

GLARNER, Fritz (1899-1972)
Swis/Amer; ptr
FORTY (statement, o.p. 1951); 2 ill
ILLINOIS 1965 209 (statement); 1 ill
MILLER 1956 28-35 (extract from a
talk: "A Visual Problem," given at
The Club 8th St., New York, 1949);
port; 7 ill
PERSONAL (statement)

GLASCO, Joseph (1925-) Amer; ptr
ILLINOIS 1959 218-219 (statement); 1 ill
MILLER 1952 33-35 (statement); 4 ill
RODMAN I 110-114 (interview)

GLASER, Milton (1929-) Amer; design
DIAMONSTEIN I 125-137 (interview);
ports

GLASGOW, Lukman (1935-) Amer;
pott, sclp
VIEWPOINT 1978 14-16 (statement); 4
ill

GLASIER, Marshall (1902-) Amer; ptr
BRITANNICA 45 (statement); port; 1 ill

GLASMEIER, Rolf (1945-) Germ; sclp
HAUSSER 64-67 (statement); 7 ill

GLASS, Philip (1937-) Amer; perf, sound
AVALANCHE no.5 26-35 (interview);
port; 3 ill
AVALANCHE no.10 43 (interview); ports
KUNST BLEIBT KUNST 362-365
(statement); 2 ill
PARACHUTE no.1 32-34 (interview); 1
ill

GLASS, Ted (Eduard Golascu) (1892-)
Amer; sclp
NAYLOR 342-343 (statement); 1 ill

GLEIZES, Albert (1881-1953) Fren; ptr
ABSTRACTION no.1 14-15 (statement);
2 ill
ABSTRACTION no.2 18 (statement); 2
ill
ABSTRACTION no.3 18 (statement); 1
ill
ABSTRACTION no.4 10 (statement); 2
ill
ABSTRACTION no.4 32 (extract from a
talk given at the Courtauld Institute of
Art, University of London, 1934)
ABSTRACTION no.5 7-8 (statement); 2
ill
CHIPP 207-216 (extract from
"Cubism," o.p. 1912/13, with Jean
Metzinger)
FRY 105-111 (essay: "Cubism," o.p.
1912/13)
FRY 172-175 ("Two Salons in 1911," c.
1944, o.p. 1957)
GUGGENHEIM II 73-74 (statement, o.p.
1912); 1 ill
LHOTE 428-433 (extract from *Du
Cubisme*, o.p. 1912/13)
POENSGEN 81-84 (extract from essay:
"Der Kubismus," o.p. 1912/13)
RAYNAL 157-163 (statement); 2 ill

SEGHERS 131-137 (extract from essay: "Cubism," o.p. 1912/13)

GLENDINNING, Peter (1951-) Amer; photo
FUGITIVE (statement); 1 ill

GLICK, John (John Parker) (1938-) Amer; pott
SHAFER 68-91 (statements); port; 29 ill
VIEWPOINT 1981 (statement); 3 ill

GLICKMAN, Maurice (1906-) Amer; sclp
100 CONTEMPORARY 62-63 (statement); port; 1 ill

GLIER, Mike ( ) Amer; ptr
FACE IT 14-15 (statement); 1 ill

GLINN, Burt (1925-) Amer; photo
CAMPBELL 156-165 (statement); port; 10 ill
LAPLANTE 22-32 (interview); port; 1 ill
WALSH 287-289 (statement); 1 ill

GLOAGUEN, Herve (1937-) Fren; photo
WALSH 289-290 (statement); 1 ill

GLOVER, Robert (1941-) Amer; ptr
LEWIS II 106 (statement); port; 1 ill

GLUCK (Hannah Gluckstein) (1895-) Brit; ptr
NAYLOR 344-345 (statement); 1 ill

GLUCKMANN, Gregory (1898-) Russ/Fren; ptr
100 CONTEMPORARY 64-65 (statement); port; 1 ill

GLUCKSTEIN, Hannah
SEE: GLUCK

GLYN, Susan ( )
REVOLUTION 112-116 (essay: "Spiritual Dimensions of Art")

GNOLI, Domenico (1933-1970) Ital; print, ptr
SKIRA 1975 28 (extract from interview with Jean-Luc Daval, o.p. 1965); 1 ill

GODFREY, Ian (1941-) pott
CAMERON E 70-77 (response); 11 ill

GODFREY, Wilhelmina (1914-) Amer; text
CONTEMPORARY AFRICAN (statement); port; 1 ill

GODLA, Joseph (1955-) Amer; wood
WOODWORKING 20-21 (statement); port; 1 ill

GODWIN, Michele ( ) Amer
EVENTS II 42-43 (statement); 1 ill

GOEDIKE, Shirl (1923-) Amer; ptr
CALIFORNIA--PAINTING 39 (statement); 1 ill
ILLINOIS 1961 51 (response); port; 1 ill

GOELLER, Charles L. (1901-1955) Amer; illus, ptr
M. H. DE YOUNG 57 (response); self port

GOEPFERT, Hermann (1926-) Germ; sclp
ART SINCE v.1 295 (statement, p.p.)

GOERG, Edouard (1893-1968) Fren; ptr
RAYNAL 165-169 (statement); 2 ill

GOERITZ, Mathias (1915-) Mexi; arch, sclp, ptr
EMANUEL I 289-290 (statement); 1 ill
IT IS no.5 40 ("A Cahier Note")
NAYLOR 345-346 (statement); 1 ill

GOLDSTEIN, Howard (1933-) Amer; ptr
GEOMETRIC (statement); 1 ill

GOLDTHWAITE, Anne Wilson (1869-1944) Amer; ptr, sclp, print
M. H. DE YOUNG 58 (response); self port

GOLDYNE, Joseph ( ) Amer; print
VISUAL v.4 no.4 12-15 (interview); 5 ill

GOLIN, Carlo ( ) perf
ART NETWORK no.2 45 (statement); 1 ill

GOLONU, Gunduz ( ) print
KATZ 175-184 (interview); port

GOLUB, Leon (1922-) Amer; ptr
ART SINCE v.2 151 (statement, o.p. 1967)
ARTFORUM v.7 no.3 4 (letter)
ART-RITE no.7 24 (statement)
EMANUEL II 343-344 (statement); 1 ill
ILLINOIS 1957 207-208 (response); 1 ill
ILLINOIS 1965 198 (statement); 1 ill
NAYLOR 347-348 (statement); 1 ill
PROFILE v.2 no.2 (interview); port; 5 ill
SELZ 76-82 (statement); 5 ill

GOLYA, Thomas J. (1940-) Amer; sclp
NOSANOW I 65-66 (statement); 2 ill

GOMEZ, Manuel Albert (1949-) Amer; sclp, metal
FAX II 221-237 (statements); port; 1 ill

GOMEZ DE KANELBA, Sita (1932-) Cuba; ptr
CUBAN (statement); 2 ill

GONCHAROVA, Natalya (1881-1962) Russ; ptr
BOWLT 54-60 ("Preface" to exhibition catalogue, o.p. 1913); port; 2 ill

BOWLT 72-78 (talk: "Cubism," given in 1912)
BOWLT 87-91 (essay: "Rayonists and Futurists: A Manifesto," o.p. 1913)
BOWLT 91-100 (essay: "Rayonist Painting," o.p. 1913); 1 ill
BOWLT 100-102 (essay: "Pictorial Rayonism," o.p. 1914)

GONDEK, Thomas G. (1944-) Amer; sclp
WISCONSIN I (statement); 1 ill

GONGORA, Leonel (1932-) Colo/Amer; ptr
ART-RITE no.6 25 (statement)
RAICES 18 (statement); 1 ill

GONZALES, Ruben E. (1923-) Amer; sclp
RAICES 53 (statement); 1 ill

GONZALEZ, Juan (1945-) Cuba; ptr
CUBAN (statement); 2 ill

GOOCH, Gerald (1933-) Amer; ptr
ILLINOIS 1967 54 (statement); 1 ill

GOODE, Joe (Jose Bueno) (1937-) Amer; sclp
ART VOICES v.5 no.4 61-62 (response); 1 ill

GOODELL, Larry ( )
CRISS-CROSS no.2 12-13 (poem: "Mom Dass")

GOODELMAN, Aaron J. (1890-) Amer; sclp
100 CONTEMPORARY 66-67 (statement); port; 1 ill

GOODMAN, Janis ( ) Amer; ptr, illus
FOUNDERS 10-11 (statement); 1 ill

GOODMAN, Percival ( ) arch
ON SITE no.5/6 80-83 (essay: "Premises for Future Planning")

GOODMAN, Sidney (1936-) Amer; ptr
GUSSOW 10-11 (letter, 1970); 1 ill
WHITNEY (statement); 1 ill

GOODNOUGH, Robert (1917-) Amer; ptr
ARTFORUM v.4 no.1 32 (statement)
ART NOW v.1 no.4 (statement); 1 ill
IT IS no.1 v.46 (statement)

GOODRICH, Susan (1933-) Amer; ptr
WISCONSIN II (statement); 1 ill

GOODWIN, Betty (1923-) Cana; sclp, envir
ARTPARK 1978 22-23 (statement); 8 ill

GOODY, Marvin E. ( ) arch
PROCESSES 9-28 (interview by Laver, Lance); 19 ill

GOODYEAR, John (1930-) Amer; sclp
GEOMETRIC (statement); 1 ill

GORCHOV, Ron (1930-) Amer; ptr
ART-RITE no.9 29-34 (group discussion)
EARLY WORK (interview with Susan Logan); 3 ill
SULTAN 59-62 (interview with Liza Bear, 1975); 1 ill

GORDIN, Sidney (1918-) Russ/Amer; ptr, sclp
HOPKINS 42-43 (statement); port; 1 ill

GORDINE, Dora ( ) sclp
OPEN AIR 1960 (statement); 1 ill

GORDON, Coco ( )
PHILLPOT (statement)

GORDON, Maxwell (1910-) Amer; ptr
ILLINOIS 1951 182 (statement); 1 ill

GORE, Arnold (1935-) Amer; print
WISCONSIN II (statement); 1 ill

GORE, Frederick (1913-) Brit; ptr
CONTEMPORARY (statement); port; 2 ill

GORELEIGH, Rex (1902-) Amer; print
FAX I 95-111 (statements); port; 1 ill

GORELICK, Boris ( ) Amer
FIRST AMERICAN 84-86 (essay: "Artists' Union Report")

GORELLA, Arwed D. (1937-) Germ; ptr
SKIRA 1975 35 (statement: "Aspekte der engagierten Kunst," 1974); 1 ill

GORIN, J. A. (1899-) Fren; ptr, sclp
ABSTRACTION no.1 16 (statement); 2 ill
ABSTRACTION no.2 19 (statement); 2 ill
ABSTRACTION no.4 11 (essay: "Vers un Art Social et Collectif Universal")
ABSTRACTION no.5 9 (essay: "But de la Plastique Constructive"); 2 ill
BANN 199-201 (essay: "The Aim of Constructive Plastic Art," o.p. 1936); 1 ill
TEMOIGNAGES I 138-145 (statement); port; 6 ill

GORKY, Arshile (Vosdanis Manoog Adoian) (1904-1948) Amer; ptr
ART SINCE v.1 156 (statement, o.p. 1941)
CHIPP 532-534 (extract from essay: "Stuart Davis," o.p. 1931); port
CHIPP 534-535 (statement, o.p. 1936)
CHIPP 535-536 (statement, 1942, o.p. 1957)

CLAUS 27-35 (statement)
JANIS I 120 (statement); 1 ill
LIPPARD 149-150 ("Garden in Sochi," p.p. in 1957, 1965)
PROTTER 242-243 (statement); 1 ill
ROSE II REVISED 107-109 (extract from essay: "Aviation: Evolution of Forms under Aerodynamic Limitations," o.p. 1957)
ROSE II REVISED 109 (letter to artist's wife, 1941, o.p. 1957)
ROSE II 138-141 (extract from essay: "Aviation: Evolution of Forms under Aerodynamic Limitations," p.p. 1957)
ROSE II 141-142 (poem: "Garden in Sochi," o.p. 1942)

GORMAN, James (1946-) Amer; pott
HERMAN 59 (statement); port; 1 ill

GOSCHL, Roland (1932-) Aust; ptr
SKIRA 1977 103 (statement); 1 ill

GOSEWITZ, Ludwig (1936-) Germ; ptr, glass
EMANUEL II 350-351 (statement); 1 ill
NAYLOR 353 (statement)

GOSSAGE, John R. (1946-) Amer; photo
KARDON 10-11, 13, 16-17, 20, 21, 24 (interview with Walter Hopps)

GOSSELIN, Louis (1947-) Cana/Fren; sclp
SKIRA 1977 14 (statement); 1 ill

GOTO, Joseph (1920-) Amer; sclp
HAAR II 14; ports; 2 ill

GOTSCH, Bob ( ) Amer; print
COMPUTER (statement); 1 ill

GOTTLIEB, Adolph (1903-1974) Amer; ptr, print
ART NOW v.1 no.7 (statement); 1 ill
ART SINCE v.1 156-157 (statements, o.p. 1947, 1955)
ART VOICES v.3 no.2 14-15 (interview with Gordon Brown); port; 5 ill
CHIPP 544-545 (statement, with Mark Rothko, o.p. 1943)
FORTY (statement, o.p. 1951); 2 ill
FRASNAY 236 (handwritten statement)
ILLINOIS 1950 177 (statement); 1 ill
ILLINOIS 1951 182 (statement); 1 ill
ILLINOIS 1955 202 (statement); 1 ill
MCCOUBREY 210-212 (letter to the *New York Times*, o.p. 1943)
MOTHERWELL 8-22 (three group discussions: "Artists' Sessions at Studio 35," New York, 1950)
NEW DECADE 35-36 (statement); 1 ill
JANIS I 119 (statement); 1 ill
JOHNSON 10-14 (letter, o.p. 1943); 1 ill
RODMAN I 87-92 (interview)
ROSE II 146 (extract from "The Ides of Art," o.p. 1947)
ROSE II REVISED 114 (extract from "The Ides of Art," o.p. 1947)
ROSE II REVISED 114-116 (essay: "On Pictographs and Symbols," o.p. 1968)
TIGER no.2 43 (statement)
TIGER no.8 52 (statement)

GOTTLIEB, Harry (1895-) Amer; print, ptr
FIRST AMERICAN 68-69 (essay: "Government in Art, Municipal Art Center")
100 CONTEMPORARY 68-69 (statement); port; 1 ill

GOTZ, Karl Otto (1914-) Germ; ptr
PREMIER BILAN 295 (statement); port

GOUGH, Robert Alan (1931-) Cana/Amer; ptr
ILLINOIS 1963 133 (statement); 1 ill
NOSANOW I 67 (statement); 2 ill

GOULDING, Timothy (1945-) Iris; ptr
KNOWLES 20-21, 69, 109 (statement); 5
ill

GOUREVITCH, Jacqueline (1933-)
Fren/Amer; ptr
ART NOW v.3 no.3 (statement); 1 ill

GOW, Isobel Dowler
SEE: DOWLER GOW, Isobel

GOWAN, James (1923-) Brit; arch
EMANUEL I 301-303 (statement); 1 ill

GOWIN, Emmet (1941-) Amer; photo
WINSTON-SALEM 23-32 (statement); 10
ill

GOWING, Lawrence (1918-) Brit; ptr
CONTEMPORARY (statement); port; 2
ill

GRABILL, Vin (1949-) Amer; video
BOSTON III (interview); 1 ill

GRADY, Dennis P. ( ) Amer; photo
BARROW 145-160 (essay: "Philosophy
and Photography in the Nineteenth
Century," o.p. 1977)

GRAEFF, Werner (1901-) arch
CONRADS 71 ("The New Engineer is
Coming," o.p. 1923)

GRAEVENITZ, Gerhard von (1934-)
Germ; sclp
KINETIC 34-35 (statement); port; 1 ill

GRAHAM, Bruce John (1925-) Amer;
arch
EMANUEL I 303-304 (statement); 1 ill

GRAHAM, Daniel H. (1942-) Amer; perf,
sclp, video

ARTFORUM v.6 no.5 30-37 (essay:
"Oldenburg's Monuments")
ART-LANGUAGE v.1 no.1 14-15 ("Poem
Schema")
KUNST BLEIBT KUNST 366-367
(statement); 3 ill
KUNST BLEIBT KUNST 413 (statement);
3 ill
LIVE no.6/7 12-17 (essay: "Semio-Sex,
New Wave Rock and the Feminine")
MEYER 126-131 (text piece); 3 ill
REALLIFE no.3 4-6 (essay: "The
Destroyed Room of Jeff Wall")
REALLIFE no.6 11-13 ("Bowwowwow,
(the Age of Piracy)")
SKIRA 1977 56 (statement); 1 ill
SKIRA 1980 99 (statement); 2 ill
STEDELIJK 124 (statement)
TRACKS v.3 no.1/2 69-75 ("Dean
Martin/Entertainment as Theater")
TRACKS v.3 no.3 52-61 ("Three
Projects for Architecture and Video,
Notes"); 7 ill

GRAHAM, David (1952-) Amer; photo
FUGITIVE (statement); 1 ill

GRAHAM, John D. (Iwan Dabrowsky)
(1881-1961) Russ/Amer; ptr
JANIS I 54 (statement); 1 ill
ROSE II 120-122 (extract from essay:
"What is the Relationship of Art to
Technique?" o.p. 1937)
ROSE II REVISED 98-100 (extract from
essay: "What is the Relationship of
Art and Technique?" o.p. 1937)

GRAHAM, Michael N. ( ) Amer; wood
MEILACH 6-7, 242 (statement); port; 5
ill

GRAHAM, Robert (1938-) Amer; ptr,
sclp
COLLABORATION 114-117 (essay:

"Human Scale at the End of the Age of Modernism"); 4 ill

GRAMATKY, Hardie (1907-1979) Amer; ptr
NORTH LIGHT 82 (statement); 1 ill

GRAND, Toni (1935-) Fren; sclp, instal
CHOIX 24 (statement); 1 ill
SKIRA 1979 63 (statement); 1 ill
SKIRA 1980 138 (statement); 2 ill

GRAND UNION (group)
AVALANCHE no.8 40-47 (text piece); 25 ill

GRANLUND, Paul (1925-) Amer; sclp
ILLINOIS 1984 (response); port; 1 ill

GRANT, James (1924-) Amer; ptr
ILLINOIS 1967 62 (statement); 1 ill

GRASEL, Friedrich (1927-) Germ; sclp
HAUSSER 70-73 (statement); 7 ill

GRASS, Peter ( ) coll
ART-RITE no.3 8-9 ("Magazine Project: Two Non-Done Works"); 1 ill
ART-RITE no.9 21-23 (interview); 4 ill
ART-RITE no.14 5, 8 (response)

GRASSI, Giorgio ( ) Ital; arch
PORPHYRIOS 42-49 (interview entitled: "The Limits of Architecture," 1977)
PORPHYRIOS 118-124 (essay: "Caso dello Studente, Chieti, Italy"); 13 ill
PORPHYRIOS 125-129 (essay: "Restoration and Extension to Castello Fagnano Olona, Italy"); 15 ill
RUSSELL F 82-83 (project proposal); 4 ill

GRAUBNER, Gotthard (1930-) Germ; ptr
EMANUEL II 355-356 (statement)

NAYLOR 358-359 (statement); 1 ill
SKIRA 1977 31 (extracts from a conversation); 1 ill

GRAU-GARRIGA, Josep (1929-) Span; ptr, sclp, text
EMANUEL II 356-357 (statement); 1 ill
NAYLOR 359-360 (statement); 1 ill
PORCEL I 101-110 (interview); 1 ill

GRAV (group)
ART SINCE v.1 296 (statements, o.p. 1966, 1967)

GRAVEROL, Jane ( ) Belg; ptr
COLLARD 126-129 (interview); port; 1 ill

GRAVES, Michael (1934-) Amer; arch
ARCHER 73-75, 97 (statement); port; 8 ill
BUILDING 42-45 (statement); 6 ill
COLLABORATION 126-129 (essay: "Bacchanal"); 5 ill
DIAMONSTEIN II 48-62 (interview); port; 5 ill
EMANUEL I 304-306 (statement); 1 ill
GA DOCUMENT no.5 4-15 (interview); ports; 4 ill
GA HOUSES no.2 8-23 (statement); 33 ill
GA HOUSES no.5 124-129 (statement); 11 ill

GRAVES, Morris (1910-) Amer; ptr
DOUZE PEINTRES (statement); 2 ill
ILLINOIS 1955 202-203 (statement); 1 ill
JANIS I 91 (statement); 1 ill
KUH 105-117 (interview); 6 ill
MILLER 1942 51-59 (statement); 10 ill
RODMAN I 8-14 (interview)

GRAVES, Nancy Stevenson (1940-) Amer; ptr, sclp
ART-RITE no.5 6 (response)

211

CELEBRATION (statement); 1 ill
KUNST BLEIBT KUNST 210-211 (statement); 2 ill
ROSE II REVISED 224 (statement, o.p. 1973)
ROSE II REVISED 225 (statement, o.p. 1974)
SCHAPIRO 25 (statement); port; 1 ill

GRAY, Clarence ( ) Amer; cart
M.H. DE YOUNG 59 (response); self port

GRAY, Cleve (1918-) Amer; ptr
ART NOW v.2 no.2 (statement); 1 ill
ILLINOIS 1951 183 (statement); 1 ill
ILLINOIS 1959 219-220 (statement)
ILLINOIS 1963 103 (statement); 1 ill

GRAZIANI, Sante (1920-) Amer; ptr
ILLINOIS 1969 40-41 (statement); 1 ill
SAO PAULO 74-75 (statement); port; 1 ill

GRCEVIC, Mladen (1918-) Yugo; photo
WALSH 300-301 (statement); 1 ill

GREAVES, Derrick (1927-) Brit; ptr
CONTEMPORARY (statement); port; 2 ill

GREEN, Alan (1932-) Brit; ptr
CONTEMPORARY (statement); port; 2 ill
EMANUEL II 361-362 (statement); 1 ill
NAYLOR 362-363 (statement); 1 ill
SKIRA 1975 102 (extract from interview with Bernard Devir, 1974); 1 ill
SKIRA 1979 51, 53 (statement); 1 ill

GREEN, Albert (1914-) Amer; pott
HERMAN 60 (statement); port; 1 ill

GREEN, Anthony (1939-) Brit; ptr
CONTEMPORARY (statement); port; 1 ill

GREEN, Denise G. (1946-) Atrl/Amer; ptr
MARSHALL 26 (statement); port; 5 ill
SHEARER 28-31 (interview); 3 ill

GREEN, Jim (1934-) Amer; coll
CALIFORNIA--COLLAGE (statement); 1 ill

GREEN, Phyllis (1950-) Cana; sclp, pott
POINT OF VIEW 12 (statement); 1 ill

GREEN, Robert H. (1930-) Amer; ptr
LEWIS I 62 (statement); port; 1 ill

GREEN, Vanalyne ( ) Amer
EVENTS II 32-33 (statement); 1 ill

GREENAMYER, George Mossman ( ) Amer; metal, sclp
HAYSTACK 23 (statement); 1 ill

GREENBERG, Allan ( ) Amer; arch
BUILDINGS 38-41 (statement); 2 ill

GREENBERG, Gloria (1932-) Amer; sclp
NAYLOR 363 (poem); 1 ill

GREENE, Balcomb (1904-) Amer; sclp, ptr
ABSTRACT 29-31, 36, 120-121 (essay: "Expression as Production"); 2 ill
ILLINOIS 1952 194-195 (statement); 1 ill
ILLINOIS 1963 109 (statement); 1 ill
JANIS I 81 (statement); 1 ill
PLASTIQUE no.3 12-14 (essay: "American Perspective"); 1 ill
RODMAN III 105-106 (statements)
ROSE II 118-120 (extract from essay: "American Perspective," o.p. 1938)
ROSE II REVISED 96-98 (extract from essay: "American Perspective," o.p. 1938)
SELZ 83-87 (statement); 3 ill

GREENE, Donald O. (1940-) Amer; ptr
LEWIS I 52 (statement); port; 2 ill

GREENE, Herbert (1929-) Amer; arch, ptr
EMANUEL I 311-312 (statement); 1 ill
HEYER 73-77 (interview); 12 ill
ILLINOIS 1965 191 (statement); 1 ill

GREENE, J. Barry (1895-) Amer; ptr
100 CONTEMPORARY 70-71 (statement); port; 1 ill

GREENE, Stephen (1918-) Amer; ptr
ART NOW v.4 no.1 (statement); 1 ill
ILLINOIS 1955 203-204 (statement); 1 ill
ILLINOIS 1957 208-209 (response); 1 ill
ILLINOIS 1961 68 (response); port; 1 ill
NEW DECADE 36-38 (statement); 2 ill

GREENFIELD, Verni ( ) Amer; pott
IRVINE 19, 87 (statement); 1 ill

GREENGOLD, Jane (1945-) Amer; ptr
BRENTANO 210-211 (statement); 1 ill

GREENHAM, Lily (1928-) Aust; sclp, light
LUMIERE (statement); port; 1 ill

GREENLY, Colin (1928-) Brit/Amer; ptr
ILLINOIS 1974 52 (statement); 1 ill

GREENSTONE, Marion (1925-) Amer; ptr
FULBRIGHT 25 (statement)

GREENWOOD, Marion (1909-) Amer; ptr
BRITANNICA 46 (statement); port; 1 ill
ZAIDENBERG 106-108 (essay: "Form and Content"); 6 ill

GREGORY, Waylande (1905-71) Amer; sclp
FIRST AMERICAN 92-93 (essay: "The Present Impasse in Sculpture")

GREGOTTI, Vittorio (1927-) Ital; arch
RUSSELL F 70-71 (project proposal); 6 ill

GREIS, Otto (1913-) Germ
PREMIER BILAN 295 (statement); port

GRENIER, Louie (1945-) Amer; video
TUCKER II 31-32 (statement); port

GREY, Alex (1953-) Amer; ptr
BOSTON III (interview); 1 ill

GREY, Roger de (1918-) Brit; ptr
CONTEMPORARY (statement); port; 2 ill

GRGEC, Petar (1933-) Yugo; ptr
TOMASEVIC 112-116 (statement); port; 2 ill

GRIEB, Toni (1918-) design, envir
KORNFELD 17 (statement); port; 4 ill

GRIFFA, Giorgio (1936-) Ital; ptr
SKIRA 1976 76 (statement); 1 ill
SKIRA 1978 78 (statement); 1 ill

GRIFFIN, George ( )
ART-RITE no.14 5, 8 (response)

GRIFFIN, Ron (1938-) Amer; sclp, ptr
LEWIS II 58 (statement); port; 3 ill

GRIFFITH, Denny (1952-) sclp
ARTPARK 1982 36-37, 46 (statement); port; 4 ill
SCULPTURE OUTSIDE (statement); 4 ill

GRIFFITH, Peg ( ) Amer
  BRAKKE   137-147   (text   piece:
  "Cognate Parallels")

GRIFFITHS, Kenneth ( ) NewZ; photo
  HOW FAMOUS 78-81 (statements); port;
  4 ill

GRIGNANI, Franco (1908-) Ital; photo
  WALSH 302-304 (statement); 1 ill

GRIGORIADIS, Mary ( ) Amer; ptr
  SCHAPIRO 26 (statement); port; 1 ill

GRIGSBY, Eugene (1918-) Amer; ptr
  LEWIS I REVISED 78 (statement); port;
  1 ill

GRILLEY, Robert L. (1920-) Amer; ptr
  ILLINOIS 1953 185 (statement); 1 ill
  WISCONSIN I (statement); 1 ill
  WISCONSIN II (statement); 1 ill

GRILLO, John (1917-) Amer; ptr
  IT IS no.3 49 (statement)

GRIMM, Lynda (1952-) Amer; pott
  HERMAN 61 (statement); port; 1 ill

GRIPPE, Peter (1912-) Amer; sclp
  ILLINOIS 1961 72-73 (response); port; 1
  ill
  MOTHERWELL   8-22   (three   group
  discussions: "Artists'   Sessions   at
  Studio 35," New York, 1950)
  TIGER no.4 78, 102 (statement); 1 ill

GRIPPI, Salvatore (1921-) Amer; ptr
  FULBRIGHT 26 (statement)

GRIPPO, Victor (1936-) Arge; sclp
  EMANUEL II 364-365 (statement); 1 ill
  NAYLOR 364-365 (statement); 1 ill

GRIS, Juan (Jose Victoriano Gonzalez)
  (1887-1927) Span; ptr
  CHIPP 274 (response, o.p. 1921)
  CHIPP 274-277 (response, o.p. 1925);
  self port; 1 ill
  FRY 162-163 ("Personal Statement,"
  o.p. 1921)
  FRY   169-171   ("Reply   to   a
  Questionnaire," o.p. 1925)
  GROHMANN 386-388 ("Briefe," 1919,
  1920, 1921, p.p. 1947)
  GROHMAN 389-390 ("Anmerkungen
  uber Meine Malerei," p.p. 1948)
  GUGGENHEIM II 70-71 (statement); 1 ill
  POENSGEN 100-102 ("Uber die
  Moglichkeiten der Malerei," 1925)
  PROTTER 217 (extract from *On the
  Possibilities of Painting*, 1924)
  RAYNAL 171-180 (statement); 2 ill
  SEGHERS 159, 193-202 (talk: "Some
  Possibilities in Painting," given in
  Paris, 1924)

GRISI, Laura (1939-) Gree/Ital; print
  SKIRA 1977 69 (statement); 1 ill
  SKIRA 1979 83 (statement); 2 ill

GROMAIRE, Marcel (1892-1971) Fren;
  ptr
  GOLDAINE 59-62 (interview); port
  RAYNAL 181-185 (statement); 2 ill

GRONBORG, Erik (1931-) Dani/Amer;
  pott, sclp
  CLARK 185-192 (essay: "Viewpoint:
  Ceramics 1977," o.p. 1977)
  HERMAN 62 (statement); port; 1 ill
  VIEWPOINT 1977 9 (statement); 3 ill

GRONDONA, Tom (1950-) Amer; arch
  LA JOLLA 46-48 (statement); port; 3 ill

GROOMS, Red (1937-) Amer; ptr, sclp,
  instal
  ART NOW v.2 no.7 (statement); 1 ill

EMANUEL II 366-367 (statement); 1 ill
KIRBY 118-120 ("a statement")
KIRBY 121-123 ("The Burning Building/ the script"); port
NAYLOR 366 (statement); 1 ill

GROPIUS, Walter (1883-1969) Germ/Amer; arch
CIRCLE 238-242 (essay: "Art Education and State," o.p. in *The Year Book of Education*, 1936)
CONRADS 46-47 ("New Ideas on Architecture," o.p. 1919)
CONRADS 49-53 ("Programme of the Staatliches Bauhaus in Weimar," o.p. 1919)
CONRADS 95-97 (extract from "Principles of Bauhaus Production (Desau)," o.p. 1926)
CONRADS 146-147 ("A Programme for City Reconstruction," o.p. 1943)
GROHMANN 468-473 ("Idee und Aufban des Staatlichen Bauhauses," p.p. 1923)
GROHMANN 473-475 ("Internationale Architektur," p.p. 1925)
HEYER 196-209 (interview); 18 ill
KEPES V 94-97 (essay: "Reorientation")
KEPES IX 62-73 (extract from "private communications" with John E. Burchard)
MIESEL 176-177 ("What is Architecture?", 1919, p.p. 1962)
NELSON 253-262 (interview with Frederick Day)
POENSGEN 94, 96 ("Grundlagen Kunstlerischer Gestaltung," 1923)

GROPPER, William (1897-) Amer; ptr
ADVERSARY 12 (extract from questionnaire, 1945)
ADVERSARY 12 (statement, o.p. 1968-69)

ART VOICES v.4 no.2 82-85 (statements); 5 ill
BRITANNICA 47 (statement); port; 1 ill
ILLINOIS 1952 195-196 (statement); 1 ill
ILLINOIS 1955 204-205 (statement); 1 ill
M. H. DE YOUNG 60 (response); self port
100 CONTEMPORARY 72-73 (statement); port; 1 ill

GROSS, Anthony (1905-) Brit; ptr, print
CONTEMPORARY (statement); port; 2 ill

GROSS, Chaim (1904-) Aust/Amer; sclp
GOODRICH 53-68 (statement); 14 ill
100 CONTEMPORARY 74-75 (statement); port; 1 ill

GROSS, Michael (1920-) Isra; ptr
SEITZ I (statement); 5 ill

GROSS, Sidney ( )
ART VOICES v.4 no.1 76 (statement); 1 ill

GROSSEN, Francoise (1945-) Swis/Amer; text
FIBER 16-17 (statement); 1 ill

GROSSMAN, Irving (1926-) Cana; arch
EMANUEL I 320-321 (statement); 1 ill

GROSSMAN, Joseph (1889-) Amer; ptr
100 CONTEMPORARY 76-77 (statement); port; 1 ill

GROSSMAN, Nancy (1940-) Amer; sclp
CELEBRATION (statement); 1 ill
NEMSER 326-355 (interview); port; 10 ill

GROSSMANN, Rudolf (1882-1941)
WINGLER 42-45 (essay: "Besuch bei Corinth," p.p.)

GROSVENOR, Robert (1937-) Amer; sclp
ARTPARK 1975 74-75 (statement); port; 1 ill

GROSZ, George (1893-1959) Germ/Amer; ptr, print
ADVERSARY 14 (statement, o.p. 1925)
BRITANNICA 48 (statement); port; 1 ill
GASSNER 573-578 (extract from *A Little Yes and a Big No*)
MIESEL 185-188 ("My New Pictures," 1921)
PROTTER 224-226 (extract from *George Grosz Drawings*)
SCHMIDT 57-58 (statement)

GROTH, John August (1908-) Amer; ptr
FIRST AMERICAN 51-53 (essay: "The Artist and His Audience, The Magazine and the Artist")

GROUNDS, Joan ( ) perf
ART NETWORK no.2 49 (statement)

GROUP OF THE FIVE (Le Groupe de Cinq) (group) perf, photo
SKIRA 1978 53 (statement); 2 ill

GROUP TALLER DE MONTEVIDEO
SEE: TALLER DE MONTEVIDEO

GROUP UNTEL (group) envir
SKIRA 1978 52-53 (statement); 1 ill

GROUPE DE CINQ
SEE: GROUP OF THE FIVE

GROUPE DE RECHERCHE D'ART VISUEL (group)
LUMIERE (statement); port; 1 ill
SEE ALSO: GRAV

GROUPE D'ETUDES D'ARCHITECTURES MOBILE

SEE: GEAM

GROW, Ronald (1934-) Amer; sclp
ILLINOIS 1965 210 (statement); 1 ill

GRUBER, Hetum (1937-) Germ; ptr, paper
SKIRA 1978 80 (extract from a letter to Dr. Manfred Schneckenburger); 1 ill
SKIRA 1980 60 (statement); 3 ill

GRUBLER, Benjamin (1948-) Amer; ptr
EVENTS I 42 (statement); 1 ill

GRUDIN, Louis ( ) ptr
ART VOICES v.4 no.1 146 (statement and poem); 1 ill

GRUEN, Victor David (1903-) Amer; arch
EMANUEL I 321-323 (statement); 1 ill

GRUMBACH, Antoine ( ) Fren; arch
ARCHITECTURES 148-153 (essay: "L'Art de Completer Les Villes"); 6 ill

GRUNBAUM, James (1909-) Amer; ptr
ILLINOIS 1953 185-186 (statement)

GRUNDER, Marianne (1926-) Swis; sclp
KORNFELD 21-22 (statement); port; 4 ill

GRUNG, Geir ( ) Norw; arch
NEWMAN 108-113 (statement); 17 ill

GRUPPE CRONICA
SEE: EQUIPO CRONICA

GRUPPE ZERO (group)
ART SINCE v.1 160 (poem, o.p. 1963)

GRUTZKE, Johannes (1937-) Germ; ptr
KUNST UND POLITIK (statement); port; 3 ill

NAYLOR 369-370 (statement); 1 ill

GRYLLS, Vaughan (1943-) Brit
SKIRA 1977 47 (statement); 1 ill

GUATTA, Mario ( ) design
DIAMONSTEIN V 48-63 (interview);
port; 9 ill

GUCCIONE, Piero ( ) ptr
CLAIR 52-53 (extract from interview
with Enzo Siciliano, 1971); 1 ill

GUDMUNDSSON, Gudmundur
SEE: ERRO

GUDMUNDSSON, Sigurdur (1942-)
Icel/Dutc; perf, sclp, photo
SKIRA 1979 34-35 (statement made to
Gjis van Tuyl); 1 ill
SLEEPING 62-71 (statement); port; 8 ill
STEDELIJK 126-127 (statement in
Dutch); 3 ill

GUEDES, Joaquim (1932-) Braz; arch
EMANUEL I 325-327 (statement); 1 ill

GUERILLA ART ACTION GROUP
(group)
KUNST UND POLITIK
("Action/Interview of the Guerilla Art
Group on Radio WBAI on 1/5/70"; in
English and German)
NAYLOR 371 (statement)

GUERIN, John (1920-) Amer; ptr
ILLINOIS 1957 209 (response); 1 ill
ILLINOIS 1959 221 (statement); 1 ill

GUERRERO, Jose (1914-) Span/Amer;
ptr
ART NOW v.2 no.8 (statement); 1 ill

GUERRIER, Raymond (1920-) Fren; ptr
PREMIER BILAN 296 (statement); port

GUETERSLOH, Albert Paris (1887-)
Aust; ptr
BREICHA 234-237 (essay: ▪Egon
Schiele,▪ o.p. 1912)

GUGLIELMI, O. Lewis (1906-1956)
Amer; ptr
BETHERS II 40 (statement); 1 ill
BRITANNICA 49 (statement); port; 1 ill
ILLINOIS 1950 178 (statement); 1 ill
ILLINOIS 1951 183-184 (statement); 1 ill
JANIS I 111 (statement); 1 ill
MILLER 1943 38-39 (statement); 2 ill

GUIDI, Virgilio (1892-) Ital; ptr
VERZOCCHI 243-247 (statement); self
port; 1 ill

GUINAN, Robert (1934-) Amer; ptr
CLAIR 54-55 (statement, 1977); 1 ill
SKIRA 1977 12 (statement); 1 ill

GUINOCHET, Francois ( )
GROH (statement)

GUINOVART, Jose (1927-) Port; ptr
SKIRA 1977 28 (statement); 1 ill

GUINOVART, Josep ( ) Span; ptr
PORCEL I 111-122 (interview); 2 ill

GUITE, Suzanne (1926/27-) Cana; sclp
CANADA 22-23 (statement); port; 1 ill

GUITET, James (1925-) Fren; ptr
RAGON 202-205 (statement)

GUITIERREZ, Louis (1933-) Amer; ptr,
sclp
ILLINOIS 1965 95 (statement); 1 ill

GUNDERSON, Barry L. (1945-) Amer;
sclp
SCULPTURE OUTSIDE (statement); 4 ill

GUNDERSON, Bruce ( ) Amer; perf
ARTPARK 1977 38-39 (statement); 3 ill

GUNDERSON/CLARK (group) Amer
BRAKKE 237-250 (text piece); 13 ill

GUNTHER, Max ( ) ptr
ART VOICES v.4 no.4 70 (statement); 1
ill

GURNEY, Eric ( ) Amer; illus
NORTH LIGHT 116-121 (statement);
port; 8 ill

GURR, Lena (1897-) Amer; ptr
100 CONTEMPORARY 78-79
(statement); port; 1 ill

GUSELLA, Ernest (1941-) Cana; video
ART-RITE no.7 11 (response)

GUSTON, Philip (1913-1980) Amer; ptr
FORTY (statement, o.p. 1951); 2 ill
IT IS no.1 44 (statement)
IT IS no.5 34-38 (group discussion)
MILLER 1956 36-43 (statement); port; 6
ill
MOMA 1959 40-43 (statement); port; 3
ill

GUTBROD, Konrad Rolf Dietrich (1910-
) Germ; arch
EMANUEL I 327-329 (statement); 1 ill

GUTTERMAN, Siegfried ( ) Amer; photo
CALIFORNIA--PHOTOGRAPHY
(statement); port; 4 ill

GUTTUSO, Renato (1912-) Ital; ptr
ART SINCE v.2 150 (statement, o.p.
1953)
KUNST UND POLITIK (statement); port;
4 ill
MARAINI 237-249 (interview)
PREMIER BILAN 297 (statement); port

VERZOCCHI 249-253 (statement); self
port; 1 ill

GUY, Joseph (1943-) Amer; paper, ptr
PAPERWORKS 12-13 (statement); 2 ill

GUZMAN, Alberto (1927-) Fren; sclp
SKIRA 1976 90 (statement); 1 ill

GWATHMEY, Charles (1938-) Amer;
arch
DIAMONSTEIN II 64-77 (interview);
port; 4 ill
EMANUEL I 329-331 (statement); 1 ill
GA DOCUMENT no.4 80-83 (statement);
15 ill

GWATHMEY, Robert (1903-) Amer; ptr
BETHERS I 230-231 (statement); 1 ill
ILLINOIS 1951 184 (statement); 1 ill
ILLINOIS 1953 186 (statement); 1 ill
ILLINOIS 1963 51 (statement); 1 ill
ILLINOIS 1965 180-181 (statement); 1 ill
PROTTER 236-237 (statement, 1963); 1
ill

GWYNNE, Patrick (1913-) Brit; arch
EMANUEL I 331-332 (statement); 1 ill

HAACKE, Hans Christoph (1936-)
Germ/Amer; sclp
ART AND TECHNOLOGY 116-117
(project proposal)
ART-RITE no.9 18 (statement)
AVALANCHE no.10 16-17 (statement)
CELANT 179-184 (statement); 5 ill
CONCEPTUAL ART 32 (statement)
DIRECTIONS I 76 (response); 1 ill
KINETIC 36-37 (statement); port; 1 ill
MEYER 132-135 (statement); 4 ill
PAOLETTI 58-63 (interview with Ralph
Emmerich); 1 ill
SKIRA 1977 75 (statement); 1 ill
SKIRA 1977 141-143 (essay: "Les
Adherents")
SKIRA 1980 91 (statement); 1 ill
STEDELIJK 128-129 (statement); 1 ill
TRACKS v.3 no.3 101-105 ("The
Constituency")
VIEW v.1 no.6 (interview); 6 ill
VISION no.3 68-73 (text piece)

HAAR, Tom ( ) Amer; print, photo
HAYSTACK 24 (statement); 1 ill

HAARDT, Georges van (1907-) Poli; ptr
SEUPHOR 185 (statement); 1 ill

HAAS, Ernst (1921-) Aust; photo
CAMPBELL 134-143 (statement); port;
13 ill
WALSH 308-309 (statement); 1 ill

HAAS, Eva (1933-) Swis; print
KORNFELD 23-24 (statement); port; 4
ill

HAAS, Richard (1936-) Amer; ptr
BELFORD 101-128 (group discussion)
COLLABORATION 136-143 (essay:
"The Great American Cemetery"); 6
ill

HABER, Shamai (1922-) Isra/Poli; sclp
SEITZ I (statement); 2 ill

HABRAKEN, Nicolaas John (1928-)
Dutc; arch
EMANUEL I 333-334 (statement)

HADFIELD, Scott (1953-) Amer; ptr
BOSTON II (statement); 1 ill

HADFIELD, Ted Lee (1950-) Amer; sclp
MICHIGAN 14-15 (statement); 2 ill

HAERER, Carol (1933-) Amer; ptr
SCHAPIRO 27 (statement); port; 1 ill

HAFIF, Marcia (1929-) Amer; ptr
SKIRA 1976 71 (statement); 1 ill

HAFNER, Dorothy (1952-) Amer; pott
HERMAN 63 (statement); port; 1 ill

HAGEN, Claude ( ) Amer
BRAKKE 148-149 (text piece: "The
Secret of the Universe")

HAGEN, Gary D. (1939-) Amer; sclp
WISCONSIN II (statement); 1 ill

HAGLER, Skeeter ( ) Amer; photo
LEEKLEY 134-139 (statement); 12 ill

HAGUE, Raoul (1905-) Amer; sclp
MILLER 1956 44-51 (statement); port; 8
ill

HAHN, Walter H. (1927-) Amer; ptr
ILLINOIS 1953 187 (statement); 1 ill

HAILEY, Jason ( ) Amer; photo
CALIFORNIA--PHOTOGRAPHY
(statement); port; 4 ill

HAINE, Desire ( ) Belg; ptr

COLLARD 130-134 (interview); port; 1 ill

HAINES, Charles Richard (1906-) Amer; ptr
CALIFORNIA--PAINTING 18 (statement); 1 ill
ILLINOIS 1950 179 (statement); 1 ill
ILLINOIS 1951 184-185 (statement); 1 ill
ILLINOIS 1961 74 (response); port; 1 ill

HAJDU, Etienne (1907-) Ruma/Fren; ptr, sclp
CHIPP 605 (statement, o.p. 1955)
EMANUEL II 379-380 (statement); 1 ill
RAGON 228-231 (statement)
RITCHIE 22-25 (statement); port; 4 ill
VINGTIEME N.S. no.9 31 (statement); 1 ill
YALE 23-24 (statement)

HAJEK, Otto Herbert (1927-) Germ; sclp
HAUSSER 74-77 (poem, 1974); 8 ill

HALASZ, Gyala
SEE: BRASSAI

HALEM, Henry (1938-) Amer; glass
GLASS v.1 10-13 (statement)
GLASS v.5 (group discussion); port; 1 ill

HALEY, John C. (1905-) Amer; ptr, sclp
BETHERS I 232-233 (statement); 1 ill
BETHERS II 86-87 (statement); 2 ill
ILLINOIS 1951 185 (statement); 1 ill
ILLINOIS 1953 187 (statement); 1 ill

HALEY, Nade ( ) sclp
ARTPARK 1981 (statement); port; 2 ill

HALFMANN, Jasper ( ) arch
RUSSELL F 101-102 (project proposal); 6 ill

HALICKA, Alice (1894-) Poli; ptr
RAYNAL 187-190 (statement); 2 ill

HALKIN, Theodore (1924-) Amer; ptr, sclp
ILLINOIS 1965 70 (statement); 1 ill

HALL, Carl (1921-) Amer; ptr
ILLINOIS 1951 185 (statement); 1 ill

HALL, Doug (1944-) Amer; ptr, video, coll
NEW VISIONS (statement); 3 ill
WINSTON-SALEM 33-41 (statement); 11 ill

HALL, Horathel Dickey (1928-) Amer; sclp, text
FAX II 314-324 (statements); port; 1 ill

HALL, John ( ) Cana; ptr
VANCOUVER (statement); 2 ill

HALL, Lee (1934-) Amer; ptr
HESS 130-146 (essay: "In the University")

HALL, Nigel (1943-) Amer; sclp
BRITISH (statement); 1 ill

HALL, Susan (1943-) Amer; ptr
SCHAPIRO 28 (statement); port; 1 ill

HALL, Walter (1949-) Amer; pott
HERMAN 64 (statement); port; 1 ill

HALL, Warren (1939-) Amer; sclp
AWARDS 4-7 (statement); 3 ill

HALL, Wes (1934-) Amer; ptr
LEWIS I REVISED 85 (statement); port; 1 ill

HALLEN, Hans (1930-) SoAf; arch
EMANUEL I 334-335 (statement); 1 ill

HALLOCK, Robert ( ) Amer; ptr, illus
MAGIC 64-67 (statement); port; 3 ill

HALPERN, Gina ( ) Amer; pott
HAYSTACK 25 (statement); 1 ill

HALPERN, Nancy ( ) Amer; text
HAYSTACK 26 (statement); 1 ill

HALPRIN, Lawrence (1916-) Amer; arch
COOPER-HEWITT I 4-6 (essay: "The Collective Perception of Cities")
COOPER-HEWITT II 44 (essay: "Urban Rituals")
EMANUEL I 335-337 (statement); 1 ill

HALSMAN, Philippe (1906-) Latv/Amer; photo
LAPLANTE 33-41 (interview); port; 1 ill

HALUPOVA, Suzana (1925-) Yugo; ptr
TOMASEVIC 117-119 (statement); port; 2 ill

HALUSKA, Andre (1947-) Amer; photo
FUGITIVE (statement); 1 ill

HALVORSEN, Liza (1949-) Amer; pott
HERMAN 65 (statement); port; 1 ill

HAMADA, Shoji (1894-) Japa; pott
ADACHI 20-23 (statement); ports; 3 ill
YAMADA 311-314 (interview with Chisaburoh Yamada, 1969)

HAMADY, Walter Samuel (1940-) Amer; photo, coll
WISCONSIN I (statement); 1 ill

HAMAYA, Hiroshi (1915-) Japa; photo
CAMPBELL 90-101 (statement); port; 12 ill
WALSH 313-315 (extract from the preface to *Landscapes of Japan*, 1964); 1 ill

HAMBLETT, Theora (1895-1977) Amer; ptr, illus
FERRIS 69-100 (statements); ports; 14 ill
SYMBOLS (statement); 1 ill

HAMBLING, Maggi (1945-) Brit; ptr
CONTEMPORARY (statement); port; 2 ill

HAMBURGER, Bernard ( ) Fren; arch
ARCHITECTURES 136-139 (essay: "La Gare D'Evry, une Structure Imaginaire"); 5 ill

HAMES, Kelly ( )
ART-RITE no.19 17-20 (group discussion)

HAMILTON, Elaine (1920-) Amer; ptr
FULBRIGHT 26-27 (statement); 1 ill

HAMILTON, Frances (1949-) Amer; ptr
BOSTON I (interview); 1 ill

HAMILTON, Frank O. (1923-) Amer; ptr
ILLINOIS 1965 65 (statement); 1 ill

HAMILTON, Leah Rinne ( ) ptr
BETHERS I 234-235 (statement); 1 ill

HAMILTON, Peter ( ) arch
GA HOUSES no.2 104-109 (statement); 14 ill

HAMILTON, Richard (1922-) Brit; ptr
ART SINCE v.2 324 (statement, o.p. 1956; letter, 1957)
ARTS YEARBOOK v.8 160-163 (interview with Eduardo Paolozzi)
CONTEMPORARY (extract from interview with Yoshiaki Toni, 1971); port; 3 ill
ENGLISH 86-91 (statement); port; 8 ill

HANSON, Duane (1925-) Amer; sclp
EMANUEL II 383-384 (statement)
JOHNSON 164-167 (interview with Linda Chase and Ted McBurnett, o.p. 1972); 1 ill
NAYLOR 382-384 (statement); 1 ill
SUPERREAL 160-161 (statement); 1 ill

HANSON, Jo ( ) Amer; instal, sclp
VISUAL v.1 no.4 21 (statement); 1 ill

HANSON, Norman Leonard (1909-) SoAf; arch
EMANUEL I 339-341 (statement); 1 ill

HANSON, Philip (1943-) Amer; ptr
ACKLAND 20-37, 64-65 (group discussion, 10/29/79); 2 ill

HARA, Hiroshi (1936-) Japa; arch
GA DOCUMENT no.4 94-117 (statements); 40 ill

HARARI, Hananiah (1912-) Amer; ptr
MILLER 1943 40 (statement); 1 ill

HARDEN, Marvin (1935-) Amer; ptr, print
FINE 227-229 (letter, 1971); 3 ill

HARDING, Noel Robert (1945-) Brit/Cana; perf, envir
SKIRA 1978 36 (statement); 5 ill

HARDING, Robert (1938-) Amer; perf
BRENTANO 222-223 (statement); 1 ill

HARDY, Andy ( ) Amer; photo
LEEKLEY 22-23 (statement); 1 ill

HARDY, Bert (1913-) Brit; photo
WALSH 318-319 (statement); 1 ill

HARDY HOLZMAN PFEIFFER ASSOCIATES (arch firm)

GA HOUSES no.5 136-141 (statement); 9 ill
SEARING 114-121 (statement); 7 ill

HARDY, Hugh Gelston (1932-) Amer; arch
COLLABORATION 96-103 (essay: "Restaurant Pavilions for Bryant Park: Musings on Variety"); 10 ill
DIAMONSTEIN II 80-102 (interview); port; 6 ill
EMANUEL I 342-344 (statement); 1 ill
ON SITE no.5/6 68-75 (essay: "The Energy of Reuse")
SEE ALSO: HARDY HOLZMAN PFEIFFER ASSOCIATES

HARE, David (1917-) Amer; sclp, ptr
ALBRIGHT-KNOX 92-93 (letter, 8/1968); 1 ill
IT IS no.5 15 ("A Talk on Sculpture")
JANIS I 122 (statement); 1 ill
JEAN 398-399 (talk given at the Maryland Institute College of Art, 1969)
LETTERS 12-13 (letter); 1 ill
MILLER 1946 24-27 (statement); 4 ill
MOTHERWELL 8-22 (three group discussions: "Artists' Sessions at Studio 35," New York, 1950)
RODMAN I 148-154 (interview)
TIGER no.4 78-79, 101 (statement); 1 ill
TRACKS v.1 no.2 42, 52 (poems: "Ants are Any Bodys," "Two Turtles")

HARE, Sharon (1950-) Amer; sclp
SCRIPPS COLLEGE (statement); 1 ill

HARGER, Stephen ( ) Amer; ptr
IRVINE 35, 80 (statement); 1 ill

HARING, Hugo (1882-1958) Germ; arch
CONRADS 103-105 (extract from talk: "Formulations Towards a

Reorientation in the Applied Arts,"
o.p. 1927)
CONRADS 126-127 (extract from "The
House as an Organic Structure," o.p.
1932)
GROHMANN 485-491 ("Wege zur
Form," p.p. 1925)

HARKAVY, Minna ( ) Amer; sclp
100 CONTEMPORARY 80-81
(statement); port; 1 ill

HARLOW, Rick (1950-) Amer; ptr
BOSTON II (statement); 1 ill
BOSTON III (interview); 1 ill

HARMAN, Fred (1902-) Amer; illus
M.H. DE YOUNG 62 (response); self port

HARMON, Lily (1912-) Amer; ptr
BRITANNICA 50 (statement); port; 1 ill
ILLINOIS 1952 197-198 (statement); 1 ill
ILLINOIS 1957 210 (response); 1 ill
ILLINOIS 1959 222-223 (statement); 1 ill
100 CONTEMPORARY 82-83
(statement); port; 1 ill

HARRINGTON, Phillip A. ( ) photo
LAPLANTE 42-52 (interview); port; 1 ill

HARRIS, Harwell Hamilton (1903-)
Amer; arch
EMANUEL I 345-348 (statement); 1 ill

HARRIS, Ian Carr ( )
PARACHUTE no.1 28-31 (statement, in
English); 4 ill

HARRIS, John T. (1908-) Amer; ptr
LEWIS I 19 (statement); port; 2 ill

HARRIS, Pamela (1940-) Amer/Cana;
photo
SCHAPIRO 30 (statement); port; 1 ill

HARRIS, Paul (1925-) Amer; sclp
SAO PAULO 76-77 (statement); port

HARRIS, Roberta (1943-) Amer; sclp
NEW VISIONS (statement); 2 ill
TEXAS 8-11 (statement); 5 ill

HARRIS, Suzanne (1942-) Amer; sclp,
envir
ARTPARK 1974 18-19 (statement); port;
2 ill
ARTPARK 1978 24-27 (statement); port;
14 ill
AVALANCHE no.5 36-45 (group
discussion); 8 ill
SKIRA 1978 121 (statement); 1 ill

HARRIS, William (1943-) Amer; pott
CONTEMPORARY AFRICAN
(statement); port; 1 ill

HARRISON, Charles ( )
ART-LANGUAGE v.3 no.2 20-30
("Pedagogical Sketchbook (AL)")
ART-LANGUAGE v.3 no.2 65-67
("Slogan Adaptation")
ART-LANGUAGE v.3 no.2 68-69 ("'Mr.
Lin Yutang Refers to "Fair Play"...?'")
ART-LANGUAGE v.3 no.2 89-92
("Utopian Prayers and Infantile
Marxism")
ART-LANGUAGE v.3 no.2 95 ("On the
Embarrassing Dangers of Banishing 12-
Tone Music")
SEE ALSO: ART AND LANGUAGE

HARRISON, Helen Mayer (1929-) Amer;
envir, sclp, instal
ARTPARK 1977 40-43 (statement); 6 ill
ARTPARK 1978 28-29 (statement); port;
5 ill
AUPING I 32-51, 98-120 (interview); 13
ill

HARRISON, Joshua ( ) Amer; envir
ARTPARK 1977 40-43 (statement); 6 ill

HARRISON, Lawrence Victor (1941-)
Amer; ptr
WISCONSIN II (statement); 1 ill

HARRISON, Liz (1947-) Brit; sclp
BRITISH (statement); 1 ill

HARRISON, Lou ( ) ptr
GRAYSON 92-93 (extract from *Lou Harrison's Music Primer*)

HARRISON, Margaret ( ) ptr, coll
BOSHIER (statement); port; 3 ill
ISSUE (statements)

HARRISON, Newton (1932-) Amer; sclp
ART AND TECHNOLOGY 118-126 (project proposal); 8 ill
ARTPARK 1977 40-43 (statement); 6 ill
ARTPARK 1978 28-29 (statement); port; 5 ill
AUPING I 32-51, 98-120 (interview); 13 ill
EMANUEL II 385-386 (statement)
KUNST BLEIBT KUNST 212-215 (statement); 1 ill
NAYLOR 384-385 (statement); port

HARRISON, Sandra ( )
ART-LANGUAGE v.3 no.2 13-19 ("'To Begin With, While I am Clearly a Marxist Sympathizer'")
ART-LANGUAGE v.3 no.2 87-88 ("My Amazed Admiration...")
ART-LANGUAGE v.3 no.2 89-92 ("Utopian Prayers and Infantile Marxism")
ART-LANGUAGE v.3 no.2 95 ("On the Embarrassing Dangers of Banishing 12-Tone Music")

HARRISON, Wallace Kirkman (1895-)
Amer; arch
EMANUEL I 348-349 (statement); 1 ill

HARRITON, Abraham (1893-) Amer; ptr
100 CONTEMPORARY 84-85 (statement); port; 1 ill

HARTELL, John A. (1902-) Amer; ptr
ILLINOIS 1951 186 (statement)

HARTIGAN, Grace (1922-) Amer; ptr
ALBRIGHT-KNOX 62-63 (letter, 7/1968); 1 ill
CELEBRATION (statement); 1 ill
EMANUEL II 386-388 (statement); 1 ill
ILLINOIS 1967 111 (statement); 1 ill
ILLINOIS 1969 182-183 (statement); 1 ill
LETTERS 14 (letter); 1 ill
MILLER 1959 (statement accompanying catalog entry for Alfred Leslie)
MUNRO 202-203 (interview)
NAYLOR 385-386 (statement); 1 ill
NEMSER 148-177 (interview); port; 6 ill
VARIAN III (statement); 1 ill

HARTLEY, Marsden (1877-1943) Amer; ptr
ARMORY SHOW 20 (extract from "Foreword to a one-man show held at the '291' Gallery in New York, o.p. 1914")
CHIPP 526-529 (essay: "Art--and the Personal Life," o.p. 1928)
CHIPP 529 (statement, 1919, o.p. 1944)
CHIPP 529-530 (statement, o.p. 1921)
CHIPP 530-531 (statement, o.p. 1937)
CHIPP 530 (statement, 1931, o.p. 1944)
FORUM 1916 64 (statement); 1 ill
GOLDWATER 469-471 (statement, 1928)
ROSE II 63-64 (statement, o.p. 1916)
ROSE II REVISED 57-58 (statement, o.p. 1916)

ROSE II REVISED 59 (extract from essay: "Art and the Personal Life," o.p. 1928)

HARTMAN, George Eitel (1936-) Amer; arch
EMANUEL I 173-175, 349-350 (statement); 2 ill

HARTMAN, Rosella ( ) Amer; ptr
ZAIDENBERG 144-147 (essay: "Animal Drawing"); 2 ill

HARTMANN, Erich (1922-) Germ/Amer; photo
ART AND TECHNOLOGY 126 (project proposal)
WALSH 319-320 (statement); 1 ill

HARTUNG, Hans (1904-) Fren; ptr
ART SINCE v.1 154 (statement, o.p. 1947)
CHARBONNIER v.1 63-72 (interview); 1 ill
CLAUS 80-86 (interview with Jurgen Claus, 1962)
FRASNAY 115-125 (statement); port; 3 ill
GOLDAINE 123-125 (interview); port
SKIRA 1975 110-111 (extract from interview with Francois Le Targat, 1974); 1 ill
VINGTIEME N.S. no.9 26-28 (statement); 1 ill
YAMADA 293-296 (interview with Tadao Takemoto, 1969)

HARTUNG, Karl (1908-) Germ; sclp
PREMIER BILAN 298 (statement); port

HARVEY, Donald E. (1941-) Amer; photo, coll
OUTSIDE II 16-17 (statement); port; 2 ill

HARVEY, James (1929-1965) Amer; ptr
FULBRIGHT 28 (statement)
YOUNG 1960 (statement); 1 ill

HARVEY, Robert (1924-) Amer; ptr
ILLINOIS 1969 59 (statement); 1 ill

HARWOOD, Janet Compere (1934-) Amer; ptr
WHITNEY (statement); 1 ill

HASEGAWA, Sabro ( ) Japa; arch
ART AND ARTIST 53-60 (essay: "My House"); 3 ill

HASELDEN, Ron (1944-) Brit; film, coll
ENGLISH 450-451 (statement); port; 3 ill

HASEN, Burton (1921-) Amer; ptr
ILLINOIS 1961 76 (response); port; 1 ill

HASKELL, Sarah D. ( ) Amer; text
HAYSTACK 27 (statement); 1 ill

HASKINS, Sam (1926-) SoAf; photo
HOW FAMOUS 164-169 (statements); port; 5 ill

HATCH, Tom (1950-) Amer; sclp
OUTSIDE I 8-11, 29 (statement); port; 3 ill

HATCHER, Brower (1942-) Amer; sclp
ILLINOIS 1974 56-57 (statement); 1 ill

HATCHER, Everett ( ) Amer; arch, design
LIFE 225-229 (interview); port

HATCHETT, Duayne (1925-) Amer; sclp
ILLINOIS 1967 50 (statement); 1 ill

HATHORN, George T. ( ) arch

GA HOUSES no.7 228-233 (statement); 21 ill

HAUER, Erwin (1926-) sclp
STRUCTURED (statement); 3 ill

HAUSMANN, Raoul (1886-1971) Aust; ptr, sclp
BANN 51-52 ("A Call for Elementarist Art," o.p. 1922)
DADA 106 ("L'Anguille")
DADA 107-108 ("L'Insigne du Poete")
PLASTIQUE no.4 7-13 (poem: "Three Little Pinetrees"); 1 ill
PLASTIQUE no.5 11-13 (statement, 1922); 2 ill

HAUSSER, Robert (1924-) Germ; photo
WALSH 324-326 (statement); 1 ill

HAVEMAN, Victor ( ) Amer; photo
CALIFORNIA--PHOTOGRAPHY (statement); port; 4 ill

HAWKES, Julian (1944-) Brit; sclp
ENGLISH 252-257 (statement); port; 5 ill

HAWLEY, Christine ( ) Brit; arch
SPIRIT 8-11 (essay: "The Avoidance of Mimicry"); 2 ill

HAXTON, Sherry (1942-) Amer; pott
HERMAN 66 (statement); port; 1 ill

HAY, Alex ( ) Amer; ptr, perf
ARTFORUM v.5 no.6 27, 29 (statement)

HAY, David ( ) Amer; pott
VIEWPOINT 1979 14-15 (statement); 5 ill

HAYAKAWA, Joanne ( ) Amer; pott
VIEWPOINT 1980 14-15 (statement); 3 ill

HAYDEN, Dolores ( ) arch
CHRYSALIS no.1 19-29 (essay: "Redesigning the Domestic Workplace")

HAYDEN, Kitty L. (1942-) Amer; ptr
LEWIS I 49 (statement); port; 2 ill

HAYDEN, Michael (1943-) Cana; film, sclp, light
ARTPARK 1975 84-85 (statement); port; 3 ill
CANADA 94-95 (statement); port; 2 ill
KUNST BLEIBT KUNST 414 (statement); 1 ill

HAYES, David V. (1931-) Amer; sclp
ILLINOIS 1965 91 (statement); 1 ill

HAYES, Lowell (1936-) Amer; coll
NOSANOW I 68-70 (statement); 2 ill

HAYES, Randy Alan (1944-) Amer; ptr, coll
GUENTHER 44-45 (statement); port; 1 ill

HAYNES, Deborah (1949-) Amer; ptr
NOSANOW II 49 (statement); 1 ill

HAYTER, Stanley William (1901-) Brit; ptr, print
FORD/VIEW v.4 no.4 126-128, 140 (essay: "Line and Space of the Imagination"); 4 ill
JANIS I 121 (statement); 1 ill
KEPES VII 71-80 (essay: "Orientation, Direction, Chierality, Velocity, and Rhythm"); 2 ill
POSSIBILITIES 76-77 ("On My Means"); 2 ill
TIGER no.8 41-45 (essay: "Interdependence of Idea and Technique in Gravure")

HAYWARD, James ( )
ART-RITE no.19 17-20 (group discussion)

HAZARD, Ben (1940-) Amer; ptr
LEWIS I REVISED 56 (statement); port; 1 ill

HAZELET, Sally Potter (1924-) Amer; ptr
FULBRIGHT 28 (statement)

HAZEN, Wayne Edmond (1945-) Amer; ptr
MICHIGAN 16-17 (statement); 1 ill

HAZLITT, Don (1948-) Amer; ptr, sclp
BRENTANO 228-229 (statement); 1 ill

HEAD, Josef (1921-) Amer; ptr
ILLINOIS 1953 188 (statement); 1 ill

HEAD, Tim (1946-) Brit; instal
ENGLISH 380-385 (statement); port; 8 ill

HEADLEY, David (1946-) Amer; ptr
CORCORAN 68-83 (interview); port; 7 ill

HEALD, Paul ( ) Amer; ptr
GUENTHER 46-47 (statement); port; 1 ill

HEALY, Anne (1939-) Amer; sclp
CELEBRATION (statement); 1 ill
HUNTER 34-37 (interview with Hugh M. Davies); 1 ill

HEARTFIELD, John (Helmut Herzfelde) (1891-1968) Germ; print, ptr, photo
SCHMIDT 67-68 (letter, 1934)
SCHMIDT 164-170 (essay: "Daumier im Reich," 1942)

HEATH, Adrian (1920-) Brit; ptr
CONTEMPORARY (statement); port; 2 ill

HEATH, David (1931-) Amer; photo
WALSH 328-329 (statement); 1 ill

HEATON, William (1918-) Amer; ptr
ILLINOIS 1959 223 (statement); 1 ill

HEBALD, Milton (1917-) Amer; sclp
ILLINOIS 1961 83 (response); port; 1 ill
ILLINOIS 1963 124 (statement); 1 ill
100 CONTEMPORARY 86-87 (statement); port; 1 ill

HECHT, J. Christopher (1950-) Amer; wood
WOODWORKING 22-23 (statement); port; 1 ill

HECHT, Zoltan ( ) Amer; ptr
100 CONTEMPORARY 88-89 (statement); port; 1 ill

HECKER, Zvi (1931-) Isra; arch
EMANUEL I 350-352 (statement); 1 ill

HEDGES, Nick (1943-) Brit; photo
WALSH 329-331 (statement); 1 ill

HEDIN, Donald M. (1920-) Amer; sclp, ptr, illus
ILLUSTRATION 94-97 (statement); port; 6 ill
MAGIC 68-71 (statement); port; 3 ill
NORTH LIGHT 130-133 (statement); port; 6 ill

HEDRICK, Robert (1930-) Cana; sclp
CANADA 70-71 (statement); port; 2 ill

HEDRICK, Wally (1928-) Amer; ptr
MILLER 1959 13-17 (statement); port; 5 ill

HEE, Hon-Chew (1906-) Amer; ptr
HAAR I 66-72 (interview with Prithwish Neogy); ports; 3 ill

HEERICH, Erwin (1922-) Germ; sclp
HAUSSER 82-83 (statement); 3 ill

HEGEDUSIC, Martin (1923-) Yugo; sclp
TOMASEVIC 120-123 (statement); port; 2 ill

HEIBEL, Axel (1936-) Germ
GROH (statement); 4 ill

HEILIGER, Bernhard (1915-) Germ; sclp
IIAUSSER 84-85 (statement); 2 ill

HEIMANN, Anne (1927-) Amer; sclp
DIRECTIONS I 76 (response); 1 ill

HEIN, Brigit (1940-) film
KUNST BLEIBT KUNST 392-393 (statement); 3 ill

HEIN, Wilhelm (1942-) film
KUNST BLEIBT KUNST 392-393 (statement); 3 ill

HEINECKEN, Robert (1931-) Amer; photo
HOWARD (interview)
TIME-LIFE III 220-221 (statements, p.p.); 2 ill
WALSH 331-332 (statement); 1 ill

HEINEMANN, Sue ( ) Amer
EVENTS II 38-39, 42-43, 44-45 (statements); 3 ill

HEINTZE, Rudy (1941-) Amer; ptr, sclp
LOGAN II 20-23 (poem); port; 5 ill

HEIZER, Michael (1944-) Amer; sclp, envir
AVALANCHE no.1 48-71 (group discussion); port; 12 ill
JOHNSON 179-184 (group discussion, o.p. 1970)
SKIRA 1980 147 (statement); 4 ill

HEJDUK, John (1929-) Amer; arch
EMANUEL I 352-354 (statement); 1 ill
RUSSELL F 109-113 (project proposal); 6 ill

HELCK, Clarence Peter (1893-) Amer; ptr
GUITAR 110-119 (interview); port; 4 ill

IIELD, Al (1928-) Amer; ptr
IT IS no.2 78 (statement)
ROSE II REVISED 190 (statement: "Art Did Not Begin in 1945," o.p. 1967)

HELD, Philip (1920-) Amer; ptr
ART VOICES v.4 no.1 81 (statement); 1 ill

HELDER, Z. Vanessa (1904-) Amer; ptr
MILLER 1943 42 (statement); 1 ill

HELIKER, John Edward (1909-) Amer; ptr
BRITANNICA 52 (statement); port; 1 ill
ILLINOIS 1951 186 (statement); 1 ill
ILLINOIS 1953 188-189 (statement); 1 ill
ILLINOIS 1955 205-206 (statement); 1 ill
ILLINOIS 1961 80-81 (response); port; 1 ill

HELION, Jean Bichier (1904-) Fren; ptr
ABSTRACTION no.1 17-18 (statement); 2 ill
ABSTRACTION no.2 20-21 (statement); 2 ill
AXIS no.2 19-24 (essay: "From Reduction to Growth"); 1 ill
AXIS no.6 9-17 (essay: "Poussin, Seurat and Double Rhythm")

EMANUEL II 398-400 (statement); 1 ill
EVANS 30-37 (essay: "Avowals and Comments"); 2 ill
EVANS 94-107 (essay: "Poussin, Seurat and Double Rhythm"); 1 ill
GUGGENHEIM II 95 (statement, o.p. 1932); 1 ill
JANIS I 74-75 (statement); 1 ill
KEPES III 148-171 (essay: "Objects for a Painter"); 16 ill
KEPES V 91 (extract from letter to Gyorgy Kepes)
KEPES IX 100-104 (statement); 3 ill
LETTERS 15 (letter); 2 ill
NAYLOR 394-395 (statement); 1 ill

HELITON, Bob (1934-) Amer; photo
LEWIS II 127 (statement); port; 2 ill

HELLER, Jules (1919-) Amer; print
VISUAL v.1 no.3 2-8 (essay: "Notes to a Young Printmaker"); port; 3 ill
VISUAL v.3 no.3 5-8 (interview)

HELLMUTH, George Francis (1907-) Amer; arch
EMANUEL I 354-356 (statement); 1 ill

HELM, Robert ( ) Amer; sclp
GUENTHER 48-49 (statement); port; 1 ill

HELMER-PETERSEN, Keld (1920-) Dani; photo
WALSH 333-334 (statement); 1 ill

HELMES, Scott ( ) Amer; coll, print
WHITE WALLS no.7 45-47 (text pieces)

HELMICK, Ralph (1952-) Amer; sclp
BOSTON I (interview); 1 ill
BOSTON III (interview); 1 ill

HELZER, Richard (1943-) Amer; metal
METALWORKS (statement); 1 ill

HEMENWAY, Audrey (1930-) Amer; sclp, envir
ARTPARK 1981 (statement); port; 3 ill

HEMINGWAY, Peter (1929-) Cana; arch
CANADIAN 56-59 (statement); 5 ill

HEMMINGS, John F. ( )
ART-LANGUAGE v.2 no.3 73-77 ("Note on Reading 1969-1972")

HENDERSON, Mike
SEE: HENDERSON, William Howard

HENDERSON, Napoleon (1943-) Amer; text
CONTEMPORARY AFRICAN (statement); port; 1 ill

HENDERSON, Nigel (1917-) Brit; photo
WALSH 334-335 (statement); 1 ill

HENDERSON, William (1941-) Brit; ptr
HAYWARD 1979 74-77 (statement); 7 ill

HENDERSON, William Howard (Mike) (1943-) Amer; ptr
LEWIS II 66 (statement); port; 3 ill

HENDRICKS, Geoffrey (1931-) Amer; perf, ptr
EMANUEL II 400-401 (statement)
NAYLOR 396-397 (statement); 1 ill

HENDRICKS, James (1938-) Amer; ptr
ILLINOIS 1969 46 (statement); 1 ill
RISENHOOVER 81-85 (interview)

HENDRICKS, Jon (1940-) Amer
ART-RITE no.6 24 (statement)
ART-RITE no.10 (letter)
ART-RITE no.11/12 ("Stop S.1 Before it Stops You")
SEE ALSO: GUERILLA ART ACTION GROUP

HENDRICKSON, Doug ( ) Amer; wood
MEILACH 250-251 (statement)

HENDRY, Ken ( ) Amer; pott
VIEWPOINT 1981 (statement); 3 ill

HENGHES (G.H. Clusmann) (1906-) sclp
LONDON BULLETIN no.13 9-10 ("My
Sculptures Bear Strange Names"); 1 ill

HENLE, Fritz (1909-) Amer; photo
WALSH 335-338 (statement); 1 ill

HENRI, Robert (1865-1929) Amer; ptr
CHIPP 520-521 (extract from essay:
"Progress in Our National Art Must
Spring from the Development of
Individuality of Ideas and Freedom of
Expression," o.p. 1909)
FORUM 1916 30-32 (essay)
GOLDWATER 398-399, 401 (xtract from
The Art Spirit)
MCCOUBREY 173-178 (essay: "The
New York Exhibition of Independent
Artists," o.p. 1910)
PROTTER 171-173 (extract from talk
given to the School of Design for
Women, Philadelphia, 1901)
ROSE II 35-36 (extract from *The Art
Spirit*)
ROSE II 36-38 (extract from talk given
at the School of Design for Women,
Philadelphia, 1901)
ROSE II 39-42 (extract from essay:
"The New York Exhibition of
Independent Artists," o.p. 1910)
ROSE II REVISED 37-40 (extract from
talk given at the School of Design for
Women, Philadelphia, 1901)

HENRICH, Biff (1953-) Amer; sclp,
envir, photo
ARTPARK 1983 30-31 (statement); 3 ill

HENRIQUEZ, Richard (1941-) Cana;
arch
CANADIAN 60-63 (statement); 5 ill

HENSELMANN, Caspar (1933-)
Germ/Amer; sclp, envir
ARTPARK 1983 32-33 (statement); 3 ill

HENSLEY, Richard (1949-) Amer; pott
HERMAN 67 (statement); port; 1 ill

HENSON, Judy Davids (1948-) Amer;
instal, video
AVANT-GARDE 22-23 (statement); 3 ill

HEPBURN, Tony (1942-) Brit/Amer;
pott
HERMAN 68 (statement); port; 1 ill
VIEWPOINT 1979 16-17 (statement); 4
ill

HEPHER, David (1935-) Brit; ptr
CONTEMPORARY (statement); port; 2
ill

HEPLER, Milton J. (1884-) Amer; ptr
SYMBOLS (statement); 1 ill

HEPPLE, Norman (1908-) Brit; ptr
BOSHIER (statement); port; 1 ill

HEPWORTH, Barbara (1903-1975) Brit
ABSTRACTION no.2 6 (statement); 2 ill
CIRCLE 113-116 (essay: "Sculpture")
FORMA 7-27 (statement); ports; 12 ill
LONDON COUNTY (statement); 1 ill
NEMSER 12-33 (interview); port; 7 ill
OPEN AIR 1954 (statement)
OPEN AIR 1960 (statement); 1 ill
QUADRUM no.10 24-26 (statements); 2
ill
READ 17-25 (statement); port; 4 ill
RODITI 90-102 (interview); port; 1 ill
TEMOIGNAGES II 22-25 (statement);
port; 8 ill

HERA (1940-) Amer; sclp
ARTPARK 1982 22-23, 44 (statement);
port; 2 ill

HERBERT, Ernest Leroy (1932-) Amer;
ptr
LEWIS II 98 (statement); port; 1 ill

HERBERT, James Arthur (1938-) Amer;
ptr
ILLINOIS 1974 58-59 (statement); 1 ill

HERBIN, Auguste (1882-1960) Fren; ptr
ABSTRACTION no.1 19 (statement); 2
ill
ABSTRACTION no.2 22 (statement); 2
ill
ABSTRACTION no.3 21 (statement); 1
ill
ABSTRACTION no.4 13-15 (statement);
1 ill
ABSTRACTION no.5 12-13 (statement);
2 ill
ART SINCE v.1 290 (statement, o.p.
1949)
FRASNAY   109-113   ("Plastic
Alphabet"); ports; 1 ill
GOLDAINE 55-58 (interview); port
TEMOIGNAGES I 146-157 (statement);
port; 8 ill

HERMAN, Josef (1911-) Poli/Brit; ptr
CONTEMPORARY (statement); port; 2
ill
NAYLOR 400-402 (statement)
RODITI 164-178 (interview); port; 1 ill

HERMES, George ( ) instal
VISUAL v.4 no.1 5-9 (interview); port; 3
ill

HEROLD, Jacques (1910-) Ruma/Fren;
ptr
DEMARNE 178-180 (interview)
PREMIER BILAN 298 (statement); port

HERON, Patrick (1920-) Brit; ptr
ARTS YEARBOOK v.6 85-87 (essay:
"The New American Painting," o.p.
1956)
ARTS YEARBOOK v.6 87-93 (essay:
"Five Americans," o.p. 1958)
ARTS YEARBOOK v.6 142-143 (essay:
"Degas: The Art of Illusionism," o.p.
1958)
NAYLOR   402-403   (extract   from
statements, 1953, 1962, 1973)

HERRAEZ GOMEZ, Fernando (1948-)
Span; photo
WALSH 339-340 (statement); 1 ill

HERRERA,   Carmen   (1915-   )
Cuba/Amer; ptr
CUBAN (statement); 2 ill

HERRING, Harry (1887-) Amer; ptr
100   CONTEMPORARY   90-91
(statement); port; 1 ill

HERRON, Ronald James (1930-) Brit;
arch
EMANUEL I 358-359 (statement); 1 ill
SPIRIT   12-15   ("Unit   6--A
Chronology"); 2 ill

HERS, Francois (1943-) Belg; photo
WALSH 340-341 (statement); 1 ill

HERSCH, Lee (1896-) Amer; ptr
PERSONAL (statement)

HERSHMAN, Lynn (1941-) Amer;
photo, coll
BATTCOCK   VI   36-39   (essay:
"Reflections on the Electric Mirror,"
p.p.)
GEORGIA 35-37, 103 (statement); port;
3 ill
GEORGIA 118-166 (group discussion:

"Artists' Convention," in Athens, GA., 1/7/1977, moderated by Jan van der Marck)
GUMPERT I 40-41 (statement); port

HERTZBERGER, Herman (1932-) Dutc; arch
EMANUEL I 359-362 (statement); 1 ill
MIKELLIDES 38-40 (essay: "Shaping the Environment"); 10 ill

HERZFELDE, Helmut
SEE: HEARTFIELD, John

HERZOG, Werner ( ) Germ; film
COTT 96-116 (interview); port

HESS, Emil (1913-) Amer; ptr
IT IS no.4 14 (statement)

HESSE, Eva (1936-1970) Amer; sclp, ptr
CELANT 56-60 (statement); 4 ill
FINCH COLLEGE (statement); port; 2 ill
GROH (statement); 1 ill
JOHNSON 188-196 (interview with Cindy Nemser, o.p. 1975); 1 ill
NEMSER 200-229 (interview); port; 8 ill
ROSE II REVISED 214-216 (extract from interview with Cindy Nemser, o.p. 1970)

HEWARD, John ( ) Cana; ptr
PARACHUTE no.1 16-21 (statement in English); 6 ill
VANCOUVER (extract from letter); 2 ill

HEYBOER, Anton (1924-) Dutc; print
STEDELIJK 132-133 (statement in Dutch); 2 ill

HEYWOOD, Peter ( ) Cana; arch
SPIRIT 88-93 (statement); 9 ill

HICKS, Leon N. (1926-) Amer; print

LEWIS I REVISED 65-66 (statement); port; 3 ill

HICKS, Margaret K. ( ) ptr
ARTISTS no.1 9-10, 12 ("Artists' Options for Supporting Their Habits")

HICKS, Sheila (1934-) Amer; text
DIAMONSTEIN IV 92-103 (interview); port; 9 ill
EMANUEL II 406 (statement)
MUNRO 362-369 (interview); port; 2 ill
NAYLOR 404-405 (statement)
SKIRA 1976 102 (statement); 1 ill

HIDALGO, Francisco ( ) Span; photo
HOW FAMOUS 194-199 (statements); port; 6 ill

HIEGEL, Hans R. (1954-) Germ; arch
SPIRIT 16-21 ("Small Manifesto 1979"); 13 ill

HIERONIM (1916-) Belg; ptr
COLLARD 136-139 (interview); port; 1 ill

HIERSOUX, Catharine (1938-) Amer; pott
HERMAN 69 (statement); port; 1 ill

HIGA, Charles E. (1933-) Amer; pott
HAAR II 19-23 (interview); ports; 2 ill

HIGBY, Wayne (1943-) Amer; pott
DIAMONSTEIN IV 104-119 (interview); port; 14 ill
HAYSTACK 28 (statement); 1 ill
WECHSLER 82-87 (statement); port; 5 ill

HIGGINS, Dick (1938-) Brit/Amer; sound, film, perf
EMANUEL II 406-407 (statement)
LIVE no.3 14 (statement)

NAYLOR 405-406 (statement)
PERFORMANCE no.1 22 (statement)

HIGGINS, Edward Ferdinand, III (1926-) Amer
CRISS-CROSS no.5 26-29 (statement); 9 ill

HIGGINS, Eugene (1874-1958) Amer; ptr
M.H. DE YOUNG 64 (response); self port

HIGGINS, George Edward (1930-) Amer; sclp
MILLER 1963 32-37 (statement); port; 7 ill

HIGGS, Joanna (1934-) Amer; ptr
KNOXVILLE (statement); port; 6 ill

HIGHSTEIN, Jene Abel (1942-) Amer; sclp
ARTPARK 1974 20-21 (statement); port; 3 ill
SKIRA 1976 106-107 (statement); 1 ill
SKIRA 1979 49 (extract from interview Jean-Paul Najar); 1 ill

HIGSBY, Wayne ( ) Amer; pott
VIEWPOINT 1977 10 (statement); 2 ill

HILBERSEIMER, Ludwig (1885-1967) arch
BANN 118-123 (essay: "Construction and Form," o.p. 1924)

HILDEBRAND, Adolf (1847-1921); Germ; sclp
THORN 92, 214, 243, 245, 246, 249, 250 (statements, p.p.)

HILER, Hilaire (1898-1966) Amer; ptr
CIRCLE no.9 55-59 (essay: "Manifesto of Psychromatic Design")

HILGER, Charles ( ) paper, sclp
VISUAL v.2 no.2 35-37 (interview); port; 1 ill
VISUAL v.3 no.4 4-6 (interview); port; 3 ill

HILL, Anthony (Redo; Rem Doxfud) (1930-) Brit; sclp
BANN 268-276 (essay: "On Constructions, Nature, and Structure," o.p. 1959); 1 ill
BOWNESS 10-11, 17, 105-107 (statement); 4 ill
EMANUEL II 407-408 (statement); 1 ill
ENGLISH 92-97 (statement); port; 7 ill
KEPES IV 162-173 (essay: "The Structural Syndrome in Constructive Art"); 8 ill
NAYLOR 406-407 (statement); 1 ill

HILL, Charles Christopher (1948-) Amer; coll, paper
AVALANCHE no.8 69 (statement); port
IRVINE 69, 84 (statement); 1 ill

HILL, James R. (1945-) Amer; ptr, sclp
OUTSIDE I 12-15, 30 (statement); port; 3 ill

HILL, Paul (1941-) Brit; photo
WALSH 341-343 (statement); 1 ill

HILL, Susan ( )
CHRYSALIS no.4 93-96 (statements)

HILLER, Susan (1940-) Brit; ptr, print, sclp
CONTEMPORARY (statement); port; 1 ill
HAYWARD 1978 46-49 (statement); 8 ill

HILLHOUSE, Jeremy ( ) Amer; ptr
CRISS-CROSS no.3 41 (statement); 1 ill

HILLIARD, John (1945-) Brit; photo
ARTIST AND CAMERA 34-35 (extract from interview with Colin Painter, o.p. 1978); 1 ill
CONTEMPORARY (statement); port; 2 ill
ENGLISH 386-391 (interview with Luca Venturi, 1974); port; 9 ill
NAYLOR 407-408 (statement); 1 ill
SKIRA 1976 31 (statement); 5 ill
SKIRA 1978 90 (statement); 1 ill
SKIRA 1980 100-101 (extract from interview with Ian Kirkwood, o.p. 1978); 1 ill
WALSH 343-344 (statement); 1 ill

HILLIER, Tristram (1905-) Brit; ptr
CONTEMPORARY (statement); port; 1 ill
READ 67-76 (statement); port; 4 ill

HILL-MONTGOMERY, Candace ( ) Amer; video
ISSUE ("Notes")

HILLSMITH, Fannie (1911-) Amer; ptr
ILLINOIS 1955 206 (statement); 1 ill
ILLINOIS 1959 223-224 (statement); 1 ill
ILLINOIS 1961 107 (response); port; 1 ill
JANIS I 100 (statement); 1 ill

HILTON, Roy (1891-) Amer; ptr
ILLINOIS 1952 198 (statement); 1 ill

HIMMEL, Christopher (1951-) Amer; wood
WOODWORKING 24-25 (statement); port; 2 ill

HINKLE, Clarence (1880-1960) Amer; ptr
BRITANNICA 54 (statement); port; 1 ill

HINMAN, Charles (1932-) Amer; sclp, ptr
ART NOW v.1 no.2 (statement); 1 ill

VARIAN II (statement); port
YOUNG 1965 (statement); 3 ill

HINTON, Alfred F. (1940-) Amer; ptr
FAX II 39-60 (statements); port; 1 ill

HINZ, Ronald Dale (1948-) Amer; paper
WISCONSIN II (statement); 1 ill

HIROMI, Fujii ( ) Japa; arch
GA HOUSES no. 4 133-144 (statement); 31 ill

HIRONS, David ( )
ART-LANGUAGE v.1 no.2 23-24 ("Moto-Spiritale")

HIRSCH, David ( ) photo, arch
ARTS YEARBOOK v.10 92-95 (essay: "XIV Triennale di Milano")

HIRSCH, Gilah Yelin (1944-) Cana; ptr
SCHAPIRO 32 (statement); port; 1 ill

HIRSCH, Joseph (1910-) Amer; ptr
BRITANNICA 55 (statement); port; 1 ill
ILLINOIS 1950 180 (statement); 1 ill
ILLINOIS 1952 198-199 (statement); 1 ill
ILLINOIS 1963 208 (statement); 1 ill
MILLER 1942 60-66 (statement); port; 8 ill
100 CONTEMPORARY 92-93 (statement); port; 1 ill

HIRSCH, Rick (1944-) Amer; pott
WECHSLER 88-93 (statement); port; 5 ill

HIRSHFIELD, Morris (1872-1946) Amer; ptr
JANIS I 94 (statement); 1 ill
JANIS II 14-39 ("My Life Biography"); port; 6 ill

HIRST, Derek (1930-) Brit; sclp, ptr
CONTEMPORARY (statement); port; 2
ill

HITCH, Stewart (1940-) Amer; ptr
LEAVITT (statement); port; 5 ill

HITCHENS, Sidney Ivon (1893-1979)
Brit; ptr
NAYLOR 409-410 (statement)
ROTHENSTEIN 56 (letter)

HNIZDOVSKY, Yakiv (Jacques) (1915-)
Ukra/Amer; ptr
ILLINOIS 1959 224 (statement); 1 ill
ILLINOIS 1961 100 (response); port; 1 ill

HO, Tao (1936-) Brit; arch
EMANUEL I 362-364 (statement); 1 ill

HOADLEY, Thomas (1949-) Amer; pott
HERMAN 70 (statement); port; 1 ill

HOAG, Paul Sterling ( ) Amer; arch
ARTFORUM v.2 no.7 23, 26-27
(statement); 5 ill

HOBBS, Joe Ferrell (1934-) Amer; sclp,
perf, envir
ARTPARK 1977 46-49 (statement); 9 ill
CRISS-CROSS no.4 14-19 (interview
with Donald Lipski and John Alberty);
8 ill

HOCH, Hannah (1889-1978); Germ; ptr
ARTS YEARBOOK v.6 28-34 (interview
with Edouard Roditi, o.p. 1959); port;
2 ill
CHIPP 396 (extract from interview with
Edouard Roditi, o.p. 1959)
SKIRA 1977 72 (statement); 1 ill

HOCK, Jean-Pierre ( ) Belg; ptr
COLLARD 140-145 (interview); port; 1
ill

HOCKNEY, David (1937-) Brit; ptr,
print
ART SINCE v.2 324 (statement, o.p.
1970)
BOSHIER (extract from interview with
Mark Glazebrook, 1970); port; 1 ill
CLAIR 56-57 (statement); 1 ill
ENGLISH 98-103 (statement); port; 9 ill
SKIRA 1975 13 (extract from interview
with Pierre Restany: "une conversation
a Paris," 7/74); 1 ill
VICTORIA 58-63 (statements); 1 ill
WEBB 375-378 (interview, 1972); 1 ill

HODGETTS, Craig (1937-) Amer; arch
COUNTERPOINT 104-117 (statements);
15 ill

HODGKIN, Howard (1932-) Brit; ptr
BOWNESS 24, 122-124 (statement); 2 ill

HODGKINS, Rosalind (1942-) Amer; ptr
TRACKS v.1 no.2 31 (statement)

HODLER, Ferdinand (1853-1918) Swis;
ptr
CHIPP 107-109 (extract from essay:
"Parallelism," o.p. 1923); 1 ill
GOLDWATER 392-394 (statement,
1900); 1 ill
THORN 37, 38, 73, 84, 117, 133, 135,
136, 157, 159, 161-163, 167, 168, 221,
285 (statements, p.p.)

HOELZEL, Adolf (1853-1934) Germ; ptr
POENSGEN 73-74
("Gesetzmassigkeiten," 1901)
POENSGEN 74 ("Harmonielehre")
THORN 285 (statement, p.p.)

HOETGER, Bernhard (1874-1949) Germ;
arch, sclp
CONRADS 107-108 ("World
Architecture," o.p. 1928)

HOFER, Karl (1878-1955) Germ; ptr
THORN 29, 32, 45-50, 52-54, 57, 62, 87, 91, 97, 107, 162, 175, 198, 207, 233, 245, 283, 291, 300, 303 (statements, p.p.)
WINGLER 35-36 (essay: "Vincent Van Gogh," p.p.)

HOFF, Margo (1912-) Amer; ptr
ILLINOIS 1951 186-187 (statement); 1 ill
ILLINOIS 1953 189 (statement); 1 ill
ILLINOIS 1955 206-207 (statement); 1 ill
ILLINOIS 1959 225 (statement); 1 ill
ILLINOIS 1961 112 (response); port; 1 ill

HOFFMAN, Eugene ( ) Amer; sclp
ILLUSTRATION 18-19 (statement); port; 2 ill

HOFFMAN, Irwin D. (1901-) Amer; ptr
100 CONTEMPORARY 94-95 (statement); port; 1 ill

HOFFMAN, Katherine ( ) Amer; ptr
WOMANART v.2 no.2 22-28 (essay: "Toward a New Humanism")

HOFFMANN, Emma (1881-) Amer; ptr
M.H. DE YOUNG 64 (statement)

HOFFMANN, Hubert ( ) Aust; arch
NEWMAN 56-63 (essay and group discussion); 14 ill

HOFFMANN, Josef (1870-1956) Aust; arch
BREICHA 209-212 (essay: "Das Arbeitsprogramm der Wiener Werkstatte," o.p. 1904); 3 ill
BREICHA 216-219 (essay: "Rede uber Otto Wagner," o.p. 1910)

HOFFMANN, Klaus ( )
GROH (statement)

HOFLEHNER, Rudolf (1916-) Aust; sclp
EMANUEL II 412-413 (statement); 1 ill

HOFMANN, Hans (1880-1966) Germ/Amer; ptr
ART SINCE v.1 157 (statement, o.p. 1959)
ART VOICES v.1 no.1 22 (interview with Roland F. Pease); port
CHIPP 536-544 (extract from *Search for the Real and Other Essays*, o.p. 1948); port; 1 ill
CHIPP 564-565, 567 (statements, o.p. 1951)
CLAUS 42-48 (statement)
FORTY (essay: "The Object in the Visual Arts--Its Function in Three-Dimensional Reality and its Two-Dimensional Pictorial Realization"); 2 ill
ILLINOIS 1951 187-188 (statement); 1 ill
ILLINOIS 1952 199-200 (statement); 1 ill
ILLINOIS 1953 189-190 (statement, accompanying NY exhibit, Nov. 1952); 1 ill
ILLINOIS 1955 (statement, p.p.); 1 ill
ILLINOIS 1959 226-227 (statement); 1 ill
ILLINOIS 1961 116-117 (response); port; 1 ill
ILLINOIS 1963 86-87 (statement); 1 ill
IT IS no.3 10 (statement)
IT IS no.4 10 (essay: "Space and Pictorial Life")
IT IS no.5 80-81 (letter: rejoinder to a letter to the editors)
JANIS I 78-79 (statement); 1 ill
KUH 118-129 (interview); 5 ill
LOCATION v.1 no.2 98 ("Photo-Critic")
MOTHERWELL 8-22 (three group discussions: "Artists' Sessions at Studio 35," New York, 1950)
PROTTER 198 ("I Condemn Dogmatism and Categorization," 1961)
ROSE II 147-149 (statement, o.p. 1955)

ROSE II 149-150 (statement, o.p. 1959)
ROSE II REVISED 116-118 (statement, o.p. 1955)
ROSE II REVISED 118-120 (statement, o.p. 1959)
ROSE II REVISED 120-121 (extract from interview with Irma B. Jaffe, o.p. 1971)
ROSE II REVISED 142-145 (group discussion, o.p. 1952)
SEUPHOR 189-190 (statement); 1 ill

HOGLE, Richard (1939-) Amer; sclp
DIRECTIONS I 76 (response); 1 ill

HOGUE, Alexandre (1898-) Amer; ptr, illus
BOSWELL 155 (statement)
BRITANNICA 56 (statement); port; 1 ill
M.H. DE YOUNG 65 (response); self port

HOIE, Claus (1911-) Norw/Amer; ptr, print
NORTH LIGHT 134-137 (statement); port; 6 ill

HOLBROOK, Hollis (1909-) Amer; ptr
ILLINOIS 1961 90 (response); port; 1 ill

HOLBROOK, Peter (1940-) Amer; ptr
ILLINOIS 1969 69 (statement); 1 ill

HOLDING, Eileen (1909-) Brit; sclp
AXIS no.3 23, 27 (essay: "London Shows"); 1 ill
AXIS no.5 27-28 (essay: "London Shows")

HOLIHAN, Michael Sean ( ) Amer; print
HAYSTACK 29 (poem); 1 ill

HOLL, Steven ( ) Amer; arch
COOPER-HEWITT II 68-69 (essay: "Anatomy of the Skyscraper")

HOLLAND, Thomas (1936-) Amer; sclp, ptr
HOPKINS 44-45 (statement); port; 1 ill
ILLINOIS 1969 105 (statement); 1 ill
VISUAL v.3 no.2 16-20 (interview); 4 ill

HOLLE, Fred ( ) Amer; illus
CALIFORNIA--DRAWING (statement); 2 ill

HOLLEIN, Hans (1934-) arch
CONRADS 181-182 ("Absolute Architecture," o.p. 1962)

HOLLEY, Lonnie B. (1950-) Amer; sclp
NOSANOW I 70-71 (statement); 2 ill

HOLLINGSWORTH, Alvin Carl (1928-) Amer; ptr
FINE 247-249 (statements, o.p. 1968, 1970); 2 ill
LEWIS II 89 (statement); port; 1 ill

HOLLINGWORTH, Keith (1937-) Amer; sclp
NAYLOR 416-417 (statement); 1 ill

HOLLIS, Douglas (1948-) Amer; sclp, sound
ARTPARK 1977 50-53 (statement); port; 10 ill
MADE FOR BUFFALO (statements); port; 2 ill

HOLMES, David V. (1945-) Amer; sclp, wood
WISCONSIN II (statement); 1 ill

HOLOMAN, Kevin ( ) Amer; arch, design
LIFE 170-173 (statement); port

HOLSTEIN, Pieter (1934-) print
REFLECTION 22-27 (interview); 16 ill

HOLT, Friso ten
SEE: TEN HOLT, Friso

HOLT, Martha (1945-) Amer; pott
WECHSLER 94-99 (statement); port; 5 ill

HOLT, Nancy Louise (1938-) Amer; film, sclp, envir
ARTPARK 1975 76-77 (statement); 3 ill
ART-RITE no.7 11, 15 (response); 1 ill
AVALANCHE no.12 6 (statement); 3 ill
EMANUEL II 415-417 (statement); 1 ill
HOUSE 52-53 (statement); 1 ill
NAYLOR 417 (statement)
SKIRA 1980 137 (statement); 3 ill

HOLTY, Carl (1900-1973) Amer; ptr
ART NOW v.1 no.8 (statement); 1 ill
ART VOICES v.4 no.4 66 (statement); 1 ill
ARTS YEARBOOK v.4 74-76 (essay: "Mondrian and Current Painting")
ILLINOIS 1963 160 (statement); 1 ill
JANIS I 76 (statement); 1 ill

HOLTZMAN, Harry (1912-) Amer; ptr
ABSTRACT 17-18, 129 (essay: "Attitude and Means"); 1 ill
IT IS no.2 78 (statement)
IT IS no.4 32-33 (essay: "The Sickness of the Cult of the Hero")

HOLZER, Jenny ( ) Amer
ISSUE (statement)

HOLZINGER, Johannes Peter (1936-) Germ; sclp
HAUSSER 68-69 (statement, o.p. 1982); 1 ill

HOMONAJ, Pal (1922-) Yugo; ptr
TOMASEVIC 124-127 (statement); port; 2 ill

HOMPSON, Davi Det (David E. Thompson) ( ) Brit
APPLE 25 (statement); 3 ill
WHITE WALLS no.8 64-67 (text piece)

HONDROGEN, Nicholas (1952-) Amer/Fren; illus
SKIRA 1976 47 (statement); 1 ill

HONE, Evie ( ) ptr
ABSTRACTION no.1 20 (statement); 2 ill

HONEGGER, Gottfried (1917-) Swis; ptr, sclp
ALBRIGHT-KNOX 238-239 (letter, 11/1968); 1 ill
EMANUEL II 417-418 (statement); 1 ill
LETTERS 16 (letter); 1 ill
NAYLOR 417-418 (statement); 1 ill
SKIRA 1976 77 (statement); 1 ill

HONEYSUCKLE, Philip
SEE: NEAGU, Paul

HOOD, Robin ( ) Amer; photo
LEEKLEY 116-117 (statement); 1 ill

HOOKER, Charlie (1953-) Brit; video, perf
HAYWARD 1979 141 (statement); 1 ill

HOOKS, Earl (1927-) Amer; sclp, ptr
FAX I 203-218 (statements); port; 2 ill

HOOPER, Jack ( ) Amer; illus
CALIFORNIA--DRAWING (statement); 2 ill

HOOVEN, Coille (1939-) Amer; pott
HERMAN 71 (statement); port; 1 ill

HOOVER, Nan (1931-) Amer; perf, video
STEDELIJK 136 (statement); 1 ill

HOPKER, Thomas (1936-) Germ; photo
CAMPBELL 124-133 (statement); port;
12 ill
WALSH 348-349 (statement); 1 ill

HOPKINS, Budd (1931-) Amer; ptr, coll,
sclp
ART NOW v.4 no.2 (statement); 1 ill
NAYLOR 418-419 (statement); 1 ill
YOUNG 1960 (statement); 2 ill

HOPKINS, Michael ( ) arch
GA HOUSES no.6 142-147 (statement);
15 ill

HOPKINS, Thurston (1913-) Brit; photo
WALSH 350 (statement)

HOPPE, William (1945-) Amer; ptr
GUENTHER 50-51 (statement); port; 1
ill

HOPPER, Edward (1882-1967) Amer; ptr
BRITANNICA 57 (statement); port; 1 ill
CRISPO II (statement); 15 ill
DOUZE PEINTRES (statement); 2 ill
FORTY (statement, o.p. 1945); 2 ill
FIFTY (statement); 1 ill
GOLDWATER 471-473 (statement, 1933)
KUH 130-142 (interview); 5 ill
RODMAN I 198-200 (interview)
ROSE II 111-112 (extract from essay:
"Charles Burchfield, American," o.p.
1928)
ROSE II REVISED 90-91 (extract from
essay: "Charles Burchfield,
American," o.p. 1928)
ROSE II REVISED 91 (extract from
essay: "Art and Life," o.p. 1953)
ROSE II REVISED 91-92 (statement, o.p.
1933)

HOPPER, Pegge (1935-) Amer; ptr
HAAR II 24-28 (interview); ports; 2 ill

HORAN, Claude (1917-) Amer; pott
HAAR II 29-35 (interview); ports; 2 ill

HORD, Donal (1902-1966) Amer; sclp
MILLER 1942 67-74 (statement); port; 6
ill

HORIUCHI, Masakazu (1911-) Japa; sclp
KUNG 164-167 (statement); port; 2 ill

HORIUCHI, Paul (1906-) Japa/Amer;
ptr
GUENTHER 52-53 (statement); port; 1
ill
ILLINOIS 1965 105 (statement); 1 ill

HORN, Rebecca (1944-) Germ; instal,
sclp, perf
EMANUEL II 419-420 (statement); 1 ill
KUNST BLEIBT KUNST 220-221
(statement); 1 ill
NAYLOR 421 (statement); 1 ill
SKIRA 1980 113 (statement); 2 ill

HOROWITZ, Frank (1889-) Amer; ptr
100 CONTEMPORARY 96-97
(statement); port; 1 ill

HOROWITZ, Ida ( ) Amer; sclp
SCHAPIRO 33 (statement); port; 1 ill

HOROWITZ, Ryszard ( ) Poli/Amer;
photo
HOW FAMOUS 200-205 (statements);
port; 7 ill

HORRELL, Deborah (1953-) Amer; pott
HERMAN 72 (statement); port; 1 ill

HORST, Horst P. (1906-) Germ/Amer;
photo
BOOTH 112-123 (interview); port; 6 ill
DIAMONSTEIN III 67-80 (interview); 5 ill

"Artists' Convention," in Athens, GA., 1/7/1977, moderated by Jan van der Marck)
KONZEPT (statements: "Variable Piece...," and "Location Piece #14")
MEYER 136-141 (statements and text pieces); 3 ill
SCHIMMEL 46-47 (statement); 2 ill
VRIES 116-119 (statement, o.p. 1970)

HUELSENBECK, Richard ( ) Amer; ptr
CHIPP 377-382, 387 (extract from essay: "En Avant Dada: A History of Dadaism," o.p. 1920); 1 ill

HUETER, James (1925-) Amer; illus, ptr
CALIFORNIA--DRAWING (statement); 2 ill

HUFF, Robert J. (1952-) Amer; sclp
SCULPTURE OUTSIDE (statement); 4 ill

HUGGINS, Victor (1936-) Amer; ptr
NOSANOW I 73-74 (statement); 1 ill

HUGHES, Lynn ( ) Cana; ptr
EVENTS II 37-38 (statement); 1 ill

HUGHES, Malcolm (1920-) Brit; ptr, sclp
CONTEMPORARY (statement); port; 2 ill
ENGLISH 110-115 (statement); port; 9 ill

HUGHES, Patrick (1939-) Brit; sclp, print, ptr
CONTEMPORARY (statement); port; 2 ill
NAYLOR 428 (statement); 1 ill

HUGHES, Richard (1926-) Brit; arch
EMANUEL I 381-382 (statement); 1 ill

HULL, Howie ( )
CRISS-CROSS no.2 3-7, 29 ("Tesla"); 2 ill

HULTBERG, John Phillip (1922-) Amer; ptr
ILLINOIS 1959 227 (statement); 1 ill
ILLINOIS 1967 56-57 (statement); 1 ill
VARIAN III (statement); 1 ill

HUM, Chi Ngih (1952-) Amer; pott
HERMAN 73 (statement); port; 1 ill

HUMPHREY, Margo (1942-) Amer; ptr, print
LEWIS I REVISED 8-10 (statement); port; 6 ill

HUMPHREY, Nene (1947-) Amer; envir, sclp
ARTPARK 1980 (statement); port; 3 ill
CRISS-CROSS no.11/12 56-57 (statement); 3 ill

HUNDERTWASSER (Friedrich Stowasser) (1928-) Aust; ptr
ART SINCE v.2 154 (statement, o.p. 1964)
CONRADS 157-160 ("Mould Manifesto Against Rationalism in Architecture," o.p. 1958)
NAYLOR 428-429 (statement); port
SKIRA 1975 60-61 (extract from interview with Jean-Luc Daval, o.p. 1967); 1 ill

HUNDT, Frances ( ) Amer; arch
COOPER-HEWITT II 98-99 (essay: "Vernacular Architecture")

HUNT, Bryan (1947-) Amer; sclp, instal
EMANUEL II 424-425 (statement); 1 ill
SHEARER 32-35 (interview); 4 ill
SKIRA 1979 48 (statement); 1 ill
VIEW v.3 no.1 (interview); 10 ill

HUNT, Martin ( ) Amer; glass
GLASS v.5 (group discussion)

HUNT, Richard (1935-) Amer; sclp
FINE 229-233 (statements, o.p. 1971); 9 ill
ILLINOIS 1963 90 (statement); 1 ill
WHITNEY (statement); 1 ill

HUNTER, Alexis (1948-) NewZ; photo, film
HAYWARD 1978 38-41 (statement); 3 ill
ISSUE (statement); 7 ill

HUNTER, Debora (1950-) Amer; photo
MCCLINTIC 70-72 (statement); 4 ill

HUNTER, Don ( ) Amer; arch, design
LIFE 7-10 (interview); port

HUNTER, Edwin (1912-) Amer; cart
M. H. DE YOUNG 68 (response); self port

HUNTER, Jan ( ) perf
ART NETWORK no.2 49 (statement)

HUNTER, John ( )
VISUAL v.1 no.1 29-30 (essay: "The Antiquarian Teenager")
VISUAL v.1 no.3 37-38 (essay: "The Antiquarian Teenager")
VISUAL v.1 no.4 31-32 (essay: "The Antiquarian Teenager")
VISUAL v.2 no.1 33-34 (essay: "The Antiquarian Teenager")
VISUAL v.2 no.2 38-39 (essay: "The Antiquarian Teenager")
VISUAL v.2 no.4 32-33 (essay: "The Antiquarian Teenager")
VISUAL v.3 no.1 39-40 (essay: "The Antiquarian Teenager")
VISUAL v.3 no.2 36-37 (essay: "The Antiquarian Teenager")
VISUAL v.3 no.3 44-45 (essay: "The Antiquarian Teenager")
VISUAL v.3 no.4 42 (essay: "The Antiquarian Teenager")
VISUAL v.4 no.1 2-4 (essay: "Eccentricity in Art...Attitudes and Aesthetics")
VISUAL v.4 no.2 35 (essay: "The Antiquarian Teenager")
VISUAL v.4 no.4 36 (essay: "The Antiquarian Teenager")

HUNTER, Mel (1927-) Amer; ptr, print
MYLAR 24-32 (statement); ports; 2 ill

HUNTER, Robert (1947-) ptr
LICHT 39-42 (statement); 3 ill

HUOT, Robert (1935-) Amer; ptr, instal, film
NAYLOR 429-430 (statement); 1 ill

HUPPI, Alfonso (1935-) Germ; sclp
HAUSSER 88-89 (statement, o.p. 1978); 1 ill

HURD, Peter (1904-) Amer; ptr, illus
BRITANNICA 58 (statement); port; 1 ill

HURN, David (1934-) Brit; photo
WALSH 364-365 (statement); 1 ill

HURRELL, Harold ( )
ART-LANGUAGE v.1 no.2 72-73 ("Notes on Atkinson's 'Concerning Interpretation of the Bainbridge/Hurrell Models'")
ART-LANGUAGE v.2 no.2 29-30 ("Interim Remarks")
ART-LANGUAGE v.3 no.2 41-43 ("Art and Language")
ART-LANGUAGE v.3 no.2 65-67 ("Slogan Adaptation")
ART-LANGUAGE v.3 no.2 68-69 ("'Mr. Lin Yutang Refers to "Fair Play"...?'")
ART-LANGUAGE v.3 no.2 93-94 ("Accidental Synopsis")

MEYER 22-25 ("Lecher System," o.p. 1970)
SEE ALSO: ART & LANGUAGE PRESS

HURSON, Michael (1941-) Amer; print, ptr
MARSHALL 32 (statement); ports; 5 ill
REALLIFE no.3 16-19 (interview with Susan Morgan); 1 ill
WHITE WALLS no.4 4-15 (essay: "Robert Moskowitz")

HURST, Ralph (1918-) Amer; sclp
ART PATRON ART 35-36 (statement); port; 1 ill

HUSARIK, Jan (1942-) Yugo; ptr
TOMASEVIC 136-139 (statement); port; 2 ill

HUTCHESON, Agnes (1955-) Brit; arch
SPIRIT 76-81 (statement); 7 ill

HUTCHINS, Maude Phelps ( ) Amer; sclp
CIRCLE no.6 67-69 (story: "Soliloquy at Dinner")

HUTCHINSON, Elizabeth ( ) Amer; ptr
CRISS-CROSS no.10 14-15 (statement); port; 2 ill

HUTCHINSON, Peter (1930-) Brit/Amer; coll, ptr, sclp
ART NOW v.1 no.4 (statement); 1 ill
BATTCOCK V 187-194 (essay: "Mannerism in the Abstract," o.p. 1966)
NAYLOR 431-432 (statement); 1 ill
ON SITE no.4 47 (statement)
SCHIMMEL 48-52 (extract from "Somewhere in that Photograph is a Work of Art"); 4 ill
SKIRA 1976 24 (statement); 1 ill

SKIRA 1979 86 (statement); 1 ill
TRACKS v.1 no.2 5-6 (story: "The Great Interplanetary Art Plot")
TRACKS v.1 no.2 58-59 ("The Art Dictator")

HUTSON, Bill (1936-) Amer; ptr
FINE 235-236, 239 (letter, 1971); 1 ill

HUXLEY-JONES, T. B. (1908-) Brit; sclp
LONDON COUNTY (statement); 1 ill

HYDE, Sarah ( ) Amer; illus, ptr
FOUNDERS 12-13 (statement); 1 ill

HYDE, Scott (1926-) Amer; photo
DUGAN 179-195 (interview, 1978); port
WALSH 366 (statement); 1 ill

HYDLER, Glenda (1951-) Amer; photo
BRENTANO 236-237 (statement); 1 ill

HYMAN, Sylvia ( ) Amer; pott, sclp
ART PATRON ART 37-38 (statement); port; 1 ill

IANNONE, Dorothy (1933-) Amer; ptr
ADLERS 44-47 (letter and interview);
port; 2 ill

ICHIMURA, Tetsuya (1930-) Japa;
photo
WALSH 367 (statement); 1 ill

IDEA, Marcel ( )
AVALANCHE no.8 34-39 (group
discussion); 14 ill

IIJIMA, Takao
SEE: AY-O

IIMURA, Takahiko (1937-) Japa/Amer;
video, perf
ART-RITE no.7 11 (response)
EMANUEL II 428-430 (statement); 1 ill
NAYLOR 434-435 (statement); 1 ill

IKEDA, Masuo (1934-) Japa/Amer;
print
KUNG 146-149 (statement); port; 2 ill

IKEGAWA, Shiro ( ) Amer; photo, coll
IRVINE 57, 80 (statement); 1 ill

IKKO
SEE: NARAHARA, Ikko

ILIC, Dragan ( ) perf
ART NETWORK no.1 31 (statement); 1
ill

IMBER, Jonathan (1950-) Amer; ptr
BOSTON I (interview); 1 ill
BOSTON III (interview); 1 ill

INDIANA, Robert (1928-) Amer; ptr,
print, sclp
ART NOW v.1 no.3 (statement); 1 ill
ART SINCE v.2 326 (statement, o.p.
1963)
DIAMONSTEIN I 151-166 (interview); 2
port
RUSSELL J 79-81 (interview with Gene
Swenson, o.p. 1963)
SAO PAULO 78-79 (statement); port; 1
ill
TRACKS v.1 no.1 6-9 ("Mother and
Father"); 2 ill
VARIAN III (statement); port

INSLEY, Will (1929-) Amer; sclp, ptr,
instal
ART NOW v.1 no.9 (statement); 1 ill
BATTCOCK V 359-363 (interview with
Elayne Varian, o.p. 1967); 1 ill
BELFORD 57-77 (group discussion)
DRAWING 69-80 (essay: "Abstract/
Buildings"); 10 ill
SYSTEMATIC 24 (statement); 1 ill
TRACKS v.1 no.1 18-37 ("The Greater
Context"); 2 ill
TRACKS v.3 no.1/2 110-123 (essay:
"Abstract Architectural Space--The
Empty Building"); 5 ill
VARIAN II (statement); port
VARIAN IV (interview); port; 2 ill

INTERNATIONAL FACTION OF
CONSTRUCTIVISTS (group)
BANN 68-69 (statement, o.p. 1922)

INTERNATIONAL LOCAL (group)
WEBER 61-77 ("Videotape"); ports

INTERSYSTEMS
SEE: HAYDEN, Michael

IPOUSTEGUY, Jean (1920-) Fren; sclp
ART SINCE v.2 149 (statement, o.p.
1963)
EMANUEL II 432-434 (statement); 1 ill
HAUSSER 90-91 (statement, 1979); 1 ill
QUADRUM no.15 107-114 (statement); 8
ill
SKIRA 1975 70-71 (statement); 1 ill

IPPOLITO, Angelo (1922-) Ital/Amer; ptr
ARTFORUM v.1 no.2 29-35 (group discussion)
IT IS no.1 47 (statement)
NOSANOW I 75 (statement); 1 ill
WHITNEY (statement); 1 ill

IRELAND, Patrick (1934-) Iris/Amer; ptr
GEORGIA 45-47, 113 (statement); port; 2 ill

IRVIN, Albert (1922-) Brit; ptr
CONTEMPORARY (statement); port; 2 ill
NAYLOR 437-438 (statement); 1 ill

IRWIN, Gwyther (1931-) Brit; ptr, coll
BOWNESS 22-23, 111-113 (statement); 2 ill
CONTEMPORARY (statement); port; 2 ill

IRWIN, Robert (1928-) Amer; light, sclp, instal
ART AND TECHNOLOGY 127-143 (project proposal)
ARTFORUM v.3 no.9 23 (statement); port
ARTFORUM v.6 no.6 4 (letter)
HOPKINS 104-105 (statement); port; 1 ill
IRVINE 51, 90 (statement); 1 ill
JOHNSON 141-144 (talk: "Set of Questions" given a symposium on "Art Education at the Higher Levels," Montreal, 1980); 1 ill
NAYLOR 438-439 (statement); 1 ill
PRADEL 41 (statement, o.p. 1982); 3 ill
PROFILE v.2 no.4 (interview); port; 1 ill
SKIRA 1978 119 (statement); 2 ill
SKIRA 1980 139 (statement); 2 ill
VISION no.1 38-39 ("Twenty Questions")

WIGHT 67-105 (interview); ports

ISAACS, Ron (1941-) Amer; ptr, wood, sclp
MEILACH 161-163 (statement); 4 ill
NOSANOW I 76 (statement); 1 ill

ISAACSON, Marcia Jean (1945-) Amer; illus
SOUTHEAST (statement); port; 4 ill

ISELI, Rolf (1934-) Swis; print, ptr
KORNFELD 25-27 (statement); port; 6 ill
SKIRA 1976 45 (statement); 1 ill
SKIRA 1979 19 (statement); 1 ill
SKIRA 1980 82 (statement); 2 ill

ISENBURGER, Eric (1902-) Germ/Amer; ptr
ILLINOIS 1959 227-228 (statement); 1 ill

ISKOWITZ, Gershon (1921-) Poli/Cana; ptr
NAYLOR 439 (statement); 1 ill

ISNARD, Vivien (1946-) Fren; ptr
SKIRA 1979 92 (statement); 1 ill

ISOBE, Yukihisa (1936-) Japa; ptr
KUNG 64-67 (statement); port; 2 ill

ISOLANI, Licio (1931-) Amer; sclp
GEOMETRIC (statement); 1 ill

ISOZAKI, Arata (1931-) Japa; arch
ARCHER 62-66, 97-98 (statement); port; 7 ill
EMANUEL I 384-385 (statement); 1 ill
GA DOCUMENT no.2 22-49 (statements); 38 ill
GA HOUSES no.1 150-155 (statement); 12 ill
RUSSELL F 56-61 (project proposal); 15 ill

ISRAEL, Frank (1945-) Amer; arch
LA JOLLA 49-53 (statement); port; 8 ill

ISTRATI, Alexandre (1915-) Ruma; ptr
PREMIER BILAN 300 (statement); port
SEUPHOR 192 (statement); 1 ill

ITTEN, Johannes (1888-1967) Swis; ptr
KEPES VIII 104-121 (essay: "The
Foundation Course at the Bauhaus")
WINGLER 79-81 (essay: "Wassily
Kandinsky--Kunst und Erziehung,"
p.p.)

ITTER, Diane Healy (1946-) Amer; text
FIBER 36-37 (statement); 1 ill

ITURBIDE, Graciela (1942-) Mexi; photo
WALSH 370-371 (statement); 1 ill

IVEY, William ( ) Amer; ptr
GUENTHER 54-55 (statement); port; 1
ill

IZQUIERDO, Manuel ( ) Span/Amer;
sclp
GUENTHER 56-57 (statement); port; 1
ill

JACCARD, Christian (1939-) Swis/Fren; text, sclp, ptr
DOUZE ANS 237-239 (statement); 2 ill
NAYLOR 440 (statement); 1 ill
SKIRA 1979 56-57 (statement); 1 ill
SKIRA 1980 51 (statement); 3 ill

JACHNA, Joseph David (1935-) Amer; photo
WALSH 374-375 (statement); 1 ill

JACKLIN, Bill (1943-) Brit; ptr
CONTEMPORARY (statement); port; 2 ill

JACKS, Robert ( ) Atrl; ptr
ART NETWORK no.1 17 (interview)

JACKSON, Anthony (1926-) Cana; arch
CANADIAN 64-65 (statement)

JACKSON, Bob ( ) Amer; photo
LEEKLEY 56-57 (statement); 1 ill

JACKSON, Daryl (1937-) Atrl; arch
EMANUEL I 386-387 (statement); 1 ill

JACKSON, David (1931-) Atrl; arch
EMANUEL I 387-389 (statement); 1 ill

JACKSON, Herb (1945-) Amer; ptr
TRANSPERSONAL 50-59 (statement); port; 4 ill

JACKSON, Martha E. (1950-) Amer; sclp, pott
CONTEMPORARY AFRICAN (statement); port; 1 ill

JACKSON, Penelope Borres ( ) Amer; metal
METALWORKS (statement); 1 ill

JACKSON, Ralph ( ) Amer; arch, design
LIFE 73-78 (interview); port

JACKSON, Richard Norris (1939-) Amer; ptr
SULTAN 3 (letter)

JACKSON, Suzanne Fitzallen (1944-) Amer; ptr
LEWIS II 91 (statement); port; 3 ill

JACKSON, Walter ( ) Amer; sclp
FINE 268-269 (letter, 1971); 1 ill

JACKSON, Ward (1928-) Amer; ptr
ART NOW v.2 no.10 (statement); 1 ill

JACOB, Pierre
SEE: TAL-COAT, Pierre

JACOBI, Lotte (1896-) Amer; photo
LIGHT 60-65 (statement); 5 ill
MITCHELL 140-157 (statement); port; self port; 15 ill
WALSH 375-377 (statement); 1 ill

JACOBS, David Theodore (1932-) Amer; sclp, sound
DIRECTIONS I 76 (response); 1 ill
GRAYSON 34-67 ("Notebook"); port; 54 ill

JACOBS, Jessica ( ) sclp, light
SCHAPIRO 34 (statement); port; 1 ill

JACOBS, Ken ( )
CRISS-CROSS no.7/8/9 106-108 ("Sunnyside Up and Stereo Images")

JACOBSEN, Hugh Newell (1929-) Amer; arch
EMANUEL I 391-392 (statement); 1 ill

JACOBSEN, Robert (1912-) Dani; sclp
PREMIER BILAN 300 (statement); port
TEMOIGNAGES I 158-165 (statement); port; 6 ill

JEFFRIES, Rosalind (1938-) Amer; ptr
FAX II 279-293 (statements); port; 1 ill
LEWIS II 30 (statement); port; 1 ill

JEFTOVIC, Dusan (1925-) Yugo; ptr
TOMASEVIC 140-144 (statement); port; 1 ill

JELINEK, Hans ( ) Aust/Amer; ptr, print
ABSTRACTION no.2 24 (statement); 2 ill
ABSTRACTION no.5 14 (statement)

JELLET, Mainie (1897-1944) Brit; ptr
ABSTRACTION no.1 22 (statement); 2 ill
ABSTRACTION no.2 25 (statement); 2 ill
ABSTRACTION no.3 25 (statement); 1 ill

JENKINS, Paul (1923-) Amer; ptr
ART VOICES v.3 no.2 5 (interview with Michel Butor, o.p. 1963); 1 ill
EMANUEL II 439, 441-443 (statement); 1 ill
ILLINOIS 1965 92-93 (statement); 1 ill
IT IS no.2 13 ("A Cahier Leaf")
IT IS no.3 77-78 ("Non-American Painting...")
IT IS no.5 40 ("A Reply to Purity")
YOUNG 1957 (statement); 1 ill

JENKINS, William ( ) Amer; photo
BARROW 51-56 ("Introduction" to *The New Topographics*, o.p. 1975)

JENNEY, Neil ( ) Amer; ptr
JOHNSON 258-260 (statement, o.p. 1978); 1 ill
MARSHALL 38 (statement); port; 5 ill
STEDELIJK 137 (statement); 1 ill

JENNINGS, Humphrey (1907-1950) Brit; ptr
JEAN 365-366 ("Reports," o.p. 1936)
LONDON BULLETIN no.1 15 ("In Magritte's Paintings...")
LONDON BULLETIN no.2 8 ("Prose Poem," in French and English)
LONDON BULLETIN no.2 22, 27-28 (essay: "The Iron Horse")
LONDON BULLETIN no.6 21-23 (essay: "Who Does That Remind You Of?"); 3 ill
LONDON BULLETIN no.12 7 (poems: "Two American Poems")
LONDON BULLETIN no.12 7-8 (essay: "The Boyhood of Byron")

JENSEN, Alfred (1903-) Amer; ptr
ART NOW v.2 no.4 (statement); 1 ill
IT IS no.4 15 (statement)
LETTERS 17 (letter); 1 ill

JENSEN, Bill ( )
ART-RITE no.9 36-38 (group discussion); port

JENSEN, Robert ( ) Amer; arch
COOPER-HEWITT I 52-53 (essay: "Dreaming of Urban Plazas")
COOPER-HEWITT II 73-74 (essay: "Big-City Downtowns")

JENSZ, David ( ) perf
ART NETWORK no.2 47 (statement)

JEPSON, Stephen ( ) pott
SHAFER 92-113 (statements); port; 23 ill

JERMAN, George ( ) Amer; photo
CALIFORNIA--PHOTOGRAPHY (statement); port; 4 ill

JERRY, Michael John (1937-) Amer;

metal
WISCONSIN I (statement); 1 ill

JESS (Jess Collins) (1923-) Amer; ptr
ILLINOIS 1974 64-65 (statement); 1 ill
RUSSELL J 61 ("A Tricky Cad")
SOME 5 (statement); 1 ill

JEVREMOVIC, Charles (1960-)
SEE: SUBTERRANEAN VIDEO

JEWELL, Dick (1951-) photo, coll
BOSHIER (statement); port; 3 ill

JILTONILRO, Avotcja (1941-) Amer;
photo
LEWIS I REVISED 131-132 (statement);
port; 2 ill

JIMENEZ, Luis A. (1940-) Amer; sclp
RAICES 38 (statement); 1 ill

JOCHEM AND RUDI (Reindent Wepko
van de Wint) (1942-) Dutc; sclp
REFLECTION 36-39 (statement); 1 ill
SKIRA 1977 112 (statement); 1 ill

JOCHIMS, Reimer (Rainer) (1935-)
Germ; ptr
ART SINCE v.1 292 (statement, o.p.
1965)
SKIRA 1977 32 (statement); 1 ill

JOE, Dale (1928-) Amer; ptr
FULBRIGHT 28-29 (statement)
YOUNG 1960 (statement); 2 ill

JOHANSEN, John MacLane (1916-)
Amer; arch
EMANUEL I 397-399 (statement); 1 ill
GA HOUSES no.3 130-153 (statement);
port; 48 ill
HEYER 336-347 (interview); 16 ill

JOHANSON, George (1928-) Amer; ptr
GUENTHER 58-59 (statement); port; 1
ill

JOHANSON, Patricia (1940-) Amer;
sclp, instal, envir
ARTFORUM v.6 no.7 4 (letter)
MUNRO 462-468 (interview); port; 3 ill
NAYLOR 448-449 (statement); 1 ill

JOHNS, Barry ( ) Amer; arch, design
LIFE 245-249 (statement); port

JOHNS, Jasper (1930-) Amer; ptr
ART NOW v.1 no.4 ("Sketchbook
Notes"); 1 ill
ART SINCE v.2 325 (statement, o.p.
1963/64)
ARTFORUM v.3 no.6 32-36 (interview
with Walter Hopps); 7 ill
ARTFORUM v.7 no.3 6 (obituary of
Marcel Duchamp)
CONCEPTUAL ART 48, 57 (statements)
JOHNSON 72-78 (extract from essay:
"Jasper Johns: Stories and Ideas,"
o.p. 1964)
JOHNSON 89-92 (extract from interview
with Gene R. Swenson, o.p. 1964)
MILLER 1959 22-27 (statement); port; 7
ill
ROSE II 165-166 (statement, o.p. 1959)
ROSE II REVISED 146-147 (statement,
o.p. 1959)
ROSE II REVISED 147-149 (extract from
interview with Gene Swenson, o.p.
1964)
ROSE II REVISED 176-178 (extract from
essay: "Notes on *According to
What?*" o.p. 1965)
RUSSELL J 82-83 (interview with Gene
Swenson, o.p. 1964)
RUSSELL J 84-85 ("Sketchbook Notes,"
o.p. 1965)

JOHNSON, Alan ( )
  SEE: ALLEY FRIENDS

JOHNSON, Benjamin Franklin (1902-1967) Amer; ptr
  ART VOICES v.4 no.2 66-73 (interview with Jacqueline Barnitz); 13 ill
  ART VOICES v.5 no.3 38 (statement); 1 ill

JOHNSON, Buffie (1912-) Amer; ptr
  CELEBRATION (statement); 1 ill
  INTERVIEWS 5-7 (interview); port; 2 ill

JOHNSON, Carl ( ) Amer
  BRAKKE 163-171 (text piece: "Sanguine Humor")

JOHNSON, Charles M. (1862-) Amer; ptr
  JANIS II 220-223 (statements); port; 1 ill

JOHNSON, Clifford ( ) ptr
  ART VOICES v.4 no.1 77 (statement); 1 ill

JOHNSON, Jerry ( ) Amer; ptr
  CRISS-CROSS no.3 14-15 (statement); port; 1 ill

JOHNSON, Larry (1935-) Amer; ptr
  YOUNG 1960 (statement); 2 ill

JOHNSON, Lester (1919-) Amer; ptr
  ART NOW v.3 no.2 (statement); 1 ill
  IT IS no.5 7 ("A Cahier Leaf")

JOHNSON, M. L. J. ( ) Amer; photo
  EVENTS I 42-43 (statement); 1 ill

JOHNSON, Marie E. (1920-) Amer; ptr, sclp
  FINE 176-177 (statements, o.p. 1970, 1971); 2 ill

LEWIS I REVISED 59-60 (statement); port; 2 ill

JOHNSON, Peter ( ) SoAf; photo
  HOW FAMOUS 112-115 (statements); port; 6 ill

JOHNSON, Philip Cortelyou (1906-) Amer; arch
  BUILDINGS 7 (statement: "Foreword")
  COOK 11-51 (interview); port; 28 ill
  COOPER-HEWITT II 22 (statement)
  GA DOCUMENT no.1 12-24 (interview with Wayne Fujii); port; 40 ill
  GA DOCUMENT no.3 22-32 (statement); 16 ill
  HEYER 278-293 (interview); 23 ill
  DIAMONSTEIN I 167-182 (interview); ports
  REVOLUTION 137-140 (statement)
  ROTH 488-501 (extract from *The International Style: Architecture Since 1922,* o.p. 1932)
  ROTH 581-585 (essay: "The Seven Crutches of Modern Architecture," o.p. 1955)
  ROTH 585-586 (letter to Jurgen Joedicke, o.p. 1961)
  RODMAN I 52-56, 60-70 (interview)

JOHNSON, Poppy (1950-) Amer; sclp
  BELFORD 27-55 (group discussion)
  SEE ALSO: GUERRILA ART ACTION GROUP

JOHNSON, Ray (1927-) Amer; coll, ptr
  ARTFORUM v.3 no.1 28-29 (interview with David Bourdon); 3 ill
  ARTFORUM v.6 no.2 51-54 (letters)
  RUSSELL J 85-87 ("extract from the New York Correspondence School")
  VARIAN I (statement); port

JOHNSON, Richard Norman (1923-) Atrl; arch

EMANUEL I 401-402 (statement); 1 ill

JOHNSON, Robert H. ( ) Amer; ptr
CALIFORNIA--PAINTING 42 (statement);
1 ill

JOHNSTON, Elena Kubler ( ) Amer
PHILLPOT (statement)

JOHNSTON, Gerry ( ) perf, ptr
ART NETWORK no.2 47 (statement)

JOHNSTON, Medford (1941-) Amer; ptr
AVANT-GARDE 24-25 (poem); 1 ill

JOHNSTON, Roy (1936-) Iris; sclp,
instal
KNOWLES 100-101 (statement); 3 ill

JOHNSTON, Steve (1956-) photo
BOSHIER (statement); port; 3 ill

JOHNSTON, Ynez (1920-) Amer; print,
ptr
AMERICAN PRINTS 29, 67 (statement);
1 ill
CELEBRATION (statement); 1 ill
ILLINOIS 1953 191 (statement)
ILLINOIS 1963 111 (statement); 1 ill

JOHNSTONE, Magnus (1952-) Amer;
ptr
BOSTON III (interview); 1 ill

JONAS, Joan (1936-) Amer; video, perf,
print
ART-RITE no.5 6 (response)
ART-RITE no.7 4 ("August 1974 Fawn
Grove, PA."); 4 ill
DAVIS 71 (statement)
EMANUEL II 448 (statement)
LIVE no.3 15-17 (statement); 1 ill
NAYLOR 451 (statement); 1 ill
PERFORMANCE no.1 23 (statement)
SKIRA 1978 40 (statement); 1 ill

STEDELIJK 140 (statement); 1 ill
VIEW v.2 no.1 (interview); port; 6 ill

JONAS, Martin (1924-) Yugo; ptr
TOMASEVIC 145-148 (statement); port;
1 ill

JONES, A. Quincy ( ) Amer; arch
HEYER 163-171 (interview); 14 ill

JONES, Allan L. (1940-) Amer; photo,
light
OUTSIDE II 20-21 (statement); port; 6
ill

JONES, Allen (1937-) Brit; ptr, sclp
ART SINCE v.2 324 (statement, o.p.
1963)
ARTFORUM v.3 no.7 19-21 (interview
with John Coplans); 3 ill
ENGLISH 122-127 (statement); port; 8
ill
WEBB 370-375 (interview, 1972); 1 ill

JONES, Benjamin Franklin (1942-)
Amer; ptr
FINE 269-271 (letter, 1970); 2 ill

JONES, Colin ( ) photo
HOW FAMOUS 32-37 (statements); port;
6 ill

JONES, Edward (1939-) Brit; arch
GA HOUSES no.6 148-151 (statement);
11 ill
PORPHYRIOS 94-101 (essay: "Schinkel
Archives Building, Berlin," with
Margot Griffin); 9 ill

JONES, Fay ( ) Amer; ptr
GUENTHER 60-61 (statement); port; 1
ill

JONES, Harold Henry (1940-) Amer;

photo
HAND COLORED 12 (statement); 1 ill
HOWARD (interview)
WALSH 381-382 (statement); 1 ill

JONES, Henry Wanton (1925-) Cana;
sclp
CANADA 62-63 (statement); port; 3 ill

JONES, Howard (1922-) Amer; sclp
ARTFORUM v.7 no.3 4 (letter)

JONES, Jerry (1947-) Amer; sclp
GEORGIA 118-166 (group discussion:
"Artists' Convention," in Athens, GA.,
1/7/1977, moderated by Jan van der
Marck)

JONES, Joe (1909-1963) Amer; ptr
BRITTANICA 59 (statement); port; 1 ill
FIRST AMERICAN 10-11 (essay:
"Repression of Art in America")
ILLINOIS 1951 188-189 (statement); 1 ill
ILLINOIS 1952 200-201 (statement); 1 ill

JONES, John Paul (1924-) Amer; ptr,
print
CALIFORNIA--PAINTING 21 (statement);
1 ill
IRVINE 47, 88-89 (statement); 1 ill

JONES, Judy V. (1949-) Amer; print
NOSANOW I 77 (statement); 2 ill

JONES, Lawrence Arthur (1910-) Amer;
ptr
FAX I 48-62 (statements); port; 2 ill

JONES, Lois Mailou (1905-) Amer; ptr
FINE 136-139 (statements, o.p. 1961,
1972); 3 ill
LEWIS I REVISED 97-98 (statement);
port; 2 ill

JONES, Marvin Harold (1940-) Amer;
ptr
RIPS (statement); 1 ill

JONES, Mary ( ) Amer; ptr
DOWNTOWN (statement); 1 ill

JONES, Otis (1946-) Amer; ptr
HOUSTON 6-9 (extract from interview
with Marti Mayo); 3 ill

JONES, Patricia (1949-) Amer; sclp
EVENTS II 32-33 (statement); 1 ill

JONES, Pirkle (1914-) Amer; photo
WALSH 382-384 (statement); 1 ill

JONES, R. Benjamin (1936-) Amer; ptr
NOSANOW I 78 (statement); 1 ill

JONES, Wendell Cooley (1899-) Amer;
ptr, illus
ZAIDENBERG 26-31 (essay: "Anatomy
of Drawing"); 6 ill

JONES-SYLVESTER, Caryl (1943-)
Amer; sclp
NOSANOW I 79-81 (statement); 6 ill

JONQUIERES, Eduardo (1918-) Arge
PREMIER BILAN 301 (statement); port

JONSSON, Olof Sune (1930-) Swed;
photo
WALSH 385-386 (statement); 1 ill

JORDAN, Eddie Jack (1925-) Amer; sclp
LEWIS I REVISED 25 (statement); port;
2 ill

JORDAN, John (1942-) Cana; photo
POINT OF VIEW 60 (statement); 1 ill

JORDAN, Lynde (1913-) Amer; metal

CONTEMPORARY AFRICAN (statement); port; 1 ill

JORDAN ROMAN, Veronique (1943-) Fren; ptr
SKIRA 1978 28 (statement); 1 ill

JORGENSEN, Robert R. (1944-) Amer; wood
WOODWORKING 30-31 (statement); port; 3 ill

JORN, Asger (1914-1973) Dani; ptr
ART SINCE v.2 150 (statement, p.p.)
GUGGENHEIM I 101 (essay: "Concerning the Actual Value of the Functionalist Concept," o.p. 1958)
GUGGENHEIM I 101 (essay: "Critique of the Organic Doctrine of Architecture," o.p. 1958)
GUGGENHEIM I 102-103 (essay: "Banalities," o.p. 1942)

JOSEPH, Cliff (1921-) Amer; ptr
LEWIS I REVISED 48 (statement); port; 1 ill

JOSEPH, Thomas ( )
ARTISTS no.1 11-12 ("Big Art--Little Art")
ARTISTS no.5 3 (letter)

JOSEPHSON, Kenneth (1932-) Amer; photo
WALSH 386-387 (statement); 1 ill

JOSIC, Alexis (1921-) Fren; arch
EMANUEL I 404-405 (statement); 1 ill

JOUBERT, Bernard (1946-) Fren; ptr, envir
SKIRA 1979 29 (statement); 1 ill

JOURNIAC, Michel (1943-) Fren; sclp, photo, perf

EMANUEL II 450-452 (statement); 1 ill
NAYLOR 454 (statement); 1 ill
SKIRA 1977 62 (statement); 3 ill

JOVANOVIC, Milisav (1935-) Yugo; ptr
TOMASEVIC 149-154 (statement); port; 2 ill

JOY, Josephine (1869-) Amer; ptr
JANIS II 200-203 (statements); port; 1 ill

JOYCE, Paul (1940-) Brit; photo
WALSH 387-388 (statement); 1 ill

JSENSTEIN, Burton (1955-) Amer; pott
HERMAN 74 (statement); port; 1 ill

JUDD, Donald (1928-) Amer; sclp
ART NOW v.1 no.1 (statement); 1 ill
ART SINCE v.1 293 (statement, o.p. 1965)
ARTS YEARBOOK v.7 21-35 (essay: "Local History")
ARTS YEARBOOK v.8 74-82 (essay: "Specific Objects")
ARTS YEARBOOK v.8 176-179 (essay: "To Encourage Sculpture")
ARTS YEARBOOK v.9 83, 91 (response); 1 ill
BATTCOCK V 148-164 (interview with Bruce Glaser, o.p. 1966); 1 ill
CONCEPTUAL ART 47, 49, 51, 52, 54, 59 (statements)
DANOFF 79, 81 (interview)
EMANUEL II 452-453 (statement)
FRASCINA 129-132 (essay: "Barnett Newman," o.p. 1970)
JOHNSON 105-109, 111 (extract from essay: "Specific Objects," o.p. 1965); 1 ill
JOHNSON 113-120 (extract from interview with Bruce Glaser, o.p. 1966)
NAYLOR 455 (statement)

ROSE II 176-180 (extract from interview with Bruce Glaser, o.p. 1966)
ROSE II REVISED 170-174 (extract from interview with Bruce Glaser, o.p. 1966)
ROSE II REVISED 178-179 (extract from essay: "Specific Objects," o.p. 1965)
VARIAN II (statement); port
VRIES 120-135 (essay: "Specific Objects," o.p. 1965)

JULES, Mervin (1912-) Amer; ptr
BRITANNICA 60 (statement); port; 1 ill
M.H. DE YOUNG 71-72 (response); self port
100 CONTEMPORARY 98-99 (statement); port; 1 ill

JULIEN, Rene ( ) Belg; ptr
COLLARD 146-149 (interview); port; 1 ill

JULLIEN-MINGUEZ, Alain (1948-) Fren; ptr
SKIRA 1978 76 (statement); 1 ill

JUMSAI, Sumet (1939-) Thai; arch
EMANUEL I 407-408 (statement); 1 ill
REVOLUTION 73-78 (essay: "Emerging New Cities Versus Old Values: The Case of Indochina")

JUNG, Dieter (1941-) Germ; ptr
SKIRA 1976 62 (statement); 1 ill

JUNG, Simonetta ( ) Belg; ptr
COLLARD 150-155 (interview); port; 1 ill

JUNGWIRTH, Martha (1940-) Aust; ptr
SANDBERG 104-107 (statement); 7 ill

JUPP, Mo (1938-) pott, sclp
CAMERON E 78-83 (response); 6 ill

JURAK, Dragutin (1911-) Yugo; ptr
TOMASEVIC 155-159 (statement); port; 2 ill

JURKIEWICZ, Zdzislaw (1931-) Poli; ptr
SANDBERG 108-111 (statement); 8 ill

JURS, Nancy (1941-) Amer; pott
HERMAN 75 (statement); port; 1 ill

JUSTIS, Gary Allen (1953-) Amer; sclp, instal, light
LOGAN I 13-16 (statement); port; 5 ill

KABAK, Robert (1930-) Amer; ptr
ILLINOIS 1959 228-229 (statement); 1 ill

KACHADOORIAN, Zubel (1924-) Amer; ptr
ILLINOIS 1959 229 (statement); 1 ill
ILLINOIS 1961 185 (response); port; 1 ill

KADISH, Katherine (1939-) Amer; ptr
NOSANOW I 82-83 (statement); 2 ill
WOMANART v.2 no.1 4-5 (statements); port; 1 ill

KADISH, Reuben ( )
IT IS no.6 7-16, 57-64, 73-75 (group discussion)

KAEP, Louis Joseph (1903-) Amer; ptr
NORTH LIGHT 80 (statement); 1 ill

KAHANE, Anne Langstadt (1926-) Aust/Cana; sclp
CANADA 44-45 (statement); port; 1 ill

KAHN, Louis Isadore (1901-1974) Russ/Amer; arch
CONRADS 169-170 ("Order is," o.p. 1955)
COOK 178-217 (interview); port; 31 ill
HEYER 388-403 (interview); 28 ill
NEWMAN 205-214 ("Talk at the Conclusion of the Otterlo Conference")
NEWMAN 214-216 (interview)
PROCESSES 29-54 (statement); 20 ill
ROTH 571-573 ("Order Is," o.p. 1955)
ROTH 574-580 (essay: "Form and Design," o.p. 1962); 1 ill

KAHN, Wolf (1927-) Germ/Amer; ptr, sclp
ART NOW v.3 no.2 (statement); 1 ill
GUSSOW 122-123 (interview, 1970 and letter, 1968); 1 ill
ILLINOIS 1957 214 (response); 1 ill
ILLINOIS 1959 230-231 (statement); 1 ill

WHITNEY (statement); 1 ill
YOUNG 1960 (statement); 2 ill

KAISER, Charles James (1939-) Amer; ptr
WISCONSIN II (statement); 1 ill

KAISER, Robert (1925-) Cana; sclp
CANADA 88-89 (statement); port; 2 ill

KAISH, Luise (1925-) Amer; sclp
ILLINOIS 1959 231-232 (statement); 1 ill
ILLINOIS 1961 141 (response); port; 1 ill

KAISH, Morton (1927-) Amer; ptr
ILLINOIS 1965 59 (statement); 1 ill

KAKS, Olle (1941-) sclp, instal, ptr
SLEEPING 82-91 (poem); port; 5 ill

KALDIS, Aristodimos ( )
IT IS no.2 36-38 ("Glossary")

KALISH, Max (1891-1945) Amer; sclp
100 CONTEMPORARY 100-101 (statement); port; 1 ill

KALISH, Muriel (1932-) Amer; ptr
ILLINOIS 1963 222 (statement); 1 ill

KALISHER, Simpson (1926-) Amer; photo
WALSH 389-390 (statement); 1 ill

KALKMANN, Hans-Werner (1940-) Germ; sclp
GROH (statement); 4 ill
NAYLOR 457-458 (statement); 1 ill

KALLAY, Karol (1926-) Czec; photo
WALSH 390-391 (statement); 1 ill

KALLEM, Herbert (1909-) Amer; sclp
ILLINOIS 1961 135 (response); port; 1 ill

KALLEM, Morris J. (1888-) Russ/Amer; ptr
100 CONTEMPORARY 102-103 (statement); port; 1 ill

KALLMANN, Gerhard Michael (1915-) Germ/Amer; arch
HEYER 256-263 (interview); 7 ill
PROCESSES 55-74 (interview by Lance Laver); 15 ill

KALLMEYER, Lothar ( ) arch
REVOLUTION 182-191 (essay: "New Tendencies in Protestant Church Building")

KALLWEIT, Richard ( ) ptr, sclp
CRISS-CROSS no.5 40-43 (statement); 4 ill
CRISS-CROSS no.10 16-17 ("The Common Ground for all this Work"); port; 1 ill

KALSI, Amarjit S. (1957-) Brit; arch
SPIRIT 68-75 (statement); 9 ill

KALTENBACH, Stephen James (1940-) Amer; light, ptr, sclp
CELANT 25-30 (statement); 12 ill
CONCEPTUAL ART 30, 32, 39, 42 (statements)
EMANUEL II 455-456 (statement)
NAYLOR 458-459 (statement); 1 ill

KALVARSKY, Eugene ( )
ART VOICES v.2 no.2 25 (essay: "Artists and Conditioned Reflexes")

KAMIHARA, Ben (1925-) Amer; ptr
GOODYEAR 58-62 (interview); 3 ill

KAMMERICHS, Klaus (1933-) Germ; sclp
SKIRA 1976 11 (statement); 2 ill

KAMROWSKI, Gerome (1914-) Amer; ptr
ILLINOIS 1952 201-202 (statement); 1 ill
JANIS I 104-105 (statement); 1 ill

KAMYS, Walter (1917-) Amer; ptr
RISENHOOVER 86-95 (interview)

KANAGA, Consuelo (1894-1978); Amer; photo
MITCHELL 158-177 (statement); ports; 18 ill

KANAGINI, Niki (Kanaginis) (1933-) Gree; instal
NAYLOR 458-460 (statement); 1 ill

KANDINSKY, Wassily (1866-1944) Russ; ptr
AXIS no.2 6 ("Line and Fish")
BERCKELAERS 167-169 (poems: "Les Promenades," "Lyrique," "Rhinoceros," "Conversation de Salon," p.p.)
BERCKELAERS 180, 182-184 (statements, 1911, 1912, 1943)
BERCKELAERS 298-300 (statement; extract from "Introduction" to 1912 exhibition catalog); 1 ill
BOWLT 17-23 (essay: "Content and Form," o.p. 1910); port; 1 ill
BOWLT 196-198 (essay: "Plan for the Physicopsychological Department of the Russian Academy of Artistic Sciences," o.p. 1923)
CHIPP 152-155 (extract from *Uber das Geistige in der Kunst*, in English, o.p. 1912); port
CHIPP 155-170 (extract from *Uber die Formfrage*, in English, o.p. 1912); 1 ill
CHIPP 346-349 (essay: "Concrete Art," o.p. 1938)
EDDY 119-120 (extract from essay, o.p. in *Der Sturm*)
EDDY 124 (statement)

KANE, John (1860-1934) Amer; ptr
DOUZE PEINTRES (statement); 2 ill
JANIS II 76-98 (statements); port; 4 ill

KANER, Felicia ( ) Amer; illus
CALIFORNIA--DRAWING (statement); 2
ill

KANN, Frederick I. (1886-) Czec/Amer;
sclp, ptr
ABSTRACT 27-28, 35, 137 (essay: "In
Defense of Abstract Art"); 1 ill
KUNG 150-153 (statement); port; 2 ill

KANOVITZ, Howard (1929-) Amer; ptr,
sclp
EMANUEL II 458-460 (statement); 1 ill
ILLINOIS 1963 178 (statement); 1 ill
NAYLOR 461-462 (statement); 1 ill

KANTOR, Morris (1896-1974) Amer; ptr
BRITANNICA 61 (statement); port; 1 ill
ILLINOIS 1950 183 (statement); 1 ill
M.H. DE YOUNG 73 (response); self port

KANTOR, Tadeusz (1915-) Poli; perf,
sclp, ptr
VISION no.2 52-55 (statement); 5 ill

KAPLAN, Joseph (1900-1980)
Russ/Amer; ptr
ILLINOIS 1951 189-190 (statement); 1 ill
ILLINOIS 1953 192 (statement); 1 ill

KAPLOWITZ, Caroline Gassner ( )
Amer; wood
MEILACH 160 (statement); 2 ill

KAPPE, Raymond ( ) arch
GA HOUSES no.1 120-149 (statement);
60 ill

KAPROW, Allan (1927-) Amer; film,
perf, ptr

ARTFORUM v.4 no.7 36-39 (essay:
"The Happenings are Dead, Long Live
the Happenings"); 11 ill
ARTFORUM v.6 no.1 4 (letter)
ARTFORUM v.6 no.5 4 (letter)
ARTFORUM v.6 no.10 32-33 (essay:
"The Shape of the Art Environment");
1 ill
ART-RITE no.7 17-18 ("Hello: Plan
and Execution")
ART-RITE no.14 5, 9 (response)
ARTS YEARBOOK v.9 94-101 ("What Is
a Museum?" conversation with Robert
Smithson)
ART VOICES v.4 no.1 46-51 (interview
with Gordon Brown); 8 ill
BATTCOCK VII 73-90 (essay: "The
Education of the Un-Artist, Part I,"
o.p. 1971)
CONCEPTUAL ART 53 (statement)
IT IS no.4 51-52 (essay: "The
Principles of Modern Art")
JOHNSON 57-58 (extract from essay:
"The Legacy of Jackson Pollock," o.p.
1958)
JOHNSON 58-65 (extract from essay:
"Happenings in the New York Art
Scene," o.p. 1961); 1 ill
KIRBY 44-52 ("a statement")
KIRBY 53-66 ("18 Happenings in 6
Parts/the script")
KIRBY 84-86 ("Coca cola, Shirley
Cannonball?/the script")
KIRBY 92-93 ("A Spring
Happening/the script")
KIRBY 105-107 ("The Courtyard/the
script"); ports
KUNST BLEIBT KUNST 416 (statement)
LIVE no.3 13 (statement)
NAYLOR 463-465 (statement)
ON SITE no.5/6 49-51 ("Travelog")
PROFILE v.1 no.5 (interview); port
ROSE II REVISED 187-189 (statement:
"The Newest Energies," o.p. 1967)

VISION no.3 26-31 (text piece, and statement)

KAPUZA, Carol ( ) Amer; sclp
ARTPARK 1980 (statement); 2 ill

KARAVAN, Dani (1930-) Isra; sclp
SKIRA 1977 108-109 (statement); 3 ill
SKIRA 1979 38-39 (statement); 2 ill

KARAWINA, Erica (1904-) Germ/Amer; ptr, glass
HAAR II 36-41 (interview); ports; 3 ill

KARDON, Dennis ( ) ptr
ART-RITE no.9 12-13 ("A Pained Expression")

KARESH, Ann Bamberger (1921-) Germ/Amer; coll, sclp
MORRIS 122-127 (statements); ports; 3 ill

KARFIOL, Bernard (1886-1952) Hung/Amer; ptr
BRITANNICA 62 (statement); port; 1 ill

KARINA, Elena ( ) Amer; pott
HERMAN 76 (statement); port; 1 ill

KARLOVEC, Gerald ( ) Amer; perf
ARTPARK 1982 18-19, 47 (statement); port; 4 ill

KARLUNG, Ake (1930-) sclp, light, instal
SEXTANT 53-71 (text pieces, in French and English); 19 ill

KARRAS, Maria (1950-) Amer; photo
ISSUE (statement); port; 2 ill

KARSCH, Joachim (1897-1945) Germ; sclp

SCHMIDT 115, 150-151, 160-161, 178-179, 194-195, 197, 206-207, (letters and statements, 1937-1945)

KARSH, Yousuf (1908-) Cana; photo
BOOTH 124-133 (interview); port; 4 ill
DANZIGER 98-111 (interview); port; 3 ill
WALSH 392-394 (statement); 1 ill

KARSKAYA, Ida (1905-) Fren; ptr, sclp, coll
SEUPHOR 197-198 (statement)

KARWELIS, Donald Charles (1934-) Amer; ptr
IRVINE 58, 82-83 (statement); 1 ill

KASIULIS, Vytautas ( ) Fren
PREMIER BILAN 301 (statement); port

KASSAK, Lajos (1887-1967) Hung; ptr, coll
NAYLOR 465-466 (statement); 1 ill

KASSIS, Barbara Meise ( )
PHILLPOT (statement)

KASTEN, Barbara (1936-) Amer; ptr, instal
SCRIPPS COLLEGE (statement); 1 ill

KASTEN, Karl Albert (1916-) Amer; ptr, sclp
BETHERS II 92-93 (statement); 3 ill
ILLINOIS 1969 162 (statement); 1 ill

KASUBA, Aleksandra (1923-) Lith/Amer
ART AND TECHNOLOGY 144-145 (project proposal); 2 ill

KATAVOLOS, William ( ) arch
CONRADS 163-164 (essay: "Organics," o.p. 1960)

KATSELAS, Tasso (1929-) Amer; arch
EMANUEL I 414-416 (statement); 1 ill

KATSIAFICAS, Diane ( ) Amer; sclp,
instal
GUENTHER 62-63 (statement); port; 1
ill

KATZ, Alex (1927-) Amer; ptr
ART NOW v.2 no.9 (statement); 1 ill
EMANUEL II 464-466 (statement); 1 ill
PROFILE v.2 no.1 (interview); port; 2 ill
STRAND 112-135 (interview); port; 21
ill
SUPERREAL 45-46, 78-79 (interview); 1
ill
YOUNG 1960 (statement); 2 ill

KATZ, Mel ( ) Amer; sclp
GUENTHER 64-65 (statement); port; 1
ill

KATZ, Paul (1942-) Amer; ptr
ART NOW v.3 no.4 (statement); 1 ill

KATZ, Raymond L. ( ) Amer; sclp
KRESGE (statement); port; 1 ill

KATZEN, Lila (1932-) Amer; sclp
CELEBRATION (statement); 1 ill
DIRECTIONS I 76 (response); 1 ill
MUNRO 225-232 (interview); port; 2 ill
NEMSER 230-265 (interview); port; 12
ill
SCHAPIRO 35 (statement); port; 1 ill

KATZMAN, Herbert (1923-) Amer; ptr
MILLER 1952 38-39 (statement); 3 ill
NEW DECADE 44-45 (statement); 2 ill
PROTTER 255-256 (statement, 1963); 1
ill

KAUFFMAN, Craig (1932-) Amer; ptr,
sclp, instal

ART VOICES v.5 no.4 61, 67 (response);
1 ill
HOPKINS 106-107 (statement); port; 1
ill
IRVINE 67, 86 (statement); 1 ill
ROSE I 50-55 (statement); 3 ill
WIGHT 107-139 (interview); ports; 6 ill

KAUFMAN, Boris ( ) Russ/Amer; film
KEPES IX 138-143 (essay: "Film
Making as an Art")

KAUFMAN, Jane A. (1938-) Amer; ptr
TUCKER I 20 (statement)

KAWAGUCHI, Tatsuo (1940-) Japa;
instal, light
EMANUEL II 467-468 (statement); 1 ill

KAWAI, Choyoshi ( )
ART-RITE no.19 17-20 (group
discussion)

KAYE, Pooh ( ) perf
LIVE no.6/7 66-69 (interview); port

KAYE, Stanton (1943-) Amer; video
ROSS 42-43 (statement)

KAYN, Hilde B. (1906-1950) Amer; ptr
BRITANNICA 63 (statement); port; 1 ill

KAYSER, Eugene (1940-) ptr
TRACKS v.1 no.3 41 (poem:
"Apologia")

KAZ, Nathaniel (1917-) Amer; sclp
ZAIDENBERG 170-174 (essay: "Good
Sculpture"); 5 ill

KAZUKI, Yasuo (1911-) Japa; ptr
KUNG 68-71 (statement); port; 3 ill

KEARNS, James (1924-) Amer; sclp, ptr
RODMAN III 84-90 (statements; letters)

KEATING, Andrew ( ) Cana; sclp, ptr
GUENTHER 66-67 (statement); port; 1 ill

KEC, Florika (1935-) Yugo; ptr
TOMASEVIC 160-162 (statement); port; 2 ill

KECK, George Fred (1895-) Amer; arch
EMANUEL I 416-418 (statement); 1 ill

KEEN, Jeff (1923-) Brit; film
ENGLISH 452-453 (statement); port; 1 ill

KEENS, David ( ) Amer; metal
METALWORKS (statement); 1 ill

KEES, Weldon (1914-) Amer; ptr
MOTHERWELL 8-22 (three group discussions: "Artists' Sessions at Studio 35," New York, 1950)

KEHOE, John D. ( ) Amer; sclp
ART PATRON ART 39-40 (statement); port; 1 ill

KEINHOLZ, Edward ( )
GUENTHER 70-71 (statement); port; 1 ill

KELLOGG, Agnes (1912-) Amer; coll
CALIFORNIA--COLLAGE (statement); 1 ill

KELLOGG, Edward (1944-) Amer; ptr
NOSANOW I 84-85 (statement); 1 ill

KELLY, Ellsworth (1923-) Amer; ptr
ART NOW v.1 no.9 (statement); 1 ill
ROSE II REVISED 165 (extract from interview with Henry Geldzahler, o.p. 1965)
STEDELIJK 142-143 (statement, o.p. 1969); 2 ill

KELLY, John ( ) Brit; photo
HOW FAMOUS 148-153 (statements); port; 6 ill

KELLY, Lee (1932-) Amer; sclp
GUENTHER 68-69 (statement); port; 1 ill

KELLY, Leon (1901-) Fren/Amer; ptr
JANIS I 108 (statement); 1 ill

KELLY, Mary (1941-) Amer; coll, ptr, print
CONTEMPORARY (statement); port; 2 ill
HAYWARD 1978 62-65 (statement); 5 ill
SKIRA 1979 70 (statement); 1 ill

KELLY, Mary (1951-) Amer/Brit
ISSUE (text piece); 2 ill

KELLY, Ray ( ) Amer; sclp
ARTPARK 1974 26-27 (statement); port; 1 ill

KELLY, Richard ( ) Amer
ARTPARK 1983 36-37 (statement); 1 ill

KELLY, Robert W. (1956-) Amer; ptr
BOSTON II (statement); 1 ill

KEMENY, Zoltan (1907-1965) Hung/Swis; sclp, ptr
ART SINCE v.2 323 (statement, o.p. 1966)
SKIRA 1975 109 (statement); 1 ill

KEMP, Renee ( ) Amer; arch, design
LIFE 232-243 (interview); port

KEMP, Roger (1908-) Atrl; ptr
DE GROEN 163-169 (interview); port

KEMPE, Fritz (1909-) Germ; photo
WALSH 396-398 (statement); 1 ill

KENNEDY, Brigid ( ) Amer; sclp, envir
ARTPARK 1977 54-57 (statement); 7 ill

KENNEDY, Peter (1945-) Atrl; ptr
DE GROEN 115-120 (interview); port

KENNINGTON, Eric (1888-1960) Brit; sclp
OPEN AIR 1960 (statement); 1 ill

KENNY, Kay ( ) Amer
EVENTS II 35-36 (statement); 1 ill

KENNY, Michael (1941-) Brit; sclp
CONTEMPORARY (statement); port; 2 ill
EMANUEL II 470-471 (statement); 1 ill
NAYLOR 473-474 (statement); 1 ill

KENT, Jane ( ) perf
ART NETWORK no.2 41 (statement)
ART NETWORK no.2 45 (statement)
ART NETWORK no.2 49 (statement)

KENT, Rockwell (1882-1971) Amer; ptr, print
BRITANNICA 64 (statement); port; 1 ill
CUMMINGS 6-23 (interview; 1969); port; 2 ill
FIRST AMERICAN 7-9 (essay: "What is Worth Fighting For")
MCCAUSLAND 65-68 (essay: "Dictators of Art")

KENYON, Colleen (1951-) Amer; photo
HAND COLORED 20 (statement); 1 ill

KEPES, Gyorgy (1906-) Hung/Amer; ptr, photo
CENTERBEAM 36, 111-112 (extract from the introduction to the dedication catalogue of C.A.V.S.); port; 3 ill
ILLINOIS 1952 202 (statement)
ILLINOIS 1965 128-129 (statement); 1 ill
JANIS I 63 (statement); 1 ill

KEPES II 1-12 (essay: "Art and Ecological Consciousness")
KEPES II 13-31 (essay: "Toward a New Environment")
KEPES II 167-197 (essay: "The Artist's Role in Environmental Self-Regulation")
KEPES VI i-vii ("Introduction")
KEPES VII i-xi ("Introduction")
KEPES VII 18-23 (essay: "Mobile Light Mural"); 4 ill
KEPES VIII i-vii ("Introduction")
KEPES IX 3-12 ("Introduction")
LIGHT 48-53 (statement); 5 ill

KERG, Theo (1909-) Fren; ptr
ABSTRACTION no.4 16-17 (statement); 2 ill

KERKAM, Earl Cavis (1890-) Amer; ptr
ILLINOIS 1963 185 (statement); 1 ill

KERMADEC, Eugene de (1899-) Fren; ptr, sclp
VINGTIEME N.S. no.10 61 ("Signes et Rythmes"); 1 ill

KERNER, Nancy ( ) Amer
BRAKKE 177-181 (text piece); 3 ill

KERTESZ, Andre (1894-) Hung/Amer; photo
BOOTH 134-144 (interview); port; 6 ill
CAMPBELL 272-283 (statement); port; 10 ill
DIAMONSTEIN III 81-92 (interview); 9 ill
HILL 44-49 (interview, 1977); port
WALSH 402-404 (statement); 1 ill

KESSEL, Dmitri (1902-) Russ/Amer; photo
TIME-LIFE VI 96-104 (essay: "Photographing Churches"); 8 ill

KESSELMAN, Malcolm ( ) ptr
REALLIFE no.7 8-9 (essay: "Paintings are More Than Medals of Honor")

KESSLER, Alan (1945-) Amer; ptr
SUPERREAL 162-163 (statement); 1 ill

KESTER, Lenard (1917-) Amer; ptr
ILLINOIS 1950 184 (statement); 1 ill
ILLINOIS 1951 190 (statement)

KETCHUM, Cavalliere (1937-) Amer; photo
WISCONSIN I (statement); 1 ill

KEVORKIAN, Richard (1937-) Amer; ptr
SOUTHEAST (statement); port; 6 ill

KEYSER, Robert Gifford (1924-) Amer; ptr
ILLINOIS 1961 115 (response); port; 1 ill

KHOSROVI, Karim (1925-) Amer; ptr
ILLINOIS 1955 210 (statement); 1 ill

KIDNER, Michael (1917-) Brit; ptr
BOWNESS 23, 63-65 (statement); 2 ill
CONTEMPORARY (statement); port; 1 ill

KIEHTREIBER, Albert
SEE: GUETERSLOH, Albert Paris

KIENBUSCH, William Austin (1914-1979) Amer; ptr
GUSSOW 90-91 (letter, 1970); 1 ill
ILLINOIS 1965 83 (statement); 1 ill
ILLINOIS 1967 74 (statement); 1 ill

KIENHOLZ, Edward (1927-) Amer; sclp, instal
ART ATTACK 4 (statement)
ART VOICES v.5 no.4 61, 63 (response); 1 ill

ARTFORUM v.1 no.5 30-34 (group discussion); port; 3 ill
STEDELIJK 146-147 (statement, o.p. 1970); 2 ill

KIESLER, Frederick J. (1896-1965) Amer; sclp, ptr, arch
CONRADS 98 ("Space City Architecture," o.p. 1926)
CONRADS 150-151 ("Magical Architecture," o.p. 1947)
IT IS no.4 27 (poem: "Frank Lloyd Wright")
LIPPARD 151-153 ("The Magic Architecture of the Hall of Superstition," o.p. 1947)
MILLER 1952 8-9 (statement); 1 ill

KIFFL, Erika (1939-) Aust; photo
WALSH 404-405 (statement); 1 ill

KIKIS, Bill ( ) Amer; arch, design
LIFE 91-114 (interview); port

KIKUTAKE, Kiyonori (1928-) Japa; arch
EMANUEL I 422-423 (statement); 1 ill

KILEY, Daniel Urban (1912-) Amer; arch
EMANUEL I 423-425 (statement); 1 ill

KILLICK, John A. (1924-1972) arch
SEE: HOWELL KILLICK PARTRIDGE AND AMIS

KILLINGER, Paul E. (1926-) Amer; wood
WOODWORKING 32-33 (statement); port; 3 ill

KILLINGSWORTH, Edward Abel (1917-) Amer; arch
EMANUEL I 425-428 (statement); 1 ill
HEYER 157-162 (interview); 13 ill

KILLIP, Chris (1946-) Brit; photo
VICTORIA 76-79 (statements)

KILLMASTER, John H. (1934-) Amer;
ptr
NOSANOW II 26-27, 51-52 (statement);
4 ill

KILMER, David ( ) Amer; ptr, illus
MAGIC 72-75 (statement); port; 3 ill

KIM, Tschang-yeul (1929-) Kore; ptr
SKIRA 1976 61 (statement); 1 ill

KIMURA, Kentaro (1928-) Japa; sclp
KUNG 168-171 (statement); port; 2 ill

KIMURA, Sueko M. (1912-) Amer; ptr
HAAR I 74-79 (interview with Prithwish
Neogy); ports; 3 ill

KING, Brian (1942-) Iris; instal, envir
KNOWLES 204-209 (statement); 8 ill

KING, Donald E. ( ) Amer; ptr
KRESGE (statement); port; 1 ill

KING, Frank (1883-1969) Amer; cart
M.H. DE YOUNG 75 (response); self port

KING, Hayward (1928-) Amer; ptr
FULBRIGHT 29 (statement)

KING, Kenneth ( ) perf
BATTCOCK I 243-250 (essay: "Toward
a Trans-Literal and Trans-Technical
Dance-Theater")
LIVE no.3 14-15 (statement)
LIVE no.4 21-22 (letter)

KING, Philip (1934-) Brit; sclp
ART AND TECHNOLOGY 146 (project
proposal)
ART SINCE v.2 323 (statement, o.p.
1966)

CHIPP 623 (statement, o.p. 1966)
CONTEMPORARY (statement; from
Australian lecture series); port; 2 ill
EMANUEL II 474-475 (statement); 1 ill
ENGLISH 258-263 (statement); port; 3
ill
NAYLOR 475-476 (statement); 1 ill
SKIRA 1975 107 (letter to Richard
Matz, 9/73); 1 ill

KING, Ray ( ) Amer; sclp, envir
ARTPARK 1980 (statement); port; 3 ill

KING, Ron ( ) Amer; text
HAYSTACK 32 (statement); 1 ill

KING, Tony (1944-) Amer; ptr
VASSAR COLLEGE (statement); 1 ill

KING, William (1925-) Amer; sclp
GOODMAN 63-65 (interview)
ILLINOIS 1957 214-215 (response); 1 ill
ILLINOIS 1963 146 (statement); 1 ill
ILLINOIS 1965 67 (statement); 1 ill

KINGMAN, Dong M. (1911-) Amer; ptr,
illus
BETHERS I 236-237 (statement); 1 ill
GUITAR 120-131 (interview); port; 4 ill
ILLINOIS 1952 202-203 (statement); 1 ill
ILLINOIS 1953 194 (statement); 1 ill

KINGREY, Kenneth (1913-) Amer;
design
HAAR II 42-48 (interview); ports; 3 ill

KINIGSTEIN, Jonah (1923-) Amer; ptr
ILLINOIS 1955 210-211 (statement); 1 ill
ILLINOIS 1957 215-216 (response); 1 ill
ILLINOIS 1959 232-233 (statement); 1 ill

KINNIARD, Richard W. (1931-) Amer;
ptr
ART PATRON ART 41-42 (statement);
port; 1 ill

HUMAN (essay: Preface to the exhibition catalog, *The Human Clay*, 1976)
LETTERS 18 (letter); 1 ill
SKIRA 1978 68-69 (statement); 1 ill
VICTORIA 80-83 (statements)

KITATSUJI, Yoshihisa (1948-) Japa; ptr, illus
EMANUEL II 481-482 (statement); 1 ill
NAYLOR 481 (statement); 1 ill

KITCHELL, Nancy Wilson (1941-) Amer; photo, print
ART-RITE no.7 25 ("Mr. Kitchell Watches While Mrs. Kitchell Writes"); 1 ill
IDENTITE 43-46 (interview with Jacques Clayssen); port
SKIRA 1977 79 (statement); 1 ill
SONDHEIM 137-156 ("Visible and Invisible"); 15 ill
TRACKS v.3 no.1/2 82-90 ("Contexts")

KIYOKAWA, Taiji (1919-) Japa/Amer; ptr
ILLINOIS 1965 66 (statement); 1 ill

KIYOMIZU, Kyubei (1922-) Japa; sclp, instal
PRADEL 16 (statement, o.p. 1982); 2 ill

KIZIK, Roger (1945-) Amer; ptr
BOSTON II (statement); 1 ill

KJARGAARD, John I. (1902-) Dani/Amer; ptr
HAAR I 83-87 (interview with Prithwish Neogy); ports; 3 ill

KLAPHECK, Konrad (1935-) Germ; ptr
ART SINCE v.2 154 (statement, o.p. 1965)
EMANUEL II 482-483 (statement); 1 ill
NAYLOR 481-483 (statement); 1 ill

SKIRA 1975 25 (statement: "La machine et moi," 1963); 1 ill

KLARER, Streng
SEE: GERSTNER, Karl

KLASEN, Peter (1935-) Germ; ptr
SKIRA 1976 61 (extract from interview with O. Kaeppelin); 1 ill

KLASSNIK, Robin (1947-) Brit; sclp, instal
NAYLOR 484-485 (statement); 1 ill

KLAVEN, Marvin (1931-) Amer; ptr
ILLINOIS 1969 79 (statement); 1 ill

KLAVUN, Betty (1916-) Amer; sclp, envir
ARTPARK 1977 60-62 (statement); 5 ill
MUNRO 456-461 (interview); port; 4 ill

KLEE, Paul (1879-1940) Swis; ptr, sclp
CHIPP 182-186 ("Creative Credo," o.p. 1920); self port
FRIEDENTHAL 205-206 (statement, o.p. 1912); 2 ill
GIEDION-WELCKER 103-110 (poems: "Letztes," "Esel," "1915," "Ende Juni," "Antwort," "Zurufe," "1926," in German); port
GOLDWATER 441-444 (journal entries, 1902, 1903; statement, 1929)
GROHMANN 432-435 ("Aus den Tagenbuchen," 1901, 1903, 1905, 1906, 1909, 1912, 1918, 1919)
GROHMANN 435-441 ("Bekenntnis," p.p. 1920)
GROTE 19 ("uber Emil Nolde," 1927)
MIESEL 80-83 ("Extracts from *The Diaries*," 1914-16)
MIESEL 83-88 ("Creative Credo," 1920)
MIESEL 149-150 (poems: "The Two Mountains," 1903, "Poem," 1906, p.p. 1962)

KLEMENT, Vera (1929-) Amer; ptr
SULTAN 79 ("Printed Thought")

KLEMMER, Robert ( )
GROH (statement); port

KLETT, Mark (1952-) Amer; photo
FUGITIVE (statement); 1 ill

KLINE, Franz (1910-1962) Amer; ptr
ART SINCE v.1 154 (extract from interview with David Sylvester, o.p. 1963)
JOHNSON 23-27 (extract from interview with David Sylvester, o.p. 1963); 1 ill
KUH 143-154 (interview); 5 ill
NEW DECADE 48-50 (statement); 2 ill
O'HARA 48-52 (interview)
PROTTER 247-248 (statements, 1955); 1 ill
RODMAN I 105-110 (interview)
ROSE II 155-158 (extract from interview with David Sylvester, o.p. 1963)
ROSE II REVISED 130-133 (extracts from interview with David Sylvester, o.p. 1963)
SIX PEINTRES (extract from "Franz Kline Talking," by Frank O'Hara, o.p. 1958); port; 2 ill

KLINGER, Max (1857-1920) print, ptr
THORN 52, 67, 69, 164, 165, 244, 325 (statements, p.p.)

KLITGAARD, Georgina (1893-) Amer; ptr
BETHERS II 96-97 (statement); 2 ill
M. H. DE YOUNG 76 (response); self port
ZAIDENBERG 148-149 (essay: "Landscape Painting"); 2 ill

KLOPHAUS, Annalies (1940-) Germ; illus
SKIRA 1976 52 (statement); 1 ill

KLOPOTAN, Franjo (1938-) Yugo; ptr
TOMASEVIC 163-168 (statement); port; self port; 1 ill

KLOSSOWSKI, Baltusz
SEE: BALTHUS

KLOSSOWSKI, Pierre (1905-) Fren; ptr
CHOIX 26 (statements); 1 ill

KLUG, Lee (1930-) Amer; photo
WISCONSIN I (statement); 1 ill

KLYUN, Ivan (1870-1942) Russ; ptr
BOWLT 114-115 (statement, o.p. 1915/16); port
BOWLT 136-138 (essay: "Primitives of the 20th Century," o.p. 1915); 1 ill
BOWLT 142-143 (essay: "Color Art," o.p. 1919)

KNAPP, Candace (1948-) Swis; sclp, ptr
O'KANE (statement); 1 ill

KNATHS, Otto Karl (1891-1971) Amer; ptr
ABSTRACT 195 (essay: "Note on Color")
ART NOW v.1 no.2 (statement); 1 ill
BETHERS I 238-239 (statement); 1 ill
BETHERS II 98-99 (statement); 2 ill
FORTY (statement); 2 ill
GOODRICH 5-20 (statements); 13 ill
ILLINOIS 1951 190-191 (statement)
ILLINOIS 1955 211 (statement); 1 ill
ILLINOIS 1957 216-217 (response); 1 ill
ILLINOIS 1961 108-109 (response); port; 1 ill
JANIS I 68 (statement); 1 ill
PERSONAL (statement)

KNEALE, Bryan (1930-) Brit; sclp
CONTEMPORARY (statement); port; 2 ill

KNEALE, Deborah (1952-) Amer; wood
WOODWORKING 34-35 (statement);
port; 3 ill

KNEE, Gina (1898-) Amer; ptr
JANIS I 98 (statement); 1 ill

KNERR, Harold H. (1882-) Amer; cart
M. H. DE YOUNG 78-79 (response); self
port

KNERR, Sallie Frost (1914-) Amer;
print, ptr
MORRIS 128-133 (statements); ports; 3
ill

KNIGHT, Frederic (1898-1973) Amer; ptr
ZAIDENBERG 111-114 (essay: "Change
and Direction in Art"); 6 ill

KNIGHT, Gwendolyn ( ) Amer; ptr, sclp
LEWIS II 83 (statement); port; 2 ill

KNIGHT, Jennie Lea (1933-) Amer; ptr
IMAGES 42-49 (interview with Clair
List); port; 5 ill

KNIGHT, Robert (1921-) Brit; ptr
NAYLOR 489-490 (statement); 1 ill

KNIGHT, Stuart ( )
ART-LANGUAGE v.1 no.4 1-5 (essay:
"Theory, Knowledge and
Hermeneutics")

KNIGIN, Michael (1942-) Amer; print
MYLAR 8-13 (statement); port; 1 ill

KNIZAK, Milan (1940-) Czec; sclp, perf
EMANUEL II 488-490 (statement); 1 ill
NAYLOR 490-491 (statement); 1 ill

KNJAZOVIC, Jan (1925-) Yugo; ptr
TOMASEVIC 169-172 (statement); port;
1 ill

KNOEBEL, David (1949-) Amer; light,
instal
BRENTANO 248-249 (statement); 1 ill

KNOWLES, Alison (1933-) Amer; perf,
ptr, print
EMANUEL II 490 (statement)
NAYLOR 491 (statement); 1 ill
SCHAPIRO 36 (statement); port; 1 ill

KNOWLES, Christopher (1959-) Amer;
perf, video, print
AVALANCHE no.11 17-21 (interview);
38 ill

KNOWLES, Edward F. (1929-) Amer;
arch
EMANUEL I 431-432 (statement); 1 ill

KNOWLES, Justin (1935-) Brit; sclp
ALLEY (statement); 1 ill

KNOWLTON, Kenneth (1931-) Amer;
print
COMPUTER (statement); 1 ill

KNUTSON, Ann (1948-) Amer; sclp,
instal, light
LOGAN I 17-20 (statement); port; 4 ill

KOBASHI, Yasuhide (1931-)
Japa/Amer; sclp
DIRECTIONS I 76 (response); 1 ill

KOBRO, Katarzyna (1898-1950) Poli;
sclp
ABSTRACTION no.2 27 (statement); 2
ill

KOCH, Albert Carl (1912-) Amer; arch
EMANUEL I 433-434 (statement); 1 ill

KOCH, Gerd (1929-) Amer; illus
CALIFORNIA--DRAWING (statement); 2
ill

KOCH, Irene (1929-) Amer; illus, ptr
CALIFORNIA--DRAWING (statement); 2 ill
CALIFORNIA--PAINTING 43 (statement); 1 ill

KOCH, John (1909-) Amer; ptr
ILLINOIS 1974 70-71 (statement); 1 ill

KOCH, Pyke (1901-) Dutc; ptr
EMANUEL II 491-492 (statement); 1 ill
NAYLOR 492-493 (statement); 1 ill

KOCH, Samuel (1887-) Amer; ptr
JANIS II 204-207 (statements); port; 1 ill

KODAMA, Hiroshi ( ) Japa; print
ADACHI 28-31 (statement); port; 5 ill

KOENIG, John Franklin (1924-) Amer; ptr, print, coll
IT IS no.2 78 (statement)

KOENIG, Pierre (1925-) Amer; arch
EMANUEL I 434-435 (statement); 1 ill

KOEPCKE, Addi ( )
ART-RITE no.8 11 (interview); port

KOHL, Barbara (1940-) Amer; paper
WISCONSIN II (statement); 1 ill

KOHLMEYER, Ida (1912-) Amer; ptr
ART PATRON ART 43-44 (statement); port; 1 ill
CELEBRATION (statement); 1 ill

KOHN, Gabriel (1910-1975) Amer; sclp
IT IS no.2 44-45 ("Dialogue Found in a Brooklyn Cellar")

KOHN, Misch (1916-) Amer; print, ptr
VISUAL v.3 no.3 9-12 (interview); port; 2 ill

KOHN, Robert (1935-) Amer; perf
OUTSIDE II 22-23 (statement and textpiece); port

KOKOSCHKA, Oskar (1886-1980) Aust; ptr
ART SINCE v.2 148 (statement, o.p. 1953)
BREICHA 238-242 (essay: "Von der Natur der Gesichte, o.p. 1912); 2 ill
CHIPP 170-174 (essay: "On the Nature of Visions," 1912) self port; 1 ill
FRIEDENTHAL 267-270 (letter to James S. Plaut, 1948); 2 ill
GROHMANN 370 ("Vom Bewusstsein der Gesichte," p.p. 1920)
GROTE 32 (statement, 1950)
HODIN 18-31 (interview)
MIESEL 98-101 ("On the Nature of Visions," originally presented as a lecture in 1912 and published in 1921)
MIESEL 101-104 ("Van Gogh's Influence on Modern Painting," 1953, English version by Oskar Kokoschka)
MIESEL 119-125 (play: "Sphinx and Strawman" 1913)
MIESEL 146 (poems: "The Saying," 1911, "Allos Makar," 1913)
PLATSCHEK 15-28 ("Der Gefesselte Kolombus," o.p. 1913); 3 ill
PROTTER 214-215 (extract from letter to Prof. Hans Tietze, 1917-18)
PROTTER 215 (statement, 1937); 1 ill
RODITI 78-89 (interview); port; 1 ill
SCHMIDT 40-43 (statement, 1933)
SCHMIDT 89-106 (essay: "Die Wahrheit," 1937)
SCHMIDT 155-159 (essay)
SCHMIDT 170-174 (essay: "Die Wahreit ist Unteilbar," 1942)
SCHMIDT 182-185 (talk: "Der Krieg, von Kindern Gesehen," given in London, 1943)
SCHMIDT 190-191, 198-199 (letters, 1943, 1944)

SCHMIDT 207-211 ("Im Tal der Todes," o.p. 1945)
STURM 10-13 (letters, 1915, 1916); 2 ill
THORN 59, 119, 204 (statements, p.p.)
WINGLER 49-50 (essay: "Edvard Munch," p.p.)

KOKUBO, Akira ( ) video
ART-RITE no.7 11-12 (response)

KOLAR, Jiri (1914-) Czec; ptr, coll, print
ART SINCE v.2 328 (statement, o.p. 1968)
EMANUEL II 494-496 (statement); 1 ill
NAYLOR 497-498 (statement); 1 ill
TRACKS v.2 no.2 27-29 (poem: "To Be Compared with Your Own Experience"; poem: "Playing at Acting")
TRACKS v.3 no.1/2 16-18 (poem: "Statue in the Air"; poem: "Cross Out or Add")

KOLAWOLE, William Lawrence Compton (1931-) Amer; ptr
LEWIS I REVISED 57 (statement); port; 1 ill

KOLIBAL, Stanislav (1925-) Czec; sclp
NAYLOR 498-499 (statement); 1 ill

KOLLHOFF, Hans F. ( ) arch
RUSSELL F 84-85 (project proposal); 4 ill

KOLLWITZ, Kathe (1867-1945) Germ; ptr, print, sclp
MIESEL 166-169 ("Journal Entries" 1916-1922, p.p. 1955)
SCHMIDT 27-31, 72, 109, 150, 154, 163-164, 186-187, 193-196, 200, 211 (letters and statements, 1933-1945)
THORN 17, 22, 25, 32, 51, 52, 59, 71, 75, 101, 102, 104, 110, 206, 207, 221, 226, 254, 255, 277, 282, 290, 309, 341, 345 (statements, p.p.)

KOLOS-VARY (1899-) Fren; ptr
NAYLOR 500 (statement); 1 ill

KOMFUT (group)
BOWLT 164-166 ("Program Declaration," o.p. 1919)

KOMODORE, Bill (1932-) Gree/Amer; ptr
ILLINOIS 1965 51 (statement); 1 ill
YOUNG 1965 (statement); 1 ill

KONSTANTINIDIS, Aris (1913-) Gree; arch
EMANUEL I 436-437 (statement); 1 ill

KOPER, Lisa ( ) Amer; coll
IRVINE 76, 84-85 (statement); 1 ill

KOPMAN, Benjamin (1887-) Russ/Amer; ptr
FIFTY (statement); port; 1 ill
100 CONTEMPORARY 110-111 (statement); port; 1 ill

KOPPE, Richard (1916-) Amer; ptr
ILLINOIS 1950 185 (statement); 1 ill
ILLINOIS 1951 191-192 (statement); 1 ill

KOPPELMAN, Chaim (1920-) Amer; print
AMERICAN PRINTS 34, 67 (statement); 1 ill

KOPRICANEC, Martin (1943-) Yugo; ptr
TOMASEVIC 173-175 (statement); port; 1 ill

KORALEK, Paul ( ) arch

SEE: AHRENDS BURTON AND KORALEK

KORMAN, Harriet (1947-) Amer; ptr
SANDBERG 118-121 (statement, handwritten); 7 ill

KORN, Arthur (1891-1978) Brit; arch
CONRADS 76-77 (essay: "Analytical and Utopian Architecture," o.p. 1923)
EMANUEL I 437-438 (statement); 1 ill

KORN, Henry James ( ) perf
CRISS-CROSS no.5 12-15 (performance transcript: "I'm Looking for a Job"); 3 ill

KOROT, Beryl (1945-) Amer; video
PARACHUTE no.8 17-18 (statement in English)

KORSMO, Arne (1900-) Norw; arch
NEWMAN 107 (statement); 4 ill

KORTLANDER, John W. (1958-) Amer; ptr
NOSANOW I 86 (statement); 1 ill

KORTLANDER, William (1925-) Amer; ptr
NOSANOW I 86-87 (statement); 1 ill

KOSICE, Gyula (1924-) Arge; sclp, light
LUMIERE (statement); port; 1 ill
NAYLOR 501-503 (statement); 1 ill
QUADRUM no.5 146-147 (statement); 3 ill

KOSLOW, Howard ( ) Amer; ptr, photo
NORTH LIGHT 138-143 (statement); port; 25 ill

KOSNICK-KLOSS, ( ) ptr
ABSTRACTION no.2 28 (statement); 2 ill

KOSSO (1920-) Isra; sclp
SEITZ I (statement); 4 ill

KOSSOFF, Leon (1926-) Brit; ptr
CONTEMPORARY (statement); port; 2 ill

KOSTELAC, Ante Josip von ( ) arch
GA HOUSES no.6 152-159 (statement); 19 ill

KOSTELANETZ, Richard ( ) Amer; print, video
ART-RITE no.14, 5, 9 (response)
CRISS-CROSS no.5 16-21 ("Notes on Numbers"); 5 ill
TRACKS v.1 no.3 42-46 ("Constructive Fiction")
WHITE WALLS no.1 33-35 ("Visual Poetry")
WHITE WALLS no.3 50-51 ("Constructivist Fiction")

KOSUTH, Joseph ( )
ARTIST AND CAMERA 38-39 (extract from talk given in Graz, Austria, 1979); 1 ill
ART-LANGUAGE v.1 no.2 1-4 (essay: "Introductory Note by the American Editor")
ART-LANGUAGE v.3 no.2 1-6 ("For Thomas Hobbes--I")
ART-LANGUAGE v.3 no.2 46-51 ("Rambling: To Partial Correspondents")
BATTCOCK II 70-101 (essay: "Art After Philosophy," o.p. 1969)
BATTCOCK II 144-148 (interview with Arthur Rose, o.p. 1969)
BELFORD 129-157 (group discussion)
CELANT 98-102 (statement); 4 ill
GROH (essay: "Art After Philosophy")
JOHNSON 134-137 (extract from essay: "Art After Philosophy," o.p. 1969)

MEYER 152-171 (essay: "Art After Philosophy," o.p. 1969); 3 ill
VRIES 136-175 (essay: "Art After Philosophy," o.p. 1969)
WHITE WALLS no.8 34 (statement)
SEE ALSO: ART AND LANGUAGE
SEE ALSO: INTERNATIONAL LOCAL

KOTANI, Setsuya (1935-) ptr
TRANSPERSONAL 60-69 (statement); port; 4 ill

KOTHE, Fritz (1916-) Germ; ptr
EMANUEL II 498-499 (statement); 1 ill
NAYLOR 505-506 (statement); 1 ill

KOTIN, Albert (1907-) Russ/Amer; ptr
IT IS no.4 30 (statement)

KOTTLER, Howard (1930-) Amer; pott
VIEWPOINT 1977 11 (statement); 3 ill

KOTZ, Suzanne (1951-) Amer; photo
MICHIGAN 18-19 (statement); 2 ill

KOUDELKA, Josef (1938-) Czec; photo
CAMPBELL 308-318 (statement); 8 ill

KOUMOUNDOUROS, Vasileios K.
SEE: KOMODORE, BILL

KOUNELLIS, Jannis (1936-) Gree; instal, envir
AVALANCHE no.5 16-25 (interview); 5 ill
CELANT 73-78 (statement); 4 ill
CHOIX 27 (statement, o.p. 1980); 1 ill
VIEW v.1 no.10 (interview); port; 9 ill

KOUTLI, Niki
SEE: KANAGINI, Niki

KOVACIC, Mijo (1935-) Yugo; ptr

TOMASEVIC 176-180 (statement); port; 1 ill

KOVETSKY, Elaine ( ) Amer; wood, paper
HAYSTACK 34 (statement); 1 ill

KOWALKE, Ron (1936-) Amer; ptr
HAAR II 49-53 (interview); ports; 2 ill

KOWALSKI, Dennis (1938-) Amer; sclp, envir
ARTPARK 1978 30-33 (statement); port; 10 ill

KOWALSKI, Piotr (1927-) Russ/Fren; sclp, instal, light
ART SINCE v.1 295 (statement, o.p. 1967)
DOUZE ANS 253-256 (extract from interview with Emmanuel Mavrommatis); port; 9 ill
LUMIERE (statement); port; 1 ill
SKIRA 1977 110-111 (statement); 3 ill

KOWALYK, Ronald (1946-) Amer; sclp
RIPS (statement); 1 ill

KOZLOFF, Joyce (1942-) Amer; instal, ptr
EMANUEL II 501-502 (statement); 1 ill
NAYLOR 507-508 (statement); 1 ill
NEW DECORATIVE 18, 32 (statement); 1 ill
SCHAPIRO 38 (extract from interview with Judy Seigel); port; 1 ill
SKIRA 1978 82 (statement); 1 ill
SULTAN 65-68 ("Thoughts on My Art"); 2 ill
VIEW v.3 no.3 (interview); port; 8 ill
VISUAL v.1 no.2 7-10 (interview); 2 ill

KOZLOV, Christine ( )
MEYER 172-173 (text piece); 1 ill

TRACKS v.3 no.3 63 ("Duchampiana")

KUCH, Elly ( ) pott
SHAFER 114-135 (statements); port; 28 ill

KUCH, Wilhelm ( ) pott
SHAFER 114-135 (statements); port; 28 ill

KUCKEI, Peter (1938-) Germ; sclp
HAUSSER 104-105 (statement); 5 ill

KUDO, Tetsumi (1935-) Japa; sclp, ptr
EMANUEL II 509-510 (statement); 1 ill
NAYLOR 512-514 (statement); 1 ill
PRADEL 24-25 (statement, o.p. 1982); port; 2 ill
SKIRA 1978 21 (statement); 1 ill

KUEHN, Frances (1943-) Amer; ptr
MILLER 74-90 (interview with Sally Swenson); 1 ill

KUEHN, Gary (1939-) Amer; sclp
GEOMETRIC (statement); 1 ill

KUHN, Bob (1920-) Amer; illus
NORTH LIGHT 144-151 (statement); port; 33 ill

KUHN, Walter Francis (1877-1949) Amer; ptr
BRITANNICA 67 (statement); port; 1 ill
MCCOUBREY 188-189 (letter to Walter Pach, 1912)
JOURNAL OF THE AAA v.5 no.4 1-6 (statements); port

KUIMSTRA, Dave ( ) Amer; arch, design
LIFE 91-114 (interview); port

KUJAC, John ( ) Amer; arch, design
LIFE 91-114 (interview); port

KULBIN, Nikolai (1868-1917) Russ; ptr
BOWLT 9, 11-17 (extract from "Free Art as the Basis of Life: Harmony and Dissonance," o.p. 1908); 2 ill

KULIK, Sharon (1951-) Amer; film, coll
ART-RITE no.14 5, 9-10 (response)
GEORGIA 57-58, 102 (statement); port; 2 ill
GEORGIA 118-166 (group discussion: "Artists' Convention," in Athens, GA, 1/7/1977, moderated by Jan van der Marck)

KUMAGAI, Morikazu (1880-) Japa; ptr
KUNG 72-75 (statement); port; 2 ill

KUMLER, Kipton C. (1940-) Amer; photo
WALSH 421-423 (statement); 1 ill

KUMP, Ernest Joseph (1911-) Amer; arch
EMANUEL I 444-446 (statement); 1 ill
HEYER 117-121 (interview); 15 ill

KUNIYOSHI, Yasuo (1893-1953) Japa/Amer; ptr
BETHERS II 100-101 (statement); 2 ill
BRITANNICA 68 (statement); port; 1 ill
FORTY (statement); 2 ill
M.H. DE YOUNG 82 (response); self port
ZAIDENBERG 97-100 (essay: "The Inner Drive"); 4 ill

KUNKEL, Michelle ( ) ptr
ARTISTS no.1 13-14 (essay: "'Feminist Art' as the Personal Experience")

KUNTZ, Roger Edward (1926-1975) Amer; ptr
CALIFORNIA--PAINTING 22 (statement); 1 ill
ILLINOIS 1955 212 (statement); 1 ill
ILLINOIS 1957 217-218 (response); 1 ill

ILLINOIS 1963 176 (statement); 1 ill

KUO, Nina ( ) Amer; photo
EVENTS I 43 (statement); 1 ill

KUPFERMAN, Lawrence (1909-) Amer;
ptr
ILLINOIS 1950 186 (statement); 1 ill
ILLINOIS 1953 195 (statement); 1 ill
ILLINOIS 1961 102 (response); port; 1 ill
MILLER 1943 43 (statement); 1 ill

KUPKA, Frantisek (1871-1957) Czec; ptr
ABSTRACTION no.1 23 (statement); 2
ill
ABSTRACTION no.2 25-26 (statement);
1 ill
ABSTRACTION no.3 28 (poem); 1 ill
LIBERMAN 45-46 (statements)
POENSGEN 86 (statement, 1913)

KUPPEL, Edmund (1947-) Germ; photo
SKIRA 1978 96 (statement); 2 ill

KUPPER, Eugene ( ) arch
GA HOUSES no.9 92-95 (statement); 8
ill

KURELEK, William (1927-) Cana; ptr
NAYLOR 516-518 (statement); 1 ill

KURHAJEC, Joseph (1938-) Amer; sclp
YOUNG 1965 (statement); 1 ill

KURIHARA, Ichiro ( ) Amer; text
HAYSTACK 35 (statement); 1 ill

KURODA, Tatsuaki ( ) Japa; wood
ADACHI 32-35 (statement); port; 3 ill

KUROKAWA, Kisho (1934-) Japa; arch
EMANUEL I 446-448 (statement); 1 ill

KUROSAKI, Akira (1937-) Japa; ptr
NAYLOR 518 (statement)

KURTZ, Bruce ( )
ART-RITE no.7 6-7 ("Shooting Star");
port

KURYLUK, Ewa (1946-) Poli/Brit; ptr
SKIRA 1978 18 (statement); 1 ill

KUSCYNSKYJ, Taras (1932-) Czec;
photo
WALSH 423-424 (statement); 1 ill

KUSHNER, Robert (1949-) Amer; instal,
ptr
APPLE 32 (statement); 2 ill
JOHNSON 250, 252-258 (interview with
Robin White, o.p. 1980); 1 ill
NEW DECORATIVE 19, 33 (statement);
1 ill
VIEW v.2 no.9/10 (interview); 31 ill

KUTTNER, Peter ( )
GROH (statement)

KUWABARA, Kineo (1913-) Japa;
photo
WALSH 425-426 (statement); 1 ill

KUWAYAMA, Tadaaki (1932-)
Japa/Amer; ptr
ART NOW v.2 no.9 (statement); 1 ill
SYSTEMATIC 24 (statement); 1 ill

KVAPIL, James (1951-) Amer; pott
HERMAN 77 (statement); port; 1 ill

LAATSCH, Gary (1956-) Amer; sclp
MICHIGAN 22-23 (statement); 2 ill

LA BARBARA, Joan ( ) perf, sound
AVALANCHE no.10 41-42 (interview);
ports

LABISSE, Felix (1905-) Fren; ptr
ART VOICES v.3 no.2 22-23 (interview
with Edouard Roditi); port; 3 ill
CHARBONNIER v.2 61-70 (interview)
GOLDAINE 174-176 (interview); port

LABLE, Eliot ( ) Amer; sclp, ptr
BRENTANO 256-257 (statement); 1 ill

LABOUNTY, John (1948-) Amer; wood
WOODWORKING 36-37 (statement);
port; 1 ill

LABOWITZ, Leslie ( ) Amer
ISSUE (statements); 19 ill

LABROT, Syl (1929-1977) Amer; photo
DUGAN 3-22 (interview, 1976); port

LACASSE, Joseph-Fernand (1894-1975)
Fren/Belg; ptr
NAYLOR 520-521 (statement); 1 ill
SEUPHOR 203-204 (statement)

LACEY, Bruce (1927-) Brit; sclp, perf
CONTEMPORARY (statement); port; 2
ill
NAYLOR 521-523 (statement); 4 ill
SKIRA 1977 60 (statement); 1 ill

LACHAISE, Gaston (1882-1935)
Fren/Amer; sclp
ROSE II 181-182 (extract from essay:
*A Comment on My Sculpture," o.p.
1928)
ROSE II REVISED 240-241 (extract from
essay: *A Comment on My
Sculpture," o.p. 1928)

LACHERT, Bohdan (1900-) Poli; arch
EMANUEL I 449-450 (statement); 1 ill

LACHOWICZ, Andrezev ( ) Poli
VISION no.2 62 (statement); 4 ill

LACY, Bill N. ( ) arch
ON SITE no.2 10, 14 (response)

LACY, Ernest (1928-) Amer; illus
CALIFORNIA--DRAWING (statement); 2
ill

LACY, Steve ( ) perf, sound
PARACHUTE no.4 24-30 (interview); 2
ill

LACY, Suzanne (1945-) Amer; perf
CHRYSALIS no.7 29-35 (essay: *The
Life and Times of Donaldina
Cameron")
ISSUE (statements); 19 ill

LADERMAN, Gabriel (1929-) Amer; ptr
GUSSOW 114-115 (interview, 1970); 1 ill

LAEMMLE, Cheryl (1947-) Amer; ptr,
instal
GUMPERT II 24-27, 33 (statement);
port; 7 ill

LAFAYE, Nell (1937-) Amer; ptr
MORRIS 140-145 (statements); ports; 3
ill

LAFFOLEY, Paul (1940-) Amer; ptr
BOSTON III (interview); 1 ill

LA FRESNAYE, Roger de (1885-1925)
Fren; ptr
RAYNAL 143-149 (statement); 3 ill

LAGLENNE, Jean-Francois (1899-)
Fren; ptr

ART D'AUJOURD'HUI v.5 26 (statement); 3 ill
RAYNAL 197-200 (statement); 2 ill

LAGRECO, Charles A. ( ) arch
GA HOUSES no.3 168-171 (statement); 11 ill

LAGZDINA, Vineta (1945-) Aust; perf
ART NETWORK no.2 49 (statement)

LAING, Gerald (1936-) Brit; ptr
SAO PAULO 82-83 (statement); port; 1 ill

LAIZEROVITZ, Daniel (1952-) Urug; photo
WALSH 428-429 (statement); 1 ill

LAKE, Suzy (1947-) Amer; photo
IDENTITE 47-49 (interview with Jacques Clayssen); port
VEHICULE (statement); 5 ill
WALSH 429-430 (statement); 1 ill

LAKICH, Lili (1944-) Amer; light, ptr
CAMERON D 57 (statement)
CHRYSALIS no.5 53-57 (statements); 4 ill

LAKOVIC, Ivan (1932-) Yugo; ptr
TOMASEVIC 181-189 (statement); port; 1 ill

LAKY, Gyorgy (1944-) Amer; text
VISUAL v.2 no.2 3-5 (essay: "On Fibers and Papers"); port

LALOUX, Gilbert ( ) Belg; ptr
COLLARD 156-160 (interview); port; 1 ill

LAM, Jennette (1911-) Amer; ptr
ILLINOIS 1961 119 (response); port; 1 ill
ILLINOIS 1963 125 (statement); 1 ill

LAM, Wilfredo (1902-) Cuba; ptr
ART SINCE v.2 153 (poem, o.p. 1960)
PREMIER BILAN 303 (statement); port

LAMANTIA, James (1923-) Amer; ptr
FULBRIGHT 31 (statement)

LAMBA, Jacquiline (1910-) Amer; ptr
JANIS I 137 (statement); 1 ill

LAMBERT, Fred ( ) Amer; perf
BRENTANO 258-259 (extract from performance, "Aerial"); 1 ill

LAMBERT, Maurice (1901-) Brit; sclp
OPEN AIR 1960 (statement); 1 ill

LAMELAS, David (1946-) Arge; film, perf, instal
EMANUEL II 519-520 (statement); 1 ill
KUNST BLEIBT KUNST 370-371 (statement); 2 ill
NAYLOR 526-527 (statement); 1 ill

LAMIS, Leroy (1925-) Amer; sclp
ILLINOIS 1965 56 (statement); 1 ill
LETTERS 19 (letter); 1 ill

LAMM, David "Blue" (1948-) Amer; ptr
NOSANOW I 89 (statement); 1 ill

LAMSWEERDE, Eugene van (1930-) Dutc; sclp
NAYLOR 527-528 (statement); 1 ill

LAN-BAR, David (1912-) Isra; ptr
SEITZ I (statement); 3 ill

LANCELEY, Colin (1938-) Atrl; sclp, ptr
NAYLOR 529-530 (statement); 1 ill
SKIRA 1978 34 (statement); 1 ill

LANDAU, S. Lev (1896-) Amer; ptr

LAPICQUE, Charles (1898-) Fren; ptr
CHARBONNIER v.1 73-82 (interview)
GOLDAINE 109-111 (interview); port
PREMIER BILAN 303 (statement); port
VINGTIEME N.S. no.4 51-54 (essay: "Voie sans Issue")

LAPIDUS, Alan ( ) Amer; arch
COOK 147-177 (interview); port; 22 ill

LAPIDUS, Morris (1902-) Amer; arch
COOK 147-177 (interview); port; 22 ill
EMANUEL I 450-452 (statement); 1 ill

LAPLANTZ, David (1944-) Amer; metal
METALWORKS (statement); 1 ill

LAPOINTE, Conrad ( ) Cana; design
ROYER 106-108 (interview, 1975)

LAPOUJADE, Robert (1921-) Fren; ptr
DADA 113-115 (statement)
PREMIER BILAN 303 (statement); port

LARDERA, Berto (1911-) Ital/Fren; sclp
EMANUEL II 523-524 (statement); 1 ill
NAYLOR 534-535 (statement); 1 ill
PREMIER BILAN 304 (statement); port
SKIRA 1977 101 (statement); 1 ill
TEMOIGNAGES I 174-181 (statement); port; 6 ill
TEMOIGNAGES II 30-33 (statement); port; 7 ill

LARIONOV, Mikhail (1881-1964) Russ/Fren; ptr
BOWLT 79-83 (essay: "Why We Paint Ourselves: A Futurist Manifesto," o.p. 1913); 1 ill
BOWLT 87-91 (essay: "Rayonists and Futurists: A Manifesto," o.p. 1913); 1 ill

LARK, Raymond (1939-) Amer; illus, ptr
LEWIS I REVISED 82-84 (statement); port; 2 ill

LA ROCCA, Ketty (1938-) Ital; illus, photo
NAYLOR 535-536 (statement)
SKIRA 1976 47 (statement); 1 ill

LA ROCHE, Lynda ( ) Amer; metal
METALWORKS (statement); 1 ill

LARSEN, Jack Lenor (1927-) Amer; text, design
DESIGN 173-179 (essay: "Textiles")
DIAMONSTEIN IV 120-133 (interview); port; 11 ill

LARSOCCHI, Eduard
SEE: NEAGU, Paul

LARSON, Gail Farris ( ) Amer; metal
METALWORKS (statement); 1 ill

LARSON, William (1942-) Amer; photo
WALSH 434-435 (statement); 1 ill

LARTIGUE, Jacques-Henri (1894-) Fren; photo
BOOTH 146-157 (interview); port; 9 ill
HILL 33-36 (interview, 1974); port
WALSH 435-437 (extract from "Journal"); 1 ill

LASANSKY, William (1938-) Amer; sclp
ILLINOIS 1963 217 (statement); 1 ill

LASCH, Pat (1944-) Amer; sclp
SKIRA 1979 108 (statement); 1 ill

LASDUN, Denys (1914-) Brit; arch
EMANUEL I 454-455 (statement); 1 ill

LASKER, Joseph L. (1918-) Amer; ptr
ILLINOIS 1951 192 (statement); 1 ill

LASSAW, Ibram (1913-) Egyp/Amer; sclp
ABSTRACT 23-24, 34, 141 (essay: "On Inventing Our Own Art"); 2 ill
ILLINOIS 1953 196-197 (statement); 1 ill
ILLINOIS 1955 213 (statement); 1 ill
IT IS no.1 26 (essay: "Remarks on the Differences between Painting and Sculpture")
IT IS no.3 52 ("A Cahier Leaf")
IT IS no.6 7-16, 57-64, 73-75 (group discussion)
MILLER 1956 64-71 (statement); port; 8 ill
MOTHERWELL 8-22 (three group discussions: "Artists' Sessions at Studio 35," New York, 1950)
NEW DECADE 50-52 (statement); 3 ill

LASSUS, Bernard (1929-) Fren; sclp, photo
LUMIERE (statement); port; 1 ill
SKIRA 1977 106 (statement); 4 ill

LASTA, Susana (1945-) Arge/Amer; ptr
RAICES 62 (statement); 1 ill

LATHAM, John (1921-) Brit; perf, sclp
CONTEMPORARY (statement); port; 2 ill
ENGLISH 134-139 (statement); port; 5 ill

LAUB, Stephen ( )
AVALANCHE no.10 24-25 (interview); 8 ill

LAUFMAN, Sidney (1891-) Amer; ptr
ILLINOIS 1951 193 (statement); 1 ill
ILLINOIS 1957 218-219 (response); 1 ill
ZAIDENBERG 61-64 (essay: "Reflections on Landscape Painting"); 6 ill

LAUFOR, Sigmund ( ) ptr
ART VOICES v.4 no.1 79 (statement); 1 ill

LAUGHLIN, Clarence John (1905-) Amer; photo
WALSH 438-440 (statement); 1 ill

LAUREN, Jilly ( ) photo
CHRYSALIS no.3 25-27 ("A Transsexual Collage"); 5 ill

LAURENS, Henri (1885-1954) Fren; sclp
GROHMANN 448-449 ("Bekenntnis," o.p. 1952)
MAYWALD (statement, in English, German, and French); ports
POENSGEN 122 ("Ausblick," 1952)

LAURENT, John Louis (1921-) Amer; ptr
ILLINOIS 1959 234-235 (statement); 1 ill

LAURY, Micha (1946-) Isra/Fren; sclp
SKIRA 1979 64-65 (statement); 1 ill

LAUTNER, John (1911-) Amer; arch
EMANUEL I 456-457 (statement); 1 ill

LAVALLE DE CARREON, Martha
SEE: CARREON, Martha Lavalle de

LAVIE, Raffie (1937-) Isra; print, ptr
SEITZ I (statement); 3 ill

LAVIER, Bertrand (1949-) Fren; print, sclp
SKIRA 1977 71 (statement); 1 ill
SKIRA 1979 69 (statement); 2 ill

LA VILLEGLE, Jacques Mahe de (1926-) Fren; print
DOUZE ANS 261-264 (statement); port; 2 ill

LAVERDIERE, Bruno ( ) Amer; sclp, envir
ARTPARK 1981 (statement); port; 2 ill

LAVRIC, Boris (1933-) Yugo; ptr
TOMASEVIC 190-192 (statement); port; 1 ill

LAW, Bob (1934-) Brit; ptr
CONTEMPORARY (statement); port; 2 ill
ENGLISH 140-145 (statement); port; 6 ill
NAYLOR 537 (statement)
SKIRA 1977 104 (statement); 1 ill

LAWRENCE, Eileen (1946-) Scot; paper, ptr
SKIRA 1978 97 (statement); 2 ill

LAWRENCE, Eleanor (1910-) Amer; photo
FRYM 164-181 (interview); port

LAWRENCE, Jacob (1917-) Amer; ptr
BETHERS I 240-241 (statement); 1 ill
FAX I 146-166 (statements); port; 2 ill
FINE 145-150 (statements, o.p. 1939, 1944, 1957, 1971); 8 ill
GUENTHER 74-75 (statement); port; 1 ill
ILLINOIS 1955 213-214 (statement); 1 ill
ILLINOIS 1959 235-236 (statement); 1 ill
ILLINOIS 1961 113 (response); port; 1 ill
LEWIS II 80 (statement); port; 2 ill
RODMAN I 204-207 (interview)

LAWRENCE, Les (1940-) Amer; pott
VIEWPOINT 1978 17-19 (statement); 4 ill

LAYCOCK, Donald (1931-) Atrl; ptr
DE GROEN 147-162 (interview); port

LEACH, Bernard (1887-) Brit; pott
CLARK 59-85 (essay: ■Towards a Standard,■ o.p. 1940); 9 ill
CLARK 86-88 (essay: ■Belief and Hope,■ o.p. 1961)
YAMADA 314-317 (interview, 1971)

LEACH, David (1910-) Brit; pott
CAMERON E 84-95 (response); 9 ill

LEACH-JONES, Alun (1936-) Atrl; ptr
DE GROEN 180-198 (interview); port

LEAL, Fernando (1897-) Mexi; ptr
STEWART 47-51 (statement); port; 4 ill

LEAPMAN, Edwina (1934-) Brit; ptr
CONTEMPORARY (statement); port; 2 ill
HAYWARD 1978 58-61 (statement); 3 ill

LEBAN, Adrienne ( ) Amer; ptr, illus
INTERVIEWS 14-16 (interview); port; 1 ill

LEBECK, Carol (1931-) Amer; pott
VIEWPOINT 1978 20-21 (statement); 4 ill

LEBENSTEIN, Jan (1930-) Poli; ptr
EMANUEL II 526-528 (statement); 1 ill

LE BOUL'CH, Jean-Pierre
SEE: BOUL'CH, Jean-Pierre Le

LE BROCQUY, Louis
SEE: BROCQUY, Louis le

LEBRUN, Rico (1900-1969) Ital/Amer; sclp, ptr
ART AND ARTIST 68-88 (selections from ■Mexican Journal,■ 1952-53); 13 ill
ARTFORUM v.1 no.11 34-36 (interview with Arthur Secunda); ports; 5 ill
FORTY (statement); 2 ill

LEE, Doris Emrich (1905-) Amer; ptr, print
BRITANNICA 69 (statement); port; 1 ill
GUITAR 132-141 (interview); port; 4 ill
ILLINOIS 1952 206-207 (statement); 1 ill
ILLINOIS 1955 214-215 (statement); 1 ill
ZAIDENBERG 76-78 (essay: "Decoration, Illustration and the Fine Arts"); 1 ill

LEE, Mark S. (1949-) Amer; ptr
NOSANOW II 54 (statement); 1 ill

LEE, Russell (1903-) Amer; photo
WALSH 442-444 (statement); 1 ill

LEE, Sarah Tomerlin ( ) design
DIAMONSTEIN V 112-127 (interview); port; 11 ill

LEE, Wesley Duke (1931-) Braz; ptr, print
ART AND TECHNOLOGY 186-192 (project proposal); 8 ill

LEEPA, Allen (1919-) Amer; ptr
BATTCOCK I 136-151 (essay: "Anti-Art and Criticism")
BATTCOCK V 200-208 (essay: "Minimal Art and Primary Meanings")
BATTCOCK VII 170-180 (essay: "Art and Self: The Morphology of Teaching Art"); port

LEESON, Loraine (1951-) Brit
ISSUE (statement); 1 ill

LEF (group-journal)
BANN 79-83 (essay: "Whom is *Lef* Alerting?" o.p. 1923)
BOWLT 199-202 ("Declaration: Comrades, Organizers of LIfe," o.p. 1923)

LE FEBURE, Jean (1930-) Cana; sclp, ptr
CANADA 42-43 (statement); port; 1 ill

LE GAC, Jean (1936-) Fren; coll, ptr
ARTIST AND CAMERA 40-41 (statements); 1 ill
DOUZE ANS 265-268 (statement); port; 2 ill
EMANUEL II 529-531 (statement); 1 ill
EUROPE 58-59 (text piece); 3 ill
NAYLOR 539-541 (statement); 1 ill
SKIRA 1975 55 ("L'alibi du Peintre" in "Pour Memoires," 1974); 1 ill
SKIRA 1977 83 (statement); 1 ill
TRACKS v.3 no.3 110-113 ("The Museum That Disappeared")

LEGER, Fernand (1881-1955) Fren; ptr
ABSTRACT 207, 210, 213-214 (essay: "Modern Architecture and Color")
ART SINCE v.1 290 (statement, o.p. 1956)
CHARBONNIER v.2 199-211 (interview)
CHIPP 277-279 (essay: "The Aesthetic of the Machine," o.p. 1924); self port
CHIPP 279-280 (essay: "A New Realism--the Object," o.p. 1926)
DUNOYER (manuscript: "Le Ballet Spectacle--L'Objet Spectacle," 1923); 1 ill
EIGHT (handwritten statement in French; statement: "New Space in Architecture" in English, French, and German); ports
EVANS 14-20 (essay: "Painting and Reality"); 2 ill
FRY 135-139 (essay: "Contemporary Achievements in Painting," o.p. 1914)
GOLDWATER 423-426 (extract from talk: "The New Realism," given in New York, 1935); 1 ill
GROHMANN 391-393 ("Aus Gesprachen," p.p.1949)

GROHMANN 390-391 ("Sehr Aktuell Sein," p.p.)
GUGGENHEIM II 68-69 (statement, o.p. 1925); 1 ill
JANIS I 129 (statement); 1 ill
KEPES V 90 ("The New Landscape")
LIBERMAN 49-52 (statements)
MAYWALD (statement, in English, German, and French; handwritten statement in French); ports
POENSGEN 117 ("Die Abstrakte Kunst und das Leben")
PROTTER 200-201 (extract from *The Writings of Fernand Leger*); 1 ill
QUADRUM no.2 77-80 (letter, in French and English)
RAYNAL 205-212 (statement); 3 ill
SEGHERS 144-147 ("Conversations with Diana Vallier")
THORN 47 (statement, p.p.)
VERDET 53-110 (interview)

LE GRICE, Malcolm (1940-) Brit; film
CRISS-CROSS no.6 42-56 (debate with Stan Brakhage); port
ENGLISH 454-455 (statement); port; 1 ill
KUNST BLEIBT KUNST 397 (statement); 1 ill

LEGUEULT, Raymond (1898-) Fren; ptr
GOLDAINE 134-137 (interview); port

LEHMAN, Irving ( ) Amer; ptr, sclp
BETHERS II 102-103 (statement); 2 ill

LEHMBRUCK, Wilhelm (1880-1919) Germ; sclp, ptr
GROHMANN 447-448 ("Uber Skulpture," p.p. 1936)
GROTE 63-64 (statement)

LEIDER, Phil ( ) Amer
IRVINE 82 (statement)

LEIDMANN, Cheyco ( ) Germ/Fren; photo
HOW FAMOUS 234-239 (statements); port; 7 ill

LEIPZIG, Arthur (1918-) Amer; photo
TIME-LIFE II 98-99 (statement); 2 ill
WALSH 444-445 (statement); 1 ill

LEIPZIG, Mel ( ) Amer; ptr
ART VOICES v.4 no.1 79 (statement); 1 ill

LEISGEN, Barbara (1940-) Belg; coll, sclp, photo
CHOIX 28 (statement, o.p. 1974); 1 ill
IDENTITE 51-54 (interview with Jacques Clayssen); port
SKIRA 1975 46 (extract from interview with Irmeline Lebeer, o.p. 1974); 3 ill
SKIRA 1978 89 (statement); 3 ill
SKIRA 1980 80-81 (statement); 3 ill

LEISGEN, Michael (1941-) Belg; sclp, coll
CHOIX 28 (statement, o.p. 1974); 1 ill
IDENTITE 51-54 (interview with Jacques Clayssen); port
SKIRA 1978 89 (statement); 3 ill
SKIRA 1980 80-81 (statement); 3 ill

LE MAIRE, Charles ( ) Amer; coll
CALIFORNIA--COLLAGE (statement); 1 ill

LEMASTER, Lynn ( )
ART-LANGUAGE v.3 no.2 1-6 ("For Thomas Hobbes--I")
ART-LANGUAGE v.3 no.2 41-43 ("Art and Language")
ART-LANGUAGE v.3 no.2 44-45 ("Community Work")
ART-LANGUAGE v.3 no.2 68-80 ("'Mr. Lin Yutang Refers to "Fair Play"...?'")

LE MOAL, Jean (1909-) Fren; ptr
CHARBONNIER v.2 71-78 (interview)

LENART, Branko (1948-) Aust; photo
WALSH 445-446 (statement); 1 ill

LENK, Thomas (1933-) Germ; print, sclp
HAUSSER 110-113 (statement, o.p. 1971); 8 ill

LENKOWSKY, Marilyn (1947-) Amer; sclp
ART-RITE no.9 29-34 (group discussion)
SHEARER 36-39 (interview); 3 ill

LENNARD, Elizabeth (1953-) Amer; photo
HAND COLORED 13, 15 (statement); 1 ill

LENNEP, Jacques (1941-) Belg; sclp, photo
COLLARD 170-174 (interview); port; 1 ill
SKIRA 1978 57 (statement); 2 ill

LENORMAND, Albert (1915-) Fren
PREMIER BILAN 304 (statement); port

LENSKI, Willi ( )
ART-RITE no.9 36-38 (group discussion); port
ART-RITE no.11/12 ("Social Realism: Or Living the Artistic Life")

LENT, Donald (1933-) Amer; print
CALIFORNIA--PRINTS (statement); 1 ill

LENT, Wayne ( ) Amer
SULTAN 71 ("Personal Statement: Concerning the Boundaries, Directions and Substance of My Art Work," 1975)

LEONARD, Joanne (1940-) Amer; photo
SCHAPIRO 43 (statement); port; 1 ill
WALSH 446-447 (statement); 1 ill

LEONARD, Jonathan Norton ( ) photo
TIME-LIFE I 12-23 (essay: "The Camera at Work")
TIME-LIFE I 140-149 (essay: "Beyond the Rainbow's Spectrum")

LEONARD, Michael (1933-) Brit; ptr
CONTEMPORARY (statement); port; 1 ill

LEONARDI, Cesare (1935-) Ital; photo
WALSH 447-448 (statement); 1 ill

LEONHARDT, Fritz (1909-) Germ; arch
EMANUEL I 463-465 (statement); 1 ill

LEONID (Leonid Berman) (1896-1976) Russ; ptr
ILLINOIS 1952 207 (statement); 1 ill

LE PARC, Julio (1928-) Arge/Fren; sclp
ART SINCE v.1 296 (statement, o.p. 1967)
LUMIERE (statement); port; 1 ill
PRADEL 168-169 (essay: "Valorization: Key Weapon for Culture Penetration")

LEPPIEN, Jean (1910-) Fren; ptr
TEMOIGNAGES I 182-189 (statement); port; 5 ill

LERMA, Jose Ramon (1930-) Amer; sclp
RAICES 34 (statement); 1 ill

LERNER, Nathan (1913-) Amer; photo
LIGHT 54-59 (statement); 5 ill

LERNER, Ralph ( ) arch
GA HOUSES no.11 108-119 (letter); 79 ill

LE ROY, Hugh (1939-) Cana; sclp
CANADA 8-9 (statement); port; 1 ill

LEROY, Louis (1941-) Amer; sclp
RAICES 33 (statement); 1 ill

LESLIE, Alfred (1927-) Amer; ptr
ART NOW v.1 no.9 (statement); 1 ill
ART VOICES v.5 no.3 37 (statement); 1 ill

LES NOUVEAU REALISTES
SEE: NEW REALISM

LESTIE, Alain (1944-) Fren; ptr
NAYLOR 546-547 (statement); 1 ill
SKIRA 1976 61 (statement); 1 ill

LETHBRIDGE, John (1948-) Atrl; sclp
DE GROEN 74-81 (interview); port

LETTICK, Birney ( ) Amer; ptr, illus
MAGIC 76-79 (statement); port; 3 ill

LE VA, Barry (1941-) Amer; sclp, instal, ptr
ARTPARK 1979 (statement); 1 ill
AVALANCHE no.3 62-75 (interview); 55 ill
CINCINNATI 16-27 (statement); 26 ill

LEVEE, John (1924-) Amer; ptr, print
ILLINOIS 1965 89 (statement); 1 ill
YOUNG 1957 (statement); 2 ill

LEVENE, Ben (1938-) Brit; ptr
CONTEMPORARY (statement); port; 2 ill

LEVEQUE, Yves (1937-) Fren; ptr
NAYLOR 547 (statement); 1 ill
SKIRA 1979 22 (statement); 1 ill

LEVERANT, Robert (1939-) Amer; photo
ART-RITE no.14 5, 10 (response)
WALSH 449 (statement); 1 ill

LEVERETT, David (1938-) Brit; ptr
EMANUEL II 537-538 (statement); 1 ill
NAYLOR 547-548 (statement); 1 ill

LEVESON, Sandra (1944-) Atrl; ptr
DE GROEN 57-62 (interview); port

LEVI, Julian (1900-) Amer; ptr
BRITANNICA 70 (statement); port; 1 ill
ILLINOIS 1957 220-221 (response)
ILLINOIS 1959 236-237 (statement); 1 ill
ILLINOIS 1961 52-53 (response); port; 1 ill
ILLINOIS 1963 220-221 (statement); 1 ill
NORTH LIGHT 152-157 (statement); ports; 6 ill
100 CONTEMPORARY 116-117 (statement); port; 1 ill

LEVI, Linda (1935-) Amer; ptr, sclp
SCHAPIRO 44 (statement); port; 1 ill

LEVINE, Jack (1915-) Amer; ptr
FIFTY (statement); 1 ill
FORTY (statement); 2 ill
FULBRIGHT 30, 32 (statement); 1 ill
ILLINOIS 1949 [unpaginated] (statement); 1 ill
ILLINOIS 1950 186-187 (statement); 1 ill
ILLINOIS 1955 215-216 (statement); 1 ill
ILLINOIS 1957 221-222 (response); 1 ill
MILLER 1942 86-92 (statement); port; 6 ill
100 CONTEMPORARY 118-119 (statement); port; 1 ill
PROTTER 251 (statement, 1952)
RODMAN I 194-197, 200-203 (interview)
SPIRITUAL 55-60 (essay: "In Praise of Knowledge")
SPIRITUAL 141-142 ("group discussion")

LEVINE, Les (1935-) Iris/Cana; instal, sclp, ptr
ART AND TECHNOLOGY 193 (project proposal)
ART-RITE no.1 1 ("Found Object")
ART-RITE no.7 26-27 ("Excerpts from a Tape: 'Artistic'")
ART-RITE no.14 30 (statement)
BATTCOCK II 194-203 ("Les Levine Replies," response to essay: The Decline and Fall of the Avant-Garde," by Robert Hughes)
BATTCOCK V 365, 368-369 (interview with Elayne Varian, o.p. 1967); 1 ill
BATTCOCK VI 76-94 (essay: "One-Gun Video Art," p.p.); 4 ill
BATTCOCK VII 11-28 (essay: "The Great American Art Machine," o.p. 1971); port; 1 ill
BELFORD 79-100 (group discussion)
CANADA 90-91 (statement); port; 2 ill
EMANUEL II 538-541 (statement); 1 ill
GEORGIA 118-166 (group discussion: "Artists' Convention," in Athens, GA, 1/7/1977, moderated by Jan van der Marck)
NAYLOR 549-551 (statement); 1 ill
ON SITE no.2 10-11 (response)
ON SITE no.4 21 (statement); 8 ill
PARACHUTE no.2 23-26 ("We Are Still Alive"); port
PARACHUTE no.8 18-19 (statement in English)
SKIRA 1977 144-145 (essay: "Utiliser l'appareil photo comme une Matraque")
SKIRA 1978 56 (statement); 1 ill
SKIRA 1980 90-91 (statement); 4 ill
VARIAN IV (interview); port; 1 ill

LEVINE, Marilyn Anne (1933-) Cana; sclp, pott
EMANUEL II 541-542 (statement); 1 ill
NAYLOR 551-552 (statement); 1 ill

LEVINE, Paula (1948-) ptr
BOSHIER (statement); port; 2 ill

LEVINE, Sherrie (1947-) Amer; photo
REALLIFE no.6 4-10 (group discussion)

LEVINSON, Joel ( ) Amer; arch, photo
GA HOUSES no.9 60-65 (statement); 9 ill
GA HOUSES no.10 7-15 (essay: "Outdoor Rooms")

LEVITT, Helen (1918-) Amer; photo
WALSH 449-451 (statement); 1 ill

LEVY, Hilda ( ) Amer; illus, ptr
CALIFORNIA--DRAWING (statement); 2 ill

LEVY, William Auerbach
SEE: AUERBACH-LEVY, William

LEW, Jeffrey ( ) Amer; sclp, ptr
AVALANCHE no.2 12-13 (interview)

LEWANDOWSKI, Edmund (1914-) Amer; ptr, print
MILLER 1943 44-45 (statement); 2 ill
WISCONSIN I (statement); 1 ill

LEWCZYNSKI, Jerzy (1924-) Poli; photo
WALSH 451-452 (statement); 1 ill

LEWICKI, James (1917-) Amer; illus, ptr
NORTH LIGHT 158-165 (statement); port; 10 ill

LEWIS, David (1922-) Amer; arch
EMANUEL I 469-471 (statement); 1 ill

LEWIS, Edward ( ) Amer; ptr
ART PATRON ART 45-46 (statement); port; 1 ill

LEWIS, Flora Carrell (1903-) Amer; ptr
JANIS II 208-212 (statements); port; 1
ill

LEWIS, Garth (1945-) Brit; ptr
CONTEMPORARY (statement); port; 2
ill

LEWIS, James E. (1923-) Amer; sclp, ptr
FAX I 219-235 (statements); port; 2 ill
FINE 177-179 (statements, o.p. 1965,
1971); 3 ill

LEWIS, Joe ( )
SEE: FASHION MODA

LEWIS, John Chapman (1920-) Amer;
ptr
ILLINOIS 1952 208 (statement); 1 ill

LEWIS, Norman Wilfred (1909-1979);
Amer; ptr
FINE 153-155 (statements, o.p. 1966); 3
ill
ILLINOIS 1950 187-188 (statement)
ILLINOIS 1951 195 (statement)
MOTHERWELL 8-22 (three group
discussions: "Artists' Sessions at
Studio 35," New York, 1950)
NAYLOR 552 (statement)

LEWIS, Samella S. (1924-) Amer; ptr,
print
LEWIS I REVISED 121-123 (statement);
port; 3 ill

LEWIS, Susan (1938-) Amer; sclp
DIRECTIONS I 76 (response); 1 ill

LEWITIN, Landes (1892-) Amer; print,
ptr
ART VOICES v.4 no.1 75 (statement); 1
ill
ILLINOIS 1963 147 (statement); 1 ill
IT IS no.1 24 ("Random Excerpts")

IT IS no.3 11 (statement)

LEWITT, Sol (1928-) Amer; sclp, ptr,
instal
ARTIST AND CAMERA 42-43 (extract
from essay: "Paragraphs on
Conceptual Art," o.p. 1967); 10 ill
ART NOW v.3 no.2 (statement); 1 ill
ARTFORUM v.5 no.10 79-83
("Paragraphs on Conceptual Art"); 1
ill
ART-LANGUAGE v.1 no.1 11-13
("Sentences on Conceptual Art")
ART-RITE no.8 17 (text piece); 1 ill
ART-RITE no.14 5, 10 (response)
AVALANCHE no.4 18-19 (text piece)
BATTCOCK II 182-183 (statement, o.p.
1970)
CHOIX 29 (letter and statement, o.p.
1970); 1 ill
CONCEPTUAL ART 47, 53, 55, 56, 58
(statements)
JOHNSON 125-127 ("Sentences on
Conceptual Art," o.p. 1969)
MEYER 174-183 ("Sentences on
Conceptual Art," o.p. 1969); 6 ill
MULLER 46-59 (statements: "On
Walldrawings" and "Sentences on
Conceptual Art," o.p. 1969); ports; 6
ill
STEDELIJK 155 (statement, o.p. 1970);
2 ill
TRACKS v.1 no.1 38-39 ("The Location
of a Line (Not Straight)"); 1 ill
VARIAN II (statement); port
VRIES 176-185 (essay: "Paragraphs on
Conceptual Art," o.p. 1967)
VRIES 186-191 ("Sentences on
Conceptual Art," o.p. 1969)

LHOTE, Andre (1885-1962) Fren; ptr,
illus
ART D'AUJOURD'HUI v.5 13-15
(statement); 10 ill
GOLDAINE 36-39 (interview); port

RAYNAL 213-217 (statement); 2 ill
SEGHERS 151-158 (essay: "Let Us Talk Painting," o.p. 1923)

L'HOTE, J. Willard (1944-) Amer; ptr
NOSANOW II 28, 55 (statement); 2 ill

LIBERMAN, Alexander (1912-) Russ/Amer; ptr, sclp
ART NOW v.1 no.1 (statement); 1 ill
LETTERS 21 (letter); 1 ill

LIBSOHN, Sol ( ) photo
TIME-LIFE II 84-85 (statement); 2 ill

LICHFIELD, Patrick ( ) Brit; photo
HOW FAMOUS 22-25 (statements); port; 4 ill

LICHTBLAU, Charlotte ( )
ARTS YEARBOOK v.10 62-67 (essay: "The Guggenheim International Award Exhibits")

LICHTENFELD, Judy Rose
SEE: DATER, Judy

LICHTENSTEIN, Roy (1923-) Amer; ptr, sclp
ART AND TECHNOLOGY 194-199 (project proposal); ports; 5 ill
ART NOW v.1 no.1 (interview); 1 ill
ART SINCE v.2 325 (extract from interview with Alan Solomon, o.p. 1966)
ARTFORUM v.2 no.4 31 (interview with John Coplans); 1 ill
ARTFORUM v.4 no.6 20-24 (group discussion); 1 ill
ARTFORUM v.5 no.9 34-39 (interview with John Coplans); 11 ill
CONCEPTUAL ART 48 (statement)
DIAMONSTEIN I 211-225 (interview); ports

JOHNSON 84-86 (extract from interview with Gene R. Swenson, o.p. 1963); 1 ill
JOHNSON 102-104 (talk given at the College Art Association, Philadelphia, 1964)
KERBER 187-188 (extract from interview with Alan Solomon, o.p. 1966)
KERBER 188 (extract from interview with David Pascal, o.p. 1966)
KERBER 189-190 (extract from interview with Raphael Sorin, o.p. 1968)
QUADRUM no.18 162-163 (interview); port
RUSSELL J 92-94 (interview with Gene Swenson, o.p. 1963)
ROSE II 167-168 (extract from interview with Gene Swenson, o.p. 1963)
ROSE II REVISED 152-153. (extract from interview with Gene Swenson, o.p. 1963)
ROSE II REVISED 153-154 (extract from interview with John Coplans, o.p. 1967)
ROSE II REVISED 187 (statement: "A Friendlier Climate," o.p. 1967)
VARIAN I (statement); port
VARIAN III (statement); port

LICHTSTEINER, Rudolf (1938-) Swis; photo
WALSH 453-454 (statement); 1 ill

LICHTY, George M. (1905-) Amer; cart
M.H. DE YOUNG 86 (response); self port

LIE, Jonas (1880-1940) Norw/Amer; ptr
BOSWELL 169-170 (statement)

LIEB, Vered (1947-) Isra; ptr
LEAVITT (statement); port; 5 ill
RE-VIEW v.1 1-4 ("Editorial")
RE-VIEW v.2/3 2-6 ("Editorial")

LIEBERMANN, Max (1847-1935) Germ; ptr, print
FRIEDENTHAL 156-158 (letter to Alfred Lichtwark, 1911); 1 ill
GOLDWATER 333-334 ("A Credo," o.p. 1922)
SCHMIDT 41 (statement, 1933)
THORN 10, 14, 19, 22, 24, 30, 31, 32, 41, 44, 46, 54-56, 58, 59, 61, 62, 66, 69, 78, 90, 96, 102, 115, 116, 131, 135, 143, 150-153, 164, 169, 171, 188, 195, 196, 198, 201, 202, 206, 218, 220, 235, 237, 239, 240, 249, 253-255, 260, 279, 280, 295, 297, 303, 304, 306, 320, 321, 326-328, 330, 333, 335, 338, 343, 345 (statements, p.p.)

LIEBERT, George ( ) Amer
BRAKKE 182-183 (statement); 1 ill

LIEBLING, Jerome (1924-) Amer; photo
TIME-LIFE II 88-89 (statement); 2 ill
WALSH 454-455 (statement); 1 ill

LIEBMAN, Marjorie ( ) Amer; ptr
ILLINOIS 1955 216 (statement); 1 ill

LIEBMANN, Gerhardt (1928-) Amer; ptr
ILLINOIS 1969 124 (statement); 1 ill

LIJN, Liliane (Liliane Segall) (1939-) Amer/Brit; sclp, light
BRITISH (statement); 1 ill
CONTEMPORARY (statement); port; 2 ill
EMANUEL II 547-549 (statement); 1 ill
HAYWARD 1978 22-25 (statement); 5 ill
LUMIERE (statement); port; 1 ill
NAYLOR 557-558 (statement); 1 ill

LIM, Chong Leat (1930-) Mala; arch
EMANUEL I 473-474 (statement); 1 ill

LIM, Kim (1936-) Chin/Brit; sclp
NAYLOR 558-559 (statement); 1 ill

LIM, William S. W. (1932-) Sing; arch
EMANUEL I 471-473 (statement); 1 ill

LIMERAT, Francis (1946-) Fren; sclp
SKIRA 1979 61 (statement); 1 ill

LIMMER, Gregory ( ) Amer; ptr
KRESGE (statement); port; 1 ill

LINAZASORO, Jose-Ignacio ( ) Span; arch
PORPHYRIOS 36-39 (essay: "Architecture as Discipline," with Miguel Garay); 9 ill
PORPHYRIOS 70-71 (essay: "Basque Pelota Court, Villafranca de Ordizia, Basque Country"); 5 ill
PORPHYRIOS 80-83 (essay: "School at Ikastola, Basque Country," with Miguel Garay); 9 ill

LINDEMAN, Nicky ( ) Amer
EVENTS II 44-45, 46-47 (statements); 2 ill

LINDENFELD, Lore ( ) Amer; text
MILLER 91-105 (interview with Sally Swenson); port; 1 ill

LINDER, Jean (1938-) Amer; sclp
DIRECTIONS I 76 (response); 1 ill

LINDNER, Richard (1901-1978) Germ/Amer; ptr
ART NOW v.2 no.10 (interview); 1 ill
ART SINCE v.2 152 (statement, o.p. 1968)
ART VOICES v.4 no.4 64-65 (statement); 3 ill
GRUEN 136-137 (statement); port
MILLER 1963 60-67 (statement); port; 6 ill

LINDQUIST, Mark (1949-) Amer; pott, sclp
HAYSTACK 37 (statement); 1 ill

LINN, Karl ( ) Amer; arch
COOPER-HEWITT I 122-123 (essay: "Cultivating Green Communities")

LINS, Lygia Pimental
SEE: CLARK, Lygia

LION, Yves ( ) Fren; arch
ARCHITECTURES 110-113 (essay: "Maintenant Construire"); 7 ill

LIPCHITZ, Jacques (1891-1973) Lith/Fren; sclp
ALBRIGHT-KNOX 174-175(letter, 1/1952); 1 ill
ARTFORUM v.1 no.12 38-40 (statements); port; 8 ill
ILLINOIS 1961 136-137 (response); port; 1 ill
ILLINOIS 1963 207 (statement); 1 ill
KUH 155-170 (interview); 10 ill
LETTERS 22 (letter); 1 ill
NELSON 263-273 (interview with Cranston Jones)
RODMAN I 130-136, 164-169 (interview)
TIGER no.4 80, 91 (statement); 1 ill

LIPPOLD, Richard (1915-) Amer; sclp
EMANUEL II 552-553 (statement); 1 ill
KEPES VI 152-164 (essay: "Illusion as Structure"); 3 ill
KEPES IX 62-73 (extract from "private communications" with John E. Burchard)
MILLER 1952 27-29 (statement); 4 ill
MOTHERWELL 8-22 (three group discussions: "Artists' Sessions at Studio 35," New York, 1950)
NAYLOR 563-564 (statement); 1 ill
NEW DECADE 53-55 (statement); 3 ill
PREMIER BILAN 305 (statement); port

QUADRUM no.14 35-46 (statements); 13 ill
TEMOIGNAGES II 42-43 (statement); port; 3 ill
TIGER no.4 79-80, 98 ("i to eye"); 1 ill

LIPSKI, Donald (1947-) Amer; sclp, envir
CRISS-CROSS no.4 14-19 (interview with Joe Hobbs and John Alberty)
CRISS-CROSS no.5 2-7 (statements); 8 ill
GUMPERT III 67-68 (statement)

LIPTON, Seymour (1903-) Amer; sclp
ALBRIGHT-KNOX 108-109 (letters, 6/1957, 7/1968, 7/1972); 1 ill
ART VOICES v.4 no.2 88-89 (statements); 1 ill
ILLINOIS 1953 198-199 (statement); 1 ill
ILLINOIS 1959 239-240 (statement); 1 ill
ILLINOIS 1963 60-61 (statement); 1 ill
LETTERS 23 (letter); 2 ill
MILLER 1956 72-77 (statement); port; 6 ill
MOTHERWELL 8-22 (three group discussions: "Artists' Sessions at Studio 35," New York, 1950)
NEW DECADE 55-57 (statement); 3 ill
TIGER no.4 80, 104 (essay: "The Web of the Unrhythmic"); 1 ill
TRACKS v.3 no.1/2 78-81 (essay: "The Grotesque and the Classical in Sculpture")

LIPTOW, Hilmar (1943-) Germ; photo, coll
SKIRA 1978 66 (statement); 1 ill

LIPTOW, Renate (1942-) Germ; photo, coll
SKIRA 1978 66 (statement); 1 ill

LIPZIN, Janis Crystal (1945-) Amer;

photo
OUTSIDE II 24-25 (statement); port; 3 ill

LISSITZKY, El (Lazar M. Lisitsky) (1890-1941) Russ; ptr, print
BANN 53-57 (essay: "The Blockade of Russia is Coming to an End," o.p. 1922)
BANN 63-64 ("Statement by the Editors of Veshch/Gegenstand/Objet" o.p. 1922)
BANN 137-147 (extract from *Russia: The Reconctruction of Architecture in the Soviet Union*, 1930)
BOWLT 151-158 (essay: "Suprematism in World Reconstruction," o.p. 1920); 2 ill
CONRADS 121-122 (essay: "Ideological Superstructure," o.p. 1929)

LITTLE, John (1907-) Amer; ptr
FRASNAY 238 (statement)
IT IS no.4 29 (statement)

LITTLE, Ken D. (1947-) Amer; pott, glass
HOUSE 58-59 (statement); 1 ill
VIEWPOINT 1979 18-19 (statement); 4 ill

LITTLETON, Harvey Kline (1922-) Amer; glass, sclp
GLASS v.1 18-19 (statement)
GLASS v.5 (group discussion); port; 1 ill
NAYLOR 566-567 (statement); 1 ill
WISCONSIN I (statement); 1 ill

LITWAK, Israel (1868-) Amer; ptr
JANIS II 138-143 (statements); port; 1 ill

LIVICK, Stephen (1945-) Cana; photo
WALSH 457 (statement); 1 ill

LIWZY, Grigory ( ) Belg; ptr
COLLARD 176-180 (interview, 1969); port; 1 ill

LLEWELYN-DAVIS, Richard (1912-) Brit; arch
EMANUEL I 475-476 (statement); 1 ill

LLOYD, Gary Marchal (1943-) Amer; video
ROSS 58-59 (interview with Glorianne Harris); port

LLOYD, Tom (1929-) Amer; sclp
FINE 222-224 (statements, o.p. 1968, 1970, 1971); 2 ill

LOBB, Vernon (1939-) Amer; sclp
DIRECTIONS I 76 (response); 1 ill

LOBE, Robert Lawrence (1945-) Amer; sclp
SHEARER 40-44 (interview); 4 ill

LOBELL, John ( ) arch
ON SITE no.5/6 38-41 (essay: "Towards a Zero Energy Architecture")

LOBELL, Mimi ( ) arch
ON SITE no.5/6 118-123 (essay: "Pickin' up the Pieces of Universal Order and Architecture")

LOCKE, Charmaine (1950-) Amer; sclp
HOUSE 60-61 (statement); 1 ill

LOCKS, Seymour (1919-) Amer; sclp
ILLINOIS 1961 125 (response); port; 1 ill

LOCKWOOD, Ward (1894-1963) Amer; ptr, illus, print
BETHERS I 242-243 (statement); 1 ill
ILLINOIS 1951 195-196 (statement); 1 ill
ILLINOIS 1955 217-218 (statement); 1 ill

ILLINOIS 1959 240-242 (statement); 1 ill

LOCSIN, Leandro V. (1928-) Fili; arch
EMANUEL I 476-478 (statement); 1 ill

LOEB, Judy ( )
VISUAL v.2 no.3 21-22 (essay: "Educating Women in the Visual Arts: An Overview"); 1 ill

LOEW, Michael (1907-) Amer; ptr
IT IS no.2 42 (statement)

LOGAN, Andrew (1945-) Brit; photo
SKIRA 1979 106 (statement); 2 ill

LOGAN, Juan (1946-) Amer; sclp
LEWIS I REVISED 51-52 (statement); port; 1 ill

LOGAN, Peter (1943-) Brit; sclp
BRITISH (statement); 1 ill

LOGEMANN, Jane Marie (1942-) Amer; ptr
ART-RITE no.14 5, 10 (response)

LOGUE, Joan (1942-) Amer; video
ROSS 118-119 (statement); 16 ill

LOHSE, Richard Paul (1902-) Swis; ptr
ART SINCE v.1 291 (statement, o.p. 1968)
BANN 277-283 (essay: "A Step Farther--New Problems in Constructive Plastic Expression," o.p. 1961)
EMANUEL II 557-558 (statement); 1 ill
KEPES IV 128-161 (essay: "Standard, Series, Module: New Problems and Tasks of Painting"); 15 ill

LOKER, John (1938-) Brit; ptr
CONTEMPORARY (statement); port; 2 ill

LOLE, Kevin ( )
ART-LANGUAGE v.2 no.1 38-50 ("Aspects of Authorities")

LOMBARDI, Judith A. R. (1948-) Amer; ptr
NOSANOW II 29, 56 (statement); 2 ill

LOMBARDO, Sergio (1939-) Ital; ptr
NAYLOR 568-569 (statement); 1 ill

LONG, Jack (1925-) Cana; arch
CANADIAN 66-69 (statement); 5 ill

LONG, Randy ( ) Amer; metal
METALWORKS (statement); 1 ill

LONG, Richard (1945-) Brit; sclp, envir, perf
ARTIST AND CAMERA 44-45 (statement); 2 ill
CHOIX 30 (statement, o.p. 1982); 1 ill
EMANUEL II 558-560 (statement); 1 ill
STEDELIJK 158-159 (statement); 3 ill

LONGO, Vincent (1923-) Amer; ptr
FULBRIGHT 32 (statement)

LONGOBARDI, Nino ( ) Ital; ptr, instal
WALDMAN 50-67 (statement); 13 ill

LONGSHORE, Willie F. (1933-) Amer; ptr
LEWIS I REVISED 93 (statement); port; 1 ill

LONGSON, Tony ( ) Brit; sclp
BRITISH (statement); 1 ill

LONGVILLE, Richard ( ) Amer; arch, design
LIFE 198-200 (interview); port

LOOS, Adolf (1870-1933) Aust; arch

BREICHA 220-224 (essay: "Ornament and Verbrechen," o.p. 1908)
CONRADS 19-24 (essay: "Ornament and Crime," o.p. 1908)

LOPEZ, Andy ( ) Amer; photo
LEEKLEY 48-49 (statement); 1 ill

LORAN, Erle (1905-) Amer; ptr
BETHERS I 244-245 (statement); 1 ill
BETHERS II 108-109 (statement); 2 ill
ILLINOIS 1952 209-210 (statement); 1 ill
ILLINOIS 1953 199-200 (statement); 1 ill
ILLINOIS 1963 171 (statement); 1 ill
ILLINOIS 1965 52-53 (statement); 1 ill

LORBER, Richard ( )
BATTCOCK VI 95-102 (essay: "Epistemological TV," o.p. 1974/75)

LORCINI, Gino (1923-) Brit/Cana; sclp
CANADA 104-105 (statement); port; 2 ill

LORD, Chip (1944-) Amer; video
NEW VISIONS (statement); 3 ill
ON SITE no.5/6 57-65 (essay: "Autorama")
SEE ALSO: ANT FARM

LORD, Sheridan (1926-) Amer; ptr
GUSSOW 149-151 (interview, 1971); 1 ill

LORIO, E. F. Goerge (1950-) Amer; pott
HERMAN 78 (statement); port; 1 ill

LOSTETTER, Alvern ( ) Amer
BRAKKE 112-128 (statement); 13 ill

LOTH, Wilhelm (1920-) Germ; sclp
NAYLOR 570-571 (statement); 1 ill

LOUGHRAN, Joyce (1954-) Amer; ptr
BOSTON II (statement); 1 ill

LOUNEMA, Risto (1939-) Finn; photo
WALSH 460-461 (statement); 1 ill

LOUW, Roelof (1935-) Brit; envir, sclp
EMANUEL II 561-562 (statement); 1 ill
PROJECTS (statement); 6 ill
TRACKS v.3 no.1/2 5-15 (essay: "Sites/Non-Sites: Smithson's Influence on Recent Landscape Projects")

LOVAK, Branko (1944-) Yugo; ptr
TOMASEVIC 193-197 (statement); port; 2 ill

LOVE, Edward (1936-) Amer; sclp
LEWIS II 100 (statement); port; 1 ill

LOVEJOY, Margot MacDonald (1930-) Cana; print, illus
COMPUTER (statement); 1 ill

LOVELESS, James K. (1935-) Amer; ptr
NOSANOW I 90 (statement); 1 ill

LOVELL, Tom (1909-) Amer; ptr, illus
MAGIC 80-83 (statement); port; 4 ill

LOVERA, James ( ) pott
VISUAL v.2 no.1 37-38 (essay: "Technical Information"); 2 ill

LOVET-LORSKI, Boris (1894-1972) Lith/Amer; sclp
ART VOICES v.2 no.4 16-17 (interview with Susan Drysdale); port; 4 ill
ART VOICES v.4 no.1 74 (statement); 1 ill

LOVETT, Wendell H. ( ) Amer; arch
GA HOUSES no.3 176-181 (statement); 14 ill
NEWMAN 48-52 (essay and group discussion); port; 6 ill

LOVING, Alvin D., Jr. (1935-) Amer; ptr
FINE 234-235 (statements, o.p. 1969, 1971); 2 ill
IMAGE COLOR FORM 18-19 (statement); 1 ill

LOVSTROM, Richard Edgar
SEE: WILFRED, Thomas

LOW, Steven ( ) film
TRACKS v.2 no.3 74-83 ("Pickup and How to Get and Keep a Job")

LOWE, Jeffrey (1952-) Brit; sclp
BRITISH (statement); 1 ill
HAYWARD 1979 118-119, 128-131 (interview with David Robson); port; 9 ill

LOWE, Peter (1938-) Brit; sclp, print
CONTEMPORARY (statement); port; 2 ill

LOWENGRUND, Margaret (1902-1957) Amer; ptr, print
ZAIDENBERG 150-153 (essay: "Fine Art and Commercial Art"); 4 ill

LOWRY, Laurence S. (1887-1976) Brit; ptr
BARBER 9-22 (interview); port

LOZOWICK, Louis (1892-1973) Amer; ptr
FIRST AMERICAN 70-71 (essay: "Government in Art, Status of the Artist in the U.S.S.R.")
MILLER 1943 47 (statement, o.p. 1930); 2 ill
100 CONTEMPORARY ix-xv (essay: "The Jew in American Plastic Art")
100 CONTEMPORARY 126-127 (statement); port; 1 ill

LU, Lucy ( ) ptr
KATZ 185-195 (interview); port; 1 ill
SKIRA 1978 117 (statement); 4 ill

LUCAS, Colin Anderson (1906-) Brit; arch
EMANUEL I 482-484 (statement); 1 ill
READ 117-124 (statement); port; 5 ill

LUCAS, David A. (1948-) Amer; ptr
NOSANOW I 91 (statement); 1 ill

LUCASSEN, Reinier (1939-) Dutc; ptr
EMANUEL II 563-564 (statement); 1 ill
NAYLOR 573-574 (statement); 1 ill
REFLECTION 28-31 (statement); 3 ill
STEDELIJK 160 (statement in Dutch); 2 ill

LUCEBERT (L. G. Swanswijk) (1924-) Dutc; ptr, print
ART SINCE v.2 151 (statement, o.p. 1963)
GUGGENHEIM I 100 (poem: "Arp," o.p. 1960)
STEDELIJK 161 (statement in Dutch); 2 ill

LUCHESSA, Gayle ( ) text
VISUAL v.2 no.2 15-18 (interview); 5 ill

LUCIER, Alvin (1931-) Amer; perf, sound
CRISS-CROSS no.3 24 (statement); 1 ill
CRISS-CROSS no.6 28 (statement); 1 ill
CRISS-CROSS no.6 29-31 (interview with Douglas Simon); 2 ill
SONDHEIM 157-177 (interview with Douglas Simon); port; 7 ill

LUCIO
SEE: MUNOZ, Lucio

LUCIONI, Luigi (1900-) Ital/Amer; ptr
BETHERS II 110-111 (statement); 2 ill

BRITANNICA 71 (statement); port; 1 ill

LUCKETT, Stephen Q. (1938-) Amer; ptr
NOSANOW I 92 (statement); 1 ill

LUDEKENS, Fred (1900-) Amer; ptr
GUITAR 142-151 (interview); port; 4 ill

LUDINS, Eugene (1904-) Russ/Amer; ptr
ILLINOIS 1957 223-224 (response); 1 ill
ZAIDENBERG 58-60 (essay: "Landscapes"); 4 ill

LUJAN, Pedro (1943-) Amer; sclp
RAICES 30 (statement); 1 ill

LUKIN, Sven (1934-) Latv/Amer; ptr, sclp
PREMIO NACIONAL 1965 58-59 (statement); port; 1 ill
VARIAN II (statement); port

LUMSDEN, Anthony ( ) Atrl/Amer; arch
BUILDINGS 34-37 (statement); 5 ill

LUND, David (1925-) Amer; ptr
FULBRIGHT 33 (statement); 1 ill
WHITNEY (statement); 1 ill
YOUNG 1960 (statement); 1 ill

LUNDBERG, Bill (1942-) Amer; film, sclp, instal
SKIRA 1980 92 (statement); 3 ill

LUNDBERG, L. G. ( ) Swed
ADLERS 17-19 (interview); ports; 2 ill

LUNDEBERG, Helen Feitelson (1908-) Amer; ptr
CELEBRATION (statement); 1 ill
HOPKINS 108-109 (statement); port; 1 ill
ILLINOIS 1950 188 (statement); 1 ill

ILLINOIS 1952 210 (statement); 1 ill
ILLINOIS 1955 218-219 (statement); 1 ill
ILLINOIS 1957 224 (response); 1 ill
ILLINOIS 1959 242 (statement); 1 ill
ILLINOIS 1965 102 (statement); 1 ill
MILLER 1942 93-96 (statement); port; 3 ill
MUNRO 170-177 (interview); port; 2 ill

LUNDIN, Norman K. (1938-) Amer; ptr
GUENTHER 76-77 (statement); port; 1 ill

LUPAS, Ana (1940-) Ruma; envir, ptr, sclp
EMANUEL II 565-567 (statement); 1 ill
NAYLOR 575-576 (statement); 1 ill

LURCAT, Jean (1892-1966) Fren; ptr
FIFIELD 255-271 (interview)
GOLDAINE 49-51 (interview); port

LURIE, Nan (1910-) Amer; ptr, print
BETHERS II 112-113 (statement); 2 ill

LUSCHER, Ingeborg (1936-) Swis; photo
NAYLOR 576-578 (statement); 1 ill

LUSKACOVA, Marketa (1944-) Czec; photo
WALSH 462 (statement); 1 ill

LUSSIER, Alvin ( ) perf, sound
PARACHUTE no.8 32-34 (interview in English); 2 ill

LUTHER, Adolf (1912-) Germ; sclp
HAUSSER 114-117 (statement); 6 ill

LUTHI, Bernhard (1938-) Swis; ptr
SKIRA 1978 104-105 (statement); 1 ill

LUTHI, Urs (1947-) Swis; perf, photo
EMANUEL II 567-568 (statement); port

IDENTITE 55-58 (interview with Jacques Clayssen); port
SANDBERG 130-133 (statement); 5 ill
SKIRA 1977 62 (statement); 6 ill
SKIRA 1980 116-117 (statement); 3 ill

LUTOMSKI, James W. (1944-) Amer; sclp
MICHIGAN 24-25 (statement); 2 ill

LUTTIKHUIZEN, Esther (1951-) Amer; sclp
MICHIGAN 26-27 (statement); 1 ill

LUTZ, Dan S. (1906-1978) Amer; ptr
BRITANNICA 73 (statement); port; 1 ill
CALIFORNIA--PAINTING 23 (statement); 1 ill
ILLINOIS 1957 224-225 (response); 1 ill

LUTZ, Winifred Ann (1942-) Amer; sclp
SCULPTURE OUTSIDE (statement); 4 ill

LUTZKE, Richard (1951-) Amer; sclp, coll
NOSANOW I 93-94 (statement); 3 ill

LUX, Theodore (1910-) Germ/Amer; ptr
MILLER 1943 46 (statement); 1 ill

LUZ, Hans (1926-) Germ; arch
EMANUEL I 494-495 (statement); 1 ill

LYE, Len (1901-) NewZ/Amer; sclp
ART AND TECHNOLOGY 200-201 (project proposal)
KINETIC 42-47 (statement: extract from "The Art That Moves"); port; 4 ill
LETTERS 24 (letter); 1 ill

LYMAN, Henry (1944-) Amer; pott
HERMAN 79 (statement); port; 1 ill

LYMAN, Susan ( ) Amer
ARTPARK 1983 40-41 (statement); port; 2 ill

LYNCH, Kevin (1918-) Amer; arch
KEPES II 108-124 (essay: "The Openness of Open Space")

LYNDON, Alice Atkinson (1935-) sclp
RUDDICK 25-37 (interview); port; 4 ill

LYNDON, Donlyn (1936-) Amer; arch
GA HOUSES no.8 8-11 (essay: "Stairs"); 19 ill
PROCESSES 75-94 (interview with Lance Laver); 15 ill

LYNDS, Clyde William (1936-) Amer; sclp, light
ILLINOIS 1969 68 (statement); 1 ill
ILLINOIS 1974 77 (statement); 1 ill

LYON, Danny (1942-) Amer; photo
WALSH 464-465 (statement); 1 ill

LYON, Robert ( ) Amer; sclp
ARTPARK 1980 (statement); port; 3 ill

LYONS, Joan (1937-) Amer; photo
DUGAN 91-99 (interview, 1976); port
WALSH 466-467 (statement); 1 ill

LYONS, Nathan (1930-) Amer; photo
BARROW 19-30 (essay: "Landscape Photography," o.p. 1962)
BARROW 31-33 ("Foreword" to *Photography 63*, o.p. 1963)
DUGAN 33-45 (interview, 1974); port
PROFILE v.2 no.5 (Sept. 1982); port; 5 ill

LYR, Claude ( ) Belg; ptr
COLLARD 182-187 (interview); port; 1 ill

LYTLE, Richard (1935-) Amer; ptr
  MILLER 1959 42-46 (statement); port; 4
  ill

LYYTIKAINEN, Olli (1949-) ptr
  SLEEPING 92-101 (statement); 24 ill

MACCARI, Mino (1898-) Ital; ptr
VERZOCCHI 255-259 (statement); self
port; 1 ill

MACDONALD, David R. (1945-) Amer;
pott
CONTEMPORARY   AFRICAN
(statement); port; 1 ill

MACDONALD, Elizabeth ( ) Amer; pott
HAYSTACK 38 (statement); 1 ill

MACDONALD, Julie (1926-) Amer; sclp
ILLINOIS 1961 94 (response); port; 1 ill

MACDONALD, Kevin John (1946-)
Amer; ptr
IMAGES 50-57 (interview with Clair
List); port; 5 ill

MACDONALD, Roberta ( ) Amer; illus
M.H. DE YOUNG 87 (response); self port

MACDONALD-WRIGHT,   Stanton
(1890-1973) Amer; ptr
CHIPP 320-321 (statement, o.p. 1916)
FORUM 1916 68 (statement); 1 ill
ILLINOIS 1950 189 (statement); 1 ill
JANIS I 39 (statement); 1 ill
ROSE II 94-95 (statement, o.p. 1916)
ROSE II REVISED 78-79 (statement, o.p.
1916)

MACENTYRE, Eduardo A. (1929-) ptr
PREMIO   NACIONAL   1965   26-27
(statement); port; 1 ill

MACGREGOR, Gregory (1941-) Amer;
photo
WALSH 468-469 (statement); 1 ill

MACHADO,   Rodolfo   (1942-   )
Arge/Amer; arch
ARCHER 68-72, 98 (statement); port; 9
ill

MACHIDA, Margo ( ) Amer; ptr
EVENTS I 44 (statement); 1 ill

MACIUNAS, George ( )
VISION no.3 52-55 (letters)

MACIVER, Loren (1909-) Amer; ptr
ART NOW v.3 no.1 (statement); 1 ill
MILLER 1946 28-33 (statement); 7 ill

MACK, Heinz (1931-) Germ; light, sclp
ART SINCE v.1 160 (statement, o.p.
1965)
EMANUEL II 572-574 (statement); 1 ill
HAUSSER 118-121 (statement); 6 ill
KINETIC 48-49 (statement); port; 2 ill
KINETISCHE (statement); 2 ill
NAYLOR 585-587 (statement); 1 ill

MACK, Mark (1949-) Aust/Amer; arch
ARCHER 24-27, 95 (statement); port; 6
ill
COUNTERPOINT 22-35 (statements); 29
ill

MACKALL, Louis ( ) Amer; arch
GA HOUSES no.8 160-171 (statement);
31 ill

MACKAY, David (1933-) Brit; arch
SEE: MARTORELL   BOHIGAS
MACKAY

MACKE, August (1887-1914) Germ; ptr
MIESEL 75-77 ("The New Program,"
o.p. 1914)
STURM 16-17 (letter, 1913); 1 ill
WINGLER 56-57 ("Nachruf," 1914)
WINGLER 58-59 (essay: "Uber
Kandinsky und Marc," p.p.)
WINGLER 59-60 (essay: "Uber Robert
Delaunay," o.p. 1912)
WINGLER 60-61 (essay: "Uber den
Kubismus," p.p.)

MACKENZIE, Ken ( ) arch
GA HOUSES no.10 162-175 (statement); 40 ill

MACKENZIE, Lucy (1952-) Brit; ptr
CONTEMPORARY (statement); port; 1 ill

MACKENZIE, Marilyn ( ) pott, sclp
VISUAL v.4 no.2 7-9 (interview); port; 3 ill

MACKENZIE, Warren (1924-) Amer; pott
HERMAN 80 (statement); port; 1 ill

MACKEY, Fletcher (1950-) Amer; sclp
O'KANE (statement); 1 ill

MACKY, Eric Spencer (1880-1958) NewZ/Amer; ptr
M.H. DE YOUNG 88 (response); self port

MACLENNAN, Alastair (1943-) Iris; perf
KNOWLES 195-199 (extract from interview); 5 ill

MACLOW, Jackson (1922-)
ART AND TECHNOLOGY 201-223 (project proposal); ports

MACNEIL, Linda ( ) Amer; metal
METALWORKS (statement); 1 ill

THE MAD DIARIST
SEE: MEW, Tommy

MADAR, Viktor (1934-) Yugo; ptr
TOMASEVIC 198-201 (statement); port; 2 ill

MADDEN, Anne (Madden-Simpson) (1932-) Brit; ptr
KNOWLES 98-99 (statement); 3 ill

NAYLOR 591-592 (statement); 1 ill

MADDOX, Conroy (1912-) Brit; ptr
LONDON BULLETIN no.18/19/20 39-43, 45 (essay: "The Object in Surrealism")

MADIGAN, Colin Frederick (1921-) Atrl; arch
EMANUEL I 502-503 (statement); 1 ill

MADSEN, Steven R. (1947-) Amer; wood
WOODWORKING 38-39 (statement); port; 2 ill

MADSON, Jack (1927-) Amer; ptr
YOUNG 1957 (statement); 2 ill

MAEYER, Marcel (1920-) Belg; ptr
SKIRA 1977 21 (statement); 1 ill

MAFAI, Mario (1902-1965) Ital; ptr
VERZOCCHI 261-265 (statement); self port; 1 ill

MAGAFAN, Ethel (1916-) Amer; ptr
FULBRIGHT 34-35 (statement); 1 ill
ILLINOIS 1961 114 (response); port; 1 ill
ZAIDENBERG 154-156 (essay: "The Problem of Retaining Spontaneity"); 2 ill

MAGAFAN, Jenne (1916-1952) Amer; ptr
ZAIDENBERG 133-135 (essay: "How Nature Provides Inspiration"); 3 ill

MAGARINOS "D", Victor (1924-) Arge; ptr
PREMIO NACIONAL 1964 30-31 (statement); port; 1 ill

MAGDALEN MARY, Sister ( ) Amer;

ptr
RODMAN I 21-26 (interview)

MAGGS, Arnaud (1926-) Cana; photo
WALSH 470-471 (statement); 1 ill

MAGNAN, Oscar Gustav (1937-)
Cuba/Amer; ptr
CUBAN (statement); 2 ill

MAGNELLI, Alberto (1888-1971) Ital;
ptr
BERCKELAERS 171-172 (poems: "Ile
San Mer," "Impots Redevables")
FRASNAY 41-51 (statement); ports; 11
ill
GOLDAINE 63-65 (interview); port
PAINTING 21 (statement); port; 1 ill
TEMOIGNAGES I 190-203 (statement);
port; 14 ill

MAGOR, Liz (1948-) Cana; sclp, instal
MISE EN SCENE 13, 94-111 (statement);
32 ill

MAGRITTE, Rene (1898-1967) Belg; ptr
ART SINCE v.2 153-154 (statement, o.p.
1954)
FORD/VIEW v.7 no.2 21-23 (essay:
"Lifeline")
FRASNAY 99-107 (handwritten
statement); ports; 3 ill
GUGGENHEIM I 104 (statement, 1963)
JEAN 237 ("Words and Images," o.p.
1929)
JEAN 360-363 ("Thought and Images,"
o.p. 1954)
LIPPARD 154-155 ("The 5
Commandments," o.p. 1925)
LIPPARD 155-156 ("Ariadne's Thread,"
o.p. 1934)
LIPPARD 156-157 (essay: "Bourgeois
Art," o.p. 1939)
LIPPARD 157-161 ("Lifeline," o.p.
1946)

LONDON BULLETIN no.12 13-14 (essay:
"L'Art Bourgeois")
LONDON BULLETIN no.17 9-12 (essay:
"Colour-Colours, or an Experiment by
Roland Penrose")
REVOLUTION SURREALISTE no.12
32-33 (text piece: "Les Mots et les
Images")
REVOLUTION SURREALISTE no.12 65,
72 ("Enquete")

MAGUBANE, Peter (1932-) SoAf; photo
TIME-LIFE IV 108-109 (statement); 1 ill
WALSH 472-473 (statement); 1 ill

MAGUIRE AND MURRAY (arch firm)
SEE: MAGUIRE, Robert

MAGUIRE, Robert ( ) Brit; arch
MIKELLIDES 122-133 (essay: "A
Conflict between Art and Life?"); 11 ill

MAGYAR, Victor
SEE: MADAR, Viktor

MAHLER, Reinhold ( ) Germ; arch
COOPER-HEWITT I 54-55 (essay:
"Pedestrian Malls")

MAHMOUD, Ben (1935-) Amer; ptr
NAYLOR 595-596 (statement); 1 ill

MAHR, Mari (1941-) Hung/NewZ; photo
WALSH 473-474 (statement); 1 ill

MAILLOL, Aristide (1861-1944) Fren;
sclp
GOLDWATER 406-408 (extract from
interview with Judith Cladel)
GROHMANN 446 ("Gesprache," p.p.
1925)
GROHMANN 447 ("Vor Einer Antiken
Venus," o.p. 1928)
MINOTAURE no.3/4 41 (statement); 1
ill

THORN 83 (statement, p.p.)

MAILMAN, Cynthia (1942-) Amer; ptr
MILLER 106-120 (interview with Sally Swenson); port; 1 ill

MAINARDI, Patricia M. (1942-) Amer; ptr
NAYLOR 596-597 (statement); 1 ill
SCHAPIRO 45 (statement); self port; 1 ill

MAINE, John (1942-) Brit; sclp
BRITISH (statement); 1 ill

MAIROVICH, Zvi (1909-) Isra; ptr
SEITZ I (statement); 3 ill

MAISEL, Jay (1931-) Amer; photo
LAPLANTE 58-65 (interview); port; 1 ill

MAISNER, Bernie (1954-) ptr
TRACKS v.3 no.1/2 54-56 ("My Molding, Flowing Conception of Image, and How it Affects the Universe")

MAJZNER, Vic (1945-) Atrl; ptr
DE GROEN 131-137 (interview); port

MAKI, Fumihiko (1928-) Japa; arch
KEPES VI 116-127 (essay: "Some Thoughts on Collective Form"); 5 ill

MAKI, Robert (1938-) Amer; sclp
GUENTHER 78-79 (statement); port; 1 ill

MAKINS, James (1946-) Amer; pott
HERMAN 81 (statement); port; 1 ill

MALAVAL, Robert (1937-) Fren; sclp
NAYLOR 597 (statement); 1 ill

MALCOLM, Scott (1952-) Amer; pott
HERMAN 82 (statement); port; 1 ill

MALDARELLI, Oronzio (1892-1963) Ital/Amer; sclp
ILLINOIS 1953 200 (statement); 1 ill

MALDONADO, Tomas (1922-) Arge; print
KEPES VIII 122-155 (essay: "Design Education")

MALECZECH, Ruth ( )
PERFORMANCE no.2 1-12 (interview); port

MALER, Leopoldo Mario (1937-) Arge; film, sclp, perf
EMANUEL II 577-578 (statement); 1 ill
HAYWARD 1978 26-29 (statement); 2 ill
NAYLOR 597-599 (statement); 1 ill
SKIRA 1977 55 (statement); 1 ill

MALEVITCH, Kasimir (1878-1935) Russ; ptr
BERCKELAERS 177 (statement)
BERKELAERS 303-304 (extract from essay, o.p. 1923)
BOWLT 111, 115-135 (essay: "From Cubism and Futurism to Suprematism: The New Painterly Realism," o.p. 1916); port; 2 ill
BOWLT 143-145 (essay: "Suprematism," o.p. 1919)
CHIPP 337-341 (essay: "Introduction to the Theory of the Additional Element in Painting," o.p. 1927)
CHIPP 341-346 (essay: "Suprematism," o.p. 1919)
CONRADS 87-88 (extract from "Suprematist Manifesto Unovis," o.p. 1924)
GOLDWATER 452-453 (statements, 1914, 1927)
GRAY 282-284 (extract from essay: "Abstract Creation and Suprematism," o.p. 1919)
GUGGENHEIM II 82-83 (statement); 1 ill

PLASTIQUE no.1 1-3 (statement, 1915-1920); 2 ill
POENSGEN 99-100 ("Die Neue Norm," o.p. 1927)
POENSGEN 105-106 ("Der Suprematismus," o.p. 1919)
PROTTER 194 (extract from "The Non-Objective World," o.p. 1927)
SEUPHOR 97-99 (extract from "The Non-Representational World," o.p. 1927)

MALINA, Frank (1912-) Amer; sclp
ART SINCE v.1 296 (statement, o.p. 1967)
LUMIERE (statement); port; 1 ill

MALLARY, Robert (1917-) Amer; sclp, ptr
ART AND TECHNOLOGY 224 (project proposal)
ARTFORUM v.2 no.7 37-39 (interview); 2 ill
COMPUTER (statements); 1 ill
ILLINOIS 1965 202 (statement); 1 ill
LOCATION v.1 no.1 58-66 ("A Self-Interview"); 4 ill
MILLER 1959 47-51 (statement); port; 5 ill

MALONE, Lois ( ) Amer; photo
IRVINE 50, 79 (statement); 1 ill

MALOOF, Sam (1916-) Amer; wood, design
DIAMONSTEIN IV 134-151 (interview); port; 17 ill

MALTHIEU, Dora ( ) Amer; illus
NORTH LIGHT 166-171 (statement); port; 10 ill

MAMBOUR, Auguste (1896-) Belg; ptr
RAYNAL 219-222 (statement); 2 ill

MAN, Felix H. (1893-) Brit; photo
WALSH 477-480 (statement); 1 ill

MAN RAY
SEE: RAY, Man

MANDEL, Howard (1917-) Amer; ptr, sclp
FULBRIGHT 34-35 (statement); 1 ill
ZAIDENBERG 121-123 (essay: "Evolving a Painting"); 3 ill

MANDELBAUM, Irva ( ) Amer; illus
PHILLPOT (statement)

MANDIC, Petar (1938-) Yugo; ptr
TOMASEVIC 202-205 (statement); port; 1 ill

MANE-KATZ (1894-1962) Fren; ptr, sclp
GOLDAINE 66-68 (interview); port

MANESSIER, Alfred (1911-) Fren; ptr, design
ART SINCE v.1 158 (statement, o.p. 1958)
CHARBONNIER v.2 79-87 (interview)
GOLDAINE 141-143 (interview); port
LIBERMAN 72 (statements)
POENSGEN 118 ("Kieseln Sind Keine Kunstwerke," 1955)
PREMIER BILAN 306 (statement); port
RITCHIE 26-30 (statement); port; 4 ill
SEUPHOR 216-217 (statement); 1 ill
VINGTIEME N.S. no.9 26 (statement)

MANGER, Barbara (1943-) Amer; sclp
WISCONSIN II (statement); 1 ill

MANGOLD, Robert Peter (1937-) Amer; ptr
CONCEPT 42-45 (statement); 1 ill
PAOLETTI 72-74 (statements, p.p.); 1 ill

ROSE II REVISED 191 (statement: "Popular Art Cannot be Avant-Garde," o.p. 1967)
SYSTEMATIC 25 (statement); 1 ill
VIEW v.1 no.7 (interview)

MANGOLD, Sylvia Plimack (1938-) Amer; ptr
CELEBRATION (statement); 1 ill
EMANUEL II 581-582 (statement); 1 ill
NAYLOR 602-603 (statement); 1 ill
PAOLETTI 75-76 (statements, p.p.); 1 ill
SCHAPIRO 46 (statement); port; 1 ill

MANGRAVITE, Peppino (1896-1978) Ital/Amer; ptr
BRITANNICA 74 (statement); port; 1 ill
ILLINOIS 1952 210-211 (statement); 1 ill
M.H. DE YOUNG 89 (response); self port
PAINTING iv ("Foreword")

MANGURIAN, Robert (1941-) Amer; arch
COUNTERPOINT 104-117 (statements); 15 ill

MANIEVICH, Abraham (1883-1942) Russ/Amer; ptr
100 CONTEMPORARY 128-129 (statement); port; 1 ill

MANN, Andy (1947-) Amer; video
ART-RITE no.7 11, 13 (response); 1 ill

MANN, David (1927-) Amer; ptr
LEWIS I REVISED 67 (statement); port; 3 ill

MANN, Story (1953-) Amer; sclp, instal, envir
ARTPARK 1978 38-41 (extract from video); port; 8 ill
IN A PICTORIAL 8-15 (statements); port; 5 ill

MANNING, Jack ( ) photo
TIME-LIFE II 90-91 (statement); 2 ill

MANNING, John (1928-) Amer; ptr
ART NOW v.3 no.2 (statement); 1 ill

MANSELL, Gordon ( ) ptr
CRISS-CROSS no.5 36-39 (essay: "Painting Context and Culture"); port; 4 ill

MANSFIELD, Alfred (1912-) Isra; arch
EMANUEL I 509-511 (statement); 1 ill

MANSHIP, Paul Howard (1885-1966) Amer; sclp
FIRST AMERICAN 19-20 (essay: "Why Established Artists Should Oppose War and Fascism")

MANSO, Leo (1914-) Amer; ptr
ILLINOIS 1951 197 (statement); 1 ill
ILLINOIS 1952 211-212 (statement)
ILLINOIS 1955 219-220 (statement); 1 ill
ILLINOIS 1957 226-227 (response); 1 ill
ILLINOIS 1959 242-243 (statement)
ILLINOIS 1965 94 (statement); 1 ill

MANTE, Harald (1936-) Germ; photo
WALSH 484-485 (statement); 1 ill

MANTEOLA, Flora (1936-) Arge; arch
SEE: MANTEOLA SANCHEZ GOMEZ SANTOS SOLSONA VINOLY

MANTEOLA SANCHEZ GOMEZ SANTOS SOLSONA VINOLY (arch firm)
EMANUEL I 511-513 (statement); 1 ill

MANTZARIS, Elly ( ) perf
ART NETWORK no.2 47 (statement)

MANZONI, Piero (1933-1963) Ital; sclp
STEDELIJK 162-163 (statement, in Italian); 4 ill

MAPPLETHORPE, Robert (1946-) Amer; photo
FIGURES 18-19 (statements: o.p. 1980, 1981); 1 ill

MAPSTON, Tim (1954-) Brit; sclp
ENGLISH 264-269 (statement); port; 8 ill

MARA, Pol (1920-) Belg; ptr
COLLARD 194-197 (interview); port; 1 ill
NAYLOR 606-607 (statement); 1 ill

MARADIAGA, Ralph (1943-) Amer; print
RAICES 20 (statement); 1 ill

MARAK, Louis (1942-) Amer; pott
HERMAN 83 (statement); port; 1 ill
VIEWPOINT 1977 13 (statement); 3 ill

MARAN, Anujka (1918-) Yugo; ptr
TOMASEVIC 206-209 (statement); port; 1 ill

MARC, Franz (1880-1916) Germ; ptr
BERCKELAERS 177 (statements, 1912, 1915)
CHIPP 178-179 (essay: "How Does a Horse See the World?," o.p. 1920); 1 ill
CHIPP 180-181 ("Aphorisms," 1914-1915, o.p. 1920)
CHIPP 181-182 (letter, 1915, o.p. 1920); 1 ill
EDDY 115 (extract from essay, o.p. in *Der Blaue Reiter*)
FRIEDENTHAL 207-208 (letters, 1907, 1915; statement, o.p. 1912); 2 ill
GOLDWATER 444-446 (statements, 1911-1912, 1915)
GROTE 40 (statements, 1911, 1912/13)
MIESEL 66-70 ("Letter to August Macke" 1911)
MIESEL 70-72 ("Germany's Savages")
MIESEL 72-74 ("Two Pictures")
MIESEL 160-164 ("In War's Purifying Fire," 1915)
POENSGEN 77-78 ("Zeichen der Zeit")
PROTTER 199 (extract from *Notes and Aphorisms*, 1912)
STURM 18-19 (letter, 1916); 1 ill
THORN 14, 15, 17, 18, 21, 22, 29, 30, 32, 45, 46, 51, 54, 79, 80, 83, 85, 86, 92, 105, 107, 110, 130, 132, 135, 146, 194, 196, 286, 291, 323, 349 (statements, p.p.)
WINGLER 51-53 (essay: "Die 'Wilden' Deutschlands," p.p.)
WINGLER 54 (essay: "Die Futuristen," p.p.)
WINGLER 54-56 (essay: "Kandinsky," p.p.)

MARCA-RELLI, Conrad (Corrado di) (1913-) Amer; ptr
ILLINOIS 1955 220 (statement); 1 ill
VARIAN I (statement); port

MARCHAND, Andre (1907-) Fren; ptr
CHARBONNIER v.1 141-151 (interview)
GOLDAINE 120-122 (interview); port
PREMIER BILAN 306 ("Notes")
YALE 66 (statement)

MARCHEGIANI, Elio (1929-) Ital; ptr, instal
NAYLOR 609-610 (statement); 1 ill

MARCHESCHI, Louis Cork (1945-) Amer; sclp, instal
LOGAN I 24-27 (statement); port; 3 ill
NAYLOR 610-611 (statement); 1 ill

MARCOUX, Alice ( ) Amer; text
HAYSTACK 40 (statement); 1 ill

MARCUS, Arron ( ) Amer; print
COMPUTER (statements); 1 ill

MARCUS, Marcia (1928-) Amer; ptr
CELEBRATION (statement); 1 ill
SCHAPIRO 47 (statement); port; 1 ill
WHITNEY (statement); self port
YOUNG 1960 (statement); 2 ill

MARDEN, Brice (1938-) Amer; ptr
ART NOW v.3 no.1 ("Three Deliberate
Greys for Jasper Johns"); 1 ill
ART-RITE no.9 39-42 (interview); port
LICHT 43-48 (statement); 4 ill
NAYLOR 611 (statement); 1 ill
PAOLETTI 77-79 (statements, p.p.); 1
ill
STEDELIJK 164-165 (statement, 1963);
2 ill
TUCKER I 20 (statement)
VIEW v.3 no.2 (interview); port; 5 ill

MARFAING, Andre (1925-) Fren; ptr
GRENIER 139-142 (interview)

MARFIA, Marcia ( ) ptr
CRISS-CROSS   no.7/8/9   48-49
("Painting"); 1 ill

MARGO, Boris (1902-) Russ/Amer; ptr,
print
ILLINOIS 1951 197-198 (statement); 1 ill
JANIS I 102 (statement); 1 ill
TIGER no.2 42-43 (statement)
TIGER   no.8   53-55   (essay: "The
Cellocut as a Graphic Medium")

MARGOLIS, Richard (1943-) Amer;
photo
WALSH 487-488 (statement); 1 ill

MARGOULIES, Berta O'Hare (1907-)
Poli/Amer; sclp
100   CONTEMPORARY   130-131
(statement); port; 1 ill

MARGULES,   DeHirsch   (1899-   )
Ruma/Amer; ptr
100   CONTEMPORARY   132-133
(statement); port; 1 ill

MARIANI, Elio (1943-) Ital; photo, coll
NAYLOR 612-613 (statement); 1 ill

MARIEN, Marcel (1920-) Belg; coll, ptr
NAYLOR   614-615   (extract   from
interview, 1967); 1 ill

MARIN, Alvaro (1946-) Span; ptr
ANGEL 103-125 (interview); port; 1 ill

MARIN, John (1870-1953) Amer; ptr
ARMORY   SHOW   24   (extract   from
"statement printed on the occasion of
his exhibition at the Photo-Secession
Gallery in 1913")
CHIPP 531-532 (extract from interview
with Dorothy Norman, o.p. 1937)
CRISPO II (statement); 18 ill
DOUZE PEINTRES (statement); 2 ill
FORTY (statement); 2 ill
FORUM 1916 72 (statement); 1 ill
GOLDWATER 466-468 (statement, 1923)
PROTTER   183-184   (extract   from   an
editorial: "The   Artist   and   the
Public," o.p. 1940)
ROSE II 64-70 (letters, 1921, 1923, 1933,
o.p. 1949)
ROSE II REVISED 59-64 (letters, 1921,
1923, 1931, 1933, o.p. 1949)
ROSE II REVISED 64 (extract from
essay: "John Marin by Himself," o.p.
1928)

MARINI, Marino (1901-) Ital; ptr, print,
sclp
RODITI 39-48 (interview); port; 2 ill
VINGTIEME N.S. no.9 36 (statement); 1
ill

MARIONI, Tom (1937-) Amer; sclp, perf
VIEW v.1 no.5 (interview); port; 12 ill
VISION no.1 8-11 ("Out Front"); 2 ill

MARISCAL, Joe ( ) Amer; pott
VIEWPOINT 1981 (statement); 3 ill

MARISOL (Marisol Escobar) (1930-)
Vene/Amer; sclp
NEMSER 178-199 (interview); port; 7 ill
QUADRUM no.18 162-164 (interview);
port

MARJANCEVIC, Mihajlo (1932-) Yugo;
ptr
TOMASEVIC 210-214 (statement); port;
2 ill

MARK, Mary Ellen (1940-) Amer; photo
WALSH 488-490 (statement); 1 ill

MARKOV, Valdimir (1877-1914) Russ;
ptr
BOWLT 23-38 (essay: "The Principles
of the New Art," o.p. 1912); 1 ill

MARKOVITZ, Sherry ( ) Amer; sclp
GUENTHER 80-81 (statement); port; 1
ill

MARKS, Carolyn ( ) sclp
VISUAL v.2 no.3 43-44 (letter)

MARKSON, Jerome (1929-) Cana; arch
EMANUEL I 516-518 (statement); 1 ill

MARLOW, Peter ( ) photo
BOSHIER (statement); port; 2 ill

MARSAN, Jean-Claude (1938-) Cana;
arch
CANADIAN 70-73 (statement); 6 ill

MARSH, Anne (1956-) Atrl; perf
ART NETWORK no.2 40-41 (statements)

ART NETWORK no.2 46 (statement)
ART NETWORK no.2 49 (statement)

MARSH, Harry (1886-) Amer; ptr
SYMBOLS (statement); 1 ill

MARSH, Reginald (1898-1954) Amer; ptr
BOSWELL 174-175 (statement)
BRITANNICA 75 (statement); port; 1 ill
ILLINOIS 1951 199 (statement); 1 ill
ROSE II 116 (extract from essay:
"Poverty, Politics, and Artists,
1930-45," o.p. 1965)
ROSE II REVISED 95 (extract from
essay: "Poverty, Politics, and Artists,
1930-1945" o.p. 1965)

MARSHA ( ) Amer; photo
IRVINE 39, 86 (statement); 1 ill

MARSHALL, Amanda (1953-) Brit; arch
SPIRIT 22-27 (statements); 15 ill

MARSHALL, Chris (1946-) Brit; sclp
BRITISH (statement); 1 ill

MARSHALL, Stuart ( )
BATTCOCK VI 103-120 (essay: "Video
Art, The Imaginary and the Parole
Vide," o.p. 1976)

MARSICANO, Nicholas (1914-) Amer;
ptr
ART NOW v.3 no.4 (statement); 1 ill
IT IS no.1 31 (essay: "Drawing the
Figure")
IT IS no.2 78 (statement)
IT IS no.4 11 (essay: "The Non-Human
Figure")

MARTENSEN, Richard (1910-)
QUADRUM no.15 98 (statement, 1951);
1 ill

MARTI, Joan ( ) Belg; ptr
COLLARD 198-202 (interview, 1969); port; 1 ill

MARTIN, Agnes (1912-) Cana/Amer; ptr
ART-RITE no.5 6-7 (response)
EMANUEL II 592-593 (statement); 1 ill
PROFILE v.1 no.2 (interview); port
STEDELIJK 166 (statement); 2 ill
VAN DER MARCK 51-52 (statement); 1 ill

MARTIN, Barry (1943-) Brit; ptr
CONTEMPORARY (statement); port; 1 ill

MARTIN, Coletta (1923-) Amer; ptr
AWARDS 8-11 (statement); 5 ill

MARTIN, David Stone (1913-) Amer; ptr, illus
BRITANNICA 76 (statement); port; 1 ill

MARTIN, Douglas (1947-) Amer; ptr
LEAVITT (statement); port; 5 ill

MARTIN, Etienne (1913-) Fren; sclp
PREMIER BILAN 306 (statement); port

MARTIN, Fletcher (1904-1979) Amer; ptr, print
BRITANNICA 77 (statement); port; 1 ill
GUITAR 152-163 (interview); port; 4 ill
MILLER 1942 97-101 (statement); port; 4 ill
ZAIDENBERG 40-43 (essay: "Composition"); 5 ill

MARTIN, Francois (1945-) Fren; ptr
SKIRA 1979 92 (statement); 1 ill

MARTIN, Fred (1927-) Amer; ptr
SOME 17 (statement); 1 ill
VISION no.1 14-15 (text piece)

MARTIN, John Lewis (1908-) Brit; arch
BANN 202-204 ("Editorial from *Circle*," o.p. 1937)
CIRCLE 215-219 (essay: "The State of Transition")
EMANUEL I 519-520 (statement); 1 ill

MARTIN, Kenneth (1905-) Brit; ptr, print, sclp
BANN 283-287 (essay: "Construction from Within," o.p. 1964); 1 ill
BOWNESS 17, 36-38 (statement); 2 ill
BRITISH (statement); 1 ill
CONTEMPORARY (statement); port; 2 ill
EMANUEL II 594-595 (statement); 1 ill
ENGLISH 152-157 (statement); port; 8 ill
NAYLOR 617-619 (statement); 1 ill
QUADRUM no.3 93-98 (statements); 8 ill

MARTIN, Knox (1923-) Amer; ptr, sclp
ART NOW v.4 no.2 (statement); 1 ill
ILLINOIS 1955 220-221 (statement); 1 ill

MARTIN, Mary (1907- 1969) Brit; sclp, ptr
BOWNESS 17, 39-41 (statement); 2 ill

MARTIN, Paul (1948-) Brit; ptr, print
RE-VIEW v.1 50-52 (statement); 2 ill

MARTIN, Ron (1943-) Cana; ptr
NAYLOR 620-621 (statement); 1 ill

MARTIN, Tony (1937-) Amer; sclp
DIRECTIONS I 77 (response); 1 ill

MARTINCEK, Martin (1913-) Czec; photo
WALSH 490-491 (statement); 1 ill

MARTINEZ, Cesar Augusto (1944-) Amer; print, ptr
RAICES 21 (statement); 1 ill

MARTINEZ, Juan (1942-) Span; ptr
SKIRA 1977 26 (statement); 1 ill

MARTINOT, Steve ( ) sclp
TRACKS v.3 no.1/2 99-101 ("A Parable")

MARTORELL BOHIGAS MACKAY (arch firm)
EMANUEL I 520-523 (statement); 1 ill

MARTORELL CODINA, Josep Maria (1925-) Span; arch
SEE: MARTORELL BOHIGAS MACKAY

MARTYL (Martyl Schweig Langsdorf) (1918-) Amer; ptr, illus
ILLINOIS 1951 199-200 (statement); 1 ill
ILLINOIS 1952 212-213 (statement)
ILLINOIS 1957 227 (response); 1 ill
ILLINOIS 1959 243-244 (statement); 1 ill
ILLINOIS 1961 120 (response); port; 1 ill

MARX, Gary (1950-) Amer; sclp
WISCONSIN II (statement); 1 ill

MARX, Suzanne
SEE: LAKE, Suzy

MARXHAUSEN, Reinhold Pieper (1922-) Amer; sclp, sound
GRAYSON 68-79 (essay: "Variations on the Theme for Listening to Door Knobs"); port; 5 ill

MARY CORITA, Sister
SEE: CORITA, Sister Mary

MASCATELLO, Tony (1947-) Amer; ptr
BRENTANO 276-277 (statement); 1 ill
LIVE no.4 25-26 (essay: "Sister Suzie Cinema")

MASON, Alden (1919-) Amer; ptr
GUENTHER 82-83 (statement); port; 1 ill

MASON, Alice Turnbull (1904-1971) Amer; ptr
ABSTRACT 19-20, 63, 143 (essay: "Concerning Plastic Significance"); 1 ill
BETHERS I 246-247 (statement); 1 ill

MASON, George (1951-) Amer; pott
HAYSTACK 41 (statement); 1 ill
HERMAN 84 (statement); port; 1 ill

MASON, Phillip (1939-) Amer; ptr, print
LEWIS I REVISED 111-112 (statement); port; 2 ill

MASON, Raymond (1922-) Brit; ptr, sclp
CLAIR 60-61 (extract from interview with Michael Brenson, 1972); 1 ill
SKIRA 1978 108 (statement); 1 ill
SKIRA 1980 72-73 (statement); 2 ill

MASON, Robert (1946-) Brit; ptr
CONTEMPORARY (statement); port; 2 ill

MASSARO, Karen T. (1944-) Dani/Amer; pott, sclp
HERMAN 85 (statement); port; 1 ill
WISCONSIN II (statement); 1 ill

MASSON, Andre (1896-) Fren; ptr, print
ART SINCE v.2 152 (statement, o.p. 1950)
ARTS YEARBOOK v.3 45 ("Foreword: Paris")
CHARBONNIER v.1 185-195 (interview)
CHIPP 436-437 (essay: "Painting is a Wager," o.p. 1941)
CHIPP 438-440 (essay: "A Crisis of the Imaginary," o.p. 1944/45); self port

EIGHT (handwritten statement in French; statement in English, French, and German); ports

FRIEDENTHAL 237-241 (letter to Henry Clifford, 1948); 4 ill

GOLDWATER 409-413 (statements, 1908)

GROHMANN 371-372 ("Aus Einem Gesprach mit Estienne," 1909)

GROHMANN 373-374 ("Gedanken uber Kunst," p.p. 1945)

LHOTE 378-384 (essay, o.p. 1937)

MAYWALD (statement in English, German, and French; handwritten statement in French); ports

PROTTER 182-183 ("About My Painting," p.p.)

SEGHERS 103-111 (extract from "Notes d'un Peintre," in English, o.p. 1908)

THORN 12, 22, 29, 111, 116, 128, 134, 161, 185, 191, 193, 302, 341, 342, 347 (statements, p.p.)

VERDET 113-132 (interview, 1948-1950)

MATISSE, Paul (1933-) Amer; sclp
DIRECTIONS I 77 (response); 1 ill

MATS B. ( )
ADLERS 39-40 (interview); port; 1 ill

MATSCHINSKY, Martin (1921-) Germ; sclp
HAUSSER 124-125 (statement, o.p. 1977); 1 ill

MATSUDA, Gonroku (1896-) Japa; lacquer
ADACHI 36-40 (statement); 4 ill

MATSUZAWA, Yutaka (1922-) Japa; ptr
NAYLOR 627-628 (statement); port; 1 ill

MATTA (ROBERTO SEBASTIAN ANTONIO MATTA ECHAURREN) (1911-) Chil; ptr
ART SINCE v.2 153 (statement, o.p. 1966)

ARTFORUM v.4 no.1 23-26 (interview with Max Kozloff); 4 ill

CHIPP 443-444 (essay: "On Emotion," o.p. 1954); port

CLAUS 35-38 (statement)

FRASNAY 259-267 (statement); port; 4 ill

GUGGENHEIM II 133 (statement); 1 ill

IT IS no.5 7 ("Letter")

JEAN 338 ("Sensitive Mathematics--Architecture of Time," o.p. 1938)

LIPPARD 167-169 (essay: "Sensitive Mathematics--Architecture of Time," o.p. 1938)

LIPPARD 169-171 (essay: "Hellucinations," o.p. 1948)

MINOTAURE no.11 43 (essay: "Mathematique Sensible--Architecture du Temps"); 1 ill

PREMIER BILAN 307 (statement); port

QUADRUM no.6 26-30 (interview with Julien Alvard); port; 6 ill

SKIRA 1975 65 (statement, 1970); 1 ill

MATTA-CLARK, Gordon (1945-1978) Amer; sclp, envir
ARTPARK 1974 28-31 (statement); port; 4 ill

AVALANCHE no.10 34-37 (interview); 8 ill

BELFORD 101-128 (group discussion)

GEORGIA 118-166 (group discussion: "Artists' Convention," in Athens, GA., 1/7/1977, moderated by Jan van der Marck)

PARACHUTE no.8 19 (statement, in English); 1 ill

SKIRA 1979 33 (statement); 7 ill

MATTER, Mercedes ( ) ptr
IT IS no.3 12-13 ("Drawing")

MATTOX, Charles (1910-) Amer; sclp, ptr
ART AND TECHNOLOGY 224 (project proposal)
KINETIC 50-51 (statement); port; 5 ill
TUCHMAN 47 (statement)

MATTSON, Henry E. (1887-1971) Swed/Amer; ptr, print
BOSWELL 175 (statement)
BRITANNICA 78 (statement); port; 1 ill

MATVEJS, Waldemars
SEE: MARKOV, Vladimir

MAUD, Zuny (1891-) Amer; ptr
100 CONTEMPORARY 134-135 (statement); port; 1 ill

MAUGERI, Concetto (1919-) Ital; ptr
VERZOCCHI 267-271 (statement); self port; 1 ill

MAURAND, Tania ( ) photo
IDENTITE 63-66, 95 (interview with Jacques Clayssen); port

MAURER, Alfred Henry (1868-1932) Amer; ptr
FORUM 1916 76 (statement); 1 ill
ROSE II 60-61 (statement, o.p. 1916)
ROSE II REVISED 53-54 (statement, o.p. 1916)

MAURI, Fabio (1926-) Ital; ptr
EMANUEL II 605-606 (statement); 1 ill

MAWDSLEY, Richard W. (1945-) Amer; metal
METALWORKS (statement); 1 ill

MAWICKE, Tran (1911-) Amer; ptr
NORTH LIGHT 84 (statement); 1 ill

MAX, Sharyn ( ) Amer; photo
PHOTOGRAHY (statement); 1 ill

MAXWELL, William (1934-) Amer; pott, ptr
LEWIS I REVISED 79-81 (statement); port; 2 ill

MAYEKAWA, Kunio (1905-) Japa; arch
EMANUEL I 528-530 (statement); 1 ill

MAYER, Edward (1942-) Amer; sclp, instal
HOUSE 62-63 (statement); 1 ill

MAYER, Rosemary (1943-) Amer; sclp, envir
INTERVIEWS 17-18 (interview); 1 ill
SONDHEIM 191-212 ("Two Years, March 1973 to January 1975"); 21 ill
TRACKS v.2 no.1 56-58 ("First Passages from a Text in Progress")
TRACKS v.2 no.3 23-36 ("Passages")
TRACKS v.3 no.1/2 82-90 ("Contexts")
WHITE WALLS no.2 6-15 ("Spell"); 7 ill
WHITE WALLS no.5 48-57 ("Those"); 7 ill
WHITE WALLS no.8 76-81 (statement); 4 ill

MAYHEW, Richard (1924-) Amer; ptr
ILLINOIS 1963 102 (statement); 1 ill
WHITNEY (statement); 1 ill

MAYNARD, Valerie J. (1937-) Amer; sclp
FAX II 97-116 (statements); port; 1 ill

MAYNE, Roger (1929-) Brit; photo
WALSH 495-496 (statement); 1 ill

MAYNE, Thom (1944-) Amer; arch
COUNTERPOINT 78-89 (statements); 34 ill
LA JOLLA 65-69 (statement); port; 12 ill

MAYO, Lynne ( ) sclp
RE-VIEW v.2/3 67-69 (statement); 4 ill

MAYR, Albert (1943-)
PARACHUTE no.1 42-43 (performance description); 3 ill

MAYS, Peter (1939-) Amer; illus
CALIFORNIA--DRAWING (statement); 2 ill

MAZA, Fernando (1936-) ptr
PREMIO NACIONAL 1965 28-29 (statement); port; 1 ill

MAZUR, Michael B. (1935-) Amer; ptr
YOUNG 1965 (statement); 2 ill

MCBANE, Kip K. ( ) arch
ON SITE no.5/6 110-113 (essay: "Los Angeles: Architecture of the Cinema")

MCBEAN, Angus (1904-) Brit; photo
WALSH 496-498 (statement); 1 ill

MCCABE, Daniel (1958-) Amer; video
BOSTON III (interview); 1 ill

MCCABE, Eamonn ( ) Brit; photo
HOW FAMOUS 130-135 (statements); port; 7 ill

MCCAFFERTY, James ( )
ART-RITE no.19 17-20 (group discussion)

MCCAFFERTY, Jay David (1948-) Amer; ptr
IRVINE 25, 89-90 (statement); 1 ill

MCCAGG, Louise ( ) Amer; print
KRESGE (statement); port; 1 ill

MCCALEBB, Howard (1947-) Amer; sclp
EVENTS I 44 (statement); 1 ill

MCCALL, Anthony (1946-) Brit/Amer; film
ENGLISH 456-457 (statement); port; 3 ill
ON SITE no. 5/6 28-29 ("Fire Cycles"); 3 ill
SEE ALSO: INTERNATIONAL LOCAL

MCCALL, Robert Theodore (1919-) Amer; ptr, illus
MAGIC 84-87 (statement); port; 3 ill

MCCARTHY, Dermot (1948-) Iris; ptr
KNOWLES 26-31 (statements); 10 ill

MCCARTHY, Paul (1945-) Amer; video
ROSS 137 (letters to and from David Ross)

MCCARTIN, Jan (1909-) Cana; ptr
ART NOW v.4 no.1 (statement); 1 ill

MCCLARD, Michael ( ) perf, video
AVALANCHE no.11 28-31 (performance transcript); 36 ill

MCCLEAN, Bruce (1944-) perf, ptr, sclp
BOSHIER (statement); port; 13 ill

MCCLEARY, Mary Fielding (1951-) Amer; paper
PAPERWORKS 20-21 (statement); 5 ill

MCCLELLAND, John ( ) ptr
NORTH LIGHT 85 (statement); 1 ill

MCCLUSKY, John D. (1914-) Amer; ptr
ILLINOIS 1959 245 (statement); 1 ill

ILLINOIS 1961 92 (response); port; 1 ill

MCCOLLUM, Allan ( ) perf
REALLIFE no.5 4-13 ("Matt Mullican's World")

MCCONNELL, Gerald ( ) Amer; sclp, ptr
ILLUSTRATION 106-112 (statement); port; 8 ill
MAGIC 88-91 (statement); port; 4 ill
NORTH LIGHT 172-177 (statement); port; 4 ill

MCCOY, Ann (1946-) Amer; ptr
EMANUEL II 606-608 (statement); 1 ill
NAYLOR 581-582 (statement)

MCCRACKEN, John (1934-) Amer; sclp, ptr
ART AND TECHNOLOGY 225 (project proposal)
DIRECTIONS I 76 (response); 1 ill
EMANUEL II 608-609 (statement)
IRVINE 48, 83 (statement); 1 ill
NAYLOR 582-583 (statement)
ROSE I 56-61 (statement); 5 ill

MCCRADY, John (1911-) Amer; ptr
BOSWELL 175-176 (statement)

MCCULLIN, Don (1935-) Brit; photo
CAMPBELL 190-201 (statement); port; 10 ill
VICTORIA 88-91 (statements)

MCCULLOUGH, David William (1945-) Amer; sclp
TEXAS 12-15 (statement); 4 ill

MCCULLOUGH, Joseph W. (1922-) Amer; ptr
ILLINOIS 1957 228 (response); 1 ill

MCCURDY, Bruce (1930-) Amer; print
CALIFORNIA--PRINTS (statement); 1 ill

MCDONALD, Rob ( ) perf
ART NETWORK no.2 43 (statement)

MCELCHERAN, William Hodd (1927-) Cana; sclp
CANADA 32-33 (statement); port; 2 ill

MCELHINNEY, Susan ( ) Amer; photo
PHOTOGRAPHY (statement); 1 ill

MCEWEN, Jean Albert (1923-) Cana; ptr
ILLINOIS 1963 72 (statement); 1 ill

MCEWEN, Rory (1932-) Brit; ptr
NAYLOR 583-584 (statement)

MCFALL, David (1919-) Brit; sclp
CONTEMPORARY (statement); port; 2 ill
LONDON COUNTY (statement); 1 ill

MCFEE, Henry Lee (1886-1953) Amer; ptr
FORUM 1916 80 (statement); 1 ill

MCGARRELL, James (1930-) Amer; print, ptr
AMERICAN PRINTS 40-41, 68 (statement); 2 ill
EMANUEL II 609-610 (statement); 1 ill
ILLINOIS 1961 105 (response); port; 1 ill
ILLINOIS 1963 174 (statement); 1 ill
NAYLOR 584-585 (statement); 1 ill
SELZ 102-105 (statement); 3 ill

MCGAUGH, Lawrence (1940-) Amer; ptr
LEWIS I REVISED 32 (statement); port; 1 ill

MCGINLEY, Connie Q. (1955-) Amer; ptr
NOSANOW II 17, 57 (statement); 2 ill

MCGOWIN, William Edward (1938-) Amer; ptr, sclp
NAYLOR 585 (statement)
SCHIMMEL 58-59 (statement); 3 ill

MCHARDY, George
SEE: COUNTY TIMES

MCHARG, Ian Lennox (1920-) Scot/Amer; arch
COOPER-HEWITT I 85 (essay: "Urban Identities")

MCILVAIN, Isabel (1943-) Amer; sclp
SUPERREAL 168-169 (statement); 1 ill

MCILVANE, Edward ( ) Amer; glass
HAYSTACK 39 (statement); 1 ill

MCINTOSH, Karl (1940-) Amer; ptr, print
LEWIS I REVISED 7 (statement); port; 3 ill

MCINTURFF, Mark ( ) arch
GA HOUSES no.11 154-157 (statements); 13 ill

MCKEEVER, Ian (1946-) Brit; ptr, envir
SKIRA 1977 46 (statement); 1 ill

MCKENNA, Stephen ( ) Amer; ptr
ART-LANGUAGE v.1 no.2 11-13 ("Notes on Marat")

MCKEOWN, Stephan (1947-) Amer; sclp
HOUSE 64-65 (statement); 1 ill

MCKINNELL, Noel Michael (1935-) Amer; arch

HEYER 256-263 (interview); 7 ill

MCLAUGHLIN, Gerald (1925-) Amer; ptr
YOUNG 1957 (statement); 1 ill

MCLAUGHLIN, John D. (1898-1976) Amer; ptr
CALIFORNIA--PAINTING 46 (statement); 1 ill
ENVIRONMENT 76-77 (statement); 1 ill
ILLINOIS 1967 102 (statement); 1 ill
NAYLOR 588-589 (statement); 1 ill

MCLEAN, Bruce (1944-) Brit; instal, perf
AVALANCHE no.2 44-53 (text piece: "King for a Day"); ports
HAYWARD 1979 13, 14, 20-23 (interview with William Furlong); 8 ill

MCLEAN, Richard Thorpe (1934-) Amer; ptr
HOPKINS 48-49 (statement); port; 1 ill
MEISEL 335-366 (statement); port; 68 ill
NAYLOR 589-590 (statement); 1 ill
SUPERREAL 134-135 (statement); 1 ill

MCMAHON, Paul ( ) perf
ART-RITE no.14 5, 10 (response)
REALLIFE no.10 12-15 (essay: "From the Permanent Collection")

MCMORDIE, Michael (1935-) Cana; arch
CANADIAN 74-75 (statement)

MCNAMARA, John (1950-) Amer; ptr
BOSTON II (statement); 1 ill
BOSTON III (interview); 1 ill

MCNAUGHTON, John W. ( ) Amer; wood
MEILACH 74-75, 154 (statement); 7 ill

MCNEIL, George (1906/8-) Amer; ptr
IT IS no.3 14-15 ("Spontaneity")

MCNEIL, William (1935-) Amer; ptr
LEWIS I 61 (statement); port; 2 ill

MCNEUR, Christopher ( )
APPLE 50 (statement); 1 ill

MCQUEEN, John (1943-) Amer; sclp,
wood, text
ARTPARK 1979 (statement); 1 ill
DIAMONSTEIN IV 152-165 (interview);
port; 13 ill

MCWHORTER, Elsie Jean (1932-)
Amer; sclp
MORRIS 158-163 (statements); ports; 3
ill

MCWILLIAM, Frederick Edward (1909-)
Iris; sclp
EMANUEL II 612-613 (statement); 1 ill
KNOWLES 128-131 (statement); 7 ill
NAYLOR 590-591 (statement); 1 ill
OPEN AIR 1960 (statement); 1 ill

MCWILLIAMS, Al (1944-) Cana; sclp,
instal
MISE EN SCENE 21, 76-93 (statement);
12 ill

MEADMORE, Clement (1929-) Amer;
sclp
NAYLOR 631 (statement)
SCULPTURE OUTSIDE (statement); 4 ill

MEARS, Ellen (1953-) Amer; text
FIBER 18, 20 (statement); 1 ill

MECHAU, Frank Albert (1903-1946)
Amer; ptr
BRITANNICA 79 (statement); port; 1 ill

MEDALLA, David (David Cortez de
Medalla y Mosqueda) (1942-) Fili; ptr,
sclp, perf
EMANUEL II 614-615 (statement)
NAYLOR 631-632 (statement)

MEDELLIN, Octavio (1908-)
Mexi/Amer; sclp
MILLER 1942 102-106 (statement); port;
5 ill

MEDINA, Ada (1948-) Amer; ptr, illus
WINSTON-SALEM 50-57 (statement); 10
ill

MEDLEY, Robert (1905-) Brit; ptr
AXIS no.8 28-29 (essay: "Hitler's Art
in Munich")
CONTEMPORARY (statement); port; 2
ill

MEEKER, Dean J. (1920-) Amer; ptr
ILLINOIS 1953 201 (statement); 1 ill

MEERT, Joseph J. P. (1905-)
Belg/Amer; ptr
ILLINOIS 1952 213-214 (statement)
ILLINOIS 1955 221 (statement); 1 ill

MEFFERD, Boyd (1941-)
ART AND TECHNOLOGY 226-235
(project proposal); ports; 5 ill

MEGERT, Christian (1936-) Swis; sclp,
print
EMANUEL II 615-616 (statement); 1 ill
KORNFELD 34-35 (statement); port; 2
ill

MEGSON, Neil Andrew
SEE: GENESIS P-ORRIDGE

MEHKEK, Martin (1936-) Yugo; ptr
TOMASEVIC 215-220 (statement); port;
2 ill

MEHTA, Ashvin (1931-) Indi; photo
WALSH 503-504 (statement); 1 ill

MEIDNER, Ludwig (1884-1966) Germ;
ptr
MIESEL 111-115 ("An Introduction to
Painting Big Cities," 1914)
MIESEL 182-184 ("Aschaffenburg
Journal," 1918)
WINGLER 31-34 (essay: "Erinnerungen
an Modigliani," p.p.)

MEIER, Richard Alan (1934-) Amer;
arch
COLLABORATION 104-107 (essay:
"Tinted Shades"); 4 ill
DIAMONSTEIN II 104-122 (interview);
port; 4 ill
EMANUEL I 535-537 (statement); 1 ill
GA DOCUMENT no.1 25-28, 36-65
(statements); 59 ill
GA HOUSES no.1 92-97 (statement); 13
ill
GA HOUSES no.5 110-123 (statement);
19 ill
SEARING 106-113 (statement); 7 ill

MEIGS, Walter (1918-) Amer; ptr
ILLINOIS 1953 202 (statement); 1 ill

MEISTERMANN, Georg (1911-) Germ;
glass
HAUSSER 126-129 (statement); 8 ill

MEITZLER, Herbert Neil (1930-) Amer;
ptr
ILLINOIS 1959 246-247 (statement); 1 ill

MEKAS, Jonas (1922-) film
PARACHUTE no.10 21-24 (interview in
English)

MELCHERT, Jim (1930-) Amer; perf
NAYLOR 633-634 (statement); 1 ill
WHITE WALLS no.5 58-67 (text piece)

MENARD, Andrew ( )
ART-LANGUAGE v.3 no.2 31-40
("Brainstorming—New York")
ART-LANGUAGE v.3 no.2 81-86
("Strategy is Political: Dear M...")

MENDEL, Mark (1947-) Amer; envir
CENTERBEAM 52-53, 114 ("Poem
On"); port; 1 ill

MENDELSOHN, Eric (1887-1953) Germ;
arch
CONRADS 54-55 (extract from talk:
"The Problem of a New Architecture,"
given 1919)
CONRADS 72-73 (extract from talk:
"Dynamics and Function," given in
1923)
CONRADS 106-107 ("Synthesis," o.p.
1928)
SCHMIDT 31, 46-47 (letters, 1933)

MENDELSOHN, John ( ) ptr
ART-RITE no.9 17 (statement); port

MENDES DA ROCHA, Paulo Archias
(1928-) Braz; arch
EMANUEL I 539-540 (statement); 1 ill

MENDIETA, Ana ( ) Cuba/Amer; ptr,
sclp
BRENTANO 278-279 (statement); 1 ill

MENKES, Sigmund (1896-) Poli/Amer;
ptr
BRITANNICA 80 (statement); port; 1 ill
ILLINOIS 1950 191-192 (statement)
ILLINOIS 1953 202 (statement); 1 ill
100 CONTEMPORARY 136-137
(statement); port; 1 ill
RAYNAL 227-229 (statement); 1 ill
ZAIDENBERG 44-47 (essay: "Color as I
See It"); 4 ill

MENSA, Carlos ( ) Span; ptr
PORCEL I 133-144 (interview); 2 ill

MENZIO, Francesco (1899-) Ital; ptr
VERZOCCHI 273-277 (statement); self
port; 1 ill

MEO, Yvonne Cole ( ) Amer; sclp
LEWIS I REVISED 104 (statement); port;
1 ill

MEREDITH, Dorothy L. (1906-) Amer;
text
WISCONSIN I (statement); 1 ill

MERIDA, Carlos (1891-) Guat; ptr
RODMAN II 149-150 (statements)

MERISIO, Pepi G. (1931-) Ital; photo
WALSH 505-506 (statement); 1 ill

MERITET, Michael (1948-) Amer; ptr
COLLABORATION 130-135 (essay:
"The Four Gates to Columbus"); 4 ill

MERKADO, Nissim (1935-) Bulg/Fren;
sclp
SKIRA 1978 114 (statement); 1 ill

MERKIN, Richard (1938-) Amer; ptr
NAYLOR 637-638 (statement); 1 ill
VARIAN I (statement); port

MERRILD, Knud (1894-1954) Dani; ptr
CIRCLE no.6 39-40, 42, 44, 46 (essay:
"A Holiday in Paint"); port; 3 ill
ILLINOIS 1952 214-215 (statement); 1 ill
MILLER 1942 107-111 (statement); port;
5 ill

MERRITT, Warren Chase (1897-) Amer;
ptr
M.H. DE YOUNG 94 (response); self port

MERZ, Mario (1925-) Ital; sclp, instal,
envir
CHOIX 31 (statement, o.p. 1982); 1 ill
MULLER 140-149 (statement); ports; 13
ill
SKIRA 1977 55 (statement); 1 ill
STEDELIJK 168-169 (statement, in
Italian); 3 ill

MESCHES, Arnold (1923-) Amer; illus
CALIFORNIA--DRAWING (statement); 2
ill

MESEJEAN, Pablo (1937-) envir
PREMIO NACIONAL 1966 28-29
(statement); port; 1 ill

MESENS, Edouard Leon Theodore
(1903-1971) Belg; ptr
JEAN 417-418 (poem: "To Put an End
to the Age of Machinery the English
Poets Make Smoke," o.p. 1944)
LONDON BULLETIN no.3 26-28, 31
(poems: "Le Mieux est l'Ennemi du
Bien," "L'Art du Portrait Implique
Toujours Certaines Concessions a la
Caricature," "Le Mari Aride")
LONDON BULLETIN no.10 19 (poem:
"Le Moyen d'En Finis")
LONDON BULLETIN no.18/19/20 20-21
(letter)
LONDON BULLETIN no.18/19/20 47
(poems: "Jeune," "Faible,"
"Amoureux," "Baiser")
QUADRUM no.16 115-122 (text piece)

MESHAK, Mara ( )
CRISS-CROSS no.1 17-18 ("Notes on a
Dream Workshop")

MESSAGER, Annette (1943-) Fren; ptr,
photo
ARTIST AND CAMERA 46-47
(statement); 2 ill
EMANUEL II 621-622 (statement); 1 ill

IDENTITE 59-62, 95 (interview with Jacques Clayssen); port
NAYLOR 639 (statement); 1 ill
SKIRA 1977 45 (statement); 3 ill
SKIRA 1979 98 (statement); 1 ill

MESSAGIER, Jean Felicien Emile (1920-) Fren; ptr
DOUZE ANS 273-275 (statement); port; 6 ill
GRENIER 145-154 (interview)
SKIRA 1976 83 (statement); 1 ill
YALE 67 (statement)

METCALFE, Eric W.
SEE: BRUTE, Dr.

METZ, Mike (1945-) Amer
SONDHEIM 213-225 (text piece: "Models"); 18 ill

METZ, Ted (1949-) Amer; pott
NOSANOW I 95 (statement); 1 ill

METZINGER, Jean (1883-) Fren; ptr
CHIPP 207-216 (extract from *Cubism*, originally published in 1912/13, with Albert Gleizes); self port
FRY 59-60 ("Notes on Painting," o.p. 1910)
FRY 68-69 ("Cubism and Tradition," o.p. 1911)
FRY 105-111 (essay: "Cubism," o.p. 1912)
LHOTE 428-433 (extract from *Du Cubisme*, o.p. 1913)
POENSGEN 81-84 ("Der Kubismus," o.p. 1912)
RAYNAL 231-235 (statement); 2 ill
SEGHERS 131-137 (essay: "Cubism," o.p. 1912)

METZKER, Ray K. (1931-) Amer; photo
DIAMONSTEIN III 93-102 (interview); 6 ill

WALSH 508-509 (statement); 1 ill

METZNER, Sheila (1939-) Amer; photo
TIME-LIFE IV 94-95 (statement); 1 ill

MEURICE, Jean-Michel (1938-) Fren; ptr
SKIRA 1975 92 (statement); 1 ill
SKIRA 1979 56-57 (statement); 1 ill

MEW, Tommy (Thomas Joseph) (1942-) Amer; ptr
NAYLOR 642-643 (statement); 1 ill

MEYBODEN, Hans (1901-1965) Germ; ptr
WINGLER 107-108 (essay: "Oskar Kokoschka das amt des Kunstlers," p.p.)

MEYER, Hannes (Hans) (1889-1954) Swis; arch
CONRADS 117-120) ("Building," o.p. 1928)

MEYER, Pedro (1935-) Span; photo
WALSH 509-510 (statement); 1 ill

MEYER, Ursula ( ) Germ/Amer; sclp
BATTCOCK V 366, 370-372 (interview with Elaine Varian, o.p. 1967); 1 ill
MEYER vii-xx ("Introduction")
VARIAN IV (interview); port; 2 ill

MEYER, Wilhelm Olaf (1935-) SoAf; arch
EMANUEL I 542-544 (statement); 1 ill

MEYEROWITZ, Joel (1938-) Amer; photo
CAMPBELL 178-189 (statement); port; 12 ill
DIAMONSTEIN III 103-116 (interview); 7 ill

MEYEROWITZ, William (1898-) Amer; ptr
100 CONTEMPORARY 138-139 (statement); port; 1 ill

MEYERS, Marshall ( ) arch
PROCESSES 31-54 (statement)

MEZA, Guillermo (1919-) Mexi; ptr
PREMIER BILAN 307 (statement); port
STEWART 152-155 (statement); port; 3 ill

MICHAEL, Lily (1912-) Amer; ptr
ILLINOIS 1952 215-216 (statement); 1 ill

MICHAEL, Peggy (1942-) Amer; photo
FUGITIVE (statement); 1 ill

MICHAELS-PAQUE, Joan (1937-) Amer; text
WISCONSIN I (statement); 1 ill
WISCONSIN II (statement); 1 ill

MICHALS, Duane (1932-) Amer; photo, print, perf
DIAMONSTEIN III 117-130 (interview); 9 ill
DUGAN 131-148 (interview, 1975); port
GEORGIA 69-71 (statement); 1 ill
HAND COLORED 13-14 (statement); 1 ill
SKIRA 1977 88 (statement); 2 ill
SKIRA 1980 102-103 (statement); 3 ill
TIME-LIFE III 218-219 (statements, p.p.); 7 ill
TIME-LIFE IV 90-91 (statement); 1 ill

MICHAUX, Henri (1899-) Belg/Fren; ptr
ART SINCE v.1 155 (poem, o.p. 1951)
CLAUS 97-102 (statement)
PLATSCHEK 117-119 ("La Cordillera de los Andes")
PLATSCHEK 121-123 ("Gebilde")
PLATSCHEK 125 ("Alphabet")
PLATSCHEK 126-130 ("Brief"); 3 ill

QUADRUM no.3 15-22 ("Vitesse et Temps"); 5 ill
SKIRA 1975 111 (statement); 1 ill
VINGTIEME N. S. no.4 47-50 (essay: "Signes"); 4 ill

MICHEL, Delbert (1938-) Amer; ptr
MICHIGAN 28-29 (statement); 2 ill

MICHELL, Roger (1947-) pott
CAMERON 96-105 (response); 10 ill

MICHELS, Douglas ( )
SEE: ANT FARM

MICHENER, Diana (1940-) Amer; photo
RUDDICK 147-161 (interview); port; 10 ill

MICHENER, Robert (1935-) Amer/Cana; ptr
AWARDS 12-15 (statement); 4 ill

MICHENER, Sally (1935-) Amer; sclp, pott
POINT OF VIEW 21 (statement); 1 ill

MICHOD, Susan (1945-) Amer; ptr
SULTAN 51-55 ("Some Thoughts on Pattern, Painting..."); 2 ill

MICUS, Edward (1925-) Germ; ptr
SKIRA 1976 68 (statement); 1 ill

MIDDAUGH, Robert (1935-) Amer; ptr
ILLINOIS 1965 78 (statement); 1 ill

MIDDLEBROOK, David (1944-) Amer; pott
VIEWPOINT 1978 22-23 (statement); 4 ill

MIDDLETON, Samuel (1927-) Amer; ptr
ILLINOIS 1959 247 (statement); 1 ill

MIDGETTE, Willard Franklin (1937-1978) Amer; ptr
ILLINOIS 1974 79-81 (statement); 8 ill
NAYLOR 644-645 (statement); 1 ill
SUPERREAL 136-137 (statement, 1977); 1 ill

MILES VAN DER ROHE, Ludwig (1886-1969) Germ/Amer; arch
CONRADS 74-75 ("Working Theses," o.p. 1923)
CONRADS 102 ("On Form in Architecture," o.p. 1927)
CONRADS 106-107 (essay: "Industrialized Building," o.p. 1924)
CONRADS 123 ("The New Era," o.p. 1930)
CONRADS 154 ("Technology and Architecture," o.p. 1950)
GROHMANN 475-479 ("Das Schone ist der Glanz des Wahren," p.p. 1950)
HEYER 26-36 (interview); 20 ill
ROTH 504-507 (talk: "Inaugural Address as Director of Architecture at Armour Institute of Technology," given in 1938)
ROTH 507-508 (talk: "Address to the Illinois Institute of Technology," given in 1950)
SCHMIDT 44 (letter, 1933)

MIGNECO, Giuseppe (1908-) Ital; ptr
VERZOCCHI 279-283 (statement); self port; 1 ill

MIHALY, Robert (1947-) Amer; sclp
SCULPTURE OUTSIDE (statement); 4 ill

MIHELIC, Polde (1923-) Yugo; ptr
TOMASEVIC 221-223 (statement); port; 1 ill

MIHICH, Velizar
SEE: VASA

MIKHAILOVSKY, Wilhelm (1942-) Russ; photo
WALSH 515-516 (statement); 1 ill

MIKI, Tomio (1937-) Japa; sclp
KUNG 172-175 (statement); port; 3 ill

MILES, Jeanne (1908-) Amer; sclp, ptr
ART NOW v.1 no.10 (statement); 1 ill

MILES, Richard ( ) Amer; sclp
ARTPARK 1980 (statement); 3 ill

MILKOWSKI, Antoni (1935-) Amer; sclp, envir
ARTPARK 1978 42-45 (statement); port; 6 ill

MILLAR, Onnie (1919-) Amer; sclp
FAX II 202-220 (statements); port; 1 ill

MILLER, Algernon (1945-) Amer; sclp, instal
EVENTS I 46 (statement); 1 ill

MILLER, Archie (1930-) Cana; sclp
CANADA 52-53 (statement); port; 3 ill

MILLER, Brenda ( ) sclp
AVALANCHE no.8 69 (statement); 1 ill

MILLER, Burr (1904-) Amer; print
MYLAR 22-23 (statement); 1 ill

MILLER, Eva Hamlin (1931-) Amer; ptr
LEWIS I 107 (statement); port; 1 ill

MILLER, Henry (1891-1980) Amer; ptr
ARTFORUM v.2 no.1 27-30 (essay: "Are We Going Anywhere?"); port; 8 ill
SEGHERS 276-279 (extract from *The Waters Reglitterized*, 1950)

MILLER, John ( ) arch
SEE: COLQUHOUN AND MILLER

MILLER, Kenneth Hayes (1876-1952)
Amer; ptr
BRITANNICA 81 (statement); port; 1 ill

MILLER, Larry (1944-) Amer; video
GEORGIA 72-74 (statement); port; 2 ill
GEORGIA 118-166 (group discussion:
"Artists' Convention," in Athens, GA.,
1/7/1977, moderated by Jan van der
Marck)

MILLER, Melissa (1951-) Amer; ptr
GUMPERT III 68-70 (statement)

MILLER, Michael J. (1954-) Amer; ptr
NOSANOW II 58-59 (statement); 1 ill

MILLER, Nachume (1949-) Amer; instal
SHEARER 45-49 (interview); 3 ill

MILLER, Richard Kidwell (1930-) Amer;
ptr
FULBRIGHT 36,37 (statement); 1 ill
VARIAN I (statement); port

MILLER, Roland ( )
SEE: CAMERON AND MILLER

MILLER, Sylvia (1942-) Amer; metal
CONTEMPORARY   AFRICAN
(statement); port; 1 ill

MILLETT, Peter ( ) Cana; ptr
GUENTHER 84-85 (statement); port; 1
ill

MILLMAN, Edward (1907-1964) Amer;
ptr
ZAIDENBERG 65-71 (essay: "The Use
of the Object in Painting"); 4 ill

MILLONZI, Victor (1915-) Amer; sclp,
light
VARIAN II (statement); port

MILLS, Lev (1940-) Amer; print
LEWIS I REVISED 110 (statement); port;
1 ill

MILNES, Robert (1948-) Amer; pott
HERMAN 88 (statement); port; 1 ill

MILOJEVIC, Dobrosav (1948-) Yugo;
ptr
TOMASEVIC 224-227 (statement); port;
2 ill

MILTON, Peter (1930-) Amer; print
VISUAL v.4 no.4 4-7 (interview); 3 ill

MINARDI, Pat ( )
WOMANART   v.1   no.3   26-27,   38
(response); port

MINASSIAN, Leone (1905-) Ital; ptr
PREMIER BILAN 308 (statement); port

MINGUZZI, Luciano (1911-) Ital; sclp
RITCHIE 90-93 (statement); port; 4 ill

MINICK, Roger (1944-) Amer; photo
FUGITIVE (statement); 1 ill
WALSH 518-519 (statement); 1 ill

MINKKINEN,   Arno   Rafael   (1945-   )
Amer; photo
WALSH 519-520 (statement); 1 ill

MINKOWITZ, Norma ( ) Amer; text
FIBER 38-39 (statement); 1 ill

MINTON, John ( )
ROTHENSTEIN 61 (letter)

MINTZ, Harry (1909-) Amer; ptr
ILLINOIS 1950 192-193 (statement); 1 ill

illus
COMPUTER (statements); 1 ill
CRONE (statement); 1 ill

MOL, Pieter Laurens (1946-) Dutc;
photo, perf
STEDELIJK 170 (statement in Dutch); 1
ill

MOLARSKY, Maurice (1885-) Amer; ptr
100 CONTEMPORARY 140-141
(statement); self port; 1 ill

MOLINARI, Guido (1933-) Czec; sclp,
ptr
CANADA 18-19 (statement); port; 2 ill
PARACHUTE no.4 31-36 (interview); 6
ill

MOLINARO, Louise (1953-) Amer; pott
HERMAN 89 (statement); port; 1 ill

MOLLER, Hans (1905-) Germ/Amer; ptr
ILLINOIS 1955 221-222 (statement); 1 ill

MOLLETT, Michael (1946-) Amer; envir
ARTISTS no.1 7-8 ("Mail Art Keeps Me
Sane," and "To Hell with the
System")

MOLNAR, Francois (1922-) Hung/Fren;
ptr
KEPES IV 204-217 (essay: "The Unit
and the Whole: Fundamental Problem
of the Plastic Arts")

MOLZAHN, Johannes (1892-1965)
Germ/Amer; ptr
JANIS I 61 (statement); 1 ill

MONDRAGON
SEE: ENRIQUE

MONDRIAN, Piet (1872-1944) Dutc; ptr

ABSTRACT 225-229, 232, 234-235
(essay: "A New Realism"); 1 ill
ABSTRACTION no.1 25 (statement); 2
ill
ABSTRACTION no.2 31 (statement); 2
ill
ART SINCE v.1 289 (statement, o.p.
1917)
BERCKELAERS 173-176 (essay:
"Plastique Pure," o.p. 1942); 1 ill
CHIPP 321-323 (essay: "Natural
Reality and Abstract Reality," o.p.
1919); self port
CHIPP 349-362 (essay: "Plastic Art
and Pure Plastic Art," o.p. 1937)
CHIPP 362-364 (statement, 1943, o.p.
1946)
CIRCLE 41-56 (essay: "Plastic and
Pure Plastic Art (Figurative Art and
Non-Figurative Art)")
FRIEDENTHAL 234-236 (letters to Theo
van Doesburg, 1915; statement, o.p.
1917); 1 ill
GOLDWATER 426-429 (statements,
1932, 1933, 1937)
GUGGENHEIM II 32-33 (essay:
"Abstract Art")
GUGGENHEIM II 54-55 (statement, o.p.
1920); 1 ill
JANIS I 128 (statement); 1 ill
POENSGEN 106-107, 109-111 ("Der
Neoplastizismus,")
PROTTER 190-191 (extract from essay:
"Plastic Art and Pure Plastic Art,"
1937)
SEUPHOR 100-104 (essay: "The New
Plastic Approach to Painting," o.p.
1917)
TRACKS v.3 no.1/2 19-43 ("Writings"
notes and fragments, some
handwritten)

MONEO, Jose Rafael (1937-) Span; arch
ARCHER 89-92, 98 (statement); port; 4
ill

EMANUEL I 551-552 (statement); 1 ill

MONET, Claude (1840-1926) Fren; ptr
GOLDWATER 313-315 (letters to Gustave Geoffroy, 1909, 1915); 1 ill

MONGRAIN, Claude (1948-) Cana; sclp
PARACHUTE no.2 20-22 (statements); 5 ill

MONK, Meredith (1942-) Amer; perf
AVALANCHE no.13 28-33 (interview); 15 ill
LIVE no.3 16 (statement)
LIVE no.4 19-20 (letter)

MONORY, Jacques (1934-) Fren; ptr
EMANUEL II 634-635 (statement); 1 ill
KUNST UND POLITIK (statement); port; 2 ill
SKIRA 1979 98 (statement); 1 ill
SKIRA 1980 84-85 (statement); 5 ill

MONRO, Nicholas (1936-) Brit; sclp
CONTEMPORARY (statement); port; 2 ill

MONROE, Arthur (1935-) Amer; ptr
LEWIS I REVISED 26 (statement); port; 1 ill

MONTA, Mozuna Kikoo (1941-) Japa; arch
EMANUEL I 552-554 (statement); 1 ill
GA HOUSES no.4 305-329 (statement); 78 ill

MONTANEZ-ORTIZ, Rafael (1934-) Amer; sclp
RAICES 23 (statement); 1 ill

MONTANO, Linda (1942-) Amer; perf
TUCKER II 34 (statement); port

MONTENEGRO, Enrique (1917-) Amer; ptr
ILLINOIS 1963 194 (statement); 1 ill

MONTES, Fernando ( ) Fren; arch
ARCHITECTURES 120-125 ("Entretien avec Richard"); 8 ill

MONTGOMERY, Evangeline J. (1933-) Amer; metal
LEWIS I REVISED 86 (statement); port; 3 ill

MONTI, Cesare (1891-) Ital; ptr
VERZOCCHI 285-289 (statement); self port; 1 ill

MOON, Jeremy (1934-1973) Brit; ptr
BOWNESS 23-24, 131-133 (statement); 2 ill
ENGLISH 164-169 (statement); port; 7 ill

MOON, Michael (1937-) Brit; ptr
CONTEMPORARY (statement); port; 2 ill
NAYLOR 656 (statement)

MOON, Sarah ( ) Fren; photo
BOOTH 158-169 (interview); port; 7 ill

MOONEY, John David (1937-) Amer; envir
ARTPARK 1982 26-29, 47 (statement); port; 6 ill

MOORE, Arthur Cotton (1935-) Amer; arch
EMANUEL I 554-555 (statement); 1 ill

MOORE, Charles T., Jr.
SEE: KRUEGER, William

MOORE, Charles W. (1925-) Amer; arch
BUILDINGS 30-33 (statement); 3 ill

MOORE, Sabra ( ) Amer; ptr
EVENTS II 26, 28-30, 40-41, 44-45 (statements); 3 ill
PHILLPOT (statement)

MOORMAN, Charlotte ( ) Amer; video
BATTCOCK VI 121-137 ("Videa, Vidiot, Videology," o.p. 1964 and 1976); 7 ill

MOOS, Max von (1903-) Swis; ptr
NAYLOR 657-658 (statement); 1 ill

MOPP, Maximilian (1885-) Aust/Amer; ptr
M.H. DE YOUNG 95 (response); self port

MORADO, Jose Chavez (Jose Chavez-Morado) (1909-) Mexi; ptr
STEWART 112-115 (statement); port; 3 ill
PREMIER BILAN 308 (statement); self port

MORALES, Armando (1927-) Nica/Amer; ptr
ILLINOIS 1965 72 (statement); 1 ill
VARIAN I (statement); port

MORAN, Douglas (1949-) Amer; sclp
HOUSE 70-71 (statement); 1 ill

MORANDI, Giorgio (1890-1964) Ital; ptr
RODITI 49-64 (interview); port; 1 ill

MORANDI, Tom ( ) Amer; sclp
GUENTHER 86-87 (statement); port; 1 ill

MORANG, Alfred (1901-1958) Amer; ptr
CIRCLE no.6 31-37 (story: "Darling Sister and the Pound of Liver")

MORATH, Inge (1923-) Aust/Amer; photo
WALSH 533-534 (statement); 1 ill

MOREHEAD, Gerry ( ) ptr, illus
REALLIFE no.5 16-18 ("Dot and Dash")

MOREHOUSE, William (1929-) Amer; ptr
ILLINOIS 1961 139 (response); port; 1 ill

MOREIRA, Jorge Machado (1904-) Braz; arch
EMANUEL I 559-561 (statement); 1 ill

MORELLET, Francois (1926-) Fren; sclp, instal, light
CHOIX 32 (statement); 1 ill
EMANUEL II 640-642 (statement); 1 ill
LUMIERE (statement); port; 2 ill
NAYLOR 659-660 (statement); 1 ill
SKIRA 1979 80 (statement); 1 ill
SKIRA 1980 95, 151 (statement); 3 ill
STEDELIJK 172-173 (statement, in French); 3 ill

MORELLI, Enzo (1896-) Ital; ptr
VERZOCCHI 291-295 (statement); self port; 1 ill

MORENI, Mattia (1920-) Ital; ptr
VERZOCCHI 297-301 (statement); self port; 1 ill

MORENO CAPDEVILA, Francisco
SEE: CAPDEVILA, Francisco Moreno

MORETTI, Carlo ( ) Ital; arch
GA HOUSES no.1 168-173 (statement); 11 ill

MORGAN, Barbara (1900-) Amer; photo, ptr
DIAMONSTEIN III 131-141 (interview); 6 ill
LIGHT 42-47 (statement); 5 ill
MITCHELL 178-198 (statement); port; 18 ill
WALSH 534-537 (statement); 1 ill

MORGAN, Cheryl ( ) Amer; arch, design
LIFE 140-145 (interview); port

MORGAN, Norma Gloria (1928-) Amer; ptr
FAX I 253-266 (statements); port; 1 ill
FINE 216-221-222 (statements and letter, 1971); 2 ill

MORGAN, Patrick H. (1904-) Amer; ptr
ILLINOIS 1952 216-217 (statement)

MORGAN, Robert C. (1943-) Amer; perf, photo
ART-RITE no.14 5, 10 (response)
ART-RITE no.19 12 (text piece: "Swim Parables")
WHITE WALLS no.9 24-36 ("Phrases and Revisions for Progress Backstroke")

MORGAN, William (1930-) Amer; arch
EMANUEL I 561-563 (statement); 1 ill

MORIGUCHI, Kako ( ) Japa; text
ADACHI 46-49 (statement); port; 5 ill

MORINAKA, Dennis ( ) Amer; wood
MEILACH 148 (statement); 3 ill

MORITA, Shiryu (1912-) Japa; ptr, calli
CLAUS 102-107 (statement)
KUNG 141-145 (statement); port; 2 ill
YAMADA 306-311 (interview with Tadao Takemoto, 1972)

MORLEY, David (1956-) Brit; arch
SPIRIT 58-63 (statement); 12 ill

MORLEY, Malcolm (1931-) Brit/Amer; ptr
BATTCOCK III 170-186 (statements, o.p. 1973); 5 ill
RUSSELL J 95 (statement)

SAO PAULO 88-89 (statement); port; 1 ill

MORLOTTI, Ennio (1910-) Ital; ptr
PAINTING 10 (statement); port; 1 ill
PREMIER BILAN 309 (statement); port
VERZOCCHI 303-307 (statement); self port; 1 ill

MORO, Peter (1911-) Brit; arch
EMANUEL I 564-566 (statement); 1 ill

MOROLES, Jesus Bautista (1950-) Amer; sclp
WINSTON-SALEM 58-65 (statement); 7 ill

MORONI, Aldo ( ) sclp, envir
ARTPARK 1978 46-49 (statement); 11 ill

MORREL, Owen (1950-) Amer; sclp
ARTPARK 1980 (statement); 4 ill

MORRIS, Adrian (1929-) Brit; ptr
HAYWARD 1978 18-21 (statement); 5 ill

MORRIS, Carl (1911-) Amer; ptr
GUENTHER 88-89 (statement); port; 1 ill
ILLINOIS 1957 229-230 (response); 1 ill
ILLINOIS 1959 249 (statement); 1 ill
ILLINOIS 1961 210 (response); port; 1 ill

MORRIS, George L. K. (1905-1975) Amer; sclp, ptr
ABSTRACT 13-14, 60, 147 (essay: "The Quest for an Abstract Tradition"); 1 ill
ABSTRACT 85-90 (essay: "The American Abstract Artists")
ABSTRACT 198-199, 201-202 (essay: "Aspects of Picture-Making")
ART NOW v.1 no.6 (statement); 1 ill
AXIS no.4 9-10 (essay: "The Gallery of Living Art, New York University")

BRITANNICA 82 (statement); port; 1 ill
ILLINOIS 1953 204 (statement); 1 ill
ILLINOIS 1965 120-121 (statement); 1 ill
PLASTIQUE no.1 12-14 (essay: "On the Abstract Tradition"); 1 ill
PLASTIQUE no.3 2-4 (essay: "A la Recherche d'une Tradition de l'Art Abstrait"); 1 ill
ROSE II 100-101 (extract from essay: "To Charles Demuth," o.p. 1938)
ROSE II 126-128 (extract from essay: "To the American Abstract Artists," o.p. 1938)

MORRIS, Hilda ( ) Amer; sclp
GUENTHER 90-91 (statement); port; 1 ill

MORRIS, Kyle Randolph (1918-1979) Amer; ptr
ILLINOIS 1955 222-223 (statement); 1 ill
ILLINOIS 1961-214 (response); port; 1 ill
IT IS no.3 25 ("A Cahier Leaf")

MORRIS, Richard Alan ( ) Amer; coll
CALIFORNIA--COLLAGE (statement)

MORRIS, Robert (1931-) Amer; sclp, ptr
ART AND TECHNOLOGY 238-240 (project proposal); port
ART NOW v.1 no.6 (statement); 1 ill
ART SINCE v.1 293 (statement, o.p. 1968)
ARTFORUM v.4 no.6 42-44 (essay: "Notes on Sculpture"); 2 ill
ARTFORUM v.5 no.2 20-23 (essay: "Notes on Sculpture, Part 2"); 1 ill
ARTFORUM v.5 no.10 24-29 ("Notes on Sculpture, Part 3"); 3 ill
ARTFORUM v.6 no.8 33-35 (essay: "Anti Form"); 2 ill
AVALANCHE no.1 12-13 (project proposal: "Pace and Process"); 12 ill
AVALANCHE no.3 30-35 (project description); 5 ill

AVALANCHE no.8 22-25 ("Exchange '73: From a Videotape"); 15 ill
BATTCOCK V 222-235 (essay: "Notes on Sculpture," o.p. 1966); 3 ill
CELANT 192-197 (statement); 5 ill
CONCEPTUAL ART 47, 50, 52 (statements)
JOHNSON 184-188 (essay: "Anti Form," o.p. 1968); 1 ill
JOHNSON 210-215 (essay: "The Present Tense of Space," o.p. 1978)
MEYER 184-185 (statement, o.p. 1970); 1 ill
ROSE II REVISED 180-182 (extract from "Notes on Sculpture," o.p. 1966)
ROSE II REVISED 212-214 (extract from "Notes on Sculpture," o.p. 1969)
RUSSELL J 94-95 (essay: "On Drawing")
STEDELIJK 174 (statement, o.p. 1972); 2 ill
TRACKS v.2 no.3 47-52 ("Cold Oracle," originally a spoken text, presented in 1974 at Leo Castelli Gallery, New York)
VRIES 192-243 (essay: "Notes on Sculpture," o.p. 1966)

MORRIS, Wright Marion (1910-) Amer; photo
WALSH 538-540 (statement); 1 ill

MORRISON, Ann K. (1929-) Cana; ptr
POINT OF VIEW 22 (statement); 1 ill

MORRISON, Art (1943-) Amer; pott
VIEWPOINT 1978 24-27 (statement); 4 ill

MORRISON, Clivia (1909-) Amer; sclp
ILLINOIS 1963 135 (statement); 1 ill

MORRISON, Robert (1939-) Amer; ptr
O'KANE (statement); 1 ill

statement: "What Abstract Art Means to Me," o.p. 1951)
CRISPO I (statemen); 18 ill
DIAMONSTEIN I 239-253 (interview); ports
FORTY (extract from talk given at the Fogg Art Museum, Cambridge, MA); 2 ill
ILLINOIS 1955 223 (statement, from the introduction to the brochure of an exhibition of sculpture by David Smith, 1950); 1 ill
ILLINOIS 1951 201-202 (statement); 1 ill
IT IS no.5 34-38 (group discussion)
JANIS I 65 (statement); 1 ill
JEAN 392-394 (extract from essay: "Notes on Chirico," o.p. 1942)
JOHNSON 27-29 (statement, o.p. 1955); 1 ill
KERBER 194 (extract from essay: "Beyond the Aesthetic," o.p. 1946)
LETTERS 26 (letter); 1 ill
MILLER 1946 34-38 (statement); 6 ill
MOTHERWELL 8-22 (three group discussions: "Artists' Sessions at Studio 35," New York, 1950)
NEW DECADE 58-59 (statement); 2 ill
O'HARA 66 (extract from television interview with Bryan Robertson, 12/15/1964)
O'HARA 68 (segment of lecture given at Yale University, 4/22/65)
PERSONAL (statement)
POSSIBILITIES 1 (preface to *Possibilities I*)
PROTTER 250 (statement, 1955)
ROSE II 129-130 (statement, o.p. 1947)
ROSE II 130-135 (extract from essay: "The Modern Painter's World," o.p. 1944)
ROSE II REVISED 103-104 (statement, o.p. 1947-48, with Harold Rosenberg)
ROSE II REVISED 104-107 (extract from essay: "The Modern Painter's World," o.p. 1944)

ROSE II REVISED 142-145 (group discussion, o.p. 1952)
SEITZ II xi-xiv ("Foreword")
SEITZ II 168-169 ("Chronology of Abstract Expressionism")
SPENCER 299-302 ("What Abstract Art Means To Me," o.p. 1951); 1 ill
TIGER no.6 46-48 (essay: "A Tour of the Sublime")
TRACKS v.1 no.1 10-16 (essay: "On the Humanism of Abstraction")

MOTONAGA, Sadamasa (1922-) Japa; ptr
KUNG 76-79 (statement); port; 3 ill

MOTOROZESKU, Marioara (1928-) Yugo; ptr
TOMASEVIC 228-230 (statement); port; 1 ill

MOTTET, Yvonne (1906-) Fren; ptr
FRASNAY 349-357 (poem); ports

MOTZKIN, Judith E. ( ) Amer; pott
HAYSTACK 44 (statement); 1 ill

MOUCHA, Miloslav (1942-) Czec/Fren; ptr
SKIRA 1976 76 (statement); 1 ill

MOULPIED, Deborah de
SEE: DE MOULPIED, Deborah

MOURAUD, Tania (1942-) Fren; ptr, instal, photo
EMANUEL II 650-651 (statement); 1 ill
NAYLOR 666-667 (statement); 1 ill
SKIRA 1979 86 (extract from essay: "Focus or the Function of Art"); 1 ill

MOURGUE, Olivier (1939-) Fren; design
DESIGN 23-26 (essay: "Design, Invention, and Fantasy"); 5 ill

MOUTON, Grover (1946-) Amer; instal
MCCLINTIC 73-75 (statement); 2 ill

MOY, Seong (1921-) Chin/Amer; ptr
ILLINOIS 1951 202 (statement)
ILLINOIS 1959 250 (statement); 1 ill

MOYA DEL PINO, Jose ( ) ptr
BETHERS II 116-117 (statement); 2 ill

MOYER, Roy (1921-) Amer; ptr
ILLINOIS 1959 251 (statement)

MOYNIHAN, Rodrigo (1910-) Brit; ptr
CONTEMPORARY (statement); port; 2 ill

MR. APOLOGY ( )
GUMPERT I 37-38 (statement); port

MR. MENTAL ( ) Amer; sclp
EVENTS I 45 (poem: "Dunce"); 1 ill

MR. PEANUT ()
SEE: PEANUT, MR.

MRAZ, Franjo (1910-) Yugo; ptr
TOMASEVIC 231-239 (statement); port; 2 ill

MUCHE, Georg (1895-) Germ; ptr
WINGLER 86-87 (essay: "Ich Habe Mit Schwitters Gemerzt," p.p.)
WINGLER 87-90 (essay: "Der Fisch des Kolumbus," p.p.)
WINGLER 90-93 (essay: "Lyonel Feininger Nachruf," p.p.)

MUDFORD, Grant (1944-) Atrl; photo
TIME-LIFE IV 96-97 (statement); 1 ill

MUEHL, Otto (1925-) Aust; sclp
EMANUEL II 651-652 (statement)
NAYLOR 667-668 (statement); 1 ill

MUELLER, Eugene (1946-) Amer; ptr
WISCONSIN I (statement); 1 ill

MUELLER, George Ludwig (1929-) Amer; ptr
ILLINOIS 1955 224-225 (statement); 1 ill

MUELLER-BRITTNAU, Willy (1938-) Swis; ptr
NAYLOR 669-670 (statement); 1 ill

MUJADEDY, Aziz ( ) ptr
KATZ 197-208 (interview); port; 1 ill

MUKAI, Ryokichi (1918-) Japa; sclp
KUNG 176-179 (statement); port; 2 ill

MULLANE, Fred ( ) photo
LAPLANTE 66-75 (interview); port; 1 ill

MULLANEY, Tom (1952-) Amer; ptr
BOSTON III (interview); 1 ill

MULLEN, Phillip Edward (1942-) Amer; ptr
ART PATRON ART 49-50 (statement); port; 1 ill

MULLER, Betsy (1955-) Amer; paper, sclp
PAPERWORKS 22-23 (statement); 4 ill

MULLER, Dody (1927-) Amer; ptr
ART NOW v.3 no.4 (statement); 1 ill

MULLER, Hans ( ) Swis; ptr
REALLIFE no.8 19-21 ("Stations," 1970, o.p. 1980)

MULLER, Hans-Walter (1935-) Germ; light
LUMIERE (statement); port; 16 ill

MULLER, Jan (1922-1958) Germ/Amer;

ptr
SELZ 106-111 (statement: from a notebook, 1956); 4 ill
YOUNG 1957 (statement); 1 ill

MULLER, Peter (1927-) Atrl; arch
EMANUEL I 571-572 (statement); 1 ill

MULLER, Robert (1920-) Swis/Fren; sclp
DOUZE ANS 285-287 (statement); port; 5 ill

MULLER-POHLE, Andreas (1951-) Germ; photo
WALSH 543 (statement); 1 ill

MULLICAN, Lee (1919-) Amer; ptr
ARTFORUM v.1 no.10 25-26 (interview); 2 ill
BARRON 38-41 (essay: "Thoughts on the Dynaton, 1976")
CALIFORNIA--PAINTING 25 (statement); 1 ill
HOPKINS 110-111 (statement); port; 1 ill
ILLINOIS 1953 205-206 (statement); 1 ill
ILLINOIS 1955 225 (statement); 1 ill
ILLINOIS 1957 231 (response); 1 ill

MUNAKATA, Shiko (1903-) Japa; print
KUNG 154-157 (statement); port; 2 ill

MUNARI, Bruno (1907-) Ital; sclp, print
KINETISCHE (statement: "Manifesto del Macchinismo," 1952)

MUNCE, Howard ( ) Amer; sclp
ILLUSTRATION 84-89 (statement); port; 5 ill

MUNCH, Edvard (1863-1944) Norw; ptr
CHIPP 114-115 (statements, 1907-1908, 1928, 1929); self port

FRIEDENTHAL 159-160 (letter to Karen Bjolstad, 1903, p.p. 1949)
PROTTER 168-169 ("The Frieze of Death,: o.p. 1918)
THORN 50, 59, 116, 155 (statements, p.p.)

MUNDT, Ernest Karl (1905-) Amer; sclp, arch
ART AND ARTIST 108-124 (essay: "Sculpture for a Public Building"); 6 ill

MUNDY, Henry (1919-) Brit; ptr
BOWNESS 19-20, 68-70 (statement); 2 ill
GUGGENHEIM I 96-97 ("Effects Used in Painting," o.p. 1961)

MUNGUIA, Roberto (1953-) Amer; paper, sclp
PAPERWORKS 24-25 (statement); 5 ill

MUNKACSI, Kurt ( ) perf, sound
AVALANCHE no.5 36-45 (group discussion); 8 ill
AVALANCHE no.10 39-41 (interview); ports

MUNOZ, Godofredo Ortega (1905-) Span; ptr
PORCEL I 145-154 (interview); port

MUNOZ, Lucio (1930-) Span; ptr
SKIRA 1977 24 (statement); 1 ill

MUNOZ DE COTE DE CARLSON, Susana
SEE: CARLSON, Susana Munoz de Cote de

MUNTADAS, Antonio (1942-) Span/Amer; photo, coll, video
SKIRA 1979 87 (statement); 3 ill

MUNTER, Gabriele (1877-1962) Germ; ptr
RODITI 130-151 (interview); port; 2 ill

MURCH, Walter Tandy (1907-1967) Cana/Amer; ptr
NEW DECADE 60-62 (statement); 3 ill
TIGER no.4 42-47 (statement); 5 ill

MURCUTT, Glenn Marcus (1936-) Atrl; arch
EMANUEL I 574 (statement); 1 ill

MUROFUSHI, Jiro ( ) Japa; arch
GA HOUSES no.8 66-81 (statement); 40 ill

MURPHY, Haas ( )
ART-RITE no.9 36-38 (group discussion); port

MURRAY, Elizabeth (1940-) Amer; ptr
EARLY WORK (interview with Allan Schwartzman); 5 ill

MURRAY, Robert Gray (1936-) Cana/Amer; sclp, ptr
ARTFORUM v.5 no.2 45-47 (interview with Barbara Rose); 6 ill
CANADA 10-11 (statement); port; 1 ill
YOUNG 1965 (statement); 2 ill

MURRAY, Stuart (1926-) Atrl; arch
EMANUEL I 575-576 (statement); 1 ill

MURRAY-WHITE, Clive (1946-) Atrl; ptr, sclp
DE GROEN 170-179 (interview); port

MUSIC, Zoran Antonio (1909-) Ital; ptr
CHARBONNIER v.2 171-179 (interview)
GOLDAINE 147-149 (interview); port
GRENIER 157-162 (interview)
PAINTING 29 (statement); port; 1 ill

MUSZYNSKA, Teresa (1937-) Poli; text
NAYLOR 677-678 (statement); 1 ill

MUTHESIUS, Hermann (1861-1927) arch
CONRADS 26-27 (extract from essay: "Aims of the Werkbund," o.p. 1911)
CONRADS 28-29 ("Werkbund Theses and Antitheses," o.p. 1914)

MUTO, LaVerne ( )
WOMANART v.1 no.1 10-11 (essay: "The American Memorial Picture--A 'Feminist' Art")

MYDANS, Carl (1907-) Amer; photo
TIME-LIFE VI 12-17 (essay: "An Expert's Advice to the Tourist Photographer")
WALSH 546-547 (statement); 1 ill

MYER, John R. ( ) arch
PROCESSES 95-114 (interview with Lance Laver); 17 ill

MYERS, Barton (1934-) Amer/Cana; arch
CANADIAN 76-79 (statement); 5 ill
EMANUEL I 576-577 (statement); 1 ill
GA HOUSES no.2 94-103 (statement); 22 ill

MYERS, Ethel (1881-1960) Amer; sclp
ARMORY SHOW 26 (statement)

MYERS, Frances (1936-) Amer; print
WISCONSIN I (statement); 1 ill
WISCONSIN II (statement); 1 ill

MYERS, Gifford Chandler (1948-) Amer; sclp
HOUSE 72-73 (statement); 1 ill

MYERS, Joel Philip (1934-) Amer; glass
GLASS v.1 14-15 (statement)
GLASS v.5 (group discussion); port; 1 ill

MYERS, Rita ( ) Amer; perf, video
AVALANCHE no.11 24-27 (interview); 5
ill

MYERS, Sharon ( ) Amer; text
HAYSTACK 45 (statement); 1 ill

MYTHOLOGIES   QUOTIDIENNES
(group)
ART SINCE v.2 327 (statement, o.p.
1964)

N. E. THING CO., LTD. (group)
VANCOUVER (dialogue); 1 ill
VIEW v.2 no.4 (interview)
SEE ALSO: BAXTER, Iain

NADEL, Leonard ( ) Amer; photo
CALIFORNIA--PHOTOGRAPHY
(statement); port; 4 ill

NAEVE, Lowell ( ) ptr
FORD/VIEW v.5 no.3 11, 23 (essay:
"Artcraft Under Security Economy")

NAGARAJAN, Tamharahalli S. (1932-)
Indi; photo
WALSH 549-550 (statement); 1 ill

NAGDI, Omar El (1921-) sclp
BIENNALE 104-105 (statement); 1 ill

NAGEL, Peter (1941-) Germ; ptr
EMANUEL II 661-662 (statement)
HAUSSER 134-135 (statement); 1 ill
NAYLOR 679-680 (statement); 1 ill

NAGLE HARTRAY (arch firm)
SEE: NAGLE, James L.

NAGLE, James L. ( ) Amer; arch
GA HOUSES no.8 37-53 (statement);
port; 50 ill

NAGLE, Ron (1939-) Amer; pott
DIAMONSTEIN IV 166-179 (interview);
port; 13 ill
WECHSLER 100-105 (statement); port;
5 ill

NAGOURNEY, Peter (1940-)
TRACKS v.3 no.3 7-9 ("The New
Pyramid," extract from *The Silver
Pharaoh*)

NAIDUS, Beverly (1953-) Amer; ptr
GUMPERT III 71-72 (statement)

ISSUE (text piece: "Occupations"); 2
ill

NAKAGAWA, Naoto (1944-) ptr
SUPERREAL 140-141 (statement); 1 ill

NAKAMURA, Kazuo (1926-) Cana; sclp
CANADA 16-17 (statement); port; 1 ill

NAKIAN, Reuben (1897-) Amer; sclp
ALBRIGHT-KNOX   114-115   (letter,
9/1968); 1 ill

NALLE, Charles (1948-) Amer; pott
HERMAN 90 (statement); port; 1 ill

NAMBU, Yoshimatsu ( ) Japa; print
ADACHI 50-52 (statement); port; 2 ill

NANGERONI, Carlo (1922-) Amer; ptr
ILLINOIS 1959 252 (statement); 1 ill

NANNUCCI, Maurizio (1939-) Ital; perf,
photo, ptr
ART-RITE no.14 5, 10 (response)
EMANUEL II 660, 662-663 (statement); 1
ill
NAYLOR 680-682 (statement); 1 ill
SKIRA 1977 49 (statement); 12 ill
SKIRA 1979 68 (statement); 1 ill

NAP, Milan (1913-) Yugo; ptr
TOMASEVIC 240-242 (statement); port;
1 ill

NAPIORKOWSKA, Danka (1946-) pott
CAMERON E 96-105 (response); 10 ill

NARAHARA, Ikko (1931-) Japa; photo
WALSH 553-555 (statement); 1 ill

NASH, David (1945-) Brit; sclp
BRITISH (statement); 1 ill

NASH, Paul (1889-1946) Brit; ptr
AXIS no.1 24-26 (essay: "For, But Not With"); 1 ill
EVANS 38-42 (essay: "The Nest of Wild Stones"); 2 ill
EVANS 108-115 (essay: "Swanage, or Seaside Surrealism"); 4 ill
FRIEDENTHAL 216-221 (letters, 1917); 2 ill
LONDON BULLETIN no.2 10 (essay: "John Piper")
LONDON BULLETIN no.11 11-12 (essay: "F. E. McWilliam")
READ 10-11 (letter)
READ 77-86 (statement); port; 5 ill
ROTHENSTEIN 60, 62 (statements, p.p.)

NASISSE, Andy (1946-) Amer; pott
NOSANOW I 99 (statement); 1 ill

NATALINI, Bob ( ) Amer; sclp
ARTPARK 1981 (statement); port; 3 ill

NATIONS, Opal L. (1941-) illus, print
TRACKS v.2 no.1 34 ("A Sandwich of Ants Between Two Words")

NATKIEL, Paul (1946-) Amer; pott
HERMAN 91 (statement); port; 1 ill

NATKIN, Robert (1930-) Amer; ptr
ART NOW v.3 no.3 (statement); 1 ill
ILLINOIS 1963 211 (statement); 1 ill
YOUNG 1960 (statement); 1 ill

NAUMAN, Bruce (1941-) Amer; ptr, sclp, photo
AVALANCHE no.2 22-31 (interview); ports; 3 ill
CELANT 90-97 (statement); 6 ill
CONCEPTUAL ART 30, 34, 37 (statements)
JOHNSON 225-232 (interview with Willoughby Sharp, o.p. 1971); 1 ill

MULLER 116-127 (statement); ports; 5 ill
ROSE II REVISED 222 (extract from interview with Joe Raffaele and Elizabeth Baker, o.p. 1967)
ROSE II REVISED 222-223 (extract from interview with Willoughby Sharp, o.p. 1970)
TUCHMAN 49 (extract from interview with Joe Raffaele)
VISION no.1 44-45 (poem: "False Silences")

NAUMOVSKI, Vangel (1924-) Yugo; ptr
TOMASEVIC 243-249 (statement); port; 2 ill

NAVARRETE, Juan Ricardo (1942-) Amer; sclp
RAICES 35 (statement); 1 ill

NAVARRO, Rafael (1940-) Span; photo
WALSH 556-557 (statement); 1 ill

NAY, Ernst Wilhelm (1902-1968) Germ; ptr
CLAUS 48-55 (statement)
POENSGEN 121 ("Kontrpunkt," 1955)
POENSGEN 122 ("Human," 1955)

NAYLOR, John Geoffrey (1928-) Brit/Amer; sclp
SOUTHEAST (statement); port; 4 ill

NAYLOR, Martin (1944-) Brit; sclp
BRITISH (statement); 1 ill

NEAGU, Paul (1938-) Ruma/Brit; ptr, sclp
CONTEMPORARY (statement); port; 2 ill
EMANUEL II 667-668 (statement); 1 ill
NAYLOR 685-686 (statement); 1 ill
SKIRA 1980 138 (statement); 1 ill

NEALS, Otto (1930-) Amer; sclp, ptr
FAX II 149-164 (statements); port; 1 ill

NECHVATAL, Joseph ( )
WHITE WALLS no.3 4-11 (handwritten statement); 1 ill

NECHVATAL, Mary Bero (1949-) Amer; text
WISCONSIN II (statement); 1 ill

NEEDHAM, Wilma ( ) Amer; sclp, envir
ARTPARK 1982 30-31, 45 (statement); port; 10 ill

NEEL, Alice (1900-) Amer; ptr
DIAMONSTEIN I 254-263 (interview); ports
GRUEN 144-146 (statement); port
KUFRIN 132-152 (interview); ports
MILLER 121-129 (interview with Sally Swenson); port; 1 ill
MUNRO 120-130 (interview); port; 2 ill
NEMSER 112-147 (interview); port; 16 ill
SCHAPIRO 50 (statement); port; 1 ill
SUPERREAL 47-48, 86-87 (interview); 1 ill

NEFF, Edwin Wallace (1895-) Amer; arch
EMANUEL I 578-579 (statement); 1 ill

NEILAND, Brendan (1941-) Brit; ptr
CONTEMPORARY (statement); port; 2 ill
NAYLOR 687-688 (statement); 1 ill

NELLENS, Roger (1937-) Belg; ptr
SKIRA 1977 16 (statement); 1 ill

NELSON, George (1908-) Amer; design, arch
DESIGN 5-10 (essay: ▪The Design Process▪)

ROSNER 251-268 (interview); port

NELSON, Marilyn (1929-) Amer; ptr
CRISS-CROSS no.10 30-31 (statement); port; 2 ill

NELSON, Patricia ( ) Amer; metal
METALWORKS (statement); 1 ill

NELSON, Paul Daniel (1895-) Amer/Fren; arch
EMANUEL I 581-582 (statement); 1 ill

NELSON, Robert (1925-) Amer; film, ptr, print
CRISS-CROSS no.4 40-45 (interview with Fred Worden); 6 ill

NELSON, Robert Allen (1925-) Amer; ptr
ILLINOIS 1967 72-73 (statement); 1 ill

NEMEC, Vernita ( ) sclp
WOMANART v.1 no.1 4-7 (essay: ▪X^{12}▪)

NEMES, Endre (1909-) Czec/Swed; ptr
NAYLOR 689-690 (statement); 1 ill

NEMOURS, Aurelie (1910-) Fren; ptr
SEUPHOR 232-233 (statement); 1 ill

NEPOTE, Alexander (1913-) Amer; ptr
ILLINOIS 1951 202-203 (statement); 1 ill
ILLINOIS 1952 218-219 (statement); 1 ill

NERI, Manuel (1930-) Amer; sclp
HOPKINS 50-51 (statement); port; 1 ill
NAYLOR 690-692 (statement); 1 ill

NERLINGER, Oskar (1893-) Germ; ptr, print
THORN 26, 67, 73 (statements, p.p.)

NERVI, Pier Luigi (1891-1979) Ital; arch
KEPES VI 96-104 (essay: ■Is Architecture Moving Toward Unchangeable Forms?■); 5 ill
KEPES VI 105-110 (essay: ■On the Design Process■); 3 ill

NESBITT, Lowell Blair (1933-) Amer; print, ptr
MYLAR 14-15 (statement); 1 ill
SAO PAULO 90-91 (statement); port; 1 ill

NESSIM, Barbara (1939-) Amer; ptr
INTERVIEWS 19-20 (interview); port; 1 ill

NETSCH, Walter (1920-) Amer; arch
KEPES IX 62-73 (extract from ■private communications■ with John E. Burchard)

NETTLES, Bea (1946-) Amer; photo
DUGAN 113-129 (interview, 1978); port
WALSH 557-558 (statement); 1 ill

NEUHAUS, Carolyn (1956-) Amer; ptr
RICKERT 1980 (statement); port; 3 ill

NEUHAUS, Eugen (1879-1963) Germ/Amer; ptr
M.H. DE YOUNG 98 (response)

NEUHAUS, Max ( ) Amer; sound
ARTPARK 1975 88-91 (statement); port; 7 ill

NEUMAN, David J. ( )
ON SITE no.5/6 44-48 (essay: ■Personal Mobility in the U.S.A.■)

NEUMAN, Robert S. (1926-) Amer; ptr
FULBRIGHT 38 (statement)
ILLINOIS 1952 219 (statement); 1 ill
ILLINOIS 1953 206-207 (statement); 1 ill

ILLINOIS 1961 123 (response); port; 1 ill
ILLINOIS 1965 130 (statement); 1 ill

NEUSTEIN, Joshua (1940-) Amer; perf, photo
NAYLOR 693-694 (statement); 3 ill

NEUSUSS, Floris M. (1937-) Germ; photo
WALSH 558-560 (statement); self port

NEUTRA, Richard J. (1892-1970) Amer; arch
CIRCLE 203-211 (essay: ■Routes of Housing Advance■); 3 ill
HEYER 138-145 (interview); 17 ill
KEPES V 82-85 (essay: ■Inner and Outer Landscape■); 1 ill

NEVADOMI, Ken (1939-) Amer; ptr
RIPS (statement); 1 ill

NEVELSON, Louise (1900-) Amer; sclp
ART NOW v.2 no.10 (statement); 1 ill
ART SINCE v.2 323 (poem, o.p. 1969)
CELEBRATION (statement); 1 ill
DIAMONSTEIN I 264-277 (interview); ports
HESS 84-85 (statement)
HUNTER 38-41 (interview with Sam Hunter); 1 ill
ILLINOIS 1963 175 (statement); 1 ill
JOHNSON 39-46 (extract from *Dawns and Dusks*, 1976); 1 ill
MUNRO 131-144 (interview); port; 4 ill
NEMSER 52-79 (interview); port; 7 ill

NEW REALISM (group)
ART SINCE v.2 326 (■First Manifesto,■ 1960, o.p. 1968)

NEWBERGER, Babette (1924-) ptr
SCHAPIRO 51 (statement); port; 1 ill
VARIAN III (statement); 1 ill

NEWBY, Christine Carol
SEE: COSEY FANNI TUTTI

NEWCOMB, W. Rock (1945-) Amer; ptr
NOSANOW II 60 (statement); 1 ill

NEWHALL, Beaumont (1908-) Amer;
photo
HILL 377-412 (interview, 1975); port

NEWMAN, Arnold (1918-) Amer; photo
BOOTH 170-184 (interview); port; 7 ill
CAMPBELL 32-43 (statement); port; 8
ill
DANZIGER 112-137 (interview); port; 3
ill
DIAMONSTEIN III 143-158 (interview); 7
ill
WALSH 560-562 (statement); 1 ill

NEWMAN, Barnett (1905-1970) Amer;
ptr
ART NOW v.1 no.3 (statement); 1 ill
ART SINCE v.1 292-293 (statement, o.p.
1962)
ARTS YEARBOOK v.9 83, 90 (response);
1 ill
ARTFORUM v.6 no.7 4 (letter)
CHIPP 550-551 (essay: "The
Ideographic Picture," o.p. 1947)
CHIPP 551-552 (essay: "The First Man
Was an Artist," o.p. 1947)
CHIPP 552-553 (essay: "The Sublime Is
Now," o.p. 1948)
CONCEPTUAL ART 46 (statement)
GUGGENHEIM I 94-95 (essay: "The
First Man was an Artist," o.p. 1947)
JOHNSON 10-14 (letter, o.p. 1943)
JOHNSON 14-15 (essay: "The
Ideographic Picture," o.p. 1947)
JOHNSON 16-19 (response to review by
Clement Greenberg, 1947, p.p. 1969); 1
ill
MOMA 1959 60-63 (statement); port; 3
ill

MOTHERWELL 8-22 (three group
discussions: "Artists' Sessions at
Studio 35," New York, 1950)
REVOLUTION 129-134 (statement)
ROSE II 145-146 (extract from essay:
"The Ideographic Picture," o.p. 1947)
ROSE II 158-160 (essay, o.p. 1948)
ROSE II REVISED 133-114 (extract from
essay: "The Ideographic Picture," o.p.
1947)
ROSE II REVISED 133-135 (statement,
o.p. 1948)
ROSE II REVISED 142-145 (group
discussion, o.p. 1952)
ROSE II REVISED 251-252 (extract from
essay: "Chartres and Jericho," o.p.
1969)
SCHNEIDER 209-233 (interview); 1 ill
SIX PEINTRES (extract from essay:
"The Ideographic Picture," o.p. 1947;
extract from essay: "The Sublime is
Now," o.p. 1948); port; 1 ill
STEDELIJK 178-179 (statement, o.p.
1971); 4 ill
TIGER no.1 57-60 (essay: "The First
Man was an Artist")
TIGER no.6 51-53 (essay: "The
Sublime is Now")
TRACKS v.1 no.1 41-42 ("The
Ideographic Picture")
TRACKS v.2 no.1 28-33 ("A Manifesto
for the Mayoral Election--New York,
1933; On the Need for Political Action
by Men of Culture")

NEWMAN, Bryan (1935-) pott
CAMERON E 106-117 (response); 15 ill

NEWMAN, Daniel (1929-) Amer; ptr
YOUNG 1960 (statement); 2 ill

NEWMAN, Oscar ( ) Amer; arch
MIKELLIDES 44-58 (essay: "Whose
Failure is Modern Architecture?"); 14
ill

NEWSUM, Floyd ( ) Amer; ptr
O'KANE (statement); 1 ill

NEWTON, Carlton (1946-) Amer; sclp, instal
LOGAN I 35-39 (statement); port

NEWTON, Gordon (1948-) Amer; sclp
SHEARER 50-53 (interview); 3 ill

NEWTON, Helmut (1920-) Germ/Atrl; photo
BOOTH 186-196 (interview); port; 4 ill

NEWTON, Kathleen Migliore ( ) Amer; ptr
EVENTS I 46-47 (statement); 1 ill

NEWTON, Richard ( ) Amer; perf
IRVINE 61, 84 (statement); 1 ill

NEY, Lancelot (1900-) Hung; ptr
SEUPHOR 233 (statement); 1 ill

NEYRA, Jose Luis (1930-) Mexi; photo
WALSH 563-564, 566 (statement); 1 ill

NICE, Don (1932-) Amer; ptr
SUPERREAL 49-50, 170-171 (interview); 1 ill

NICHOLAS, Donna Lee (1938-) Amer; pott
WECHSLER 106-111 (statement); port; 5 ill

NICHOLAS, Thomas Andrew (1934-) Amer; ptr
NORTH LIGHT 190-195 (interview with William Fletcher); port; 4 ill

NICHOLS, Dale William (1904-) Amer; ptr
BRITANNICA 83 (statement); port; 1 ill

NICHOLS, Dean ( ) Amer; perf
BRENTANO 258-259 (extract from performance: "Aerial"); 1 ill

NICHOLS, Hobart ( ) ptr
BETHERS I 248-249 (statement); 1 ill

NICHOLSON, Ben (1894-) Brit; ptr
BANN 202 204 ("Editorial from *Circle*," o.p. 1937)
CIRCLE 75 ("Quotations")
GUGGENHEIM II 143-146 (essay: "Notes on Abstract Art," o.p. 1941)
READ 87-94 (statement); port; 3 ill
ROTHENSTEIN 60-61 (statement, p.p.)

NICHOLSON, Winifred (1893-) Brit; ptr
CIRCLE 57-60 (essay: "Unknown Colour")

NICOLA (1937-) Moro/Belg; envir, perf
SKIRA 1977 61 (statement); 1 ill

NICOLESCU, Alec ( ) Amer
BRENTANO 284-285 (text piece); 1 ill

NICOLSON, Annabel (1946-) Brit; film
ENGLISH 458-459 (statement); 2 ill

NIEMEYER, Oscar (1907-) Braz; arch
EMANUEL I 588-589 (statement); 1 ill

NIERHOFF, Ansgar (1941-) Germ; sclp
NAYLOR 698-699 (statement); 1 ill

NIESE, Henry Ernst (1924-) Amer; ptr
WHITNEY (statement); 1 ill
YOUNG 1960 (statement); 2 ill

NIEUWENHUIS, Cesar Domela
SEE: DOMELA, Cesar

NIEVA, Francisco (1924-) Span
PREMIER BILAN 310 (statement); port

NIIZUMA, Minoru (1930-) Japa/Amer; sclp
EMANUEL II 677-678 (statement); 1 ill
LETTERS 27 (letter); 1 ill
NAYLOR 701 (statement); 1 ill

NIKSIC, Radovan ( ) Yugo; arch
NEWMAN 202-204 (essay); 4 ill

NILAND, David L. ( ) arch
GA HOUSES no.13 70-75 (interview); ports; 12 ill

NISSLMULLER, Manfred (1940-) Aust; ptr
SKIRA 1977 21 (statement); 1 ill

NIVOLA, Constantino (1911-) Ital/Amer; sclp
IT IS no.1 28 (essay: "Remarks on the Differences between Painting and Sculpture")

NIVOLLET, Pierre (1946-) Fren; ptr
SKIRA 1979 71 (statement); 1 ill
SKIRA 1980 56 (statement); 2 ill

NOBLE, Jean-Francois ( ) Fren; photo
IDENTITE 67-69 (interview with Jacques Clayssen); port

NOBLE, Richard ( ) photo
TIME-LIFE IV 82-83 (statement); 1 ill

NOBLET, Jocelyn de (1936-) Fren; sclp
SKIRA 1976 97 (statement); 1 ill

NOE, Jerry Lee (1940-) Amer; sclp, light, ptr
ARTPARK 1975 92-93 (statement); port; 4 ill
NOSANOW I 100 (statement); 1 ill
SOUTHEAST (statement); port; 6 ill

NOEFER, Werner (1937-) Germ; photo
NAYLOR 702-703 (statement)

NOGUCHI, Isamu (1904-) Japa/Amer; sclp
ART NOW v.3 no.1 (statement); 1 ill
CUMMINGS 102-122 (interview, 1973); port; 2 ill
HUGHES 25-26 (essay: "On Washi")
IT IS no.6 77-80, 109-113 (group discussion)
KUH 171-187 (interview); 7 ill
MILLER 1946 39-43 (statement); 7 ill
PREMIER BILAN 311 (statement); port
TIGER no.4 81, 95 (statement); 1 ill
YAMADA 289-293 (interview with Chisaburoh Yamada, 1976)

NOLAN, Anne ( ) Amer; print
KRESGE (statement); port; 1 ill

NOLAN, Sidney (1917-) Atrl; ptr
BARBER 83-100 (interview); port

NOLAND, Kenneth C. (1924-) Amer; ptr
ART SINCE v.1 293 (statement, o.p. 1968)
CUMMINGS 136-153 (interview, 1971); port; 2 ill
JOHNSON 47, 49-50 (statement, o.p. 1968); 1 ill
TUCKER I 8 (extract from interview with Philip Leider, o.p. 1968)
VISUAL v.3 no.4 13-16 (group discussion)

NOLDE, Emil (1867-1956) Germ; ptr, print
CHIPP 146-151 (extract from *Jahre der Kampfe*, in English, o.p. 1934); self port
GROTE 13 (statements, 1901, 1906); 1 ill

MIESEL 31-41 ("Work in Nine Parts," 1911-1912)
MIESEL 209-210 (letter, 1938)
MIESEL 210-211 ("The Second War")
PROTTER 179 ("Reflections," p.p.)
SCHMIDT 44, 152-153 (letters, 1933, 1938)
THORN 9, 10, 13, 16, 18, 19, 21, 24, 26, 65, 66, 83, 89, 108, 155, 161, 179, 194, 195, 200, 202, 203, 204, 207-209, 225, 232, 234, 236, 237, 242, 245, 250, 253, 254, 256, 257, 276, 279, 291, 298, 299, 303, 307-309, 320, 323, 325, 326, 331, 333 (statements, p.p.)
WINGLER 48 (letter, 1922)

NOLEN, John (1869-1937) Amer; arch
ROTH 445-451 (essay: "City Making," o.p. 1909)

NOMMO, Issac (1940-) Amer; ptr
LEWIS II 41 (statement); port; 1 ill

NONAS, Richard ( )
ART-RITE no.14 5, 10-11 (response)
PARACHUTE no.8 19 (statement, in English); 1 ill
PARACHUTE no.9 4-7 (interview, in English); 7 ill

NORDFELDT, B. J. O. (1878-1955) Swed/Amer; ptr
M.H. DE YOUNG 99 (response); self port

NORFLEET, Barbara (1926-) Amer; photo
BOSTON III (interview); 1 ill

NORFLEET, Gail (1947-) Amer; paper, coll
PAPERWORKS 28-29 (statement); 4 ill

NORGAARD, Bjorn (1947-) sclp
SLEEPING 102-111 (statement); port; 25 ill

NORMAN, Dorothy (1905-) Amer; photo
ART VOICES v.2 no.10 16 (poem: "Fantasy for Living Painters and Dead"); 1 ill

NORMAN, Emile (1918-) Amer; sclp
ILLINOIS 1961 142 (response); port; 1 ill

NORMAN, Irving (1910-) Amer; ptr
ILLINOIS 1957 231-232 (response); 1 ill
VISUAL v.1 no.1 15-19 (interview); port; 3 ill

NORRIS, Ben (1910-) Amer; ptr
HAAR I 93-94 (interview with Prithwish Neogy); ports; 4 ill

NORRIS, Norman (1932-) Brit; ptr
HAYWARD 1979 48-49 (statement); 2 ill

NORTON, Ann (1915-) Amer; sclp
SKIRA 1979 114, 116 (statement); 1 ill

NORTON, Charles ( ) Amer; photo
PHOTOGRAHY (statement); 1 ill

NORTON, Rob Roy, Jr. (1948-) Amer; ptr
VASSAR COLLEGE (statement)

NOTHHELFER, Gabriele (1945-) Germ; photo
WALSH 570-571 (statement); 1 ill

NOTHHELFER, Helmut (1945-) Germ; photo
WALSH 570-571 (statement); 1 ill

NOTKIN, Richard T. (1948-) Amer; pott, sclp
HERMAN 92 (statement); port; 1 ill

NOTTINGHAM, Walter G. (1930-) Amer; text

WISCONSIN I (statement); 1 ill

NOUVEL, Jean ( ) Fren; arch
ARCHITECTURES 160-163 (essay: "Oser L'Ornament"); 7 ill

NOVAK, Ladislav (1925-) ptr
SKIRA 1975 67 ("des notes sur l'art" 1966); 1 ill

NOVATI, Marco (1895-) Ital; ptr
VERZOCCHI 309-313 (statement); self port; 1 ill

NOVELLO, Giuseppe (1897-) Ital; ptr
VERZOCCHI 315-319 (statement); self port; 1 ill

THE NOVEMBER GROUP (group)
MIESEL 169-171 ("Manifesto" 1918)

NOVIK, Jennie (1892-) ptr
SYMBOLS (statement); 1 ill

NOVROS, David (1941-) Amer; ptr
TUCKER I 14 (statement)

NOWICKI, Matthew (1910-1950) Poli/Amer; arch
ROTH 558-564 (essay: "Composition in Modern Architecture," o.p. 1949); 1 ill
ROTH 564-569 (essay: "Origins and Trends in Modern Architecture," o.p. 1951)

NUGENT, Barbara ( ) ptr
CHRYSALIS no.6 39-43 (statement); 6 ill

NUGENT, Bob ( ) Amer; sclp, paper
VISUAL v.2 no.2 6-10 (interview); 3 ill

NUNLEY, Robert ( ) Amer; print
COMPUTER (statement); 1 ill

NUSBERG, Lev (1936-) Russ; sclp, light
SANDBERG 142-145 (statement); 7 ill

NUZUM, Thomas (1942-) Amer; ptr
MICHIGAN 32-33 (statement); 2 ill

NYST, Jacques-Louis (1942-) Belg; photo
SKIRA 1977 93 (statement); 1 ill
SKIRA 1979 27, 117 (statement); 1 ill

O. M. A. (arch firm)
RUSSELL F 72-75 (project proposal); 10 ill
RUSSELL F 88-90 (project proposal); 5 ill

OBERMAYR, Lorna (1924-) Amer; paper
NOSANOW II 61 (statement); 1 ill

OBEY, Trudell Mimms ( ) Amer; ptr, sclp
FAX II 131-148 (statements); port; 1 ill

OBLOWITZ, Michael ( ) film
REALLIFE no.6 36 ("Belmondo is Belmondo")

OCAMPO, Miguel (1922-) Arge/Amer; ptr
PREMIER BILAN 311 (statement); port

OCHIKUBO, Tetsuo (1923-1975) Amer; ptr, print
HAAR II 54-58 (interview); ports; 2 ill

OCHSNER, Ernest V. (1944-) Amer; ptr
REGIONALISM 12-13 (statement); port; 1 ill

OCKENGA, Starr (1938-) Amer; photo
FUGITIVE (statement); 1 ill

OCTOBER--ASSOCIATION OF ARTISTIC LABOR (group)
BOWLT 273-279 ("Declaration," o.p. 1928)

ODDNER, Georg (1923-) Swed; photo
WALSH 573-574 (statement); 1 ill

O'DOHERTY, Brian (1934-) Iris/Amer; sclp
BATTCOCK V 251-255 (essay: "Minus Plato," o.p. 1966)

BATTCOCK V 366, 372-374 (interview with Elayne Varian, o.p. 1967); 1 ill
VARIAN IV (interview); port; 2 ill

OESTERLEN, Dieter (1911-) Germ; arch
EMANUEL I 592-594 (statement); 1 ill

OF, George F. (1876-1954) Amer; ptr
FORUM 1916 (statement); 1 ill

OGINZ, Richard (1944-) Amer; sclp
DOWNTOWN (statement); 1 ill

O'GORMAN, Juan (1905-) Span; arch, ptr
RODMAN II 19-21, 26-27, 84-86 (statements)

O'HANLON, Richard (1906-) Amer; sclp, ptr
SOME 43 (statement); 1 ill

OHARA, Ken (1942-) Japa; photo
WALSH 574-575 (statement); 1 ill

O'HARA, Sheila (1953-) Amer; text
FIBER 19, 21 (statement); 1 ill

OHASHI, Yutaka (1923-) Amer; sclp, ptr
ART VOICES v.4 no.4 71 (statement); 1 ill
ILLINOIS 1961 138 (response); port; 1 ill

OHLSON, Doug (1936-) Amer; ptr
TUCKER I 10 (statement)

OHTAKA, Masato (1923-) Japa; arch
KEPES VI 116-127 (essay: "Some Thoughts on Collective Form"); 5 ill

OJI, Helen (1950-) Amer; ptr
GUMPERT III 72-73 (statement)

OKA, Shikanosuke (1898-) Japa; ptr
KUNG 80-83 (statement); port; 2 ill

OKABE, Shigeo (1912-) Japa; ptr
KUNG 84-87 (statement); port; 3 ill

OKADA, Frank Sumio ( ) Amer; ptr
GUENTHER 92-93 (statement); port; 1
ill

OKADA, Kenzo (1902-) Japa/Amer; ptr
ART NOW v.1 no.4 (statement); 1 ill
RODMAN I 94-96 (interview)
YAMADA 300-303 (interview with
Michiaki Kawakita, 1969)

OKADA, Shin'ichi (1928-) Japa; arch
EMANUEL I 595-597 (statement); 1 ill

OKAMOTO, Shinjiro (1933-) Japa; ptr
KUNG 88-91 (statement); port; 2 ill

OKAMOTO, Taio ( ) Japa; ptr
ABSTRACTION no.5 21 (statement); 1
ill

OKAMOTO, Taro (1911-) Japa/Fren;
ptr
PREMIER BILAN 311 (statement); port

OKAMURA, Arthur (1932-) Amer; ptr
ILLINOIS 1955 226 (statement)
ILLINOIS 1959 252-253 (statement); 1 ill
ILLINOIS 1963 179 (statement); 1 ill
WHITNEY (statement); 1 ill

OKASHI, Avshalom (1916-) Isra; ptr
SEITZ I (statement); 2 ill

O'KEEFFE, Georgia (1887-) Amer; ptr
ALBRIGHT-KNOX 404-405 (letter,
10/1968); 1 ill
KUH 188-203 (interview); 8 ill
LETTERS 28 (letter); 1 ill

ROSE II 59-60 (extract from interview
with Katharine Kuh, o.p. 1960)
ROSE II REVISED 54-55 (extract of
interview with Katharine Kuh, o.p.
1960)
SPENCER 251-252 (essay: "About
Myself," o.p. 1939); 1 ill

O'KELLY, Alanna (1955-) Iris; sclp,
envir
KNOWLES 210-211 (statement); 4 ill

OKUBO, Mine ( ) ptr
BETHERS I 250-251 (statement); 1 ill

OKUMURA, Shigeo (1937-) Amer; ptr
SYMBOLS (statement); 1 ill

OKWUMABUA, Constance (1947-)
Amer; ptr
LEWIS I REVISED 115 (statement); port;
1 ill

OLDENBURG, Claes (1929-)
Swed/Amer; perf, sclp, ptr
ART AND TECHNOLOGY 241-269
(project proposal); ports; 37 ill
ART NOW v.1 no.8 (statement); 1 ill
ART SINCE v.2 326 (statement, o.p.
1970)
ARTFORUM v.4 no.5 32-33 ("Extracts
from the Studio Notes (1962-64)")
port; 2 ill
ARTFORUM v.4 no.6 20-24 (group
discussion); 1 ill
ARTFORUM v.7 no.2 19 (letter)
ARTS YEARBOOK v.9 83, 88 (response);
1 ill
CHIPP 585-587 (extract from group
discussion with Bruce Glaser, o.p.
1966)
CHOIX 33 (statement); 1 ill
CRISS-CROSS no.3 20-23 (interview
with Genevieve Freeman, 1975); port;
1 ill

IT IS no.6 77-80, 109-113 (group discussion)
JOHNSON 68-70 (statement, o.p. 1965)
JOHNSON 97-102 ("I am for an Art..." o.p. 1967); 1 ill
JOHNSON 201-207 (interview with Paul Carroll, o.p. 1969); 1 ill
KERBER 196-197 (extract from interview with Robert Pincus-Witten, o.p. 1963, in English and German)
KIRBY 200-203 ("a statement")
KIRBY 204-206 ("Injun/the script")
KIRBY 220-222 ("World's Fair II/the script")
KIRBY 234-240 ("Gayety/the script")
KIRBY 262-271 ("Autobodys/the script"); port
MILLER 1963 74-79 (from a statement for *Environments Situations Spaces* exhibition catalog, Martha Jackson Gallery, 1961); port; 8 ill
ROSE II 166-167 (statement, o.p. 1961)
ROSE II REVISED 151-152 (statement, o.p. 1961)
ROSE II REVISED 193-195 (extract from essay: "America: War and Sex, Etc.," o.p. 1967)
RUSSELL J 95-96 (essay: "On the Bedroom")
RUSSELL J 97-99 ("I am for an Art..." o.p. 1967)
SAO PAULO 92-93 (statement); port
TRACKS v.2 no.1 5-10 ("A History of the *Double-Nose/Purse/ Punching-Bag/Ashtray* Multiple")
VARIAN I (statement); port
VISION no.1 5-7 (interview with Kathan Brown); ports

OLDFIELD, Alan (1943-) Atrl; ptr
DE GROEN 47-56 (interview); port

OLESZKO, Pat ( ) Amer; perf
ARTPARK 1976 166-169 (statement); port; 7 ill

OLITSKI, Jules (1922-) Russ/Amer; ptr
ART NOW v.1 no.5 ("On Sculpture" p.p.); 1 ill
ARTFORUM v.5 no.5 20-21 (statement); 4 ill
JOHNSON 50-52 (essay: "Painting in Color," o.p. 1967)
ROSE II 172 (statement, o.p. 1966)
ROSE II REVISED 165-166 (statement, o.p. 1966)
SKIRA 1975 99 (statement: extract from *Catalogue de la Biennale de Venise,* o.p. 1966); 1 ill
TUCKER I 20 (statement)

OLIVEIRA, Nathan (1928-) Amer; ptr
HOPKINS 52-53 (statement); port; 1 ill
SELZ 112-116 (statement); 4 ill

OLIVER, Betty ( ) Amer; paper
HAYSTACK 46 (statement); 1 ill

OLIVER, Kermit (1943-) Amer; ptr
FAX II 117-130 (statements); port; 1 ill

OLIVER, Richard B. ( ) Amer; arch
COOPER-HEWITT I 58-59 (essay: "Images of Special Places")
COOPER-HEWITT II 55-56 (essay: "Regional Architectural Styles")

OLIVIER, Olivier O. (1931-) Fren; ptr
SKIRA 1977 13 (statement)
SKIRA 1978 27 (statement); 1 ill
SKIRA 1980 68-69 (statement); 2 ill

OLIVIERI, Claudio (1934-) Ital; ptr
EMANUEL II 696-697 (statement); 1 ill
NAYLOR 712 (statement)

OLLMAN, Arthur (1947-) Amer; photo
FUGITIVE (statement); 1 ill

OLSON, Charles (1951-) Amer; pott
HERMAN 93 (statement); port; 1 ill

OLTVEDT, Carl ( ) Amer; ptr
KRESGE (statement); port; 1 ill

OMMER, Uwe ( ) Germ; photo
HOW FAMOUS 160-163 (statements); port; 4 ill

ONCU, Ana (1932-) Yugo; ptr
TOMASEVIC 250-252 (statement); port; 2 ill

O'NEILL, Desmond ( ) photo
BOSHIER (statement); port; 13 ill

ONOSATO, Toshinobu (1912-) Japa; ptr
EMANUEL II 697 (statement)
KUNG 92-95 (statement); port; 2 ill
NAYLOR 713-714 (statement)

ONSLOW-FORD, Gordon Max (1912-) Brit/Amer; ptr
BARRON 42-44 (essay: "Reflections on the Dynaton Exhibition 25 Years Later"); 2 ill
ILLINOIS 1963 91 (statement); 1 ill
LIPPARD 177-179 (essay: "The Painter Looks Within Himself," o.p. 1940)
LONDON BULLETIN no.18/19/20 10 (essay: "The Worden Giantess of Henry Moore")
LONDON BULLETIN no.18/19/20 30-31 (essay: "The Painter Looks Within Himself")
SOME 19 (statement); 1 ill

ONTANI, Luigi ( ) Ital; ptr
NAYLOR 714 (statement); 1 ill

OPALKA, Roman (1931-) Poli; ptr, perf, photo
EMANUEL II 699-700 (statement); 1 ill
NAYLOR 715 (statement); 1 ill
SKIRA 1976 51-52 (statement); 1 ill
SKIRA 1980 110 (statement); 2 ill
VISION no.2 60-61 (statement)

OPPENHEIM, Dennis (1938-) Amer; sclp, instal, envir
ART NOW v.1 no.1 (statement); 1 ill
ARTPARK 1975 94-95 (statement); port; 4 ill
ART-RITE no.7 20 ("Rehearsal for 5 Hour Slump"); 3 ill
AVALANCHE no.1 48-71 (group discussion); port; 10 ill
AVALANCHE no.2 96-99 (group discussion)
AVALANCHE no.9 14-15 (interview); 4 ill
BELFORD 79-100 (group discussion)
CELANT 126-132 (statement); 5 ill
COMPUTER (statement); 1 ill
CONCEPTUAL ART 30, 38, 40, 45 (statements)
EARLY WORK (interview with Allan Schwartzman); 8 ill
FOX 66-75 (statement); 10 ill
JOHNSON 179-184 (group discussion, o.p. 1970)
PARACHUTE no.9 30-33 (interview, in English); 4 ill
SKIRA 1975 47 (extract from interview with Irmeline Lebeer, o.p. 1973); 1 ill
SKIRA 1977 58-59 (statement); 3 ill
SKIRA 1978 54 (statement); 1 ill
SKIRA 1980 140-141 (extract from interview with Dany Bloch, p.p.); 2 ill
SONDHEIM 246-266 (transcript of notebooks: "Catalyst 1967-1974"); 24 ill

OPPO, Cipriano Efisio (1890-) Ital; ptr
VERZOCCHI 321-325 (statement); self port; 1 ill

O'REILLY, Edward (1950-) Amer; pott
HERMAN 94 (statement); port; 1 ill

ORITZ, Ralph (1934-) Amer; sclp
YOUNG 1965 (statement); 2 ill

ORKIN, Ruth (1921-) Amer; photo
LAPLANTE 76-88 (interview); port; 1 ill
TIME-LIFE II 94-95 (statement); 1 ill

ORLANDO, Felipe ( )
TIGER no.2 44 (statement)

ORNITZ, Don ( ) Amer; photo
CALIFORNIA--PHOTOGRAPHY
(statement); port; 4 ill

O'ROURKE, Barry ( ) Amer; photo
CALIFORNIA--PHOTOGRAPHY
(statement); port; 4 ill

OROZCO, Jose Clemente (1883-1949)
Mexi; print, ptr
ADVERSARY 17 (statement, o.p. 1942)
ADVERSARY 18 (extract from
interview, o.p. 1946)
ADVERSARY 19 (manifesto, issued in
1922)
GOLDWATER 477-479 (statement, 1934)
PREMIER BILAN 312 (statement); self
port
STEWART 16-20 (statement); port; 2 ill

ORR, Eric (1939-) Amer; ptr
HOUSE 74-75 (statement); 1 ill

ORTEGA DE DIEZ DE SOLLANO,
Dolores
SEE: DIEZ DE SOLLANO, Dolores
Ortega de

ORTELLI, Gottardo (1938-) Ital; ptr
SKIRA 1976 70 (statement); 1 ill

ORTIZ BADILLO, Fernando
SEE: BADILLO, Fernando Ortiz

ORTIZ MONASTERIO, Pablo (1952-)
Mexi; photo
WALSH 577-578 (statement); 1 ill

ORTMAN, George (1926-) Amer; ptr,
sclp, print
ILLINOIS 1965 57 (statement); 1 ill
LETTERS 29 (letter); 1 ill
VARIAN I (statement); port
VARIAN III (statement); port
YOUNG 1960 (statement); 2 ill

ORTNER, Jorg ( )
CLAIR 62-63 (extract from letter); 1 ill

OSAWA, Shosuke (1903-) Japa; ptr
KUNG 96-99 (statement); port; 2 ill

OSBORN, Robert (1904-) Amer; illus,
ptr
KEPES I 184-199 ("The Hangover"); 23
ill

OSBORNE, Danny (1949-) Iris; ptr
KNOWLES 22-23 (statement); 3 ill

OSCAR, Charles (1923-) Amer; ptr
FULBRIGHT 38 (statement)
ILLINOIS 1955 227 (statement); 1 ill

OSSIPOFF, Vladimir (1907-)
Russ/Amer; arch
HAAR II 59-63 (interview); ports; 2 ill

OSSORIO, Alfonso (1916-) Fili/Amer;
ptr
VARIAN I (statement); port

OST (group)
SEE: SOCIETY OF EASEL ARTISTS

OSTER, Gerald (1918-) Amer; ptr, print
ART VOICES v.4 no.2 93 (statement); 1
ill

OSTROW, Saul (1947-)
CONCEPTUAL ART 35 (statement)

OSTROWSKY, Abbo (1889-) Russ/Amer; ptr
100 CONTEMPORARY 142-143 (statement); port; 1 ill

OSVER, Arthur (1912-) Amer; ptr
BETHERS II 120-121 (statement); 2 ill
ILLINOIS 1951 203-204 (statement); 1 ill
ILLINOIS 1952 219-220 (statement)
ILLINOIS 1955 227 (statement); 1 ill
ILLINOIS 1957 233-234 (response); 1 ill
ILLINOIS 1959 253-254 (statement); 1 ill
ILLINOIS 1961 149 (response); port; 1 ill

OTERO REYES, Ariosto
SEE: ARIOSTO

OTIS, James ( )
CRISS-CROSS 7/8/9 6-9 ("Binary Trees")

OTIS, Jeanne (1940-) Amer; pott
HERMAN 95 (statement); port; 1 ill
VIEWPOINT 1981 (statement); 3 ill

OTNES, Fred (1925-) Amer; illus
ILLUSTRATION 14-17 (statement); port; 2 ill

OTTH, Jean (1940-) Swis; photo
SKIRA 1976 14-15 (statement); 2 ill

OUBRE, Hayward Louis, Jr. ( ) Amer; ptr, illus
LEWIS I REVISED 96 (statement); port; 1 ill

OUDOT, Roland (1897-) Fren; print, ptr
GOLDAINE 150-152 (interview); port
RAYNAL 245-247 (statement); 2 ill

OUELLET, Jean (1922-) Cana; arch
CANADIAN 80-83 (statement); 4 ill

OUTTERBRIDGE, John Wilfred (1933-) Amer; sclp, ptr
FAX II 294-313 (statements); port; 1 ill
LEWIS I REVISED 23 (statement); port; 1 ill

OVENDEN, Graham (1943-) Brit; ptr
CONTEMPORARY (statement); port; 2 ill

OWEN, Beverly ( ) Amer; illus
BRENTANO 298-299 (statement); 1 ill

OWENS, Bill (1938-) Amer; photo
WALSH 581-582 (statement); 1 ill

OWENS, Craig ( )
REALLIFE no.6 4-10 (group discussion)

OYAMADA, Jiro (1914-) Japa; ptr
KUNG 100-103 (statement); port; 2 ill

OZENFANT, Amedee (1886-1966) Fren/Amer; ptr
EVANS 43-51 (essay: "Serial Art"); 2 ill
FORD/VIEW v.2 no.1 31 (letter to Charles H. Ford)
FRY 171-172 ("Towards the Crystal," o.p. 1925)
JANIS I 138 (statement); 1 ill
POENSGEN 103 ("Kunst und Erkenntnis," 1931)
RAYNAL 249-254 (statement); 2 ill

PABEL, Hilmar (1910-) Germ; photo
WALSH 583, 585 (statement); 1 ill

PACE, Lorenzo (1943-) Amer; sclp
LEWIS I REVISED 47 (statement); 2 ill

PACH, Walter (1883-1958) Amer; ptr,
print
ARMORY SHOW 27 (statement)

PACHECO, Maria Luisa (1919-)
Boli/Amer; ptr
ILLINOIS 1963 67 (statement); 1 ill

PACHNER, William (1915-) Czec/Amer;
ptr, print
ZAIDENBERG 136-140 (essay: "The
Basis of Art"); 7 ill

PACKARD, Sandra ( )
VISUAL v.2 no.3 18-20 (essay: "Uphill
Struggle: Women in Art Academe")

PADOVANO, Anthony John (1933-)
Amer; sclp
YOUNG 1965 (statement); 2 ill

PAEFFGEN, C. O. (1933-) Germ; sclp,
ptr
KUNST UND POLITIK (statement); port;
4 ill

PAGELS, Elaine ( )
ART-RITE no.11/12 ("The Gospel of
Mary Magdalene")

PAGES, Bernard (1940-) Fren; sclp,
envir
CHOIX 34 (statement); 1 ill
SKIRA 1979 64-65 (statement); 1 ill

PAIDOLA, Anton
SEE: NEAGU, Paul

PAIK, Nam June (1932-) Kore/Amer;
video
ART-RITE no.7 11, 14 (response); port
BATTCOCK VI 121-137 ("Videa, Vidiot,
Videology," o.p. 1964 and 1976); 7 ill
BELFORD 1-25 (group discussion)
DAVIS 38-47 (statement: "The Video
Synthesizer and Beyond"); port
TRACKS v.3 no.3 50-51 (story)

PAILTHORPE, Grace W. ( ) ptr
LONDON BULLETIN no.7 10-16 (essay:
"The Scientific Aspect of Surrealism")
LONDON BULLETIN no.17 22-23 (letter:
"Letter to the Editors")

PAINTERS, The
SEE: JOCHEM AND RUDI

PAJAUD, William E. (1925-) Amer; ptr
LEWIS I REVISED 68-69 (statement);
port; 4 ill

PAKENHAM, Jack (1938-) Iris; ptr
KNOWLES 52-53 (statement); 3 ill

PALEN, Wolfgang (1905-1959)
LIPPARD 180-183 (extract from
"Surprise and Inspiration," o.p. 1945)

PALESTINE, Charlemagne (1945-)
APPLE 46 (statement)
ART-RITE no.10 (statement)
GEORGIA 118-166 (group discussion:
"Artists' Convention," in Athens, GA.,
1/7/1977, moderated by Jan van der
Marck)
PARACHUTE no.5 4-9 (interview, in
English); 2 ill
TRACKS v.3 no.3 45-49 ("Conversation
with Teddy")

PALEY, Albert (1944-) Amer; metal
DIAMONSTEIN IV 180-195 (interview);
port; 11 ill

photo
VISUAL v.1 no.4 3-5 (group discussion)
WALSH 587-588 (statement); 1 ill

PAPPAS, Marilyn R. (1931-) Amer;
paper
HAYSTACK 47 (statement); 1 ill

PAPSDORF, Frederick (1887-) Amer;
ptr
MILLER 1943 48 (statement); 1 ill

PARANT, Jean-Luc (1944-) Fren; photo
SKIRA 1979 47 (statement); 1 ill

PARDI, Gianfranco (1933-) Ital; sclp,
instal
SKIRA 1979 74 (statement); 1 ill

PARDO, Julio M., III (1955-) Amer; pott
RICKERT 1980 (statement); port; 3 ill

PARIS, Harold (1925-1979) Amer; sclp,
print, paper
ILLINOIS 1969 120-121 (statement); 1 ill
VISUAL v.3 no.4 7-9 (interview); 3 ill

PARISH, Tom (1933-) Amer; ptr
ILLINOIS 1969 82 (statement); 1 ill

PARISI, Ico (1916-) Ital; sclp, ptr
NAYLOR 729-730 (statement); 1 ill

PARISOT, Christian (1948-) Fren; ptr
SKIRA 1980 65 (statement); 2 ill

PARK, David (1911-1960) Amer; ptr
ILLINOIS 1952 220 (statement)
ILLINOIS 1957 234 (response); 1 ill
ILLINOIS 1959 254-255 (statement); 1 ill

PARKER, Alfred Charles (1906-) Amer;
ptr
GUITAR 164-173 (interview); port; 4 ill

PARKER, Bart ( ) Amer; photo
VISUAL v.1 no.4 3-5 (group discussion)

PARKER, James (1933-) Amer; ptr
TUCKER I 10 (statement)

PARKER, Lucinda ( ) Amer; ptr
GUENTHER 94-95 (statement); port; 1
ill

PARKER, Olivia (1941-) Amer; photo
WALSH 588-589 (statement); 1 ill

PARKER, Raymond (1922-) Amer; ptr
ART NOW v.2 no.10 (statement); 1 ill
ILLINOIS 1961 124 (response); port; 1 ill
IT IS no.1 20 (essay: "Direct
Painting")
IT IS no.2 8-9 ("Intent Painting")
REVIEW v.2/3 86-93 (statement); 3 ill

PARKER, Robert Andrew (1927-) Amer;
ptr
WHITNEY (statement); 1 ill
YOUNG 1957 (statement); 2 ill

PARKIN, John Cresswell (1922-) Cana;
arch
CANADIAN 84-87 (statement); 5 ill
EMANUEL I 606-608 (statement); 1 ill

PARKINSON, Norman (1913-) Brit;
photo
WALSH 590-591 (statement); 1 ill

PARKS, Carrie Anne ( ) Amer; sclp, pott
KRESGE (statement); port; 1 ill

PARKS, James Dallas (1907-) Amer; ptr
LEWIS I REVISED 87 (statement); port;
1 ill

PARMEGGIANI, Carlo (1927-1964) Ital;
ptr

VERZOCCHI 327-331 (statement); self port; 1 ill

PARMENTIER, Michel (1938-) Fren; ptr
DOUZE ANS 293-296 (statement); port; 1 ill

PARMIGGIANI, Claudio (1943-) Ital; sclp, ptr
SKIRA 1978 85 (statement); 1 ill

PARR, Mike (1945-) Atrl; photo, instal
BIENNALE 70-71, 73 (statement); 4 ill
EMANUEL II 715-716 (statement); 1 ill

PARRISH, David (1939-) Amer; ptr
SUPERREAL 172-173 (statement); 1 ill

PARROTT, Alice Kagawa (1929-) Amer; text
HAAR II 64-68 (interview); ports; 2 ill

PARSONS, Bruce ( ) Cana; ptr
VANCOUVER (statement); 2 ill

PARTCH, Harry (1901-1974) Amer; sclp, sound
GRAYSON 88-91 (essay: "No Barriers," 1952; and extract from "Monophonic Just Intonation," 1967); port

PARTRIDGE, David (1919-) Cana; sclp, ptr, print
CANADA 74-75 (statement); port; 2 ill
EMANUEL II 716-718 (statement); 1 ill
NAYLOR 731-732 (statement)

PARTRIDGE, John A. (1924-) Brit; arch
SEE: HOWELL KILLICK PARTRIDGE AND AMIS

PARTRIDGE, Roi (1888-) Amer; ptr, photo, print
M.H. DE YOUNG 100 (response)

PASCHKE, Ed (1939-) Amer; ptr, illus
ACKLAND 20-37, 70-71 (group discussion 10/29/79); 2 ill
ILLINOIS 1974 95 (statement); 1 ill
PROFILE v.3 no.5 (interview); ports; 10 ill

PASMORE, Victor (1908-) Brit; ptr, sclp
EMANUEL II 718-721 (statement); 1 ill
LETTERS 30 (letter); 1 ill

PASQUALE, Carol De ( )
WOMANART v.1 no.3 8-11 ("Dialogues with Nancy Spero")

PASQUE, Aubin ( ) Belg; ptr
COLLARD 204-209 (interview); port; 1 ill

PASSANTINO, George Christopher ( ) Amer; ptr
DAUGHERTY 30-47 (statements); ports; 2 ill

PASSMORE, George
SEE: GILBERT AND GEORGE

PATELLI, Paolo ( )
GROH (statement); 2 ill

PATERNOSTO, Cesar (1931-) Arge/Amer; ptr
PREMIO NACIONAL 1966 32-33 (statement); port; 1 ill

PATKAI, Ervin (1937-) Hung/Fren; sclp
SKIRA 1977 104 (statement); 1 ill

PATTISON, Abbott (1916-) Amer; sclp, ptr
ILLINOIS 1959 255-256 (statement); 1 ill
ILLINOIS 1961 130 (response); port; 1 ill
ILLINOIS 1963 214 (statement); 1 ill

PAVIA, Phillip (1912-) Amer; sclp
ILLINOIS 1961 217 (response); port; 1 ill
IT IS no.1 2-5 (essay: "The Problem as the Subject-Matter")
IT IS no.1 6-7 (essay: "Polemics")
IT IS no.2 4-6 (essay: "The Second Space: The American Sense of Space on Space")
IT IS no.4 4-6 (essay: "Excavations in Non-History")
IT IS no.4 79-80 ("An Open Letter to Leslie Katz, Publisher of *Arts Magazine*")
IT IS no.5 8-11 (essay: "The Unwanted Title: Abstract Expressionism")
IT IS no.5 51-56 (group discussion)
IT IS no.5 82-84 (essay: "Advice to Future Polemicists, Subject: Hilton Kramer's Non-Art Criticism")
IT IS no.6 7-16, 57-64, 73-75 (group discussion)
IT IS no.6 77-80, 109-113 (group discussion)

PAWLEY, Martin ( ) arch
ON SITE no.2 10, 12 (response)

PAXTON, Steve ( ) perf
AVALANCHE no.12 26-30 (interview); 11 ill

PAYSSE-REYES, Mario (1913-) Urug; arch
EMANUEL I 609-611 (statement); 1 ill

PEACOCK, Clifton (1953-) Amer; ptr
BOSTON I (interview); 1 ill
BOSTON III (interview); 1 ill

PEAKE, Channing (1910-) Amer; ptr
CALIFORNIA--PAINTING 26 (statement); 1 ill
ILLINOIS 1953 207-208 (statement)
ILLINOIS 1955 227-228 (statement); 1 ill

PEANUT, Mr. ( )
AVALANCHE no.8 34-39 (group discussion); 14 ill

PEARLSTEIN, Philip (1924-) Amer; ptr, print
ART NOW v.3 no.1 (statement); 1 ill
ART VOICES v.5 no.3 40 (statement); 1 ill
ARTS YEARBOOK v.7 129-132 (essay: "Whose Painting Is It Anyway?")
CUMMINGS 154-171 (interview, 1972); port; 2 ill
ILLINOIS 1965 75 (statement); 1 ill
ILLINOIS 1969 142 (statement); 1 ill
ROSE II REVISED 189-190 (statement: "The Romantic Self-Image Is Gone," o.p. 1967)
STRAND 88-111 (interview); port; 20 ill
SUPERREAL 37-40, 88-89 (essay: "A Concept of New Realism"); 1 ill

PEARSON, John (1940-) Brit/Amer; ptr
NAYLOR 736 (statement); 1 ill

PEARSON, Ralph M. (1883-1958) Amer; ptr
FIRST AMERICAN 55-58 (essay: "The Art Museums, Imposing Monuments to Our National Divorce from the Arts")

PEARSON, Ronald Hayes ( ) Amer; metal
HAYSTACK 49 (statement); 1 ill

PEARSON, Stephen (1946-) Amer; sclp, envir
HOUSE 76-77 (statement); 1 ill

PECHSTEIN, Max (1881-1955) Germ; ptr
MIESEL 178-180 ("What We Want," 1919)
MIESEL 180-181 ("Creative Credo," 1920)

PECIURA, Auste ( )
WHITE WALLS no.5 76-79 (text piece)

PECK, Richard ( ) perf, sound
AVALANCHE no.10 40 (interview); ports

PECK, Robin (1950-) Cana; sclp, ptr
REALLIFE no.7 29 (essay: "The Extinction of Sculpture")

PECNIK, Greta (1924-) Yugo; ptr
TOMASEVIC 256-259 (statement); port; 2 ill

PEDERSEN, Carl-Henning (1913-) Dani; ptr
GUGGENHEIM I 98-99 (essay: "Abstract Art or Imaginary Art—An Artist's Work," o.p. 1943)
GUGGENHEIM I 99-100 (poem: "The Strange Night," o.p. 1949)

PEERY, Laura (1952-) Amer; pott
HERMAN 97 (statement); port; 1 ill

PEI, I. M. (Icoh Ming) (1917-) Chin/Amer; arch
DIAMONSTEIN I 278-290 (interview); ports
DIAMONSTEIN II 144-162 (interview); port; 5 ill
HEYER 308-323 (interview); 32 ill

PEICHL, Gustav (1928-) Aust; arch
EMANUEL I 612-613 (statement); 1 ill
RUSSELL F 40-41 (project proposal); 4 ill

PEIRCE, Waldo (1884-1970) Amer; ptr
BRITANNICA 85 (statement); port; 1 ill

PEIRE, Luc (1916-) Belg; ptr
SKIRA 1976 76 (statement); 1 ill

PEISER, Mark Curtis (1938-) Amer; sclp, glass
ARTPARK 1979 (statement); port
GLASS v.5 (group discussion)

PELLECCHIA, Anthony ( ) arch
PROCESSES 31-54 (statement)

PELLEW, John C. (1903-) Brit/Amer; ptr
NORTH LIGHT 80 (statement); 1 ill

PELLI, Cesar (1926-) Arge/Amer; arch
COLLABORATION 118-125 (essay: "The Hexagonal Room: A Door, Two Windows, and Three Paintings"); 15 ill
COOPER-HEWITT II 25 (statement)
DIAMONSTEIN II 164-182 (interview); port; 6 ill
EMANUEL I 613-615 (statement); 1 ill
SEARING 78-85 (statement); 6 ill

PENA, Feliciano (1915-) Mexi; ptr
STEWART 138-141 (statement); port; self port; 3 ill

PENA, Ganghegui Luis (1926-) Span; arch
EMANUEL I 615-616 (statement); 1 ill

PENALBA, Alicia (1913-) Arge; sclp
EMANUEL II 723-725 (statement); 1 ill
LETTERS 31 (letter); 1 ill
NAYLOR 738-740 (statement); 1 ill
PREMIER BILAN 313 (statement); port
QUADRUM no.17 71-76 (essay: "Reflexions sur la Sculpture"); 6 ill
SKIRA 1976 88 (statement); 1 ill

PENCK, A. R. (1939-) Germ; ptr
CHOIX 36 (statement, o.p. 1979); 1 ill
PRADEL 92 (statement); port; 3 ill

PENNEY, J. James (1910-) Amer; ptr
ILLINOIS 1951 205 (statement); 1 ill

PENNIE, Michael (1936-) Brit; sclp
BRITISH (statement); 1 ill

PENONE, Giuseppe (1947-) Ital; ptr, sclp, photo
CELANT 10, 168-173 (statement); 18 ill
CHOIX 37 (statement, o.p. 1982); 2 ill
IDENTITE 75-77 (interview with Jacques Clayssen); port
KUNST BLEIBT KUNST 278-279 (statement); 2 ill
MURS 13-14 (statement); 1 ill
SKIRA 1977 51 (statement); 1 ill
SKIRA 1978 87 (statement); 1 ill
STEDELIJK 187 (statement, in Italian); 1 ill
WALDMAN 88-105 (statement); 13 ill

PENROSE, Roland (1900-) Brit; ptr
LONDON BULLETIN no.2 24 ("The Transparent Mirror")
LONDON BULLETIN no.7 16-22 (extract from "The Road is Wider Than Long")
LONDON BULLETIN no.8/9 50-56 (extract from "The Road is Wider Than Long")

PENTEADO, Fabio (1929-) Braz; arch
EMANUEL I 616-618 (statement); 1 ill

PENTTILA, Timo (1931-) Finn; arch
EMANUEL I 618-619 (statement); 1 ill

PEPPER, Beverly (1924-) Amer; sclp, ptr, envir
ALBRIGHT-KNOX 104-105 (letter, 3/1969); 1 ill
CELEBRATION (statement); 1 ill
DIAMONSTEIN I 291-304 (interview); ports
EMANUEL II 726-727 (statement); 1 ill
LETTERS 32 (letter); 1 ill
MUNRO 345-354 (interview); ports; 2 ill
NAYLOR 741-742 (statement); 1 ill

SKIRA 1978 127 (statement); 1 ill
SKIRA 1980 139 (statement); 2 ill

PERDURABO, S. S. ( )
ART-RITE no.8 12 ("A Serious Proposal for Nelson Rockefeller"); 1 ill

PEREIRA, Irene Rice (1907-1971) Amer; ptr
ART VOICES v.4 no.2 80-81 (letter to the editor); 1 ill
BETHERS I 252-253 (statement); 1 ill
FORTY (statement); 2 ill
ILLINOIS 1955 228-229 (statement); 1 ill
JANIS I 71 (statement); 1 ill
KEPES IX 62-73 (extract from "private communications" with John E. Burchard)
MILLER 1946 44-48 (statement); 6 ill
PERSONAL (statement)
SEUPHOR 239-240 (statement)

PERESS, Gilles (1946-) Fren; photo
WALSH 594-596 (statement); 1 ill

PEREZ, Vincent (1938-) Amer; ptr
ILLINOIS 1969 164 (statement); 1 ill

PERICAUD, Jean-Pierre (1938-) Fren; ptr
SKIRA 1976 72 (statement); 1 ill

PERILLI, Achille (1927-) Ital; ptr
EMANUEL II 727-729 (statement); 1 ill
NAYLOR 742-744 (statement); 1 ill
PAINTING 24 (statement); port; 1 ill

PERKINS, Angela L. (1948-) Amer; ptr
LEWIS I 49 (statement); port; 1 ill

PERKINS, Lawrence Bradford (1907-) Amer; arch
EMANUEL I 621-622 (statement); 1 ill

PERLIN, Bernard (1918-) Amer; ptr
FULBRIGHT 39 (statement); 1 ill
ILLINOIS 1955 229-230 (statement); 1 ill
NEW DECADE 62-64 (statement); 3 ill
RODMAN I 185-188 (interview)

PERREAULT, John (1937-) Amer; perf
BATTCOCK II 135-139 (essay: "It's Only Words," o.p. 1971)
BATTCOCK V 256-262 (essay: "Minimal Abstracts," o.p. 1967)
MEYER 200-201 (statement)

PERRY, James Robert (1950-) Amer; sclp
WISCONSIN II (statement); 1 ill

PESKIN, Roger (1943-) Amer; sclp
ART NOW v.4 no.1 (statement); 1 ill

PETER, R. Max (1923-) Amer; paper
NOSANOW II 30-31, 62 (statement); 3 ill

PETER, Steve (1953-) Amer; ptr
WISCONSIN II (statement); 1 ill

PETERDI, Gabor (1915-) Hung/Amer; print
AMERICAN PRINTS 45, 69 (statement); 1 ill

PETERNELJ, Joze-Mausar (1927-) Yugo; ptr
TOMASEVIC 260-262 (statement); port; 1 ill

PETERNELJ, Konrad (1936-) Yugo; ptr
TOMASEVIC 263-265 (statement); port; 1 ill

PETERS, Mary Ann ( ) Amer; ptr
GUENTHER 96-97 (statement); port; 1 ill

PETERS, Richard C. ( ) Amer; arch
GA HOUSES no.7 143-149 (essay: "Lighting for Moore"); port

PETERSEN, Asmus (1928-) sclp
KUNST UND POLITIK (statement, with H. J. Breuste); port; 1 ill

PETERSEN, Roland Conrad (1926-) Dani/Amer; ptr
ILLINOIS 1961 122 (response); port; 1 ill
ILLINOIS 1963 183 (statement); 1 ill
ILLINOIS 1969 48 (statement); 1 ill
VARIAN III (statement); port

PETERSON, Jon (1945-) Amer; sclp, envir, ptr
DOWNTOWN (statement); 1 ill
HOUSE 78-79 (statement); 1 ill

PETERSON, Susan ( ) Amer; arch, design
LIFE 175-196 (interview); port

PETERSSON, Bertil ( ) perf
AVALANCHE no.13 7 (statement); 2 ill

PETHERBRIDGE, Deanna (1939-) SoAf/Brit; ptr, illus
SKIRA 1978 110-111 (statement); 1 ill
SKIRA 1979 93 (statement); 1 ill

PETHICK, Jerry (1935-) Cana; sclp, instal
MISE EN SCENE 13, 21, 112-129 (interview with Scott Watson); 12 ill

PETRANOVIC, Tomislav-Rvat (1934-) Yugo; ptr
TOMASEVIC 266-270 (statement); port; 2 ill

PETTERSEN, Arvid (1943-) ptr
SLEEPING 122-131 (statement); port; 6 ill

PETTIBONE, Shirley ( ) Amer; ptr
IRVINE 38, 81 (statement); 1 ill

PEVSNER, Antoine (1886-1962) Russ/Fren; sclp, ptr
ABSTRACTION no.1 27 (statement); 2 ill
ABSTRACTION no.2 34-35 (statement); 2 ill
BANN 3-11 ("The Realistic Manifesto," o.p. 1920, with Naum Gabo)
BOWLT 208-214 ("The Realistic Manifesto," o.p. 1920, with Naum Gabo); 1 ill
CHIPP 325-330 ("The Realistic Manifesto," o.p. 1920, with Naum Gabo)
CONRADS 56 ("Basic Principles of Construction," o.p. 1920)
GOLDWATER 454-455 (statement, 1920)
GUGGENHEIM II 138 ("Realistic Manifesto," o.p. 1920, with Naum Gabo)
POENSGEN 91-92 ("Aus dem Realistischen Manifest," o.p. 1920)
TEMOIGNAGES I 212-221 (statement); port; 7 ill
VINGTIEME v.1 no.5/6 47 (extract from letter)
VINGTIEME N.S. no.12 13-17, 94 (essay: "La Science Tue la Poesie" in French and English); 4 ill
VINGTIEME N.S. no.13 44-45 (extract from letter, o.p. 1939); 1 ill

PEVZNER, Naum Neemia
SEE: GABO, Naum

PEVZNER, Noton
SEE: PEVSNER, Antoine

PEZOLD, Friederike (1945-) Aust; envir
SKIRA 1978 38-39 (statement); 2 ill

PFAFF, Judy (1946-) Amer; sclp, instal
JOHNSON 264-266 (statement, o.p. 1981); 1 ill
MCCLINTIC 24-27 (statement); 3 ill

PFAFFE, Wolfgang (1950-) Germ; print
SKIRA 1977 91 (statement); 1 ill

PFAHL, John (1939-) Amer; photo
ARTPARK 1975 96-97 (statement); port; 5 ill
FUGITIVE (statement); 1 ill SKIRA 1979 17 (statement); 1 ill
WALSH 599-600 (statement); 1 ill

PFAHLER, Georg Karl (1926-) Germ; ptr, sclp, instal
HAUSSER 142-143 (statement, 1970); 8 ill

PHIL GLASS ENSEMBLE (group)
SEE: GLASS, Phil

PHILIPP, Robert (1895-) Amer; ptr
BETHERS II 122-123 (statement); 2 ill
BRITANNICA 86 (statement); port; 1 ill

PHILIPP, Werner (1897-) Amer; ptr
M.H. DE YOUNG 103 (response)

PHILLIPS, Anne (1943-) Amer; sclp, instal
SCRIPPS COLLEGE (statement); 1 ill

PHILLIPS, Bertrand D. (1938-) Amer; ptr
FAX II 79-96 (statements); port; 1 ill
LEWIS I REVISED 38 (statement); port; 1 ill

PHILLIPS, Helen Elizabeth (1913-) Amer; sclp
TIGER no.4 81, 94 (statement); 1 ill

PHILLIPS, James (1929-) Amer; ptr
FULBRIGHT 40 (statement)
WHITNEY (statement); 1 ill
YOUNG 1957 (statement); 2 ill

PHILLIPS, Liz ( ) Amer; sound, instal
ARTPARK 1974 34-35 (statement); port;
1 ill

PHILLIPS, Mary Walker (1923-) Amer;
text
FIBER 52-53 (statement); 1 ill

PHILLIPS, Tom (1937-) ptr
ENGLISH 170-175 (statement); port; 8
ill
NAYLOR 748-749 (statement); 1 ill
SKIRA 1976 78-79 (statement); 1 ill

PIANO, Renzo (1937-) Ital; arch
EMANUEL I 626-627 (statement); 1 ill

PIAUBERT, Jean (1900-) Fren; ptr
FRASNAY 167-177 (statement); ports; 4
ill

PICABIA, Francis (1879-1953) Fren; ptr
ARMORY SHOW 28 (extract from "his
foreword for a one-man show held at
'291' Gallery in New York in 1913")
BERCKELAERS 170-171 (poems: "Ou
Bien," "Affaire de Gout," "Vestiaire,"
p.p.)
CHARBONNIER v.1 131-140 (interview)
DADA 65-66 ("Poeme inedit")
DUNOYER (poem); 1 ill
EDDY 82 (statement)
EDDY 95-96 (extract from interview,
o.p. in *New York Tribune*)
EDDY 96-97 (extract from interview)
EDDY 97-98 (statement)
GIEDION-WELCKER 89-96 (poems:
"Pensees' sans Langage," 1919,
"Unique Eunuque," 1920, "Thalassa

dans le Desert," 1940, "Chanson
Finale," 1940, in French); self port
GUGGENHEIM II 60-61 (statement); 1 ill
JEAN 66-67 ("Aphorisms," p.p.); port
JEAN 68-69 ("May Day," o.p. 1920)
LIPPARD   184-186   ("Cerebral
Undulations," o.p. 1922)
LIPPARD 187 ("Entr'acte," o.p. 1927)
REVOLUTION   SURREALISTE   no.12
(poems: "Mon   Ame,"   "Poeme
d'Esperance,"   "De   l'Autre   Cote,"
"L'Enfant," "Curiosite")
TRACKS v.1 no.2 7 (story: "5 Minute
Intermission," o.p. 1920)

PICARD, Lil ( ) Amer; coll, perf
ART VOICES v.4 no.1 80 (statement); 1
ill
ART-RITE no.9 4-5 ("Lil Picard
Remembers")
ARTS YEARBOOK v.10 78-81 (essay:
"Kunstmarkt and Prospect '68")
SCHAPIRO 53 (statement); port; 1 ill

PICASSO, Pablo (1881-1973) Span/Fren;
ptr, print, sclp
ADVERSARY   10   (extract   from
statement given to Simone Tery, o.p.
1945)
ADVERSARY 10 (poem: "The Dream
and Lie of Franco")
ADVERSARY 15 (statement, issued in
May or June 1937 at the time of an
exhibition of Spanish war posters in
New York)
ART SINCE v.2 148 (statement, o.p.
1935)
CHIPP 263-266 (statement, o.p. 1923);
self port
CHIPP 266 (statement: "On *Les
Demoiselles d'Avignon*," 1933, o.p.
1952)
CHIPP 266-273 (interview with
Christian Zervos, o.p. 1935); ports

PICKETT, Vic ( ) Amer; sclp
ART PATRON ART 51-52 (statement);
port; 1 ill

PICKHARDT, Carl E. (1908-) Amer; ptr
ILLINOIS 1951 206-207 (statement); 1 ill

PICTON, Tom ( ) photo
VICTORIA 100-103 (statements)

PIENE, Otto (1928-) Germ/Amer; ptr,
light, envir
ALBRIGHT-KNOX 242-243 (letter,
11/1968); 1 ill
ART AND TECHNOLOGY 322-323
(project proposal)
ART SINCE v.1 160 (statement, o.p.
1961)
CENTERBEAM 10 ("Recognition, In
Praise of 'Centerbeam'")
CENTERBEAM 13 ("Massachusetts
Institute of Technology Center for
Advanced Visual Studies")
CENTERBEAM 16, 19
("Acknowledgements" with Elizabeth
Goldring)
CENTERBEAM 20-24, 119-120
("Centerbeam"); ports; 8 ill
EMANUEL II 739-741 (statement); 1 ill
GUGGENHEIM I 97 (essay: "Darkness
and Light," o.p. 1960)
GUGGENHEIM I 97 (statement, o.p.
1961)
HAUSSER 146-147 (statement, o.p.
1965); 1 ill
LETTERS 33 (letter); 1 ill
NAYLOR 754-756 (statement); 1 ill
TECHNOLOGIES (essay: "Technology
for Art"; statements); port; 20 ill
VARIAN II (statement); port

PIERCE, Bruce ( ) Amer; ptr
ARTISTS no.1 15-16 ("High Plains
Drifter").

PIERSOL, Virginia ( ) perf, film
APPLE 47 (statement); 1 ill
AVALANCHE no.12 6 (statement); 4 ill

PIERZGAISKI, Ireneusz (1929-) Poli;
instal
SANDBERG 154-157 (statement); 3 ill

PIETILA, Reima (1923-) Finn; arch
EMANUEL I 628-629 (statement); 1 ill

PIGNON, Edouard (1905-) Fren; ptr
CHARBONNIER v.2 189-197 (interview)
GOLDAINE 116-119 (interview); port
RITCHIE 31-34 (statement); port; 3 ill

PIJUAN, Juan Hernandez (1931-) Span;
ptr
SANDBERG 162-163 (statement); 2 ill
SKIRA 1976 68 (statement); 1 ill

PILCHER, Don (1942-) Amer; pott
HERMAN 98 (statement); port; 1 ill

PILKINGTON, Philip ( )
ART-LANGUAGE v.2 no.1 38-50
("Aspects of Authorities")
ART-LANGUAGE v.2 no.3 12-17
("Models and Indexes: Fringe
Benefits")
ART-LANGUAGE v.2 no.3 18-33
("Bibliotherapy")
ART-LANGUAGE v.3 no.2 1-6 ("For
Thomas Hobbes--I")
ART-LANGUAGE v.3 no.2 44-45
("Community Work")
ART-LANGUAGE v.3 no.2 52-58
("Vulgar and Popular Opinions")
ART-LANGUAGE v.3 no.2 59-62 ("Little
Grey Rabbit Goes to Sea")
ART-LANGUAGE v.3 no.2 63-64
("Overview The Paradox of a Heap of
Stones")
ART-LANGUAGE v.3 no.2 89-92

("Utopian Prayers and Infantile Marxism")

PILLET, Edgar (1912-) Fren; ptr
TEMOIGNAGES I 222-231 (statement); port; 10 ill

PINCEMIN, Jean-Pierre (1944-) Fren; ptr
SKIRA 1977 36 (statement); 1 ill

PINCHBECK, Peter (1940-) Amer; ptr
LEAVITT (statement); port; 5 ill

PINDELL, Howardena Doreen (1943-) Amer; ptr
ART-RITE no.6 25 (statement)
CELEBRATION (statement); 1 ill
INTERVIEWS 21-23 (interview); port; 2 ill
MILLER 130-156 (interview with Sally Swenson); port; 1 ill
NAYLOR 758-759 (extract from interview Marina Urbach); 1 ill
SCHAPIRO 54 (statement); port; 1 ill

PINE, Michael (1928-) Cana; sclp
CANADA 60-61 (statement); port; 1 ill

PINEDA, Marianna (1925-) Amer; sclp
ILLINOIS 1957 235 (response); 1 ill

PINKERTON, Clayton David (1931-) Amer; ptr
ILLINOIS 1967 176 (statement); 1 ill
ILLINOIS 1969 167 (statement); 1 ill

PINKNEY, Elliott (1934-) Amer; sclp
LEWIS I REVISED 64 (statement); port; 1 ill

PINTARIC, Josip (1927-) Yugo; ptr
TOMASEVIC 271-275 (statement); port; 1 ill

PINTO, Jody (1942-) Amer; sclp
ARTPARK 1975 98-99 (statement); port; 4 ill
QUINTESSENCE 14-27 (project proposal); ports; 25 ill

PIPER, Adrian (1948-) Amer; ptr
ART-RITE no.6 24 (statement)
ART-RITE no.14 5, 11-12 (response)
ART-RITE no.14 30 (statement)
CONCEPTUAL ART 36 (statement)
EVENTS I 47 (statement); self port
INTERVIEWS 24-27 (interview); port; 1 ill
ISSUE ("Some Political Self-Reflections"); 3 ill
MEYER 202-203 (text piece)
PAOLETTI 82-84 (statements, p.p.); 1 ill
SCHAPIRO 55 ("Notes on the Mythic Being, March, 1974"); port; 1 ill
SONDHEIM 267-269 ("Notes on The Mythic Being, I, March 1974")
SONDHEIM 270-289 ("Notes on The Mythic Being, II, January 1975"); 10 ill

PIPER, John (1903-) Brit; ptr
AXIS no.6 30-31 (essay: "Picasso Belongs Where?")
AXIS no.7 5-9 (essay: "England's Climate" with Geoffrey Grigson)
AXIS no.8 5-7 (essay: "Prehistory from the Air")
BARBER 55-68 (interview); port
EVANS 68-73 (essay: "Lost, A Valuable Object"); 2 ill
EVANS 116-125 (essay: "England's Early Sculptors")
PREMIER BILAN 313 (statement); port
ROTHENSTEIN 59 (statement, p.p.)
VINGTIEME v.1 no.3 41 (essay: "Abstraction on the Beach"); 1 ill

PIPPIN, Horace (1888-1946) Amer; ptr
BRITANNICA 87 (statement); port; 1 ill

FINE 112-120 (statements, o.p. 1972); 8 ill
JANIS II 186-191 ("My Life's Story"); port; 1 ill

PIQUERAS, Jorge (1925-) Peru/Fren; sclp
SKIRA 1976 94 (statement); 1 ill

PIRANDELLO, Fausto (1899-) Ital; ptr
VERZOCCHI 333-337 (statement); self port; 1 ill

PISANI, Vettor (1935-) Ital; instal
WALDMAN 106-127 (statement, in Italian); port; 15 ill

PISANO, Al ( ) Amer; sclp
ILLUSTRATION 50-53 (statement); port; 6 ill

PISSARRO, Camille (1830-1903) Fren; ptr
FRIEDENTHAL 148-149 (letters to Lucien Pissarro, 1900, 1903, p.p. 1950)
GOLDWATER 319 (statement, 1900)

PISTOLETTO, Michelangelo (1933-) Ital; instal
SKIRA 1975 16 (extract of interview with Marella Bandini, "Notiziario Arte Contemporanea," *Daedalo*, Turin, 3/73); 1 ill

PITCHFORTH, Roland Vivian (1895-) Brit; ptr
CONTEMPORARY (statement); port; 2 ill

PITTMAN, Hobson (1900-1972) ptr
BRITANNICA 88 (statement); port; 1 ill
M.H. DE YOUNG 104 (response); self port

PIZZINATO, Armando (1910-) Ital; ptr
VERZOCCHI 339-343 (statement); self port; 1 ill

PLACKMAN, Carl J. (1943-) Brit; instal, sclp
BRITISH (statement); 1 ill
CONTEMPORARY (statement); port; 2 ill
ENGLISH 284-289 (statement); port; 4 ill
SANDBERG 164-167 (statement); 10 ill

PLAGENS, Peter (1941-) Amer; ptr
TRACKS v.1 no.3 33-40 ("Subway Orbit")

PLATE, Walter (1925-1972) Amer; ptr
ILLINOIS 1959 256 (statement); 1 ill

PLATNER, Warren ( ) design
DIAMONSTEIN V 128-143 (interview); port; 11 ill

PLATSCHEK, Hans (1923-) Germ; ptr
CLAUS 121-128 (statement)

PLAZY, Gilles (1942-) Fren; ptr
SKIRA 1979 50 (statement); 1 ill

PLEMELJ, Anton (1923-) Yugo; ptr
TOMASEVIC 276-279 (statement); port; 2 ill

PLESSI, Fabrizio (1940-) Ital; sclp, photo
SKIRA 1976 16 (statement); 2 ill

PLETOS, Nancy ( ) Amer; sclp
BRAKKE 8-34 (statements); ports; 14 ill

PLOETZ, Gregory (1949-) Amer; ptr
TEXAS 16-19 (statement); 8 ill

PLUMB, John (1927-) Brit; ptr
CONTEMPORARY (statement); port; 2
ill

PLUNKETT, Edward C. (1939-) Iris;
illus
SKIRA 1976 46 (statement); 1 ill

POAG, James (1954-) Amer; ptr
GUMPERT III 73 (statement)

POE, Amos ( ) perf
REALLIFE no.6 28-31 (interview with
David Robbins); 1 ill

POEHLMANN, Joanna (1932-) Amer;
ptr
WISCONSIN I (statement); 1 ill
WISCONSIN II (statement); 1 ill

POELZIG, Hans (1869-1936) Germ; arch
CONRADS 14-17 (essay: "Fermentation
in Architecture," o.p. 1906)

POHL, Louis G. (1915-) Amer; ptr
HAAR I 96-102 (interview with
Prithwish Neogy); 3 ill

POIRIER, Anne (1942-) Fren; sclp,
photo
EMANUEL II 744-746 (statement); 1 ill
EUROPE 30, 68-69 ("Symmetry--
Reflection--Depth of the Great Black
Necropolis," in English and French); 1
ill
IDENTITE 79-82 (interview with
Jacques Clayssen); port
KUNST BLEIBT KUNST 280-283
(statement, in French and German); 4
ill
PARACHUTE no.8 19-20 (statement)
SKIRA 1976 30 (statement); 1 ill
SKIRA 1980 120, 152 (statement); 3 ill

POIRIER, Patrick (1942-) Fren; print,
sclp
EMANUEL II 744-746 (statement); 1 ill
EUROPE 30, 68-69 ("Symmetry--
Reflection--Depth of the Great Black
Necropolis," in English and French); 1
ill
IDENTITE 79-82 (interview with
Jacques Clayssen); port
KUNST BLEIBT KUNST 280-283
(statement, in French and German); 4
ill
PARACHUTE no.8 19-20 (statement)
SKIRA 1976 30 (statement); 1 ill
SKIRA 1980 120, 152 (statement); 3 ill

POLIAKOFF, Serge (1906-) Russ/Fren;
ptr
GOLDAINE 83-85 (interview); port
POENSGEN 123 ("Zur Frage des
Publikums," 1921)
PREMIER BILAN 314 (statement); port
RAGON 160-166 (statement)
TEMOIGNAGES I 232-239 (statement);
port; 6 ill
VINGTIEME N.S. no.9 29 (statement)
YALE 68 (statement)

POLIERI, Jacques ( )
QUADRUM no.8 166-168 (interview with
Andre Veinstein); 6 ill

POLLACK, Reginald (1924-) Amer; ptr
ILLINOIS 1965 87 (statement); 1 ill

POLLARO, Paul (1921-) Fren; ptr,
photo, print
VARIAN I (statement); port

POLLOCK, Jackson (1912-1956) Amer;
ptr
ART SINCE v.1 153 (statements, o.p.
1944, 1950)
ARTFORUM v.5 no.9 16-23 (statements,

in the essay: "The Genesis of Jackson Pollock: 1912 to 1943" by Francis V. O'Connor); 12 ill

CHIPP 546-548 (statements, o.p. 1944, 1947, 1948); port

CLAUS 56-65 (statement)

DOUZE PEINTRES (statement); 2 ill

FRIEDENTHAL 271-272 (statements, o.p. 1947, 1951); 1 ill

JANIS I 112-113 (statement); 1 ill

JOHNSON 1-4 (statement, o.p. 1944); 1 ill

JOHNSON 4-5 ("My Painting," o.p. 1947/48)

JOHNSON 5-10 (extract from interview with W. William Wright, 1950, p.p. 1967); 1 ill

MCCOUBREY 212-213 (statements, o.p. 1944, 1947)

PERSONAL (statement)

POSSIBILITIES 78-83 ("My Painting..."); 6 ill

PROTTER 249 (statement, 1947)

RODMAN I 76-87 (interview)

ROSE II 151-152 (statement, o.p. 1944)

ROSE II 152 ("My Painting," o.p. 1947)

ROSE II REVISED 122-123 (statement, o.p. 1944)

ROSE II REVISED 123 (extract from "My Painting," o.p. 1947-48)

ROSE II REVISED 124-125 (statement, p.p. 1972)

SEGHERS 280-281 (statements, o.p. 1944, 1947-48)

SEGHERS· 281-282 (extract from interview with Selden Rodman, o.p. 1957)

SEUPHOR 244-245 (statement); 1 ill

SIX PEINTRES (statement, o.p. 1947/48); port; 2 ill

SPENCER 296-298 (statement, o.p. 1944); 1 ill

POLONSKY, Arthur (1925-) Amer; ptr
ILLINOIS 1951 207 (statement)

POLONYI, Charles ( ) Hung; arch
NEWMAN 42-47 (essay); port; 15 ill

POLSHEK, James Stewart (1930-) Amer; arch
DIAMONSTEIN II 185-205 (interview); port; 4 ill
EMANUEL I 632-634 (statement); 1 ill

POMAR, Julio (1926-) Port; ptr
PREMIER BILAN 314 (statement); port

POMODORO, Arnaldo (1926-) Ital; sclp
HUNTER 42-45 (extract from interview with Sam Hunter, o.p. 1974); 1 ill
SKIRA 1977 100 (statement); 2 ill

POMPILI, Lucian Octavius ( ) pott
VIEWPOINT 1978 28-29 (statement); 4 ill

PONCE DE LEON, Michael (1922-) Amer; print, ptr
AMERICAN PRINTS 47, 69 (statement); 1 ill

PONCELET, Maurice Georges (1897-) Fren; ptr
COLLARD 210-213 (interview); port; 1 ill

PONTOREAU, Daniel (1947-) Fren; sclp
SKIRA 1979 59 (statement); 3 ill

POOLE, Leslie (1942-) Cana; coll, ptr
POINT OF VIEW 24 (statement); 1 ill

POOR, Anne (1918-) Amer; ptr
GUSSOW 92-93 (interview, 1970); 1 ill

POOR, Henry Varnum (1888-1970) Amer; ptr
FIFTY (statement); port; 1 ill
GUSSOW 127-129 (interview, 1970); 1 ill

POPE, Terry (1941-) Brit; sclp
CONTEMPORARY (statement); port; 1
ill
HAYWARD 1978 88-91 (statement); 3 ill

POPOV, Georgije (1944-) Yugo; ptr
TOMASEVIC 280-282 (statement); port;
1 ill

POPOVA, Lyubov (1889-1924) Russ; ptr
BOWLT 146-148 (statement, o.p. 1919);
1 ill

POPOVIC, Zoran ( ) Yugo
VISION no.2 23-24 (essay: "For Self-
Management Art")

P-ORRIDGE, Genesis
SEE: GENESIS P-ORRIDGE

PORRO, Ricardo ( ) Fren; arch
ARCHITECTURES 164-169 (essay:
"Porro par Porro"); 7 ill

PORTER, David (1912-) Amer; ptr
ILLINOIS 1952 221 (statement)
ILLINOIS 1961 166 (response); port; 1 ill

PORTER, Eliot F. (1901-) Amer; photo
HILL 237-252 (interview, 1975); port
WALSH 603-605 (statement); 1 ill

PORTER, Fairfield (1907-1975) Amer;
ptr
ART NOW v.1 no.6 (statement); 1 ill
ART VOICES v.4 no.1 22-23 (essay:
"Against Idealism," o.p. 1964)
CUMMINGS 124-135 (interview, 1968);
port; 2 ill
GUSSOW 144-145 (interview, 1970; and
letter, 1968); 1 ill
IT IS no.2 28-29 ("The Short Review")
SEITZ III 143 (extract from *School of
New York*, o.p. 1959)

PORTER, George ( ) Amer; sclp, illus
ILLUSTRATION 20-23 (statement); port;
5 ill

PORTER, James F. ( ) Amer; arch
GA HOUSES no.3 172-175 (statement); 9
ill

PORTER, Katherine (1941-) Amer; ptr
GUMPERT III 73-74 (statement)

PORTER, Robert ( ) Amer; sclp, envir
ARTPARK 1978 50-51 (statement); 6 ill

PORTIS, Michael (1950-) Amer; video
ROSS 68-69 (statement); 2 ill

PORTLAND, Jack (1946-) Amer; ptr
GUENTHER 98-99 (statement); port; 1
ill

PORTMAN, John C. (1924-) Amer; arch
DIAMONSTEIN II 208-228 (interview);
port; 4 ill

PORTNOFF, Alexander (1887-)
Russ/Amer; sclp
100 CONTEMPORARY 144-145
(statement); port; 1 ill

PORTWAY, Douglas O. (1922-) Brit;
ptr, illus
CONTEMPORARY (statement); port; 2
ill
NAYLOR 772-773 (statement); 1 ill

PORTZAMPARC, Christian de ( ) Fren;
arch
ARCHITECTURES 154-159 (essay: "Le
Symbolique et L'Utilitaire"); 9 ill

POSAVEC-DOLENC, Tereza (1935-)
Yugo; ptr
TOMASEVIC 283-285 (statement); port;
1 ill

POSKA, Roland (1938-) Amer; ptr
WISCONSIN I (statement); 1 ill

POST WOLCOTT, Marion (1910-)
Amer; photo
WALSH 606-607 (statement); 1 ill

POTOK, Charlotte (1930-) Amer; pott
HERMAN 99 (statement); port; 1 ill

POTT, Carl (1906-) Germ; design
DESIGN 151-153 (essay: "Metalwork")

POTTER, Mary (1900-) Brit; ptr
CONTEMPORARY (statement); port; 2
ill

POU, F. Alyson (1952-) Amer; film
AVANT-GARDE 28-29 (statement); 6 ill

POUGNY, Jean
SEE: PUNI, IVAN

POULIN, Roland ( ) Cana; sclp, instal
ARTPARK 1977 68-69 (statement); 4 ill
PARACHUTE no.1 24-27 (statement); 4
ill

POULOS, Basilios (1941-) Amer; ptr
TEXAS 20-23 (statement); 4 ill

POUSETTE-DART, Richard (1916-)
Amer; ptr
ILLINOIS 1952 221-222 (extract from
talk given at the School of the Museum
of Fine Arts, Boston, 1951); 1 ill
ILLINOIS 1953 209 (statement); 1 ill
MOTHERWELL 8-22 (three group
discussions: "Artists' Sessions at
Studio 35," New York, 1950)
NEW DECADE 69-71 (extract from talk
given at the School of the Museum of
Fine Arts, Boston, 1951); 4 ill
PERSONAL (statement)

POVOLNI, Mihal (1935-) Yugo; ptr
TOMASEVIC 286-288 (statement); port;
1 ill

POVORINA, Alexandra (1886-)
Russ/Germ; ptr
ABSTRACTION no.2 35 (statement); 2
ill
ABSTRACTION no.4 24 (statement); 2
ill

POWELL, Arnold Joseph Philip (1921-)
Brit; arch
EMANUEL I 641-642 (statement); 1 ill

POWELL, Geoffrey (1920-) Brit; arch
SEE: CHAMBERLIN POWELL AND
BON

POWELL, Michael ( ) film
REALLIFE no.7 12-14 (interview)

POWELL, Richard ( ) arch
GA HOUSES no.9 42-43 (statement);
port

POWER, John Wardell (1881-) Atrl; ptr
ABSTRACTION no.1 28 (statement); 2
ill
ABSTRACTION no.2 36 (statement); 2
ill
ABSTRACTION no.3 34 (statement); 1
ill

POWER, Mark (1937-) Amer; photo
FRALIN 10-11, 32-33 (statement); 1 ill
PHOTOGRAPHY (statement); 1 ill

POZZATTI, Rudy O. (1925-) Amer;
print, sclp, ptr
AMERICAN PRINTS 48, 69 (statement);
1 ill
FULBRIGHT 40 (statement)
ILLINOIS 1957 235-236 (response); 1 ill
RISENHOOVER 111-122 (interview)

YOUNG 1960 (statement); 2 ill

POZZI, Lucio (1935-) Ital; ptr, sclp, print
ART-RITE no.3 14-15 (letter)
ART-RITE no.9 7-8 ("Painting Matters")
ART-RITE no.14 5, 12 (response)
EMANUEL II 754-755 (statement); 1 ill
NAYLOR 776-778 (statement); 1 ill
SKIRA 1978 114 (statement); 2 ill
SKIRA 1979 70 (statement); 1 ill
TRACKS v.1 no.3 75-81 ("Instruction Manual")
WEBER 35-57 ("A Continuous Discussion"); ports
WHITE WALLS no.2 46-53 (handwritten text piece)
WHITE WALLS no.5 80-84 (text piece)

PRADEL, Jean-Louis ( ) Fren; ptr
SKIRA 1977 103 (statement); 2 ill

PRAMPOLINI, Enrico (1894-) Ital; ptr
ABSTRACTION no.2 36-37 (statement); 2 ill
ABSTRACTION no.3 36 (statement); 2 ill
APOLLONIO 115-118 ("Chromophony-- the Colours of Sounds," o.p. 1913)
APOLLONIO 181-183 ("The Futurist 'Atmosphere-Structure'--Basis for an Architecture," o.p. 1914-15)
APOLLONIO 200-202 ("The Futurist Stage (Manifesto)" o.p. 1915)
VERZOCCHI 345-349 (statement); self port; 1 ill

PRANGE, Sally Bowen (1927-) Amer; pott
HERMAN 100 (statement); port; 1 ill

PRANTL, Karl (1923-) Aust; sclp, envir
HAUSSER 150-151 (statement, o.p. 1976); 1 ill

PRASSINOS, Mario (1916-) Gree; ptr, text
CHARBONNIER v.1 107-117 (interview)
EMANUEL II 755-757 (statement); 1 ill
GOLDAINE 177-179 (interview); port
VINGTIEME N.S. no.7 84 (interview with Jean Lescure); 2 ill

PRATT, James Reece (1927-) Amer; arch
EMANUEL I 642-644 (statement); 1 ill

PRATT, Mary (1935-) Cana; ptr
GRAHAM 53-66 (statement); 12 ill

PREDMORE, Jessie ( ) Amer; ptr
JANIS II 213-215 (statements); port; 1 ill

PREECE, Lawrence W. (1942-) Brit; ptr, print
SKIRA 1979 29 (statement); 1 ill

PREETORIUS, Emil (1883-) Germ; print
THORN 10, 29, 31, 32, 43, 46, 50, 51, 52, 55, 58, 79, 83-86, 91, 102, 150, 175, 182, 201, 203, 204, 245, 279, 282, 285, 291, 301, 303, 326 (statements, p.p.)

PRENDERGAST, Maurice (1859-1924) Amer; ptr
CRISPO II (statement, 1905); 14 ill

PRENT, Mark (1947-) Amer; sclp, envir, instal
EMANUEL II 757-758 (statement); 1 ill
NAYLOR 780-781 (statement); 1 ill

PRESSER, Josef (1907-1967) Amer; ptr, print
ZAIDENBERG 141-143 (essay: "The Nature of the Artist"); 4 ill

PRESSET, Henri (1928-) Swis; sclp
SKIRA 1975 112-113 (extract from interview with Jean-Luc Daval, 1973); 1 ill

PRESSMANE, Joseph (1904-) Poli/Fren
PREMIER BILAN 315 (statement); port

PRESTINI, James (1908-) Amer; sclp, design
ILLINOIS 1969 115 (statement); 1 ill
ILLINOIS 1974 98-99 (statement); 1 ill

PRESTON, Astrid (1945-) Amer; ptr
CELEBRATION (statement); 1 ill

PRESTOPINO, Gregorio (1907-) Amer; ptr
ILLINOIS 1951 208 (statement); 1 ill
ILLINOIS 1952 222 (statement); 1 ill
ILLINOIS 1955 231 (statement); 1 ill

PREUSSER, Robert (1919-) Amer; ptr
KEPES VIII 208-219 (essay: "Visual Education for Science and Engineering Students")

PRICE, Cedric (1934-) Brit; arch
EMANUEL I 644-645 (statement); 1 ill

PRICE, Clayton S. (1874-1950) Amer; ptr
JANIS I 67 (statement); 1 ill

PRICE, Jonathan ( )
BELFORD 129-157 (group discussion)

PRICE, Ken (1935-) Amer; pott, sclp
WECHSLER 112-117 (statement); port; 5 ill

PRICE, Leslie (1945-) Amer; ptr
LEWIS II 101 (statement); port; 1 ill

PRINCE, Douglas D. (1943-) Amer; photo
WALSH 608-610 (statement); 1 ill

PRINCE, Richard Edmund (1949-) Cana; sclp, ptr
FACE IT 16-17 (statement); 1 ill
REALLIFE no.3 2-3 ("Primary Transfers")
REALLIFE no.4 29-31 ("Menthol Pictures")
TRACKS v.2 no.3 41-46 ("Eleven Conversations")
WHITE WALLS no.2 2-5 ("Author's Note")
WHITE WALLS no.4 2-3 ("Moving by Wading more than Swimming")

PRINI, Emilio ( ) Ital
CELANT 211-218 (statement, in Italian); port; 18 ill

PROBST, Joachim (1913-) Amer; ptr
ILLINOIS 1959 256-257 (statement); 1 ill

PROCKTOR, Patrick (1936-) Brit; ptr
BARBER 145-158 (interview); port
CONTEMPORARY (extract from essay: "A Return to Watercolour," o.p. 1967); port; 2 ill

PROCTOR, Jody (1943-) Amer; video
NEW VISIONS (statement); 3 ill

PRODUCTIVIST GROUP (group)
BANN 18-20 ("Program of the Productivist Group," o.p. 1920)

PROESCH, Gilbert
SEE: GILBERT AND GEORGE

PROHASKA, Ray (1901-) Yugo/Amer; ptr, illus
ILLINOIS 1953 210 (statement); 1 ill

NORTH LIGHT 196-201 (statement); ports; 2 ill

PROJECTIONIST GROUP (group)
BOWLT 240-241 ("Our Primary Slogans," o.p. 1924)

PRONKO, Jane ( ) Amer; ptr
REGIONALISM 14-15 (statement); port; 1 ill

PROSEK, Josef (1923-) Czec; photo
WALSH 610 (statement); 1 ill

PROSS, Lester F. (1924-) Amer; ptr
NOSANOW I 103 (statement); 1 ill

PROUVE, Jean (1901-) Fren; arch
EMANUEL I 645-646 (statement); 1 ill

PROVAN, Sara (1917-) Amer; ptr
ILLINOIS 1953 210-211 (statement); 1 ill

PROVISOR, Janis ( ) Amer; ptr
OUTSIDE I 20-23, 31 (statement); port; 3 ill

PRUS, Victor (1917-) Cana; arch
EMANUEL I 646-648 (statement); 1 ill

PRUTCH, Joseph G. (1946-) Amer; wood
WOODWORKING 40-41 (statement); port; 2 ill

PUENTE, Alejandro (1933-) sclp
PREMIO NACIONAL 1966 34-35 (extract from interview with Saul Yurkievich); port; 1 ill

PUGH, Valerie (1952-) Cana; pott, sclp
POINT OF VIEW 26 (statement); 1 ill

PUJA, Florika (1920-) Yugo; ptr

TOMASEVIC 289-291 (statement); port; 2 ill

PULSA (group)
ART AND TECHNOLOGY 275 (project proposal)

PUMA, Fernando (1919-) Amer; ptr
ILLINOIS 1952 222-223 (statement); 1 ill

PUNCHATZ, Don Ivan ( ) Amer; illus
ILLUSTRATION 98-100 (statement); port; 2 ill

PUNI, Ivan (1894-1956) Russ; ptr
BANN 51-52 ("A Call for Elementarist Art," o.p. 1922)
BOWLT 112-113 (statement, o.p. 1915-16); port; 1 ill

PURCELL, Ann (1941-) Amer; ptr
CORCORAN 84-98 (statement and interview); port; 14 ill

PURCELL, Rosamond Wolff (1942-) Amer; photo
WALSH 610-612 (statement); 1 ill

PURIFOY, Noah (1917-) Amer, sclp
LEWIS II 68 (statement); port; 2 ill

PURRMANN, Hans (1880-1966) Germ; ptr
SCHMIDT 72-73 (letter, 1935)

PURYEAR, Martin (1941-) Amer; sclp
SHEARER 54-57 (interview); 3 ill

PYE, William (1938-) Brit; sclp
CONTEMPORARY (statement); port; 2 ill
NAYLOR 783 (statement); 1 ill

QUANCHI, Leo (1892-) Amer; ptr
ILLINOIS 1951 208 (statement); 1 ill

QUARONI, Ludovico (1911-) Ital; arch
EMANUEL I 651-652 (statement); 1 ill

QUAYTMAN, Harvey (1937-) Amer; ptr
ART NOW v.2 no.5 (statement); 1 ill
NAYLOR 784-785 (statement); 1 ill
TUCKER I 16 ("10 Thoughts on Color")

QUENTIN, Bernard (1923-) Fren; ptr
PREMIER BILAN 315 (statement); port
SEUPHOR 247 (statement); 1 ill

QUIGLEY, Rob Wellington ( ) Amer;
arch
LA JOLLA 75-77 (statement); port; 4 ill

QUINN, Jalal ( ) ptr
CRISS-CROSS no.7/8/9 92-95 (poem); 9
ill

QUIRT, Walter W. (1902-1968) Amer;
ptr
ILLINOIS 1952 223-224 (statement); 1 ill
JANIS I 112 (statement); 1 ill

QUISTGAARD, Jens (1919-) Dani;
design
DESIGN 197-199 (essay: "Wood")

RABAN, William (1948-) Brit; film
ENGLISH 460-461 (statement); port; 1 ill
KUNST BLEIBT KUNST 400-401 (statement); 1 ill

RABASCALL, Joan (1935-) Span; coll, print
NAYLOR 785-786 (statement); 1 ill
SKIRA 1977 73 (statement); 2 ill

RABINOWITCH, David (1943-) Cana; sclp
KUNST BLEIBT KUNST 290-293 (statement); 3 ill
SKIRA 1979 28, 117 ("Preliminary Thoughts on the Construction of Scale: Ten Queries and Replies"); 1 ill

RABINOWITCH, Royden Leslie (1943-) Cana; sclp
SKIRA 1978 120-121 (statement); 2 ill

RABUZIN, Ivan (1919-) Yugo; ptr
TOMASEVIC 292-301 (statement); port; 2 ill

RACHEL, Vaughan (1933-) Amer; photo
SCHAPIRO 56 (statement); port; 1 ill

RACITI, Cherie (1942-) Amer; ptr, instal, sclp
SCRIPPS COLLEGE (statement); 1 ill

RACZ, Andre (1916-) Amer; ptr, print
JANIS I 104 (statement); 1 ill
TIGER no.8 47-51 (essay: "Techniques are Born of Spiritual Necessity")

RADCLIFFE, John (1940-) Amer; photo
FRALIN 24-25, 40-41 (statement); 1 ill

RADULOVIC, Savo (1911-) Yugo/Amer; ptr
FULBRIGHT 41 (statement); 1 ill

RADY, Elsa (1943-) Amer; pott
HERMAN 101 (statement); port; 1 ill

RADZIWILL, Franz (1895-) Germ; ptr, print
THORN 54 (statement, p.p.)

RAFFAELE, Joseph (1933-) Amer; ptr
ARTHUR 98-113 (interview); port; 14 ill
BATTCOCK III 212-222 (interview with Gene R. Swenson, o.p. 1966); 6 ill
EMANUEL II 764-765 (statement); 1 ill
HOPKINS 54-55 (statement); port; 1 ill
ILLINOIS 1974 100-101 (extract from letter to Marion Greenstone, 1973); 1 ill
NAYLOR 787-788 (statement); 1 ill
SAO PAULO 94-95 (statements and excerpts from letters); port
VARIAN I (statement); port

RAFFO, Steve ( ) ptr
BETHERS II 126-127 (statement); 2 ill

RAFOLS-CASAMADA, Albert (1923-) Span; ptr
SKIRA 1979 54 (statement); 1 ill

RAGAZZINI, Vincenzo (1934-) Ital; photo
WALSH 613-614 (statement); 1 ill

RAHMMINGS, Keith ( )
WHITE WALLS no.4 16-17 ("Five Hundred Words or so")

RAIKEN, Laupin
SEE: GUERILLA ART ACTION GROUP

RAIMOND-DITYVON, Claude (1937-) Fren; photo
WALSH 614-615 (statement); 1 ill

RAIN, Charles Whedon (1911-) Amer;
ptr
ILLINOIS 1951 209 (statement); 1 ill
ILLINOIS 1953 211-212 (statement); 1 ill
ILLINOIS 1957 237 (response); 1 ill
MILLER 1943 49 (statement); 1 ill

RAINER, Arnulf (1929-) Aust; ptr,
photo
EMANUEL II 765-768 (statement); 1 ill
IDENTITE 83-86 (interview with
Jacques Clayssen); port
NAYLOR 789-790 (statement); 1 ill

RAINER, Roland (1910-) Aust; arch
EMANUEL I 653-654 (statement); 1 ill

RAINER, Yvonne (1934-) Amer; film,
perf
AVALANCHE no.5 46-59 (statements
and interview); 30 ill
KUNST BLEIBT KUNST 376-377
(statement); 2 ill
LIVE no.4 18-19 (letter)
PARACHUTE no.10 45-49 (interview, in
English)
STEDELIJK 190 ("Objects Dances"); 1
ill

RAJZIK, Jaroslav (1940-) Czec; photo
WALSH 615-616 (statement); 1 ill

RAMBERG, Christina (1946-) Amer; ptr
ACKLAND 20-37, 72-73 (group
discussion 10/29/79); 2 ill

RAMIREZ, Dora (1925-) ptr
ANGEL 127-145 (interview); port; 1 ill

RAMIREZ CHAVARRIA, Jose
SEE: CHAVARRIA, Jose Ramirez

RAMIREZ VAZQUEZ, Pedro (1919-)
Mexi; arch
BAYON 130-153 (interview); 26 ill

EMANUEL I 654-655 (statement); 1 ill

RAMOS, Federico Manuel Peralta (1939-
) ptr
PREMIO NACIONAL 1965 32-33
(statement); port; 1 ill

RAMOS, Mel (1935-) Amer; ptr
ART NOW v.3 no.1 (statement); 1 ill
EMANUEL II 768-769 (statement); 1 ill
HOPKINS 56-57 (statement); port; 1 ill
NAYLOR 790-792 (statement); 1 ill

RAMS, Dieter (1932-) Germ; design
DESIGN 81-85 (essay: "Appliances")

RAMSDEN, Mel (1944-) Brit
ART-LANGUAGE v.1 no.2 84-88 ("Notes
on Genealogies")
ART-LANGUAGE v.1 no.3 1-3 ("The
Society for Theoretical Art and
Analyses Proceedings")
ART-LANGUAGE v.1 no.3 4-6 (essay:
"Art-Inquiry")
ART-LANGUAGE v.1 no.3 29 (essay: "A
Preliminary Proposal for the Directing
of Perception")
ART-LANGUAGE v.2 no.1 28-37 ("Four
Wages of Sense")
ART-LANGUAGE v.2 no.2 1-10 (essay:
"Some Questions on the
Characterization of Questions")
ART-LANGUAGE v.2 no.2 21-28 (essay:
"Art Language and Art-Language")
ART-LANGUAGE v.2 no.3 38-52 (essay:
"Frameworks and Phantoms")
ART-LANGUAGE v.2 no.3 53-72 (essay:
"Problems of Art and Language
Space")
ART-LANGUAGE v.3 no.1 1-110 ("Draft
for an Anti-Textbook")
ART-LANGUAGE v.3 no.2 31-40
("Brainstorming--New York")
ART-LANGUAGE v.3 no.2 81-86
("Strategy is Political: Dear M...")

ART-LANGUAGE v.3 no.2 89-92 ("Utopian Prayers and Infantile Marxism")
ART-LANGUAGE v.3 no.3 129-130 (letter)
MEYER 96-103 ("Excerpts from the Grammarian," o.p. 1971)
VRIES 90-95 (essay: "The Role of Language," o.p. 1969)
VRIES 96-103 (essay: "Some Notes on Practice and Theory," o.p. 1969)
VRIES 104-115 (talk: "The Artist as Victim," given in Melbourne, 1972)
SEE ALSO: SOCIETY FOR THEORETICAL ART AND ANALYSES

RANALLI, George ( ) arch
GA HOUSES no.12 108-111 (statement); 27 ill

RANCILLAC, Bernard (1931-) Fren; ptr
KUNST UND POLITIK (statement); port; 3 ill
SKIRA 1976 62-63 (statement); 1 ill

RAND, Glenn (1944-) Amer; photo
FUGITIVE (statement); 1 ill

RAND, Paul (1914-) design, print
KEPES VIII 156-174 (essay: "Design and the Play Instinct")
KEPES IX 127-135 (essay: "Advertisement: Ad Vivum ad Hominem?"); 1 ill

RANDOLPH, Larry ( ) Amer; arch, design
LIFE 121-138 (interview); port

RANKINE, Terry ( ) Amer; arch
EMANUEL I 133-135 (statement); 1 ill

RANNEFELD, James
SEE: JAWAR

RAPOPORT, Sid ( ) photo, print
DUGAN 215-220 (interview, 1978)

RAPOPORT, Sonya ( ) Amer; coll, print
ZEITLIN (statement)

RAPPOPORT, Janet (1916-) Amer; instal, ptr
AWARDS 16-19 (statement); port; 7 ill

RAPSON, Ralph (1914-) Amer; arch
EMANUEL I 655-657 (statement); 1 ill
HEYER 55-59 (interview); 16 ill

RASIC, Milan (1931-) Yugo; ptr
TOMASEVIC 302-307 (statement); port; 1 ill

RASKIN, Jeff (1943-) Amer
ART AND TECHNOLOGY 276-278 (project proposal); 3 ill

RASKIN, Saul (1878-) Russ/Amer; ptr
100 CONTEMPORARY 146-147 (statement); port; 1 ill

RATHSACK, Lawrence P. (1920-) Amer; ptr
WISCONSIN I (statement); 1 ill
WISCONSIN II (statement); 1 ill

RATKAI, George S. (1907-) Amer; sclp, ptr
ILLINOIS 1951 209-210 (statement); 1 ill
ILLINOIS 1953 212 (statement); 1 ill
ILLINOIS 1955 231 (statement); 1 ill
ILLINOIS 1957 237-238 (response); 1 ill

RATTNER, Abraham (1895-1978) Amer; ptr
BRITANNICA 89 (statement); port; 1 ill
GOODRICH 37-52 (statement); 12 ill
ILLINOIS 1951 210 (statement); 1 ill
ILLINOIS 1957 238-240 (response); 1 ill
ILLINOIS 1963 126 (statement); 1 ill

MINOTAURE no.5 27-29 ("Danses--Horisons"); 33 ill

REVOLUTION SURREALISTE no.11 32-40 (group discussion: "Recherches sur la Sexualite")

SEITZ III 48-49 (Preface from *One Hundred Objects of My Affection*); 3 ill

TIME-LIFE III 130-131 (statements, p.p.); 2 ill

VINGTIEME v.1 no.2 16-19 ("La Photographie qui Console"); 5 ill

RAY, Robert D. (1924-1976) Amer; print, ptr
ILLINOIS 1957 240-241 (response); 1 ill
ILLINOIS 1959 258 (statement); 1 ill

RAY, Ruth (1919-1977) Amer; ptr
ILLINOIS 1959 259 (statement); 1 ill

RAYMOND, Lilo (1922-) Germ/Amer; photo
WALSH 618-619 (statement); 1 ill

RAYMOND, Marie (1908-) Fren; ptr
TEMOIGNAGES I 240-245 (statement); port; 5 ill

RAYNAUD, Jean-Pierre (1939-) Fren; sclp, print
ART SINCE v.2 328 (statement, o.p. 1968)
DOUZE ANS 297-299 (statement); port; 5 ill
SKIRA 1978 72 (statement); 1 ill

RAYNOR, Vivien ( ) ptr
ARTS YEARBOOK v.7 46-55 (essay: "Critic for a Day")
ARTS YEARBOOK v.8 116-120 (essay: "Costantino Nivola")

RAYSSE, Martial (1936-) Fren; ptr, sclp
BATTCOCK V 400-401 (statement)

STEDELIJK 193-194 (statement, in French); 4 ill

READ, Edie (1949-) Amer; sclp
BOSTON I (interview); 1 ill

READ, Mark Woodward (1950-) Amer; sclp, metal
MICHIGAN 34-35 (statement); 1 ill

READ, Simon (1949-) Brit; photo
ARTIST AND CAMERA 50-51 (statement); 5 ill

REALIDAD, Equipo
SEE: EQUIPO REALIDAD

REBAY, Hilla (1890-) Amer; ptr
FRASCINA 145-148 (essay: "The Beauty of Non-Objectivity," o.p. 1937)

REDDIX, Roscoe (1933-) Amer; ptr
LEWIS II 40 (statement); port; 1 ill

REDER, Bernard (1897-1963) Aust/Amer; sclp, arch, print
ILLINOIS 1953 213 (statement); 1 ill
ILLINOIS 1961 188-189 (response); port; 1 ill

REDERER, Franz (1899-) Swis/Amer; ptr
ILLINOIS 1952 225-226 (statement); 1 ill
M.H. DE YOUNG 108 (response); self port

REDFERN, David (1947-) Brit; ptr
BOSHIER (statement); port; 2 ill

REDO, Rem Doxfud
SEE: HILL, Anthony

REDON, Odilon (1840-1916) Fren; ptr, print

CHIPP 116-119 ("Suggestive Art," 1909); self port
CHIPP 119-120 (statement, o.p. 1922)
TIGER no.8 64-72 (essay: "On Lithography," o.p. 1915)

REED, David (1946-) Amer; ptr
ART-RITE no.9 9 ("On Jumping;" "On Intermediate Cases")
ART-RITE no.9 29-34 (group discussion)
GUMPERT IV 36-39, 45-46 (statement); port; 3 ill
RE-VIEW v.2/3 20-23 (statement); 3 ill

REED, Jerry (1949-) Amer; ptr
LEWIS II 93 (statement); port; 1 ill

REED, Orrel P. (1921-) Amer; ptr
CALIFORNIA--PAINTING 47 (statement); 1 ill

REEDY, Robert T. (1952-) Amer; pott
NOSANOW I 104 (statement); 2 ill

REFREGIER, Anton (1905-) Russ/Amer; ptr
BRITANNICA 90 (statement); port; 1 ill
ILLINOIS 1951 210-211 (statement); 1 ill
ZAIDENBERG 36-39 (essay: "Line"); 6 ill

REGINATO, Peter (1945-) Amer; sclp
NAYLOR 798-799 (statement); 1 ill

REHWINKEL, Charles (1943-) Amer; ptr
BRENTANO 308-309 (statement); 1 ill

REICH, Don (1931-) Amer; ptr
ILLINOIS 1959 260 (statement); 1 ill
ILLINOIS 1961 158 (response); port; 1 ill

REICH, Murray (1932-) ptr
TUCKER I 8 (statement)

REICH, Steve (1936-) Amer; print, perf, sound
PARACHUTE no.2 27-29 (statement, in English); port
VIEW v.1 no.4 (interview); port; 6 ill

REICHEK, Jesse (1916-) Amer; print, ptr
ART AND TECHNOLOGY 289-295 (project proposal); port; 2 ill

REICHEU, Bernard ( ) Fren; arch
ARCHITECTURES 140-143 (essay: "L'Art du Fondu Enchaine," with Philippe Robert); 8 ill

REICHMAN, Fred (1925-) Amer; ptr
HOPKINS 58-59 (statement); port; 1 ill

REID, Charles (1936-) Amer; ptr
DAUGHERTY 48-65 (statements); ports; 2 ill

REID, Leslie (1947-) Cana; photo, ptr, print
GRAHAM 67-77 (statement); 5 ill

REID, Richard ( ) arch
GA HOUSES no.11 108-119 (letter); 79 ill

REID, Robert G. ( ) Amer; sclp
ART PATRON ART 53-54 (statement); port; 1 ill

REID, Terry ( )
ART NETWORK no.1 9 (letter)
ART NETWORK no.1 42 (statement)

REID, William (1927-) Amer; ptr
LEWIS I 50 (statement); port

REIF, David (1941-) Amer; ptr
REGIONALISM 16-17 (statement); port; 1 ill

REIGL, Judit (1923-) Hung/Fren; ptr
SKIRA 1976 74 (statement); 1 ill

REIMANN, William (1935-) Amer; sclp
STRUCTURED (statement); 3 ill
YOUNG 1965 (statement); 1 ill

REINDEER WERK (group) perf
AVALANCHE no.13 5 (statement); 1 ill

REINGARDT-KARLSTROM, Ragnhild (
) Swed/Amer; sclp, envir
ARTPARK 1983 42-43 (statement); 1 ill

REINHARDT, Ad (1913-1967) Amer; ptr
ART SINCE v.1 292 (statements, o.p.
1957, 1967)
ART VOICES v.4 no.2 86-87 ("39 Art
Planks"); 2 ill
ARTFORUM v.4 no.7 34-35 (statements,
1960, 1965); 1 ill
BATTCOCK I 199-209 (statements, o.p.
1957, 1962, 1963, 1964)
CONCEPTUAL ART 46, 51, 52, 54, 59
(statements)
CRISPO I (statement); 13 ill
GASSNER 595 ("The Last Word (A
Description of a Canvas Called
Abstract Painting)")
ILLINOIS 1952 226-227 (statement)
IT IS no.1 42 (statement)
IT IS no.2 76-77 ("All-Over Painting")
IT IS no.4 25 ("Seven Quotes")
IT IS no.5 34-38 (group discussion)
JANIS I 82 (statement); 1 ill
JOHNSON 31-35 ("Art-as-Art," o.p.
1962); 1 ill
KEPES I 180-183 (poem: "Art in Art is
Art as Art")
MILLER 1963 80-86 (various
statements, 1955-1963); port; 2 ill
MOTHERWELL 8-22 (three group
discussions: "Artists' Sessions at
Studio 35" New York, 1950)
NEW DECADE 72-74 (statement); 3 ill

RODMAN I 98-99 (interview)
ROSE II 160-162 (extract from essay:
"Art-as-Art," o.p. 1962)
ROSE II REVISED 137-139 (extract from
essay: "Art-as-Art," o.p. 1962)
ROSE II REVISED 142-145 (group
discussion, o.p. 1952)
ROSE II REVISED 200-204 (extract from
talk given to the College Art
Association, New York, 1960)
TRACKS v.1 no.1 9, 42, 48, 58, 62
(postcards to Joan Washburn)
TRACKS v.1 no.3 29-31 (postcards to
Eleanor Ward, Elaine de Kooning, and
Betty Parsons)

REINHARDT, Siegfried Gerhard (1925-)
Germ/Amer; ptr
ILLINOIS 1957 241 (response); 1 ill
YOUNG 1960 (statement); 2 ill

REISMAN, Philip (1904-) Amer; ptr
100 CONTEMPORARY 150-151
(statement); port; 1 ill

REISS, Lionel S. (1894-) Amer; ptr
100 CONTEMPORARY 148-149
(statement); port; 1 ill

REISS, Roland (1929-) Amer; sclp, instal
HOUSE 80-81 (statement); 1 ill
VISUAL v.4 no.3 4-7 (interview); 3 ill

REITZENSTEIN, Reinhard (1949-)
Germ/Cana; photo
VANCOUVER (statement); 3 ill

REMINGTON, Deborah (1935-) Amer;
ptr
CELEBRATION (statement); 1 ill
ILLINOIS 1967 166 (statement); 1 ill
IMAGE COLOR FORM 20-21 (statement);
1 ill
NAYLOR 800-801 (statement); 1 ill
SCHAPIRO 57 (statement); port; 1 ill

RENART, Emilio J. (1925-) sclp
PREMIO NACIONAL 1964 36-37 (statement); port; 1 ill
PREMIO NACIONAL 1965 62-63 (statement); port; 1 ill

RENNELS, Sig ( ) Amer; sclp
ARTPARK 1976 172-173 (statement); 5 ill

RENNIE, Bill (1953-) Cana; sclp, pott
POINT OF VIEW 28 (statement); 1 ill

RENOIR, Pierre Auguste (1841-1919) Fren; ptr
GOLDWATER 322 (statement, 1915)

RENOUF, Edda (1943-) Amer; sclp, ptr, print
EMANUEL II 775 (statement)
NAYLOR 801 (statement)
PARACHUTE no.9 25-29 (interview and statement, in English); 5 ill
SKIRA 1979 51-52 (statement); 1 ill

RENTERIA, Philip (1947-) Amer; ptr
TEXAS 24-27 (statement); 7 ill

RENTON, Andrew (1917-) Brit; arch
EMANUEL I 663-664 (statement); 1 ill

REPIN, Ilya (Elias) (1844-1930) Russ; ptr
THORN 319 (statement, p.p.)

REPNIK, Anton (1935-) Yugo; ptr
TOMASEVIC 308-310 (statement); port; 1 ill

REQUICHOT, Bernard (1929-1961) Fren; sclp
DOUZE ANS 305-308 (statement); port; 5 ill

REQUILLART, Bruno (1947-) Fren;
photo
WALSH 622-623 (statement); 1 ill

RESIKA, Paul (1928-) Amer; ptr
GUSSOW 46-47 (interview, 1970); 1 ill

RESNICK, Marcia Aylene (1950-) Amer; photo
ART-RITE no.14 5, 12-13 (response)

RESNICK, Milton (1917-) Russ/Amer; ptr
IT IS no.1 43 (statement)
IT IS no.3 78 ("Non-American Painting...")

RESSLER, Robert (1954-) Amer; sclp
SCULPTURE OUTSIDE (statement); 4 ill

RET, Etienne (1900-) Fren/Amer; ptr
BRITANNICA 91 (statement); port; 1 ill
M.H. DE YOUNG 109 (response); self port

RETH, Alfred (1884-1966) Fren; ptr
ABSTRACTION no.2 24, 33 (statement); 2 ill
BERCKELAERS 309-311 (statement); port; 1 ill
TEMOIGNAGES I 246-255 (statement); port; 8 ill

REUSCH, Erich (1925-) Germ; sclp
EMANUEL II 775-776 (statement); 1 ill
HAUSSER 152-155 (STATEMENT); 6 ILL
SKIRA 1977 115 (statement); 1 ill

REUSENS, Robert (1909-) Belg; photo
WALSH 624 (statement); 1 ill

REUTERSWARD, Carl Frederik (1934-) Swed; photo, ptr
ADLERS 42-43 (interview); port; 1 ill
SKIRA 1977 17 (statement); 1 ill

SKIRA 1978 47 (statement); port; 3 ill

REXROTH, Nancy (1946-) Amer; photo
PHOTOGRAPHY (statement); 1 ill
WALSH 625-626 (statement); 1 ill

REYHER, Max (1862-) Amer; ptr
JANIS II 150-153 (statements); port; 1
ill

REYNAL, Jeanne (1903-) Amer; sclp,
ptr
ART NOW v.4 no.1 (statement); 1 ill
ILLINOIS 1951 211-212 (statement)
IT IS no.4 26 (essay: "Mosaic is
Light")
MUNRO 178-188 (interview); ports; 2 ill

REYNIER, Yves (1946-) Fren; coll
CHOIX 41 (statement, o.p. 1982); 1 ill

REYNOLDS, Alan Munro (1926-) Brit;
sclp, ptr
CONTEMPORARY (statement); port; 2
ill

REYNOLDS, Jim E. (1938-) Amer; ptr
EVENTS I 48 (statement); 1 ill

REYNOLDS, Steve ( ) Amer; pott
VIEWPOINT 1980 16-17 (statement); 3
ill

REZVANI, Serge (1928-) Fren; ptr, print
PREMIER BILAN 315 (statement); port

RHAYE, Yves ( ) Belg; sclp
COLLARD 220-226 (interview); port; 1
ill

RHOADS, George (1926-)
PROTTER 256-258 (statement, 1963); 1
ill

RHODEN, John W. (1918-) Amer; sclp
ILLINOIS 1959 260-261 (statement); 1 ill

RIBAK, Louis Leon (1903-) Amer; ptr
ILLINOIS 1959 261-262 (statement); 1 ill
100 CONTEMPORARY 152-153
(statement); port; 1 ill

RIBE, Angels (1943-) Span; perf
SKIRA 1978 39 (statement); 1 ill

RICCI, Leonardo (1918-) arch
KEPES III 108-119 (essay: "Form, the
Tangible Expression of a Reality")

RICE, Chuck (1955-) Cana; photo
POINT OF VIEW 64 (statement); 1 ill

RICH, Don (1941-) Amer; sclp
ILLINOIS 1974 104 (statement); 1 ill

RICH, Linda G. (1949-) Amer; photo
WISCONSIN I (statement); 1 ill

RICHARD SHEPPARD ROBSON AND
PARTNERS (arch firm)
EMANUEL I 666-667 (statement); 1 ill

RICHARDS, Bruce ( ) Amer; ptr
IRVINE 60, 83-84 (statement); 1 ill

RICHARDS, Ceri (1903-1971) Brit; ptr
BARBER 23-35 (interview); port
BOWNESS 16, 31-33 (statement); 2 ill

RICHARDS, Walter DuBois (1907-)
Amer; ptr
NORTH LIGHT 85 (statement); 1 ill

RICHARDSON, Constance Coleman
(1905-) ptr
GUSSOW 139-141 (letter, 1971); 1 ill
M.H. DE YOUNG 110 (response); self
port

RICKSON, Gary A. (1942-) Amer; ptr
FINE 271-272 (letter, 1971); 2 ill
LEWIS I REVISED 3-4 (statement); port;
1 ill

RIDABOCK, Ray Budd (1904-1970)
Amer; ptr
NORTH LIGHT 82 (statement); 1 ill

RIDDLE, John Thomas (1933-) Amer;
sclp
LEWIS II 49 (statement); port; 1 ill

RIFFLE, David L. (1947-) Amer; ptr
NOSANOW I 105 (statement); 1 ill

RIFKA, Judy ( ) Amer; illus, ptr
ART-RITE no.9 38-38 (group discussion;
port
ART-RITE no.11/12 ("Social Realism:
Or Living the Artistic Life")

RIGGLE, Alan Merrick (1934-) Amer;
ptr
ILLINOIS 1969 92 (statement); 1 ill

RILEY, Bridget L. (1931-) Brit; ptr,
print
ART NETWORK no.1 2 (interview); port
EMANUEL II 782-783 (statement); 1 ill
HESS 82-83 (statement)
NAYLOR 807-809 (statement); 1 ill

RILEY, Kenneth (1919-) Amer; ptr, illus
MAGIC 96-99 (statement); port; 4 ill

RIMBERT, Rene (1896-) Fren; ptr
PREMIER BILAN 316 (statement); port

RIMINGTON, Alexander Wallace
(1854-1918) Brit; print
EDDY 140-141 (statement)

RINGGOLD, Faith (1934-) Amer; ptr,
sclp, text

FAX I 188-202 (statements); port; 1 ill
FINE 208-210 (statements, o.p. 1969,
1970); 1 ill
MILLER 157-175 (interview with Sally
Swenson); port; 1 ill
MUNRO 409-416 (interview); port
NAYLOR 809-810 (statement); 1 ill

RINKE, Klaus (1939-) Germ; perf
AVALANCHE no.2 54-57 (text piece); 13
ill
PARACHUTE no.8 20-21 (statement, in
English); 2 ill
SKIRA 1980 112 (extract from interview
with Erika Billeter); 3 ill

RIOPELLE, Jean-Paul (1923-) Cana; ptr
SCHNEIDER 99-118 (interview); 1 ill

RIPPON, Tom Michael (1954-) Amer;
sclp, pott
VIEWPOINT 1979 20-21 (statement); 4
ill

RISLEY, Mary Kring ( ) Amer; pott
HAYSTACK 52 (statement); 1 ill

RISTIC, Petar (1927-) Yugo; ptr
TOMASEVIC 311-314 (statement); port;
2 ill

RITTERBUSCH, Klaus (1947-) Germ;
photo
SKIRA 1976 16-17 (statement); 4 ill

RIVA, Umberto ( ) Ital; arch
GA HOUSES no.6 168-171 (statement);
17 ill

RIVERA, Diego (1886-1957) Mexi; ptr
ADVERSARY 19 (manifesto, issued in
1922)
DICCIONARIO v.3 479-480 (statement
on the artist Arturo Estrada)
GOLDWATER 475-477 (statement, 1929)

ARCHITECTURES 140-143 (essay: "L'Art du Fondu Enchaine," with Bernard Reicheu); 8 ill

ROBERTO, Mauricio (1942-) Braz; arch
EMANUEL I 671-674 (statement); 1 ill

ROBERTO ARCHITECTS (arch firm)
SEE: ROBERTO, Mauricio

ROBERTS, Priscilla (1916-) Amer; ptr
BETHERS I 254-255 (statement); 1 ill
ILLINOIS 1961 165 (response); port; 1 ill

ROBERTS, Sarah ( ) Amer; illus
CALIFORNIA--DRAWING (statement); 2 ill

ROBERTSON, Anna Mary
SEE: MOSES, Grandma

ROBERTSON, Jaquelin Taylor (1933-) Amer; arch
EMANUEL I 676-677 (statement)
RUSSELL F 91-93 (project proposal); 6 ill

ROBERTSON, Kip (1947-) Amer; glass, sclp
NOSANOW II 63 (statement); 1 ill

ROBERTSON, Lethia (1940-) Amer; text
CONTEMPORARY AFRICAN (statement); port; 1 ill

ROBINSON, Boardman (1876-1952) Cana/Amer; ptr
M.H. DE YOUNG 112 (response); self port
SAYLER 314-317 (essay: "Learning by Working on the Job")

ROBINSON, Leo ( ) Amer; ptr
DOWNTOWN (statement); 1 ill

ROBINSON, Walter ( ) Amer; ptr
REALLIFE no.10 25 (story: "The Sunrise")

ROBISON, Patrick (1950-) Amer; pott, sclp
WISCONSIN II (statement); 1 ill

ROBSON, Geoffrey ( ) Brit; arch
SEE: RICHARD SHEPPARD ROBSON AND PARTNERS

ROCHA, Dolores
SEE: DOLORES

ROCHE, Jim (1943-) Amer; envir, sclp, ptr
ARTPARK 1975 100-103 (statement); port; 3 ill
ARTPARK 1976 174-177 (statement); port; 8 ill
AVALANCHE no.13 14-17 (interview; and transcript of performance); ports

ROCHE, Kevin (1922-) Iris/Amer; arch
COOK 52-89 (interview); port; 36 ill
HEYER 355-361 (interview); 14 ill

ROCKBURNE, Dorothea ( ) Cana/Amer; ptr
EARLY WORK (interview with Marcia Tucker); 3 ill
LICHT 49-55 (statement); 5 ill
PAOLETTI 88-89 (statements, p.p.); 1 ill

ROCKLIN, Raymond (1922-) Amer; sclp
WHITNEY (statement); 1 ill
YOUNG 1957 (statement); 2 ill

ROCKWELL, Norman (1894-1978) Amer; ptr
GUITAR 174-183 (interview); port; 4 ill

RODCHENKO, Aleksandr (1891-1956)
Russ; sclp
BOWLT 148-151 (statement, o.p. 1919)
BOWLT 250-254 (essay: "Against the
Synthetic Portrait, For the Snapshot,"
o.p. 1928); port

RODDY, Mike (1948-) Amer; sclp, instal
LOGAN I 30-35 (statement); 4 ill

RODEN, Mary (1952-) Iris; ptr
KNOWLES 45 (statement); 1 ill

RODGER, George (1908-) Brit; photo
HILL 50-73 (interview, 1973); port
WALSH 634-636 (statement); 1 ill

RODIA, Sam (Simon) (1879-1965)
Ital/Amer; sclp, arch, envir
ARTFORUM v.1 no.11 32-33 (interview
with Kate T. Steinitz); port; 2 ill
SEITZ III 77-80 (statement); 6 ill

RODRIGUEZ, Fabio (1950-) photo
BIENNALE 100-102 (statement); 1 ill

ROEHR, Peter (1944-1968) Germ; film
VRIES 244-247 (statements, o.p. 1971,
1972)

ROEMHILD, Janet (1919-) Amer; ptr
M.H. DE YOUNG 113 (response)

ROESCH, Kurt F. (1905-) Germ/Amer;
ptr
ILLINOIS 1950 199-200 (statement)
ILLINOIS 1951 212-213 (statement); 1 ill
ILLINOIS 1955 233 (statement)
JANIS I 68-69 (statement); 1 ill

ROETENBERG, Ephraim
SEE: FIMA

ROGERS, Archibald Coleman (1917-)
Amer; arch

EMANUEL I 679-680 (extract from
novel: *Monticello Fault*); 1 ill

ROGERS, Barbara Joan (1937-) Amer;
ptr
ILLINOIS 1974 105 (statement); 1 ill

ROGERS, Bob ( ) pott
CLARK 110-115 (essay: "Reflections on
Freedom and Ceramics," o.p. 1975)

ROGERS, Brenda (1940-) Amer; ptr
LEWIS I REVISED 63 (statement); port;
2 ill

ROGERS, Charles D. (1935-) Amer; ptr
LEWIS I REVISED 63 (statement); port;
2 ill

ROGERS, Ernesto N. (1909-) arch
KEPES I 242-251 (essay: "The Image:
The Architect's Inalienable Vision")
NEWMAN 76-79, 218-221 (group
discussion)
NEWMAN 92-97 (essay and group
discussion); 19 ill

ROGERS, Howard ( ) Amer; sclp
ILLUSTRATION 82 (statement); port; 1
ill

ROGERS, Mary (1929-) Brit; pott
CAMERON E 126-135 (response); 11 ill

ROGERS, Michael (1954-) Amer; ptr
NOSANOW I 106 (statement); 1 ill

ROGERS, Richard (1933-) Amer; arch
EMANUEL I 681-682 (statement); 1 ill

ROGGE, Cornelius (1932-) Dutc; sclp
NAYLOR 816 (statement)

ROGGE, Edward (1941-) Amer; ptr
NOSANOW I 107 (statement); 1 ill

ROGOVIN, Milton (1909-) Amer; photo
WALSH 637-638 (statement); 1 ill

ROGOWAY, Alfred (1905-) Amer; ptr
ILLINOIS 1953 214 (statement); 1 ill
ILLINOIS 1955 233 (statement); 1 ill

ROHLFS, Christian (1849-1938) Germ;
ptr
SCHMIDT 114-115 (statement, 1937)

ROHM, Robert (1934-) Amer; sclp, envir
ARTPARK 1977 74-76 (statement); 6 ill
NAYLOR 816-817 (statement); 1 ill

ROITER, Fulvio (1926-) Ital; photo
WALSH 638-639, 641 (statement); 1 ill

ROLFE, Nigel (1950-) Iris; perf
KNOWLES 188-191 (statement); 4 ill

ROLLINS, Bernard Hassel ( ) Amer; ptr
LEWIS II 48 (statement); port; 1 ill

ROMAN, Veronique Jordan
SEE: JORDAN ROMAN, Veronique

ROMANO, Emanuel Glicen (1897-)
Ital/Amer; ptr
100 CONTEMPORARY 154-155
(statement); port; 1 ill

ROMANO, Umberto Roberto (1906-)
Ital/Amer; ptr, sclp
BRITANNICA 92 (statement); port; 1 ill
ILLINOIS 1951 213 (statement); 1 ill

ROMBERG, Osvaldo (1938-) Arge; ptr,
print
EMANUEL II 790-791 (statement); 1 ill
NAYLOR 817-818 (statement); self port
SKIRA 1978 70 (extract from interview
with Zalmona Ygal); 1 ill
SKIRA 1980 123 (statement); 3 ill

ROME, Richard (1943-) Brit; sclp
HAYWARD 1979 119, 132-135 (interview
with David Robson); port; 8 ill

ROMEDA, Bruno (1929-) Ital; sclp
NAYLOR 819 (statement); 1 ill

ROMERO, Frank (1941-) Amer; ptr
RAICES 45 (statement); 1 ill

RONALD, William (1926-) Cana/Amer;
ptr
ILLINOIS 1961 170 (response); port; 1 ill
IT IS no.3 78 ("Non-American
Painting...")
NAYLOR 819-820 (statement); port

RONIS, Willy (1910-) Fren; photo
WALSH 640-642 (statement); 1 ill

ROOBJEE, Piero (1945-) Belg; ptr
NAYLOR 820-821 (statement); 1 ill

ROOSKENS, Anton (1906-1976) Dutc;
ptr
NAYLOR 821-820 (statement); 1 ill

ROSAI, Ottone (1895-) Ital; ptr
VERZOCCHI 351-355 (statement); self
port; 1 ill

ROSANDER, Russell (1947-) Amer; coll
NOSANOW II 64 (statement); 1 ill

ROSAS, Mel (1950-) Amer; ptr
MICHIGAN 36-37 (statement); 1 ill

ROSATI, James (1912-) Amer; sclp
ART NOW v.2 no.9 (interview); 1 ill
IT IS no.5 51-56 (group discussion)
IT IS no.6 7-16, 57-64, 73-75 (group
discussion)

ROSE, Arthur (1921-) Amer; sclp

LEWIS I REVISED 22 (statement); port; 1 ill

ROSE, Herman (1909-) Amer; ptr
FIFTY (statement); port; 1 ill
MILLER 1952 40-41 (statement); 3 ill

ROSE, Peter (1943-) Cana; arch
CANADIAN 88-91 (statement); 5 ill

ROSE, Thomas Albert (1942-) Amer; ptr, sclp
MCCLINTIC 48-51 (statement); 4 ill

ROSEN, Carol ( )
PHILLPOT (statement)

ROSEN, Sandy (1944-) Amer; instal
OUTSIDE II 30-31 (statement); port; 3 ill

ROSENBACH, Ulrike (1943-) Germ; video, perf
ART-RITE no.7 11, 13 (response); 1 ill
AVALANCHE no.9 10-11 (statement); port; 4 ill
KUNST BLEIBT KUNST 420 (statement); 1 ill
SKIRA 1977 65 (statement); port; 1 ill
SKIRA 1978 40 (statement); 2 ill
SKIRA 1980 115 (statement); 4 ill
STEDELIJK 196 (statement in German); 1 ill

ROSENBAUM, Art (1938-) Amer; ptr
NOSANOW I 109-110 (statement); 2 ill

ROSENBERG, Joan (1942-) Amer; pott
HERMAN 104 (statement); port; 1 ill

ROSENBERG, Samuel (1896-) Amer; ptr
BRITANNICA 93 (statement); port; 1 ill
ILLINOIS 1952 227 (statement); 1 ill

ROSENBLATT, Phyllis G. ( ) ptr
CRISS-CROSS no.10 34-35 ("About the Work of Phyllis G. Rosenblatt"); port; 1 ill

ROSENBLUM, Jay (1933-) Amer; ptr
ART NOW v.3 no.2 (statement); 1 ill

ROSENBLUM, Walter (1919-) Amer; photo
WALSH 642-643 (statement); 1 ill

ROSENBOOM, David (1947-) Cana; sclp, envir, sound
GRAYSON 127-131 (essay: "Vancouver Piece"); port; 2 ill

ROSENBORG, Ralph M. (1913-) Amer; ptr
ABSTRACT 25-26, 65, 153 (essay: "Non-Objective Expression"); 1 ill
ILLINOIS 1955 233-234 (statement); 1 ill
JANIS I 92 (statement); 1 ill
MOTHERWELL 8-22 (three group discussions: "Artists' Sessions at Studio 35," New York, 1950)

ROSENQUIST, James (1933-) Amer; ptr
ALBRIGHT-KNOX 380-381 (letter, 6/1969); 1 ill
ART NOW v.1 no.2 (statement); 1 ill
ART SINCE v.2 325-326 (statement, o.p. 1965)
ARTS YEARBOOK v.9 83-87 (response); 1 ill
BATTCOCK IV 57-65 (statements; interview with Gene R. Swenson, o.p. 1965); 2 ill
JOHNSON 94-97 (extract from interview with Gene R. Swenson, o.p. 1963); 1 ill
MILLER 1963 87-93 (statement); port; 6 ill
ROSE II REVISED 156-157 (extract from interview with Gene R. Swenson, o.p. 1963)

RUSSELL J 104-110 (interview with Gene Swenson, o.p. 1965)
RUSSELL J 110-112 (interview with Gene Swenson, o.p. 1963)

ROSENTHAL, Bernard (1914-) Amer; sclp
ILLINOIS 1955 234-235 (statement); 1 ill
IT IS no.6 7-16, 57-64, 73-75 (group discussion)
RODMAN I 26-28 (interview)

ROSENTHAL, Doris Charash (1895-1971) Amer; ptr
BRITANNICA 94 (statement); port; 1 ill
M.H. DE YOUNG 114 (response); self port

ROSENTHAL, Philip ( ) design
DESIGN 27-30 (essay: "Design for Market")

ROSENTHAL, Rachel (1926-) Amer; ptr
PERFORMANCE no.2 26-31 (interview); port; 10 ill

ROSENTHAL, Stephen (1935-) Amer; ptr
DRAWING 135-142 (statement); 7 ill

ROSER, Ce (Cecilia) ( ) Amer; ptr, video
WOMANART v.1 no.3 26, 34-35 (response); port

ROSLER, Martha ( ) Amer; video
ISSUE (essay); 5 ill

ROSOMAN, Leonard (1913-) Brit; ptr
CONTEMPORARY (statement); port; 2 ill

ROSS, Alexander (1908-) Scot/Amer; ptr
NORTH LIGHT 84 (statement); 1 ill

ROSS, Charles (1937-) Amer; sclp, instal, light
ART NOW v.3 no.3 (statement); 1 ill
BATTCOCK V 374-375, 377-378 (interview with Elayne Varian, o.p. 1967); 1 ill
DIRECTIONS I 77 (response); 1 ill
EMANUEL II 793-794 (statement); 1 ill
NAYLOR 824-825 (statement); 1 ill
ON SITE no.5/6 24-25 ("Sunlight Convergence/Solar Burn"); 5 ill
VARIAN IV (interview); port; 2 ill

ROSS, Hal ( ) Amer; metal
METALWORKS (statement); 1 ill

ROSS, Michael Franklin ( ) Amer; arch
LA JOLLA 78-79 (statement); port; 4 ill

ROSSI, Aldo (1931-) Ital; arch
PORPHYRIOS 18-21 (essay: "The Greek Order," o.p. 1959)
PORPHYRIOS 110-113 (essay: "Modena Cemetary, Italy"); 9 ill
RUSSELL F 94-97 (project proposal); 11 ill

ROSSI, Barbara (1940-) Amer; ptr, print
ACKLAND 20-37, 76-77 (group discussion, 10/29/79); 3 ill

ROSSO, Medardo (1858-1928) Ital; sclp
THORN 41, 50, 175, 299 (statements, p.p.)

ROSZAK, Theodore J. (1907-) Poli/Amer; sclp
ART VOICES v.4 no.2 90 (statement); 1 ill
CHIPP 568 (statement, o.p. 1952)
DOUZE PEINTRES (statement); 2 ill
ILLINOIS 1955 235-236 (statement, from a radio talk entitled "Modern Sculpture and American Legend," 1953); 1 ill

ILLINOIS 1963 198 (statement); 1 ill
MILLER 1946 58-61 (statement); 6 ill
QUADRUM no.2 49-60 (essay: *In Pursuit of an Image*); 8 ill
SELZ 134-140 (statement); 4 ill

ROT, Dieter
SEE: ROTH, Dieter

ROTH, Alfred (1903-) Swis; arch
EMANUEL I 688-689 (statement); 1 ill

ROTH, Dieter (1930-) Swis; ptr
EMANUEL II 797-800 (statement)
KINETISCHE (statement); port; 2 ill
NAYLOR 827-829 (statement)
STEDELIJK 197 (statement in German); 1 ill

ROTH, Frank (1936-) Amer; ptr
ILLINOIS 1965 82 (statement); 1 ill
YOUNG 1960 (statement); 2 ill

ROTHBLATT, Abe ( ) Amer; envir
ARTPARK 1976 178-179 (statement); port; 5 ill

ROTHENBERG, David ( ) Amer; sound, light
GRAYSON 138-141 (essay: *Visual Music--A New Art Form*); 1 ill

ROTHENBERG, Susan (1945-) Amer; ptr
MARSHALL 56 (statement); port; 5 ill

ROTHENSTEIN, Michael (1908-) Brit; ptr, print
ROTHENSTEIN 57, 60-61 (extracts from Notebook)

ROTHKO, Mark (1903-1970) Russ/Amer; ptr
ART SINCE v.1 156 (statements, o.p. 1951, 1958)

CHIPP 544-545 (letter, o.p. 1943, with Adolph Gottlieb)
CHIPP 548-549 (essay: *The Romantics Were Prompted,* o.p. 1947)
JANIS I 118 (statement); 1 ill
JOHNSON 10-14 (letter, o.p. 1943); 1 ill
MCCOUBREY 210-212 (letter to the *New York Times*, o.p. 1943)
MILLER 1952 18-20 (statement); 3 ill
PERSONAL (statement)
POSSIBILITIES 84-86, 89-90, 93 (essay: *The Romantics Were Prompted*); 8 ill
PROTTER 238 (extract from essay, 1947)
RODMAN I 92-94 (interview)
ROSE II 143-145 (statement, o.p. 1947)
ROSE II 160 (statement, o.p. 1951)
ROSE II REVISED 111-113 (statement, o.p. 1947-48)
ROSE II REVISED 136 (statement, o.p. 1951)
ROSE II REVISED 136-137 (statement, o.p. 1945)
ROSE II REVISED 137 (statement, o.p. 1949)
SIX PEINTRES (statement, o.p. 1949); port; 1 ill
TIGER no.2 44 (statement)
TIGER no.9 109-114 (statement); 5 ill

ROTHMAN, Jerry (1933-) Amer; pott
HERMAN 105 (statement); port; 1 ill

ROTHROCK, James (1946-) Amer; pott
HERMAN 106 (statement); port; 1 ill

ROTHSCHILD, H. D. (1907-) Amer; ptr
MILLER 1943 50 (statement); self port; 2 ill

ROTHSCHILD, Lincoln (1902-) Amer; sclp

MCCAUSLAND 42-52 (essay: "Industrial Artists-in-Residence")

ROTHSTEIN, Arthur (1915-) Amer; photo
WALSH 644-646 (statement); 1 ill

ROTONDI, Michael (1949-) Amer; arch
COUNTERPOINT 78-89 (statements); 34 ill
LA JOLLA 65-69 (statement); port; 12 ill

ROUALDES, Michel (1937-) Fren; illus
SKIRA 1976 54-55 (statement); 1 ill

ROUAN, Francois (1943-) Fren; ptr
CHOIX 43 (statement, o.p. 1982); 1 ill
SKIRA 1979 91 (statement); 1 ill

ROUAULT, Georges (1871-1958) Fren; ptr
CHARBONNIER v.2 89-97 (interview, 1950)
GOLDWATER 414-415 (statements, 1937); 1 ill
LIBERMAN 25-26 (statements)
MAYWALD (handwritten poem); ports
MINOTAURE no.3/4 114 ("Enquete")
PROTTER 187-190 (statements, o.p. 1947)
SEGHERS 247-250 (statement, p.p.)
THORN 105 (statement, p.p.)

ROUBILLOTTE, Paul (1875-) Fren; ptr
ABSTRACTION no.3 38 (statement); 2 ill

ROUGEMONT, Guy (1935-) Fren; sclp
SKIRA 1979 35 (statement); 1 ill

ROUSSEAU, Henri (1844-1910) Fren; ptr
CHIPP 129 (letter, 1910, o.p. 1914)
CHIPP 129 (poem: inscription for *The Dream*, 1910)

GIEDION-WELCKER 25-28 (poems: "Un Philosophe," "La Pensee Philosophique," "Reve," in French); self port
GOLDWATER 403-404 (letter, 1910); 1 ill

ROUSSEAU-MURPHY, Shirley ( ) Amer; coll
CALIFORNIA--COLLAGE (statement); 1 ill

ROUVRE, Yves (1910-) Fren; ptr
YALE 70 (statement)

ROUX, Guillermo (1929-) Arge; ptr
SKIRA 1978 26 (statement); 1 ill

ROYCE, Richard ( ) sclp
VISUAL v.4 no.4 8-11 (interview); 3 ill

ROYER, Dorothy (1911-) Amer; illus
CALIFORNIA--DRAWING (statement); 2 ill

ROZANOVA, Olga (1886-1918) Russ; coll
BOWLT 102-111 (essay: "The Bases of the New Creation and the Reasons Why it is Misunderstood," o.p. 1913); port; 1 ill
BOWLT 148 (extract from essay, o.p. 1918)

RUBEN, Richards (1925-) Amer; ptr
CALIFORNIA--PAINTING 27 (statement); 1 ill
LEAVITT (statement); port; 5 ill

RUBENSTEIN, Meridel (1948-) Amer; photo
WALSH 646-647 (statement); 1 ill

RUBIN, Michael ( ) arch
GA HOUSES no.11 128-129 (statements); 6 ill

RUBIN, Reuben (1893-) Ruma/Isra; ptr
100 CONTEMPORARY 158-159
(statement); port; 1 ill

RUBINGTON, Norman (1921-) Amer;
ptr, sclp
ILLINOIS 1955 236 (statement); 1 ill
ILLINOIS 1959 264-265 (statement); 1 ill

RUBINSTEIN, Eva (1933-) Arge/Amer;
photo
LAPLANTE 89-99 (interview); port; 1 ill
WALSH 648-649 (statement); 1 ill

RUBLE, John ( ) Amer; arch
GA DOCUMENT no.4 88-89 (statement);
9 ill
LA JOLLA 58-64 (statement); port; 9 ill

RUCKRIEM, Ulrich (1938-) Germ; sclp
AVALANCHE no.3 42-51 (interview); 12
ill
CHOIX 44 (statement); 1 ill
MCCLINTIC 28-29 (statement); 2 ill

RUDA, Edwin (1922-) Amer; sclp, ptr
ARTFORUM v.6 no.8 50-53 (essay:
"Jack Krueger: Frontiers of Zero")
ILLINOIS 1967 71 (statement); 1 ill
ILLINOIS 1974 106-107 (statement); 1 ill
LEAVITT (statement); port; 5 ill
SYSTEMATIC 25 (statement); 1 ill

RUDOLPH, Paul Marvin (1918-) Amer;
arch
COOK 90-121 (interview); port; 23 ill
ARCHER 86-88, 99 (statement); port; 7
ill
GA HOUSES no.5 100-109 (statement);
14 ill
HEYER 294-307 (interview); 15 ill

RUELLAN, Andree (1905-) Amer; ptr
BRITANNICA 95 (statement); port; 1 ill
ILLINOIS 1957 242 (response); 1 ill

ZAIDENBERG 115-117 (essay: "The
World of Personal Vision"); 5 ill

RUGG, Matt (1935-) Brit; sclp
BRITISH (statement); 1 ill

RUHLMAN, Jill (1944-) Amer; pott
HERMAN 107 (statement); port; 1 ill

RUHNAU, Werner ( ) arch
CONRADS 171 ("Project for an Aerial
Architecture," o.p. 1960)

RUHTENBERG, Cornelis (1923-)
Latv/Amer; ptr
ILLINOIS 1953 215 (statement)

RUITER, Jean ( ) Dutc; photo, print
HOW FAMOUS 184-187 (statements);
port; 5 ill

RUIZ, Pierre ( ) Amer; perf, sound
BRENTANO 314-315 (statement); 1 ill

RUIZ CHAMIZO, Juan
SEE: CHAMIZO, Juan Ruiz

RUNDLE, Elyssa (1934-) ptr
TRACKS v.1 no.3 32 (poem: "Biopsy
Report")

RUSCHA, Edward (1937-) Amer; photo,
ptr
ART VOICES v.5 no.4 61, 68 (response);
1 ill
ARTFORUM v.3 no.5 24-25 (interview
with John Coplans); port
AVALANCHE no.7 30-39 (interview);
ports
CONCEPTUAL ART 35 (statement)
EMANUEL II 803-805 (statement); 1 ill
HOPKINS 112-113 (statement); port; 1
ill
MEYER 206-209 (extract from interview
with John Coplans, o.p. 1965); 8 ill

NAYLOR 833-835 (statement); 1 ill
WALSH 650-651 (statement); 1 ill

RUSH, Kent (1948-) Amer; coll
PAPERWORKS 32-33 (statement); 4 ill

RUSHTON, David ( )
ART-LANGUAGE v.2 no.1 38-50
("Aspects of Authorities")
ART-LANGUAGE v.2 no.3 12-17
("Models and Indexes: Fringe
Benefits")
ART-LANGUAGE v.2 no.3 18-33
("Bibliotherapy")
ART-LANGUAGE v.3 no.2 7-12 ("A
Review of Styles")
ART-LANGUAGE v.3 no.2 46-51
("Rambling: To Partial
Correspondents")
ART-LANGUAGE v.3 no.2 89-92
("Utopian Prayers and Infantile
Marxism")

RUSSELL, Alfred (1920-) Amer; ptr
ILLINOIS 1952 228 (statement); 1 ill
ILLINOIS 1953 215-216 (statement); 1 ill
IT IS no.5 31-32 (essay: "Toward
Meta-Form")

RUSSELL, Bruce (1946-) Brit; illus, ptr
HAYWARD 1979 78-81 (statement); 9 ill

RUSSELL, Frank J. (1921-) Amer; ptr
ILLINOIS 1953 216 (statement); 1 ill

RUSSELL, George Gordon, Jr. (1932-)
Amer; ptr
ILLINOIS 1957 243 (response); 1 ill

RUSSELL, John (1931-) Amer; photo
LEWIS II 130 (statement); port; 2 ill

RUSSELL, Laura (1949-) Amer; illus
PAPERWORKS 34-35 (statement); 4 ill

RUSSELL, Morgan (1886-1953) Amer;
ptr
BARRON 13-18 (extracts from letters)
FORUM 1916 92 (statement); 1 ill
GALLERY STUDIES I 4-10 (statements,
letters, interviews; interspersed in
essay: "Morgan Russell's Synchromy
in Orange: To Form" by Gail Levin);
11 ill

RUSSELL, Shirley Marie Hopper (1886-)
Amer; print, ptr
HAAR I 104-111 (interview with
Prithwish Neogy); ports; 3 ill

RUSSO, Alexander Peter (1922-) Amer;
ptr
FULBRIGHT 43 (statement)
ILLINOIS 1957 243-244 (response); 1 ill

RUSSO, Marialba (1947-) Ital; photo
WALSH 651-652 (statement); 1 ill

RUSSO, Michele (1909-) Amer; ptr
GUENTHER 100-101 (statement); port;
1 ill

RUSSOLO, Luigi (1885-1947) Ital; ptr
APOLLONIO 24-27 ("Manifesto of the
Futurist Painters," o.p. 1910)
APOLLONIO 27-31 ("Futurist
Paintings: Technical Manifesto," o.p.
1910)
APOLLONIO 45-50 ("The Exhibitors to
the Public," o.p. 1912)
APOLLONIO 74-76, 85-88 (extract from
"The Art of Noices," o.p. 1913)
CHIPP 289-293 ("Futurist Painting:
Technical Manifesto," o.p. 1910)
CHIPP 294-298 ("The Exhibitors to the
Public," o.p. 1912)
GUGGENHEIM II 135-137 ("Manifesto of
the Futurist Painters," o.p. 1910)

RUTAULT, Claude (1941-) Fren; ptr, print
MURS 14-15 (statement); 1 ill
SKIRA 1978 73 (statement); 1 ill

RUTHENBECK, Reiner (1937-) Germ; instal, sclp, photo
AVALANCHE no.13 19-23 (interview, in English and German); 16 ill
EMANUEL II 805-806 (statement); 1 ill
SKIRA 1976 12 (statement); 1 ill

RUTKOVSKY, Fran Cutrell ( ) Amer; text
HAYSTACK 53 (statement); 1 ill

RUTKOWSKI, Rita (1932-) Amer; ptr
FULBRIGHT 42-43 (statement); 1 ill

RUUSUVUORI, Aarno (1925-) Finn; arch
EMANUEL I 694 (statement); 1 ill

RUVOLO, Felix (1912-) Amer; ptr
ILLINOIS 1951 214-215 (statement); 1 ill
ILLINOIS 1953 217-218 (statement); 1 ill

RYAN, Anne (1889-1954) Amer; ptr, print, coll
CRISPO I (statement); 15 ill
TIGER no.8 55-56 (statement)

RYDER, Albert Pinkham (1847-1917) Amer; ptr
MCCOUBREY 186-188 ("Paragraphs from the Studio of a Recluse," 1905)

RYDINGSVARD, Ursala von ( ) sclp, envir
ARTPARK 1979 (statement); 1 ill

RYKWERT, Joseph ( ) Poli/Brit; arch
ARCHER 46-50, 99 (statement); port; 6 ill

RYMAN, Robert (1930-) Amer; ptr
ART NOW v.3 no.3 (statement); 1 ill
CHOIX 45 (statement, o.p. 1971); 1 ill
DIAMONSTEIN I 330-340 (interview); ports
SKIRA 1980 59 (statement); 3 ill
STEDELIJK 200-201 (statement); 3 ill

RYZACK, Michael ( ) Amer; ptr
ART PATRON ART 57-58 (statement, o.p. 1977); port; 1 ill

SAAR, Betye (1926-) Amer; sclp, print, ptr
HOPKINS 114-115 (statement); port; 1 ill
LEWIS I REVISED 35-37 (statement); port; 2 ill
MILLER 176-184 (interview with Sally Swenson); port
MUNRO 355-361 (interview); port; 1 ill
SCHAPIRO 59 (statement); port; 1 ill
KRESGE (statement); port; 1 ill

SAARINEN, Eero (1910-1961) Finn/Amer; arch
HEYER 348-354 (interview); 9 ill
ROTH 570-571 (statement, 1959, o.p. 1962)

SACCARO, John M. (1913-) ptr
SOME 20 (statement); 1 ill

SACKS, Cal ( ) Amer; ptr
ILLUSTRATION 72-75 (statement); port; 4 ill
NORTH LIGHT 202-205 (statement); port; 6 ill

SADEK, George (1928-) Czec; arch
ON SITE no.2 10-11 (response)

SADLEY, Wojciech (1932-) Poli; text, sclp
NAYLOR 837-838 (statement); 1 ill

SADUN, Piero (1919-) Ital; ptr
PAINTING 36 (statement); port; 1 ill

SAETTI, Bruno (1902-) Ital; ptr
VERZOCCHI 357-361 (statement); self port; 1 ill

SAGE, Kay (1898-1963) Amer; ptr
ILLINOIS 1951 215 (statement)
ILLINOIS 1959 265 (statement); 1 ill

SAHNER, Mindi ( ) Amer; pott
HAYSTACK 54 (statement); 1 ill

ST. EOM (1908-) Amer; ptr
SYMBOLS (statement); 1 ill

ST. GERMAIN, Patrick (1947-) Amer; illus
MICHIGAN 38-39 (statement); 2 ill

SAINT-PHALLE, Niki de (1930-) Fren; ptr, coll, sclp
ART VOICES v.4 no.4 86-89 (interview with Edouard Roditi); ports

SAINT-PIERRE, Georges ( ) Cana; ptr
ROYER 115-119 (interview, 1975)

SAITO, Yoshishige (1904-) Japa; print, ptr
KUNG 104-107 (statement); port; 2 ill

SAITOWITZ, Stanley (1948-) SoAf; arch
COUNTERPOINT 90-103 (statements); 30 ill
GA HOUSES no.10 54-73 (statements); 66 ill

SAKOGUCHI, Ben (1938-) Amer; print
CALIFORNIA--PRINTS (statement); 1 ill

SALADINO, John F. ( ) design
DIAMONSTEIN V 144-159 (interview); port; 13 ill

SALEMME, Attilio (1911-1955) Amer; ptr
ILLINOIS 1955 236-237 (statement); 1 ill
NEW DECADE 77-79 (statement); 3 ill
PERSONAL (statement)

SALERNO, Charles (1916-) Amer; sclp
ILLINOIS 1953 218 (statement); 1 ill

SALERNO, Nina (1954-) Amer; video
TUCKER II 36-37 (statement); port

SALICRUP, Fernando ( ) Amer
EVENTS I 31 (text piece)

SALIETTI, Alberto (1892-) Ital; ptr
VERZOCCHI 363-367 (statement); self
port; 1 ill

SALINAS, Fernando (1930-) Cuba; arch
BAYON 88-107 (interview); 22 ill

SALINAS MENDEZ, Angel
SEE: ANGEL

SALLE, David (1952-) Amer; ptr, perf,
instal
FIGURES 22-23 (statements, o.p. 1979,
1980); 1 ill
REALLIFE no.6 4-10 (group discussion);
1 ill

SALLES, Francis (1928-) Fren; ptr
YALE 70 (statement)

SALMONA, Rogelio ( ) Colo; arch
BAYON 62-87 (interview); port; 20 ill

SALON DE LA JEUNE PEINTURE
(group)
ART SINCE v.2 328 (statement, o.p.
1966)

SALOTTI, Gian Dominico ( ) Ital; arch
REVOLUTION 196-203 (essay: "Sacred
Space: Observations on Some New
Italian Churches")

SALT, John (1937-) Brit; ptr, photo
MEISEL 367-398 (statement); port; 89
ill

SALTER, Peter ( ) Brit; arch
SPIRIT 50-57 (statement); 7 ill

SALTONSTALL, Nathaniel ( ) arch
ART VOICES v.1 no.2 21 (interview);
port; 1 ill

SALVADORI, Aldo (1905-) Ital; ptr
VERZOCCHI 369-373 (statement); self
port; 1 ill

SALVATI AND TRESOLDI (arch firm)
GA HOUSES no.1 174-185 (statement);
23 ill

SAMARAS, Lucas (1936-) Gree/Amer;
sclp
ART NOW v.2 no.8 (statement); 1 ill
ARTFORUM v.5 no.239-244 (interview
with Alan Solomon); port; 12 ill
ARTFORUM v.6 no.4 26-27 ("An
Explanatory Dissection of Seeing"); 4
ill
ARTFORUM v.7 no.2 54-57 (essay: "A
Reconstituted Diary, Greece, 1967")
CUMMINGS 196-218 (interview, 1968);
port; 2 ill
DIAMONSTEIN I 341-353 (interview);
ports
LETTERS 36-40 (letter); 9 ill

SAMPLE, Paul Starrett (1896-1974)
Amer; ptr
BOSWELL 187 (statement)
BRITANNICA 96 (statement); port; 1 ill
ILLINOIS 1952 229-230 (statement)

SAMPSON, Frank (1928-) Amer; ptr
REGIONALISM 18-19 (statement); port;
1 ill

SAMS, Anastasis ( ) Amer; ptr
O'KANE (poem); 1 ill

SAMUELS, Edward (1941-) Amer; sclp,
ptr
DIRECTIONS I 77 (response); 1 ill

SAMUELS, Florence ( ) Amer; text
HAYSTACK 55 (statement); 1 ill

SAMUELS, Isadore ( ) Amer; photo
HAYSTACK 56 (statement); 1 ill

SANCHEZ, Fabian (1935-) Peru/Fren;
ptr
SKIRA 1978 21 (statement); 1 ill

SANCHEZ, Juan (1954-) Amer; ptr, coll
EVENTS I 50 (statement); 1 ill

SANCHEZ GOMEZ, Javier (1936-) arch
SEE: MANTEOLA SANCHEZ
GOMEZ SANTOS SOLSONA
VINOLY

SANCHEZ MONTOYA, Carmen
SEE: CARMEN

SANDBACK, Fred (1943-) Amer; sclp,
instal
DRAWING 145-156 (statement, o.p.
1975); 10 ill

SANDELS, Karl (1906-) Swed; photo
WALSH 656-657 (statement); 1 ill

SANDERS, Har (1929-) Dutc; ptr
NAYLOR 842-843 (statement); 1 ill

SANDERS, Joop (1922-) Dutc/Amer;
sclp
DIRECTIONS I 77 (response); 1 ill

SANDERS-TURNER, Carolyn C. (1947-
) Amer; ptr
NOSANOW I 111 (statement); 1 ill

SANDLE, Michael (1936-) Amer; sclp,
ptr
CONTEMPORARY (statement); port; 2
ill
EMANUEL II 813-814 (statement)

HAYWARD 1978 50-53 (statement); 5 ill
NAYLOR 843-844 (statement); 1 ill

SANDOVAL, Arturo Alonzo (1942-) text
FIBER 14-15 (statement); 1 ill

SANDMAN, Jo (1931-) Amer; ptr
BOSTON II (statement); 1 ill

SANEJOUAND, Jean-Michel (1934-)
Fren; sclp, film, instal
DOUZE ANS 321-323 (extract from
Introduction aux Espaces Concrets,
edited by Mathias Fels); port; 4 ill
EMANUEL II 814-815 (statement); 1 ill
NAYLOR 844-845 (statement); 1 ill
SKIRA 1977 112 (statement); 1 ill

SANT'ELIA, Antonio (1888-1916) Ital;
arch
APOLLONIO 160, 169-172 (*Manifesto
of Futurist Architecture,* o.p. 1914)
CONRADS 34-38 (essay: *Futurist
Architecture,* o.p. 1914); 1 ill

SANTO, Patsy (1893-) Amer; ptr
JANIS II 144-149 (statements); port; 1
ill

SANTOMASO, Giuseppe (1907-) Ital;
ptr
PAINTING 44 (statement); port; 1 ill
PREMIER BILAN 317 (statement); port
VERZOCCHI 375-379 (statement); self
port; 1 ill

SANTOS, Alfonso Lorenzo
SEE: ALFONSO LORENZO, Santos

SANTOS, Josefa (1931-) Arge; arch
SEE: MANTEOLA SANCHEZ
GOMEZ SANTOS SOLSONA
VINOLY

SANTOS, Rene ( ) Amer; ptr
FACE IT 18-19 (statement); 1 ill

SARET, Alan Daniel (1944-) Amer;
envir, sclp, ptr
ARTPARK 1975 106-109 (statement); 7
ill
ART-RITE no.11/12 ("The Ghosthouse
of @1 @el at Artpark"; "The
Regiomantrine Decision")
AVALANCHE no.2 12-13 (interview)
AVALANCHE no.12 8 (poem); 6 ill
AVALANCHE no.12 9-11 (interview); 7
ill
BRENTANO 318-319 (statement); 1 ill
GEORGIA 82-85, 105, 116 (statement);
port; 5 ill
GEORGIA 118-166 (group discussion:
"Artists' Convention," in Athens, GA.,
1/7/1977, moderated by Jan van der
Marck)

SARFATI, Alain ( ) Fren; arch
ARCHITECTURES 132-135 (essay:
"Reference...Brique et Pierre"); 8 ill

SARGENT, John Singer (1856-1925) ptr
CRISPO II (statement); 14 ill

SARKIS (Zabunyan) (1938-) Turk;
photo, ptr, envir
IDENTITE 87-89 (interview with
Jacques Clayssen); port
SKIRA 1977 54 (extracts from an
interview); 1 ill
SKIRA 1979 106-107 (statement); 1 ill

SARNACKI, Michael (1950-) Amer;
photo
FUGITIVE (statement); 1 ill

SARTORIS, Alberto (1901-) Ital; arch
CIRCLE 212-214 (essay: "Colour in
Interior Architecture")

SASLOW, Herbert (1920-) Amer; ptr
ILLINOIS 1955 237-238 (statement); 1 ill
ILLINOIS 1957 244-245 (response); 1 ill
ILLINOIS 1959 265-266 (statement)

SASSU, Aligi (1912-) Ital; ptr
VERZOCCHI 381-385 (statement); self
port; 1 ill

SATIN, Clair Jeanine ( ) Amer; ptr
PHILLPOT (statement)

SATO, Mamoru (1937-) Amer; sclp
HAAR II 69-73 (statement); ports; 2 ill

SATO, Norie (1949-) Japa/Amer; ptr,
video, instal
GUENTHER 102-103 (statement); port;
1 ill

SATO, Tadashi (1923-) Amer; ptr, sclp
HAAR I 112-119 (interview with
Prithwish Neogy); ports; 3 ill

SATORU, Abe (1926-) sclp
ILLINOIS 1961 153 (response); port; 1 ill

SAUDEK, Jan (1935-) Czec; photo
WALSH 660-661 (statement); 1 ill

SAUER, Dick (1942-) Amer; text
WISCONSIN I (statement); 1 ill

SAUER, Greta (1909-) Aust
PREMIER BILAN 318 (statement); port

SAUER, Louis (1928-) Amer; arch
EMANUEL I 710-712 (statement); 1 ill

SAUER, Michel (1949-) Germ; photo,
ptr, instal
SKIRA 1976 17 (statement); 1 ill
SKIRA 1978 56 (statement); 2 ill

SAUL, Peter (1934-) Amer; ptr
ILLINOIS 1974 108-109 (statement); 1 ill

SAULNIER, Emmanuel (1952-) Fren;
ptr, illus
MURS 15 (statement); 1 ill

SAUNDERS, Boyd (1937-) Amer; print
MORRIS 188-193 (statements); ports; 1
ill

SAUNDERS, David (1954-) Amer; ptr,
sclp, instal
FACE IT 20-21 (statement); 1 ill
IN A PICTORIAL 24-31 (statements);
port; 5 ill

SAUNDERS, Raymond (1934-) Amer;
ptr
FINE 262-263 (statements, o.p. 1967); 1
ill
HOPKINS 62-63 (statement); port; 1 ill

SAUPIQUE, Georges Laurent (1889-)
Fren; sclp
ART D'AUJOURD'HUI v.4 8-9
(statement); 4 ill

SAURA, Antonio (1930-) Span; ptr
CLAUS 117-121 (statement)
PORCEL I 155-166 (interview); 2 ill
SKIRA 1975 77 (statement); 1 ill
SKIRA 1978 60 (statement); 1 ill

SAVAGE, Juta (1940-) Amer; pott
HERMAN 108 (statement); port; 1 ill

SAVAGE, Naomi (1927-) Amer; photo
SCHAPIRO 60 (statement); port; 1 ill

SAVAGE, Whitney Lee (1928-) Amer;
ptr, design
ILLINOIS 1967 150 (statement); 1 ill

SAVELLI, Angelo (1911-) Ital/Amer;
ptr, print, sclp
EMANUEL II 818-819 (statement)
NAYLOR 848-849 (statement)
TRACKS v.1 no.1 5 (poem)

SAVIC, Krsta (1931-) Yugo; ptr
TOMASEVIC 315-317 (statement); port;
2 ill

SAVIN, Maurice (1894-) Fren; ptr
GOLDAINE 69-71 (interview); port

SAWADA, Miho ( ) Japa/Cana; sclp,
envir
ARTPARK 1983 44-45 (statement); 3 ill

SAX, Ursula (1935-) Germ; sclp, instal
HAUSSER 160-161 (statement, o.p.
1979); 1 ill

SAXE, Adrian (1943-) Amer; pott
HERMAN 109 (statement); port; 1 ill

SAXE, Henry (1937-) Cana; sclp, instal
PARACHUTE no.3 4-10 (interview, in
English); 7 ill

SAXON, Charles (1920-) Amer; illus,
cart
NORTH LIGHT 206-213 (statement);
port; 21 ill

SAYTOUR, Patrick (1935-) Fren; sclp,
ptr
SKIRA 1979 105 (statement); 1 ill

SCANGA, Italo (1932-) Ital/Amer;
instal, sclp, print
AVALANCHE no.3 36-41 (statement);
ports
BRENTANO 324-325 (statement); 1 ill
NAYLOR 850-852 (statement); 1 ill
VIEW v.3 no.5 (interview); port; 9 ill
WISCONSIN I (statement); 1 ill

SCARFE, Gerald (1936-) cart
 BOSHIER (statement); port; 1 ill

SCARLETT, Rolph (1890-) Amer; ptr
 ILLINOIS 1953 218-219 (statement); 1 ill

SCARPITTA, Salvatore (1919-) Amer;
 ptr, sclp
 FRASNAY 238 (statement)

SCHAARE, Harry J. (1922-) Amer; ptr,
 illus
 MAGIC 100-103 (statement); port; 5 ill

SCHAD, Christian (1894-1982) Germ;
 photo
 WALSH 663-664 (statement); 1 ill

SCHADEBURG, Jurgen (1931-) photo
 BOSHIER (statement); port; 8 ill

SCHAFER, R. Murray (1933-) Cana;
 sound
 GRAYSON 98-125 (essay: "The
 Graphics of Musical Thought"); port;
 30 ill

SCHAIBLE, Mike ( ) design
 DIAMONSTEIN V 32-47 (interview);
 port; 9 ill

SCHANKER, Louis (1903-) Amer; ptr,
 print
 ILLINOIS 1957 245 (response); 1 ill
 TIGER no.8 45-47 (statement)

SCHAPIRO, Miriam (1923-) Amer; coll,
 ptr
 CELEBRATION (statement); 1 ill
 EMANUEL II 823-825 (statement)
 ILLINOIS 1961 203 (response); port; 1 ill
 JOHNSON 246-249 (extract from essay:
 "Notes from a Conversation on Art,
 Feminism, and Work," o.p. 1977); 1 ill
 MUNRO 272-281 (interview); ports; 2 ill

NEW DECORATIVE 21, 42-44
 (statement); 3 ill
 RUDDICK 283-305 (interview); port; 7
 ill
 SCHAPIRO 61 (statement); 1 ill
 SKIRA 1980 46-47 (statement); 3 ill
 VISUAL v.1 no.2 19-21 (statements); 2
 ill
 WOMANART v.1 no.3 4-7 (essay: "At
 Long Last: An Historical View of Art
 Made by Women")
 WOMANART v.1 no.3 26, 30 (response);
 port

SCHARF, William (1927-) Amer; ptr
 ILLINOIS 1961 200 (response); port; 1 ill

SCHARFENBERG, Bruce (1949-) Amer;
 sclp, ptr
 MICHIGAN 40-41 (statement); 2 ill

SCHARFF, Edwin (1887-1955) Germ;
 sclp
 SCHMIDT 47 (letter, 1933)

SCHAROUN, Hans (1893-1972) Germ;
 arch
 GROHMANN 491-499 ("Vom Wesen der
 Stadt zur Idee und zur Gestalt
 Berlins," p.p. 1950)

SCHARY, Saul (1904-1978) Amer; ptr,
 illus
 FIRST AMERICAN 60-62 (essay:
 "Tendencies in American Art")

SCHAUFFELEN, Konrad Baldur ( )
 GROH (statement); 1 ill

SCHEDEL SCHAUWECKER, Erika
 SEE: ERIKA

SCHEERBART, Paul (1863-1915) arch
 CONRADS 32-33 (extract from essay:
 "Glass Architecture," o.p. 1914)

SCHERR, Mary Ann ( ) Amer; metal
DIAMONSTEIN IV 196-209 (interview);
port; 15 ill

SCHIFANO, Mario (1934-) Ital; ptr, film
MARAINI 89-93 (interview)

SCHIFFRIN, Herbert (1944-) Amer; ptr
LEAVITT (statement); port; 5 ill

SCHIRM, David ( ) Amer; ptr
DOWNTOWN (statement); 1 ill

SCHLATTMAN, Craig (1949-) Amer;
photo, instal
GUMPERT III 75 (statement)

SCHLEETER, Howard B. (1903-) Amer;
ptr, illus
BRITANNICA 97 (statement); port; 1 ill

SCHLEMMER, Oskar (1888-1943) Germ;
ptr, sclp
CONRADS 68-70 ("Manifesto for the
First Bauhaus Exhibition," o.p. 1923);
1 ill
GROHMANN 413-415 ("Buhne und
Mensch," p.p. 1924)
GROHMANN 415-416 ("Analyse eines
Bildes," p.p. 1928)
POENSGEN 84-85 ("Kubismus und
Mystik," 1913/15)
POENSGEN 85 ("Abstraktion des
Sichtbaren," 1915/16)
POENSGEN 85 ("Die Kunst--Eine Neue
Religion," 1917/18)
POENSGEN 86 (statement, 1918)
SCHMIDT· 27, 35, 48-49, 72-73, 76-77,
153-154, 163 (letters, 1933-1940)
WINGLER 96-100 (essay: "Otto Meyer-
Amden," p.p.)

SCHLEY, Evander Duer Van (1941-)
Cana/Amer; photo

AVALANCHE no.7 22-23 (interview);
port

SCHMIDT, Hans ( ) arch
CONRADS 115-116 ("ABC Demands the
Dictatorship of the Machine," o.p.
1928)

SCHMIDT, Julius (1923-) Amer; sclp
ILLINOIS 1959 266-267 (statement); 1 ill
ILLINOIS 1963 108 (statement); 1 ill
MILLER 1959 64-69 (statement); port; 8
ill

SCHMIDT, Katherine Shubert
(1898-1978) Amer; ptr
CUMMINGS 64-81 (interview, 1969); self
port; 2 ill
FIRST AMERICAN 87-89 (essay: "The
Rental Policy")
M.H. DE YOUNG 117 (response); self
port

SCHMIDT, Michael (1945-) Germ; photo
WALSH 666-667 (statement); 1 ill

SCHMIDT-ROTTLUFF, Karl
(1884-1976) Germ; ptr
MIESEL 28-29 ("The New Program"
1914)
SCHMIDT 45 (letter, 1933)

SCHMIT, Tomas (1943-) Germ; sclp
NAYLOR 856 (statement)

SCHNABEL, David (1924-) Amer; ptr
CALIFORNIA--PAINTING 48 (statement);
1 ill

SCHNABEL, Day (1905-) Aust/Amer;
sclp, ptr
TEMOIGNAGES I 256-263 (statement);
port; 4 ill
TEMOIGNAGES II 34-37 (statement);
port; 8 ill

SCHNABEL, Duane (1945-) Amer; ptr
NOSANOW II 36, 65 (statement); 2 ill

SCHNABEL, Julian (1951-) Amer; ptr
ART-RITE no.9 19 (extract from interview); ports
REALLIFE no.6 4-10 (group discussion); 1 ill

SCHNACKENBERG, Roy (1934-) Amer; ptr, sclp
ILLINOIS 1965 114 (statement); 1 ill
ILLINOIS 1967 104-105 (statement); 1 ill

SCHNEEMANN, Carolee (1939-) Amer; perf, ptr, film
ART-RITE no.14 5, 13 (response)
BELFORD 27-55 (group discussion)
NAYLOR 856-858 (statement)
PERFORMANCE no.1 8-15 (interview with Robert Coe); 5 ill
SCHAPIRO 62 (statement); port; 1 ill
WEBER 143-175 ("ABC--We Print Anything--In the Cards"); 47 ill

SCHNEIDER, Gerard (1896-) Swis/Fren; ptr
PREMIER BILAN 318 (statement); port
RAGON 167-174 (statement)
SEUPHOR. 258-259 (statement); 1 ill
SKIRA 1976 82 (statement); 1 ill

SCHNEIDER, Richard (1937-) Amer; sclp, pott
RIPS (statement); 1 ill

SCHNITZLER, Max (1903-) Poli/Amer; ptr
JANIS I 66 (statement); 1 ill

SCHOEN, Eugene (1880-1957) Amer; arch, design
SAYLER 330-333 (essay: "Form and Color in the Home")

SCHOFFER, Nicolas (1912-) Hung/Fren; sclp
ART SINCE v.1 294 (statements, o.p. 1963)
BANN 248-257 (essay: "Spatiodynamism, Luminodynamism, and Chronodynamism," o.p. 1960)
EMANUEL II 828-830 (statement); 1 ill
HAUSSER 162-163 (statement, o.p. 1963); 1 ill
LUMIERE (statement); port; 1 ill
TEMOIGNAGES II 38-41 (statement); port; 7 ill

SCHONBRUN, Adele Y. (1941-) Amer; pott
HERMAN 110 (statement); port; 1 ill

SCHONZEIT, Ben (1942-) Amer; ptr
IMAGE COLOR FORM 22-23 (statement); 1 ill
SUPERREAL 51-52, 176-177 (interview); 1 ill

SCHOONHOVEN, Terry (1945-) Amer; ptr
HOUSE 88-89 (statement); 1 ill

SCHOOP, Ulrich (1903-) Germ; sclp
ABSTRACTION no.3 43 (statement); 1 ill

SCHOTTLANDER, Bernard (1924-) Brit; sclp
NAYLOR 859-860 (statement); 1 ill

SCHOTZ, Benno (1891-) Brit; sclp
LONDON COUNTY (statement); 1 ill

SCHRAG, Karl (1912-) Germ/Amer; ptr
GUSSOW 100-101 (letter, 1968); 1 ill

SCHRAGENHEIM, Arthur A. ( ) arch
REVOLUTION 191-195 (essay: "The

Problem of Planning Synagogues in Modern Israel")

SCHREIBER, Georges (1904-1977) Belg/Amer; ptr, illus, print
BRITANNICA 98 (statement); port; 1 ill

SCHREIBER-MILICEVIC, Tania
SEE: TANIA

SCHREIER, Curtis ( )
SEE: ANT FARM

SCHROEDER, John ( ) Amer; ptr, sclp
DOWNTOWN (statement); 1 ill

SCHUELER, Jon (1916-) Amer; ptr
IT IS no.5 12-14 ("A Letter About the Sky")

SCHULDT ( )
GROH (statement); 1 ill

SCHULE, Don ( ) Amer; wood
MEILACH 147 (statement); 3 ill

SCHULEIN, Julius W. (1881-) Amer; ptr
ILLINOIS 1952 230-231 (statement); 1 ill

SCHULITZ, Helmut ( ) Amer; arch
GA HOUSES no.2 68-73 (statement); 10 ill

SCHULMAN, Norman (1924-) Amer; pott
HERMAN 111 (statement); port; 1 ill

SCHULT, HA (1939-) Germ; photo, envir, perf
NAYLOR 860-862 (statement); 1 ill
SKIRA 1977 47 (statement); 1 ill
SKIRA 1978 50 (statement); 3 ill

SCHULTZE, Bernard (1915-) Germ; ptr, sclp
EMANUEL II 832-834 (statement); 1 ill
PREMIER BILAN 318 (statement); port

SCHULTZE, Klaus (1927-) Germ; sclp
SKIRA 1977 105 (statement); 1 ill

SCHULZ, Herbert ( ) Germ; photo
HOW FAMOUS 52-57 (statements); port; 10 ill

SCHULZE, Paul (1934-) Amer; glass
GLASS v.5 (group discussion)

SCHULZE, Wolfgang
SEE: WOLS, Otto

SCHULZE-FIELITZ, Echkhard (1929-) arch
CONRADS 175-176 (essay: "The Space City," o.p. 1960)

SCHUMACHER, Emil (1915-) Germ; ptr
ART SINCE v.1 158 (statement, o.p. 1959)
EMANUEL II 834-836 (statement); 1 ill

SCHURMANN, Wilhelm (1946-) Germ; photo
WALSH 670-671 (statement); 1 ill

SCHWALB, Susan (1944-) Amer; print
MILLER 185-201 (interview with Sally Swenson); port; 1 ill
WOMANART v.2 no.3 9-11 (essay: "Notes from Houston")

SCHWARTZ, Aubrey (1928-) Amer; ptr
YOUNG 1957 (statement); 3 ill

SCHWARTZ, Barbara (1948-) Amer; envir, sclp
ARTPARK 1976 180-181 (statement); port; 5 ill
ART-RITE no.9 29-34 (group discussion)

SCHWARTZ, Buky (1932-) Isra/Amer; video, instal
ARTPARK 1983 46-47 (statement); 2 ill
CRISS-CROSS no.7/8/9 50-55 (statements); 6 ill

SCHWARTZ, Randy ( ) Amer; arch, design
LIFE 251-266 (interview); port

SCHWARTZ, William Samuel (1896-) Russ/Amer; ptr
BRITANNICA 99 (statement); port; 1 ill
ILLINOIS 1950 203-204 (statement); 1 ill
100 CONTEMPORARY 162-163 (statement); port; 1 ill

SCHWARZ, Martin (1946-) Swis; ptr
SKIRA 1976 60 (statement); 1 ill

SCHWARZKOGLER, Rudolf (1940-1969) Aust; ptr
NAYLOR 863 (statement)

SCHWEBLER, Yuri ( ) sclp, envir
ARTPARK 1976 182-183 (statement); port; 3 ill
ON SITE no.5/6 124-125 (statement); 3 ill

SCHWEIG, Martyl
SEE: MARTYL

SCHWEIKHER, Paul (1903-) Amer; arch
EMANUEL I 727-729 (statement); 1 ill

SCHWITTERS, Kurt (1887-1948) Germ; ptr, coll
ABSTRACTION no.1 33 (statement); 2 ill
ABSTRACTION no.2 41 (statement); 2 ill
BERCKELAERS 180 (statement, 1924)
CHIPP 382-384 (extract from "Merz," o.p. 1921); 1 ill
GIEDION-WELCKER 179-190 (poems: "Portrat Rudolf Blumner," 1919, "Portrat Herwath Walden," "Wir," 1919, "Portrat Nell Walden," 1919, "Lanke tr gl," 1922, "Entspannung," 1919, "An Franz Marc," 1921, "Die Rabenblute," 1921, "Denaturierte Poesie," 1922, "An Anna Blume," 1922, "An Eine Zeichnung Marc Chagalls," 1922, "Basel," 1922, in German; "A Eve Mafleur," in French)
PLASTIQUE no.4 22-23 (poems: "Kleines Gedicht fur Grosse Stotterer," "Die Liebe"); 1 ill
PLATSCHEK 59 ("An Eine Zeichnung Marc Chagall")
PLATSCHEK 60-67 ("An Alle Buhnen der Welt," o.p. 1919)
PLATSCHEK 68 ("Teufel in Not")
POENSGEN 103-104 ("Die Malerei," 1919)
PROTTER 218 (extract from *The Notes of Kurt Schwitters*)
SEITZ III 50-57 (statement, o.p. 1920); 10 ill
THORN 83 (statement, p.p.)

SCIALOJA, Toti (1914-) Ital; ptr
PAINTING 3 (statement); port; 1 ill

SCORDIA, Antonio (1918-) Ital; ptr
PAINTING 39 (statement); port; 1 ill

SCOTT, Michael (1905-) Iris; arch
EMANUEL I 729-731 (statement); 1 ill

SCOTT, Tim (1937-) Brit; sclp
NAYLOR 864-865 (statement); 1 ill

SCOTT, Vivian (1940-) Amer; ptr
ILLINOIS 1974 112 (statement); 1 ill

SCOTT, William
SEE: FASHION MODA

SCOTT, William (1913-) Scot; ptr
RITCHIE 74-77 (statement); port; 4 ill

SCOTT BROWN, Denise (1931-) Amer;
arch
COOK 247-266 (interview); port; 14 ill
EMANUEL I 731-733 (statement); 1 ill
ON SITE no.5/6 100-107 (interview)

SCREMINI, Clara
SEE: TALLER DE MONTEVIDEO

SCURIS, Stephanie (1931-) Gree/Amer;
sclp
STRUCTURED (statement); 3 ill

SEBRING, Ellen (1953-) Amer; video
BOSTON III (interview); 1 ill

SEDESTROM, Robert (1935-) Amer;
pott
HERMAN 112 (statement); port; 1 ill

SEDGLEY, Peter (1930-) Brit; instal, ptr
EMANUEL II 839-840 (statement); 1 ill
NAYLOR 866-867 (statement)

SEELIG, Warren (1946-) Amer; text
FIBER 60-61 (statement); 1 ill

SEERY, John (1941-) Amer; ptr
IMAGE COLOR FORM 24-25 (statement);
1 ill

SEGAL, George (1924-) Amer; sclp
ART NOW v.2 no.6 (statement); 1 ill
ARTFORUM v.3 no.2 26-29 (interview
with Henry Geldzahler); 7 ill
DIAMONSTEIN I 354-366 (interview);
ports
GALLERY STUDIES I 11-17 (interview

with Christopher B. Crosman & Nancy
Miller); 4 ill
HOUSE 86-87 (statement); 1 ill
IT IS no.6 77-80, 109-113 (group
discussion)
KERBER (extract from interview with
Sidney Tillim, o.p. 1963, in English
and German)
PRADEL 21 (extracts from interviews,
1982); 3 ill
QUADRUM no.18 162-164 (interview);
port
QUADRUM no.19 118-126 (interview); 9
ill
ROSE II REVISED 192-193 (statement:
"Everyone Shares a Stew of Ideas,"
o.p. 1967)
SAO PAULO 102-103 (extract from talk
given at Albright-Knox Gallery,
Buffalo, NY, 2/28/1967); port

SEGAL, Walter ( ) Brit; arch
MIKELLIDES 171-175 (essay: "The
Housing Crisis in Western Europe:
Britain: Assessment and Options")

SEGALL, Liliane
SEE: LIJN, Liliane

SEGALOVE, Ilene (1950-) Amer; video
ROSS 78-87 (statement); 30 ill

SEGONZAC, Andre Dunoyer de
(1884-1974) Fren; ptr
CHARBONNIER v.2 131-144 (interview)
GOLDAINE 30-32 (interview); port
LHOTE 408-411 (statements, o.p. 1929)

SEIBERT, Garfield (1881-) Amer; ptr
ILLINOIS 1959 267-268 (statement); 1 ill
ILLINOIS 1963 210 (statement); 1 ill

SEIDLER, Harry (1923-) Atrl; arch
EMANUEL I 734-736 (statement); 1 ill

GA HOUSES no.2 152-157 (statement); 14 ill

SEIFERT, Ivan (1926-) Fren; arch
EMANUEL I 736-737 (statement); 1 ill

SEIFERT, Robin (1910-) Brit; arch
EMANUEL I 737-739 (statement); 1 ill

SEKLER, Edward F. (1920-) Aust/Amer; arch
KEPES VI 89-95 (essay: "Structure, Construction, Tectonics")
KEPES IX 74-78 (essay: "The City and the Arts")
NEWMAN 186-189 (essay); port; 14 ill

SEKULA, Sonia (1918-) Amer; ptr
ILLINOIS 1952 231 (statement)

SEKULIC, Sava (1902-) Yugo; ptr
TOMASEVIC 318-321 (statement); port; 2 ill

SELDIN, Jacob (1892-) Russ/Amer; ptr
100 CONTEMPORARY 164-165 (statement); port; 1 ill

SELEY, Jason (1919-) Amer; sclp
MILLER 1963 94-99 (statement); port; 7 ill
RISENHOOVER 140-152 (interview)

SELF, Colin (1941-) Brit; sclp, ptr, coll
KUNST UND POLITIK (statement); port; 2 ill
NAYLOR 869-870 (statement)
RUSSELL J 113-114 (statement, o.p. 1967)

SELF, Jim ( ) perf
LIVE no.6/7 70-73 (interview); port

SELIGER, Charles (1926-) Amer; ptr
ILLINOIS 1965 182 (statement); 1 ill

PERSONAL (statement)

SELIGMANN, Kurt L. (1900-1962) Swis/Amer; ptr
ABSTRACTION no.1 31 (statement); 2 ill
ABSTRACTION no.2 (poem); 2 ill
FORD/VIEW v.1 no.7/8 3 ("An Eye for a Tooth")
FORD/VIEW v.1 no.11/12 3 ("Magic Circles")
FORD/VIEW v.2 no.2 (essay: "It's Easy to Criticize")
FORD/VIEW v.4 no.1 24-25 (essay: "Oedipus and the Forbidden Fruit")
FORD/VIEW v.4 no.4 129 ("Microcosmological Chart of Man"); 1 ill
FORD/VIEW v.5 no.5 6-8 (essay: "Heritage of the Accursed")
FORD/VIEW v.7 no.1 15-17 (essay: "Magic and the Arts")
ILLINOIS 1950 204-205 (statement); 1 ill
ILLINOIS 1952 231 (statement); 1 ill
JANIS I 144 (statement); 1 ill
JEAN 411 (extract from interview with James Johnson Sweeney, o.p. 1946)
LIPPARD 199-203 (essay: "Magic and the Arts," o.p. 1946)
MINOTAURE no.12/13 66-69 ("Entretien avec un Tsimshian")
TIGER no.6 46, 87-92 (statement); 5 ill
TIGER no.9 61-67 (essay: "The Hollow of the Night")
VINGTIEME v.1 no.2 22-24 ("Imageries Cinghalaises")

SELLERS, David ( ) arch
GA HOUSES no.12 74-87 (statement); port; 31 ill

SEMAK, Michael (1934-) Cana; photo
WALSH 672-674 (statement); 1 ill

SEMEGHINI, Pio (1878-) Ital; ptr
VERZOCCHI 387-391 (statement); self
port; 1 ill

SEMMEL, Joan (1932-) Amer; ptr
NAYLOR 871-872 (statement); 1 ill
SCHAPIRO 63 (statement); port; 1 ill
WOMANART v.2 no.2 14-21, 29
(interview); ports

SEMSER, Charles (1922-) Amer; ptr
ILLINOIS 1953 219-220 (statement)
ILLINOIS 1955 239 (statement); 1 ill

SEN, Ranjan (1941-) Cana; ptr
POINT OF VIEW 31 (statement); 1 ill

SENATE, The (group) Amer; video, perf
BOSTON III (interview); 1 ill

SENDAK, Maurice (1928-) Amer; illus
COTT 188-219 (interview); port; 1 ill

SENGSTACKE, Robert (1943-) Amer;
photo
LEWIS I REVISED 133-134 (statement);
port; 2 ill

SENNHAUSER, John (1907-)
Swis/Amer; ptr
ILLINOIS 1953 220 (statement); 1 ill

SEPESHY, Zoltan (1898-) Hung/Amer;
ptr
BETHERS II 128-129 (statement); 2 ill
BRITANNICA 100 (statement); port; 1
ill
M.H. DE YOUNG 119 (response); self
port

SERISAWA, Sueo (1910-) Japa/Amer;
ptr
CALIFORNIA--PAINTING 28 (statement);
1 ill

SERPA, Bob ( ) paper
VISUAL v.2 no.2 33-35 (interview); port
VISUAL v.3 no.4 41 (essay: "Technical
Information"); port

SERPAN, Jaroslav (1922-) Czec/Fren;
ptr
ART SINCE v.1 159 (statement, o.p.
1965)
CLAUS 91-97 (statement)
PREMIER BILAN 319 (statement); port

SERRA, Richard (1939-) Amer; ptr, sclp,
video
ART AND TECHNOLOGY 298-305
(project proposal); 9 ill
ART NOW v.3 no.3 (statement); 1 ill
ART-RITE no.7 5 ("Text: Television
Delivers People")
AVALANCHE no.2 20-21 (statements);
14 ill
AVALANCHE no.8 14-15 (interview); 2
ill
AVALANCHE no.9 26-28 (interview); 3
ill
CELANT 219-224 (statement); 5 ill
COLLABORATION 156-159 (essay:
"Connections"); 8 ill
DAVIS 104-107 (interview with Liza
Bear); port
HAUSSER 166-167 (extract from
interview with Lucie Borden, o.p.
1978); 1 ill
JOHNSON 201-210 (extract from essay:
"Shift," edited by Rosalind Krauss,
o.p. 1973); 1 ill
ROSE II REVISED 223, 252-254 (extracts
from essay: "Play It Again Sam," o.p.
1970)

SERRA-BADUE, Daniel (1914-)
Cuba/Amer; ptr
CUBAN (statement); self port; 2 ill

sclp
ILLINOIS 1967 127 (statement); 1 ill

SHADBOLT, Jack (1909-) Brit/Cana;
ptr
ART AND ARTIST 195-206 (essay:
"Picture in Process"); 4 ill
POINT OF VIEW 32 (statement); 1 ill

SHAFFER, Mary (1947-) Amer; glass,
sclp
AVALANCHE no.13 6 (statement); 1 ill
DIAMONSTEIN IV 210-223 (interview);
port; 14 ill

SHAFFER, Richard (1947-) Amer; ptr
SUPERREAL 52-53 (interview)
SUPERREAL 94-95 (statement); 1 ill

SHAHN, Ben (1898-1969) Amer; ptr
ADVERSARY 14-15 (extract from "Ben
Shahn: Painter of America," by
Selden Rodman, o.p. 1952)
ART SINCE v.2 148 (statement, o.p.
1959)
DOUZE PEINTRES (statement); 2 ill
FAMOUS v.1 166-169 (statement); 4 ill
FORTY (extract from talk given at
Harvard University, Cambridge, MA);
2 ill
GUITAR 184-195 (interview); port; 4 ill
ILLINOIS 1955 239-241 (statement); 1 ill
ILLINOIS 1959 268-269 (statement); 1 ill
KUH 204-218 (interview); 9 ill
MILLER 1943 52-53 (statement); 2 ill
REVOLUTION 135-136 (statement)
RODMAN I 189-193, 221-228 (interview)

SHANNON, Joe (1933-) Amer; ptr
IMAGES 58-65 (interview by Clair List);
port; 5 ill

SHANNONHOUSE, Sandra (1947-)
Amer; pott
HERMAN 113 (statement); port; 1 ill

SHAPIRO, David (1916-) Amer; ptr
FULBRIGHT 44-45 (statement); 1 ill

SHAPIRO, Howard-Yana ( ) pott
VIEWPOINT 1981 (statement); 3 ill

SHAPIRO, Joel (1941-) Amer; sclp
AVALANCHE no.12 15-19 (interview);
38 ill
EARLY WORK (interview with Susan
Logan); 4 ill
HOUSE 90-91 (statement, o.p. 1982); 1
ill

SHAPIRO, Seymour (1927-) Amer; ptr
ILLINOIS 1963 199 (statement); 1 ill

SHARITS, Paul Jeffrey (1943-) Amer;
film, instal
ARTPARK 1975 110-111 (statement);
port; 6 ill
DRAWING 171-180 (statement, 1976); 9
ill
GEORGIA 86-91, 110 (statement); port;
4 ill
GEORGIA 118-166 (group discussion:
"Artists' Convention," in Athens, GA.,
1/7/1977, moderated by Jan van der
Marck)
STEDELIJK 208 (statement, o.p. 1976);
1 ill

SHARON, Miriam (1944-) Isra
ISSUE (statements); 4 ill

SHARP, Anne (1943-) Amer; ptr
ARTPARK 1980 (statement); 1 ill

SHARP, John (1911-) Amer; ptr
ILLINOIS 1952 232 (statement); 1 ill

SHARP, Willoughby (1936-) Amer;
video, sclp, film
ART-RITE no.7 11, 14 (response); 1 ill

AVALANCHE no.9 16-17 (interview); 3 ill
BATTCOCK V 317-358 (essay: "Luminism and Kineticism," o.p. 1967)
KUNST BLEIBT KUNST 422 (statement); 1 ill

SHARRER, Honore (1920-) Amer; ptr
MILLER 1946 62-65 (statement); 4 ill
NEW DECADE 79-81 (statement); 2 ill

SHAW, Charles Green (1892-1974) Amer; sclp, ptr
ABSTRACT 9-11 (essay: "A Word to the Objector"); 1 ill
PLASTIQUE no.3 28-29 (essay: "The Plastic Polygon"); 1 ill

SHAW, Jeffrey (1944-) Atrl; film
EMANUEL II 849-850 (statement); 1 ill

SHAW, Kaete Brittin (1945-) Amer; pott
HERMAN 114 (statement); port; 1 ill

SHAW, Karen ( ) Amer
BRENTANO 332-333 (statement); 1 ill

SHAW, Richard Blake (1941-) Amer; pott, sclp
HERMAN 115 (statement); port; 1 ill
HOPKINS 64-65 (statement); port; 1 ill
HOUSE 92-93 (statement); 1 ill

SHAW, Rod ( )
ART NETWORK no.1 24 (interview)

SHAWCROFT, Barbara (1930-) Amer; paper
HAYSTACK 58 (statement); 1 ill

SHAWN, Nelson ( ) Amer; photo
CALIFORNIA--PHOTOGRAPHY (statement); port; 4 ill

SHEA, Judith (1948-) Amer; text
ARTPARK 1974 36-37 (statement); port; 1 ill
ARTPARK 1975 112-113 (statement); port; 1 ill

SHEEHAN, Maura ( ) Amer; sclp, envir
DOWNTOWN (statement); 1 ill

SHEELER, Charles (1883-1965) Amer; ptr
ARMORY SHOW 31 (statement)
BRITANNICA 101 (statement); port; 1 ill
FORTY (statement); 2 ill
FORUM 1916 96 (statement); 1 ill
GOLDWATER 473-474 (statement, 1916)
ILLINOIS 1949 (unpaginated) (statement)
ILLINOIS 1957 247 (response); 1 ill
ILLINOIS 1959 270 (statement); 1 ill
JOURNAL OF THE AAA v.5 no.2 1-4 (statements); port
ROSE II 95-96 (statement, o.p. 1916)
ROSE II REVISED 79-81 (statement, o.p. 1916)
ROSE II REVISED 81 (statement, o.p. 1939)
ROSE II REVISED 81-82 ("Cathedrals and Factories," o.p. 1938)

SHEETS, James ( ) Amer; ptr
IRVINE 14, 79-80 (statement); 1 ill

SHEETS, Millard Owen (1907-) Amer; ptr
BRITANNICA 102 (statement); port; 1 ill
CALIFORNIA--PAINTING 29 (statement); 1 ill

SHEFFER, Glen ( ) film
WHITE WALLS no.9 14-15 ("Cheerleaders from the Black

Lagoon," "Icon Teen: A Turn (Her/He) View")

SHELLY, Mary (1950-) Amer; ptr, coll
NOSANOW I 112 (statement); 1 ill

SHELTON, Christopher (1933-) Amer; sclp, ptr
FINE 226-227 (letter, 1971); 1 ill

SHELTON, Peter (1951-) Amer; sclp
ARTPARK 1980 (statement); 5 ill

SHEMI, Yehiel (1922-) Isra; sclp
SEITZ I (statement, o.p. 1957); 3 ill

SHEMTOV, Igael (1952-) Isra; photo
WALSH 681-682 (statement); 1 ill

SHEPPARD, Richard ( ) Brit; arch
SEE: RICHARD SHEPPARD ROBSON AND PARTNERS

SHER, Cathy Lynn (1949-) Amer; sclp, pott
NOSANOW II 32-33, 66 (statement); 3 ill

SHERIDAN, Noel (1936-) Iris
KNOWLES 202-203 (text piece); 1 ill

SHERIDAN, Sonia Landy (1925-) Amer; print, photo
COMPUTER (statement); 1 ill

SHERMAN, Cindy (1954-) Amer; photo
FACE IT 22-23 (statement); 1 ill

SHERMAN, Sarai (1922-) Amer; ptr
FULBRIGHT 44 (statement)
ILLINOIS 1955 241-242 (statement); 1 ill
ILLINOIS 1961 194 (response); port; 1 ill

SHERMAN, Stuart (1945-) Amer; perf
APPLE 51 (statement); 1 ill

SHERMAN, Tom (1947-) Cana; video
PARACHUTE no.9 17-21 (statement, in English)

SHERWIN, Guy (1948-) Brit; film
ENGLISH 464-465 (statement); port; 1 ill

SHEVCHENKO, Aleksandr (1882-1948) Russ; ptr
BOWLT 41-54 (extract from *Neoprimitivism: Its Theory, Its Potentials, Its Achievements*, o.p. 1913); 2 ill

SHIBLEY, Bob ( ) arch, design
LIFE 55-71 (interview); port

SHIELDS, Alan J. (1944-) Amer; sclp, ptr
IMAGE COLOR FORM 26-27 (statement); 1 ill

SHIELDS, William S., Jr. ( ) Amer; sclp
ILLUSTRATION 42-45 (statement); port; 4 ill

SHIM, Moon-Seup (1942-) Kore; sclp
NAYLOR 880-881 (statement); 1 ill

SHIMIZU, Kotaro ( ) Japa; print
ADACHI 53-55 (statement); port; 4 ill

SHINEMAN, Larry (1943-) Amer; ptr
OUTSIDE II 32-33 (statement); port; 4 ill

SHINN, Everett (1876-1953) Amer; ptr
BRITANNICA 103 (statement); port; 1 ill
JOURNAL OF THE AAA v.6 no.2 1-12 (essay: "George Luks")

SHINODA, Morio (1931-) Japa; sclp
KUNG 180-183 (statement); port; 2 ill

SHINOHARA, Kazuo (1925-) Japa; arch
EMANUEL I 745-746 (statement); 1 ill

SHIOMI, Mieko (1938-) Japa
NAYLOR 881 (statement); port

SHIPMAN, Dru ( ) photo
VISUAL v.1 no.4 3-5 (group discussion)

SHIRAGA, Kazuo (1924-) Japa; ptr
KUNG 108-111 (statement); port; 2 ill

SHIRAKAWA, Yoshikazu (1935-) Japa; photo
WALSH 683-684 (statement); 1 ill

SHIRAS, Myrnas ( )
CRISS-CROSS no.5 48-53 ("Professional Artist's Resume Kit"); port; 7 ill

SHIRK, Helen ( ) Amer; metal
METALWORKS (statement); 1 ill

SHIVES, Arnold (1943-) Cana; ptr
POINT OF VIEW 33 (statement); 1 ill

SHONO, Shounsai ( ) Japa
ADACHI 56-59 (statement); port; 3 ill

SHORR, Harriet (1939-) Amer; ptr
TRACKS v.2 no.3 68-69 (poem: "Dancing with Grandin")

SHOSTAK, Edwin Bennett (1941-) Amer; sclp
NAYLOR 881-882 (statement); 1 ill

SHOTTENKIRK, Dena ( )
REALLIFE no.10 22-24 (essay: "More Positions than Modernism Ever Dreamt of")

SHTERENBERG, David (1881-1948) Russ; ptr

BANN 70-72 ("Foreword" to the *Catalogue of the First Exhibition of Russian Art*, Berlin, 1922)
BOWLT 186-190 (essay: "Our Task," o.p. 1920); port; 1 ill

SHULKIN, Anatol (1901-1961) Russ/Amer; ptr
ILLINOIS 1950 206 (statement); 1 ill

SHURTLEFF, Cheryl K. (1947-) Amer; ptr
NOSANOW II 34-35, 67 (statement); 3 ill

SHUTT, Ken (1928-) Amer; sclp
HAAR II 74-78 (interview); ports; 2 ill

SIBLEY, Andrew (1933-) Atrl; ptr
DE GROEN 1-20 (interview); port

SICARD, Pierre (1900-) Amer; ptr
ILLINOIS 1957 247-248 (response); 1 ill

SICKERT, Walter Richard (1860-1942) Brit; ptr
FRIEDENTHAL 189-192 (letter to *ArtNews*, 1910); 1 ill
GOLDWATER 394-395, 397 (statements, 1911, 1916, 1922)

SIEFF, Jeanloup (1933-) Fren; photo
HOW FAMOUS 218-223 (statements); port; 8 ill
WALSH 686-687 (statement); 1 ill

SIEGEL, Irene (1932-) Amer; ptr, print
NAYLOR 882-883 (statement); 1 ill

SIEGEL, Robert ( ) arch
GA DOCUMENT no.4 80-83 (statement); 15 ill

SIEGRIEST, Louis B. (1899-) Amer; ptr
HOPKINS 66-67 (statement); port; 1 ill
ILLINOIS 1963 169 (statement); 1 ill

SOME 21 (statement); 1 ill

SIEGRIEST, Lundy (1925-) Amer; ptr
ILLINOIS 1953 222-223 (statement); 1 ill
ILLINOIS 1955 242-243 (statement); 1 ill
ILLINOIS 1961 195 (response); port; 1 ill
YOUNG 1957 (statement); 2 ill

SIGLER, Hollis (1948-) Amer; ptr
PROFILE v.3 no.2 (interview); port; 4 ill

SIGNAC, Paul (1863-1935) Fren; ptr
LHOTE 367-375 (essay: "L'Education
de l'Oeil," o.p. 1911)
SCHMIDT 68 (letter, 1934)
SEGHERS 17-32 (essay: "The
Contribution of the Neoimpressionists;
The Divided Touch," p.p.)
THORN 41, 200, 205, 233 (statements,
p.p.)

SIJAKOVIC, Dorde (1901-) Yugo; ptr
TOMASEVIC 353-356 (statement); port;
1 ill

SILBERBERG, Sally (1945-) Amer; pott
HERMAN 116 (statement); port; 1 ill

SILLS, Thomas Albert (1914-) Amer; ptr
FINE 158, 160, 167 (statements, o.p.
1970); 2 ill

SILVA, Carlos Alberto da (1934-) Port;
pott, ptr, sclp
PREMIO NACIONAL 1965 40-41
(statement); port; 1 ill

SILVER, Thomas C. (1942-) Amer; sclp
RIPS (statement); 1 ill

SILVERMAN, Melvin Frank (1931-1966)
Amer; ptr
ILLINOIS 1965 98 (statement); 1 ill

SILVETTI, Jorge (1942-) Arge/Amer;
arch
ARCHER 68-72, 99 (statement); port; 9
ill

SIMA, Josef (1891-) Czec; ptr
GRENIER 165-173 (interview)

SIMKIN, Phillips M. (1944-) Amer; perf,
sclp, envir
ARTPARK 1975 114-115 (statement);
port; 10 ill
ARTPARK 1976 184-185 (statement); 6
ill

SIMMONS, Laurie (1949-) Amer; photo
FIGURES 30-31 (statement); 1 ill

SIMON, Jewel Woodard (1911-) Amer;
print, ptr
LEWIS I REVISED 108 (statement); port;
1 ill

SIMON, Mark ( ) Amer; arch
GA HOUSES no.7 76-77 (essay: "The
Halcyon Days of Now or the Desperate
Hours"); port
GA HOUSES no.13 112-117, 130-141
(statements); 36 ill

SIMONDS, Charles (1945-) Amer; sclp,
pott
ARTPARK 1974 38-41 (statement); 6 ill
COLLABORATION 144-151 (essay:
"Ellis Island: Gateway to America");
6 ill
EMANUEL II 852-854 (statement); 1 ill
HOUSE 94-95 (statement, o.p. 1982); 1
ill
NAYLOR 884 (statement); 1 ill
ON SITE no.4 32-33 (statement); 3 ill
QUINTESSENCE 50-60 (statement);
ports; 21 ill
SKIRA 1979 112-113 (statement); 2 ill
SKIRA 1980 121 (statement); 3 ill

SONDHEIM 290-311 *"Selected Works"); 12 ill

SIMONDS, John Ormsbee (1913-) Amer; arch
EMANUEL I 747-749 (statement); 1 ill
REVOLUTION 140-144 (essay: "A Search for Quality")

SIMONETTI, Gianni-Emilio (1940-) Ital; ptr
SKIRA 1977 22 (statement); 1 ill

SIMONETTI, Naomi Castillo (1943-) Amer; photo
RAICES 74 (statement); 1 ill

SIMONIAN, Judith E. ( ) Amer; ptr, envir
DOWNTOWN (statement); 1 ill

SIMONS, Harvey Low (1940-) Amer; ptr
BOSTON III (interview); 1 ill

SIMOUNET, Roland ( ) Fren; arch
ARCHITECTURES 92-97 (essay: "Intuition et Rationalite"); 6 ill

SIMPSON, David (1928-) Amer; ptr
ILLINOIS 1963 66 (statement); 1 ill
MILLER 1963 100-105 (statement); port; 5 ill

SIMPSON, Gregg (1947-) Cana; video
POINT OF VIEW 47 (statement); 1 ill

SIMPSON, Kenn (1926-) Amer; print
LEWIS I REVISED 90 (statement); port; 1 ill

SIMPSON, Merton D. (1928-) Amer; ptr
MORRIS 200-205 (statements); ports; 4 ill

SINA, Alejandro (1945-) Chil/Amer; envir, sclp, light
CENTERBEAM 71, 121-122 ("Neon-Argon Line"); port; 5 ill
TECHNOLOGIES (statement); port; 15 ill

SINDEN, Tony ( ) Brit; film, instal
HAYWARD 1979 15-18 (interview with William Furlong)
HAYWARD 1979 28-31 (statement); 11 ill

SINGER, Burr Friedman ( ) Amer; illus
CALIFORNIA--DRAWING (statement); 2 ill

SINGER, Gerard (1929-) Fren; sclp
SKIRA 1977 104 (statement); 1 ill

SINGER, Michael (1945-) Amer; sclp, envir
AUPING I 51-65, 122-132 (interview); 12 ill

SINGH, Patwant ( ) arch
REVOLUTION 69-73 (essay: "The Real Challenge")

SINGIER, Gustave (1909-) Belg; ptr
CHARBONNIER v.1 19-28 (interview)
VINGTIEME N.S. no.7 48-50 (interview with Guy Wheelen); 4 ill

SINTENIS, Renee Weiss (1888-1965) Germ; sclp
SCHMIDT 46 (letter, 1933)

SIPORIN, Mitchell (1910-1976) Amer; ptr
BRITANNICA 104 (statement); port; 1 ill
ILLINOIS 1951 216 (statement)
MILLER 1942 112-117 (statement); port; 4 ill

SLEIGH, Sylvia ( ) Brit/Amer; ptr
ART-RITE no.5 7 (response)
ART-RITE no.11/12 (poem: "The Song of Lilith"); 1 ill
SCHAPIRO 65 (statement); port; 1 ill
WOMANART v.1 no.2 12-13 (essay: "Laura Knight as a War Artist")
WOMANART v.1 no.3 51 (essay: "Realists Choose Realists")

SLEVOGT, Max (1868-1932) Germ; ptr, print, illus
THORN 200, 209, 309, 340 (statements, p.p.)

SLICK, John Colburn (1946-) Amer; sclp
MICHIGAN 42-43 (statement); 2 ill

SLIVKA, David ( ) Amer; sclp
IT IS no.5 51-56 (group discussion)
IT IS no.6 7-16, 57-64, 73-75 (group discussion)

SLOAN, John (1871-1951) Amer; ptr
FORTY (statement); 2 ill
GOLDWATER 401-402 (extract from *The Gist of Art*, o.p. 1939)
ROSE II 42-43 (extract from *The Gist of Art*, o.p. 1939)
ROSE II REVISED 40-41 (extract from *The Gist of Art*, o.p. 1939)
SAYLER 318-321 (essay: "Art Is, Was, and Ever Will Be")

SLOBODKIN, Louis (1903-) Amer; sclp
100 CONTEMPORARY 168-169 (statement); port; 1 ill

SMAJIC, Petar (1910-) Yugo; sclp
TOMASEVIC 331-334 (statement); port; 1 ill

SMIGROD, Claudia (1949-) Amer; photo
FRALIN 30-31, 43 (statement); 1 ill

SMITH, Alexis Patricia Anne (1949-) Amer; video
ROSS 24-27 (statement); 4 ill
WHITE WALLS no.6 46-51 (text piece)

SMITH, Alfred James (1948-) Amer; sclp
CONTEMPORARY AFRICAN (statement); port; 1 ill
FAX II 181-201 (statements); port; 1 ill

SMITH, Arenzo (1939-) Amer; ptr
LEWIS II 60 (statement); port; 1 ill

SMITH, Arthur (1923-) Amer; metal
CONTEMPORARY AFRICAN (statement); port; 1 ill

SMITH, Barbara T. (1931-) Amer; perf, sclp, video
AVALANCHE no.13 4-5 (statement); 1 ill
IRVINE 32, 79 (statement); 1 ill
SCHAPIRO 66 (statement); port
STEDELIJK 209 (statement); 1 ill

SMITH, Bradley ( ) Amer; sclp
IRVINE 56, 85 (statement); 1 ill

SMITH, Charles ( ) Brit; ptr
PERSONAL (statement)

SMITH, Christina Yvonne ( ) Amer; metal
METALWORKS (statement); 1 ill

SMITH, Damballah ( ) Amer; text
LEWIS I REVISED 101-102 (statement); port; 2 ill

SMITH, David (1906-1965) Amer; sclp
ADVERSARY II (statement, o.p. 1940)
CHIPP 576-578 ("Notes on My Work," o.p. 1960); port
DOUZE PEINTRES (statement); 2 ill
JOHNSON 36-39 (extract from *David Smith by David Smith*, 1968); 1 ill

JOURNAL OF THE AAA v.8 no.2 1-11 (statements); port; 2 ill
JOURNAL OF THE AAA v.8 no.2 11-16 ("Memories to Myself"); 2 ill
KUH 219-234 (interview); 10 ill
MOTHERWELL 8-22 (three group discussions: "Artists' Sessions at Studio 35," New York, 1950)
POSSIBILITIES 24-26, 30, 33, 37 ("I Have Never Looked at a Landscape"); 8 ill
RODMAN I 126-130 (interview)
ROSE II 185-186 (extract from "A Symposium on Art and Religion," o.p. 1953)
ROSE II 186-189 (extract from essay: "Thoughts on Sculpture," o.p. 1954)
ROSE II 190-192 (extract from essay: "Second Thoughts on Sculpture," o.p. 1954)
ROSE II REVISED 244-245 (extract from "A Symposium on Art and Religion," o.p. 1953)
ROSE II REVISED 245-248 (extract from essay: "Thoughts on Sculpture," o.p. 1954)
ROSE II REVISED 249-251 (extract from essay: "Second Thoughts on Sculpture," o.p. 1954)
SPENCER 303-306 ("Thoughts on Sculpture," o.p. 1954); 1 ill
TIGER no.4 81-82, 100 (poem: "The Golden Eagle--a Recital"); 1 ill

SMITH, Edith M. T. (1925-) Amer; ptr
ILLINOIS 1955 243-244 (statement); 1 ill

SMITH, George H. (1942-) Amer; sclp, envir
ARTPARK 1976 186-187 (statement); 3 ill
LEWIS II 22 (statement); port; 1 ill

SMITH, Hassel W., Jr. (1915-) AMer; ptr

ARTFORUM v.1 no.2 29-35 (group discussion)
ENVIRONMENT 102-103 (statement); 1 ill
SOME 23 (statement); 1 ill

SMITH, Henry Holmes (1909-) Amer; photo
HILL 132-159 (interview, 1975); port

SMITH, Howard (1928-) Amer; print
LEWIS II 115 (statement); port; 2 ill

SMITH, Ivor (1926-) Brit; arch
EMANUEL I 756-758 (statement); 1 ill

SMITH, Jack (1928-) Brit; perf, ptr
ART-RITE no.6 19 (extract from talk given in New York; extract from performance); ports
BARBER 101-113 (interview); port
CONTEMPORARY (statement); port; 2 ill

SMITH, Joan (1946-) Iris; sclp
KNOWLES 132-135, 183 (statement); ports; 7 ill

SMITH, John Ivor (1927-) Brit/Cana; sclp
CANADA 20-21 (statement); port; 1 ill

SMITH, Judson DeJonge (1880-1962) Amer; ptr
ZAIDENBERG 86-89 (essay: "Random Thoughts on Non-Objective Painting"); 4 ill

SMITH, June (1934-) Amer; coll
CALIFORNIA--COLLAGE (statement); 1 ill

SMITH, Keith (1938-) Amer; photo
DUGAN 79-90 (interview, 1976); port
WALSH 700-701 (statement); 1 ill

KEPES II 222-232 ("The Spiral Jetty");
9 ill
ON SITE no.2 10, 13 (response)
ON SITE no.4 26-31 (interview); 8 ill
ROSE II REVISED 261-264 (extract from
essay: "Entropy and the New
Monuments," o.p. 1966)
VARIAN II (statement); port

SMULLIN, Frank ( ) Amer; print
COMPUTER (statement); 1 ill

SMYTH, David (1943-) Amer; sclp
TRACKS v.1 no.1 17 (poem)

SMYTH, Ned (1948-) Amer; instal, ptr,
sclp
REALLIFE no.8 25-28 (interview); 2 ill

SNELGROVE, Walter H. (1924-) Amer;
ptr
ILLINOIS 1965 111 (statement); 1 ill

SNELSON, Kenneth (1927-) Amer; sclp
ART VOICES v.5 no.3 82-83 (essay:
"How Primary is Structure?"); 4 ill
ARTFORUM v.5 no.7 46-49 (interview
with John Coplans); 9 ill
BELFORD 57-77 (group discussion)
HAUSSER 168-169 (extract from
interview with Angela Schneider, o.p.
1977); 1 ill
NAYLOR 891-892 (statement); 1 ill

SNIDER, Jenny (1944-) Amer; ptr
SHEARER 58-61 (interview); 3 ill
SULTAN 37-38 ("Artist Outfoxed by
Death")

SNODGRASS, Cindy (1952-) Amer; sclp,
text, envir
ARTPARK 1981 (statement); port; 2 ill

SNOW, Michael (1929-) Cana; sclp,
photo, film

CANADA 12-13 (statement); port; 1 ill
PARACHUTE no.3 27-29 (statements, in
English)
PARACHUTE no.4 39 (letter)
STEDELIJK 210 (statement, o.p. 1979);
1 ill
VANCOUVER (letter); 1 ill
WALSH 704-705 (statement); 1 ill

SNOW, Vivian Douglas (1927-) Amer;
ptr
FULBRIGHT 45 (statement)
ILLINOIS 1967 70 (statement); 1 ill

SNOWBALL, Crystall
SEE: SCHNEEMANN, Carolee

SNOWDON, Lord (Armstrong-Jones,
Antony Charles Robert) (1930-) Brit;
photo
DANZIGER 138-153 (interview); port; 4
ill

SNYDER, Joan (1940-) Amer; sclp
NAYLOR 893-894 (statement); 1 ill
SCHAPIRO 67 (statement); port; 1 ill

SNYDER, Kit-Yin Tieng ( ) Chin/Amer;
sclp, envir
ARTPARK 1983 48-49 (statement); port;
1 ill
HOUSE 96-97 (statement); 2 ill

SNYERS, Alain (1951-) Fren
SEE: GROUPE UNTEL

SOBEL, Janet (1894-) Amer; ptr
JANIS I 96-97 (statement); 1 ill

SOBRINO, Francisco (1932-) Span; sclp
LUMIERE (statement); port; 1 ill

SOCIETY FOR THEORETICAL ART
AND ANALYSES (group)

CONCEPTUAL ART 21-22 (essay: "Real Premise" by Ian Burn)
CONCEPTUAL ART 22-25 (essay: "Elements in Reference to" by Roger Cutforth)
CONCEPTUAL ART 26-28 (essay: "Inquiry #5" by Mel Ramsden)

SOCIETY OF EASEL ARTISTS (group)
BOWLT 279-281 ("Platform," o.p. 1929/33)

SOFFICI, Ardengo (1879-) Ital; ptr
APOLLONIO 134-135 ("The Subject in Futurist Painting," o.p. 1914)
VERZOCCHI 405-409 (statement); self port; 1 ill

SOGLOW, Otto (1900-1975) Amer; cart
M.H. DE YOUNG 123 (response); self port

SOKOL, Jan (1909-) Yugo; ptr
TOMASEVIC 335-337 (statement); port; 1 ill

SOKOLOWSKI, Linda Robinson (1943-) Amer; ptr
NOSANOW I 114-115 (statement); 2 ill

SOLBES, Rafael (1940-)
SEE: EQUIPO CRONICA

SOLDATE, Joe ( ) pott
VIEWPOINT 1979 22-23 (statement); 3 ill

SOLDNER, Paul Edmund (1921-) Amer; pott
VIEWPOINT 1980 20-21 (statement); 4 ill

SOLEM, Elmo John (1933-) Amer; print
CALIFORNIA--PRINTS (statement); 1 ill

SOLERI, Paolo (1919-) Ital/Amer; arch
EMANUEL I 761-762 (statement); 1 ill
HEYER 78-83 (interview); 14 ill
ON SITE no.2 10, 13 (response)

SOLMAN, Joseph (1909-) Russ/Amer; ptr
JANIS I 84 (statement); 1 ill

SOLOMON, Daniel (1939-) Amer; arch
GA HOUSES no.11 58-65 (statement); 16 ill
LA JOLLA 87-91 (statement); port; 6 ill

SOLOMON, Hyde (1911-) Amer; ptr
ART NOW v.3 no.1 (statement); 1 ill
ILLINOIS 1963 83 (statement); 1 ill

SOLOMON, Syd (1917-) Amer; ptr
FAMOUS v.1 178-179 (statement); 3 ill
GUITAR 196-205 (interview); port; 4 ill

SOLON, Louis Marc Emanuel ( ) pott
CLARK 28-44 (essay: "The Revival of the Art of Faience Painting," o.p. 1903)

SOLOTAROFF, Moi ( ) Amer; ptr
100 CONTEMPORARY 170-171 (statement); port; 1 ill

SOLSONA, Justos Jorge (1931-) Arge; arch
SEE: MANTEOLA SANCHEZ GOMEZ SANTOS SOLSONA VINOLY

SOLTAN, Jerzy ( ) Poli; arch
NEWMAN 197-201 (essay); port; 13 ill

SOMAINI, Francesco (1926-) Ital; print
SKIRA 1977 107 (statement); 1 ill

SOMMER, Ed (1932-) Swis; sclp
NAYLOR 895-896 (statement); 1 ill

SOMMER, Frederick (1905-) Ital/Amer; photo
DIAMONSTEIN III 167-178 (interview); 5 ill

SOMVILLE, Roger ( ) Belg; ptr
COLLARD 228-233 (interview); port; 1 ill

SONDERBORG, Kurt R. H. (1923-) Dani; ptr
ART SINCE v.1 155 (statements, o.p. 1959, 1960)

SONDHEIM, Alan (1943-) Amer; envir, video
ART-RITE no.14 30 (statement)
CRISS-CROSS no.7/8/9 10-15 ("W")
PROJECTS (statement); 4 ill
SCHIMMEL 8-13 (essay: "Give Me an 'N'")
TRACKS v.2 no.2 32-44 ("Seventy-four Characteristics of the World"; "The Characteristics of the World")

SONENBERG, Jack (1925-) Cana/Amer; ptr
ILLINOIS 1963 70 (statement); 1 ill
VARIAN III (statement); port

SONFIST, Alan (1946-) Amer; envir, sclp, video
ARTPARK 1975 118-119 (statement); port
AUPING I 66-82, 133-145; 13 ill
BELFORD 79-100 (group discussion)
EMANUEL II 864-866 (statement); 1 ill
KUNST BLEIBT KUNST 320-323 (statement); 3 ill
MADE FOR BUFFALO (statements); ports
NAYLOR 897-899 (statement); 1 ill
ON SITE no.4 38-40 (statement); 6 ill
SKIRA 1978 86 (statement); 1 ill
SKIRA 1980 129 (statement); 3 ill

TRACKS v.3 no.1/2 44-47 ("Natural Phenomena as Public Monuments")

SONNABEND, Yolanda (1935-) Brit; ptr
SKIRA 1979 97 (statement); 1 ill

SONNEMAN, Eve (1946-) Amer; photo, film
ART-RITE no.6 25 (statement)

SONNIER, Keith (1941-) Amer; sclp, video, instal
AVALANCHE no.5 36-45 (group discussion); 8 ill
AVALANCHE no.9 24-25 (interview)
BRENTANO 340-341 (statement)
CELANT 162-167 (statement); 5 ill
FIVE 16-19 (interview with Calvin Harlan, 11/1976); 3 ill
PARACHUTE no.6 25-28 (interview, in English); 3 ill

SOPPELAND, Mark (1952-) Amer
RIPS (statement)

SORENSEN, William Louis ( )
GROH (statement)

SORG, Christian (1941-) Fren; ptr
SKIRA 1978 75 (statement); 1 ill
SKIRA 1980 57 (statement: from "Documents sur" nos.2/3, 4/5); 4 ill

SORGE, Peter (1937-) Germ; print
SKIRA 1975 75 (statement, 1972); 1 ill

SORGEL, Herman ( )
GROHMANN 459-463 ("Entstehung des Architektonischen Kunstwerkes," p.p. 1921)

SORIANO, Juan (1919-) Mexi; ptr
STEWART 148-151 (statement); port; 2 ill

SORIANO, Raphael ( ) Amer; arch
HEYER 130-136 (interview); 18 ill

SOTO, Jesus-Raphael (1923-)
Vene/Fren; sclp
ART SINCE v.1 294 (statement, o.p.
1967)
LUMIERE (statement); port; 1 ill
SKIRA 1975 78-79 (extract from
interview with Claude-Louis Renard,
1974); 1 ill

SOTTSASS, Ettore, Jr. (1917-) Ital;
design
DESIGN 3-4 (interview)

SOUKOP, Willi (1907-) Aust/Brit; sclp
CONTEMPORARY (statement); port; 2
ill

SOULANGES, Pierre (1919-) Fren; ptr
ART SINCE v.1 158 (statement, o.p.
1963)
CHARBONNIER v.1 153-158 (interview)
GOLDAINE 168-170 (interview); port
GRENIER 177-182 (interview)
QUADRUM no.8 95-106 (statements); 6
ill
RAGON 174-182 (statement)
RITCHIE 39-43 (statements, 1950-1953);
port; 5 ill
SCHNEIDER 47-64 (interview); 1 ill
VINGTIEME N.S. no.9 36 (statement)

SOUSA, Ernesto de (1921-) Port; video
BIENNALE 168-169 (statement)

SOUTHWORTH, Ella (1872-) Amer; ptr
JANIS II 174-177 (statements); port; 1
ill

SOUTINE, Chaim (1894-1943)
Russ/Fren; ptr
PROTTER 231 (extract from letter to
Zborowski, 1923)

SOUVERBIE, Jean (1891-) Fren; ptr
ART D'AUJOURD'HUI v.4 7 (statement);
5 ill

SOVAK, Pravoslav (1926-) Czec; print
KUNST UND POLITIK (statement); port;
6 ill

SOVIAK, Harry (1935-) Amer; ptr
VARIAN I (statement); port

SOVIK, Edward A. ( ) arch
REVOLUTION 230-232 (essay:
"Metaphors: A Photographic Essay on
Religious Architecture")

SOYER, Isaac (1902-) Russ/Amer; ptr
FIFTY (statement); port; 1 ill
M.H. DE YOUNG 125 (response); self
port
100 CONTEMPORARY 172-173
(statement); port; 1 ill

SOYER, Moses (1899-) Russ/Amer; ptr
100 CONTEMPORARY 174-175
(statement); port; 1 ill

SOYER, Raphael (1899-) Russ/Amer;
ptr
BRITANNICA 107 (statement); port; 1
ill
DIAMONSTEIN I 367-380 (interview);
ports
FIFTY (statement); self port; 1 ill
100 CONTEMPORARY 176-177
(statement); port; 1 ill
ROSNER 279-287 (interview); port
SUPERREAL 54-55, 98-99 (interview); 1
ill

SPADARI, Giangiacomo (1938-) Ital; ptr
KUNST UND POLITIK (statement, with
Paolo Baratella); port; 1 ill
SKIRA 1976 65 (statement); 1 ill

SPAFFORD, Michael Charles (1935-) Amer; ptr
GUENTHER 106-107 (statement); port; 1 ill

SPAGNULO, Giuseppe (1936-) Ital; sclp
NAYLOR 904 (statement); 1 ill
SKIRA 1976 104-105 (statement); 1 ill

SPARKS, Gregory L. (1957-) Amer; pott
CONTEMPORARY AFRICAN (statement); port; 1 ill

SPASIC, Ceda (1922-) Yugo; ptr
TOMASEVIC 338-340 (statement); port; 1 ill

SPATARU, Mircea (1938-) Ruma; sclp
NAYLOR 904-906 (statement); 1 ill

SPEAR, Laurinda ( ) arch
GA DOCUMENT no.7 4-14 (interview); port; 6 ill
SEE ALSO: ARQUITECTONICA

SPECTOR, Buzz ( ) Amer; sclp, illus
WHITE WALLS no.1 iii (editorial statement)
WHITE WALLS no.3 29-34 ("Jacob's Ladder"); 4 ill
WHITE WALLS no.5 2-5 (essay: "Words as Images")

SPEER, Albert (1905-) Germ; arch
EMANUEL I 766-767 (statement); 1 ill

SPEICHER, Eugene (1883-1962) Amer; ptr
BRITANNICA 108 (statement); port; 1 ill
ZAIDENBERG 72-73 (essay: "Painting a Portrait")
ZAIDENBERG 74-75 (essay: "My Method of Painting"); 5 ill

SPEIGHT, Francis (1896-) Amer; ptr
BRITANNICA 109 (statement); port; 1 ill

SPENCER, Jean (1942-) Brit; ptr
CONTEMPORARY (statement); port; 2 ill

SPENCER, Niles (1893-1952) Amer; ptr
ILLINOIS 1952 233-234 (statement); 1 ill

SPENCER, Sharon (1943-) Amer; print, pott
CONTEMPORARY AFRICAN (statement); port; 1 ill

SPENDER, Humphrey (1910-) Brit; photo
WALSH 711-713 (statement); 1 ill

SPERO, Nancy (1926-) Amer; ptr, coll
ART-RITE no.9 18 (statement)
EMANUEL II 873-875 (statement); 1 ill
GUMPERT III 77-79 (statement)
INTERVIEWS 28-29 (interview); port; 1 ill
MILLER 202-212 (interview with Sally Swenson); port
NAYLOR 907-908 (statement); 1 ill
PROFILE v.3 no.1 (interview); port; 5 ill
SCHAPIRO 68 (statement); port; 1 ill
WOMANART v.1 no.3 8-11 (interview with Carol De Pasquale); port; 4 ill
WOMANART v.1 no.3 26, 31, 36 (response); port

SPEYER, Nora ( ) ptr
SCHAPIRO 69 (statement); port; 1 ill

SPIEGEL, Laurie ( ) ptr
REALLIFE no.3 14 (statements)

SPIEGELMAN, Lon H. ( ) Amer; illus
ARTISTS no.1 7-8 ("Mail Art Keeps Me

Sane," and "To Hell with the System")

SPIERS, Raymond (1934-) Cana; sclp
CANADA 66-67 (statement); port; 1 ill

SPIVAK, Laurie ( ) Amer; metal
METALWORKS (statement); 1 ill

SPLETH, Tom (1946-) Amer; pott
HERMAN 117 (statement); port; 1 ill

SPLICHAL, Jan (1929-) Czec; photo
WALSH 712, 714 (statement); 1 ill

SPOERRI, Daniel (1930-) Ruma; sclp
STEDELIJK 212-213 (statement, in German, 1960); 3 ill

SPOFFORTH, John (1931-) Amer; sclp
NOSANOW I 116 (statement)
SCULPTURE OUTSIDE (statement); 4 ill

SPOHN, Clay E. (1898-1977) Amer; ptr
ILLINOIS 1953 224-225 (statement); 1 ill

SPRUANCE, Benton (1904-1967) Amer; ptr, print
BETHERS II 130-131 (statement); 2 ill

SPRUCE, Everett (1907-) Amer; ptr
MILLER 1942 118-122 (statement); port; 4 ill

SPURIS, Egons (1931-) Latv; photo
WALSH 714-716 (statement); 1 ill

SQUIER, Jack (1927-) Amer; sclp
RISENHOOVER 163-170 (interview)

SQUIRES, Graham (1956-) Brit; arch
SPIRIT 94-96 (statement); 2 ill

SRAGOW, Ellen ( )
ART-RITE no.14 5, 13-14 (response)

STAAKMAN, Ray (1941-) Dutc; sclp, instal
NAYLOR 909-910 (statement); 1 ill

STACKHOUSE, Robert ( ) Amer; sclp, envir
ARTPARK 1977 77-79 (statement); port; 4 ill

STADLER, Albert (1923-) Amer; ptr
ART NOW v.3 no.2 (statement); 1 ill

STAECK, Klaus (1938-) Germ; print, coll
EMANUEL II 877-878 (statement); 1 ill
KUNST BLEIBT KUNST 324-327 (statement); 5 ill
KUNST UND POLITIK (statement); port; 6 ill
NAYLOR 910-911 (statement); 1 ill
SKIRA 1977 75 (statement); 1 ill

STAEL, Nicolas de (1914-1955) Russ/Fren; ptr
ART SINCE v.1 158 (statement, o.p. 1964)
TEMOIGNAGES I 264-269 (statement); port; 6 ill

STAHL, Ben (Albert) (1910-) Amer; ptr
GUITAR 206-215 (interview); port; 4 ill

STAHLY, Francois (1911-) Swis/Fren; sclp
PREMIER BILAN 321 (statement); port
RAGON 226-228 (statement)
YALE 22-23 (statement)

STAIGER, Paul (1941-) Amer; ptr, photo
VISUAL v.1 no.4 13-16 (interview); 2 ill

STALEY, Earl (1938-) Amer; ptr
MCCLINTIC 52-55 (statement); 4 ill

STAM, Mart ( ) arch
CONRADS 115-116 ("ABC Demands the Dictatorship of the Machine," o.p. 1928)

STAMATY, Stanley (1916-1979) Amer; cart
M.H. DE YOUNG 128 (response); self port

STAMERRA, Joanne ( ) Amer; photo
WOMANART v.1 no.1 12-13 (essay: "Erasing Sexism from MOMA")

STAMOS, Theodoros (1922-) Amer; sclp, ptr
ART NOW v.2 no.3 (statement); 1 ill
ILLINOIS 1950 208 (statement); 1 ill
ILLINOIS 1951 217 (statement)
ILLINOIS 1955 244 (statement); 1 ill
ILLINOIS 1961 88-89 (response); port; 1 ill
ILLINOIS 1965 172-173 (statement); 1 ill
IT IS no.3 27 (statement)
MOMA 1959 72-75 (statement); port; 3 ill
NEW DECADES 82-84 (statement); 3 ill
TIGER no.2 43, 68 (statement)
TUCKER I 8 (statement)
WHITNEY (statement); 1 ill

STAMPER, Wilson (1912-) Amer; ptr
HAAR I 120-127 (interview with Prithwish Neogy); ports; 3 ill

STAMPFLI, Peter (1937-) Swis; ptr
EMANUEL II 878-879 (statement); 1 ill
NAYLOR 912-913 (statement); 1 ill

STAMSTA, Jean (1936-) Amer; sclp, text
WISCONSIN I (statement); 1 ill

STANCZAK, Julian (1928-) Poli/Amer; ptr
ILLINOIS 1965 194 (statement); 1 ill
ILLINOIS 1969 185 (statement)
ILLINOIS 1974 114-115 (statement); 1 ill

STANGE, Richard ( )
SEE: ALLEY FRIENDS

STANISAVLJEVIC, Dragisa (1921-) Yugo; sclp
TOMASEVIC 341-344 (statement); port; 2 ill

STANISAVLJEVIC, Milan (1944-) Yugo; sclp
TOMASEVIC 345-349 (statement); port; 1 ill

STANKIEWICZ, Richard (1922-) Amer; sclp
ARTS YEARBOOK v.8 156-159 (essay: "An Open Situation"); 4 ill
CHIPP 576 (statement, o.p. 1959)
LETTERS 41 (letter); 1 ill
MILLER 1959 70-75 (statement); port; 7 ill
WHITNEY (statement); 1 ill
YOUNG 1957 (statement); 2 ill

STANLEY, Robert (1932-) Amer; ptr
NAYLOR 913-914 (statement); 1 ill

STANSBURY, Peter ( )
ART-RITE no.14 5, 14 (response)

STARK, Jack Gage (1882-1950) Amer; ptr
BRITANNICA 110 (statement); port; 1 ill

STARK, Robert (1939-) Amer; ptr
NOSANOW I 117-118 (statement); 2 ill

STARK, Ronald C. (1944-) Amer; photo,

ptr
PHOTOGRAPHY (statement); 1 ill

STARK, Shirley (1927-) Amer; sclp
FAX II 19-38 (statements); port; 1 ill

STARKEY, Peter (1945-) pott
CAMERON E 136-143 (response); 8 ill

STARR, Steve ( ) Amer; photo
LEEKLEY 72-73 (statement); 1 ill

STASACK, Edward A. (1929-) Amer;
ptr
HAAR I 128-135 (interview with
Prithwish Neogy); ports; 3 ill
ILLINOIS 1961 184 (response); port; 1 ill
ILLINOIS 1963 154 (statement); 1 ill

STAUFFACHER-SOLOMON, Barbara (
) Amer; arch
LA JOLLA 87-91 (statement); port; 6 ill

STAVENITZ, Alexander R. ( ) Amer; ptr
FIRST AMERICAN 80-83 (essay:
"Economic Status of the Artist
Today")

STAZEWSKI, Henryk (1894-) Poli; ptr
ABSTRACTION no.1 34 (statement); 2
ill
ABSTRACTION no.2 39, 42 (statement);
2 ill

STECHA, Pavel (1944-) Czec; photo
WALSH 716-717 (statement); 1 ill

STEELE, Chris (1948-) Amer; ptr
OUTSIDE II 34-35 (statement); port; 3
ill

STEELE, Jeffrey (1931-) Brit; ptr
EMANUEL II 882-884 (statement); 1 ill
NAYLOR 915-916 (statement); 1 ill

STEELE-PERKINS, Chris (1947-) Brit;
photo
VICTORIA 112-115 (statements)

STEEN, William (1949-) Amer; ptr
TEXAS 28-31 (statement); 6 ill

STEFANELLI, Joe (1921-) Amer; ptr
ILLINOIS 1961 177 (response); port; 1 ill

STEICHEN, Edward (1879-1973) Amer;
photo
KEPES IX 136-137 (essay: "On
Photography")
NELSON 35-43 (interview with Wayne
Miller)
ROSNER 311-317 (interview); port

STEIN, Joel (1926-) Fren; sclp
LUMIERE (statement); port; 1 ill

STEIN, Richard G. ( ) arch
ON SITE no.5/6 30 (essay:
"Architectural Prospects")

STEIN, Walter (1924-) Amer; ptr
ILLINOIS 1952 234 (statement); 1 ill

STEINBERG, Richard ( ) photo
TIME-LIFE IV 88-89 (statement); 1 ill

STEINBERG, Saul (1914-) Ruma/Amer;
illus, cart
KEPES IX 124-126 (statement); 3 ill
RODMAN I 181-185 (interview)
SCHNEIDER 81-98 (interview); 5 ill

STEINER, Ralph (1899-) Amer; photo
WALSH 721-722 (statement); 1 ill

STEINER, Sherry L. M. ( )
WOMANART v.2 no.1 4-5 (statements);
port; 1 ill

STEINHAUSER, Judith (1941-) Amer; photo
HAND COLORED 21 (statement); 1 ill

STEIR, Pat ( ) Amer; print, ptr
PAOLETTI 96-97 (statements, p.p.); 1 ill
PROFILE v.1 no.6 (interview); port
VIEW v.1 no.3 (interview); ports; 13 ill

STELLA, Frank (1936-) Amer; ptr, sclp
ART SINCE v.1 293 (statement, o.p. 1966/67)
ARTFORUM v.6 no.5 6 (letter)
ART-RITE no.1 4 ("Over the Edge"); 1 ill
BATTCOCK V 148-164 (interview with Bruce Glaser, o.p. 1966); 1 ill
COLLABORATION 104-107 (essay: "Tinted Shades"); 4 ill
CONCEPTUAL ART 51 (statement)
JOHNSON 113-120 (extract from interview with Bruce Glaser, o.p. 1966); 1 ill
ROSE II 176-180 (extract from interview with Bruce Glaser, o.p. 1966)
ROSE II REVISED 170-174 (extract from interview with Bruce Glaser, o.p. 1966)

STELLA, Joseph (1877-1946) Ital/Amer; ptr
ROSE II 60-62 (essay, o.p. 1921)
ROSE II REVISED 56-57 (essay, o.p. 1921)

STEMATSKY, Avigdor (1908-) Isra; ptr
SEITZ I (statement); 5 ill

STEMBERA, Petr (1945-) Czec; sclp, perf
GROH (statement); 4 ill
LIVE no.4 29 (letter); 2 ill
NAYLOR 919-920 (statement); 1 ill
VISION no.2 42-43 (essay, o.p. 1970); 2 ill

STENVERT, Curt (1920-) Aust; sclp
KUNST UND POLITIK (statement); port; 3 ill

STEPANOVA, Varvara (1894-1958) Russ; print
BOWLT 139 (essay: "Concerning My Graphics at the Exhibition," o.p. 1919)
BOWLT 140-142 (essay: "Nonobjective Creation," o.p. 1919); port

STEPHAN, John (1906-) Amer; ptr
IT IS no.3 34-35 (book review: *Wassily Kandinsky Life and Work* by Will Grohman)
IT IS no.4 49-50 (essay: "Concerning Social Realism, Revivals and Ghosts")
TIGER no.2 45-46 (statement)
TIGER no.6 56 (essay: "The Myth is Sublimity")
TIGER no.9 68 ("Night")

STEPHEN, Douglas Cruden (1923-) Brit; arch
EMANUEL I 771-773 (statement); 1 ill

STEPHENSON, Ian (1934-) Brit; ptr
BOWNESS 22, 134-135 (statement); 2 ill
CONTEMPORARY (statement); port; 2 ill
ENGLISH 188-193 (statement); port; 6 ill
NAYLOR 923-924 (statement); 1 ill

STEPHENSON, John (1929-) Amer; sclp, pott
VIEWPOINT 1981 (statement); 3 ill

STEPPAT, Leo (1910-1964) Amer; sclp
ILLINOIS 1955 244-245 (statement)

STERN, Irene ( ) Amer; photo
INTERVIEWS 30-33 (interview); port; 1 ill

STERN, Robert A. M. (1939-) Amer; arch, design
BUILDINGS 26-29 (statement); 3 ill
COLLABORATION 114-117 (essay: "Human Scale at the End of the Age of Modernism"); 4 ill
COOPER-HEWITT II 75-77 (essay: "Toward an Urban Suburbia, Once Again")
DIAMONSTEIN II 230-253 (interview); port; 4 ill
DIAMONSTEIN V 160-175 (interview); port; 13 ill
EMANUEL I 773-775 (statement); 1 ill
GA HOUSES no.1 36-77 (statement); port; 122 ill
GA HOUSES no.5 4-7 (essay: "Not Space but...Room"); 13 ill
GA HOUSES no.6 92-105 (statement); 40 ill
ROTH 648-666 (essay: "The Doubles of Post-Modernism," o.p. 1980)

STERN, Rudi (1936-) sclp
DIRECTIONS I 75 (response); 1 ill

STERNBERG, Harry (1904-) Amer; print, ptr
FIRST AMERICAN 54 (essay: "The Artist and his Audience, Graphic Art")
100 CONTEMPORARY 180-181 (statement); port; 1 ill

STERNE, Hedda (1916-) Russ/Amer; ptr
ILLINOIS 1950 208 (statement)
ILLINOIS 1961 191 (response); port; 1 ill
ILLINOIS 1965 188-189 (statement); 1 ill
MOTHERWELL 8-22 (three group discussions: "Artists' Sessions at Studio 35," New York, 1950)
MUNRO 95-97 (interview)
TIGER no.2 44-45 (statement)

STERNE, Maurice (1878-1957) Amer; ptr
BRITANNICA 111 (statement); port; 1 ill
100 CONTEMPORARY 178-179 (statement); port; 1 ill

STERRENBURG, Joan (1941-) Amer; text
FIBER 43, 45 (statement); 1 ill

STERRITT, Coleen ( ) Amer; sclp
DOWNTOWN (statement); 1 ill

STETTNER, Bill ( ) photo
LAPLANTE 100-108 (interview); port; 1 ill

STETTNER, Louis J. (1922-) Amer; photo
WALSH 725, 727 (statement); 1 ill

STEVENS, Edward John, Jr. (1923-) Amer; ptr
ILLINOIS 1952 234-235 (statement); 1 ill
ILLINOIS 1953 225-226 (statement); 1 ill
ILLINOIS 1959 271-272 (statement); 1 ill

STEVENS, May (1924-) Amer; ptr
ART-RITE no.6 24 (statement)
ART-RITE no.7 24 (letter)
INTERVIEWS 34-36 (interview); port; 1 ill
MILLER 213-227 (interview with Sally Swenson); port
NAYLOR 924-925 (statement); 1 ill
RUDDICK 103-116 (interview); port; 5 ill
TRACKS v.1 no.2 6 (poem: "Sitting Still")
TRACKS v.1 no.2 39-41 ("Two Prosepoems for Old Women")
WOMANART v.1 no.1 8-9 (essay: "Whitney Protests")

STEVENS, Michael K. (1945-) Amer;
wood
MEILACH 186 (statement); 3 ill

STEVENS, Nelson L. (1938-) Amer; ptr
LEWIS II 34 (statement); port; 2 ill

STEVENS, Walter H. (1927-) Amer; ptr
KNOXVILLE (statement); port; 7 ill

STEVENSON, A. Brockie (1919-) Amer;
ptr
IMAGES 66-73 (interview with Clair
List); port; 5 ill

STEVENSON, Harold (1929-) Amer; ptr
EMANUEL II 890-891 (statement); 1 ill

STEVENSON, Robert Bruce (1924-)
Amer; sclp
TUCHMAN 52 (extract from the artist's
dissertation, 6/65)

STEWART, F. Clark (1942-) Amer; ptr,
coll
NOSANOW I 119 (statement); 1 ill

STEWART, Leora Klaymer ( ) Amer;
text
FIBER 56-57 (statement); 1 ill

STEWART, William (1938-) Amer; ptr
NAYLOR 926-927 (statement); 1 ill

STEZAKER, John (1949-) Brit; photo
ART-RITE no.14 30 (statement)
ENGLISH 398-405 (statement); port; 5
ill
KUNST BLEIBT KUNST 328-331
(statement); 1 ill

STIEGLITZ, Alfred (1864-1946) Amer;
photo
FORUM 1916 35 (essay)

ROSE II 48-49 (extracts from "Writings
and Conversations of Alfred Stieglitz,"
by Dorothy Norman, o.p. 1947)
ROSE II REVISED 45-46 (extracts from
"Writings and Conversations with
Alfred Stieglitz," by Dorothy Norman,
o.p. 1947)

STILL, Clyfford (1904-1980) Amer; ptr
ART SINCE v.1 156 (statements, o.p.
1952, 1961)
ARTFORUM v.2 no.6 30-35 ("An Open
Letter to an Art Critic"); 7 ill
ARTFORUM v.2 no.8 4 (letter)
CHIPP 574-576 (statement, o.p. 1959)
MILLER 1952 21-23 (statement); 3 ill
ROSE II REVISED 139-142 (statement,
o.p. 1966)
SEUPHOR 268-269 (statement); 1 ill

STILLMAN AND EASTWICK-FIELD
(arch firm)
EMANUEL I 776-777 (statement); 1 ill

STILLMAN, Ary (1891-) Russ/Amer
100 CONTEMPORARY 182-183
(statement); port; 1 ill

STILLMAN, John (1920-) Brit; arch
SEE: STILLMAN AND EASTWICK-
FIELD

STIRLING, James (1926-) Brit; arch
EMANUEL I 777-779 (statement); 1 ill
RUSSELL F 62-63 (project proposal); 3
ill

STITT, Andre (1958-) Iris; perf
KNOWLES 213 ("Notes to Ye
Declaration of Rights"); 2 ill

STOCKHAUSEN, Karlheinz (1928-)
sound
ART AND TECHNOLOGY 322 (project
proposal)

STONE, Edward Durell (1902-1978)
Amer; arch
HEYER 172-183 (interview); 20 ill

STONE, Sylvia (1928-) Amer; sclp
ART-RITE no.5 7 (response)
HESS 90-92 (statement)
MUNRO 334-344 (interview); ports; 2 ill

STONIER, Ron ( ) Cana; ptr
POINT OF VIEW 34 (statement); 1 ill

STOUMEN, Lou ( ) AMer; photo
TIME-LIFE IV 104-105 (statement); 1 ill

STOWASSER, Friedrich
SEE: HUNDERTWASSER,
Friedensreich

STRAND, Paul (1890-1976) Amer; photo
HILL 1-8 (interview, 1974); port

STRATTON, Dorothy King ( ) Amer;
illus, ptr
CALIFORNIA--DRAWING (statement); 2
ill

STRAUTMANIS, Edvins (1933-)
Latv/Amer; sclp
ILLINOIS 1969 180 (statement); 1 ill

STRAYER, Donald (1934-) photo
LAPLANTE 109-116 (interview); port; 1
ill

STREBELLE, Olivier (1927-) Belg; sclp
SKIRA 1977 16 (statement); 1 ill

STRECKER, Bernhard (1940-) Germ;
sclp
HAUSSER 104-105 (statement); 5 ill

STREETER, Tal (1934-) Amer; sclp,
envir

ARTPARK 1978 56-59 (statement); 11
ill
NAYLOR 927-928 (statement)

STREICHMAN, Yeheskiel (1906-) Isra;
ptr
SEITZ I (statement); 3 ill

STRIDER, Majorie (1934-) Amer; sclp,
ptr
ARTPARK 1976 188-189 (statement);
port; 2 ill
BRENTANO 344-345 (statement); 1 ill
CELEBRATION (statement); 1 ill
HESS 93-95 (statement)
NAYLOR 928-929 (statement); 1 ill
SCHAPIRO 71 (statement); port; 1 ill

STRIEBEL, John H. (1892-) ptr
M.H. DE YOUNG 130-131 (response); self
port

STROBEL, Thomas C. (1931-) Amer;
ptr
ILLINOIS 1969 67 (statement); 1 ill

STROMBOTNE, James (1934-) Amer;
ptr
ILLINOIS 1961 181 (response); port; 1 ill
YOUNG 1960 (statement); 2 ill

STROMSTEN, Amy ( ) Amer; photo
MILLER 228-245 (interview with Sally
Swenson); port; 1 ill

STROSAHL, William (1910-) Amer; ptr
NORTH LIGHT 81 (statement); 1 ill

STROUD, Peter Anthony (1921-) Amer;
ptr
ARTFORUM v.4 no.7 20-23 (interview
with John Coplans); 5 ill

STRZEMINSKI, Vladislav (1893-1952)
Poli; ptr

ABSTRACTION no.1 35 (statement); 2 ill

ABSTRACTION no.2 40, 44 (statement); 2 ill

STUART, Michelle (1938-) Amer; envir, ptr, sclp
ARTPARK 1975 122-123 (statement); port; 3 ill
EMANUEL II 892-894 (statement); 1 ill
INTERVIEWS 37-39 (interview); port; 1 ill
MCCLINTIC 56-59 (statement); 4 ill
MUNRO 438-446 (interview); ports; 3 ill
NAYLOR 929-930 (statement); 1 ill
PHILLPOT (statement)
PROFILE v.3 no.3 (interview); port; 6 ill
SCHAPIRO 72 (statement); port; 1 ill
SKIRA 1978 35 (statement); 1 ill
SKIRA 1979 109 (statement); 1 ill
WHITE WALLS no.5 96-99 ("Correspondences")
WOMANART v.1 no.3 26, 29 (response); port

STUBBING, Tony (1921-) Brit; ptr
NAYLOR 930-931 (statement); 1 ill

STUBBINS, Hugh Asher, Jr. (1912-) Amer; arch
EMANUEL I 782-785 (statement); 1 ill
HEYER 216-223 (interview); 18 ill

STUDER, Harold (1942-) illus
KORNFIELD 48-49 (statement); port; 4 ill

STUDLEY, Dick (1950-) Amer; pott
HERMAN 120 (statement); port; 1 ill

STUHL, Michelle Hope (1957-) Amer; glass, sclp
WISCONSIN II (statement); 1 ill

STURGEON, John Floyd (1946-) Amer; video
ROSS 28-31 (statement); 8 ill

STURTEVANT, Elaine F. (1930-) Amer; ptr
NAYLOR 931-932 (statement); 1 ill

STUSSY, Jan (1921-) Amer; ptr
CALIFORNIA--PAINTING 50 (statement); 1 ill
ILLINOIS 1965 208 (statement); 1 ill

SUAREZ, Aurorina
SEE: AURORINA

SUBA, Miklos (1880-) Hung/Amer; ptr
MILLER 1943 56 (statement); 1 ill

SUBERO, Oswaldo (1934-) ptr, sclp
BIENNALE 206, 208 (statement); 1 ill

SUBIRACHS, Josep Maria (1927-) Span; sclp
PORCEL I 167-176 (interview); 2 ill

SUBLETT, Carl C. (1919-) Amer; ptr
KNOXVILLE (statement); port; 10 ill

SUBTERRANEAN VIDEO (group) video
BOSTON III (interview); 1 ill

SUDA, Issei (1940-) Japa; photo
WALSH 734-735 (statement); 1 ill

SUDA, Kunitaro (1891-1961) Japa; ptr
KUNG 112-115 (statement); port; 2 ill

SUDRE, Jean-Pierre (1921-) Fren; photo
WALSH 737-738 (statement); 1 ill

SUEYOSHI, Hiroshi (1946-) Amer; pott
HERMAN 121 (statement); port; 1 ill

SUGA, Kishio (1944-) Japa; sclp, instal
EMANUEL II 894-895 (statement); 1 ill
NAYLOR 932-933 (statement); 1 ill

SUGARMAN, George (1912-) Amer; sclp
ART NOW v.1 no.1 (statement); 1 ill
ARTS YEARBOOK v.8 150-155 (group discussion led by Bruce Glaser)
EMANUEL II 896-897 (statement); 1 ill
IT IS no.3 49 (statement)
IT IS no.6 77-80, 109-113 (group discussion)
NAYLOR 934-935 (statement); 1 ill

SUGARMAN, Judith W. ( ) Amer; paper
HAYSTACK 60 (statement); 1 ill

SUGASAWARA, George ( ) Amer; photo
CALIFORNIA--PHOTOGRAPHY (statement); port; 4 ill

SUGIMATA, Tadashi (1914-) Japa; ptr
KUNG 116-119 (statement); port; 2 ill

SUHR, William (1896-) Germ/Amer; ptr
M.H. DE YOUNG 132 (response); self port

SUICIDE, Alan ( )
ART-RITE no.1 3 ("Downhome Organic Technology"); port

SUKENICK, Ronald ( )
CRISS-CROSS no.6 36-41 ("Endless Short Story: Five and Ten")

SULLIVAN, Ann ( ) arch, design
LIFE 1-5 (statement); port

SULLIVAN, Francoise ( ) Cana; sclp
CANADA 86-87 (statement); port; 2 ill

SULLIVAN, Louis (1865-1924) Amer; arch

ROSE II 193-195 (extract from essay: "The Young Men in Architecture," o.p. 1939)
ROSE II 195-199 (extract from *Kindergarten Chats and Other Writings*, o.p. 1901)
ROTH 346-356 (extracts from *Kindergarten Chats* o.p. 1901)
ROTH 356-364 (extract from *The Autobiography of an Idea*, o.p. 1922); 1 ill
SPENCER 196-201 (extracts from *The Autobiography of an Idea*, o.p.1922)

SULLIVAN, Patrick J. (1894-1967) Amer; ptr
JANIS II 53-75 (statements, letters; "History: P. J. Sullivan,"); port; 4 ill
MILLER 1943 54-55 (statement); 2 ill

SULLIVAN, Terry (1946-) Amer; perf
TUCKER II 38 (statement); port

SUMMERFORD, Ben L. (1924-) Amer; ptr
FULBRIGHT 46 (statement)

SUMMERS, Elaine ( )
LIVE no.3 12-13 (statement); 1 ill

SUNG, Woo Chun (1935-) ptr
ILLINOIS 1967 67 (statement); 1 ill

SUREDA, Andre (1872-1930) Fren; ptr
ART D'AUJOURD'HUI v.4 5 (statement); 6 ill

SURLS, James (1943-) Amer; sclp
ARTPARK 1976 190-191 (statement); port; 3 ill
HOUSE 98-99 (statement); 1 ill
O'KANE (statement); 1 ill

SUSCHITZKY, Wolfgang (1912-) Brit;

photo
WALSH 739-740 (statement); 1 ill

SUTHERLAND, Graham (1903-1980) Brit; ptr
ALBRIGHT-KNOX 151, 153 (letter, 9/1968); 1 ill
ART SINCE v.2 148 (statement, o.p. 1953)
BARBER 37-53 (interview); port
BOWNESS 16, 34-35 (statement); 1 ill
CONTEMPORARY (extract from talk given in Hamburg, 1974); port; 3 ill
EIGHT (handwritten statement in English; statement in English, French and German); ports
EVANS 89-93 (essay: "An English Stone Landmark"); 4 ill
LETTERS 42 (letter); 1 ill
PREMIER BILAN 321 (statement); port
ROTHENSTEIN 56, 58, 61-62 (letters; transcript of talk)

SUTKUS, Antanas (1939-) Lith; photo
WALSH 740-741 (statement); 1 ill

SUTTON, Philip (1928-) Brit; ptr
BARBER 115-127 (interview); port

SUZAR, Jolynn ( )
ART-RITE no.19 17-20 (group discussion)

SVANBERG, Max Walter (1912-) Swed; ptr
ART SINCE v.2 153 (statement, o.p. 1959)

SVETINA, Joze (1934-) Yugo; ptr
TOMASEVIC 350-352 (statement); port; 1 ill

SWAIN, Robert (1940-) Amer; ptr
ART NOW v.1 no.9 (statement); 1 ill
TUCKER I 10 (statement)

SWALE, Suzan (1946-) Brit; ptr
SKIRA 1979 102 (statement); 1 ill

SWAN, Douglas (1935-) Amer/Germ; ptr
SKIRA 1979 97 (statement); 1 ill

SWANNELL, John ( ) Brit; photo
HOW FAMOUS 46-51 (statements); port; 11 ill

SWANSWIJK, L. G.
SEE: LUCEBERT

SWARTWOOD, Marilyn ( ) ptr
CRISS-CROSS no.7/8/9 90-91 (statement); 2 ill

SWARZ, Sahl (1912-) Amer; sclp
ILLINOIS 1961 167 (response); port; 1 ill
ILLINOIS 1963 182 (statement); 1 ill

SWEET, Roger ( ) Amer; sclp
IRVINE 59, 85 (statement); 1 ill

SWIDZINSKI, Jan ( )
PARACHUTE no.5 22-25 (essay: "Art as a Contextual Art," in English)

SWIFT, Dick (1918-) Amer; print, illus
CALIFORNIA--DRAWING (statement); 2 ill

SWINDELL, Geoffrey (1945-) Brit; pott
CAMERON E 144-155 (response); 13 ill

SWINDEN, Albert (1901-) AMer; ptr
ABSTRACT 12 70, 163 (essay: "On Simplification"); 1 ill

SWINTON, George (1917-) Aust/Cana; ptr
ART VOICES v.4 no.1 133-135 (statements); 3 ill

SYMONS, Patrick (1925-) Brit; ptr
CONTEMPORARY (statement); port; 1
ill
HAYWARD 1979 50-53 (statement); 8 ill

SYNDICATE OF TECHNICAL
WORKERS, PAINTERS, AND
SCULPTORS (group)
CHIPP 461-462 ("Manifesto," o.p. 1922)

SZABO, Steve (1940-) Amer; photo
PHOTOGRAPHY (statement); 1 ill

SZAFRAN, Gene ( ) Amer; sclp
ILLUSTRATION 101-103 (statement);
port; 3 ill

SZAFRAN, Sam (1934-) Fren; ptr
CLAIR 64-65 (statement, 1970); 1 ill
DOUZE ANS 337-339 (statement); 4 ill

SZCZUKA, Mieczyslaw (1898-) Poli;
photo
WALSH 743-744 (statement); 1 ill

SZE TO, Lap (1949-) Chin; ptr
IN SITU 133-143 (statement); 9 ill

SZEEMANN, Harold ( ) ptr
SKIRA 1975 53 (extract from interview
Otto Hahn o.p. 1974); 1 ill

SZENES, Arped (1897-) Hung; ptr
GRENIER 185-192 (interview)

SZILASI, Gabor (1928-) Cana; photo
WALSH 746-747 (statement); 1 ill

SZYMKOWICZ, Charles (1948-) Belg;
ptr
COLLARD 238-241 (interview, 1970);
port; 1 ill

TABACK, Simms (1932-) Amer; illus
ILLUSTRATION 83 (statement); port; 1
ill

TAC (arch firm)
EMANUEL I 807-810 (statement); 1 ill

TACHA, Athena (1936-) Gree/Amer;
sclp
JOHNSON 215-221 (extract from essay:
"Rhythm as Form," o.p. 1978); 1 ill

TADINI, Emilio (1927-) Ital; ptr
SKIRA 1976 67 (statement); 1 ill
SKIRA 1979 100 (statement); 1 ill

TADLOCK, Thomas (1941-) Amer; sclp,
light
YOUNG 1965 (statement); 1 ill

TAFURI, Manfredo ( ) arch
FRAMPTON 57-58 (essay:
"Architecture and Poverty")
PORPHYRIOS 6-17 (essay: "Classical
Melancholies," o.p. 1980)

TAHARA, Keiichi (1951-) Japa; photo
WALSH 749-750 (statement); 1 ill

TAILLIBERT, Roger (1926-) Fren; arch
EMANUEL I 791-793 (statement); 1 ill

TAKAEZU, Toshiko (1922-) Amer; pott
HAAR II 79-84 (interview); ports; 2 ill

TAKAL, Peter (1905-) Ruma/Amer;
illus, ptr
ART VOICES v.4 no.1 80 (statement); 1
ill

TAKEHARA, John (1929-) Amer; pott
HERMAN 123 (statement); port; 1 ill

TAKEYAMA, Minoru (1934-) Japa; arch
EMANUEL I 792-795 (statement); 1 ill

TAKIAS, George ( ) Amer; envir
ARTPARK 1976 192-195 (statement); 6
ill

TAKIS (Panoyotis Vassilakis) (1925-)
Gree/Fren; sclp
ART AND TECHNOLOGY 324-325
(project proposal); 1 ill
CHOIX 46 (statement, o.p. 1968); 1 ill
EMANUEL II 904-906 (statement); 1 ill
KINETIC 58-63 (extract from interview
with Guy Brett); port; 5 ill
LUMIERE (statement); port; 1 ill
NAYLOR 943-945 (statement); 1 ill
PRADEL 94 (extract from interview
with Alfred Pacquement, o.p. 1982); 2
ill

TAL COAT, Pierre (1905-) Fren; ptr
CHARBONNIER v.2 17-24 (interview)
EMANUEL II 906-907 (statement); 1 ill
GOLDAINE 112-115 (interview); port
SKIRA 1975 96 (statement:
"Dialogue"); 1 ill

TALKINGTON, Lester ( ) photo
TIME-LIFE II 106 (statement); 1 ill

THE TALLER (group)
SEE: TALLER DE MONTEVIDEO

TALLER DE MONTEVIDEO (Armando
Bergallo, Hector Vilche, Gorki Bollar,
Clara Scremini) (group)
NAYLOR 946-947 (statement); 1 ill

TALLEY, Dan R. (1951-) Amer; video
AVANT-GARDE 32-33 (text piece)

TALPIN, Robert ( ) Amer; sclp
ARTPARK 1981 (statement); port; 1 ill

TAM, Reuben (1916-) Amer; ptr
BETHERS II 132-133 (statement); 2 ill

GUSSOW 63-67 (letter, 1968 & poems); 2 ill
HAAR II 85-89 (interview); ports; 2 ill
ILLINOIS 1953 226-227 (statement); 1 ill
ILLINOIS 1955 245-246 (statement)
ILLINOIS 1959 272-273 (statement); 1 ill
ILLINOIS 1961 129 (response); port; 1 ill
ILLINOIS 1965 58 (statement); 1 ill

TAMAYO, Rufino (1899-) Mexi; ptr
PREMIER BILAN 322 (statement); port
RODMAN II 216-219, 220-225 (statements)
TIGER no.1 61-66 (statement); 6 ill

TAMBELLINI, Aldo (1930-) Amer; video
BOSTON III (interview); 1 ill

TAMBLYN, Christine ( ) Amer; perf
BRAKKE 252-270 (interview with Auste)

TAMBURI, Orfeo (1910-) Ital; ptr
VERZOCCHI 411-415 (statement); self port; 1 ill

TAMIR, Moshe (1924-) Isra; ptr
SEITZ I (statement); 3 ill

TANAKA, Kazumi (1948-) Cana; photo
POINT OF VIEW 65 (statement); 1 ill

TANGE, Kenzo (1913-) Japa; arch
NEWMAN 170-185 (essay); port; 18 ill
NEWMAN 218-221 (group discussion)
YAMADA 287-289 (interview, 1969)

TANGEN, Dieter ( )
GROH (statement); 3 ill

TANGUY, Yves (1900-1955) Fren/Amer; ptr
ILLINOIS 1953 227 (statement); 1 ill
JEAN 294-295 ("Weights and Colors," o.p. 1931)

JEAN 412 (extract from interview with James Johnson Sweeney, o.p. 1946)
LIPPARD 204-206 (essay: "Weights and Colors," o.p. 1931)
LONDON BULLETIN no.4/5 33-35 (text piece: "In the Margin of Cross Words")
REVOLUTION SURREALISTE no.11 32-40 (group discussion: "Recherches sur la Sexualite")
SURREALISME no.3 27 ("Poids et Couleurs"); 3 ill
SURREALISME no.6 10-23 ("Recherches Experimentales" (questions and responses))

TANIA (Schreiber-Milicevic) (1924-) Poli/Amer; ptr
ILLINOIS 1963 115 (statement); 1 ill

TANIGUCHI, Y. ( ) Japa; arch
GA HOUSES no.1 156-161 (statement); 12 ill

TANNER, James (1941-) Amer; sclp, pott
CONTEMPORARY AFRICAN (statement); port; 1 ill

TANNING, Dorothea (1910-) Amer; ptr
JANIS I 107 (statement); 1 ill
SKIRA 1975 64 (extract from interview with Alain Jourrfoy, 3/74); 1 ill

TAPIES, Antoni (1923-) Span; ptr
ART SINCE v.1 155 (statement, o.p. 1963)
CLAUS 136-141 (statement)
PORCEL I 177-188 (interview); 2 ill
SKIRA 1975 112-113 (extract from "La Vocation de la Forme," o.p. 1973); 1 ill
SKIRA 1976 85 (statement); 1 ill

TARDI, Carla (1948-) Amer; ptr
CAMERON D 59-60 (statement)

TARNAUD, Claude (1922-) ptr
EXPOSICION (statement); port; 1 ill

TARNOSKI, Virginia (1931-) Amer; ptr
SYMBOLS (statement); 1 ill

TAS, Filip Josef (1918-) Belg; photo
WALSH 750-751 (statement); 1 ill

TATLIN, Vladimir (1885-1953) Russ; sclp
BANN 11-14 ("The Work Ahead of Us," o.p. 1920); 1 ill
BANN 112-115 (essay: "On Zangezi," o.p. 1923)
BANN 170-174 (essay: "Art Out into Technology," o.p. 1933)
BOWLT 205-206 (essay: "The Work Ahead of Us," o.p. 1920)

TAUBES, Frederic (1900-) Poli/Amer; ptr
BRITANNICA 112 (statement); port; 1 ill
ILLINOIS 1957 249 (response); 1 ill
M.H. DE YOUNG 135 (response); self port

TAULE, Antoni (1945-) Span; ptr
SKIRA 1976 62-63 (statement); 1 ill

TAUSS, Herb ( ) Amer; sclp
ILLUSTRATION 104-105 (statement); port; 1 ill

TAUT, Bruno (1880-1938) Germ; arch
CONRADS 41-43 ("A Program for Architecture," o.p. 1918)
CONRADS 47 ("New Ideas on Architecture," o.p. 1919)
CONRADS 57-58 ("Down with Seriousism!," o.p. 1920)
CONRADS 63 ("Daybreak," o.p. 1921)

TAVENNER, Patricia (1941-) Amer; print, photo, coll

SCHAPIRO 73 (statement); 2 ill

TAWNEY, Lenore ( ) Amer; text
FIBER 50-51 (poem); 1 ill
MUNRO 325-333 (interview); ports; 3 ill

TAYLOR, Della Brown (1922-) Amer; text, pott
CONTEMPORARY AFRICAN (statement); port; 1 ill
LEWIS I REVISED 103 (statement); port; 1 ill

TAYLOR, John Williams (1897-) Amer; ptr
BETHERS II 134-135 (statement); 2 ill
ZAIDENBERG 109-110 (essay: "A Well-Made Picture"); 4 ill

TAYLOR, Richard (1902-) Amer; ptr
M.H. DE YOUNG 137 (response); self port

TAYLOR, Rod (1932-) Amer; sclp
LEWIS II 94 (statement); port; 2 ill

TAYLOR, Wendy (1945-) Brit; sclp
BRITISH (statement); 1 ill
CONTEMPORARY (statement); port; 2 ill
NAYLOR 951-952 (statement); 1 ill

TCHAKALIAN, Sam (1929-) Brit; ptr
TUCKER I 14 (statement)

TCHELITCHEW, Pavel (1898-1957) Russ/Amer; ptr
RAYNAL 291-294 (statement); 2 ill
RODITI 103-129 (interview); port; 1 ill

TEAKEL, Wendy ( ) perf
ART NETWORK no.2 47 (statement)

TEALEAF, Glenson
SEE: DOUGLAS, Edward

TEASON, William ( ) Amer; ptr, illus
MAGIC 104-107 (statement); port; 5 ill

TEGARDEN, Terry ( ) ptr
CRISS-CROSS no.6 24-27 (statement); 3 ill

TEIXIDOR, Jorge (1941-) Span; ptr
SKIRA 1977 30 (statement); 1 ill

TEJADO DE ANGLES, Fela
SEE: ANGLES

TELEMAQUE, Herve (1937-) Fren; ptr
EMANUEL II 913-914 (statement); 1 ill
KUNST UND POLITIK (statement); port; 2 ill
NAYLOR 953-954 (statement); 1 ill
SKIRA 1977 16 (statement); 1 ill

TELEWISSEN (group) film
KUNST BLEIBT KUNST 423 (statement); 1 ill

TELSON, Bob ( ) perf, sound
AVALANCHE no.10 40-41 (interview); ports

TEMKIN, Merle ( ) Amer; sclp, envir
ARTPARK 1981 (statement); port; 1 ill

TENEAU, Peter ( ) Amer; sclp, instal
GUENTHER 108-109 (statement); port; 1 ill

TEN HOLT, Friso (1921-) Dutc; ptr, illus
WHELDON 150-159 (interview with John Berger); port

TENNENT, Madge (1889-1972) Amer; ptr
HAAR I 9-13 (interview with Prithwish Neogy); port; 4 ill

TERAOKA, Masami (1936-) Japa; ptr
VISUAL v.4 no.3 8-11 (interview); 4 ill

TERRAZAS, Eduardo (1936-) Mexi; arch
KEPES II 198-207 (essay: "Creation of Environment: Mexico 68")

TERRY, Evelyn (1946-) Amer; print
LEWIS I REVISED 105-106 (statement); port; 2 ill

TERRY, Quinlan (1937-) Brit; arch
ARCHER 28-33, 99 (statement); port; 10 ill

TESKE, Edmund (1911-) Amer; photo
WALSH 751-753 (statement); 1 ill

TESTA, Clorindo (1923-) Arge; arch
BAYON 10-37 (interview); port; 28 ill

TEYRAL, Hazel J. (1918-) Brit/Amer; ptr
ILLINOIS 1949 (unpaginated) (statement); 1 ill

THENOT, Jean-Paul (1943-) Fren; video, photo
NAYLOR 955-956 (statement); 1 ill
SKIRA 1976 21 (statement); 3 ill

THEODOROS (1931-) Gree; sclp
NAYLOR 956 (statement); 1 ill

THERIAULT, Normand ( )
PARACHUTE no.1 4-7 (interview); port

THIBEAU ( ) photo
IDENTITE 91-94 (interview with Jacques Clayssen); port

THIEBAUD, Wayne (1920-) Amer; ptr
ARTHUR 114-129 (interview); port; 21 ill

HOPKINS 68-69 (statement); port; 1 ill
ILLINOIS 1965 168-169 (statement); 1 ill
SAO PAULO 104-105 (extract from "A Painter's Personal View of Eroticism," o.p. 1966); port; 1 ill
STRAND 180-199 (interview); port; 18 ill
VISUAL v.3 no.2 12-15 (interview); port; 4 ill

THIELER, Fred (1916-) Germ; ptr
HAUSSER 170-173 (statement, 1962, o.p. 1976); 5 ill

THIOLAT, Dominique (1946-) Fren; ptr
SKIRA 1976 72 (statement); 1 ill

THIRY, Paul (1904-) Amer; arch
EMANUEL I 810-812 (statement); 1 ill

THOA, Choua (1943-) text
KATZ 137-148 (interview); port

THODE, Joachim (1942-) Germ; photo
SKIRA 1979 16 (statement); 2 ill

THOGMARTIN, Jon ( )
CRISS-CROSS no.10 26-29 (statement); port; 11 ill

THOM, Ronald James (1923-) Cana; arch
EMANUEL I 812-814 (statement); 1 ill

THOMAN, Marta ( ) print
VISUAL v.1 no.3 17-19 (essay: "Etching"); port; 2 ill

THOMAS, Alma Woodsey (1891-) Amer; ptr
CELEBRATION (statement); 1 ill
FINE 151-153 (statements, o.p. 1970); 1 ill
MUNRO 189-197 (interview); port; 2 ill

THOMAS, Gloria (1945-) Amer
WINSTON-SALEM 70-75 (statement); 6 ill

THOMAS, James ("Son Ford") (1926-) Amer; sclp
FERRIS 133-156 (statements); ports; 11 ill

THOMAS, John (1927-) Amer; ptr
ILLINOIS 1961 164 (response); port; 1 ill
ILLINOIS 1963 58 (statement); 1 ill
ILLINOIS 1965 203 (statement); 1 ill

THOMAS, Lew (1932-) Amer; photo, sclp, instal
VISUAL v.1 no.4 6-9 (interview); 3 ill

THOMAS, Ron ( ) Amer; arch, design
LIFE 147-168 (interview); port

THOMKINS, Andre (1930-) Swis; ptr
ADLERS 36-38 (interview); port; 3 ill

THOMPSON, Benjamin (1918-) Amer; arch
EMANUEL I 814-816 (statement); 1 ill
HEYER 210-215 (interview); 14 ill

THOMPSON, Brian (1950-) Brit; sclp
BRITISH (statement); 1 ill

THOMPSON, Cindy ( ) Amer; arch, design
LIFE 28-49 (interview); port

THOMPSON, David E.
SEE: HOMPSON, Davi Det

THOMPSON, Michael ( ) Cana; ptr
ART-LANGUAGE v.1 no.2 77-83 ("Conceptual Art: Category and Action")

THOMPSON, Phyllis (1946-) Amer; print
ARTPARK 1975 124-125 (statement); port; 1 ill

THOMPSON, Robert (1936-1966) Amer; ptr
FINE 243-244 (statements, o.p. 1967, 1969); 1 ill

THOMSON, Chris ( ) Brit; photo
HOW FAMOUS 154-159 (statements); port; 7 ill

THON, William (1906-) Amer; ptr
ILLINOIS 1952 235-236 (statement); 1 ill

THORNE, Joan (1943-) Amer; ptr, illus
RE-VIEW v.1 5-8 (statement); 3 ill
RE-VIEW v.2/3 124-129 (poem: "Traveler"); 5 ill

THORNTON, John ( ) Brit; photo
HOW FAMOUS 206-211 (statements); port; 8 ill

THRALL, Arthur (1926-) Amer; print, ptr
WISCONSIN II (statement); 1 ill

THRASHER, Joe W. (1934-) Amer; sclp
NOSANOW I 120 (statement); 1 ill

THUBRON, Harry (1915-) Brit; ptr
CONTEMPORARY (statement); port; 2 ill

TICE, George Andrew (1938-) Amer; photo
DUGAN 149-167 (interview, 1975); port

TICKEL, William (1953-) Amer; wood
WOODWORKING 44-45 (statement); port; 2 ill

TIFFANY, Jackson (1925-) Amer; photo, print
WISCONSIN II (statement); 1 ill

TIGERMAN, Stanley (1930-) Amer; arch
BUILDINGS 22-25 (statement); 6 ill
COLLABORATION 136-143 (essay: "The Great American Cemetery"); 6 ill
EMANUEL I 816-817 (statement); 1 ill
GA HOUSES no.6 18, 20-56 (statement; and essay: "Stanley Tigerman on Frank O. Gehry" p.56); 98 ill
GA HOUSES no.12 160-165 (statement); 12 ill

TIHANYI, Ludwig (Lajos) (1885-1938) Hung/Fren; ptr
ABSTRACTION no.3 43 (statement); 1 ill

TILBURY, John ( ) perf, sound
PARACHUTE no.9 37-38 (interview, in English)

TILLIM, Sidney (1925-) Amer; ptr
ART NOW v.2 no.7 (statement); 1 ill
ARTS YEARBOOK v.3 148-151 (essay: "Ellsworth Kelley")
ARTS YEARBOOK v.6 74-75 (essay: "The Nude in American Art," o.p. 1961)
ARTS YEARBOOK v.6 106-111 (essay: "What Happened to Geometry?" o.p. 1959)
ARTS YEARBOOK v.6 118-120 (essay: "The Paintings of Edwin Dickinson," o.p. 1961)
ARTS YEARBOOK v.7 56-59 (essay: "Notes of a New York Critic")
EMANUEL II 916-917 (statement); 1 ill
NAYLOR 957-958 (statement); 1 ill
ROSE II 175-176 (extract from essay: "Optical Art: Pending or Ending?" o.p. 1965)

ROSE II REVISED 265-267 (extract from essay: "Earthworks and the New Picturesque," o.p. 1968)

TILLOTSON, Edmund (1941-) Brit; sclp
BRITISH (statement); 1 ill

TILSON, Joe (1928-) Brit; sclp, print, coll
ART SINCE v.2 324 (statement, o.p. 1970)
ENGLISH 194-199 (statement); port; 6 ill
KUNST UND POLITIK (statement); port; 4 ill

TIMM, Wayne (1936-) Amer; ptr
SOUTHEAST (statement); port; 6 ill

TIMOCK, George (1945-) Amer; pott
WECHSLER 118-123 (statement); port; 5 ill

TINDLE, David (1932-) Brit; ptr
CONTEMPORARY (statement); port; 2 ill
EMANUEL II 919-920 (statement); 1 ill

TING, Walasse (1929-) Chin/Amer; ptr
ART NOW v.1 no.10 (poem); 1 ill
NAYLOR 959-960 (statement)

TINGUELY, Jean (1925-) Swis; sclp
ART SINCE v.1 194-295 (statement, o.p. 1967)
LUMIERE (statement); port; 1 ill
SKIRA 1975 14 (statement: extract from "L'Art est revolte," o.p. 1967); 1 ill
TOMKINS 145-187 (statements); port; 3 ill

TIPS, Jan (1942-) Amer; paper, ptr
PAPERWORKS 36-37 (statement); 5 ill

TISCHLER, Victor (1891-) Aust/Amer; ptr
100 CONTEMPORARY 184-185 (statement); port; 1 ill

TISDALL, Caroline ( ) photo
VICTORIA 116-119 (statements)

TISNIKAR, Joze (1928-) Yugo; ptr
TOMASEVIC 357-360 (statement); port; self port

TITUS-CARMEL, Gerard (1941-) Fren; ptr, illus, print
CHOIX 47 (statement, o.p. 1980/81); 1 ill
EMANUEL II 920-922 (statement); 1 ill
NAYLOR 961-962 (statement); 1 ill
SKIRA 1975 29 (extract from "La strategie du dessin," 1973); 1 ill
SKIRA 1980 79 (statement); 3 ill

TOBAS, Christian (1944-) Fren; coll
NAYLOR 962-963 (statement); 1 ill

TOBEY, Alton (1914-) Amer; ptr, illus
GOODMAN 60-63 (interview)

TOBEY, Mark (1890-1976) Amer; ptr
ART SINCE v.1 153 (statement, o.p. 1960)
CLAUS 87-91 (statement)
FORD/VIEW v.3 no.4 125 (story: "Cymbals")
FRASNAY 141-149 (statement); ports; 2 ill
ILLINOIS 1951 218-219 (statement); 1 ill
JANIS I 98-99 (statement); 1 ill
KUH 235-248 (interview); 7 ill
MILLER 1946 70-75 (statement); 6 ill
MOTHERWELL 24-37 (group discussion: "The Western Round Table on Modern Art," San Francisco, 1949)
MOTHERWELL 145 (statement)

TONELLO, Fernando (1943-1975) Ital; illus
SKIRA 1976 40 (statement); 1 ill

TONEY, Anthony (1913-) Amer; ptr
ILLINOIS 1950 211-212 (statement)
ILLINOIS 1951 219-220 (statement); 1 ill
ILLINOIS 1952 236 (statement)
ILLINOIS 1955 248-249 (statement)

TONGIANI, Vito (1940-) Ital; ptr
CLAIR 66-67 (extract from interview, 1978); 1 ill
SKIRA 1980 67 (extract from interview with Michel Suret-Canale); 2 ill

TOOKER, George (1920-) Amer; ptr
NEW DECADE 87-89 (statement); 3 ill
RODMAN I 207-211 (interview)

TOOMING, Peeter (1939-) Esto; photo
WALSH 755-756 (statement); 1 ill

TOPLJAK, Petar (1948-) Yugo; ptr
TOMASEVIC 361-364 (statement); port; 1 ill

TORAL, Mario (1945-) Chil/Amer; ptr, print
KATZ 163-173 (interview); port; 1 ill
RAICES 59 (statement); 1 ill

TORFFIELD, Marvin (1943-) Amer; envir
PROJECTS (statement); 1 ill

TORM, Fernando (1944-) Span/Amer; photo
BRENTANO 348-349 (poem, in Spanish); 1 ill

TORONI, Niele (1937-) Swis; ptr
EUROPE 74-75 (statement); 1 ill
MURS 15 (statement); 1 ill

TORRE, Susana (1944-) Amer; arch
COLLABORATION 144-151 (essay: "Ellis Island: Gateway to America"); 6 ill

TORREANO, John Francis (1941-) Amer; ptr
ART-RITE no.9 29-34 (group discussion)

TORRENCE, Vivian (1945-) Amer; ptr, coll
REGIONALISM 20-21 (statement); port; 1 ill

TORRES, Francesco ( ) perf, instal
ON SITE no.5/6 96 (statement); 4 ill

TORRES, John, Jr. (1939-) Amer; sclp
FAX I 283-299 (statements); port; 1 ill

TORRES-GARCIA, Joaquin (1874-1949) Urug/Span; ptr
BANN 194-199 ("The Constructive Art Group—Joint Collaborative Work," o.p. 1933)

TORROJA, Eduardo ( ) Span; arch
ART AND ARTIST 219-228 (essay: "Notes on Structural Expression,"); 2 ill

TOSI, Arturo (1871-) Ital; ptr
VERZOCCHI 423-427 (statement); self port; 1 ill

TOTH, Carl (1947-) Amer; photo
HAND COLORED 17 (statement); 1 ill

TOTTEN, Doris ( ) sclp
ART VOICES v.4 no.1 78 (statement); 1 ill

TOUBES, Xavier ( ) Amer; pott
HAYSTACK 61 (statement); 1 ill

TOUCHAGUES, Louis (1893-) Fren; ptr
GOLDAINE 89-91 (interview); port

TOULMIN-ROTHE, Ann ( ) Amer; ptr
DAUGHERTY 106-127 (statements); ports; 2 ill

TOURNEUR, Renault ( ) Amer; ptr
JANIS II 182-185 (statements); 1 ill

TOUSIGNANT, Claude (1932-) Cana; ptr
EMANUEL II 929-930 (statement); 1 ill
NAYLOR 971-972 (statement); 1 ill

TOUZENIS, Georges (1947-) Gree/Fren; illus
SKIRA 1976 54 (statement); 1 ill

TOVISH, Harold (1921-) Amer; sclp
ILLINOIS 1961 147 (response); port; 1 ill
ILLINOIS 1969 75 (statement); 1 ill
NAYLOR 972 (statement)

TOWN, Harold (1924-) Amer; ptr
ILLINOIS 1965 84-85 (statement); 1 ill

TOWNLEY, Hugh (1923-) Amer; sclp
ILLINOIS 1961 156 (response); port; 1 ill

TOWNS, Elaine (1937-) Amer; ptr
LEWIS I REVISED 31 (statement); port; 1 ill

TOY, Richard Horton Beauclerc (1911-) NewZ; arch
EMANUEL I 820-821 (statement); 1 ill

TOZZI, Claudio (1944-) Braz; ptr
SKIRA 1977 15 (statement); 1 ill

TRACY, Michael (1943-) Amer; instal
PAPERWORKS 38-39 (statement); 3 ill
WHITE WALLS no.4 24-36 (statement); 8 ill

TRAEGER, Tessa ( ) Brit; photo
HOW FAMOUS 172-175 (statements); port; 5 ill

TRAKAS, George (1944-) Cana/Amer; envir, sclp
AVALANCHE no.3 54-61 (extracts from notebooks, 1964-1971); 9 ill
PROJECTS (statements); 9 ill

TRAPP, David L. (1949-) Amer; wood
WOODWORKING 46-47 (statement); port; 2 ill

TRAUB, Charles Henry (1945-) Amer; photo
WALSH 759, 761-762 (statement); 1 ill

TRBULJAK, Goran (1948-) Yugo; ptr
NAYLOR 974 (statement)

TREIBER, Richard (1940-) Amer; sclp
ILLINOIS 1969 134 (statement); 1 ill

TREIMAN, Joyce Wahl (1922-) Amer; ptr
ILLINOIS 1951 220-221 (statement); 1 ill
ILLINOIS 1952 237 (statement); 1 ill
ILLINOIS 1957 250 (response); 1 ill
ILLINOIS 1961 163 (response); port; 1 ill
ILLINOIS 1963 196-197 (statement); 1 ill
ILLINOIS 1974 120-121 (statement); 1 ill
VISUAL v.3 no.2 4-7 (interview); self port; 4 ill
YOUNG 1957 (statement); 1 ill

TREMAGLIO, Richard C. ( ) arch
PROCESSES 115-140 (interview with Lance Laver); 19 ill

TREMLETT, David (1945-) Brit; ptr
AVALANCHE no.3 10-17 (interview); port; 20 ill

TREMONTO, Roxie ( ) Amer
SULTAN 27-30 ("Prelude/Theme" and "The Mind Seducing Pettiness")

TRESS, Arthur (1940-) Amer; photo
WALSH 762-763 (statement); 1 ill

TREVELYAN, Julian ( ) ptr
EVANS 58-61 (essay: "Mythos"); 2 ill
LONDON BULLETIN no.10 24 (letter)
LONDON BULLETIN no.12 9-10 (essay: "John Tunnard")

TREVINO, Jesse C. (1946-) Amer; ptr
SUPERREAL 146-147 (statement); 1 ill

TREVINO, Rudy R. (1945-) Amer; ptr
RAICES 40 (statement); 1 ill

TRIER, Hann (1915-) Germ; ptr
HAUSSER 174-175 (statement, o.p. 1981); 3 ill

TRIVIGNO, Pat (1922-) Amer; ptr
ILLINOIS 1950 212-213 (statement); 1 ill
ILLINOIS 1961 159 (response); port; 1 ill

TROKES, Heinz (1913-) Germ; ptr
GROHMANN 441-443 ("Der Surrealismus," p.p. 1946/47)
WINGLER 112-114 (essay: "Flecken, Flecken, Hommage a Wols," p.p.)

TROLLER, Fred (1930-) Amer; sclp
YOUNG 1965 (statement); 1 ill

TROMKA, Abram ( ) Amer; ptr
100 CONTEMPORARY 188-189 (statement); port; 1 ill

TROOSTWYK, David (1929-) Brit; sclp
BRITISH (statement); 1 ill

TROTMAN, Bob ( ) Amer; wood
MEILACH 95 (statement); 3 ill

TROTTA, Antonio (1937-) Arge; ptr, sclp
SKIRA 1977 20 (statement); 1 ill
SKIRA 1979 43 (statement); 1 ill

TROUILLE, Clovis (1889-) Fren; ptr, sclp, envir
EMANUEL II 935 (statement)
NAYLOR 976-978 (statement); 1 ill

TROWBRIDGE, David ( )
ART-RITE no.19 17-20 (group discussion)

TROWBRIDGE, Gail (1900-) Amer; print, ptr
CALIFORNIA--PRINTS (statement); 1 ill

TROY, David C. (1936-) Amer
TUCKER II 39 (statement); port

TRUAX, Karen (1946-) Amer; photo
HAND COLORED 18-19 (statement); 1 ill

TRUCK, Fred ( )
ART-RITE no.14 5, 14 (response)

TRUCKERBROD, Joan ( ) Amer; print
COMPUTER (statement); 1 ill

TRUE, David (1942-) Amer; ptr
MARSHALL 62 (statement); port; 5 ill

TRUE, Shirley (1940-) Amer; photo
FRALIN 20-21, 38-39 (statement); 3 ill

TRUITT, Anne Dean (1921-) Amer; sclp
MUNRO 314-324 (interview); port; 2 ill

TSCHACBASOV, Nahum (1899-) Russ/Amer; ptr, print
ILLINOIS 1955 249-250 (statement); 1 ill
ILLINOIS 1957 251 (response); 1 ill
100 CONTEMPORARY 186-187 (statement); port; 1 ill

ZAIDENBERG 101-105 (essay: "Fear of Influences"); 5 ill

TSCHICHOLD, Jan (1902-) Swis; print
AXIS no.2 16-18 (essay: "On Ben Nicholson's Reliefs")
CIRCLE 249-255 (essay: "New Typography"); 5 ill

TSCHINKEL, Paul ( ) video
ART-RITE no.7 11, 13 (response)

TSCHUMI, Bernard (1944-) Swis; arch
ARCHER 42-45, 100 (statement); port; 7 ill

TSENG YU-HO (Betty Tseng Yu-Ho Ecke) (1923-)Chin/Amer; ptr
ILLINOIS 1959 273-274 (statement); 1 ill
ILLINOIS 1961 176 (statement); port; 1 ill

TSOCLIS, Costa (1930-) Gree; print
EMANUEL II 936-937 (statement); 1 ill

TSUCHIDA, Hiromi (1939-) Japa; photo
WALSH 763-764 (statement); 1 ill

TSUJI, Shindo (1910-) Japa; sclp
KUNG 184-187 (statement); port; 2 ill

TSURU KAYABA, Ayako
SEE: AYAKO

TSURUOKA, Masao (1907-) Japa; ptr
KUNG 124-127 (statement); port; 2 ill

TSUTAKAWA, George (1910-) Amer; sclp
GUENTHER 112-113 (statement); port; 1 ill

TUCHOLKE, Christel-Anthony (1941-) Amer; ptr
WISCONSIN I (statement); 1 ill

TUCKER, Curtis (1939-) Amer; pott
CONTEMPORARY AFRICAN (statement); port; 1 ill

TUCKER, Nicolas (1948-) Brit; photo
WALSH 764-765 (statement); 1 ill

TUCKER, William (1935-) Brit; sclp, illus
TRACKS v.1 no.3 5-27 (essay: "Space Illusion Sculpture," originally given as three talks at St. Martin's School of Art, London); 1 ill

TUCKER, Yvonne (1941-) Amer; pott
CONTEMPORARU AFRICAN (statement); port; 1 ill

TUDOR, David (1926-) Amer; perf, sound, instal
STEDELIJK 217 (statement); 1 ill

TULL, Charlene (1945-) Amer; ptr
LEWIS II 24 (statement); port; 1 ill

TULLIS, Garner ( ) Amer; print, ptr
VISUAL v.3 no.4 13-16 (group discussion)

TUMARKIN, Yigael (1933-) Isra; ptr, sclp
SEITZ I (statement); 4 ill

TURBEVILLE, Deborah (1937-) Amer; photo
WALSH 766-768 (statement); 1 ill

TURCATO, Giulio (1912-) Ital; ptr
EMANUEL II 940-942 (statement); 1 ill
NAYLOR 981-983 (statement); 1 ill
PAINTING 1 (statement); port; 1 ill
VERZOCCHI 429-433 (statement); self port; 1 ill

TURNBULL, William (1922-) Scot; sclp, ptr
ALLEY (statement); 1 ill
GUGGENHEIM I 96 ("Head Semantic," o.p. 1960)
GUGGENHEIM I 96 (statement, o.p. 1963)

TURNBULL, William, Jr. (1935-) Amer; arch
EMANUEL I 822-825 (statement); 1 ill
GA HOUSES no.1 98-103 (statement); 13 ill
LA JOLLA 92-95 (statement); port; 10 ill

TURNER, Lynn (1943-) Amer; pott
HERMAN 125 (statement); port; 1 ill

TURNER, Maggie ( ) Amer; sclp, pott
ART NETWORK no.3/4 29 (essay)

TURNER, Othar (1908-) Amer; wood
FERRIS 157-174 (statements); ports

TURNER, Peter ( ) photo
VICTORIA 120-123 (statements)

TURNER, Rene ( )
ARTISTS no.3 9-10 ("Erotic Art")

TURNER, Richard (1936-) Cana; sclp, print
CANADA 46-47 (statement); port; 2 ill

TURNER, Richard (1943-) Amer; sclp, envir
HOUSE 100-101 (statement); 1 ill

TURNER, Robert ( ) Amer; pott
HAYSTACK 63 (statement); 1 ill

TURNER, Tom (1945-) Amer; pott
HERMAN 127 (statement); port; 1 ill

TURRELL, James Archie (1943-) Amer; sclp
ART AND TECHNOLOGY 127-143 (project proposal)

TUSQUETS, Guillen Oscar (1941-) Span; arch
EMANUEL I 825 (statement)

TUTTLE, Richard (1941-) Amer; sclp, ptr
CINCINNATI 38-49 ("Conversations with the Work and the Artist," by Dorothy Alexander); 15 ill
MURS 16 (statement, in French and English); 1 ill

TWIGGS, Leo F. (1934-) Amer; text
FAX II 325-344 (statements); port; 1 ill
LEWIS II 88 (statement); port; 2 ill

TWORKOV, Jack (1900-1977) Poli/Amer; ptr, illus
ALBRIGHT-KNOX 52-53 (letter, 7/1968); 1 ill
ART NOW v.2 no.4 (statement); 1 ill
ILLINOIS 1961 216 (response); port; 1 ill
ILLINOIS 1974 122-123 (statement); 1 ill
IT IS no.1 25 (essay: "Journal")
IT IS no.2 15 (statement)
IT IS no.4 12-13 ("Four Excerpts from a Journal")
IT IS no.5 4-6 (essay: "Color")
IT IS no.5 34-38 (group discussion)
LETTERS 43 (letter); 1 ill
NAYLOR 985-986 (statement); 1 ill
SULTAN 83-84 ("Provincetown," 7/15/75)

TYLER, Alfred (1933-) Amer; illus
LEWIS II 79 (statement); port; 1 ill

TYLER, Anna (1933-) Amer; print
LEWIS II 32 (statement); port; 2 ill

TYRRELL, Brinsley (1941-) Amer; sclp
SCULPTURE OUTSIDE (statement); 4 ill

TYSHLER, Alexander Grigorievich
(1898-) Russ; ptr
NAYLOR 986 (statement); 1 ill

UBAC, Rodolphe Raoul (1910-)
Belg/Fren; ptr
CHARBONNIER v.2 159-169 (interview)
DADA 81 (statement, on Francis
Picabia)
GOLDAINE 153-156 (interview); port
GRENIER 195-200 (interview)
VINGTIEME N.S. no.9 29 (statement); 1
ill
VINGTIEME N.S. no.10 51-52 (essay:
"Mes Gravures")

UECKER, Gunther (1930-) Germ; sclp
ART SINCE v.1 160 (statement, o.p.
1965)
EMANUEL II 948-949 (statement); 1 ill
HAUSSER 178-181 (statement, 1973,
o.p. 1981); 8 ill
NAYLOR 987-988 (statement); 1 ill
SKIRA 1979 82 (statement); 1 ill
STEDELIJK 220 (statement, in
German); 2 ill

UEDA, Shoji (1913-) Japa; photo
WALSH 769-770 (statement); 1 ill

UELSMANN, Jerry Norman (1934-)
Amer; photo
HOWARD (interview)

UHLMANN, Hans (1900-1975) Germ;
illus, sclp
CHIPP 606 (statement, o.p. 1955)
HAUSSER 182-183 (statement, o.p.
1974); 2 ill
RITCHIE 44-47 (statement); port; 4 ill
SKIRA 1976 48 (statement); 1 ill

UITTI, Frances-Marie ( ) perf, sound
STEDELIJK 221 (statement); port

UKELES, Mierle Laderman (1939-)
Amer
ISSUE ("Touch Sanitation"); 1 ill

ULOVEC, Vladimir (1945-) Cana; photo
POINT OF VIEW 66 (statement); 1 ill

ULRICHS, Timm (1940-) Germ; ptr,
perf
KUNST BLEIBT KUNST 332-335
(statement); 2 ill
SKIRA 1980 113 (statement); 7 ill

UMLAUF, Charles (1911-) Amer; sclp
ILLINOIS 1963 218 (statement); 1 ill

UNCINI, Giuseppe (1929-) Ital; sclp
SKIRA 1979 26 (statement); 1 ill

UNGAR, Nancy ( )
WOMANART v.2 no.3 15-18, 27-30
(essay: "Tenth Street Revisited")

UNGER, Mary Ann (1945-) Amer; sclp
CRISS-CROSS no.7/8/9 16-19
("Hexagonal Quintet"); 4 ill
CRISS-CROSS no.10 20-23 (essay: "I am
Interested in Structure"); port; 3 ill

UNGERS, Oswald Mathias ( ) arch
CONRADS 165-166 ("Towards a New
Architecture," o.p. 1960)
ON SITE no.5/6 52-55 (essay: "A
Subjective Study of the L.A. Freeway
Grid")
RUSSELL F 80-81 (project proposal); 6
ill
RUSSELL F 114 (project proposal); 6 ill

UNSWORTH, Ken (1931-) Atrl; sclp,
instal
EMANUEL II 952-954 (extract from
interview); 1 ill

UNTERSEHER, Chris (1943-) Amer;
pott
HERMAN 128 (statement); port; 1 ill

UNTRACHT, Oppi A. J. ( ) metal
ROSNER 207-221 (interview); port

UPSHUR, Bernard (1936-) Amer; print
LEWIS II 77 (statement); port; 2 ill

URBAN, Albert (1909-1959) Amer; ptr,
print
ILLINOIS 1950 213-214 (statement)
ILLINOIS 1959 275 (statement); 1 ill

URBAN, Janos (1934-) Hung/Swis; film,
video
GROH (statement); 2 ill
NAYLOR 991-992 (statement); 1 ill

URBAN, Joao Aristeu (1943-) Braz;
photo
WALSH 776-777 (statement); 1 ill

URBAN, Reva (1925-) Amer; ptr
VARIAN III (statement); port

URIBE, Juan Camilo (1945-) Span; ptr
ANGEL 147-165 (interview); port; 1 ill

URIBURU, Nicolas Garcia (1937-) Arge;
ptr
EMANUEL II 954-955 (statement); 1 ill

URQUHART, Tony (1934-) Cana; sclp,
ptr
CANADA 40-41 (statement); port; 2 ill
NAYLOR 993-995 (statement); 1 ill

US, Valta (1944-) Amer; ptr
BOSTON III (interview); 1 ill

USAMI, Keiji (1940-) Japa; ptr
NAYLOR 995 (statement); 1 ill

UTRILLO, Maurice (1883-1955) Fren; ptr
MAYWALD (handwritten statement in
French); ports

UYTENBOGAARDT, Roelof S. (1933-)
SoAf; arch
EMANUEL I 830-831 (statement); 1 ill

UZZLE, Burk (1938-) Amer; photo
CAMPBELL 44-55 (statement); port; 13
ill
DIAMONSTEIN III 23-38 (interview); 12
ill
WALSH 777-778 (statement); 1 ill

VAGNETTI, Gianni (1898-) Ital; ptr
VERZOCCHI 435-439 (statement); self
port; 1 ill

VALDERRAMA, Francisco ( ) Span; sclp
ANGEL 169-181 (interview); port; 1 ill

VALDES, Manuel (1942-) Span; ptr
SEE: EQUIPO CRONICA

VALDES DE SOLA, Berta Carlota
SEE: CARLOTA, Bertha

VALDOVIN, Rogelio Ruiz (1934-) Amer;
sclp
RAICES 24 (statement); 1 ill

VALENTI, Italo (1912-) Ital; ptr
VERZOCCHI 441-445 (statement); self
port; 1 ill

VALENTIN, Helene ( ) Amer; photo
ARTPARK 1976 196-197 (statement);
port; 10 ill

VALENTINE, DeWain (1936-) Amer;
sclp
HOPKINS 118-119 (statement); port; 1
ill

VALERIO, James Robert (1938-) Amer;
ptr
ARTHUR 130-143 (interview); port; 21
ill
SUPERREAL 56-57, 178-179 (interview);
1 ill

VALLEDOR, Leo ( ) Amer; ptr
HOPKINS 70-71 (statement); port; 1 ill

VALLEJO, Anibal (1945-) Span; ptr
ANGEL 183-203 (interview); port; 1 ill

VALLEJO DE BROZON, Guadalupe
SEE: BROZON, Guadalupe Vallejo de

VALMIER, Georges (1885-1937) Fren;
ptr
ABSTRACTION no.2 47 (statement); 2
ill

VALOCH, Jiri (1946-) Czec; ptr
EMANUEL II 958-959 (statement); 1 ill
NAYLOR 997-998 (statement)

VAN AMEN, Woody (1936-) Dutc; sclp
EMANUEL II 959-960 (statement); 1 ill

VANCE, Florestee (1940-) Amer; ptr
LEWIS II 17 (statement); port; 1 ill

VAN DALEN, Anton (1938-) ptr
ART NOW v.4 no.1 (statement); 1 ill

VAN DEN ENDE, Jaap (1944-) Dutc;
ptr
NAYLOR 998-999 (statement); 1 ill

VAN DER BEEK, Edward Stanley (1927-
) Amer; sclp, film, video
ARTPARK 1975 126-127 (statement);
port; 1 ill
DAVIS 58-62 (statement: "Social
Imagistics")
REVOLUTION 219-228 (poem: "Movies,
Disposable Art, Synthetic Media and
Artificial Intelligence")

VANDERCAM, Serge ( ) Belg; sclp
COLLARD 242-248 (interview); port; 1
ill

VAN DER ELSKEN, Edward
SEE: ELSKEN, Edward van der

VAN DER HEYDEN, Jacob Cornelis
Johan (1928-) Dutc; ptr
EMANUEL II 960-961 (statement); 1 ill
NAYLOR 999-1000 (statement); 1 ill

VANDER LEE, Jana (1945-) Amer; text
O'KANE (statement); 1 ill

VAN DER RYN, Sim ( ) Amer; arch
COOPER-HEWITT II 132-134 (essay: "Sustainable Cities")

VANDER SLUIS, George (1915-) Amer; ptr
FULBRIGHT 46-47 (statement); 1 ill
ILLINOIS 1961 190 (response); port; 1 ill

VAN DE VELDE, Henry Clemens (1863-1957) Belg; ptr, arch, design
CONRADS 13 ("Programme," o.p. 1903)
CONRADS 18 ("Credo," o.p. 1907)
CONRADS 29-31 ("Werkbund Theses and Antitheses," o.p. 1914)
CONRADS 152-153 (extract from "Forms," o.p. 1949)
GROHMANN 456 ("Das Organische," o.p. 1902)
GROHMANN 457 ("Das Moralische und das Technische," o.p. 1902)

VAN DUINWYK, George Paul (1941-) Amer; metal
METALWORKS (statement); 1 ill

VAN ELK, Ger
SEE: ELK, Ger van

VAN EYCK, Aldo (1918-) Dutc; arch
EMANUEL I 842-843, 845 (statement); 1 ill
NEWMAN 26-35 (essay); port; 19 ill
NEWMAN 169, 197 (group discussion)
NEWMAN 216-217 ("Talk at the Conclusion of the Otterlo Conference")

VAN FLEET, Ellen ( )
SCHAPIRO 74 (statement); port; 1 ill

VAN GINKEL, Blanche Lemco ( ) Cana; arch
NEWMAN 102-106 (essay); 9 ill

VAN HAARDT, Georges (1907-) Fren; ptr
YALE 73 (statement)

VAN HOOK, David H. (1923-) Amer; ptr
ART PATRON ART 59-60 (statement); port; 1 ill
MORRIS 206-211 (statements); ports; 2 ill

VAN KONINGSBRUGGEN, Rob (1948-) Dutc; ptr
EMANUEL II 965 (statement); 1 ill

VAN LEAR, Robin ( ) Amer; wood
MEILACH 165, 167 (statement); 3 ill

VAN MUNSTER, Jan (1939-) Belg; sclp, light
EMANUEL II 965-967 (statement); 1 ill

VANN, Marsha ( )
CRISS-CROSS no.7/8/9 46-47 ("Interweavings"); 2 ill

VAN NOSTRAND, Bruce ( ) Amer; coll
CALIFORNIA--COLLAGE (statement); 1 ill

VAN NOSTRAND, Mary ( ) Amer; coll
CALIFORNIA--COLLAGE (statement); 1 ill

VAN SAUN, John ( ) perf
AVALANCHE no.2 16-17 (statement); 4 ill

VAN SCHLEY, Evander Duer (1941-) Amer; photo
NAYLOR 1003 (statement)

VEREECKE, Amand ( ) Belg; ptr
COLLARD 250-254 (interview); port; 1
ill

VERHEYEN, Jef (1932-) Belg; ptr
SKIRA 1978 76 (statement); 1 ill

VERLANGIERI, Michael John ( )
ARTISTS no.3 7-9 ("Handmade Paper")
ARTISTS no.4 8-10 ("On Creativity")

VERONESI, Luigi M. (1908-) Ital; photo
WALSH 785-787 (statement); 1 ill

VERSTOCKT, Marc (1930-) Belg; ptr,
sclp
GROH (statement); 2 ill

VESCI, Eva (1930-) Hung/Cana; arch
EMANUEL I 846-848 (statement); 1 ill

VESPIGNANI, Renzo (1924-) Ital; ptr,
illus
ART VOICES v.4 no.4 96-97 (interview
with Joan Silleck); 2 ill

VESSA, Michael (1948-) Amer; ptr,
envir
SKIRA 1978 116 (extract from interview
with Alexandra Schwartz); 1 ill

VESTAL, David (1924-) Amer; photo
WALSH 787-788 (statement); 1 ill

VEZELAY, Paule (Mrs. Watson-
Williams) (1893-) Brit; ptr
ABSTRACTION no.3 48 (statement); 1
ill
NAYLOR 1012-1013 (statement); 1 ill

VIALLAT, Claude (1936-) Fren; ptr,
sclp, instal
CHOIX 48 (statement, o.p. 1982); 1 ill
DOUZE ANS 369-372 (statement); 5 ill
PRADEL 93 (statement, o.p. 1982); 3 ill

SKIRA 1976 73 (statement); 1 ill
SKIRA 1979 56-57 (statement); 1 ill
SKIRA 1980 45 (statement); 1 ill

VICENTE, Esteban (1903-) Span/Amer;
ptr, sclp, coll
ILLINOIS 1952 238 (statement); 1 ill
ILLINOIS 1953 228-229 (statement); 1 ill
IT IS no.1 41 (statement)
LOCATION v.1 no.2 62-74 (essay:
"Painting Should be Poor"); port; 7 ill

VICKREY, Robert Remsen (1926-)
Amer; illus, ptr
ILLINOIS 1955 250 (statement); 1 ill
MAGIC 108-111 (statement); port; 3 ill
NEW DECADE 89-91 (statement); 3 ill

VICTORIA, Theodosius (1942-) Amer;
sclp, ptr
DIRECTIONS I 77 (response); 1 ill

VIEILLARD, Roger (1907-) Fren; print
PREMIER BILAN 326 (statement); port

VIEIRA DA SILVA, Marie-Helene (1908-
) Port/Fren; ptr
ART SINCE v.1 158 (statement, o.p.
1960)
CHARBONNIER v.2 51-60 (interview)
GOLDAINE 189-191 (interview); port
PREMIER BILAN 326 (statement); port
RITCHIE 102-105 (statement); port; 4 ill
SCHNEIDER 158-174 (interview); 1 ill

VIGNELLI, Lella ( ) design
DIAMONSTEIN V 176-191 (interview);
port; 12 ill

VIGNELLI, Massimo ( ) design
DIAMONSTEIN V 176-191 (interview);
port; 12 ill

VILADECAUS, Joan-Pere (1948-) Port;

sclp
SKIRA 1978 58 (statement); 1 ill

VILCHE, Hector
SEE: TALLER DE MONTEVIDEO

VILLAGRAN GARCIA, Jose (1901-)
Mexi; arch
EMANUEL I 850-852 (statement); 1 ill

VILLALBA, Dario (1939-) Span; sclp,
ptr, instal
EMANUEL II 978-979 (poem); 1 ill
NAYLOR 1014-1016 (statement); 1 ill
SKIRA 1976 95 (statement); 1 ill

VILLANUEVA, Carlos Raul (1900-)
Vene; arch
BAYON 214-231 (interview); port; 20 ill

VILLEGLE, Jacques de la (1926-) Fren;
ptr, coll, print
NAYLOR 1016-1017 (statement); 1 ill

VILLEROUX, Albert de ( ) Belg; ptr
COLLARD 256-260 (interview); port; 1
ill

VILLON, Jacques (Gaston Duchamp)
(1875-1963) Fren; ptr
ABSTRACTION no.2 47-48 (statement);
2 ill
CHARBONNIER v.1 83-93 (interview)
GOLDAINE 12-14 (interview); port
LIBERMAN 52-57 (statements)
MAYWALD (statement, in English,
German, and French); ports
PROTTER 192-194 (extract from
Reflections on Painting, 1950)
SEGHERS 257-258 (statement, p.p.)
VINGTIEME N.S. no.4 30-32 (essay: "La
Creation Artistique"); 3 ill
VINGTIEME N.S. no.9 23 (statement)
VINGTIEME N.S. no.12 16-24, 94

(interview with Yvon Taillandier, in
French and English); 13 ill

VILMOUTH, Jean-Luc (1952-) Fren;
sclp, instal
CHOIX 49 (statement, o.p. 1982); 1 ill

VILUMSOUS, Alex ( ) Amer; illus
CALIFORNIA--DRAWING (statement); 2
ill

VINAY, Jean (1907-) Fren; ptr
PREMIER BILAN 327 (statement); self
port

VINER, Frank Lincoln (1937-) Amer;
sclp, instal
DIRECTIONS I 77 (response); 1 ill
NAYLOR 1017-1018 (statement); 1 ill

VINOLY, Rafael (1944-) Arge; arch
SEE: MANTEOLA SANCHEZ
GOMEZ SANTOS SOLSONA
VINOLY

VIS, Jerry ( ) instal, perf
APPLE 24, 26 (statements); 4 ill

VISEUX, Claude (1927-) Fren; sclp
SKIRA 1976 89 (statement); 1 ill

VISSER'T HOOFT, Martha H. (1906-)
Amer; ptr
ILLINOIS 1952 239 (statement); 1 ill

VITTORINI, Umberto (1890-) Ital; ptr
VERZOCCHI 459-463 (statement); self
port; 1 ill

VIVONA, Linda (1940-) Amer; ptr
VARIAN I (statement); port

VLAMINCK, Maurice de (1876-1958)
Fren; ptr

CHIPP 144-145 ("Prefatory Letter," o.p. 1923); self port
LHOTE 413-425 (essays, o.p. 1942)
LIBERMAN 28-30 (statements)
RAYNAL 313-317 (statement); 3 ill

VOELCKER, John ( ) arch
NEWMAN 157-159 (essay); 10 ill

VOGEL, Donald S. (1917-) Amer; ptr
ILLINOIS 1957 253 (response); 1 ill

VOGEL, Karel (1897-) sclp
OPEN AIR 1960 (statement); 2 ill

VOGEL, Peter (1939-) Germ; ptr
GROH (statement); 3 ill

VOGELER, Heinrich (1872-1942) Germ; ptr
MIESEL 156-159 ("A Painter's Experience," 1938)

VOGELGESANG, Klaus (1945-) Germ; ptr, illus
SKIRA 1978 21 (statement); 1 ill

VOGL, Harold ( ) film, ptr
TRACKS v.3 no.1/2 94-98 ("What a Journey (Horror Trip to Poland)"); port

VOGT, Chrisitan (1946-) Swis; photo
SKIRA 1976 18 (statement); 1 ill

VOIERS, Leslie ( ) Amer; text
HAYSTACK 64 (statement); 1 ill

VOLLEY, Nicholas (1950-) Brit; ptr
HAYWARD 1979 58-61 (statement); 8 ill

VOLTI, Antoniucci (1915-) Ital/ Fren
PREMIER BILAN 327 (statement); port

VON EUER, Judith A. (1938-) Amer; print
CALIFORNIA--PRINTS (statement); 1 ill

VON GAGREN, Verena (1946-) Germ; photo
WALSH 792 (statement)

VON GERKAN, Meinhard (1935-) Germ; arch
EMANUEL I 855-856 (statement); 1 ill

VON RINGELHEIM, Paul (1938-) Aust/Amer; sclp
ILLINOIS 1965 147 (statement); 1 ill

VON SCHLEGELL, David (1920-) Amer; ptr, sclp
ILLINOIS 1957 253-254 (response); 1 ill

VON SCHMIDT, Harold (1893-) Amer; ptr
GUITAR 216-225 (interview); port; 4 ill
NORTH LIGHT 220-227 (statement); ports; 7 ill

VORDEMBERGE-GILDEWART, Friedrich (1899-1963) Germ/Dutc; ptr
ABSTRACTION no.2 49 (statement); 1 ill

VOSS, Jan (1936-) Germ; ptr
EMANUEL II 983-985 (statement); 1 ill
SKIRA 1979 90 (statement); 1 ill

VOSTELL, Wolf (1932-) Germ; ptr, sclp, perf
ART SINCE v.2 323 (statement, o.p. 1968)
ART VOICES v.5 no.3 84-87 (text piece)
EMANUEL II 985-987 (statement); 1 ill
KUNST UND POLITIK (statement; and text of "Rebellion der Verneinung," radio happening, 6/29/69); port; 4 ill

PARACHUTE no.8 20-21 (statement, in English); 1 ill
SKIRA 1977 52-53 (statement); 6 ill
SKIRA 1980 111 (statement); 1 ill

VOULKOS, Peter (1924-) Amer; pott, sclp
HOPKINS 72-73 (statement); port; 1 ill
VISUAL v.2 no.4 12-16 (interview); 4 ill

VULLIAMY, Gerard (1909-) Swis/Fren; ptr
ABSTRACTION no.2 50 (statement); 2 ill
GRENIER 203-211 (interview)

VYTLACIL, Vaclav (1892-) Amer; ptr
ILLINOIS 1951 221 (statement); 1 ill

WACHSMANN, Konrad (1901-) arch
CONRADS 156 ("Seven Theses," o.p. 1957)

WADDY, Ruth G. (1909-) Amer; ptr, print
LEWIS I REVISED 124-126 (statement); port; 4 ill

WADE, Eugene
SEE: EDA, Eugene

WADE, Robert Schrope (1943-) Amer; sclp, envir, ptr
ARTPARK 1978 60-63 (statement); port; 9 ill
NAYLOR 1023-1024 (statement); 1 ill
SKIRA 1978 66 (statement); 1 ill

WADSWORTH, Edward Alexander (1889-1949) Brit; ptr, print
GOLDWATER 458-459 (statement, 1933)
READ 95-104 (statement); port; 4 ill

WAGNER, Martin ( ) arch
CONRADS 146-147 ("A Programme for City Reconstruction," o.p. 1943)

WAGNER, Otto (1841-1918) Aust; arch
BREICHA 213-215 (essay: "Nachruf auf Joseph M. Olbrich," o.p. 1908)

WAITZKIN, Stella ( ) Amer; sclp, ptr
PHILLPOT (statement)

WAKAE, Kanji (1944-) Japa; sclp, instal
NAYLOR 1025 (statement); 1 ill

WAKELY, Shelagh (1932-) Brit; sclp
CONTEMPORARY (statement); port; 3 ill

WAKITA, Kazu (1908-) Japa; ptr
KUNG 128-131 (statement); port; 2 ill

WALD, Sylvia (1914-) Amer; print
AMERICAN PRINTS 58, 71 (statement); 1 ill

WALDBERG, Isabelle (1917-) Swis; sclp
PREMIER BILAN 327 (statement); port

WALDECK, Charles (1943-) Amer; sclp
DIRECTIONS I 77 (response); 1 ill

WALDMAN, Paul (1936-) Amer; ptr
VARIAN I (statement); port

WALDMAN, Peter ( ) arch
GA HOUSES no.10 74-75 (essay)
GA HOUSES no.10 76-93 (statements); 51 ill

WALKER, Derek (1931-) Brit; arch
EMANUEL I 860-862 (statement); 1 ill

WALKER, Harold Todd (1917-) Amer; photo
WALSH 793-795 (statement); 1 ill

WALKER, James Faure (1948-) Brit; ptr
HAYWARD 1979 70-73 (statement); 6 ill

WALKER, John (1939-) Brit; ptr
ART NOW v.3 no.4 (statement); 1 ill
SKIRA 1979 23 (extract from interview, o.p. 1978); 1 ill

WALKER, Larry (1935-) Amer; ptr
LEWIS I REVISED 74 (statement); port; 1 ill

WALKER, Ron ( ) Amer; photo
PHOTOGRAPHY (statement); 1 ill

WALKER, Wendy (1951-) print, illus
TRACKS v.2 no.2 5-7 ("Brief Tales, The Succession, The Betrothal, The Illuminated Book")

WALKER, William (1927-) Amer; ptr
LEWIS II 120 (statement); port; 3 ill

WALKOWITZ, Abraham (1878-1965) Russ/Amer; ptr
FIFTY (statement); port; 1 ill
FORUM 1916 100 (statement); 1 ill
JANIS I 44 (statement); 1 ill
JOURNAL OF THE AAA v.9 no.1 10-17 (interview with Abraham Lerner and Bartlett Cowdrey); ports
100 CONTEMPORARY 190-191 (statement); port; 1 ill
ROSE II 57-58 (statement, o.p. 1916)
ROSE II REVISED 53 (statement, o.p. 1916)

WALL, Jeff (1946-) Cana; photo
MCCLINTIC 30-32 (statement); 2 ill

WALL, Jeff ( )
REALLIFE no.3 4-6 (statements); 1 ill

WALLACE, Andre (1947-) Brit; sclp
BRITISH (statement); 1 ill

WALLACE, Don (1922-) Cana; sclp
CANADA 96-97 (statement); port; 1 ill

WALLACE, George (1920-) Iris/Cana; sclp
CANADA 28-29 (statement); port; 4 ill

WALLACE, Ian ( ) Cana; photo
POINT OF VIEW 36 (statement); 1 ill

WALLACE, Jim ( ) photo
LAPLANTE 117-125 (interview); port; 1 ill

WALLACE, Joan ( )
REALLIFE no.6 32, 36 (essay: "Something About Art")

WALLEEN, Hans (1902-) Amer; ptr
NORTH LIGHT 83 (statement); 1 ill

WALLET, Taf (1902-) Belg; ptr
COLLARD 262-265 (interview); port; 1 ill

WALLS, Bobby (1948-) Amer; print
LEWIS I REVISED 113-114 (statement); port; 2 ill

WALLS, Dedra M. (1950-) Amer; coll
WISCONSIN II (statement); 1 ill

WALTERS, Carl (1883-1955) Amer; ptr, sclp
ZAIDENBERG 175-176 (essay: "There are no Words for Art"); 1 ill

WALTHER, Franz Erhard (1939-) Germ; sclp, envir
AVALANCHE no.4 34-41 (project proposal); 16 ill
CELANT 10, 174-178 (statement); 13 ill
EMANUEL II 993-994 (statement); 1 ill
KUNST BLEIBT KUNST 380-381 (statement); 12 ill
SKIRA 1978 120 (statement); 3 ill

WARASHINA, M. Patricia (Patti) (1940-) Amer; pott
GUENTHER 114-115 (statement); port; 1 ill
VIEWPOINT 1978 30-31(statement); 4 ill
WECHSLER 124-129 (statement); port; 5 ill

WARD, Carole (1943-) Amer; metal
LEWIS II 46 (statement); port; 1 ill

WARD, John (1917-) Brit; ptr
CONTEMPORARY (statement); port; 2 ill
VISUAL v.1 no.4 3-5 (group discussion)

WARD, Lynd Kendall (1905-) Amer; illus, print
FIRST AMERICAN 38-41 (essay: "Race, Nationality and Art")
MCCAUSLAND 69-78 (essay: "The Book Artist")

WARHOL. Andy (1928-) Amer; ptr
ART SINCE v.2 325 (statement, o.p. 1963)
ARTFORUM v.4 no.6 20-24 (group discussion); 1 ill
DANOFF 79, 81 (interview)
KERBER 214 (extract from interview with Gretchen Berg, o.p. 1967, in English and German)
JOHNSON 86-89 (extract from interview with Gene R. Swenson, o.p. 1963); 1 ill
ROSE II REVISED 155-156 (extract from interview with Gene Swenson, o.p. 1963)
RUSSELL J 116-119 (interview with Gene Swenson, o.p. 1963)

WARNECKE, John Carl (1919-) Amer; arch
EMANUEL I 865-867 (statement); 1 ill
HEYER 122-129 (interview); 21 ill

WARNER, Betty G. (1921-) Amer; ptr
NOSANOW I 126 (statement); 1 ill

WARNER, Deborah ( ) Amer; text
FIBER 62-63 (statement); 1 ill

WARNER, Elsa ( ) Amer; coll
CALIFORNIA--COLLAGE (statement); 1 ill

WARNER, Pat (1939-) Amer; paper
PAPERWORKS 40-41 (statement); 5 ill

WARNER, Pecolia (1901-) Amer; text
FERRIS 175-191 (statements); ports; 4 ill

WARREN, Guy (1921-) Atrl; ptr
DE GROEN 203-210 (interview); port

WARSHAW, Howard (1920-) Amer; ptr
ARTFORUM v.2 no.1 34-35 ("Response, Howard Warshaw on Don Factor"); 4 ill
CALIFORNIA--PAINTING 30 (statement); 1 ill
ILLINOIS 1951 221-222 (statement); 1 ill
ILLINOIS 1959 276-277 (statement, o.p. 1958); 1 ill

WASHINGTON, Mary Parks (1926-) Amer; ptr
LEWIS I REVISED 58 (statement); port; 1 ill

WASSERMAN, Burton (1929-) Amer; sclp, ptr
GEOMETRIC (statement); 1 ill

WASSERMAN, Cary (1939-) Amer; photo
WALSH 797-798 (statement); 1 ill

WATANABE, Youji (1923-) Japa; arch
EMANUEL I 868-871 (statement); 1 ill

WATKINS, Franklin C. (1894-1972) Amer; ptr
ILLINOIS 1959 277 (statement); 1 ill

WATKINS, James (1925-) Amer; ptr
LEWIS I REVISED 91 (statement); port; 1 ill

WATSON, Bruce (1925-) Cana; sclp
CANADA 92-93 (statement); port; 1 ill

WATSON, Genna (1948-) Amer; sclp, coll
IMAGES 74-80 (interview with Clair List); port; 5 ill

WATSON, Jenny (1951-) Atrl; sclp
DE GROEN 21-25 (interview); port

WATSON, Robert (1923-) Amer; ptr
ILLINOIS 1955 250-251 (statement); 1 ill

WATTENWYL, Peter von (1942-) envir
KORNFELD 54-55 (interview with Walter Voegeli); port; 2 ill

WATTS, Robert (1923-) Amer; perf, instal
ART AND TECHNOLOGY 338 (project proposal)

WAUGH, Frederick Judd (1861-1940) Amer; ptr
BRITANNICA 114 (statement); port; 1 ill

WAUTERS, Jef ( ) Belg; ptr
COLLARD 266-269 (interview); port; 1 ill

WAWIRKA, Julie (1954-) Amer; ptr
NOSANOW II 68-69 (statement); 2 ill

WAY, Jeff ( ) Amer; ptr
FACE IT 24-25 (statement); 1 ill

WAYNE, June C. (1918-) Amer; ptr, print
ILLINOIS 1951 222-223 (statement)
ILLINOIS 1953 229-230 (statement); 1 ill
ILLINOIS 1955 251-252 (statement); 1 ill
ILLINOIS 1957 254-255 (response); 1 ill
MUNRO 282-288 (interview); port; 3 ill
RODMAN I 28-31 (interview)
RODMAN III 109-112 (statements)
VISUAL v.2 no.3 4-8 (interview); 4 ill

WAYTT, Richard (1955-) Amer; ptr
LEWIS II 21 (statement); port; 1 ill

WAX, Bea ( ) pott
VISUAL v.2 no.1 3-4 (statements)

WEARDEN, Clifford (1920-) Brit; arch
EMANUEL I 871-872 (statement); 1 ill

WEARE, Shane ( ) print
VISUAL v.3 no.3 13-16 (interview); 4 ill

WEARIN, Catherine Norah (1954-) Amer; wood
WOODWORKING 48-49 (statement); port; 2 ill

WEAVER, James ( )
ARTISTS no.2 17, 20 ("MOMA/Reno")

WEBB, Alex ( ) photo
TIME-LIFE IV 110-111 (statement); 1 ill

WEBB, Charles Clayton
SEE: WEBB, Todd

WEBB, Paul (1902-) Amer; cart
M.H. DE YOUNG 142 (response); self port

WEBB, Todd (1905-) Amer; photo
WALSH 798-799 (statement); 1 ill

WEBER, Hugo (1918-1971) Swis; ptr
ILLINOIS 1950 215 (statement)
SEUPHOR 287 (statement)

WEBER, Idelle Lois (1932-) Amer; ptr, sclp
CELEBRATION (statement); 1 ill
SUPERREAL 57-58, 148-149 (interview); 1 ill

WEBER, Max (1881-1961) Amer; ptr
BRITANNICA 115 (statement); port; 1 ill
FIFTY (statement); port; 1 ill

WEINRIB, David ( )
ARTS YEARBOOK v.8 150-155 (group discussion led by Bruce Glaser)

WEINSTEIN, Richard S. (1932-) Amer; arch
COOPER-HEWITT II 26 (statement)
DIAMONSTEIN II 208-228 (interview); port; 2 ill
EMANUEL I 877 (statement)

WEISBERG, Ruth ( ) print
VISUAL v.3 no.3 23-26 (essay: "All of the News that Fits the Print; An Ecology of Southern California Printmaking")

WEISS, Edward H. ( ) ptr
ART VOICES v.5 no.3 50-54 (statements); port; 9 ill

WEISS, Harvey (1922-) Amer; sclp
ILLINOIS 1961 187 (response); port; 1 ill
ILLINOIS 1963 56 (statement); 1 ill
NORTH LIGHT 232-237 (statement); port; 8 ill

WEISS, Hugh (1925-) Amer; ptr
ILLINOIS 1953 230-231 (statement); 1 ill

WEISS, Murray (1926-) Amer; photo
WISCONSIN II (statement); 1 ill

WEJCHERT, Alexandra (1920-) Poli/Iris; sclp
KNOWLES 150-151 (statement); 4 ill

WEJCHERT, Hanna (1920-) Poli; arch
EMANUEL I 877-879 (statement); port

WEJCHERT, Kaximierz (1912-) Poli; arch
EMANUEL I 877-879 (statement); port

WELCH, Roger (1946-) Amer; sclp, video, film
APPLE 30 (statement); 2 ill
ART-RITE no.7 11, 17 (response); 1 ill
GEORGIA 118-166 (group discussion: "Artists' Convention," in Athens, GA., 1/7/1977, moderated by Jan van der Marck)
KUNST BLEIBT KUNST 346-347 (statement); 2 ill
NAYLOR 1034-1035 (statement); 1 ill
TRACKS v.1 no.2 60-64 ("On Recorded History (Part I)")

WELLIVER, Neil (1929-) Amer; ptr
ARTHUR 144-157 (interview); port; 16 ill
ILLINOIS 1965 63 (statement); 1 ill
STRAND 200-227 (interview); port; 22 ill

WELLS, Cady (1904-1954) Amer; ptr
ILLINOIS 1952 240 (statement); 1 ill

WELLS, David (1955-) Amer; sclp
LOGAN II 28-31 (poem); port; 5 ill

WELLS, John Clayworth Spencer (1907-) Brit; ptr
BOWNESS 17, 42-43 (statement); 1 ill

WELLS, Sue (1952-) photo
BOSHIER (statement); port; 3 ill

WELPOTT, Jack (1923-) Amer; photo
WALSH 803-805 (statement); 1 ill

WELSBY, Chris ( ) Brit; film
ENGLISH 466-467 (statement); port; 1 ill

WELTON, Roland (1919-) Amer; ptr
LEWIS I REVISED 30 (statement); port; 3 ill

WENDT, Francois W. (1919-)
Germ/Fren
PREMIER BILAN 328 (statement); port

WENGENROTH, Stow (1906-1978)
Amer; ptr, print
MILLER 1943 57 (statement); 1 ill

WENGER, John (1889-) Russ/Amer; ptr
100 CONTEMPORARY 194-195
(statement); port; 1 ill

WERNER, Nat (1908-) Amer; sclp
100 CONTEMPORARY 196-197
(statement); port; 1 ill

WERNER, Theodor (1886-) Germ; ptr
RITCHIE 48-51 (statement); port; 4 ill

WERRO, Roland (1926-) Swis; sclp, ptr
KORNFELD 56-57 (statement); port; 4
ill
NAYLOR 1035-1036 (statement); 1 ill

WERY, Marthe ( )
PARACHUTE no.8 21 (statement)

WESCHKE, Karl Martin (1925-) Germ;
ptr
CONTEMPORARY (statement); port; 2
ill
NAYLOR 1037-1038 (statement); 1 ill

WESELER, Gunter (1930-) Germ; instal,
sclp
NAYLOR 1038-1039 (statement); 1 ill

WESLER, Hugh R. (Huff) (1947-) Amer;
sclp
WISCONSIN II (statement); 1 ill

WESSELMANN, Tom (1931-) Amer;
coll, ptr, print
ART SINCE v.2 326 (statement, o.p.
1964)

ART VOICES v.5 no.3 39 (statement); 1
ill
ART VOICES v.5 no.3 46-49
(statements); ports; 7 ill
CRISPO I (statement); 18 ill
JOHNSON 92-94 (extract from interview
with Gene R. Swenson, o.p. 1963); 1 ill
RUSSELL J 119-120 (extract from
interview with Gene Swenson, o.p.
1963)

WESSELS, Glenn ( ) ptr
BETHERS I 258-259 (statement); 1 ill
BETHERS II 136-137 (statement); 2 ill

WEST, Pennerton ( )
PERSONAL (statement)

WESTON, Brett (1911-) Amer; photo
DANZIGER 154-175 (interview); port; 3
ill
HILL 211-223 (interview, 1975); port

WESTON, Edward (1886-1958) Amer;
photo
TIME-LIFE IV 16 (statement, p.p.)

WESTPFAHL, Conrad (1891-) Germ;
ptr
WINGLER 110-111 (essay: "Zu
Lithographien von Ernst Wilhelm
Nay," p.p.)

WESTWOOD, Bryan (1930-) Atrl; ptr
DE GROEN 26-31 (interview); port

WEWERKA, Stefan (1928-) Germ; illus
ADLERS 24-29 (interview); ports; 5 ill

WEXLER, George (1925-) Amer; ptr
GUSSOW 116-117 (interview, 1970); 1 ill

WHARTON, Margaret (1943-) Amer;
sclp

ARTPARK 1976 200-201 (statement); 4 ill

WHEELER, Charles (1892-) sclp
LONDON COUNTY (statement); 1 ill

WHEELER, Doug (1939-) Amer; instal, ptr
NAYLOR 1041 (statement)

WHEELER, Steve ( ) print
TIGER no.8 61-62 (statement)

WHITAKER, Richard ( ) arch
GA HOUSES no.7 7-11 (essay: "Connections"); ports

WHITCOMB, Jon (1906-) Amer; ptr, illus
GUITAR 226-235 (interview); port; 4 ill

WHITE, Amos ( ) Amer; pott
LEWIS I REVISED 53 (statement); port; 1 ill

WHITE, Charles Wilbert (1918-1979) Amer; print, ptr
FAX I 63-78 (statements); port; 2 ill
FINE 170-175 (statements, o.p. 1970, 1971); 7 ill

WHITE, Ed ( ) Brit; photo
HOW FAMOUS 176-179 (statements); port; 4 ill

WHITE, Francis Robert (1907-) Amer; ptr
FIRST AMERICAN 90-92 (essay: "Revolt in the Country")

WHITE, Jon (1938-) ptr
TRACKS v.3 no.3 62 (poem)

WHITE, Minor (1908-1976) Amer; photo
DANZIGER 14-35 (interview); port; 3 ill

HILL 338-376 (interview, 1975); port
TIME-LIFE IV 17 (statement, p.p.)

WHITEMAN, Edward Russell (1938-) Amer; ptr, coll
ART PATRON ART 63-64 (statement); port; 1 ill

WHITEN, Colette (1945-) Cana; sclp, film
GRAHAM 79-89 (statement); 4 ill

WHITEN, Tim ( ) Amer; sclp, envir
ARTPARK 1977 80-83 (statement); port; 6 ill

WHITING, Jim (1951-) Brit; sclp, perf
HAYWARD 1979 18-19, 32-35 (interview with William Furlong); 6 ill

WHITLOCK, An (1944-) Cana; sclp
ARTPARK 1975 130-131 (statement); port; 4 ill
GRAHAM 91-102 (statement); 8 ill

WHITMAN, Deborah ( ) Amer; sclp, instal
EVENTS I 50-51 (statement); 1 ill

WHITMAN, Robert (1935-) Amer; perf, ptr
ART AND TEHNOLOGY 340-358 (project proposal); port; 18 ill
ARTFORUM v.5 no.6 26-27 (statement)
JOHNSON 70-71 (statement, o.p. 1965); 1 ill
KIRBY 134-136 ("a statement")
KIRBY 137-138 ("The American Moon/the script"); port

WHITNEY, James ( ) film, ptr
CIRCLE no.10 4-10 (essay: "Audio Visual Music")

IMAGE COLOR FORM 28-29 (statement); 1 ill
SCHIMMEL 81-84 (statement); 6 ill
TUCHMAN 52 (extract from interview with Joe Raffaele)
VIEW v.2 no.2 (interview); port; 9 ill
WHITE WALLS no.5 100-103 (text piece)
WHITNEY (statement); 1 ill
YOUNG 1960 (statement); 2 ill

WILFORD, Michael ( ) arch
RUSSELL F 62-63 (project proposal); 3 ill

WILFRED, Thomas (Richard Edgar Loustrom) (1889-1968) Dani/Amer; sclp, light
MILLER 1952 30-32 (statement); port; 6 ill

WILGUS, Beverly ( ) Amer; photo
PHOTOGRAPHY (statement); 1 ill

WILKE, Hannah (1940-) Amer; perf, video, sclp
ART-RITE no.5 7 (response)
ART-RITE no.7 11 (response)
RE-VIEW v.1 41-42 (transcript of videotape performance); 1 ill
SCHAPIRO 76 (statement); 1 ill
VISUAL v.2 no.4 17-20 (interview); port; 3 ill

WILKINS, Jim ( ) Amer; arch, design
LIFE 91-114 (interview); port

WILL, Philip, Jr. (1906-) Amer; arch
EMANUEL 1 881-882 (statement); 1 ill

WILLAR, Fred (1939-) Cana; sclp
CANADA 54-55 (statement); port; 2 ill

WILLATS, Stephen (1943-) Brit; print
ARTIST AND CAMERA 56-57 (statement); 2 ill

GROH (statement); 1 ill
NAYLOR 1045-1047 (statement); 1 ill

WILLENBECHER, John (1936-) Amer; sclp
VARIAN II (statement); port

WILLEQUET, Andre ( ) Belg; sclp
COLLARD 270-274 (interview); port; 1 ill

WILLER, Jim (1921-) Brit/Cana; sclp
CANADA 64-65 (statement); port; 1 ill

WILLERVAL, Jean (1924-) Fren; arch
EMANUEL 1 882-884 (statement); 1 ill

WILLIAMS, Acquaetta (1950-) Amer; glass, sclp
CONTEMPORARY AFRICAN (statement); 2 ill
WISCONSIN II (statement); 1 ill

WILLIAMS, Amanico (1913-) Arge; arch
EMANUEL 1 884-886 (statement); 1 ill

WILLIAMS, Chester Lee (1944-) Amer; sclp
CONTEMPORARY AFRICAN (statement); port; 1 ill

WILLIAMS, Dan (1942-) Amer; photo
LEWIS I REVISED 127-128 (statement); port; 2 ill

WILLIAMS, Danny (1950-) Amer; ptr
SHEARER 62-65 (statement); 3 ill

WILLIAMS, George Blackstone ( ) Amer; print
IRVINE 62, 87-88 (statement); 1 ill

WILLIAMS, Gluyas (1888-) Amer; cart
M.H. DE YOUNG 144 (response); self port

WILLIAMS, Grace ( ) Amer
EVENTS I 51 (statement); 1 ill

WILLIAMS, Guy (1932-) Amer; ptr
IRVINE 88 (statement)

WILLIAMS, Hiram Draper (1917-)
Amer; ptr
ILLINOIS 1963 168 (statement); 1 ill

WILLIAMS, Jean (1916-) Amer; text
HAAR II 91-95 (interview); ports; 2 ill

WILLIAMS, Judy (1940-) Cana; ptr, sclp
POINT OF VIEW 37 (statement); 1 ill

WILLIAMS, Laura G. (1915-) Amer; ptr
LEWIS I 17 (statement); port; 3 ill

WILLIAMS, Meghan ( )
ART-RITE no.19 17-20 (group discussion)

WILLIAMS, Rick (1943-) Cana; ptr
POINT OF VIEW 38 (statement); 1 ill

WILLIAMS, Vern ( ) Amer; arch, design
LIFE 12-26 (interview); port

WILLIAMS, William T. (1942-) Amer; ptr
TUCKER I 10 (statement)

WILLIAMSON, Clara McDonald (1875-1976) Amer; ptr
ILLINOIS 1953 232 (statement); 1 ill
ILLINOIS 1957 257-258 (response); 1 ill

WILLIS, Andrew Mitchell (1948-) Amer; ptr
NOSANOW I 127 (statement); 1 ill

WILLIS, Luster (1913-) Amer; ptr, wood
FERRIS 193-212 (statements); ports; 16 ill

WILLIS, Stirling (1946-) Amer; ptr
CELEBRATION (statement); 1 ill

WILLOUGHBY, Bob ( ) Amer; photo
CALIFORNIA--PHOTOGRAPHY (statement); port; 4 ill

WILMARTH, Christopher (1943-) Amer; sclp
NAYLOR 1048 (statement)

WILMARTH, Susan (1942-) ptr
TRANSPERSONAL 80-89 (statement); port; 4 ill

WILLS, Thornton (1936-) Amer; ptr
LEAVITT (statement); port; 5 ill
RE-VIEW v.1 53-57 (statement); 4 ill
RE-VIEW v.2/3 46-51 (statement); ports; 5 ill

WILS, Lydia ( ) Belg; ptr
COLLARD 276-279 (interview); port; 1 ill

WILSON, Bryan (1927-) Amer; ptr
SOME 28 (statement); 1 ill

WILSON, Charles ( ) Amer
BRAKKE 36-61 (text piece); 24 ill

WILSON, Colin St. John (1922-) Brit; arch
EMANUEL I 890-891 (statement); 1 ill

WILSON, Crawford R. (1957-) Amer; ptr
RICKERT 1980 (statement); port; 3 ill

WILSON, David (1947-) Atrl; sclp
DE GROEN 138-146 (interview); port

WILSON, Frank Avray ( ) ptr
QUADRUM no.14 103-108 (statements); 5 ill

■The Stratford Fragments: Extravisionary Perceptions Based on Articulation, Definition, and Wheels■); 9 ill

WINKLER, Bernhard ( ) Germ; arch
COOPER-HEWITT I 54-55 (essay: ■Pedestrian Malls■)

WINKLER, Ralph
SEE: PENCK, A. R.

WINNEWISSER, Rolf (1949-) Swis; print, sclp
NAYLOR 1051-1052 (statement); 1 ill
SANDBERG 198-201 (statement); 4 ill
SKIRA 1978 29 (statement); 1 ill
SKIRA 1980 124 (statement); 4 ill

WINOGRAND, Garry (1928-) Amer; photo
DIAMONSTEIN III 179-191 (interview); 8 ill

WINOKUR, Paula (1935-) Amer; pott, sclp
HERMAN 131 (statement); port; 1 ill

WINSLOW, John Randolph (1938-) Amer; ptr
SUPERREAL 59-60 (interview)
SUPERREAL 108-109 (statement); 1 ill

WINSOR, V. Jacqueline (Jackie) (1941-) Cana/Amer; sclp, ptr
AVALANCHE no.4 10-17 (interview); port; 19 ill
MUNRO 431-437 (interview); port; 3 ill

WINT, Reindert Wepko van de
SEE: JOCHEM and RUDI

WINTER, Fritz (1905-) Germ; ptr
RITCHIE 52-55 (statement); port; 4 ill
SEUPHOR 290 (statement)

WINTERS, Denny (1907-) Amer; ptr
ZAIDENBERG 128-130 (essay: ■The Subjective Interpretation of Reality■); 5 ill

WINTERS, Robin ( )
ART-RITE no.14 5, 14 (response)
AVALANCHE no.11 11-15 (interview); 12 ill

WINZER, Icke (1937-) Germ; ptr
NAYLOR 1051-1053 (statement); 1 ill

WISE, Kelly (1932-) Amer; photo
WALSH 819-821 (statement); 1 ill

WISE CIOBOTARU, Gillian (1936-) Brit; ptr
NAYLOR 1054-1055 (statement); 1 ill

WISHAW, Anthony (1930-) Brit; ptr
CONTEMPORARY (statement); port; 2 ill

WISNOSKY, John (1940-) Amer; ptr
HAAR II 96-100 (interview); ports; 2 ill

WITKIN, Jerome Paul (1939-) Amer; ptr, sclp
SUPERREAL 106-107 (statement); 1 ill

WITT, Bill ( ) photo
TIME-LIFE II 104-105 (statement); 1 ill

WIXON, Scott (1948-) Amer; ptr
SHEARER 66-70 (interview); 3 ill

WOELFFER, Emerson S. (1914-) Amer, ptr, coll
ARTFORUM v.1 no.10 24-25 (interview); 4 ill
HOPKINS 120-121 (statement); port; 1 ill
ILLINOIS 1959 281 (statement); 1 ill

WOELL, J. Fred (1934-) Amer; metal
WISCONSIN I (statement); 1 ill

WOFFORD, Philip (1935-) Amer; ptr
ART NOW v.2 no.3 (statement); 1 ill
ILLINOIS 1974 131 (statement); 1 ill

WOGENSCKY, Andre ( ) arch
NEWMAN 128-131 (statement, in French); port; 7 ill
NEWMAN 147-149 (group discussion)

WOJCKIK, Gary Thomas (1945-) Amer; sclp
ILLINOIS 1969 177 (statement); 1 ill

WOLF, Sue ( ) pott
VISUAL v.2 no.1 9-12 (interview); 5 ill

WOLFE, Jack (1924-) Amer; ptr
BOSTON III (interview); 1 ill
YOUNG 1957 (statement); 1 ill

WOLFE, Townsend Durant (1935-) Amer; ptr
MORRIS 212-217 (statements); ports; 3 ill

WOLFF, Adolf (1887-1943) Belg/Amer; sclp
100 CONTEMPORARY 200-201 (poem: "The Artists"); port; 1 ill

WOLFF, Dee I. (1948-) Amer; coll, ptr
PAPERWORKS 42-43 (statement); 7 ill

WOLFF, Gustav (1886-1934) Germ; sclp
THORN 93 (statement, p.p.)

WOLFF, Robert Jay (1905-1978) Amer; ptr, sclp
ABSTRACT 15-16, 49, 173 (essay: "Toward a Direct Vision"); 1 ill
ILLINOIS 1957 258-259 (response); 1 ill
JANIS I 57 (statement); 1 ill

KEPES VIII 220-230 (essay: "Visual Intelligence in General Education")

WOLS (Otto Alfred Schultze-Battmann) (1913-1951) Germ; ptr
ART SINCE v.1 153 (poem, o.p. 1958)
CLAUS 107-112 (statement)
PREMIER BILAN 328 (statement); port

WONG, Jackson Chack Sang (1930-) Chin; arch
EMANUEL I 894-895 (statement); 1 ill

WONG, Paul ( ) Cana; photo, video
POINT OF VIEW 59 (statement); 1 ill

WONNER, Paul John (1920-) Amer; ptr
HOPKINS 76-77 (statement); port; 1 ill
ILLINOIS 1961 208 (response); port; 1 ill

WOOD, Alan (1935-) Cana; ptr
POINT OF VIEW 39 (statement); 1 ill

WOOD, Bernardine (1924-) Amer; ptr
ILLINOIS 1957 259 (response); 1 ill

WOOD, Grant (1892-1942) Amer; ptr
BRITANNICA 116 (statement); port; 1 ill

WOOD, Paul ( )
ART-LANGUAGE v.3 no.2 7-12 ("A Review of Styles")
ART-LANGUAGE v.3 no.2 46-51 ("Rambling: To Partial Correspondents")
ART-LANGUAGE v.3 no.2 89-92 ("Utopian Prayers and Infantile Marxism")

WOOD, Susan ( ) Amer; pott
HAYSTACK 65 (statement); 1 ill

WOOD, Viola (1949-) Amer; pott

CONTEMPORARY AFRICAN (statement); port; 1 ill

WOODHAM, Derrick (1940-) Amer; sclp
EMANUEL II 1016-1018 (statement); 1 ill
NAYLOR 1056-1057 (statement); 1 ill

WOODMAN, Elizabeth (Betty) (1930-) Amer; pott
HERMAN 132 (statement); port; 1 ill
WECHSLER 130-135 (statement); port; 5 ill

WOODMAN, George ( ) Amer; ptr
CRISS-CROSS no.3 25 (statement); 1 ill
CRISS-CROSS no.6 4-7 (statement); 5 ill
CRISS-CROSS no.10 6-7 (essay: "Pattern")
CRISS-CROSS no.10 40-41 (statement); port; 1 ill

WOODS, Conrad (1932-) Amer; ptr
ILLINOIS 1959 281 (statement); 1 ill

WOODS, S. John ( ) ptr
LONDON BULLETIN no.7 27-28 (essay: "A National People's Theatre")
LONDON BULLETIN no.11 13-15 (essay: "Who's Been Frightened by the Big Bang?")

WOODY, Thomas Howard (1935-) Amer; perf, sclp
ARTPARK 1976 202-203 (statement); 4 ill
MORRIS 218-223 (statements); ports; 3 ill

WOOLLEY, Kenneth Frank (1933-) Atrl; arch
EMANUEL I 896-898 (statement); 1 ill

WOOSTER, Ann-Sargent ( )

WOMANART v.2 no.1 6-9, 33-34 (essay: "19th Century American Printmakers")

WORDEN, Fred ( ) film
CRISS-CROSS no.10 24-25 (statement); port; 1 ill
CRISS-CROSS no.13 31-32 (essay: "Seeing/Thinking")

WORK COUNCIL FOR ART (group)
CONRADS 44-45 ("Under the Wing of a Great Architecture," o.p. 1919)

WORTH, Don (1924-) Amer; photo
WALSH 823-824 (statement); 1 ill

WORTH, Margarita( ) Amer; sclp
ILLINOIS 1953 232-233 (statement); 1 ill

WOSTAN (Stanislas Wojcieszynski) (1915-) Poli; sclp, ptr
QUADRUM no.16 83-90 (poems); 10 ill

WOTRUBA, Fritz (1907-) Aust; sclp
ALBRIGHT-KNOX 189-190 (letter, 10/1968); 1 ill
ART SINCE v.2 150 (statement, o.p. 1967)
LETTERS 44-46 (letter); 4 ill
SELZ 146-149 (statement); 3 ill

WRAGG, Gary (1946-) Brit; ptr
CONTEMPORARY (statement); port; 2 ill
HAYWARD 1979 82-85 (statement); 10 ill

WRAY, Dick (1933-) Amer; ptr
TEXAS 36-39 (statement); 4 ill

WREN, Bernie (1917-) Cana; ptr
POINT OF VIEW 40 (statement); 1 ill

XCERON, Jean (1890-1967) Gree/Amer;
ptr
BETHERS II 143 (statement); 1 ill
ILLINOIS 1950 216-217 (statement); 1 ill
ILLINOIS 1951 224 (statement); 1 ill
ILLINOIS 1957 259-260 (response); 1 ill

XENAKIS, Constantin (1931-) Gree; sclp
LUMIERE (statement); port; 1 ill

XOCHITIOTZIN, Desiderio Hernandez
(1947-) Mexi; ptr
STEWART 156-159 (statement); port; 2
ill

YACOE, Donald (1923-) Amer; ptr
CALIFORNIA--PAINTING 51 (statement);
1 ill

YAGHJIAN, Edmund K. (1904-) Amer;
ptr
MORRIS 230-235 (statements); ports; 1
ill

YALTER, Nil (1938-) Turk/Fren; instal
ISSUE (statement, in French); 7 ill
KUNST BLEIBT KUNST 348-351
(statement, in French and German); 8
ill

YAMAGUCHI, Takeo (1902-) Japa; ptr
KUNG 132-135 (statement); port; 2 ill

YAMAGUCHI, Takako ( ) Amer; ptr
DOWNTOWN (statement); 1 ill

YAMAMOTO, Norkio (1929-) Amer; ptr
YOUNG 1960 (statement); 1 ill

YAMASAKI, Minoru (1912-) Amer; arch
EMANUEL I 910-912 (statement); 1 ill
HEYER 184-195 (interview); 17 ill

YAMASHITA, Mike ( ) Amer; photo
HOW FAMOUS 88-93 (statements); port;
7 ill

YAN
SEE: DIEUZAIDE, Jean

YANG, Hanford ( ) Amer; arch
ART VOICES v.4 no.4 21-24 (interview
with Gordon Brown)
BELFORD 57-77 (group discussion)

YARMOLINSKY, Sirpa (1940-) Finn;
text
FIBER 40-41 (statement); 1 ill

YARWOOD, Walter (1917-) Cana; sclp
CANADA 82-83 (statement); port; 2 ill

YATES, Marie (1940-) Brit; photo
ISSUE (statement)
SKIRA 1976 26 (statement); 2 ill

YATES, Sharon Deborah (1942-) Amer;
ptr
GUSSOW 50-52 ("Journal," 1970); 1 ill

YERXA, Thomas (1923-) Amer; ptr
WHITNEY (statement); 1 ill

YHAP, Laetitia (1941-) Brit; ptr
CONTEMPORARY (statement); port; 2
ill

YOSHIDA, Kenji (1924-) Japa; ptr
EMANUEL II 1025 (statement); 1 ill
NAYLOR 1064 (statement)

YOSHIDA, Masaji (1917-) Japa; print,
wood
KUNG 158-161 (statement); port; 2 ill

YOSHIDA, Ray Kakuo (1930-) Amer;
ptr
ACKLAND 20-37, 52-53 (group
discussion 10/29/79); 1 ill

YOSHIHARA, Jiro (1905-) Japa; ptr
KUNG 136-139 (statement); port; 3 ill

YOSHIMURA, Fumio (1926-)
Japa/Amer; ptr, sclp
NAYLOR 1064-1065 (statement); 1 ill

YOSIZAKA, Takamasa (1917-) Japa;
arch
EMANUEL I 915-916 (statement); 1 ill

YOUDELMAN, Nancy (1948-) Amer;
sclp, instal
SCRIPPS COLLEGE (statement); 1 ill

VISUAL v.3 no.2 24 (statement); 1 ill

YOUDELMAN, Rachel ( )
ART-RITE no.14 5, 14 (response)

YOUNG, Bernard (1952-) Amer; ptr
LEWIS I REVISED 55 (statement); port;
1 ill

YOUNG, Charles Alexander (1930-)
Amer; ptr
LEWIS II 8 (statement); port; 1 ill

YOUNG, John Chin (1909-) Amer; ptr
HAAR I 144-150 (interview with
Prithwish Neogy); ports; 3 ill

YOUNG, Mahonri Mackintosh
(1877-1957) Amer; ptr, sclp
SAYLER 322-326 (essay: "The Sculptor
Waits on the Architect")

YOUNG, Milton (1935-) Amer; ptr, sclp
LEWIS II 96 (statement); port; 2 ill

YOUNG, Peter (1940-) Amer; ptr
ART NOW v.1 no.5 (statement); 1 ill

YOUNGER, Robert (1947-) Amer; sclp,
envir, instal
ARTPARK 1978 64-67 (statement); port;
7 ill
GUMPERT III 80-81 (statement)

YOUNGERMAN, Jack (1926-) Amer;
ptr, illus
ART NOW v.2 no.1 (statement); 1 ill
ARTFORUM v.4 no.5 27-31 (interview
with Barbara Rose); 10 ill
ILLINOIS 1965 175 (statement); 1 ill

YOUNGMAN, William R. (1927-) Amer;
sclp
ILLINOIS 1961 201 (response); port; 1 ill

YRISARRY, Mario (1933-) Phil/Amer;
ptr
CRISS-CROSS no.6 12-15 (poem, o.p.
1974; poem, 1978); 2 ill
NAYLOR 1066-1067 (statement); 1 ill
TRACKS v.1 no.1 40 (poem)
TUCKER I 18 (statement)

YUDELL, Buzz (Robert) ( ) Amer; arch
GA DOCUMENT no.4 88-89 (statement);
9 ill
GA HOUSES no.7 112-119 (essay:
"Moore in Progress"); port
LA JOLLA 58-64 (statement); port; 9 ill

YU-HO, Tseng (1924-) Chin/Amer; ptr
HAAR I 138-143 (interview with
Prithwish Neogy); ports; 3 ill

YUNKERS, Adja (1900-) Latv/Amer;
print, ptr
ART NOW v.2 no.6 (statement); 1 ill
ILLINOIS 1961 207 (response); port; 1 ill
IT IS no.4 28 (statement)
TIGER no.8 52-53 (statement)

YVARAL (Jean Pierre Vasarely) (1934-)
Fren; sclp, ptr
LUMIERE (statement); port; 1 ill
NAYLOR 1068-1069 (statement); 1 ill

ZABLOCKI, Wojciech (1930-) Poli; arch
EMANUEL I 917-918 (statement); 1 ill

ZABLUDOVSKY, Abraham (1924-) Mexi; arch
EMANUEL I 918-920 (statement); 1 ill

ZACH, Jan (1914-) Czec/Amer; sclp, ptr
CANADA 56-57 (statement); port; 2 ill

ZAIDENBERG, Arthur ( ) Amer; sclp, illus, ptr
ZAIDENBERG 32-35 (essay: "Drawing"); 3 ill

ZACK, Leon (1892-) Russ; ptr
GRENIER 215-231 (interview)

ZADKINE, Ossip (1890-1967) Fren; sclp
FORD/VIEW v.4 no.1 17 (statement); port
FORD/VIEW v.4 no.2 42-44 (essay: "The Minotaure Lost and Found")
FRASNAY 65-79 (poem); ports; 8 ill
GOLDWATER 429-431 (statement, 1944)
TIGER no.4 83-84, 90 ("Prolegomenes to Sculpture" and "Forms"); 1 ill
VINGTIEME v.1 no.2 29-30 (essay: "La Colonne Dorique")
WHELDON 29-37 (interview with Bernard Williams); port

ZAJAC, Jack (1929-) Amer; print, ptr
AMERICAN PRINTS 60, 71 (statement); 1 ill
ARTFORUM v.1 no.1 30-32 (statements); port; 3 ill
CALIFORNIA--PAINTING 52 (statement); 1 ill
ILLINOIS 1952 241 (statement); 1 ill
ILLINOIS 1961 206 (response); port; 1 ill
YOUNG 1957 (statement); 2 ill

ZAK, Helena (1954-) Swed/Iris; instal, sclp
KNOWLES 178-179 ("The Nuancer"); 3 ill

ZAKANITCH, Robert S. (Zakanych) (1935-) Amer; ptr
ILLINOIS 1969 173 (statement); 1 ill
NEW DECORATIVE 22-23, 52-54 (statement); 3 ill
TUCKER I 14 (statement)

ZAKARIAN, Robert (1938-) Amer; sclp
DIRECTIONS I 77 (response); 1 ill

ZALENSKI, Joan ( ) Amer; sclp
ARTPARK 1977 84-87 (statement); port; 7 ill

ZALMAR (1925-) Amer; ptr
ILLINOIS 1951 224-225 (statement); 1 ill

ZAMBONINI, Giuseppe ( ) arch
GA HOUSES no.13 162-167 (statements); 19 ill

ZAMIR, Batya (1942-) Amer; perf
BRENTANO 366-367 (statement); 1 ill
INTERVIEWS 40-42 (interview); port

ZAMMITT, Norman (1931-) Amer; ptr
HOPKINS 121-123 (statement); port; 1 ill

ZAN FAGNA (1929-) Amer; illus
CALIFORNIA--DRAWING (statement); 2 ill

ZANARTU, Enrique (1921-) Chil; ptr, print
PREMIER BILAN 328 (statement); port

ZANGS, Herbert (1924-) Germ; ptr, coll
SKIRA 1976 69 (statement); 1 ill

ZIVKOVIC, Bogosav (1920-) Yugo; sclp, print
TOMASEVIC 383-389 (statement); port; 3 ill

ZOBEL, Fernando (1924-) Span; ptr
NAYLOR 1074-1075 (statement); 1 ill

ZOGBAUM, Wilfrid M. (1915-1965) Amer; sclp
ARTFORUM v.1 no.2 29-35 (group discussion)
IT IS no.1 27 (essay: "Remarks on the Differences between Painting and Sculpture")
IT IS no.5 51-56 (group discussion)

ZOOG, Trina ( ) instal, ptr
CRISS-CROSS no.11/12 (statement); 5 ill

ZORACH, William (1887-1966) Lith/Amer; sclp
ARMORY SHOW 34 (statement)
BRUMME 8-12 ("Introduction")
FIFTY (statement); port; 1 ill
FORUM 1916 104 (statement); 1 ill
ILLINOIS 1955 254-255 (statement); 1 ill
ILLINOIS 1959 282-283 (statement); 1 ill
ILLINOIS 1961 204-205 (response); port; 1 ill
ILLINOIS 1965 160-161 (statement); 1 ill
100 CONTEMPORARY 204-205 (statement); port; 1 ill

ZORIO, Gilberto (1944-) Ital; ptr, sclp
CELANT 185-191 (statement); 6 ill
WALDMAN 128-143 (statement); 11 ill

ZOX, Holly ( ) Amer
EVENTS II 32-33, 40-41, 44-45 (statements); 3 ill

ZOX, Larry (1936-) Amer; ptr
ART NOW v.1 no.2 (statement); 1 ill

ROSE II REVISED 189 (statement: "Removing the Camouflage and Exposing the Foundation," o.p. 1967)
SYSTEMATIC 25 (statement); 1 ill
TUCKER I 14 (statement)

ZSCHOKKE, Alexander (Zschocke) ( ) Swis; sclp
ART AND ARTIST 61-68 (essay: "An Encounter with Paul Klee," o.p. 1948)

ZSISSLY (Malvin Marr Albright) (1897-) Amer; sclp, ptr
M.H. DE YOUNG 150 (response); self port
MILLER 1943 60-61 (statement); 2 ill

ZUCKER, Barbara Marion (1940-) Amer; sclp, envir
ARTPARK 1978 72-75 (statement); port; 11 ill
BRENTANO 370-371 (statement); 1 ill
INTERVIEWS 43-46 (interview); port; 1 ill
SCHAPIRO 78 (statement); port; 1 ill

ZUCKER, Jacques (1900-) Amer; ptr
100 CONTEMPORARY 206-207 (statement); port; 1 ill

ZUCKER, Joseph I. (Joe) (1941-) Amer; ptr
MARSHALL 68, 93 (statement); port; 5 ill

ZUNIGA, Francisco (1911-) Mexi; sclp
STEWART 134-137 (statement); port; 3 ill

ZURLO, Donald (1934-) Amer; light, sclp
GEOMETRIC (statement); 1 ill

ZWACK, Michael ( ) Amer; envir, ptr,

film
ARTPARK 1976 206-207 (statement);
port; 4 ill
FACE IT 26-27 (statement); 1 ill